Africa

Africa

*Dilemmas of
Development and Change*

edited by

Peter Lewis

Westview Press
A Member of Perseus Books, L.L.C.

To the memories of Carl Rosberg,
whose dedicated teaching and insightful scholarship
inspired generations of students,

and Claude Ake,
whose penetrating views and personal fellowship
are greatly missed

Copyright © 1998 by Westview Press, A Member of Perseus Books, L.L.C.

Published in 1998 in the United States of America by Westview Press, 5500 Central Avenue, Boulder, Colorado 80301-2877, and in the United Kingdom by Westview Press, 12 Hid's Copse Road, Cumnor Hill, Oxford OX2 9JJ

Library of Congress Cataloging-in-Publication Data
Lewis, Peter.
  Africa : dilemmas of development and change / Peter Lewis.
    p.   cm.
  Includes bibliographical references and index.
  ISBN 0-8133-2754-7 (hardcover). — ISBN 0-8133-2755-5 (pbk.)
    1. Africa—Economic conditions—1960– 2. Africa—Social conditions. 3. Africa—Politics and government—1960– I. Title.
HC800.L483   1998
306'.096—dc21   98-13688
                                                                      CIP

The paper used in this publication meets the requirements of the American National Standard for Permanence of Paper for Printed Library Materials Z39.48-1984.

10   9   8   7   6   5   4   3   2   1

Contents

v

Acknowledgments

I would like to offer thanks to the many authors and publishers who graciously gave permission for the publication of these selections. Special recognition is due to my research assistant, Michael Gonzales, whose patience, care, and resourcefulness enabled the completion of this volume. The staff at Westview Press has also been helpful and congenial throughout this project, and they have my gratitude.

Peter Lewis

Introduction:
Development and Change
in Africa

Africa south of the Sahara encompasses some forty-eight countries with more than 600 million people. Although these states reflect great variety in their territories, populations, cultures, resources, and historical legacies, the diversity of this region should not obscure the common problems and challenges evident during four decades of postindependence development. The search for stable and legitimate government, the quest for unity among heterogeneous societies, and the aspiration for economic attainment have been perennial themes since the end of the colonial era. African countries have worked toward these goals with varying degrees of success, yet the region as a whole has experienced some of the most formidable—indeed, often intractable—problems in the developing world. Scholars and analysts have examined Africa's travails through different conceptual prisms, yielding an assortment of prescriptions for policy and strategy. Their debates have evolved in response to changing trends on the continent.

This book surveys the enduring themes and current challenges of development in sub-Saharan Africa. The readings include many classic works on African political and economic development, along with important writings on emerging issues in the region. The selections focus mainly on broader comparative questions, rather than descriptions of specific countries or areas. Readers familiar with Africa will find a concise review of the leading concepts, controversies, and questions in African studies over the past two decades. Those who are new to African affairs will find a general introduction to salient issues and ideas. I hope that all readers will find this an engaging selection of writings on this complex region.

By way of introduction, this chapter provides a brief historical overview of Africa's developmental challenges and a survey of the leading conceptual approaches to the region. I will review the colonial legacy in Africa, the pivotal moment of decolonization, and the central challenges encountered by postindependence regimes and describe the lead-

1

ing schools of thought that have influenced the analysis of African development in recent decades. The chapter concludes with a note on the rationale guiding the selection of readings and an outline of the book's organization.

The Historical Context

Although I cannot do justice here to the broad sweep of African history, it is important to point out the great heterogeneity and rich heritage of African societies before the advent of colonialism.[1] In the centuries prior to European rule, Africa was home to both large centralized empires and smaller segmentary communities, as well as an array of other political entities. Cooperation, conflict, alliance, and rivalry among peoples could all be found within the region. Although precolonial economies were overwhelmingly agrarian, pastoralism, trade, crafts, and mining also contributed to the livelihoods of many populations. Islam and Christianity were evident in some areas, and many parts of the continent had regular contact with European, Middle Eastern, and South Asian cultures.

The colonial legacy had a formative impact on African states.[2] As traumatic and far-reaching as colonialism may appear, however, we should not yield to the view that foreign rule completely effaced existing structures and practices. To the contrary, it is evident that colonial interventions produced widely disparate effects. Indigenous societies were utterly transformed by some aspects of foreign control, yet they adapted, resisted, or evaded other influences. Thus contemporary Africa reflects the lineage of both its precolonial institutions and successive historical changes, among which the disruptive elements of colonialism are prominent.

European involvement in Africa began in the late fifteenth century, although formal colonization was not established in most areas for another three hundred years. The odious slave trade, which peaked between the seventeenth and nineteenth centuries, was organized mainly by European commercial networks in collaboration with dispersed local intermediaries. Prompted by the combined pressures of industrial capitalism and strategic rivalries in Europe, leading European powers began to demarcate their interests in Africa during the latter half of the nineteenth century. By 1870 a "scramble for Africa" was underway, as competing powers struggled for a foothold on the continent. By 1885, Europe's powers, both the dominant and the Johnny-come-lately, had ratified their respective claims on the continent at the Berlin Conference.

European imperial domination created new territorial boundaries, political relationships, social strata, and economic structures. Among the most pronounced features of colonial rule was the creation of new states.

Colonial territories were formally demarcated, and control was instituted by civil and military administrations. Colonial rule introduced a central bureaucratic form of authority that had never been experienced in many areas. The new states were arbitrarily defined, often with little correspondence to precolonial divisions of culture, politics, or commerce. Several ethnic groups could be incorporated within a single colonial territory, or a single group could be split by two (or more) colonies.

The colonies were extensively integrated into the global economy. Commercial production and trade penetrated into the interior as infrastructure opened up the hinterland. The growth of export and import activities created broader linkages between world markets, foreign capital, and dispersed rural communities. The expansion of commodity production and the development of open economies created problems of dependence and vulnerability, as African societies were increasingly exposed to outside economic forces. Investments in enterprise and infrastructure during the latter decades of colonial rule fostered additional economic transformations, especially in the areas of manufacturing and primary commodity exports.

Africa was profoundly affected by new cultural and social currents. The colonial powers typically cultivated a cultural mythology through a European lingua franca, education, and symbols of identity. Although most Africans did not readily identify with the culture of the colonizers, these new influences had far-reaching effects on colonial societies. Urbanization, formal education, and the migration of peoples led to greater interaction among groups and ideas. Social change gave rise to a new stratum of elites—many with unique education and skills—who ultimately usurped the traditional authority of their elders. Missionary activities were a major impetus to Christianity in many countries, although new avenues of communication also facilitated the expansion of Islam. By the middle of the twentieth century, the spread of such ideas as democracy, egalitarianism, socialism, and self-determination created powerful intellectual currents throughout the continent, exerting a subversive effect on the maintenance of colonial rule.

Finally, Africa became enmeshed in an international state system. African countries came under the jurisdiction of international law, and their external affairs were defined by predominant standards of global diplomacy. They were also powerfully impacted by the strategic and security objectives of the major world powers. Even during the period of colonial rule, African interstate relations were transformed into broader international relations, with all the risks and opportunities attendant upon this new status.

The decline of empire progressed rapidly after World War II.[3] Dissipated by the war, the European powers confronted a growing tide of anticolonial nationalism even as their domestic constituencies evinced greater ambivalence toward the colonial enterprise. Initiatives to reform or modify the colonial system proved ineffectual, and by 1960 Africa joined the prevailing global movement toward independence.

The newly independent political systems were shaped, in large part, by the specific characteristics of their struggles against and settlements with the respective colonial powers. Many countries attained sovereignty through a process of negotiation between colonial officials and a relatively small nationalist elite. The resultant governments were typically conservative, inviting limited popular involvement. In several other territories, the independence struggle was advanced by militant popular movements, often guided by magnetic and ideologically inspired leaders. This commonly yielded populist regimes with ambitious agendas for change and a bent toward the mobilization of mass constituencies. A few colonies were governed by settler regimes whose intransigence provoked armed struggles against foreign rule. After prolonged efforts to attain liberation, these movements frequently established governments with a revolutionary profile.

Challenges of Development

The independent states of Africa have confronted a series of fundamental developmental tasks that in many respects echo the historical experiences of other regions. The first of these has been the project of state building.[4] African countries have faced the difficulties of constructing effective public authority, establishing viable state institutions, and creating responsive and legitimate agents of governance. Attaining security and managing conflict are also integral features of state consolidation. Building public power requires much more than the installation of new governmental structures, indeed, it involves the very character of relations between rulers and citizens.

A second common challenge is the task of nation building. Many African countries have experienced the travails of forging unified political communities from plural states. Because of the arbitrary basis of colonial boundaries, newly independent states inherited diverse populations that often became fractious as disparate groups contended for resources and identity. The difficulties of managing competition and strife among ethnic communities and promoting common symbols and identities have placed substantial demands upon governments throughout the region.

Economic development presents a third overarching task for African states, who have to cope with the myriad challenges of growth and structural transformation in low-income agrarian economies. They have also grappled with external dependence and a marginal position in world markets. Regimes have pursued various means to promote a diversified productive base and to make inroads against poverty and inequality. Many governments have been equally intent on modifying patterns of trade and regulating international transactions.

These developmental challenges have been reflected in regional strategies and problems since independence. As the wave of decolonization swept over Africa in 1960, many people had high expectations for the newly independent states. Colonial rule bequeathed weak economic and political foundations to most countries, yet there was a widely shared view that abundant resources, human energies, and political innovation could offer a sound basis for development. The popular mobilization of the nationalist era provided substantial legitimacy to the fledgling governments, and an array of dynamic leaders commanded broad respect and loyalty. The new rulers experimented with a variety of ideologies and strategies for development, while many sought a distinctive regional identity for Africa in the global arena.

Signs of disenchantment were manifest quickly, however, as much of the region succumbed to authoritarian rule, internal division, and instability. Participatory institutions were curtailed in many countries as political leaders created single-party regimes and personal dictatorships. Even as 1960 was called the year of independence, 1966 became known as the year of the coup d'état after several governments were toppled by military intervention. Disquieting signs of ethnic discord were also evident in a series of civil conflicts, secessionist challenges, and political antipathies. The seeming unity and purpose of the independence moment was soon replaced by the disarray of factional struggle.

New sources of interstate conflict and ideological rivalry in Africa appeared in the 1970s alongside growing international intervention and a deceleration of economic development. A "second generation" of socialist states emerged mid-decade, when several countries embraced Marxist-Leninist doctrine, eclipsing the populist and African socialist models of the independence era. Regional or local strife erupted in the southern and eastern zones of the continent and in the Horn of Africa. Many of these hostilities attracted the interest and intervention of the major powers, bringing Africa into prominence as a major arena of Cold War rivalry. These developments unfolded against a backdrop of waning economic performance, as oil price shocks and domestic policy problems led to a significant slowdown in growth.

The 1980s were bracketed by crisis. At the beginning of the decade, Africa experienced a steep regional economic decline. Dozens of countries experienced stagnant growth, dwindling production and trade, widening domestic poverty, and burgeoning foreign debt. Confronted with acute fiscal problems, many governments turned for support to the

World Bank and the International Monetary Fund. With the sponsorship of these international financial institutions, a majority of African states pursued economic reform programs that yielded tentative recovery for many of them. Yet the social and political effects of adjustment and the role of donors in the region provoked substantial controversy.

At the close of the decade, the region experienced a dramatic political transformation as African regimes were confronted with concerted pressures for democratization. The end of the Cold War disrupted the external alliances and rivalries that had long stabilized many governments. A combination of domestic opposition and global influence induced a majority of regimes to either liberalize their political systems or concede a transition to democratic rule. The ensuing political shifts proved beneficial to some countries but detrimental for a number of others. Most of the region's military and single-party states shifted toward some form of competitive politics, although in several instances regime change yielded new instability or increased conflict.

These historic currents yielded different trajectories for African countries in the 1990s. States such as Ghana and Uganda sought recovery from the ruinous political and economic circumstances of the preceding decades. South Africa, Namibia, and Mozambique ended longstanding conflicts and embarked upon democratic beginnings. Benin, Malawi, Mali, and several other countries also gravitated toward a democratic path. On the other hand, many states including Nigeria, Togo, Cameroon, and Niger remained mired in authoritarian rule. Still others, notably Somalia, Liberia, Rwanda, and Zaire (now Democratic Republic of Congo), experienced civil catastrophe or state collapse. As the millenium draws to a close, Africa reflects greater intraregional diversity than at any time since independence. Across the continent, growth has contended with stagnation, democracy with dictatorship, and stability with turmoil.

Structure, Change, and Choice: Theories of Development

Since the era of independence, analysis and debate have produced various views of development. These approaches offer very different perspectives on the sources of underdevelopment and the prospects for change in Africa.[5] Modernization theory was the earliest attempt to provide a comprehensive explanation of progress or stagnation in the former colonies. The modernization perspective, elaborated by Western social scientists in the 1950s and 1960s, regards the developing countries as endeavoring to "catch up" to the advanced industrialized states.

Drawing upon the historical lessons of European development, modernization theorists offer an archetypal model of modernity, counterposed to a generic image of traditional society.[6] Modern societies are identified as industrialized, mass consumption economies, reflecting high levels of technological development and innovation. Their social and economic structures are characterized by specialization and complex interdependence. Frequently, modern society is also described as democratic, with a premium on individual rights and popular engagement in politics. By contrast, this model describes traditional societies as having simpler technology and lower productivity. Most modernization theories identify as traditional those economies based on agriculture, with a comparatively rudimentary division of labor and relative stasis in their economic and social structures. They are mainly hierarchical polities, reflecting the primacy of customary authority. In the view of modernization theory, the reasons for these differences and the potential for change reside in different forms of cultural and social organization. Modern societies embody individualism, a preference for abstract principles, pragmatism, and the rule of law. Traditional societies are oriented toward collectivism, stereotyped social roles, the dominance of inherited tradition, and the rule of custom.

Modernization theory not only poses a dichotomy between traditional and modern societies, it also indicates a unidirectional pattern of change, from traditional to modern attributes. It views modernization as an integral package of transformation, driven by the related influences of education, communications, trade, migration, urbanization, and economic growth. The theory recognizes that, once certain elements of the process are set in motion, it is difficult to arrest modernization, or to limit the extent of change in society. This creates abundant stresses and tensions in modernizing societies, as different spheres of economy, society, and politics are transformed at different rates. But solving the problem of modernization is primarily a question of comprehending western patterns of change and managing the strains and conflicts in the process.

Scholars in the developing countries soon dissented from this view. Beginning in the 1960s, they presented a radical critique of modernization perspectives. Their point of departure was the observation that developing countries have a separate history from industrial capitalist states, as Third World states were dominated by Western imperialism for at least a century before independence and attained independence in a world already stratified and dominated by the advanced industrialized powers. They criticise modernization theorists for ignoring the international context of change.

Dependency theory, or underdevelopment theory, is premised on the struggle between North and South in a stratified world. Dependency theorists present a single international model in which two spheres—core and periphery—interact in an unequal relationship. In this perspective, the core countries of the North grow wealthy by exploiting and subordinating the resources, markets, and labor of the peripheral countries of the South. The underdevelopment of Third World countries is attributable mainly to the structure of the international system. Dependency theorists disparage modernization theory's emphasis on cultural and social forces in development, stressing instead the primacy of economic and political factors. In dependency theory, the structures of dependency are elaborated through several processes and institutions. The unequal terms of trade between industrial exporters in the core and primary commodity producers in the periphery constitute a fundamental economic imbalance. The role of multinational corporations in shaping investment, trade, consumption, and labor markets in the developing world form another important mechanism of dependence. The elites in Third World countries commonly appear as active collaborators with foreign elements in constructing dependency relations. Moreover, the direct political and military interventions of core states sustain international inequalities.

Dependency theorists argue that the chronic underdevelopment and poverty in Third World countries can only be explained in global terms, and that the primary objective for developing states is to change their relation to the international system. They admonish countries of the South to minimize exploitive linkages with Northern states and take collective action to change the dynamics of the international system.

By the 1980s, many critics challenged the premises of dependency theory, especially its preoccupation with external constraints on change. More generally, there was a reaction to prevailing theories that viewed African governments as essentially marginal to the development process, whether caught up in an evolutionary path of modernization or constrained by global structures of capitalism. Instead, many analysts came to focus on the state, an emphasis that highlights the importance of domestic political capabilities in the development process.[7] State-centric analyses start from the simple premise that governments and public institutions have a decisive role in managing domestic change and international interactions. Although all countries face constraints and challenges, the qualities of leadership and government determine the relative abilities to surmount such difficulties.

State-centric analysis proceeds from the distinction between the state and society. The state embodies the formally constituted public institutions of coercion, bureaucracy, and infrastructure, as distinct from the private and particular interests of societal groups. The state can provide important public goods such as security, law and order, infrastructure, and selected market institutions. States can also structure social relations through the establishment of property rights, the reinforcement of social hierarchies, and mediation among different groups and strata.

In comparing the performance of different state structures, we can observe that certain states may assert relative autonomy from their constituent societies. The interests of state elites may take precedence over pressures from specific domestic or external interests. The comparative autonomy of states conditions their success in meeting long-term developmental goals. Governments also reflect varying capacities in pursuing important objectives. State capacity reflects the ability to gain compliance from society, to organize diverse interests, and to influence various actors. State capacity is broader than mere coercive power, referring also to qualities of administration, the coherence of leadership, and the legitimacy of government.

State-centric analysts have acknowledged that modernization pressures and external dependency create challenges for states, yet they stress that strong states are better equipped to cope with such obstacles.[8] The state-centric perspective emphasizes that even weak states have considerable leverage over domestic society and external linkages. From the vantage of state theory, key issues in African development have been the comparative weakness of African states and identifying outlets for improving the capacity of governing institutions.

However appropriate the focus on the state, in many instances it has been overemphasized or misplaced. By the mid-1980s, there was growing recognition of the independent role of societal groups in the region's political dynamics. The frailties of state institutions and the limited capabilities of ruling elites in Africa suggested that social networks, interest groups, and an evolving realm of associational life merited equal attention as significant political factors. A number of analysts have argued for a shift away from state-centric analysis, toward a perspective encompassing state-society relations.[9] In this view, politics is regarded as a process of reciprocal interaction between governments and societal groups. While state elites seek to establish authority and control over their constituent societies, social groups also endeavor to influence state policy and resource allocations. Elements of many societies also attempt to evade or resist the reach of central authorities. State-society relations embody an often contentious interaction over the control of resources and power.

An Eclectic View

The readings presented here offer a frankly eclectic view of states, societies, and economies in contemporary Africa. Naturally enough, the selections reflect my own biases, derived mainly from the traditions of historical sociology and theories of political development.[10] This vantage focuses on domestic social and political factors, rather than international linkages, as central factors in the process of change. It also stresses the importance of contingency and choice alongside the evident structural influences on development. It is necessary to recognize the social forces and economic constraints surrounding any political regime, but an understanding of developmental outcomes requires that we also pay attention to the quality of institutions, the design of public policy, and the autonomous role of leaders. Ultimately, we can only understand the course of change in Africa and the disparate fortunes within the region by examining the initiatives of political actors within the limitations consigned by history and resources.

Plan of the Book

This book is organized around a series of developmental issues and analytical themes. The first three sections address perennial questions regarding states, societies, and political action. Part 1 takes up the nature of state power and political leadership, focusing on the historical construction of African states, the modes of political control in the region, and the character of political elites. Part 2 turns to the relations between states and social groups, examining the nature of political legitimacy and the avenues of participation or withdrawal pursued by various popular sectors. Part 3 looks more closely at issues of social stratification: class, ethnicity and gender. The meaning of these divisions in African settings and the political significance of different forms of inequality is the common thread among these articles.

The last two sections survey the region's evolving challenges of political reform and economic transition. Part 4 focuses on recent movement toward political liberalization and democratic transition in Africa. The chapters assess the progress of democratization, the nature of political change in various countries, and the prospects for enduring democratic rule. Part 5 considers the dilemmas of regional economic failure and recovery. The debates over economic development, the background of economic crisis, and the challenges of reform are discussed.

Notes

1. For a general introduction see John Iliffe, *Africans: The History of a Continent* (Cambridge: Cambridge University Press, 1995).

2. M. Crawford Young, *The African Colonial State in Comparative Perspective* (New Haven: Yale University Press, 1994).

3. D. K. Fieldhouse, *Black Africa 1945–1980: Economic Decolonization and Arrested Development* (London: Unwin Hyman, 1986).

4. This scheme is derived from the model outlined by James Coleman et al., *Crises and Sequences in Political Development* (Princeton: Princeton University Press, 1971).

5. Alvin Y. So, *Social Change and Development: Modernization, Dependency, and World-System Theories* (Newbury Park, Calif.: Sage Publications, 1990); Naomi Chazan, Robert Mortimer, John Ravenhill, and Donald Rothchild, *Politics and Society in Contemporary Africa*, 2d ed. (Boulder: Lynne Rienner Publishers, 1992).

6. Cyril E. Black, *The Dynamics of Modernization* (New York: Harper and Row, 1966); W. W. Rostow, *The Stages of Economic Growth* (Cambridge: Cambridge University Press, 1962).

7. Peter Evans, Dietrich Rueschemeyer, and Theda Skocpol, eds., *Bringing the State Back In* (Cambridge: Cambridge University Press, 1985).

8. Tony Smith, "The Underdevelopment of Development Literature: The Case of Dependency Theory," *World Politics* 31 (January 1979): 247–288.

9. Joel Migdal, Atul Kohli, and Vivienne Shue, eds., *State Power and Social Forces: Domination and Transformation in the Third World* (Cambridge: Cambridge University Press, 1994); Donald Rothchild and Naomi Chazan, eds., *The Precarious Balance: State and Society in Africa* (Boulder: Westview Press, 1988).

10. For a concise review of these perspectives, see Anthony Giddens, *Capitalism and Modern Social Theory* (New York: Cambridge University Press, 1971); and Myron Weiner and Samuel P. Huntington, ed., *Understanding Political Development* (Boston: Little, Brown, 1987).

Suggestions for Further Reading

Apter, David, and Carl Rosberg, eds. *Political Development and the New Realism in Sub-Saharan Africa*. Charlottesville: University Press of Virginia, 1994.

Berg, Robert J., and Jennifer Seymour Whitaker, eds. *Strategies for African Development*. Berkeley and Los Angeles: University of California Press, 1985.

Chazan, Naomi, Robert Mortimer, John Ravenhill, and Donald Rothchild. *Politics and Society in Contemporary Africa*. 2d ed. Boulder: Lynne Rienner Publishers, 1992.

Coleman, James, et al. *Crises and Sequences in Political Development*. Princeton: Princeton University Press, 1971.

Fieldhouse, D. K. *Black Africa 1945–1980: Economic Decolonization and Arrested Development*. London: Unwin Hyman, 1986.

Hodder-Williams, Richard. *An Introduction to the Politics of Tropical Africa*. London: George Allen and Unwin, 1984.

Iliffe, John. *Africans: The History of a Continent*. Cambridge: Cambridge University Press, 1995.

Migdal, Joel, Atul Kohli, and Vivienne Shue, eds. *State Power and Social Forces: Domination and Transformation in the Third World*. Cambridge: Cambridge University Press, 1994.

Weiner, Myron, and Samuel P. Huntington, eds. *Understanding Political Development*. Boston: Little, Brown, 1987.

Young, M. Crawford. *The African Colonial State in Comparative Perspective*. New Haven: Yale University Press, 1994.

Part One

States and Leadership

The study of African politics has shifted in light of changing perspectives on development and new assessments of governance. At first, theories of modernization and political development prompted attention to central institutions and discrete political processes. Throughout the 1960s and 1970s, writers sought to understand African bureaucracies, military establishments, and political parties in tandem with a focus on corruption, civil-military interactions, political participation, and patron-client relations. The role of ideology was also accentuated during this period, as analysts gave considerable attention to the distinctions among various political regimes and doctrines.

With the growing prevalence of state-centric approaches, there was an effort to build upon these earlier studies by elaborating broader comparative features of political power and capacity in Africa. This new generation of political studies centered on the general aspects of politics that cut across ideology and regime type, including the social foundation of ruling groups, the qualities and capabilities of political institutions, and the strategies of political control pursued by various governments. This work is guided by two assumptions: that there are specific and enduring elements that are fundamental to politics in the region and that an appreciation of these characteristics is essential to understanding processes of continuity and change.

During much of the postindependence era, weak authoritarian regimes have been prevalent throughout Africa. Despite the variety of leadership forms, ideologies, and political institutions, most of the region's governments have been politically restrictive and autocratic. African leaders have exercised considerable leeway in the use of power, and they have not generally been accountable to electorates or other organized constituencies. At the same time, African states have reflected very limited capacities in fulfilling basic functions or advancing developmental goals.

The concentration of authority and the frailties of government control are integrally related.

The legacy of colonial state creation and the challenges of political consolidation provided the foundations of African political development. The colonial state was an alien imposition on African societies, authoritarian by nature and usually distant from its subjects. At the same time, colonial administration was often thin on the ground, and there was not an intensive bureaucratic presence in many territories. While colonial authorities did exercise stable rule and provided some basic public goods, they were commonly experienced by their subjects as illegitimate and predatory. Not surprisingly, Africans typically regarded the colonial state as an intrusive presence to be evaded or exploited whenever possible.

This inheritance created basic problems for the establishment of effective governments after independence. The new leaders faced manifold difficulties in gathering stable governing coalitions, fostering durable institutions, and extending substantial control over the mass of their populations. The emergent governing formulas typically blended traditional modes of authority with institutional forms inherited from the colonial regime. These strategies often stabilized nascent political elites, yet they were less effective in building sound governing structures.

The readings in this section address basic features of political authority and control in the postindependence era. The authors elaborate several important themes, including the nature of leadership and institutions in African political systems, the construction of the region's ruling groups, and the relation of governing elites to their supporting constituencies. These analyses provide insights into the ways that African regimes have been constituted and sustained and the implications of political domination for other spheres of development. This focus on the politics of the center provides a starting point for exploring the broader scope of relations between citizens and rulers.

Robert Jackson's and Carl Rosberg's discussion of personal rule in Africa highlights the tendency toward the concentration of authority into the hands of individual leaders and the corresponding erosion of institutional sources of power. The region's political leaders have pursued different modes and styles of governance, but the relative autonomy of individual leaders and the comparative weakness of formal organizations and the rule of law have been hallmarks of African politics in the decades since independence. The syndrome of personal rule has fostered a basic dilemma of political institutionalization in the region.

Richard Joseph provides a further vantage on the nature of elite control and the disposition of state resources. Observing the ambiguous boundaries between the public and private realms in Nigeria, he outlines a pattern of "prebendal" politics, in which nominally public resources are appropriated for personal and community ends. As both a mode of political coalition-building and an attitude toward state assets, prebendalism has had debilitating effects on both political stability and economic growth.

In the section's final reading, Richard Sandbrook considers how ruling groups have been comprised in Africa. He explains the ubiquitous role of patron-client relations in building political networks and solidifying regimes. The article also stresses the importance of factional division as a source of dissension in African governments. While patron-client linkages often provide the building blocks of political control, this form of alliance carries inherent weaknesses and hazards.

1

Personal Rule:
Theory and Practice in Africa

Robert H. Jackson and
Carl G. Rosberg

When I say "politics," . . . it [is] not a question of the art of governing the
State for the public welfare in the general framework of laws and regulations. *It is [a] question of politician politics: the struggles of clans—not
even [ideological] tendencies—to place well oneself, one's relatives, and one's
clients in the* cursus honorum, *that is the race for preferments.*
                                    —Leopold Sedar Senghor

The Image of Personal Rule

Personal rule has been a compelling facet of politics at least since the time
of Machiavelli. It is the image not of a ruler but of a type of rulership.[1]
Personal rule is a dynamic world of political will and activity that is
shaped less by institutions or impersonal social forces than by personal
authorities and power; it is a world, therefore, of uncertainty, suspicion,
rumor, agitation, intrigue, and sometimes fear, as well as of stratagem,
diplomacy, conspiracy, dependency, reward, and threat. In other words,
personal rule is a distinctive type of political system in which the rivalries
and struggles of powerful and wilful men, rather than impersonal institutions, ideologies, public policies, or class interests, are fundamental in
shaping political life. Indicators of personal regimes in sub-Saharan
Africa are coups, plots, factionalism, purges, rehabilitations, clientelism,
corruption, succession maneuvers, and similar activities which have been

Reprinted with permission from *Comparative Politics* (July 1984): 421–442.

significant and recurring features of political life during the past two decades. Furthermore, there is no indication that such activities are about to decline in political importance. Whereas these features are usually seen as merely the defects of an otherwise established political order—whether capitalist, socialist, military, civilian, or whatever—we are inclined to regard them much more as the integral elements of a distinctive political system to which we have given the term "personal rule."[2]

It is ironic that in the twentieth century a novel form of "presidential monarchy" has appeared in many countries of the Third World. The irony consists in the contradiction of what is perhaps the major tendency in the evolution of the modern state during the past several centuries: the transformation of political legitimacy from the authority of kings to the mandate of the people.[3] What has happened in the Third World and especially in Africa was not expected to happen. When colonial rule was rapidly coming to an end in the 1950s and 1960s, it was hoped that independent African countries would adopt some form of democracy, be it liberal-democratic or socialist or some indigenous variant.[4] Instead of democracy, however, various forms of autocracy appeared.

> Fifteen years ago, scholarly writings on the New States . . . were full of discussions of parties, parliaments, and elections. A great deal seemed to turn on whether these institutions were viable in the Third World and what adjustments in them . . . might prove necessary to make them so. Today, nothing in those writings seems more passe, relic of a different time. Marcos, Suharto, Ne Win, al-Bakr, Sadat, Gaddafi, Boumedienne, Hassan, Houphouet, Amin, Mobutu may be doing their countries good or harm, promoting their peoples' advantage or oppressing them, but they are not guiding them to democracy. They are autocrats, and it is as autocrats, and not as preludes to liberalism (or, for that matter, to totalitarianism), that they, and the governments they dominate, must be judged and understood.[5]

There is a related methodological irony in this unforeseen historical development of presidential monarchy. At about the same time that students of politics were discarding the traditional tools of political theory, biography, and history that had proved of some value in the study of statecraft and were adopting the modern tools of sociology—thereby acknowledging that modern politics are mass, social politics in which governments interact with national populations or large classes or groups within them—political systems appeared in the Third World in which social politics were practically nonexistent and ruling politicians were remarkably free from the constraints of democratic institutions or social demands.[6] Therefore, despite the crucial importance of sociological explanations of politics—in which society is at least as important as the state; quantity or political weight counts for more than quality or political skill; impersonal social process is more significant than individual political practice; and little room, if any, is left for the analysis of rulership or leadership as such—in the Third World, and certainly in Africa, we continue to encounter prominent politicians who act as if the principle of popular legitimacy had not been invented and national societies did not exist.

Political sociologists are justified in their criticisms of the "great man" theories of some historians, and we do not wish to suggest either that rulers are wholly independent actors or that biography is the most suitable approach in studying rulership. But the "little man" and certainly the "invisible man" theories of social politics can also be criticized, especially in those societies, as in Africa, where the image of the "big man" is deeply embedded in the political culture and politics is often a vertical network of personal, patron-client relations.[7] If we are to deal with rulership in sociological terms—that is, in theoretical and not merely descriptive terms—we are obliged to regard political life as "a dialectic of power and structure, a web of possibilities for agents, whose nature is both active and structured, to make choices and pursue strategies within given limits, which in consequence expand and contract over time."[8] Therefore, in terms of methodology the image of personal rule draws our attention not only to rulers and their activities, but also to the political networks, circumstances, and predicaments in which they are entangled and from which they can never entirely extricate themselves.

Political images can often be sharpened by the careful selection of terms with which they are designated. If the terms "social politics" or "public politics" are apt for designating the political life of nation-states in which a popular mandate is the principle of legitimacy and politics is a "sociological activity . . . of preserving a community grown too complicated for either tradition alone or pure arbitrary rule to preserve it without the undue use of coercion," then perhaps Bernard Crick's term "palace politics" captures the largely personal, private, and elitist characteristics of political life in the autocracies that have emerged in Africa and elsewhere during the past several decades.[9] In this essay we present a theory of personal rule and its integral practices in independent African countries.

A Theory of Personal Rule

In the introductory remarks we have hinted at the main characteristics of personal rule. To understand its distinctive character we must first set aside some central sociological assumptions about the nature of the modern state, including the following: (1) the modern state's legitimacy ultimately rests upon, and its government interacts on a continuous basis with, an underlying national society and its constituent groups and classes; (2) the relations of society and government concern primarily group demands or class interests, ideal or material, calling forth public laws and policies which in turn provoke policies which in turn provoke new demands and so forth; (3) the institutional and policy biases of government reflect the power and privilege of classes and groups in society; and (4) the activity of government policymaking is at once social (in attempting to address societal demands) and technical (in attempting to apply the knowledge of the policy sciences, including especially economics, to deal with policymaking problems).[10]

The assumptions of personal rule are quite different, and an instructive way to approach them is to recall the concept of rulership in Machiavelli's masterpiece, *The Prince*.[11] Machiavelli assumes that the Prince is a self-interested, rational actor who desires to acquire and hold a principality. But the principality is not a national society of mobilizable groups and classes whose interests command the attention of the Prince; and the Prince is not primarily concerned to promote the welfare and conciliate the conflicts of an underlying national society upon which his legitimacy depends. Rather, the principality is a political entity which is acted upon—ruled—by the Prince and may be capable of occasional political reaction—such as rebellion—but it is not integrated with the government and has few political interests other than to be left unexploited and in peace. "As long as he does not rob the great majority of their property or their honour, they remain content. He then has to contend only with the restlessness of a few, and that can be dealt with easily and in a variety of ways."[12]

Personal rule is an elitist political system composed of the privileged and powerful few in which the many are usually unmobilized, unorganized, and therefore relatively powerless to command the attention and action of government. The system favors the ruler and his allies and clients: its essential activity involves gaining access to a personal regime's patronage or displacing the ruler and perhaps his regime and installing another. As an elitist system, personal politics concerns cooperation and rivalry among leaders and factions within the political class only and not among broader social classes or groups.[13] Consequently, the political process in personal regimes is primarily asocial insofar as it is largely indifferent to the interests, concerns, and problems of social strata beyond the political class. Personal politics is not public politics: it is not a "sociological activity" in Crick's meaning of the term, nor is personal governance significantly technical in practice. Although it may employ technocrats and proclaim socioeconomic plans and policies—including national development plans—its concrete activities are rarely guided by such impersonal criteria. Rather, government and administration are likely to be highly personal and permeated with patronage and corruption.

As already indicated, personal rule is a form of elite politics. However, it does not rest upon established constitutional rules and practices (including traditions) that effectively regulate the activities of the political class—especially the ruler—and is therefore distinguished from constitutional rule. Established and effective political institutions are largely absent from regimes of personal rule. In defining a political "institution" we follow Rawls.

> By an institution I shall understand a public system of rules which defines offices and positions with their rights and duties, powers and immunities, and the like. These rules specify certain forms of action as permissible, others as forbidden. . . . An institution may be thought of in two ways: first as an abstract . . . system of rules; and second, as the . . . [realized] actions specified by these rules. . . . A person taking part in an [real] institution knows what the rules demand of him and of the others. He also knows that the others know this and that they know that he knows this, and so on.[14]

Most contemporary Black African states have abstract political institutions, but they do not have them in the concrete, or realized, sense specified by Rawls. Institutional rules do not effectively govern the behavior of most leaders most of the time. Individuals do not perform political actions in an institutionally required way in the awareness that others expect it and that risks and difficulties would arise if they failed to do so. Political conduct is governed by the awareness that constitutional rules or administrative regulations can, and probably ought, to be evaded. The real norms that affect political and administrative action are not rooted in state institutions and organizations but in friendship, kinship, factional alliance, ethnic fellowship—that is, norms that are frequently at odds with the rules of state institutions and organizations and which tend to undermine them rather than reinforce or support them.[15] Political action in personal regimes is thus strongly affected by expediency and necessity. What an actor can do is more strongly affected by the resources at his disposal than by the office he occupies. What an actor must do is more strongly affected by particularistic norms—that is, obligations and attachments to friends, kin, factional allies, clansmen, ethnic fellows—than by state rules and regulations.

Personal rule is a form of monopolistic rather than pluralistic politics. Personal regimes consist primarily of the internecine struggles of powerful individuals, civilian or military, for power and place and secondarily of the actions of outsiders who desire to enter the monopoly, influence members within it, or displace it with their own personal regime. Politics tend to be closed to public participation and observation and even to be secretive—hence "palace politics." Personal rivalry within the monopoly for the ruler's favor gives rise to clandestine political activities, while challenges to the regime from without can often assume the character of political conspiracy since general political liberties are usually withheld by law or are not allowed in practice.[16] Political stability in all regimes depends ultimately on the ability and willingness of powerful men to regulate their conflicts and forebear from using violence, but, as pointed out, leaders in personal regimes do not have legitimate and effective institutions to assist them in this endeavor. Furthermore, personal regimes are neither highly organized nor effective monopolies that penetrate and control society. They are a type of authoritarianism, autocratic or oligarchic but not bureaucratic. African regimes rarely have the character of bureaucratic authoritarianism, which is a prominent feature of many Latin American countries,[17] and only a few have come close to being single-party democracies.

Personal politics involve almost exclusively the activities of "big men" who are a considerable distance from the ordinary people. As indicated, "the people," "the public," "the nation," "the national interest," "public opinion," and similar collectivities are abstractions that have little effect on political life. Individuals figure very prominently in politics while social collectivities figure very little. Personal politics express the conflicting appetites, desires, ambitions, aversions, hopes, and fears of a relatively small number of leaders who seek access to the resources and honors of the state and care little about questions of political ideology or public policy except as these affect their political situation and that of their associates, clients, and supporters. In African autocracies there are no elections to be won by actively promoting social or economic programs. Where elections are occasionally held, they are typically intraparty affairs in which big men—current or aspiring—vie with each other in promising benefits for local electorates; there is little to be gained from advocating national programs that reflect ideological viewpoints or require technical expertise.[18] Indeed, if there is an official ideology, it is not likely to be a subject of political debate.

Models and Metaphors for Theorizing About Personal Rule

In thinking and writing about personal rule, we have confronted the methodological problem of finding appropriate heuristics that can reveal the distinctive characteristics of such political systems and guide empirical studies of them. None of the usual models employed in comparative and African politics, which postulate social politics, is very suitable. And, while none of the following models and metaphors is entirely adequate by itself in capturing the character of personal rule, each has proved to be useful in exploring different features and facets of it in Black Africa.

Politics as a Competitive Game

This is a very widespread model of politics where actors are at the forefront of the analysis. A "game" indicates an orderly activity involving rules, authorities, players, skills, stratagems, prizes, uncertainty, and luck. Order is provided primarily by legitimate and effective rules. "Rules are an essential part of games: indeed, in a sense a game *is* a set of rules, for it can only be defined by a statement of these rules."[19] Thus in a game the competition among players and teams is kept within acceptable bounds by their acceptance of the rules and the authorities who enforce them. Scholars who employ this metaphor (such as Bailey) find it instructive to substitute "politics" for "game," "politicians" for "players," "parties" or "factions" for "teams," and so forth.

This model reveals some interesting features and facets of personal rule. Unlike institutional or constitutional government, personal rule lacks legitimate and effective rules and authorities that keep the game orderly. Personal regimes are far more dependent than institutional regimes on the co-operation, self-restraint, and good will of politicians and factions if the "game" is to remain orderly and not deteriorate into a fight. Political order depends far more on informal, "pragmatic" rules—what we prefer to call "practices"—that politicians accept out of self-interest rather than moral or legal obligation.[20] (For a definition and discussion of "practices," see below.) Of course, the limitation of pragmatic rules in keeping political competition orderly is precisely their pragmatism: if they are no longer useful, politicians will readily discard them. And if there are no legitimate and effective formal institutions to serve as backstops when this happens, only the players themselves can prevent politics from deteriorating into a fight.

African politics resembles a game without legitimate and effective institutional rules: most African states have not succeeded in becoming institutionalized in a formal-legal sense, and political life is highly dependent on the politicians and factions to keep it civil and non-violent. However, some political players, particularly soldiers, are often presented with a situation in which they have far more to gain than to lose by violating any tacit understandings that prohibit the threat or use of armed force in politics. Indeed, in some African countries the military *coup d'état* has become the most frequent type of political practice.

Politics as a Stage Play

This metaphor is not as familiar as the previous one, but it is similar in that it too can be used to explore the important distinction between personal rule and institutional government. Here politicians are likened to actors cast in different roles which they attempt to perform with whatever talent and skill they possess. Plays (i.e., politics) are performed before audiences, and a great play is one with an outstanding script and talented actors who can capture and hold the attention of an audience by playing upon its sympathy, curiosity, amusement, righteousness, anger, and other emotions. But plays are not the improvisations of players; they are the scripts of playwrights. "A play depends on its actors . . . as well as on its author. What the audience sees is an interpretation of the script."[21] Some playwrights are more gifted, some plays more popular, some performances more successful, and some performers more talented than others. Whereas all these elements are necessary for a play to be successful, a play would be impossible without a script. Scripts are to plays what rules are to games. In comparing "institutions" to "plays," Ridley argues that "political institutions are not merely endowed with a script but the script, in one way or another, generally embodies the meaning of the institution. . . . Institutions . . . are the script rather than the play."[22]

In applying this metaphor to politics, we can consider rulers and other leaders as actors in a national political drama that is ultimately defined by its political offices and institutions, that is, by parliamentary democracy, cabinet government, congressional government, federalism, democratic centralism, and so forth. Great leaders are like great actors: they give a commanding performance and create affection and support among an audience. By the same token, unsuccessful leaders are like novice or apprentice actors who aspire to give a commanding performance but are not fully aware of the possibilities and limitations of their offices (roles), owing primarily to their lack of political experience and "talent," which include energy, resourcefulness, and luck. If they cannot learn how to perform their roles successfully, it is unlikely that they will remain in them for very long.

Leaders in personal regimes differ from leaders in institutionalized regimes not in lacking a script—as indicated, institutions are present in the abstract although not in the realized sense—but in disregarding it and preferring, or finding it expedient or necessary, to improvise distinctive political roles. Personal leaders do not usually perform the roles assigned to them by the constitution. If they do, it is not unlikely that they have arbitrarily changed the constitution to accommodate their preferred personal roles rather than attempted to draw their roles from the script, which is the way of constitutional government.

In many African countries political improvisation predominates. Some African rulers succeeded in creating for themselves the office of "life president" (Kwame Nkrumah, Kamazu Banda, Idi Amin, Francisco Macias Nguema, and Jean-Bedél Bokassa, who went on to crown himself "emperor"). Is it an exaggeration to suggest, as one writer has, that President Mobutu Sese Seko of Zaire has succeeded in becoming a de facto "king"?[23] Successful African rulers are those who have created an elevated political role for themselves which is acknowledged (if not always appreciated) by other leaders and the wider audience, for example, Leopold Senghor, Félix Houphouët-Boigny, Sékou Touré, Jomo Kenyatta, Julius Nyerere, Ahmadou Ahidjo, Omar Bongo, and Gaafar Numeiri. Not only are these political actors self-taught, but also their roles are self-made. In most cases it is still unclear whether their personally tailored roles will become distinctive offices (defined by a "constitutional script") that are widely regarded as legitimate and can be occupied by succeeding politicians. In a few cases there are signs of such a development, as for example in the 1978 succession of Daniel arap Moi to the presidency of Kenya on the death of Kenyatta. However, for every successful political improviser in African politics there has been an unsuccessful one, usually a novice on the political stage. Some of these political amateurs, but by no means all, have been soldiers who gained power by armed force but could not hold it owing to limited political skill.

Commanding the Ship of State

The metaphor of the ruler as commander of the ship of state is as old as political philosophy and as new as cybernetics.[24] Historically and etymologically, the predominant idea in this metaphor is government as the art of the steersman.[25] In addition to the idea of steering (and navigation), the metaphor evokes an image of seamanship: a ruler is responsible not only for guiding government toward its goals, but also for keeping it afloat, steady, and on an even keel.[26]

Of these two images the first seems to us to be far more prominent and influential at present. In the Third World and certainly in Africa a predominant idea is the rationalist concept of governing as promoting, planning, guiding, managing, and coordinating the activities, not only of government agencies, but also of diverse social and economic organizations so as to move a country in the direction of greater national prosperity and welfare. It is the central idea of the planning and administrative state and of the policy sciences that stand behind such a state.[27] There is little doubt in our minds that the concept of governing as an activity of guiding a nation toward preselected, largely socioeconomic goals is the primary standard against which contemporary governments are appraised. The Third World is not different from the First and Second Worlds in understanding government primarily in terms of purpose, enterprise, and management. However, it is very different in imposing on governments with extremely limited resources, capacities, discipline, and authority a task that is comparatively far more burdensome and is unlikely to result in significant progress at least in the short and medium terms.

Personal rule can be explored in terms of the contrasting ideas of political steering and political seamanship. Most African rulers speak—and many endeavor to act—in a manner consistent with the idea of steering and navigation. At least officially government is held to be an instrumental agency of public policy where "the word 'policy' can be taken to refer to the principles that govern action directed towards given ends."[28] The proclamation of national goals and of plans and policies with which to pursue them is central to their political style. The idea of steering is especially characteristic of avowed socialist rulers, such as Nkrumah, Touré, Nyerere, and Modibo Keita. The articulate Nyerere provides excellent examples of the vocabulary of political steering in his speeches and writing. Perhaps this is nowhere more evident than in the first sentence of "The Arusha Declaration," which reads: "The policy of TANU [the Tanganyika African National Union] is to build a socialist state."[29] In a speech to explain the meaning of the declaration to students at the University of Dar es Salaam, Nyerere began by saying that "the Arusha Declaration is a declaration of intent. . . . It states the goal towards which TANU will be leading the people of Tanzania, and it indicates the direction of development."[30]

Lest it be assumed that only socialist rulers use the language of political steering, we hasten to add that most nonsocialist rulers in Africa and elsewhere speak in similar terms. This is the predominant language of late twentieth-century governance, and it is spoken virtually everywhere, regardless of the official ideologies of regimes. It is the idiom of modern liberalism as well as of socialism; Americans are no less fluent in it than are Swedes or Russians. The idea of purpose is independent of the content of a particular purpose: a government is no less purposive if it seeks to promote capitalist development rather than socialist development. Furthermore, this is the technological language of the policy sciences. In a world that understands governments primarily as purposive, problem-solving, progress-creating agencies, merely for a regime to avow a socially valid purpose might garner it some legitimacy. Of course a problem of credibility arises if declarations and resolutions repeatedly fail to be followed by concrete actions and discernible progress. This is the legitimacy problem of modern government, and it is not confined by any means only to African or even Third World governments.[31]

In many Black African countries the concrete practices of governance much more closely approximate the image of political seamanship, however. We find rulers who are not nearly as preoccupied with the problem of going somewhere as with the task of keeping themselves and their regimes afloat: they are trying to survive in a political world of great uncertainty and often turbulence. Many are in danger of capsizing as a result of either poor seamanship or stormy political weather, and many others have gone to the bottom owing to either their own misadventures or the efforts of others. In most African countries the military is feared rather like a hostile submarine is feared by the captain of a merchantman. Unlike their counterparts in constitutional states, a personal ruler who is striving to survive and a rival leader who desires to replace him are not usually afforded institutional protection to complete a term of office or legal guarantees of a chance to compete for the right to rule.

In consequence, African personal rulers are more likely to be old-fashioned, conservative system-maintainers rather than progressive nation-builders. Among the most successful of such rulers are the great survivors of contemporary African politics: Senghor, Touré, Houphouët-Boigny, Kenyatta, Numeiri, Kenneth Kaunda, Mobutu, Ahidjo, Bongo, Banda. Even Nyerere, one of the few African rulers who has earnestly and persistently striven to conduct his government in terms of the modern criteria of political and economic development, is also a survivor. We are inclined to believe that most African regimes appear inadequate probably owing to their rulers' preoccupation with political survival—not an unusual disposition among politicians—which is often purchased at the expense of a concern for socioeconomic development, let alone its realization. But if these regimes are to be appraised, it seems more reasonable to appraise them in terms of the criteria of legitimacy that their practices invoke. These are the criteria not of political navigation but of political seamanship—namely political order, stability, and civility. Although many African governments will be found wanting by such standards as well, unlike the criteria of modern rationalism—which, when applied, leave all but a very few African countries in one large, undifferentiated category of "underdevelopment"—those of political seamanship at least enable us to draw some important distinctions among African personal regimes. For example, they enable us to distinguish the more orderly and civil rule of a Senghor, a Nyerere, or a Kenyatta from the more abusive rule of a Mobutu or a Bokassa—to say nothing of a Macias or an Amin—and, more important, to seek an explanation of such distinctions.

Some Characteristic Practices of Personal Regimes in Sub-Saharan Africa

Largely by utilizing indigenous political-cultural materials readily at hand as well as by accommodating the necessity of pragmatism, many African politicians have improvised a makeshift polity that is not modeled on any design and lacks effective institutions but is characterized by a number of distinctive practices.[32]

By "practices" we mean activities in which political actors are commonly engaged. As such, they are recognized and frequently used ways of pursuing one's power or security goals. It is important and useful to distinguish political "practices" from social "processes": while the former are the activities of political actors, the latter are the operations of a more impersonal social system. It is also necessary to distinguish between "practices" and "institutions": like all practices, those of personal rule are entirely pragmatic and carry no legitimacy or value that is independent of their effective uses, unlike formal political institutions and procedures which are valued not only for what they enable but also for their own sake.

Among the most important practices in personal regimes are conspiracy, factional politics and clientelism, corruption, purges and rehabilitations, and succession maneuvers. We do not regard these as the necessary "functions" of personal political systems, but we do regard them as the kinds of political behavior one might expect in countries in which formal institutions are ineffective. Not all of these practices contribute to political order, stability, and civility; in fact, some of them, such as conspiracy, are harmful to the provision of such political goods. However, taken together, they appear to accurately characterize the kind of politics to which politicians in the great majority of sub-Saharan countries have resorted over the past two decades.

These practices have been widely noted—and often deplored—in the study of contemporary African politics. Indeed, they have been the subjects of considerable commentary, and an already sizable literature deals with some of them, such as coups and corruption. However (as we have noted), as yet there has been little inclination to view them as integral elements of a distinctive type of political system, personal rule. Instead, they have usually been viewed from the rationalist perspective as shortcomings in the endeavor to establish modern social politics and policy government in Black Africa. As indicated, we are inclined to regard such practices as the very essence of political and governmental conduct in most countries south of the Sahara. While it is evident that most contemporary African states have not acquired the rationalist characteristics of social politics and policy government, they nevertheless have become something more than can adequately be described in terms merely of the absence of such characteristics. The political system of personal rule and its distinctive practices are the reality of what they have become.

Before we begin to examine the distinctive political practices of personal rule in Black Africa, it may be appropriate to remind ourselves of the obvious fact that all political systems, and not only systems of personal rule, consist of persons and systems of personal relationships. Political institutions that are effective—that is, those which are not simply unrealized, abstract rules—always give rise to informal relationships and practices that enable them to work: "To each of the legal organs of the state corresponds, more or less exactly, a social system, which consists in effect of persons brought together by legal relationships, existing together in social relationships."[33] Thus the House of Commons is not only a primary political institution of Great Britain but also the "best club in London."[34] In contrast, in contemporary African regimes of personal rule we find informal social systems that have evolved not out of sympathy and loyalty to the formal political institutions but out of indifference or antagonism to them. The personal system has displaced rather than augmented the legal system of rule; where a concern for legality has been displayed, it has always been dependent on the interests of powerful individuals rather than the other way about. (Why this has happened is a question we address briefly in the conclusion.)

Political Conspiracy

Individuals or groups usually resort to conspiratorial politics either when they are deprived of a fair opportunity to compete openly for government positions or when they believe they cannot win by open competition. In contemporary Black African countries both conditions have frequently been present, and coups and plots have emerged as characteristic political practices. By 1983 there had been at least fifty successful coups since the end of colonial rule in twenty-three countries, and many others that were unsuccessful. By definition a coup is an unlawful action, an action in violation of constitutional rules. Similarly, to engage in political plotting is to undertake actions such as scheming and spying aimed at displacing a ruler or leader—or protecting him. There have been widespread reports of plotting in Black Africa, including bogus as well as genuine plots, by rulers as well as by their opponents. Plotting is generally associated with conspiracies against rulers and regimes, but it has been alleged that at least one African despot—Touré of Guinea—has governed "by plot."[35] While it is impossible to know with certainty how widespread such practices have been owing to their secretive nature, there is little doubt that many African politicians have engaged in them.

The relationship of weak political institutions and the prevalence of coups has been given considerable attention by political scientists.[36] The absence of effective institutional restraints is undoubtedly a critical consideration which disposes ambitious individuals or groups with access to power to contemplate and engage in unlawful bids for political control. In contemporary Black Africa, as elsewhere in the Third World, members of the military, or factions within it, have found themselves in a position to contemplate political intervention. During the initial postindependence years, African soldiers were less disposed to intervene, probably owing more to their inexperience and peripheral position in the state than to the strength of political institutions. But with the passing of time and the increasing contravention of constitutional rules by civilian rulers, the self-restraint of soldiers has declined, and their political ambitions have increased. By the second half of the 1960s they had become less hesitant to assert their power. In place of constitutional-democratic government, there appeared contrary expectations and practices in which the checks on powerholders became merely the power of others or personal loyalty to one's supporters. Politically ambitious African soldiers who were lacking in loyalty to the ruler and his regime and who in addition possessed more than sufficient power to take command of the government became disposed to intervene in politics. Once some successful coups had been perpetrated, others were contemplated and attempted. It is perhaps understandable that in such circumstances it was not long before the coup was established as a recognized political practice which was most frequently—but not exclusively—engaged in by soldiers. Today military rulers are as common in sub-Saharan Africa as civilian ones. Indeed, they have been for some time. However, the distinction between military and civilian rule—which has received much attention in African political studies—is probably less important than the fact that *both* soldiers and civilians are attempting to rule without the benefit of effective institutions and that *both* have been victims of coups.

Factional Politics and Clientelism

The politics of faction has been evident in African political life throughout the independence era, especially as political pluralism declined, and political monopoly increased in the years immediately following independence.[37] By "factional politics" we mean jockeying and maneuvering to influence a ruler and to increase one's political advantage or security in a regime, an inherently nonviolent political activity (unlike conspiratorial politics, which may involve violence). By its nature, factionalism tends to be an internal competition for power and position within a group rather than an open contest among groups. Under political monopoly, factionalism is ordinarily the prevalent form of nonviolent politics because open, legitimate political competition based on parties is forbidden. When a factional struggle is transformed into a public, nonviolent contest which is governed by rules of some kind, factions in effect have become parties. To our knowledge this has never happened in contemporary African politics, undoubtedly owing to the fact that open political competition has seldom been permitted. Moreover, a factional struggle may deteriorate into violent conflict and civil warfare; this has happened in Chad, Burundi, post-Amin Uganda, and Ethiopia following the overthrow of Emperor Haile Selassie in 1974.

It is to factional politics (and clientelism) that Senghor is referring in employing the term "politician politics." Ordinarily, the objects—the prizes and spoils—of factional politics are government positions and the patronage they control.[38] The less autocratic and the more diplomatic and tolerant a personal ruler is, the more likely factional politics is a common practice in his regime. Outstanding examples of politics based on faction (and also clientelism) are Senghor's sagacious rule in Senegal (1960–80),

Kenyatta's courtly but stern governance in Kenya (1963–78), William Tolbert's paternalist style in Liberia (1971–80), Numeiri's adroit and resolute rule in Sudan (1969–present), and Kaunda's somewhat self-indulgent and utopian pursuit of socialism in Zambia (1964–present). By comparison, in a few highly autocratic regimes there has tended to be less factional politics because the ruler is sufficiently strong and confident to attempt to dominate the state without sharing power with other leaders if he so desires. Such is definitely the case in Banda's Malawi and Ahidjo's Cameroon; these two rulers have displayed a type of personal regime reminiscent of European absolutism, where the country is virtually the ruler's estate and the government is his personal apparatus to deploy and direct as he wishes without consulting anyone. Thus while factional politics is practiced widely in sub-Saharan Africa, it is by no means practiced everywhere or to the same extent.

Closely related to factionalism in idea and expression is the practice of clientelism. The image of clientelism is one of extensive chains of patron-client ties extending usually from the center of a personal regime, that is, from the ruler to his lieutenants, clients, and other followers, and through them to their followers, and so on. The substance and conditions of such ties can be conceived of as the intermingling of two factors: the resources of patronage (which can be used to satisfy wants and needs and can be allocated by patrons to clients) and personal loyalty (which is an affective relationship that helps to sustain dyadic relations during times of resource scarcity).[39] Clientelism is primarily personal: unlike institutions, individual patron-client linkages are contingent upon the persons in a relationship and ordinarily cannot outlast them. A change of ruler or leader—as a result of a successful coup or assassination plot, for instance—can alter greatly both an existing clientelist pattern and the political fortunes of those entangled in it. When Tom Mboya and Josiah Kariuki, each a "big man" in Kenyan politics, were assassinated (Mboya in 1969 and Kariuki in 1975), the political fortunes not only of personal clients and followers but also of clans and large segments of ethnic communities were adversely affected. Clientelist relations are the outcome of a stratagem of pursuing power and position by securing the support of others in exchange for patronage (or vice versa) in societies in which democratic political organizations and interest groups are weak or nonexistent.

Political Corruption

Unlike clientelism, corruption is an unlawful practice; it is the disregard of the rules and requirements of one's office for the sake of a personal advantage, such as a bribe. While corruption occurs whenever officials accept bribes, corrupt governments can develop only where such practices are widespread and are sustained by social attitudes: it is more difficult and offensive to be corrupt in Sweden than in Italy. Where corruption is widely practiced, it is evidence of the weakness of public institutions and the strength of private appetites and desires as determinants of political and administrative behavior.[40]

Corruption is a widely noted practice in contemporary African states.[41] In addition to the weakness of civil and political institutions, the incidence of corrupt behavior in personal regimes depends greatly on the conduct of those leaders who are in the best position to be corrupt. If a ruler and other prominent leaders strenuously oppose corruption, are able to police it, and refuse to engage in corrupt practices themselves, then it may not be as prevalent. This is clearly the case in Banda's Malawi, where such practices have been kept in check. But if the ruler or other prominent leaders indulge in such practices themselves, then the demonstration effect upon the rest of the country can be profound because such practices can reinforce existing social expectations in which family, friends, associates, clients, clansmen, and tribesmen have a higher claim on a public official's conduct than do government rules and regulations.

In some African countries corruption has been virtually "a way of life," for example in Ghana, Sierra Leone, Liberia, Amin's Uganda, Bokassa's Central African Empire, Nigeria, and Zaire. In these countries the expectation of corruption is probably more difficult for officials to ignore than the institutional regulations which prohibit such practices. Nigeria's pervasive corruption has been viewed as part and parcel of "the present accepted value system of Nigerian society."[42] Nonetheless, it is probably Zaire which enjoys the dubious status of being the most thoroughly corrupt country in sub-Saharan Africa. Corruption is so extensive that observers have virtually had to invent new phrases to describe it; it is termed a "structural fact," and Zaire is referred to as "an extortionist culture" in which bribery is common and has been described as "economic mugging."[43] Probably the most corrupt individual of all is the ruler, Mobutu, who is reputed to be one of the world's richest men and to have amassed an enormous fortune (in the billions of dollars) by personally appropriating or misusing the funds of the Bank of Zaire, the state trading companies, and other government agencies.[44] What Mobutu debases on a vast scale, lesser leaders debase on a diminishing scale from the upper levels of government to the lower ones, where soldiers and minor officials act virtually as if they possess "a license to steal."[45] Zaire is an extreme case of a country where government is personally appropriated by the governors.

Political Purges and Rehabilitations

Like factionalism, purges and rehabilitations are entangled with political monopoly. A purge is an action which expels from an organization members who are accused of disloyalty, disobedience, or excessive independence. If there is but one political organization in a country to which all politicians must belong, the threat or use of expulsion may be a method of controlling them, while offers of rehabilitation may reduce their temptation to conspire against the regime from outside the ruling group. In most African countries the political monopoly is a monopoly not only of power but also of wealth and status; there is no comparable source of privilege outside of politics. Therefore, to be deprived of membership in the ruling monopoly of an African country or to be restored to membership is to have one's life and fortune dramatically altered. For politicians everywhere the political wilderness is a lonely place; for African politicians it is also a misfortune.

With the decline of political pluralism and the rise of political monopoly in sub-Saharan Africa in the past two decades, there has been a corresponding increase in purges and rehabilitations as rulers have endeavored to maintain control of their regimes. Such practices were in evidence in Nkrumah's Ghana soon after his Convention People's Party (CPP) acquired its political monopoly in 1960.[46] In autocratic Malawi these practices have been a jealously guarded prerogative of the ruler, Dr. Banda. Since 1964 he has not hesitated to exercise his prerogative, and during this period there has been a consistent emphasis on the requirement of absolute obedience and devotion of all politicians to the ruler.[47] In a few countries leading politicians have been purged for a lack of expressed ideological fervor, as in Guinea, where Touré has periodically removed notables from his regime on these grounds, and in Congo-Brazzaville, where a "purge commission" with the authority to remove cadres who failed to meet contrived standards of "socialist" behavior was established in 1975.[48]

Succession Maneuvers

The ultimate prize in most regimes is the attainment of rulership. In multi-party democracies the allocation of the prize is determined by rules: the president or prime minister has won his party's nomination and a general election contested with other parties, or he has succeeded to office in accordance with constitutional provisions. In contrast, in personal regimes the struggle of rulers to maintain their position or to pass it on to a designated successor, and the efforts of other leaders to become the ruler or to prevent their rivals from attaining rulership, is a direct struggle of power and skill unmediated by political institutions. Therefore, uncertainty always surrounds the question: "Who shall rule and for how long?" For elites the prospect of succession is likely to be a catastrophic destabilizing political issue because the regime is tied to the ruler. When he loses his ability to rule or passes from the scene, his regime can be jeopardized; a change of ruler might augur a change of regime. "Succession" is the replacement of a ruler who has died, become incapacitated, or resigned; it differs from a change of ruler by election, a termination of office, or a reconstitution of a country after an interlude of unconstitutional rule. In personal regimes succession is an important problem precisely because the rules governing succession—like all constitutional rules in personal regimes—lack legitimacy and therefore the predictable capacity to shape political behavior.

Succession uncertainties have affected politics in some African personal regimes, although perhaps not to the extent that the theory of personal rule would lead us to expect. Furthermore, there have been several, albeit qualified, constitutional successions. The uncertainty of who would succeed Kenyatta and whether the succession would be peaceful or violent affected Kenyan politics for a decade prior to his death in 1978. As it happened, the succession of Vice-President Moi to the presidency was orderly and appeared to comply with constitutional procedures, an indication that Kenyan politics is becoming institutionalized at least in this respect. The succession of Vice-President Tolbert to the Liberian presidency following the death of President William Tubman in 1971 also complied with constitutional provisions. In 1983 there appeared to be a possibility of a constitutional succession in Tanzania, where Nyerere has declared his wish to leave the presidency by 1985, when elections are scheduled. However, if he is still alive and in good health the personal legitimacy of Nyerere himself, rather than the constitutional rules, may be the deciding factor in an orderly succession. Such was the case in Senegal, where Senghor took the step—extremely unusual in African politics—of voluntarily resigning his office on December 31, 1980, and passing it on to his prime minister and protege, Abdou Diouf. The succession had the quality of being orchestrated by Senghor insofar as he had arranged a revision of the constitution in 1976 to make the prime minister, who is appointed by the president, the automatic successor to the presidency.[49] Senghor's example may have been followed by Ahmadou Ahidjo, the autocratic ruler of the Cameroons for more than two decades, who resigned from the presidency in November 1982 and was succeeded by his own nominee, prime minister Paul Biya.[50] Therefore, the Senegalese and Cameroonian successions more nearly correspond to the model of the "dauphin," in which the ruler manipulates constitutional procedures to arrange for a successor of his own choosing, than to the model of a fully institutional succession. The dauphin model was also apparent in Gabon, where ailing President Leon M'Ba created a vice-presidency in 1966, designated its incumbent the rightful successor, and appointed a loyal and capable lieutenant, Bongo, to the post. (Bongo became president in 1967.)

Conditions of Personal Rule

In conclusion, let us explore two questions. First, what conditions appear to be the most important in encouraging and sustaining the practices of personal governance in sub-Saharan Africa? All political systems are provisional; they are all built on sand, not on the rock of Gibraltar. Personal rule is no exception. It is dependent on the inclination and ability of people, particularly politicians, to understand and utilize its practices. Second, since personal rule is the converse of institutional government and since political institutions in the great majority of sub-Saharan countries are present formally as abstract rules but not substantively as effective restraints on political behavior, it is important to ask what conditions discourage the realization of concrete political institutions in these countries and what the prospects are of changing them.

Neither of these questions is easy to answer, and we have the space to offer only some suggestions as to the direction in which we believe answers might be found. It is somewhat easier to conjecture an answer to the first question because the practices of personal rule are essentially pragmatic and can be understood in terms of a rational politician who must operate in a country in which state institutions are merely forms and duties other than those of his office compete with self-interest as a claim to his conduct. In other words, the practices of personal rule are the sort in which a rational politician would engage if he found himself in a world in which the official rules and regulations of the state were not well understood or appreciated and were poorly enforced, and if he knew that others were aware of this and were not likely to conform to the rules in their own conduct. In such circumstances political and administrative conduct would be shaped by a combination of expediency and whatever obligations were owed to family, friends, allies, clansmen, tribesmen, and any other moral community to which an actor belonged. Most African politicians and administrators find themselves in more or less such circumstances.

At the center of any answer to the second question there must be an explanation as to why personal, arbitrary rule has not been widely condemned as political misconduct in sub-Saharan Africa. Why has personal rule not become sufficiently established as misconduct to effectively discourage the kinds of practices that we have reviewed in this essay and to encourage the realization of institutional rules and regulations? These questions are difficult to formulate, let alone answer, but if an answer is to be found, it will probably be connected with the widely acknowledged arbitrariness of most African states and its political and sociological roots.

In political terms, almost every sub-Saharan African state was the successor of a geographically identical, preexisting colonial entity. From the perspective of the European colonial powers a colony was not arbitrary. It was an extension of the sovereignty of the metropole, and its officials were subject to imperial policy and colonial regulations; far from being arbitrary rulers, colonial officials were considered responsible servants. However, from the perspective of subject Africans, colonial government was essentially arbitrary. It was imposed from outside and worked in accordance with alien and unfamiliar rules and regulations, in disregard, often in ignorance, of indigenous institutions. The British in effect acknowledged that colonial rule was arbitrary in their practice of indirect rule, but even indirect rule could not cancel the fundamental political reality that colonialism was essentially the imposition of government by an external, superior power.

The African states were arbitrary entities in sociological terms as well. It is well known that the size and shape of almost every sub-Saharan country was the result of boundaries arbitrarily drawn by colonialists who rarely acknowledged, or were not even aware of, the preexisting boundaries of traditional African societies. (Even if they had been aware of such boundaries, the traditional political systems were usually too small to be viable as separate colonial entities.) Consequently, there were no territory-wide traditional institutions that could be resurrected at independence and used to identify legitimate conduct and condemn misconduct by a state's new rulers. (It must be acknowledged that even if such institutions had existed, most of the new leaders, who were usually intellectuals, would very likely have been as hostile to them as they were to the traditional institutions that existed at the subnational level. However, in some cases such institutions might have been sufficiently strong to command the reluctant compliance of the new rulers.)

Sociologically, most African countries are multiethnic societies with populations that are sharply divided along racial, cultural, linguistic, religious, and similar lines of cleavage. Most are composed of several and some of many different traditional societies, each with distinctive institutions to which members of other traditional societies are not only detached but also disinclined, if not actually opposed. Multiethnic societies are not confined to sub-Saharan Africa, but they appear to be a characteristic of most new states. Roth suggests that

> one of the major reasons for the predominance of personal rulership over legal-rational legislation and administration in the new states seems to lie in a social, cultural, and political homogeneity of such magnitude that a more or less viable complementary and countervailing pluralism of the Western type, with its strong but not exclusive components of universality, does not appear feasible.[51]

Roth sees the divided plural society as an impediment to the realization of modern, rational-legal institutions. But it is no less an impediment to the realization of traditional institutions or any other kind of general political institutions. All institutions that are realized in conduct must rest upon some kind of general understanding and acknowledgment by most of the people who live under them.

The attempts by the colonial authorities—very belated in the case of Belgium and Spain, and scarcely undertaken in the case of Portugal—to introduce modern political institutions as an essential stage of decolonization were not successful owing to the political and sociological impediments we have noted. British parliamentarianism and French republicanism were as alien to most Africans as colonial bureaucracy. Indeed, they were probably more difficult to understand since they are inherently less pragmatic and rational and more exotic and ritualistic in their rules and offices. It is easy for the forms and rites of (for example) parliamentary government to be mistaken for its substance, which is what happened not infrequently in some African countries before the forms too were discarded or fundamentally altered to suit the interests of those in power.

Imported European political institutions had no greater inherent capacity to overcome the centrifugal effects of sub-Saharan Africa's multiethnic societies than did any other institutions. The British were sensitive to this sociological problem, as indicated by their preference both for bicameral legislatures (with upper chambers to give representation to traditional rulers) and for federalism. Nonetheless, the checkered history of federalism in Nigeria, where politicians have striven to make it work, suggests that federalism, like any other national political institution, requires a commitment of the parts for the whole, of the whole for the parts, and of each part for each other part. In no sub-Saharan country to date has federalism proved to be a workable and durable institutional arrangement, although the Nigerians must be given full marks for persevering in efforts to make it a reality and not merely a formality in their political life. In short, the borrowing of institutional forms from abroad—even the most widely admired models—in no way guarantees their substantiation in political conduct.

In regard to changing the conditions that presently encourage personal rule and obstruct the realization of institutional government in sub-Saharan Africa, there seems to be very little prospect, if any, of altering the political and sociological conditions mentioned above, at least in the short and medium terms. Such fundamental change is a long-term historical process. But if institutional development is to occur in the foreseeable future, it will very likely begin at the top and not at the bottom of African political systems. It is not inconceivable—and there is some evidence to support the contention—that rulers and other leading politicians might begin to value the limited security of official tenure more highly than the uncertain possession of personal power and, beyond this, the greater stability and order attainable only under institutional government. Periodic attempts to reconstitutionalize some states which had been ruled by soldiers, as in Ghana (1969 and 1979), Nigeria (1979), and Upper Volta (1978), are evidence. However, wholesale attempts at constitutional engineering hold out less promise of success owing precisely to their very ambitious character: they literally ask leaders and their followers to transform their political attitudes and behavior overnight. Institutionalization in politics is a transformation involving piecemeal social engineering and time.[52]

A less improbable course of political institutionalization in sub-Saharan Africa is the incremental steps taken by some rulers and their associates to find acceptable and workable procedures to organize political competition and to prevent violence and other political evils. Constitutional rules of succession tend to be accepted for preventive reasons: leaders who face the prospect of a succession may fear the threat of uncertainty, dislocation, violence, bloodshed, and other hazards more than they desire the prize of becoming the successor or his associate. This "negative" political rationality, which we usually associate with the political theory of Hobbes, is also evident in electoral institutionalization in sub-Saharan Africa.[53] For example, in Senegal under the prudent and judicious rule of Senghor the one-party system was liberalized in the late 1970s to allow other parties to compete openly with Senghor's party, but only under labels approved by the regime with Senghor's party preempting the most popular "democratic socialist" label. This experiment in "guided" democratization apparently reflected Senghor's conviction that a de facto one-party system—such as had existed from 1963 to 1976 in Senegal, with its numerous and various ethnic and ideological tendencies—invited conspiratorial politics and threatened national stability.[54] But the success of Senegalese liberalization to date probably must be attributed to Senghor and to his successor, President Abdou Diouf, who in 1981 accepted the challenge of governing a multi-party democracy.

Senegal is a fascinating experiment in moving from a party monopoly to a multi-party state and would reward study by political scientists who are interested in political institutionalization. But to date it is unique and has not inspired imitation by other African rulers. A more typical path of electoral development in sub-Saharan Africa is the encouragement of institutionalized competition within a ruling party. Kenya and Tanzania are good examples of this tendency. Kenya is probably the most unrestricted of Africa's one-party democracies, where elections regularly result in a high level of participation and a large turnover of elected politicians. In the November 1979 general election, more than 740 candidates competed for 158 elected parliamentary seats in the national assembly; seventy-two incumbent MPs, including seven ministers and fifteen assistant ministers, were defeated.[55] Similar results have occurred in previous Kenyan elections and also in Tanzanian elections, although the latter are more strictly controlled and do not exhibit the freewheeling character of Kenyan one-party democracy. Neither of these countries has suffered a successful military coup, which reinforces our impression that they have established the beginnings of a democratic tradition during their two decades of independence. The Kenyan experiment is the more impressive of the two, since that country has also experienced a presidential succession following the death of the founding father, Jomo Kenyatta, in 1978. Nyerere has been at the helm since Tanzania's independence in 1961 and lends his personal authority to that country's political procedures. The real test for the Tanzanian experiment will occur after Nyerere exits from the political stage that he has dominated for so long. These experiments in expanded political choice have more recently encouraged others in Zambia, Ivory Coast, Sierra Leone, Malawi, and Gabon. This may indicate that one-party democracy is better suited than multi-party democracy to the personal and communal idioms of African politics.

These African political experiments suggest the following conclusions, one practical and the other theoretical. First, democracy can be promoted by inventive political practitioners as well as by favorable socioeconomic processes, and the former do not necessarily have to wait upon the latter. Statesmen are to political development what entrepreneurs are to economic development. Indeed, they may be more important insofar as political development is less dependent on material resources and consists essentially in appropriate inclinations and conduct. Political development may be within the reach of countries such as those in sub-Saharan Africa, which are as yet too poor in resources to achieve much in the way of substantial economic development. Second, politics can therefore be understood theoretically as a (constructive and destructive) human activity as well as an impersonal process, and can be studied profitably in terms of choice, will, action, opposition, obligation, compulsion, persuasion, possession, and other elements of individual and intersocial volition, that is, in terms of neo-classical political theory.

Notes

1. Only a few recent political science studies have centered upon rulership. Two important general statements are Dankwart A. Rustow, ed., *Philosophers and Kings: Studies in Leadership* (New York: George Braziller, 1970), and W. Howard Wriggins, *The Ruler's Imperative: Strategies for Political Survival in Asia and Africa* (New York: Columbia University Press, 1969). Among the more important African studies are Henry Bretton, *The Rise and Fall of Kwame Nkrumah: A Study of Personal Rule in Africa* (New York: Praeger, 1966); John R. Cartwright, *Political Leadership in Sierra Leone* (Toronto: University of Toronto Press, 1978); Rene Lemarchand, ed., *African*

Kingships in Perspective: Political Change and Modernization in Monarchical Settings (London: Frank Cass & Co., 1977); Christopher Clapham, "Imperial Leadership in Ethiopia," *African Affairs*, 68 (April 1969); and Ali A. Mazrui, "Leadership in Africa: Obote of Uganda," *International Journal*, 25 (Summer 1970), 538–64.

2. This essay attempts to develop the theory of personal rule contained in our study entitled *Personal Rule in Black Africa: Prince, Autocrat, Prophet, Tyrant* (Berkeley: University of California Press, 1982).

3. This is the central theme of Reinhard Bendix's *Kings or People: Power and the Mandate to Rule* (Berkeley: University of California Press, 1980).

4. The contrasting ideas in these variants of contemporary democracy are succinctly set out in C. B. Macpherson, *The Real World of Democracy* (Toronto: Canadian Broadcasting Corporation, 1965).

5. Clifford Geertz, "The Judging of Nations: Some Comments on the Assessment of Regimes in the New States," *European Journal of Sociology*, 18 (1977), 252. While autocracy was not expected to prevail against democracy, it was sometimes recognized as a possibility given the magnitude of the problems of state-building facing African leaders: "The problems of stabilization and modernization that African leaders face are equivalent in magnitude to past crises in the West. It is from this perspective that we must view prospects for democracy in Africa. . . . Many developing countries have had to rely upon autocratic leadership when nascent democratic institutions have been unable to govern effectively." Carl G. Rosberg, Jr., "Democracy and the New African States," in Kenneth Kirkwood, ed., *African Affairs* (London: Chatto & Windus, 1963), No. 2, p. 53.

6. Very influential in the basic change of academic orientation was Gabriel A. Almond and James S. Coleman, eds., *The Politics of the Developing Areas* (Princeton: Princeton University Press, 1960).

7. See Robert M. Price, "Politics and Culture in Contemporary Ghana: The Big Man-Small Boy Syndrome," *Journal of African Studies*, 1 (Summer 1974), 173–204; Richard Sandbrook, "Patrons, Clients, and Factions: New Dimensions of Conflict Analysis in Africa," *Canadian Journal of Political Science*, 5 (March 1972), 104–19; and Rene Lemarchand, "Political Clientelism and Ethnicity in Tropical Africa: Competing Solidarities in Nation-Building," *American Political Science Review*, 66 (March 1972), 68–90.

8. Steven Lukes, *Essays in Social Theory* (New York: Columbia University Press, 1977), p. 29.

9. Bernard Crick, *In Defence of Politics* (Harmondsworth: Penguin Books, 1964), pp. 20–24.

10. This model is captured brilliantly in historical terms by Gianfranco Poggi, *The Development of the Modern State: A Sociological Introduction* (Stanford: Stanford University Press, 1978), chs. 5 and 6.

11. Niccolo Macchiavelli, *The Prince*, trans. by George Bull (Harmondsworth: Penguin Books, 1961).

12. Ibid., p. 102.

13. Robert H. Jackson, "Political Stratification in Tropical Africa," *Canadian Journal of African Studies*, 7 (1973), 381–400.

14. John Rawls, *A Theory of Justice* (Cambridge, Mass.: Harvard University Press, 1971), pp. 55–56.

15. The literature on political clientelism is useful in understanding personal rule, although there is a tendency to emphasize structure at the expense of actors and behavior and therefore to understate the uncertainty, instability, and choice inherent in personal rule. For an outstanding volume of recent essays, see Steffan W. Schmidt, James C. Scott, Carl Landé, and Laura Guasti, eds., *Friends, Followers and Factions: A Reader in Political Clientelism* (Berkeley: University of California Press, 1977); also see a comprehensive review in S. N. Eisenstadt and Louis Romigu, "Patron-Client Relations as a Model of Structuring Social Exchange," *Comparative Studies in Society and History: An International Quarterly,* 22 (January 1980), 42–77.

16. Machiavelli devotes a long discourse to conspiracies in *The Discourses,* ed. by Bernard Crick (Harmondsworth: Penguin Books, 1976), pp. 398–424.

17. See David Collier, ed., *The New Authoritarianism in Latin America* (Princeton: Princeton University Press, 1979), and Guillermo A. O'Donnell, *Modernization and Bureaucratic-Authoritarianism: Studies of South American Politics* (Berkeley: Institute of International Studies, 1973).

18. A tendency toward the making of promises to local electorates has been noted even in socialist Tanzania, where personalism and specifically such practices as patronage, nepotism, and corruption are officially condemned. See Goran Hyden and Colin Leys, "Elections and Politics in Single-Party Systems: The Case of Kenya and Tanzania," *British Journal of Political Science,* 2 (October 1972), 416.

19. F. G. Bailey, *Stragems and Spoils: A Social Anthropology of Politics* (Toronto: Copp Clark Publishing Co., 1969), p. 1.

20. Ibid., p. 3.

21. F. F. Ridley, *The Study of Government: Political Science and Public Administration* (London: George Allen & Unwin, 1975), p. 40.

22. Ibid., p. 41; also see F. F. Ridley, "Political Institutions: The Script Not the Play," *Political Studies,* 23, 243–58.

23. V. S. Naipaul, "A New King for the Congo," *New York Review of Books,* June 16, 1975, pp. 19–25.

24. For the use of the metaphor in a cybernetic approach to governing (i.e., steering and feedback), see Karl W. Deutsch, *The Nerves of Government: Models of Political Communication and Control* (New York: Free Press, 1966), ch. 11.

25. The Greek root of "govern" is *kubernan,* "to steer" *Oxford Dictionary of English Etymology,* ed. by C. T. Onions (Oxford: Clarendon Press, 1976), p. 407.

26. This image is taken from Michael Oakeshott, *Rationalism in Politics and Other Essays* (London: Methuen & Co., 1962), p. 127. In his most recent work it has become one of two dominant images of the modern state in western political thought: that of *universitas,* or a common-purpose, "enterprise association," and that of *societas,* or a non-purposive "civil association." See his *On Human Conduct* (Oxford: Clarendon Press, 1975), pp. 185–326.

27. Fritz Morstein Marx, *The Administrative State* (Chicago: University of Chicago Press, 1957); Daniel Lerner and Harold D. Lasswell, eds., *The Policy Sciences* (Stanford: Stanford University Press, 1965).

28. Richard M. Titmus, *Social Policy: An Introduction* (New York: Pantheon Books, 1974), p. 23. The idea of "policy government" is explored in Robert H. Jackson, *Plural Societies and New States: A Conceptual Analysis,* Research Series No. 30 (Berkeley: Institute of International Studies., 1977), pp. 27–35.

29. Julius K. Nyerere, *Freedom and Socialism/Uhuru na Ujamaa* (Dar es Salaam: Oxford University Press, 1968), p. 231.

30. Ibid., p. 315.

31. See James Cornford, ed., *The Failure of the State* (London: Croom Helm, 1975).

32. For an interesting analysis of the necessity of pragmatism or prudence in politics, see R. L. Nichols and D. M. White, "Politics Proper: On Action and Prudence," *Ethics*, 89 (July 1979), 372–84.

33. W. J. M. Mackenzie, *Politics and Social Science* (Harmondsworth: Penguin Books, 1967), p. 347.

34. Ibid.

35. See Ladipo Adamolekun in *Afriscope*, 5 (March 1975), 45.

36. See especially Samuel P. Huntington, *Political Order in Changing Societies* (New Haven: Yale University Press, 1968), ch. 2; Claude E. Welch, Jr., "Soldier and State in Africa," *Journal of Modern African Studies*, 5 (November 1967), 305–22; and Samuel Decalo, *Coups and Army Rule in Africa: Studies in Military Style* (New Haven: Yale University Press, 1976).

37. See, for example, Donald B. Cruise O'Brien, *Saints and Politicians: Essays in the Organization of a Senegalese Peasant Society* (London: Cambridge University Press, 1975); Jonathan S. Barker, "Political Factionalism in Senegal," *Canadian Journal of African Studies*, 7 (1973), 287–303; J. M. Lee, "Clan Loyalties and Socialist Doctrine in the People's Republic of Congo," *The World Today*, 27 (January 1971), 40–46; Dennis L. Dresang, "Ethnic Politics, Representative Bureaucracy and Development Administration: The Zambian Case," *American Political Science Review*, 68 (December 1974), 1605–17; and Richard Stren, "Factional Politics and Control in Mombasa, 1960–1969," *Canadian Journal of African Studies*, 4 (Winter 1970), 33–56.

38. O'Brien, p. 149.

39. See Carl H. Landé, "The Dyadic Basis of Clientelism," in Schmidt et al., eds., pp. xiii–xxxvii.

40. Huntington, pp. 59–71.

41. For two explanations of the attractions of corruption as a practice, see Opoku Acheampong, "Corruption: A Basis for Security?," *West Africa* (January 5, 1976); and "The Battle of Corruption," ibid. (February 8, 1982). For an excellent case study from which many generalizations can be drawn, see Victor T. Le Vine, *Political Corruption: The Ghana Case* (Stanford: Hoover Institution, 1975).

42. Colin Legum, ed., *Africa Contemporary Record: Annual Survey and Documents, 1971–72* (New York: Africana Publishing Co., 1972), p. B653.

43. Ghislain C. Kabwit, "Zaire; The Roots of the Continuing Crisis," *Journal of Modern African Studies*, 17 (1979), 397.

44. See Crawford Young, "Zaire: The Unending Crisis," *Foreign Affairs*, 57 (Fall 1978), 173; and "Political and Economic Situation in Zaire—Fall 1981," Hearing before the Subcommittee on Africa of the Committee on Foreign Affairs, House of Representatives, September 15, 1981 (Washington, D.C.: U.S. Government Printing Office, 1982), esp. pp. 4–6.

45. Kabwit, "Zaire: The Roots of the Continuing Crisis," p. 399.

46. See David E. Apter, *Ghana in Transition*, 2nd ed. (Princeton: Princeton University Press, 1972), p. 348.

47. See Legum, ed., *Africa Contemporary Record, 1973–74.* pp. B210–11; and ibid., 1974–75, p. B233.

48. See ibid., 1975–76, p. B471.

49. See the account in ibid., 1980–81, pp. B592–93.

50. *Africa Research Bulletin: Political, Social, and Cultural Series,* 19 (December 15, 1982), 6647C–6650B.

51. Guenther Roth, "Personal Rulership, Patrimonialism, Empire-Building in New States," *World Politics,* 20 (January 1968), 203.

52. Huntington, pp. 13–14; and Karl Popper, *The Open Society and Its Enemies,* vol. 1 (Princeton: Princeton University Press, 1967).

53. Thomas Hobbes, *Leviathan,* ed. by Michael Oakeshott (New York: Collier Books, 1962), chs. 13 and 17.

54. See a seminal article by William J. Foltz, "Social Structure and Political Behavior of Senegalese Elites," in Schmidt et al., eds., pp. 242–49.

55. *African Research Bulletin: Political, Social, and Cultural Series,* 16 (December 15, 1979), 5466.

2

Class, State, and Prebendal Politics in Nigeria

Richard A. Joseph

The expulsion of well over a million unregistered aliens from Nigeria in January 1983 abruptly conveyed to world opinion that the country was in the throes of a severe crisis. This action was soon followed by the decision of the Nigerian government to cut the posted price of its crude oil in the hope that the steady decline in export earnings could be halted. These drastic measures, however, should be seen as consequences of a deeper crisis in the political and economic order which can be temporarily palliated, but not resolved, by such sudden initiatives. I shall examine several aspects of this deeper crisis, such as the shift to a mono-mineral export economy, the socio-economic proclivities of the dominant class, the considerable expansion in the state's economic role, and the distinct pattern of competition for access to public resources in all sectors of Nigerian society. The sense of dissatisfaction with the achievements of Nigeria's Second Republic, and the mounting concern about its viability, will be shown to reflect the combined effects of these fundamental problems.

In a statement which is certain to be cited frequently because of its blunt acknowledgement of the unremitting public tensions in Nigeria, Claude Ake exclaimed:

> The crux of the problem is the overpoliticisation of social life . . . We are intoxicated with politics: the premium on political power is so high that we are prone to take the most extreme measures to win and to maintain political power.[1]

Reprinted with permission from the *Journal of Commonwealth and Comparative Politics*, Vol. 21, No. 3, 21–38, published by Frank Cass & Company, Ilford, Essex IG2 7HH, England. © Frank Cass & Co Ltd.

Ake's sharp critique calls to mind the condemnation of W. Arthur Lewis of the destructive winners-take-all politics that swept post-colonial Africa shortly after independence. Ake's strictures also echo the more recent commentary by General Murtala Muhammed, Nigeria's military ruler for seven months in 1975–76, that during the First Republic "winning elections became a life and death struggle which justifies all means—fair or foul".[2]

In this paper I shall put forward an analytical framework which enables me to examine and discuss in a systematic way the major components of Nigeria's political economy and society. The arguments presented will be drawn from a book in progress in which a concerted attempt is being made to explain the dynamics of the Nigerian socio-political system. At times, I shall only be able to sketch my more fully-developed arguments. The point of departure is that the self-destructive tendencies of this system must be thoroughly understood if ways can ever be devised to escape its debilitating cycle of political renewal and decay. The existence of many of these practices in other African countries will enable me to draw on the commentaries of a wide range of writers who have addressed various dimensions of this predicament.

The Nigerian State: Overdeveloped and Underdeveloped

Central to the deepening crisis in Nigeria is the ambivalent nature of state power, inherited from the colonial era, and expanded considerably since independence in ways which have deepened this ambivalence. I use the term "ambivalence" here to cover the range of contradictory features in both the structure of this state power and the uses to which it has been put. Even for scholars who may not wish to adopt the special features of Hamza Alavi's model of the overdeveloped post-colonial state, that model is still of general utility in its portrayal of how countries in the capitalist periphery were bequeathed state apparatuses that could be deemed overdeveloped in relation to the general level of the economy.[3]

The key agencies in the expansion of the state's economic role in Nigeria were the marketing boards of the post-1945 era which Douglas Rimmer has aptly described as instruments "for collectivizing savings".[4] There was a pattern of continuity in practice from the British to the independence governments in the utilisation of these savings to finance a plethora of development agencies. At no time in this process was an appropriate theory formulated setting limits to the increasing role of the state in the country's economy. The use of these resources eventually came to be determined on the basis of persistent political conflicts among individuals, groups, and factions over welfare schemes, fixed capital formation, the recurrent expenditures of governing parties, "development" loans, and the acquisition of state property at derisory prices.[5]

It is necessary to go back to the colonial, and especially the terminal colonial, period to understand the ways in which contemporary African states have continued, rather than created *de novo,* certain statist economic practices.[6] Nigeria, for example, has never known a liberal *laissez-faire* state in economic matters. Such ideological strictures were often left behind in the European metropolis by colonial officers, one of whose main duties was ensuring the economic rentability of the colonial enterprise. As one of Nigeria's foremost economists, Ojetunji Aboyade, put it: "Forced to depend on its own internally-generated resources to finance its administrative needs, the colonial government could not afford just to keep the ring as a passive referee for the capitalist operators."[7] The colonial state therefore adopted an interventionist posture which quickly went beyond the provision of such basic physical and social infrastructures as railways, roads, schools, and hospitals.

As early as the 1920s government-owned cotton ginneries and rice-hulling factories were established. Public collieries, stone quarries, and even saw-milling and furniture factories proliferated during the inter-war years.[8] The real heyday for the establishment of public enterprises came during the 1945–60 period, with the government's commitment to rapid economic development coinciding, as mentioned above, with the accumulation of investible cash surpluses in the agricultural marketing boards.[9] The Nigerian state, at the regional as well as federal levels, therefore pursued the establishment of "directly productive enterprises that were intended to be run as profitable ventures",[10] despite the formal commitment to promoting the development of a private enterprise economy. By the mid-1960s, Aboyade tells us, these public enterprises ranged "from farm organisations to manufacturing, from municipal transport to mining, from housing to multi-purpose power, and from trading to banking and insurance".[11]

The period of military rule was characterised by considerable expansion of the economic role of the state. Tom Forrest has demonstrated the extent of the increase in number, kind, and operating budgets of Nigerian state corporations during the 1970s.[12] He estimates that federal expenditures, which accounted for 12 per cent of GDP in 1966, amounted to 36 per cent in 1977. These figures closely correlate with Pius Okigbo's calculations of 9.2 per cent in 1962 and 39 per cent in 1974.[13] With the proliferation of more investment corporations at the federal and state levels to match the buoyant oil revenues after the civil war, public industrial investment in Nigeria came to exceed private investment, both domestic and foreign.[14] By 1975, Forrest estimates that the Nigerian state owned 38 per cent of the total equity in large-scale industry.[15] Yet, instead of this massive expansion of the public sector yielding a socialised economy along Fabian lines, as desired by Aboyade, or a state capitalist system in which public authorities exercised greater autonomy, the conclusion of leading students of these developments is that the vulnerability and fragility of the Nigerian state increased *pari passu* with the expansion of its economic activities. By "vulnerability" is meant the degree to which individuals and private concerns were able to block, alter, or circumvent state policies to suit their own interests.[16]

The vast expansion of Nigeria's oil economy during the 1970s, and the gradual nationalisation of this industry, had major consequences for the country's political and economic life that will be felt throughout the present decade. Between 1970 and 1977, federal revenues jumped almost ten-fold, from ₦756 millions to ₦7,070.[17] During that period, total government expenditures multiplied to keep pace with the swelling treasury, with current spending increasing from ₦774 millions to ₦3,574 and outlays for capital formation from ₦99 millions to a sum nearly fifty times greater at ₦4,913. By the time the military leader, General Olusegun Obasanjo, called a halt to this spiralling disbursement of national revenue in 1978, it was virtually too late: a new class of Nigerian entrepreneurs—disparagingly termed "drone capitalists" by Akeredolu-Ale—had consolidated itself in both the public and the (nominally) private sectors.[18] Of particular importance to our analysis is the recognition that when the state itself becomes the key distributor of financial resources—and this in the absence of any socialist or even state capitalist ideology—all governmental projects become the object of intense pressures to convert them into means of individual and group accumulation.[19]

Several points can be drawn from this discussion. Access to the Nigerian state, from the colonial period to the present, has become increasingly central to the social struggle for control of scarce (and occasionally abundant) resources. One can speak paradoxically of the overdeveloped as well as underdeveloped nature of the Nigerian state by drawing attention to the ways in which the "softness", "corruption", and "indiscipline" which characterise the daily conduct of public affairs is fostered by the emergence of the state as the central focus or vortex of the struggle for advancement at all levels and from all sections of Nigerian society.[20] Procedural rules governing the conduct of state business become fig leaves behind which a range of informal mechanisms and strategies are employed to achieve access to the public till or to procure valuable licences to import, build, borrow, or exchange. We do not mean to assert the uniqueness of Nigeria or other African countries in the avoidance or evasion of formal governmental procedures. We are merely affirming the priority, or even decisiveness, of such approaches and their detrimental effect on the functioning of the swollen state apparatus.

At this point in analyses of Nigerian political society interpreters veer sharply in differing directions. Few are likely to dispute Ake's linking of the highly conflictual nature of Nigerian politics to the great expansion of the public sector:

> As things stand now, the Nigerian state appears to intervene everywhere and to own virtually everything including access to status and wealth. Inevitably a desperate struggle to win control of state power ensues since this control means for all practical purposes being all powerful and owning everything. Politics becomes warfare, a matter of life or death.[21]

Yet the factors which are either stressed or played down to explain these statist and political outcomes vary greatly among commentators. In the ensuing sections I shall outline my understanding of the societal matrix in Nigeria and show how it sustains a debilitating set of political attitudes and practices. My main aim is to help advance the formulation of new and appropriate theoretical frameworks at a critical juncture in the history of the most populous African nation.

Class Formation: Fragmentary and Diffuse

That a Nigerian bourgeoisie has emerged during the course of the past half-century, and that it has expanded greatly in size in recent decades, should be a matter beyond much dispute.[22] Available evidence regarding property ownership, access to public resources via party channels, institutional entrenchment in chambers of commerce, governmental corporations and supervisory agencies, and the partial but insightful evidence from investigatory commissions demonstrate the variety of avenues which have facilitated private accumulation in Nigeria and the collaboration among members of this bourgeoisie to further their mutual interests.[23] If we were to go on from such a statement, however, and analyse what is assumed to be class politics in Nigeria, we would be making a jump that is not fully warranted. Dennis Austin's distinction between the existence of a political class, and the absence of class politics in Ghana, has some relevance to Nigeria.[24] There is a need to explain a similar distinction between the obvious features of class action in Nigeria, and the absence of a "clear development of class-based politics", as has been noted by a significant number of students of that country.[25]

In discussing the emergence of a dominant class in Nigeria, and its further consolidation during the military era, Forrest outlines the many ways in which the oil-boom and the expansion of the state sector provided conditions favourable for the private accumulation of wealth. He and other writers emphasise the ways in which the indigenisation programme of the 1970s enhanced "the accumulation and concentration of wealth amongst the bureaucratic, professional and intermediate classes".[26] Yet the very context of that accumulation, which includes multinational penetration and manipulation of an essentially *rentier* state, militates against the "growing coherence of bourgeois interests" that Forrest also claims to recognise.[27] There is a contradiction that must be recognised between a system whose investible capital is diverted into discretionary consumption and real estate speculation and one which can be said to reflect "the growing coherence of bourgeois interests". Indeed, if the latter process were taking place, Nigeria would be far better able politically and economically to withstand the steady drop in state revenues since the final years of the Obasanjo regime. As Bala Usman contended, Nigeria would suffer if its fate were entrusted to the country's bourgeoisie after 1979 because the latter's rapacious economic activities impelled it to fragment and abuse state power.[28] The commentaries which now inundate the press, Nigerian and international, clearly reflect the correctness of such predictions:

> The self-styled businessmen and women, forwarding and backwarding agents, general contractors and Mr. Fix-alls, have seized upon the state of corruption "in high places" to perpetrate even more heinous crimes against the nation.[29]

The general point is that a class whose formation, and sustenance, has become closely tied to the privatising of public resources is a class which is doubly at risk. First, the relative ease of appropriation via state agencies militates against the establishment of a strong independent economic base outside the public sector. Forrest and Biersteker do not fully agree on this point. Biersteker sees much of the privatised wealth being squandered or diverted into non-productive activities, while Forrest points to the expansion of distributive trades, of local assemblage of consumer goods, and of a perceptible shift to manufacture in some sectors (i.e., Kano).[30] Second, the masking of a certain amount of private consumption as government consumption means that the reduction of state budgetary allocations since 1979 has constricted what had been the prime channels of class accumulation. The reduction of these available funds will render the privatisation of public wealth more socially unacceptable as the squeeze is felt throughout the economy. The shrinkage of the economy thus accentuates the problem of class formation in Nigeria which, according to several scholars, has produced a bourgeoisie which is profoundly deficient.[31] "Drone capitalists" may be able to fatten themselves on oil-generated wealth, to paraphrase Akeredolu-Ale;[32] their consumerist and compradorial proclivities, however, will prevent them from shifting to really productive activities as long as sufficient oil income can be siphoned off.

Thus a serious dilemma of Nigeria's Second Republic derives from the fact that its operative principle is the accession to positions of state power by bourgeois and aspirant bourgeois elements who are often quite adept at milking the very source which they are historically expected to strengthen and fructify. Under civilian government, according to Enukora Joe Okoli, there is such a general acquiescence to bribery that "one could even say . . . it has gained official recognition".[33] Even President Shehu Shagari, after having approved ₦200 million in supplementary allocations to the state governments so they could meet the overdue salaries of their employees, was moved to comment acidly that a number of these governments "were still in default because the money they received had changed hands".[34] Thus, while one can definitely agree that a Nigerian bourgeoisie exists, it is equally true that this class has an economic orientation and a set of priorities that render it fundamentally incapable of ruling without squeezing dry the arteries of the state itself.

Ethnicity and Clientelism

An understanding of the vertical dimensions of political and social mobilisation in Nigeria can help explain why the dominant class in Nigeria is unable to rule effectively, even in its own interests. To undertake such an analysis, I must shift emphasis from the assumed causal primacy of class action and consider the determining character of conflicts which are conducted on a sectional basis. One of the greatest stumbling blocks in the analysis of contemporary African politics has been the zero-sum debate between class and ethnic models of social conflict. Scholars have for too long felt it necessary to adopt primarily one or the other. For a while Richard Sklar's explanation of the contribution of class formation to ethnic mobilisation was a satisfactory way of combining the two.[35] On the basis of the common experiences of many African countries, it is clear that such an analysis must now be broadened to include other dynamics.

Ethnicity, to use the language of Abner Cohen, has become "one type of political grouping within the framework of the modern state".[36] Such a grouping is called into being as a result of the keen struggle ". . . over new strategic positions within the structure of the new state".[37] There now exist a number of cogent discussions of the capacity of ethnic groups to serve as functional or interest groups in their own right.[38] Anyone who has to deal directly with the ways in which Nigerians, and other Africans, at all levels of the social hierarchy seek to mobilise or evoke sectional identities— whether of ethnicity, locality, or religion—in pursuit of the most basic goods and services would find it difficult to maintain that such identities are solely a reflection and instrument of bourgeois class formation.[39]

For authors to uphold claims for the class nature of Nigerian politics and state policy, it is often necessary for them to play down the importance of these vertical networks. Such a tendency can be seen in Forrest's contention:

> A class alliance has formed between foreign capital and bureaucratic and managerial elements of the bourgeoisie. These class forces may be weakened and obscured by sectional and distributional conflicts, but it is they, in the absence of any independent industrial bourgeoisie, which largely determine the character, effectiveness and limits of state policy.[40]

In our formulation, "sectional and distributional conflicts" will be seen as doing much more than just weakening and obscuring the action of class forces.

A number of recent studies can be cited to demonstrate what this author regards as an unnecessary polarisation in the analysis of class and ethnicity in Africa. Larry Diamond, for example, is unable to free himself from the viewpoint that ethnicity is essentially a consequence of bourgeois class formation, and that the former will give way to the latter commensurate with increasing "contradictions between classes".[41] Goran Hyden, on the other hand, goes to the opposite extreme, rendering the African bourgeoisie as captives of communal groups which are generated, not from the former's class action, but rather from various social and affective networks which coalesce to offer political support in exchange for social welfare benefits.[42] In general Hyden is correct in emphasising the significant input from the popular masses in sustaining the sectional pattern of socio-political conflicts in Africa. I also agree with him on the need to develop appropriate language for discussing the ways in which ethnicity forms "an integral part of Africa's contemporary political economy".[43] Indeed, the following discussion addresses that need to a certain extent.

Deeply imprinted in western scholarship is the expectation that affective identities eventually give way to more "functional" ones. In the case of tropical Africa, we can now strongly assert that in the struggle for survival and advancement such identities also take on a functional, instrumental and interest-based cast. Moreover, the advantages offered by ethnic groups in "combining interest with an affective tie" can hardly be matched by other organisational forms.[44] David Parkin calls attention to the adaptation of kinship to serve "as an excellent medium" for communicating and insulating political messages "from observation by other ethnic groups",[45] and Crawford Young provides a general overview that captures this new understanding:

> The rapid growth of cities creates social arenas where competition for survival is intense, and where the consciousness of other groups locked in combat for the same resources deepens.
> The importance of scarcity of resources and competition for status in the crystallisation of contemporary identities can hardly be overstated.[46]

Yet a recognition that the affective nature of ethnic ties can co-exist, and indeed enhance, their functional and instrumental capacities, must be buttressed by the recognition that an even more fundamental and pervasive mechanism is at work in sustaining them, namely that of clientelism. The grid of Nigerian political society is an intricate and expanding network of patron-client ties, which serve to link communities in a pyramidal manner. At the summit of such networks can be found individual office-holders in the federal and state capitals. Haroun Adamu vividly captures the clientelistic norms of political and economic life:

> A young businessman, whose contact with various groups in the state is tops, would like to know from me whether those in authority over there in Lagos are aware that they in Bauchi have no representation in the Federal Government.
> "What do you mean?" I asked.
> "It is that simple", he said, "we have no one in the Supreme Military Council; we have no one in the National Council of State and we have no one in the Federal Executive Council".
> "Would the state have fared any better if you had anyone in those bodies?" I countered.
> "Sure. When I come to Lagos on business, I do not have anyone to go to with my problems to help me solve them. That's the difference".[47]

Clientelistic networks also link individuals at different levels within public and private institutions. Central to these relationships is the exchange of various kinds of patronage for assistance, support, and loyalty. The "mercenary" nature of such ties need not contradict the shared ethnic identity between patron and client where they exist.[48] Indeed, as Robert Bates aptly put it, "the language of relationships" and "the sense of obligation" are themselves broadened to reflect the widening circles of "kinship" necessitated by the pursuit of jobs, permits, and finance.[49]

Analyses of Nigerian politics must take into account the spatial as well as vertical dimensions of what can be termed ethno-clientelism. The basic dyadic (two-person) relationship that reflects patron-client ties can operate among persons who share, as well as those who do not share, a common ethnic or other communal identity.[50] Moreover, clientelistic relations have served in Africa to reinforce and even promote ethnic clustering as individuals provide the conduit for the transmission of resources from their own patrons downwards while ensuring in exchange the support of a reliable constituency. Therefore, ethnic communities complement the former regions and now federal states of Nigeria as informal constituencies of the nation.

I do not need to emphasise the determining force of "territory and community rather than class and occupation" as Henry Bienen suggests, because my model acknowledges a non-contradictory interplay between class formation and ethnic conflict via the mediating mechanism of clientelism.[51] Without such an understanding, one cannot grasp the ways in which the disproportionate access to goods and services between individuals of high and low socio-economic status are legitimised in Nigerian society. Nigerian writers are adept at portraying this subtle commingling of individual procurement with communal advancement, as in the remarks of Honourable Nanga in Chinua Achebe's novel, *A Man of the People:*

> I think you are wasting your talent here. I want you to come to the capital and take up a strategic post in the civil service. We shouldn't leave everything to the highland tribes. My secretary is from there; our people must press for their fair share of the national cake.[52]

Too much academic writing on Africa today is weakened because of the reluctance of scholars to grapple with the pervasive normative expectations, shared by bourgeois, *petit bourgeois*, and plebeian alike, that the struggle for a share of public goods will be conducted and assessed along ethnic and other sectional lines.[53] Such expectations, and the actions they foster, do not preclude egoistic appropriations by individuals or mutual exchanges among members of the dominant class.

Clientelism, and more broadly ethno-clientelism, provide the linkages between village and provincial or state capitals in Africa. Despite the apparent sharp discontinuities in economic benefits and life-styles between those at the centre and the periphery of the statist distributional system, the former can be shown to be linked to the latter through a pyramiding "of ethno-clientelistic networks".[54] A political broker or entrepreneur in Nigeria stands—or struggles to stand—at the apex of one of these pyramids. Consequently, much of Nigerian party formation has consisted of a fierce competition to recruit the men and women whose affiliation can mean the inclusion of a community of followers varying from a handful of villages to the block vote of an ethno-linguistic group.[55]

This basic pattern seems to be a notable feature of party politics during the Second Republic. Larry Diamond tells of the jockeying for positions and power since 1979 via the formation of sectional caucuses within parties.[56] He describes the NPN, as I did during its formative stage, as "a loose coalition of many diverse ethnic groups"[57] and points to the new options enjoyed by minority groups to barter their political affiliations.[58] These practices reflect the strategic brokering role that can be fulfilled by federal, state, and local politicians on behalf of vertically mobilised groups. Individual personalities in Nigeria play a commanding political role. The struggle by a variety of political groups in 1978–79 to win the affiliation of Dr Nnamdi Azikiwe was done in the full knowledge that he would bring with him the greater majority of Igbo voters. The same can be said of a variety of other "political patrons", such as Joseph Tarka of the Tiv. Ethno-clientelism, reflecting the fundamental behaviour pattern in Nigerian social life of individuals seeking out their kinfolk for patronage or support, must be part of any satisfactory analysis of wider political and economic activities.

The Theory of Prebendal Politics

There is a certain logic to Nigerian political behaviour and to the fashioning of formal and informal political alliances, although this behaviour inevitably contributes to a serious crisis in the legitimacy and effectiveness of governmental authorities. I have adopted, and then elaborated, the notion of prebendal politics to refer to this prevalent pattern of socio-political behaviour, and its attendant norms, whose features are now familiar to many students of contemporary Nigeria.

The term prebend or prebendal is little used in contemporary social science analysis. Its first general application was made by Max Weber, as the following account indicates:

> . . . prebend was originally an ecclesiastical term signifying the stipend drawn from land granted to a canon from a cathedral estate. Weber used this to mean "allowances in kind" or "right to use of land in return for services" where these allowances or rights are not granted on hereditary principles.[59]

In general historical usage, therefore, the term prebend refers to offices of feudal states which could be obtained through services rendered to a lord or monarch, or through outright purchase by supplicants and then administered to generate income for their possessors. Max Weber discussed both prebends and a prebendal organisation of office.[60]

In my adaptation of this concept to Nigerian politics, as well as many other peripheral capitalist nations, the term prebendal refers to patterns of political behaviour which reflect as their justifying principle that the offices of the existing state may be competed for and then utilised for the personal benefit of office-holders as well as that of their reference or support group. To a significant extent, the "state" in such a context is perceived as a congeries of offices susceptible to individual *cum* communal appropriation. The statutory purposes of such offices become a matter of secondary concern however much that purpose might have been codified in law or other regulations or even periodically cited during competitions to fill them.

Many former as well as contemporary students of Nigeria have made the fundamental observations which are embraced by my terminology, although no attempt has previously been made to carry such observations to the level of a general theory of the country's politics and society.[61] Robert Cohen contributed a relevant assessment of Nigeria's First Republic:

> . . . behind the liberal facade of formal political institutions and debate lay a series of vicious struggles over the allocation and distribution of political of-

fices, the award of contracts, positions in the corporations and state boards, and the distribution of social and economic benefits.[62]

Such an interpretation is carried forward by Williams and Turner when they describe Nigerian politics as being essentially "the process of gaining control of public resources for private ends". The term "private" here is immediately and appropriately broadened to "private/communal": "The competition for access to resources in Nigeria has taken place predominantly between ethnically-defined constituencies. These constituencies were not simply given, but are defined in the process of political competition itself".[63] Douglas Rimmer comes the closest among contemporary students of Nigeria to my understanding of what I now consider to be a qualitatively unique form of statist and clientelist political behaviour:

> Either directly or through the medium of the parties, men in authority benefitted their supporters and home communities by provisions of amenities, misappropriations of funds, and nepotism in appointments. They received fealty and delivered largesse.[64]
>
> . . . public economic power and patronage were valued mainly as instruments of distribution . . . Appointments to public office (particularly ministerial and in the public corporations) were therefore decisive, and the dominant purpose of electoral activity was to control such preferment.[65]

What the theory of prebendal politics brings to the study of Nigeria, and that of other countries to which it will be seen to apply, is a framework for understanding the mutually reinforcing nature of several dimensions of political, social, and economic behaviour which are often discussed singly or in sub-sets but rarely as parts of a new system of power in the context of peripheral capitalism. Moreover, such a system can be seen to be eventually self-destructive. The numerous parallels between the outcome of Nigerian electoral politics since 1979 and those experienced in the 1950s and 1960s evoke the well-founded fear that it will suffer the same ultimate fate.[66]

The centrality of the Nigerian state in the distribution of desired goods and services renders it a kind of "market", to use Terisa Turner's expression.[67] Competition for such benefits, we would contend, reflects a combination of individualistic, class, and communal motivations. Some writers distinguish egoistic from solidaristic graft, others prefer to use the language of class accumulation.[68] For me, all three axes of social action are evident, although the mal-distribution of state-derived resources tends to be legitimised in terms of the conflicts between ethnic or geographic sections of the population.

The politics of competition over the allocation of resources, or what in Nigeria is called "the national cake", has as its most dire consequence the transformation of the offices of the state into prebends. The higher (in political terms) the office, the larger its budget, the wider its array of jobs, the greater its control of permits and contracts—these are the factors which determine the fierceness of the competition for such an office. The intensity of political conflict in Nigeria, which most commentators regard as the greatest threat to its constitutional democracy, can now be more fully understood in terms of prebendal attitudes to governmental office.

Since Nigeria has changed in recent decades from civilian to military rule and then back to a competitive civilian political system, it may be asked what implications such changes have for the prebendal nature of political life? Moreover, what about the shift from an agricultural export economy to one predominantly of petroleum export? Finally, what can we learn of the current struggle to evolve a "working democracy" which might avoid the bitter strains of what Ake referred to as the "over-politicisation of social life"? Let us consider each of these questions in terms of prebendalism.

The wide array of policy departures which Nigeria's military regimes were able to undertake—the creation of new states, an indigenisation programme in industry and commerce, the nationalisation of oil production, a land-use decree—reflect the degree to which a military-bureaucratic elite during the 1970s was able to act in an authoritative and often unilateral manner to execute policy and institute reforms. The tendency to assess government appointments and the allocation of public funds along communal lines, however, persisted throughout the period of military rule, and these pressures could be partly contained because of the government's monopolization of collective force and authority.[69] The transition to a constitutional civilian system, and the entrenchment in the 1979 Constitution of the requirement that the country's "federal character" be reflected in all governmental appointments and disbursements, converted what had for long been an informal norm of political competition into a directive principle of state policy.[70]

The shift from agricultural export to that of petroleum contributed to both the multiplication and centralisation of public revenues. The widespread tendency throughout Africa of using "official positions to distribute public resources through unofficial channels", or even to convert "state offices into businesses", reached its apogee in Nigeria as was reflected in the great cement scandal that—along with a host of other cases of misuse of government for private gain—contributed to the downfall of the Gowon regime in 1975.[71] What a study of the gross figures of government expenditure during the military years seems to suggest is that egoistic graft, or private and class accumulation through public channels, took priority over "solidaristic graft" or distribution to ethnic collectivities.[72]

One of the apparent consequences of combined military and bureaucratic rule in the 1970s is that higher state officials, through "triangular relationships" with foreign and domestic businessmen, were able to appropriate public funds in ways which shielded such disbursements from the pressures for distribution to subordinate strata within ethnic constituencies.[73] With the return to competitive party politics after 1978, these constraints to the full flowering of prebendal politics were removed. The winning of elections calls for heavy investment by aspirant candidates and their parties in Nigeria, and the recouping of such investments cannot be done without the simultaneous distribution of public resources to sectional constituencies. At a time of a sharp drop in export earnings, however, the Nigerian treasury cannot satisfy these combined sets of demands. Thus the Nigerian system has entered a prolonged period of crisis since the dominant class elements will not temper their greed to make possible a sufficient downward flow of resources. Demoralisation and anxiety consequently permeate the society.[74]

The dual legitimisation of prebendal politics in Nigeria has been that an individual's sectional support group should obtain tangible benefits from the former's exploitation of his or her public office, and also that a certain pride will be taken by these sectional clients in the magnificence of the patron's life-style. These expectations constitute normative principles of democratic representation—of both sharing in the spoils and vicariously rejoicing in the material success of one's kinsfolk among the elites—which will not be found in political science textbooks. That is prebendal politics when it "works". It cannot, however, work even to such a degree in post-military Nigeria because the civilians were bequeathed a shrinking economy perched on the declining fortunes of petroleum export. The unhappy consequence of this inheritance is that the state will be squeezed beyond the point of financial exhaustion, i.e., into growing international indebtedness; and those who achieve public positions will find themselves violently assailed for their abuse of office while being simultaneously prevailed upon to procure some benefits for their artificially expanded networks of sectional supporters.

The culmination of such a deepening crisis can be seen in fires which are widely believed to have been deliberately started in government buildings to destroy evidence of corruption: the Foreign Ministry in 1981, the headquarters of the Federal Capital Authority in Abuja in 1982, and the 32-story External Telecommunications building in Lagos in 1983.[75] The twisted logic of this social system we have been describing appears to be reaching a fatal and even cruel consummation: offices of the state are dutifully filled via elections or appointments in ways which satisfy constitutional guidelines regarding the federal character of Nigeria. These offices are not, however, merely occupied but rather appropriated for a certain length of time and quickly exploited in a variety of formal and informal ways. However, if it happens that such misconduct is on the verge of being uncovered and publicised, the appropriate course of action is now to put to the torch the entire building housing the offices themselves.

Here we have the worst aspect of a long-standing attitude towards public property in Nigeria forming an inflammatory compound with the worst side of privatisation: "a government office is public, it therefore belongs to no-one"; "it has, through election or appointment become mine, and thus ours"; "we can therefore use it, abuse it, and now even eliminate it, as suits our interests". Most Nigerians, it should be pointed out, deplore and condemn this ruinous cycle of thought and action. They have, however, found no way of escaping its destructive logic, despite the detailed provisions to ensure the accountability of public officials that were written into the 1979 Constitution.

Conclusion

Beyond the many institutional reforms that were incorporated into Nigeria's Second Republic, ways must be found to protect the state-power itself from being prebendalised and then squeezed of its resources to satisfy the unceasing struggle among massed communities and their (self-serving) patrons for access to the public till. Goran Hyden's suggestion is that the state bureaucracy must relinquish control of the market and allow the latter to expand according to its own dymanics.[76] He believes that such a change would facilitate the emergence of a genuine capitalist bourgeoisie because of the lessened need for entrepreneurs to rest in a parasitic way on the state.[77] Such a solution appears less feasible in Nigeria as long as the oil continues to flow and the option remains of siphoning off substantial sums for personal accumulation and consumption.

There also remains the pressing need to break some of the links in the chain that connects the pursuit by individuals of excessive material rewards with the pursuit of more basic goods and amenities by members of their "solidary group". Hyden's suggestion that horizontal linkages among persons will not take precedence over vertical ones unless a vigorous market economy comes to supplant what we, following Turner, would call the state-as-a-market, might sound like a step backward to many ears. But if increasing statism in the context of peripheral capitalism, complicated by mono-mineral export, only fosters the prebendalising of state-power, what other alternative can one suggest? Some would answer "revolutionary socialism", others a new "corrective" military regime. A final group might counsel greater patience in the hope that the current crisis would itself generate a new set of political norms, practices, and party structures and thus preclude the need to divest the state of its acquired "commanding heights" in the economy. Whichever of these options is finally adopted, there should be little doubt that the cost to Nigerians will be high and that the choices to be made by those who exercise public power will require the tapping of new reserves of goodwill, foresight, and probity.

Notes

1. See *West Africa*, 25 May 1981, 1162–3 for excerpts from Ake's address to the annual meeting of the Nigerian Political Science Association.

2. W. Arthur Lewis, *Politics in West Africa* (Toronto and New York, 1965), 65–84. For General Muhammad's remarks, see *Report of the Constitution Drafting Committee Containing the Draft Constitution* (Lagos, 1976), xii.

3. Hamza Alavi, "The State in Post-Colonial Societies—Pakistan and Bangladesh", *New Left Review*, 74 (1972).

4. Douglas Rimmer, "Development in Nigeria: An Overview" in Henry Bienen and V. P. Diejomaoh (eds), *The Political Economy of Income Distribution in Nigeria* (New York and London, 1981), 31.

5. Sayre P. Schatz documents this chaotic pattern of the distribution of state financial resources in *Nigerian Capitalism* (Berkeley and Los Angeles, 1977), 151–250.

6. For relevant remarks concerning the state in Zambia, see Robert H. Bates, "Modernization, Ethnic Competition and the Rationality of Politics in Contemporary Africa" in Donald Rothchild and Victor A. Olorunsola (eds), *State versus Ethnic Claims: African Policy Dilemmas* (Boulder, Colorado, 1983), 158.

7. O. Aboyade, "Nigerian Public Enterprises as an Organizational Dilemma" in Paul Collins (ed), *Administration for Development in Nigeria* (Lagos, 1980), 89.

8. *Ibid.*, 85–6.

9. This period has been well-covered in several works. See, in particular, Gerald K. Helleiner, *Peasant Agriculture, Government and Economic Growth in Nigeria* (Illinois, 1966), and Peter Kilby, *Industrialization in an Open Economy* (Cambridge, 1969).

10. Schatz, *op. cit.*, 5.

11. Aboyade, *op. cit.*, 86.

12. Tom Forrest, "State Capital in Nigeria", Conference on the African Bourgeoisie: The Development of Capitalism in Nigeria, Kenya and the Ivory Coast, Dakar, December 1980, 10. To appear in Paul Lubeck (ed), *The African Bourgeoisie: The Development of Capitalism in Nigeria, Kenya and the Ivory Coast*, forthcoming.

13. *Ibid.*, 8; and P.N.C. Okigbo, "Ideological Perspectives of Public Sector Role in Nigerian Economy" in *Public Sector Role in Nigerian Development*, Proceedings of the Nigerian Economic Society Annual Conference, Lagos, February 1978, 9.

14. Tom Forrest, "Recent Developments in Nigerian Industrialisation" in Martin Fransman (ed), *Industry and Accumulation in Africa* (London, 1982), 335.

15. Forrest, "State Capital in Nigeria", 30.

16. O. Aboyade, "Indigenizing Foreign Enterprises: Some Lessons from the Nigerian Enterprise Promotion Decree", in O. Teriba and M.O. Kayode (eds), *Industrial Development in Nigeria* (Ibadan, 1977) and Tom Biersteker, "Indigenization and the African Bourgeoisie: Dependent Development in an African Context", Conference on the African Bourgeoisie, Dakar, 1980. To appear in Lubeck, *The African Bourgeoisie*.

17. These statistics are drawn from Forrest, "State Capital in Nigeria", p. 9. For an overview of the consequences of the oil boom in Nigeria, see Richard A. Joseph, "Affluence and Underdevelopment: The Nigerian Experience", *Journal of Modern African Studies,* 16 (1978), 221–239.

18. E. O. Akeredolu-Ale, "Some Thoughts on the Indigenisation Process and the Quality of Nigerian Capitalism, in *Nigeria's Indigenisation Policy. Proceedings of the Nigerian Economic Society Symposium* (Ibadan, 1975), 72.

19. The Reports of the Investigation Panels established to probe the actions of public officials after the retirement exercise of 1975–76 provide interesting, though incomplete, accounts of this process of accumulation. These have been published by the Ministry of Information, Lagos, between 1976 and 1978.

20. This general argument is made in strong and sweeping terms for much of post-colonial Africa by Goran Hyden in "Problems and Prospects of State Coherence" in Rothchild and Olorunsola, *State Versus Ethnic Claims,* 67–84.

21. Ake, *op. cit.*

22. See the cited works of Forrest and Biersteker, as well as Ankie Hoogvelt, "Indigenisation and Foreign Capital: Industrialisation in Nigeria", *Review of African Political Economy,* 14 (1979), 36–55; and Segun Osoba, "The Deepening Crisis of the Nigerian Bourgeoisie", *Review of African Political Economy,* 13 (1979), 63–77.

23. For a general study, see Gavin Williams (ed), *Nigeria: Economy and Society* (London, 1976).

24. Dennis Austin, "Introduction" in Dennis Austin and Robin Luckham (eds), *Politicians and Soldiers in Ghana 1966–1972* (London, 1975), 11.

25. See, for example, Henry Bienen, "The Politics of Income Distribution: Institutions, Class, and Ethnicity" in Bienen and Diejomaoh, *op. cit.,* 162.

26. Forrest, "Recent Developments in Nigerian Industrialisation", 337; Biersteker, *op. cit.;* and E.O. Akeredolu-Ale, "Some Thoughts on the Indigenisation Process and the Quality of Nigerian Capitalism", in *Nigeria's Indigenisation Policy,* Proceedings of the Nigerian Economic Society, Ibadan, 1974, 68–76.

27. Forrest, "State Capital in Nigeria", 31.

28. Yusufu Bala Usman, *For the Liberation of Nigeria* (London and Port-of-Spain, 1979), 59–77.

29. Enukora Joe Okoli, "Corruption in High Places", *West Africa,* 24 January 1983, 191.

30. Biersteker, *op. cit.,* 37 and Forrest, "Recent Developments in Nigerian Industrialisation", 339. Further on Kano, see Paul Lubeck, "Labour in Kano since the Petroleum Boom", *Review of African Political Economy,* 13 (1979).

31. Osoba, *op. cit.*

32. E. O. Akeredolu-Ale. *Underdevelopment* (Ibadan, 1975), 75.

33. Okoli, *op. cit.*

34. Lagos Radio Broadcast, 5 April 1983.

35. See, in particular, Richard Sklar, *Nigerian Political Parties: Power in an Emergent African Nation* (Princeton, 1963), and "Political Science and National Integration: A Radical Approach", *Journal of Modern African Studies,* 5 (1967), 6.

36. Abner Cohen, *Two-Dimensional Man: An essay on the anthropology of power and symbolism in complex society* (Berkeley and Los Angeles, 1974), 87.

37. *Ibid.,* 96–7.

38. See for example, David Parkin, *The Cultural Definition of Political Response: Lineal Destiny Among the Luo* (London and New York, 1978); Bates, *op. cit.;* and Elliott P. Skinner, "Competition within Ethnic Systems in Africa" in Leo A. Despres (ed), *Ethnicity and Resource Competition in Plural Societies* (The Hague and Paris, 1975). For a general, cross-national study, see M. Crawford Young, *The Politics of Cultural Pluralism* (Madison, Wisconsin, 1976).

39. For a general essay which emphasises the "situational" dimension of ethnicity, see Nelson Kasfir, "Explaining Ethnic Political Participation", *World Politics,* 31 (1979), 345–364.

40. Forrest, "Recent Developments in Nigerian Industrialisation", 341. Any of a number of other progressive writers could have been cited here. We cite Forrest because of our considerable respect for his painstaking research and careful writing.

41. Larry Diamond, "Social Change and Political Conflict in Nigeria's Second Republic" in I. William Zartman (ed), *The Political Economy of Nigeria* (New York, 1983), 30. In a sweeping and informative article, "Cleavage, Conflict, and Anxiety in the Second Nigerian Republic", *Journal of Modern African Studies,* 20 (1983), 629–68, Diamond explains and analyses the major political events and social dynamics of Nigeria since the transition to civilian rule in 1979. On an appropriate occasion, I shall extend this discussion to show how Diamond's insistence on the contemporary importance of non-ethnic cleavages—class, personalities, ideological, and between "the people and the politicians"—can be reconciled with his acknowledgement that ethnicity still remains the "most basic source of cleavage and conflict" (658).

42. Hyden, *op. cit.,* 70–71.

43. *Ibid.,* 70.

44. Daniel Bell, cited by M. Crawford Young in "Patterns of Social Conflict: State, Class, and Ethnicity", *Daedalus,* 111 (1982), 92.

45. David Parkin, "Congregational and Interpersonal Ideologies in Political Ethnicity" in Abner Cohen (ed), *Urban Ethnicity* (London, 1974), 120.

46. Young, *op. cit.,* 89.

47. Haroun Adamu, writing in the *Sunday Times* (Lagos), June 1977.

48. Richard Sandbrook, "Patrons, Clients and Factions: New Dimensions of Conflict Analysis in Africa", *Canadian Journal of Political Science,* 5 (1972), 111.

49. Bates, *op. cit.,* 160. I do not follow Bates, however, in seeing a need to call the pursuit of "valued goods" in contemporary Africa the pursuit of "modernity" or as part of the process of "modernisation".

50. The literature on political clientelism is now quite extensive. For a collection of relevant papers, see S.N. Eisenstadt and René Lemarchand, *Political Clientelism, Patronage and Development* (Beverly Hills and London, 1981).

51. Bienen, *op. cit.,* 144.

52. (New York, 1969), 11.

53. See, for example, Morris Szeftel's analysis which coincides with ours in several ways, "Political Graft and the Spoils System in Zambia—the State as a Resource in Itself", *Review of African Political Economy,* 24 (1982).

54. See Sandbrook, *op. cit.,* and the many articles on this subject by René Lemarchand, including "Political Clientelism and Ethnicity in Tropical Africa: Competing Solidarities in Nation-Building" in *The American Political Science Re-*

view, 66 (1972). It is important that our awareness of the wide differences in power and resources between the dominant strata and the peasantry (or rural dwellers) do not blind us to the less visible clientelistic (and affective) mechanisms and shared norms regarding distributional conflicts which unite them. Of course, the salience of the latter phenomena will vary among African countries.

55. See Richard Joseph, "Political Parties and Ideology in Nigeria", *Review of African Political Economy*, 13 (1979), and "The Ethnic Trap: Notes on the Nigerian Campaign and Elections (1978–79)", *Issue*, 11 (1981), 17–23.

56. Diamond, "Cleavage, Conflict, and Anxiety", 638.

57. *Ibid.*, 658–9.

58. *Ibid.*, 664.

59. Brian Turner, "Feudalism and Prebendalism" in *For Weber: Essays on the Sociology of Fate* (Boston, London, and Henley, 1981), 208.

60. For the most relevant passages, see Max Weber, "Bureaucracy" in H. H. Gerth and C. Wright Mills (ed and trans), *From Max Weber: Essays in Sociology* (London, 1948), 207; and Talcott Parsons (ed), *Max Weber, The Theory of Social and Economic Organization* (London, 1964), 342–9.

61. The closest approximation is the discussion of Nigeria as a "conglomerate society" and as having a pervasive "system of rewards" by Ken Post and Michael Vickers in their *Structure and Conflict in Nigeria 1960–1966* (London, 1973). This theoretical framework was never widely adopted partly because of certain flaws in its formulation.

62. Robin Cohen, *Labour and Politics in Nigeria* (London, 1974), 28.

63. Gavin Williams and Terisa Turner, "Nigeria" in John Dunn (ed), *West African States: Failure and Promise* (Cambridge, 1978), 133, 134.

64. Rimmer, *op. cit.*, 45.

65. *Ibid.*, 48.

66. The basis of these fears is outlined in Diamond, "Cleavage, Conflict, and Anxiety in the Second Nigerian Republic".

67. Terisa Turner, "Multinational Corporations and the Instability of the Nigerian State", *Review of African Political Economy*, 5 (1976), 63–79.

68. For the former, see Rimmer, *op. cit.* and, for the latter, Forrest, "Recent Developments in Nigerian Industrialisation", 340 and Szeftel, *op. cit.*

69. For a discussion of these pressures, see Habibu A. Sani, "An Ex-Insider's Overview of the Civil Service (1966–1977)", *The Nigerian Journal of Public Affairs*, 6 (1976), 87–9), and Brigadier David M. Jemibewon, *A Combatant in Government* (Ibadan, 1978), 91–2.

70. Sam Egite Oyovbaire in "Structural Change and Political Process in Nigeria", *African Affairs*, 82 (1983), 19, discusses how a constitutional provision to assure distributional equity has become debased in practice: "federal character is federal discrimination". While seeking to provide the best protection against ethnic domination, the drafters of the 1979 Constitution also gave constitutional legitimacy to the subsequent pursuit of governmental benefits by "indigenes" over the claims of those adjudged "non-indigenes" at all levels of the political system.

71. See respectively, Hyden, *op. cit.*, 79; Szeftel, *op. cit.*, 11–12; and, for the cement crisis, Thomas J. Biersteker, *Distortion or Development: Contending Perspectives on the Multinational Corporation* (Cambridge, 1978).

72. See Douglas Rimmer's analysis of the relevant statistics, *op. cit.*, 62–3.

73. Terisa Turner, "The Working of the Nigerian Oil Corporation" in Collins, *Administration for Development in Nigeria*, 124–5.

74. See Diamond's discussion of the widespread disaffection engendered by the excessive corruption and extravagance, and the consequent failure to meet the basic needs of the masses of the people. "Cleavage, Conflict, and Anxiety", 657–8.

75. For a highly comical, yet all too accurate, portrayal of the behaviour of corrupt government officials and their pattern of destructive behaviour when confronted with the threat of discovery, see Femi Osofisan's play, *Who's Afraid of Solarin?* (Ibadan, 1978).

76. Hyden, *op. cit.*, 76–7.

77. *Ibid.*, 77–8. Diamond also concludes on a similar note, although what can be called his prior "class critique" differs strikingly from Hyden's "class defence". Diamond sees the hope of Nigeria's democracy as resting on "the development of a genuinely pluralistic economic structure, one which affords opportunities for upward mobility and accumulation of wealth based on honest initiative and enterprise". "Conflict, Cleavage, and Anxiety", 668. Much fuller discussion and analysis of the dynamic interplay between statism, class formation, and the market in contemporary Africa are clearly required.

3

Patrons, Clients, and Factions: New Dimensions of Conflict Analysis in Africa

Richard Sandbrook

I

While it is undoubtedly true that African political life frequently constitutes an "almost institutionless arena with conflict and disorder as its
most prominent features" and that African régimes face, as a result, a certain "inevitability of instability," we still do not possess a conceptual apparatus capable of fully comprehending these realities.[1] Analysts have
most often sought to come to grips with this political experience by focusing on cleavages between social classes, occupations, generations (in
studies of bureaucracies), and ethnic-regional grouping. But there is another salient political cleavage, seldom systematically explored in studies
of African politics, in which the lines of division do not coincide with
identifiable social categories. I refer to "factional" cleavages. Factionalism
is a form of conflict which, far from uniting people of the same social category (social class, occupation, generation, ethnic group, etc.) in defence
of their *collective* welfare, unites people of *different* social categories with
the aim of advancing the participants' *individual* (usually material) interests. Although the blatantly mercenary basis of factions and their associated patron-client networks makes them an unedifying and even dangerous subject for research, knowledge of their operation, I will argue, is
crucial to an understanding of many conflict situations in African countries.

Reprinted with permission from the *Canadian Journal of Political Science* Vol. 5, No. 1
(March 1972): 104–119.

Most treatments of African politics have explained political conflict in terms of ethnic antagonisms. At an earlier stage of African studies, "tribalism" was usually cited as responsible for turmoil in polyethnic societies. Recently, a more complex view has gained widespread currency: "tribe" is now conceived, not as a primordial loyalty causing political conflict, but as itself a dependent variable, a loyalty or identity which is politicized only under certain specifiable conditions. Conflicts in which people from different tribes are ranged against each other are generally the result of much more than merely cultural differences and traditional hostilities. Rather, solidarity on the basis of cultural-linguistic affinity becomes salient in a situation of competition over the distribution of wealth, power, and jobs in poor countries composed of disparate peoples. A symbiotic relationship emerges between politicians, who wish to advance their own positions, and their "people," who fear political domination and economic exploitation by a culturally distinct group allegedly organized for these ends. A politician thus gains a tribal power base by successfully manipulating the appropriate cultural symbols and by articulating and advancing his people's collective aspirations (which he himself probably helped arouse). This general approach to "tribalism" is, of course, well known by now, having been the subject of a plethora of recent articles.[2]

While the ethnic conflict models are definitely helpful in understanding African political realities, they are often deficient in two respects. First, their emphasis on cleavage between cultural-linguistic groupings tends to underrate the degree of inter-ethnic co-operation evident in many new states. As Donald Rothchild has ably argued, some ethnic conflict models need to be supplemented with a focus on ethnic bargaining, the process by which the constituent ethnic groups in a country are reconciled to continued coexistence.[3] Where integration has to be achieved in the absence of a broad consensus on goals and values, as in Africa, the political authorities must rely on some combination of repression and accommodation to maintain order. However, reliance solely on repression as a long-term policy or in relation to large ethnic groups is unlikely, owing to the paucity of coercive power at the disposal of African régimes. Hence, integration often depends on bargains worked out at the highest political levels, whereby the foremost ethnic leaders are co-opted into the privileged sector while their peoples obtain a fair share of the national economic pie. Mutual self-interest is the one sure basis of inter-ethnic co-operation in a situation of minimal moral consensus. In this environment patron-client ties linking the leaders and sub-leaders of various ethnic groups tend to proliferate. I will return to this point in the concluding section.

A second shortcoming of ethnic conflict models is their inability to explain some forms of *intra*-ethnic conflict.[4] It is clear that, to the extent that intra-tribal cleavages occur along clan or lineage lines, we simply have the politicization of smaller-scale ascriptive ties. Often, however, intra-tribal politics are more complicated than this, in that competing patrons seek clients with their own followings within the same clan or lineage. In this situation, the allied concepts of patron-client network and faction are useful in explaining the mode of conflict. In short, both inter-tribal co-operation and intra-tribal conflict are to some extent explicable in terms of patron-client politics.

A somewhat competing, and less popular, model of political cleavages focuses on social classes as the prime conflict units. Variants of this model have been adopted both by Marxists with an intellectual commitment to class analysis, and by other scholars who have reacted against the more naïve formulations of "tribal" analysis or have desired to introduce a socially critical dimension into their analyses. Richard Sklar, who has written an influential article entitled "Political Science and National Integration—A Radical Approach," apparently would belong in the latter category.[5] His article, though stimulating, illustrates the difficulties encountered in applying class analysis to the understanding of African political life. Sklar argues, in a much quoted passage, that "tribal movements may be created and instigated to action by the new men of power in furtherance of their own special interests which are, time and again, the constitutive interests of emerging social classes. Tribalism then becomes a mask for class privilege."[6] If his rejection of tribalism as an independent explanatory factor is persuasive, his advocacy of class analysis is less so. "An approach in terms of class analysis," he claims, "does not necessarily imply the existence of major class conflict. Class formation would appear to be more significant than class conflict as a form of class action in contemporary Africa. Intra-class conflict is supremely important."[7]

But what kind of class analysis is this? Does it make sense to advocate class analysis and then suggest that, since there is not much discernible class conflict, researchers should instead study class formation, even though *intra*-class conflict is "supremely important"? An obvious question arises: if intra-class conflict is so manifest, what is the evidence of class formation? Moreover, class formation cannot in practice be so neatly separated from class conflict, since a class forms, that is, gains consciousness, precisely through conflict relations with another class or other classes. Social class shapes the attitudes and actions of its members only to the extent that individuals occupying similar economic roles recognize their common interests vis-à-vis an antagonistic grouping.[8] Without this inter-relation of classes, a class represents nothing more than a category imposed by the observer. Finally, Sklar, in emphasizing the high incidence of intra-class conflict, is actually alluding to the prevalence of factionalism in African countries. This factionalism, I will later contend, vitiates class consciousness by linking individuals of different socio-economic strata in a common cause.

A more fruitful approach would begin the class analysis at the base of the social hierarchy rather than at its peak. Concentration on the extension and entrenchment of the privileges of the new men of power frequently diverts attention away from developments in the countryside where, after all, the bulk of the population resides. The neo-colonial class model, as usually conceived, assumes that the rural population will be increasingly impoverished, pushed off the land, or proletarianized.[9] In fact, this may not be the trend in Africa, at least in the short run. As Colin Leys has cogently argued in the case of Kenya, what is developing is a *peasant* society with a rather peripheral modern, capitalist sector and an urban élite which extracts a portion of the economic surplus produced by the peasantry.[10] African peasants, of course, generally exhibit very low "class-ness," since they, like peasants elsewhere, are divided by particularistic loyalties to tribe, clan, and village. The peasantry is therefore not so much a "class" as a "society," a distinctive pattern of social and economic life.[11] The analyst has to understand this distinctive pattern, but he should also assess, on the basis of such indicators as local riots, assaults on government officials, and mass refusals to pay taxes or repay loans, the degree of peasant class consciousness and the potential for class conflict in the future.

One advantage of peasantry as a concept is the advancement of cross-national comparisons between black Africa and other regions of the world. While tribe and tribalism are concepts whose applicability is largely restricted to Africa, the peasantry is a phenomenon which is studied in Southeast Asia, South Asia, Southern Europe, and Latin America. Since studies of the peasantry in these other regions have frequently referred to patron-client networks as a characteristic mode of political organization,[12] we would also expect to discover such structures in African peasant societies too. Before we can proceed further on this point, however, a brief discussion of terminology is necessary.

II

We can begin to unravel the various meanings of such terms as patron-clientship, patronage, and political machine in the social sciences by reference to a trenchant article by Alex Weingrod entitled "Patrons, Patronage and Political Parties."[13] Weingrod contends that social anthropologists and political scientists use the term patronage in very different senses. For the anthropologist, he maintains, patronage (or patron-clientship) refers to a particular kind of inter-personal relationship. It is, first, a relationship that develops between two persons unequal in status, wealth, and influence, the archetype being the relationship between a landowner and a peasant working on his land. Second, the formation and maintenance of the relationship depends upon reciprocity in the exchange of goods and services: the patron offers economic benefits or protection against the exactions of the authorities, while the client reciprocates with more intangible assets, such as demonstrations of esteem, information on the machinations of a patron's enemies, and political support (such as voting for him or joining his faction in some political arena).[14] Finally, patronage, for the anthropologist, is a personal relationship, based on face-to-face contact.

In contrast, the political scientist—according to Weingrod—uses patronage to refer to "the ways in which party politicians distribute public jobs or special favours in exchange for electoral support . . . [and] . . . seek to turn public institutions and public resources to their own ends."[15] Hence, patronage for the political scientist is seen as tied to the electoral interests of a formally organized group, a political party, while the term for the anthropologist refers to a type of dyadic relationship unrelated to the formal system of government.

The sort of political party that Weingrod has in mind in his discussion of the political scientist's use of patronage is often referred to as a political machine. Although the latter term was first used to explain late nineteenth-century electoral politics in the United States, several writers have argued for its usefulness in understanding political life in the very different circumstances of contemporary Africa.[16] This view has been disputed on the grounds that political machines can only arise where mobilizing voters behind particular candidates is essential to control of government, whereas, in tropical Africa, electoral competition is either non-existent or subject to manipulation.[17] The question then is whether the existence of reasonably free elections is the *sine qua non* of machine politics. I think not. Nineteenth-century America was certainly an historically important case of the conditions under which this type of organization can emerge. But machine-like organizations, depending almost exclusively on particularistic, material rewards to maintain or extend political support, can form even in non-electoral systems, though in this case their reach will probably not extend beyond the élite.[18]

There is, however, a second, more substantial, difficulty with the term which, in my view, detracts considerably from its usefulness in the African context. A political machine is a type of formal organization—generally a political party. Yet, personal alliance networks in many underdeveloped countries, far from being restricted within organizational boundaries, characteristically cut across these boundaries to link individuals in different organizational and territorial arenas.[19] In many African countries the governing party became after independence merely one more arena within which members of the élite competed for precedence and political resources. In these circumstances I prefer the term patron-client network to political machine, so that I can then give priority to the personal relationships developed rather than to the existence of an organization called a governing party. I would then consider jobs in the public sector, licences, government contracts, government loans, and development funds as new sorts of political resources available to certain patrons in the government who can use them in forming linkages with clients among the politically relevant strata of the population, linkages which may have little connection with any political party.

A patron-client network is thus an extended series of patron-client relationships (that is, dyadic relationships characterized by unequal status, reciprocity, and personal contact) arranged hierarchically. All linkages eventually lead to the central ego, but few individuals in the hierarchy have any lateral contact with others at the same level. Such informal hierarchies based on personal, self-interested ties are, of course, not unique to the new states but are a generic feature of all régimes, where they exist within bureaucracies ostensibly organized on impersonal and universalistic criteria.[20] However, patron-client networks are generally more prevalent and pervasive where civil societies have not yet been created and where national integration is very low. Where a society's impersonal, legal guarantees of physical security, status, and wealth are relatively weak or nonexistent, individuals often seek personal substitutes by attaching themselves to "big men" capable of providing protection and even advancement. In the words of one writer, a patron-client dyad is a "personal security mechanism."[21] Patron-client ties also flourish where ethnic cleavages are deep but leaders of the various groups must associate together in order to achieve their common purposes. Where there is considerable insulation and separation between the various cultural-linguistic groupings, patrons emerge to bridge the gaps through personal linkages, and to link the periphery to the centre.[22]

Indeed, one of the advantages of studying patron-client networks is the possibility of linking more closely studies of politics at the centre with those of local politics, whether carried out by anthropologists or political scientists. Those studying national politics must usually refer to the local bases of support of national political figures. This will involve discovering which local political leaders the national figure recruits from amongst the competing patrons and brokers. These local patrons will often recruit further subleaders, generally choosing those who can assemble small followings from amongst their kin, occupational colleagues, or associates in a prominent local voluntary association (such as an agricultural co-operative, for example). The latter transactions can only be documented by those carrying out research in a particular locality. It is likely, however, that the pattern discovered by J. R. Pollock in Sierra Leone will hold true in many countries also:

> · The local Patron operates by gaining the support of certain groups of persons within the local area in town and village by promising to represent their

interests and helping them directly in many small ways. He can then use the position thus created to gain the patronage of someone more influential than himself within the Party organization promising him the support of his own clients. This step may be repeated up the scale of influence before it reaches the national politician who is operating on a much wider scale and within a set of issues and conflicts that are often quite different.[23]

Patron-client pyramids often cut across organizational as well as regional boundaries, as political rivals compete for access to new political resources. When powerful political leaders seek to recruit officers in the army, the labour movement, statutory corporations, tribal unions, or co-operative societies, political conflict tends to spill over into these supposedly apolitical bodies. But once we begin to talk about political conflict, we must turn from clientage networks to the closely related concepts of faction and factionalism.

III

Faction—like patronage—is a concept that is frequently used in differing senses by anthropologists and political scientists. The two senses, however, are not incompatible.

Although anthropologists have certainly not been unanimous in their conception of "faction," it has most usually been defined by them as a quasi-group arising out of, and organized for, conflict within a village or other small-scale social unit, the members of the faction being recruited personally by a leader or sub-leaders across caste, class, or kinship lines on the basis of material advantages. Some anthropologists state that followers can be recruited on the basis of ethnic and religious loyalties, personal attachment, and common hostilities, as well as material self-interest. All view factions as political forms in that their aim is to augment a leader's power and prestige within local arenas.[24]

Political scientists, reflecting the different structural context in which they have carried out their research, have generally conceived of factions as conflict units operating within, and struggling for control of, formal organizations—usually, in practice, political parties. Rival ambitions are frequently seen as the foci about which factional alignments arise, though factionalism may have policy or ideological implications. Indeed, factions within a political party dedicated to a well-articulated ideology will necessarily seek to legitimate their existence by reference to an ideological doctrine that they are striving to defend against "deviationists." Most political science writings on the subject agree that, while they are inherently unstable, factions may persist for some time. But the longer they continue in discernible form the more likely they are to attain the status of a corporate group, with an internal division of labour. At this point, a faction has transformed itself into something more permanent, perhaps a "sub-party."[25]

Political scientists, in contrast to anthropologists, thus tend to conceive of faction, as of patronage, in the context of formal organizations. But there is no incompatibility between the two views if one thinks of a faction as a particular kind of conflict unit operating within *political arenas,* rather than within small-scale social entities or organizations, *per se.*[26] A faction may therefore be defined very broadly as a segment of a clientage network organized to compete with a unit or units of similar type within one or more political arenas. It is a coalition of self-interested followers recruited personally by or on behalf of a leader, who is in conflict with another leader or leaders. To the extent that the persons surrounding the leader feel bound to him by such moral ties as friendship, kinship, or ideological commitment, rather than merely by mutual self-interest, they constitute a more stable core or clique.[27]

While a patron-client network constitutes an informal hierarchy, often cutting across both organizational and regional units, a faction is that segment of the network eligible to compete within a particular organizational or territorial arena. Although factionalism at the local level and in strategic organizations is almost never solely a function of conflict at the centre, it can often be usefully interpreted in this larger context. As Richard Stren has remarked about politics in Mombasa, Kenya: "The weakness of party machinery at both local and national levels has given more weight to personal alliances in Kenyan politics. Conflicts at the national level are easily transmitted to local political arenas . . . To be successful locally, ambitious leaders had to have a clear idea of the existing patterns of informal national alliances and had then to calculate their strategies accordingly."[28] In order to increase their prestige and political resources, political leaders at the centre thus often seek to advance their own followers, or to undermine those of their opponents, within certain strategic localities and organizations. In doing so, these politicians exacerbate factionalism at the local level and politicize many supposedly apolitical bodies.

Consider some examples. The army, to the extent that it monopolizes armed force, remains the most crucial organization in the calculations of civilian régimes in tropical Africa. Military coups are, of course, endemic in this part of the third world. And the evidence, though fragmentary, suggests that many coups are partly a consequence of the mode of political competition which precedes them. As Samuel Huntington has written: "The effort to answer the question, 'What characteristics of the military establishment of the new nation facilitate its involvement in domestic politics?' is misdirected because the most important causes of military in-

tervention in politics are not military but political and reflect not the social and organizational characteristics of the military establishment but
the political and institutional structure of society."[29]

Generalizing from experience in the Middle East and North Africa, another writer has concluded that one condition contributing to frequent
military interventions in politics is frequent intervention by politicians
into the army, seeking powerful allies. Factional struggles within civilian
(political) structures "spill over" into the military politicizing the organization and eventually prompting the army or a faction within it to overthrow the civilian government.[30] This has certainly been a pattern in tropical Africa. J. M. Lee, for example, has sought to link the high incidence of
military intervention in this region with the weakness or absence of "civil
order." The actions of politicians are not circumscribed by established
"rules of the game," which a significant proportion of the populace are
committed to uphold. The consequential insecurity of political leaders
prompts them develop their own "clientage systems," in which "leaders
secure places of profit, contracts, or more extensive resources for their followers, who in return demonstrate their support."[31] But the problem with
this mode of political competition is that it is difficult to restrict within
specified boundaries: "Armies and police forces themselves were vulnerable to outside interference. Warring factions could seek support for their
opposing causes within the ranks of the army. Unless elaborate precau-
tions were taken, any leader who wished to further his cause might well
look for support among soldiers and policemen especially if they contained members of his own tribe or region."[32] Since support within the
army may provide a national political leader with a short-cut to power,
this organization sometimes becomes a locus of political conflict which
destroys its cohesion. Such a process in Uganda led the Army Commander (and present military head of the government), General Idi Amin, to
post the following notice on the main gate of his army headquarters: "Out
of bounds to politicians."

Other supposedly apolitical organizations that are sometimes drawn
into political strife include tribal unions, co-operative societies, and trade
unions.[33] These bodies assume considerable political importance in tropical Africa mainly because of their mass memberships and independent
sources of funds. They are, moreover, often led by men with evident political ambitions. Politics, in underdeveloped countries, is the main avenue of upward mobility; yet few, if any, of these countries contain political systems capable of absorbing the large number of politically
ambitious individuals who emerge with the broadening of political participation. However large parliaments, however many county and municipal councillors, party officials, chiefs, district commissioners, etc., there is
a continual pressure from ambitious outsiders to gain political positions.

In this situation such voluntary associations and other organizations (for example, statutory corporations) as do exist are pressed into the role of supplementary structures for the attainment of status, power, and high salaries. Associational leadership provides ambitious individuals with the opportunity to exercise and develop their political skills, to gain publicity and prestige, and perhaps to use the financial and other resources attached to their offices to make their way in politics. Owing to the general absence of vigilant or informed memberships, leaders of organizations such as the ones mentioned above are seldom deterred from exploiting their official positions for personal ends by apprehension of their members' reactions.

One common consequence of this conjunction of weakly institutionalized organizations commanding impressive political resources and an organizational leadership many of whom nurture political ambitions is predictable. Politicians can easily be drawn into, or initiate, leadership rivalries as they seek to extend their own organizational support or eliminate that of their opponents. In either case, political conflict disrupts the activities of voluntary associations by creating or exacerbating factionalism.

This was certainly the pattern in Kenya, the site of my own research, where patron-client networks emanating from the governing élite have penetrated, among other associations, the trade union movement.[34] I found that the reality of trade union life at the top levels is as much factional struggles for union and political power as it is industrial struggles with employers for enhanced terms and conditions of service.

Space does not permit a description of the complex contours of clientelist politics in Kenya beyond a few elliptical assertions. Until his assassination in July 1969, Tom Mboya was one of the main protagonists in factional conflicts within central political arenas. He had originally built his power on the basis of his control of the trade union movement, a control which he had largely retained through clients after he relinquished formal leadership of the Kenya Federation of Labour in 1962. Initially, Mboya's main opponent at the centre was another Luo politician, Oginga Odinga. After Odinga led a breakaway group out of the governing party in 1966, the principal opposition to Mboya in the power struggle shifted to a coalition of Kikuyu and Kalenjin cabinet ministers. President Jomo Kenyatta remained neutral in many of these contests among his lieutenants, though he had intervened in the earlier period against Mboya, before switching, in 1965–6, to back Mboya's coalition of "conservatives" against Odinga's "radicals."[35]

Factionalism at the centre spilled over to create or worsen factionalism in various local political arenas[36] and within various associations—particularly trade unions—as the main contenders sought to extend their patron-client networks throughout the country. Between 1960 and 1970 the

Kenyan union movement was convulsed by five phases of widespread factional conflict, the last four of which were tied to power struggles within the governing party. Why Mboya's political enemies expended so much effort to capture control of the labour movement can only be understood in the light of the resources controlled by union leaders and the use Mboya made of them for political advantage.

In less developed countries, both political leaders and union officials stand to benefit from entering into patron-client relations with each other. Trade union office—particularly in a large union—is highly prized in a country like Kenya where there exist few alternative opportunities to obtain status, power, and comparatively high salaries or allowances. In addition, many union leaders hope to use their unions as a "ladder" (to use the Kenyan colloquial term) to attain political office, where the real rewards lie. To achieve their ambitions, union leaders—or contenders for union office—frequently seek to attach themselves to a nationally prominent politician or his sub-leader within the national trade union federation. Aspiring union leaders expect their patrons to provide them with financial and occasionally personal campaign assistance to maintain or advance their trade union positions. They also expect to receive their share of whatever spoils become available through their patrons' political victories—particularly positions on public boards—and generally bask in the reflected glory of their *samaki wakubwa* (Swahili for "big fish").

What do political leaders stand to gain from acting as patrons to leaders in the national union federation and, through these, with leaders of affiliated unions? First, there has always been a lot of talk in Kenya about the Kenya Federation of Labour (KFL) and its successor, the Central Organization of Trade Unions (Kenya) (COTU), being used as surreptitious transmission belts for foreign funds to certain political leaders. While these allegations are impossible to prove, there is likely some element of truth in them, given the extent to which "Cold War" rivalries had spilled over into Kenyan politics and trade unionism by the mid-1960s. Second, before the right to strike was severely restricted by the Trade Disputes Act, 1965, politicians with influence in the labour movement gained prestige flowing from their supposed capacity to instigate strikes.

Third, it is convenient for cabinet ministers to have followers heading voluntary associations who can be relied upon to deliver public denunciations of rivals within the cabinet. While it is improper for a minister to criticize publicly one of his colleagues, it is sometimes permissible for a leader of the national union federation, for example, to do so. When Mboya reliquished day-to-day leadership of the labour movement in April 1962, in order to become labour minister, he left in command his own nominee. (In fact Mboya's hold on the national union federation was not broken by his political enemies until February 1969.) During the period 1962–9, KFL and COTU officials often launched attacks, directly or by implication, on prominent political leaders. In August 1962, union leaders even publicly denounced Kenyatta for "undemocratic actions" and "irresponsible statements."[37]

Finally, and most significantly, the trade union movement in Kenya represents a polyethnic, territory-wide, organizational network invaluable to any politician seeking to extend his influence throughout the country. There are a variety of appointed positions at the national union federation level, in the headquarters' staff of affiliated unions, and even at the union branch level. To the extent that the actual distribution of power in the labour movement is from the top downwards, rather from the bottom upwards as union constitutions prescribe, the patron at the top can ensure that many appointed and "elected" officials are personally loyal to himself. Since many trade unionists within the head offices and branches of the national union federation and individual trade unions are politically active within their localities, he who controls the labour movement can probably swing the support of a significant proportion of these ambitious and politically skilled individuals. Their active support is an invaluable asset in election campaigns or intra-party contests.

This, then, is the context in which union leaders have involved their unions in political power struggles. These leaders have usually managed to avoid censure or rebuke for entering into patron-client relations with politicians owing to the weakly institutionalized nature of trade unions. Elucidation of this rather cryptic statement will take us beyond the description of factionalism to its explanation and implications, the subject of the following and final section.

IV

Factionalism is a form of conflict over access to wealth, power, and status, frequently with only minor ideological and policy implications, in which members of the conflict units are recruited on the basis of mercenary ties. The study of factionalism *per se* is thus not particularly edifying. There is a danger for the researcher in becoming so fascinated by the intricacies of factional dynamics—by the more ingenious stratagems and the more endearing or outrageous participants—that he may ignore important questions in favour of describing this scheming and manoeuvring. Important questions I take to be those directed to the social, economic, and political conditions and consequences of this mode of political conflict.

One such question, which has already been alluded to, relates to the extent of institutionalization as both a condition and a consequence of pervasive factionalism. An "institution" may be defined as a stable, valued, recurring pattern of behaviour. According to Samuel Huntington, the level of institutionalization of any organization or procedeure can be measured by its adaptability, complexity, autonomy, and coherence.[38] Although there is difficulty in operationalizing these criteria, many underdeveloped countries would have few strong institutions no matter what indicators were used.

Most trade unions in Kenya, for example, have manifested very little complexity, autonomy, or coherence, and have existed for too short a period to demonstrate adaptability. Since the participation of the bulk of union members is limited to the monthly deduction of union dues from their wages, and since few members appear to understand how their unions are supposed to operate, it is hardly surprising that union members do not yet regard these organizations as their own. Consequently, union leaders have been relatively free to use their offices for personal advancement. Their involvement in political struggles has inevitably prompted politicians to intervene in trade union affairs to safeguard their own interests. The result has been that political conflict has increased the instability of union leadership and decreased the organizational autonomy of trade unions. In short, politically inspired factionalism in trade unions has been a consequence of, and a further cause for, their low degree of institutionalization.

It should be emphasized that institutionalization is not a mysterious process which proceeds independently of human volition; it can be promoted by an enlightened leadership. The importance of leadership can be illustrated by contrasting the roles of Presidents Kenyatta and Nyerere within their own countries. In Tanzania, President Nyerere has invested a lot of energy in building political institutions that would permit the orderly operation of the political system even in his absence. His concern for the health of the Tanganyikan African National Union (TANU), the governing party, is epitomized by his decision to leave the prime ministership in 1962 to engage in party organizational activities. Although TANU remains a decentralized and imperfectly bureaucraticized party, it, unlike most others in Africa, retains a real presence at the regional, district, and local levels, and continues to carry out important functions.[39]

Kenyatta, on the other hand, has not sought to institutionalize his personal authority. True, he was faced with a more intractable situation at independence than was Nyerere: the Kenya African National Union (KANU) did not command as widespread popular support as TANU; divisions among cultural-linguistic groups were deeper and more persistent; and powerful "tribal bosses" were a much more prominent feature in Kenya than Tanzania. But, granting all this, it is still the case that Kenyatta has never attempted to formulate and implement an independent role for KANU. As one observer has remarked, "Kenyatta has consistently created an image of himself similar to that of a prince free from the normal bonds of party politics, and who is conscious of the gossip in the city: 'After Kenyatta, who?' By being the centre of attention he has managed to insert his own brand of leadership quite independent of the party he leads."[40] President Kenyatta rules the country through a Provincial Administration composed at the highest levels of officials who are personally loyal to him. Far from seeking to transform clientelism, Kenyatta has elevated it into his *modus operandi* of politics by establishing himself as the "Grand Patron" and "Ultimate Arbiter" of factional conflict, whether in central or local political arenas or within organizations. In this respect he fills a role which closely resembles that ascribed to King Hassan II of Morocco:

> The entire political élite is the field of action for the alliance-building of the king, and he maintains a number of clientele groups of which he is the patron. Although certain segments of the élite identify their interests more closely than others with those of the throne, the king consistently tries to promote the notion that all segments of the élite constitute a large family, subject to political differences, but essentially united in approval of the direct role of the monarchy in politics. If there is any one discernible rule to the game of politics in Morocco whose violation is followed by immediate sanctions, it is this: the person of the king, the monarchical institution, and the powers it has arrogated for itself are in no way to be attacked or criticized directly and in public.[41]

I would argue, furthermore, that Kenyatta's assumption of the role of presidential-monarch is not merely a consequence of his personality and preferences, but is rather a normal adaptation to the realities of a nonegalitarian yet basically classless peasant society.[42] Nyerere is the exception in his leadership style, not Kenyatta—or Houphouet-Boigny, Nkrumah, Mobutu, Banda, and Hassan II, to name a few other leaders who have adopted the presidential-monarch role.

A second question worth examining concerns the implications of clientelist politics for the publicly enunciated goal of "nation-building." Nation-building—whatever the specific content of that term—requires hard work and sacrifice for the collective good. Clientelism, however, both reflects and produces loyalties based on self-interest and material incentives. The frantic competition for new resources breeds nepotism and corruption among the élite—and a corrupted élite is incapable of eliciting sacrifice or even hard work from those further down on the social scale. The problem about corruption is that, "to the extent that the official public morality of a society is more or less systematically subverted, especially if the leadership is involved in it, it becomes useless as a tool for getting things done, and this is expensive in any society where resources are scarce."[43] A nation cannot be built in an atmosphere of widespread cynicism.

An alternative leadership strategy is to seek to suppress the ethic of self-interest by means of, firstly, exemplary selfless behaviour on the part of the political élite and, secondly, a socialist ideology of the collective good. One is of little use without the other. But both together allow the leadership legitimately to employ coercion against those who exhibit an attitude of "enrichissez-vous." There are, of course, a host of difficulties in the way of successfully eliciting support behind a quasi-puritanical ideology. Chief among these are the unintegrated nature of most African countries, widespread poverty which makes bribery so easy, the absence of a revolutionary experience, and concomitant absence of a committed socialist cadre, and subversive activities by foreign powers. All these conditions favour a clientelist mode of politics.

A third question concerns the relationship between national integration and clientelist politics. As indicated in the introductory section, ethnic cooperation in a plural society often depends to a large degree on bargains and compromise worked out at the top of the political structure. These bargains may frequently be contingent on the reciprocity established by means of patron-client ties linking leaders of the various ethnic groups. In addition, clientelist politics aids national integration to the extent that factionalism within a "tribe" throws up competing tribal bosses, who enter into clientage relations with different outsiders. Ethnic cleavages are, in this case, blurred by factional cleavages at the national level. Needless to say, however, if an ethnic group perceives an external threat to its collective interests or existence, it will close ranks, causing external patron-client linkages to be broken off.[44]

A second aspect of the problem of national integration is the relationship between class formation and clientelist politics. Politicians, to succeed, must obviously offer those inducements that are appropriate to the loyalty patterns of their constituents. Machine politicians, who offered personal material benefits and services in exchange for electoral support, flourished in the cities of the United States before occupational and class loyalties had overlaid ethnic divisions. Machine politics became less effective when occupational and class interests emerged in the process of economic growth. Inducements were then more appropriately offered as general legislation than as individual benefits. As workers, for example, begin to appreciate their broad, long-term interests, they increasingly demand legislation that meets these interests in exchange for support, instead of individual rewards.[45]

Most tropical African countries have not yet reached the stage where horizontal loyalties based on class have vitiated the vertical solidarity of tribe or origin. The reasons for the feebleness of class consciousness in Africa have often been enumerated; these include the strengthening of tribal identity owing to the differential impact of modernization among the various cultural-linguistic groupings, the rural orientation of many urban inhabitants, and continued links between urban and rural dwellers.[46] More basically, class conflict is unlikely to emerge in a situation where the relatively underprivileged believe they may one day share in the privileges of the élite, many of whom were yesterday struggling teachers, traders, and trade unionists. The son of a poor farmer often still hopes to obtain a good education and a well-paid job or office, even though his chances of success are rapidly diminishing. At some point there is bound to be a general recognition that the opportunities for upward mobility are minimal. At the moment, however, there is no evidence that the unemployed and other disadvantaged segments of society regard their salvation as dependent upon a transformation of the structure of society and the economy through collective action. Instead, "individual frustrations are expressed through charges of tribalism and corruption, of witchcraft and sorcery. Action lies in developing one's own relationships with influential patrons and in seeking from supernatural agencies protection against evil forces and support in one's aspirations."[47]

Where class consciousness is weak, individuals may thus try to improve their situation by means of individual actions, through the mechanism of patron-clientship. Conversely, clientelist politics, emphasizing vertical, personal linkages, may impede the development of class loyalties. This, at any rate, is the conclusion arrived at by writers studying politics in countries as diverse as India and the Philippines.[48] In Africa this whole subject remains to be studied; we may speculate, however, that, here too, class conflict will be forestalled by the creation of patron-client structures linking the "have-nots" to the "haves."

Notes

1. The first quotation is from Aristide Zolberg, "The Structure of Political Conflict in the New States of Tropical Africa," *American Political Science Review,* LXII, no 1 (1968), 70; the second is the title of an article by J. O'Connell in the *Journal of Modern African Studies,* v, 2 (1967).

2. See especially P. H. Gulliver, "Introduction," in Gulliver, ed., *Tradition and Transition in East Africa: Studies of the Tribal Factor in the Modern Era* (Los Angeles, 1969); Colin Legum, "Tribal Survival in the Modern African Political System," *Journal of Asian and African Studies,* v, nos 1–2 (Jan.–April 1970); A. A. Mazrui, "Violent Contiguity and the Politics of Retribalization in Africa," *Journal of International Affairs,* XXIII, no 1 (1969); and Paul Mercier, "On the Meaning of Tribalism in Black Africa," in Pierre van den Berghe, ed., *Africa: Social Problems of Change and Conflict* (San Francisco, 1965). For a more abstract and complex model of ethnic conflict based on the concept of the "plural society," see the chapters by Leo Kuper and M. G. Smith in their edited volume, *Pluralism in Africa* (Los Angeles, 1969).

3. "Ethnicity and Conflict Resolution," *World Politics,* XXII, no 4 (1970), 602.

4. A point made by James C. Scott in the context of Southeast Asia. See his "Patron-Client Politics and Political Change," paper delivered at the Annual

Meeting of the American Political Science Association, Los Angeles, Sept. 1970, p. 2.

5. Sklar's article appeared in *Journal of Modern African Studies*, v, no 1 (1967), 1–11.

6. *Ibid.*, 6.

7. *Ibid.*, 7.

8. As Marx noted in a discussion of the development of the bourgeoisie during the feudal period, "the separate individuals form a class only in so far as they have to carry on a common battle against another class; otherwise they are on hostile terms with each other as competitors." Karl Marx and Friedrich Engels, *The German Ideology* (New York, 1939), 49. For a persuasive analysis of working-class formation on the basis of a common struggle, see E. P. Thompson, *The Making of the English Working Class* (London, 1964).

9. See Giovanni Arrighi and John Saul, "Nationalism and Revolution in Sub-Saharan Africa," in Ralph Miliband and John Saville, eds., *The Socialist Register, 1969* (London, 1969), 169; Szymon Chodak, "Social Classes in Sub-Saharan Africa," *Africana Bulletin*, IV (1966), 45–6; and Kwame Nkrumah, *Class Struggle in Africa* (New York, 1970), esp. pp. 10–12.

10. "Politics in Kenya: The Development of Peasant Society," *British Journal of Political Science*, I, no 3 (1971).

11. The dual position of the peasantry as a class and as a society is illuminated by Teodor Shanin, "The Peasantry as a Political Factor," *Sociological Review*, XIV, no 1 (1966), 6–10.

12. John Duncan Powell, "Peasant Society and Clientelist Politics," *American Political Science Review*, LXIV (June 1970), 411–12.

13. Weingrod's article appeared in *Comparative Studies in Society and History*, X (July, 1968).

14. Cf. Eric Wolf, "Kinship, Friendship and Patron-Client Relationships in Complex Societies," in Michael Banton, ed., *Social Anthropology of Complex Societies* (London, 1966), 16.

15. Weingrod, "Patrons," 379.

16. See especially A. R. Zolberg, *Creating Political Order: The Party-States of West Africa* (Chicago, 1966), 122–3, and Henry Bienen, "One-Party Systems in Africa," in Samuel Huntington and C. H. Moore, eds., *Authoritarian Politics in Modern Society* (New York, 1970) 115.

17. James C. Scott, "Corruption, Machine Politics and Political Change," *American Political Science Review*, LXII (Dec. 1969), 1143.

18. I am indebted for this point to Professor Colin Leys.

19. This point will be discussed further below.

20. See, for example, Franz Borkenau, "Getting at the Facts behind the Soviet Facade," *Commentary*, XVII (April 1954), 393–400; Carl A. Linden, *Khrushchev and the Soviet Leadership, 1957–64* (Baltimore, 1966); and Sidney I. Ploss, *Conflict and Decision-making in Soviet Russia* (Princeton, 1965).

21. Scott, "Patron-Client Politics," 19.

22. Weingrod, "Patrons," 382, and Scott, *ibid.*, 19.

23. "The Organization of Patronage in the Changing Scale of Society: A Study of a Developing Region in Temne Country," unpublished paper, presented at the University of Western Ontario, May 1971, p. 12.

24. For excellent, critical surveys of the anthropological literature on factionalism, see two currently unpublished articles by Janet Bujra entitled "Factions and Factionalism: A Reappraisal" and "A Comparative Analysis of Factions and Factionalism" (both Nairobi, April 1970). See also Fred Bailey, *Stratagems and Spoils* (Oxford, 1969), 51–2; and R. W. Nicholas, "Factions: A Comparative Analysis," in Michael Banton, ed., *Political Systems and the Distribution of Power* (London, 1965), 27–9.

25. See H. Lasswell, "Faction," *Encyclopedia of the Social Sciences,* ed. E. R. A. Seligman and A. Johnson (New York, 1931), 49; Raphael Zariski, "Party Factions and Comparative Analysis," *Midwest Journal of Political Science,* IV (Feb. 1960), 33–6; S. D. Johnston, "A Comparative Analysis of Intra-Party Factionalism in Israel and Japan," *Western Political Quarterly,* XXI (June 1967), 291; V. O. Key, *Politics, Parties and Pressure Groups,* (5th ed., New York, 1964), 291–5; Carl H. Landé, *Leaders, Factions and Parties: The Structure of Philippine Politics* (Monograph Series no 6, Yale University South-East Asia Studies Program, 1965), 16–25; Joseph Nyomarkay, *Charisma and Factionalism in the Nazi Party* (Minneapolis, 1967), 35; and Paul Brass, *Factional Politics in an Indian State* (Berkeley, 1965), 54–6.

26. A "political arena" is an observable locus of competition for some prize, generally wealth, power, or status. See Bailey, *Stratagems and Spoils,* 86–110.

27. Bailey, for example, uses "core" in this sense. See *ibid.,* 45.

28. "Factional Politics and Central Control in Mombasa, 1960–1969," *Canadian Journal of African Studies,* IV (Winter 1970), 52–3. For similar analyses of the impact of conflicts between national political figures on local factionalism in Murang'a and South Nyanza Districts, Kenya, see Geoff Lamb, "Politics and Administration in Murang'a District, Kenya," unpublished D PHIL dissertation, University of Sussex, 1970; and W. O. Oyugi, "The Ndhiwa By-Elections," *East Africa Journal,* VII (Oct. 1970), esp. pp. 4–6.

29. *Political Order in Changing Societies* (New Haven and London, 1968), 194.

30. Amos Perlmutter, "The Praetorian State and the Praetorian Army," *Comparative Politics,* I (April 1969), 390. See also P. B. Springer, "Disunity and Disorder: Factional Politics in the Argentine Military," in Henry Bienen, ed., *The Military Intervenes* (New York, 1968), 145–68; and J. B. Crowley, "Japanese Army Factionalism in the Early 1930's," *Journal of Asian Studies,* XXI (May 1962), 72–91.

31. Lee, *African Armies and Civil Order* (London, 1969), 56.

32. *Ibid.,* 72.

33. On the interrelation between political conflict and factionalism within agricultural co-operatives, see, for example, Joan Vincent, "Local Co-operatives and Parochial Politics in Uganda," *Journal of Commonwealth Political Studies,* VIII (March 1970), 3–17; and G. B. Lamb, "Coffee, Co-operatives and Politics in Murang'a District, Kenya," unpublished paper, University of Sussex, 1968. The case of trade unions is considered further below.

34. For an extended analysis of this phenomenon, see my article "Patrons, Clients and Unions: The Labour Movement and Political Conflict in Kenya," *Journal of Commonwealth Political Studies,* IX (March 1972).

35. The most comprehensive source on recent Kenyan politics is Cherry Gertzel, *The Politics of Independent Kenya, 1963–1968* (London, 1970).

36. *Ibid.,* 61.

37. See, for example, *East African Standard,* Aug. 20 and 24, 1962.

38. *Political Order in Changing Societies,* 12–24.

39. Henry Bienen, *Tanzania: Party Transformation and Economic Development,* (expanded ed., Princeton, 1970), esp. pp. 449–58.

40. John Okumu, "Charisma and Politics in Kenya," *East Africa Journal,* v (Feb. 1968), 16. See also K. Good, "Kenyatta and the Organization of KANU," *Canadian Journal of African Studies,* II (1968), 132.

41. John Waterbury, *The Commander of the Faithful: The Moroccan Political Elite—A Study in Segmented Politics* (London, 1970), 149.

42. The term "presidential-monarch" has been used by David Apter. See his *The Politics of Modernization* (Chicago, 1965), 307, 410–11. See also A. A. Mazrui, "The Monarchical Tendency in African Political Culture," *British Journal of Sociology,* XVIII, no 3 (1967), 231–50.

43. Colin Leys, "What Is the Problem about Corruption?" *Journal of Modern African Studies,* III no 2 (1965), 228.

44. See Scott, "Patron-Client Politics," 23, where he makes some similar points in the context of Southeast Asia; see also R. Lemarchand's excellent article, "Political Clientelism and Ethnicity: Competing Solidarities in Nation-building," *American Political Science Review,* LXVI (March 1972).

45. Scott, "Corruption, Machine Politics and Political Change," 1146–8.

46. See Basil Davidson, "The Outlook for Africa," in Miliband and Saville, eds., *The Socialist Register, 1966* (New York, 1966), 193–219; S. Andreski, "Emergent Classes," in his *The African Predicament* (London, 1968); Peter Gutkind, "The Poor in Urban Africa," in Warner Bloomberg and H. J. Schmandt, eds., *Power, Poverty and Urban Policy* (New York, 1968), esp. pp. 388–92.

47. P. C. Lloyd, *Africa in Social Change* (Harmondsworth, 1967), 317. Generalizing about the urban poor in the third world, Joan Nelson argues that they seldom engage in collective political action to better their miserable circumstances. Since "the most urgent needs of the poor are intensely individual," they often seek relief or assistance by attaching themselves to better-established individuals or organizations. See her "The Urban Poor: Disruption or Political Integration in Third World Cities?" *World Politics,* XXII, no 3 (1970), esp. p. 406.

48. See Hamza Alavi, "Peasants and Revolution," in Miliband and Saville, eds., *The Socialist Register, 1965* (London, 1965), 274, and Carl Landé, "Networks and Groups in South-east Asia," paper presented to the South-east Asia Development Advisory Group, New York, March 1970, p. 36.

Suggestions for Further Reading

Bayart, Jean-Francois. *The State in Africa: The Politics of the Belly.* London: Longman, 1993.

Bienen, Henry. "Political Parties and Political Machines in Africa." In *The State of the Nations,* ed. Michael F. Lofchie. Berkeley and Los Angeles: University of California Press, 1971.

Callaghy, Thomas. *The State-Society Struggle: Zaire in Comparative Perspective.* New York: Columbia University Press, 1984.

Chabal, Patrick, ed. *Political Domination in Africa*. London: Cambridge University Press, 1986.

Clapham, Christopher. *Third World Politics: An Introduction*. Madison: University of Wisconsin Press, 1985.

Collier, Ruth Berins. *Regimes in Tropical Africa*. Berkeley and Los Angeles: University of California Press, 1982.

Decalo, Samuel. *Coups and Army Rule in Africa*. New Haven: Yale University Press, 1975.

Eisenstadt, S. N., and Rene Lemarchand, eds. *Political Clientelism, Patronage, and Development*. Beverly Hills, Calif.: Sage Publications, 1981.

Ergas, Zaki, ed. *The African State in Transition*. London: Macmillan, 1987.

Evans, Peter, Dietrich Rueschemeyer, and Theda Skocpol, eds. *Bringing the State Back In*. Cambridge: Cambridge University Press, 1985.

Huntington, Samuel P. *Political Order in Changing Societies*. New Haven: Yale University Press, 1968.

Jackson, Robert, and Carl Rosberg, eds. *Personal Rule in Black Africa: Prince, Autocrat, Prophet, Tyrant*. Berkeley and Los Angeles: University of California Press, 1984.

Keller, Edmond J., and Donald Rothchild, eds. *Afro-Marxist Regimes*. Boulder: Lynne Rienner Publishers, 1987.

Krasner, Stephen D. "Approaches to the State: Alternative Conceptions of Historical Dynamics." *Comparative Politics* 16, no. 2 (1984), 223–246.

Migdal, Joel. *Strong Societies and Weak States: State-Society Relations and State Capabilities in the Third World*. Princeton: Princeton University Press, 1988.

Rothchild, Donald, and Naomi Chazan, eds. *The Precarious Balance: State and Society in Africa*. Boulder: Westview Press, 1987.

Zolberg, Aristide. *Creating Political Order: The Party States of West Africa*. Chicago: Rand McNally, 1966.

Part Two

State, Society, and Participation

The strategies of ruling elites and the structures of government form only part of the total fabric of politics. Participation at the grass roots comprises an essential element of governance that complements the actions of the state. The attributes of power and the guiding tensions of political life arise from the interactions of states and their constituent societies. Questions of legitimacy, sovereignty, stability, and distribution are negotiated through myriad associations among governments and citizens. Public welfare is an essential quality of development, and the relative opportunities and resources of popular sectors are integral to evaluating the nature of African polities.

This section considers African political development from a societal perspective, offering a broad perspective on state-society relations. The nature of political legitimacy and participation are common themes, as the authors seek to reconcile the evident vitality of social organization and community life with the weakness of civic bonds in most African countries. The relations between citizens and governments in Africa have been shaped by the colonial experience as well as the ruling strategies of postindependence regimes.

The remote and exploitive character of the colonial state reinforced an aversion among rural societies toward most forms of central authority. In the decades since independence, ambivalent relations between the capital and the hinterland have persisted. Even as they brandish new symbols of legitimacy, nationalist elites have commonly discouraged popular involvement in politics and have discriminated economically against the rural areas. In the cities, a combination of political containment and economic frustration has also served to foster disaffection. Independent African regimes have pursued a range of strategies toward popular constituencies ranging from corporatist regulation to benign neglect, to overt repression. Few countries, however, have developed effective channels for popular expression or representation.

As state capabilities waned in the 1970s and 1980s, the lack of services and basic public functions aggravated popular alienation from many regimes. In many instances, communities and social groups turned to independent networks or associations to meet their basic needs. Sometimes associational life could serve as a vehicle of active protest or political opposition. Often these coping strategies fostered political estrangement and withdrawal from a common civic arena. The diverse forms of participation in different countries significantly influenced patterns of stability and change.

In a widely influential article, Peter Ekeh describes two separate publics in Africa, one civic and one private. This separation originated in the colonial era, as the imperial state lacked any moral link to the affairs of households and localities. One legacy of colonialism has been an implicit ethical distinction between allegiance to the state and observance of communal or familial norms. In consequence, civic loyalties have been fragile in many African political systems.

The effects of authoritarianism and state decline have fostered a retreat from politics in many countries, as communities and social groups seek to limit their contact with government officials and withdraw to the private realm. Victor Azarya and Naomi Chazan observe a range of relations between state and society, and they explain the process of disengagement by citizens in two West African states.

Although channels of formal participation are often limited, a wide array of associations and social networks have nonetheless flourished in many African countries. Some observers have regarded nongovernmental groupings as constituents of a coherent civil society, yet this idea remains controversial in African settings. In the final selection, Peter Lewis discusses the meaning of civil society in comparative perspective, describing the evolution of associational life and participation in Africa.

4

Colonialism and the Two Publics in Africa: A Theoretical Statement

Peter P. Ekeh

This paper argues that the experiences of colonialism in Africa have led to the emergence of a unique historical configuration in modern post-colonial Africa: the existence of two publics instead of one public, as in the West. Many of Africa's political problems are due to the dialectical relationships between the two publics. I shall characterize these two publics and attempt to explain some of Africa's political features within the matrix of these publics. In order to give some empirical content to the distinction drawn here, I shall illustrate the issues raised with examples from Nigeria.

The Private Realm, the Public Realm, and Societal Morality

Perhaps the best definition of politics is the oldest one: politics refer to the activities of individuals insofar as they impinge on the public realm made up of the collective interests of the citizenry. As Wolin (1960: 2–3) has pointed out, 'one of the essential qualities of what is political, and one that has powerfully shaped the view of political theorists about their subject-matter, is its relationship to what is "public"'. The distinction between the private realm and the public realm delimits the scope of politics. Not all the everyday activities of an individual are political. To the extent that he acts in his household or practices his religion in his home, he is acting in the private realm. Furthermore, the distinction tells us when changes do take place and may define the characteristics of political regimes. The publicization of the private realm—that is, the conversion of private activities and resources into material for the public realm—is characteristic of absolutist regimes. On the other hand, the privatization of the public realm—that is, the 'sublimation' of politics in which what is traditionally private swallows up the public realm—may well, as Wolin (1960) contends, be a major characteristic of the age of organization.

But the distinction between the public and private realms as used over the centuries has acquired a peculiar Western connotation, which may be identified as follows: the private realm and the public realm have a common *moral* foundation. Generalized morality in society informs both the private realm and the public realm. That is, what is considered morally wrong in the private realm is also considered morally wrong in the public realm. Similarly, what is considered morally right in the private realm is also considered morally right in the public realm. For centuries, generalized Christian beliefs have provided a common moral fountain for the private and the public realms in Western society. There are anomic exceptions, of course. For instance, the strong appeal of Banfield's *The Moral Basis of a Backward Society* is that it provides a striking case of an exception in which the same morality does not govern the private and the public realms. But this is a case where the exception proves the rule. Banfield's (1958) observation of amoral politics in the southern Italian village has drawn so much attention precisely because it violates the Western norm of politics without reproach.

When one moves across Western society to Africa, at least, one sees that the total extension of the Western conception of politics in terms of a monolithic public realm morally bound to the private realm can only be made at conceptual and theoretical peril. There is a private realm in Africa. But this private realm is differentially associated with the public realm in terms of morality. In fact there are two public realms in post-colonial Africa, with different types of moral linkages to the private realm. At one level is the public realm in which primordial groupings, ties, and sentiments influence and determine the individual's public behavior. I shall call this the primordial public because it is closely identified with primordial groupings, sentiments, and activities, which nevertheless impinge on the public interest. *The primordial public is moral and operates on the same moral imperatives as the private realm.* On the other hand, there is a public realm which is historically associated with the colonial administration and which has become identified with popular politics in post-colonial Africa. It is based on civil structures: the military, the civil service, the police, etc. Its chief characteristic is that it has no *moral* linkages with the private realm. I shall call this the civic public. *The civic public in Africa is amoral and lacks the generalized moral imperatives operative in the private realm and in the primordial public.*[1] The most outstanding characteristic of African politics is that the same political actors simultaneously operate in the primordial and the civic publics. The dialectical relationship between the two publics foments the unique political issues that have come to characterize African politics. The two publics are amenable to observation. But they will gain their full meaning in the context of a theory of African politics. Having identified the two publics, there are two lines of theoretical approach that one can attempt. The first is politico-historical: how did this unique political configuration emerge in Africa? The second is sociological: how does the operation of the publics affect African politics? I shall discuss both theories in this paper.

Ideologies of Legitimation and the Emergence of the Two Publics

Modern African politics are in large measure a product of the colonial experience. Pre-colonial political structures were important in determining the response of various traditional political structures to colonial interference. But the colonial experience itself has had a massive impact on modern Africa. It is to the colonial experience that any valid conceptualization of the unique nature of African politics must look.[2]

In fact, we can still narrow the issue and focus on the two critical bourgeois groups that influenced colonial Africa and continue to influence post-colonial African politics. These are the cadre of colonial administrators, mostly drawn from the rising bourgeois class in Europe, and the African bourgeois class born out of the colonial experience itself. It is my contention that the emergence and the structures of the two publics owe their origin first and foremost to these two groups, especially to their ideological formulations intended to legitimate their rule of the ordinary African. This is not to say that the ordinary African had nothing to do with the emergence of the two publics. He was the target of the intellectual workmanship of the two bourgeois groups in their formulation of ideologies.

It is chiefly to emphasize the lack of firm legitimacy on their part that I have used the term 'bourgeois' to characterize these groups. The term connotes the newness of a privileged class which may wield much power, but have little authority; which may have a lot of economic influence, but enjoy little political acceptance. I have not, unlike Hodgkin (1956), preferred the term middle class because it connotes (*a*) that those thus referred to have established value linkages with the other layers of their society, and (*b*) that the class thus referred to occupies a middle layer in a social stratification system. In my view, the European colonial rulers of Africa and their African successors in the post-colonial period do not fit readily into the same social stratification system with other segments of the societies they ruled and now rule. The African bourgeois class especially does not have an upper class, an aristocracy, over and above it, although it does have a defeated traditional aristocracy whose bases of power have been weakened by the importation of foreign techniques of governance. Nor have I used the term African 'elites' because it connotes to me a class of men who enjoy autonomy in the formation of their values and in their decision-making processes, independent of external sources. The emergent ruling class in Africa clearly lacks such autonomy.

Because of the repeated use of the term 'ideologies' in this essay, it would seem fair to the reader to explain as clearly as possible the use of the term, and the context of that use. By 'ideologies' I refer to unconscious distortions or perversions of truth by intellectuals in advancing points of view that favor or benefit the interests of particular groups for which the intellectuals act as spokesmen. That is, ideologies are interest-begotten theories. The invention of aesthetically appealing interest-begotten theories, or ideologies, that detract from scientific truth is, as Werner Stark (1958) has emphasized, different from socially determined thought in which the writer's cultural world view and his more immediate social background condition and define his perception of social reality. It is when bias in favor of an identifiable group is introduced into theories that I refer to them as ideologies. Needless to add, this specialized usage leans on a tradition of the conceptualization of ideology as an abnormal element in social theory construction—so fully expounded by Werner Stark (1958)—rather than on Mannheim's broad view of ideologies as constituting essential elements in social theories.

My view of ideologies does not then imply a Marxist or Paretean assumption of pan-ideologism—that is, the assertion that all ideas and theories in society are biased in favor of either the ruling class or the emerging class. My position does imply that the particular groups that benefit from ideological distortions of truth must be identified in any analysis that claims perversion and abuse of scientific truth. My assumption—that is, the unexamined hypothesis in this analysis—is that ideological distortions and abuse of truth usually indicate a degree of insecurity on the part of the group promoting such ideologies. This is the case with the European bourgeoisie, not only in the eighteenth and nineteenth centuries in Europe, but also in the colonial administration of Africa. A sense of insecurity also dominates the emergent African bourgeoisie.

The European bourgeois class of course has a well known history in domestic European economic and political life. Not so well known is its influence in the European expansion to Africa. Although the history of the 'scramble' for Africa is filled with the names of nobility, the motive force of the expansion must ultimately be traced to the rise of the bourgeoisie in Europe:

The central inner-European event of the imperialist period [between 1884 and 1914 and ending with the scramble for Africa] was the political emancipation of the bourgeoisie, which up to then had been the first class in history to achieve economic preeminence without aspiring to political rule. The bourgeoisie had developed within, and together with the nation-state (Arendt, 1951:123).

Imperialism was born when the ruling class in capitalist production came up against national limitations to its economic expansion. The bourgeois turned to politics out of economic necessity; for if it did not want to give up the capitalist system whose inherent law is constant growth, it had to impose this law upon its home governments and to proclaim expansion to be an ultimate political goal of foreign policy (Arendt, 1951:126).

In large part, the European expansion to, and colonization of, Africa must be seen as a result of the bourgeois attempt to acquire political power, via colonization, that would be commensurate with, and further consolidate, its economic power at home.[3] Arendt (1951:133) was pointing to an important matter in colonization when she remarked that 'The conflict between the representatives of the imperial "factor" [i.e., the home government] and the colonial administrators [largely recruited from the ranks of the bourgeoisie] runs like a red thread through the history of British imperialism.' As Hobson (1902:46) so bitterly complained, 'Although the new Imperialism has been bad business for the nation, it has been good business for certain classes and certain trades within the nation.' The British bourgeoisie, like some other European bourgeois classes, who gained the most from expansion and colonization, attempted to justify such imperial expansion as being beneficial to all the colonizing nations and to every taxpayer in them. I call the theories that emerged from such rationalization and justifications addressed to the taxpayers and citizens of the colonizing nations *imperial ideologies*.[4] Although they constitute an important area that must be examined in any intellectual history of colonialism in Africa, I shall not deal directly with such imperial ideologies in this essay.

The European bourgeois colonizers of Africa were also confronted with formidable problems in their conquest and rule. Although their superior technology plus the fact that African political life had been softened by the slave trade that ravaged the continent in the previous three centuries facilitated their conquest, the successful colonization of Africa was achieved more by the colonizers' ideological justification of their rule than by the sheer brutality of arms. I shall call the ideologies invented by the colonizing Europeans to persuade Africans that colonization was in the interest of Africans *colonial ideologies*. The impact of these colonial ideologies on the emergence of the two publics in Africa is of major concern for me in this essay.

In the course of colonization a new bourgeois class emerged in Africa composed of Africans who acquired Western education in the hands of the colonizers, and their missionary collaborators, and who accordingly were the most exposed to European colonial ideologies of all groups of Africans. In many ways the drama of colonialism is the history of the clash between the European colonizers and this emergent bourgeois class. Although native to Africa, the African bourgeois class depends on colonialism for its legitimacy. It accepts the principles implicit in colonialism but it rejects the foreign personnel that ruled Africa. It claims to be competent enough to rule, but it has no traditional legitimacy. In order to *replace* the colonizers and rule its own people it has invented a number of interest-begotten theories to justify that rule. I shall call the ideologies advanced by this new emergent bourgeois class in Africa *African bourgeois ideologies of legitimation.* Their impact on the development of the two publics in Africa is also of major concern for me in this essay.

Colonial Ideologies of Legitimation

The late nineteenth- and early twentieth-century European colonization of Africa owes a measure of its effectiveness to the ideological justifications of the efforts of the colonizers. The more successful colonizers, particularly the British and the French, attempted to create ideologies that not only backhandedly justified their penetration into Africa but also justified to their fellow countrymen their continuing actions. In addition, and more to our point here, they also tried to persuade Africans to accept European rule as beneficial. These latter attempts aimed at colonized Africans are what I have called *colonial ideologies.* They were wrought jointly by the colonial administrators and their close collaborators in the colonial enterprise, the Christian missionaries.[5] What were the ideologies invoked by the colonizers to legitimate their rule of Africa?

The Backwardness of the African Past.   One of the most successful ideologies used to explain the necessity of colonial rule was the heavy emphasis placed on what was described as a backward ahistorical past. Africans, according to this view, should be ashamed of their past; the only important thing is in the present. Missionaries openly told Africans that ancestor-worship was bad and they should cut themselves loose from their 'evil' past and embrace the present in the new symbolisms of Christianity and Western culture. Indeed, Africans were virtually told that the colonizers and missionaries came to save them, sometimes in spite of themselves, from their past.

The point of emphasis here of course is the ideological distortion of what is after all a partially correct observation, namely that Africa was and is, in many ways, backward. 'Nowhere', Warner Stark (1958:50) once warned, 'are [ideological influences] more dangerous than where they make use of, and abuse, undeniable scientific truths.' That abuse is what is at issue here. It consisted of defaming the African past—including important city-state civilizations—and exaggerating the achievement of the African present. Africans who were 'Western' educated—and they mattered in the colonial situations in Africa—were sharply differentiated from the 'natives' on the principle that the former were those of the 'Europeanized' present and the natives belonged to the backward past.

The Lack of Contributions by Africans to the Building of Africa. A related ideological weapon employed by the colonial administrators in emphasizing the necessity of their rule in Africa consisted of down-grading the contribution by Africans to the building of African nations and to history generally. History is to a large extent the selective emphasis of events from a national point of view. Americans talk a great deal about their relations to England; but it would be a rare American teacher or writer who says that England built or founded the U.S. In colonial, and even in postcolonial, Africa, the emphasis on contributions made by the colonizers to the building of Africa is extravagantly presented in favor of colonialism. The essence of colonial history is the demonstration of the massive importance of the European 'intervention' in Africa and of the 'fact' that African contributions to the building of Africa have relevance only when seen in the context of a wider and more significant contribution of the European colonizers. Every schoolboy in colonial Africa, and many in postcolonial Africa, read in history books that Africa and especially its important landmarks and waterways were 'discovered' by European explorers. The mental outlook here is important. To say that River Niger or Kano was discovered by European explorers is to invite the African to see his own people from the point of view of the European. Many Western educated Africans took this point of view. As Jahoda (1961:115) puts it, the Western educated African 'now comes to look at Africans and African culture to some extent through the eyes of those European educators who determined the manner and content of the teaching he received'.

Again, of course, it enhanced the legitimacy of Europeans to downgrade African contributions to the building of Africa and hence to make the European colonizer a benevolent ruler who graciously filled a void and brought Africa 'into light and history'. The most effective vehicle here is the teaching of colonial history, although the very use of the language of the colonizers as the medium of education has much the same effect of legitimating foreign rule. Mungo Park, an adventurer, becomes a 'discoverer' in colonial history taught in British colonized nations.[6] A rather sensitive African historian once complained that Bishop Ajayi-Crowther's—the first Nigerian bishop's—contribution to the documentation of history was underrepresented: 'Crowther's narrative is an important document on the early stages of the Yoruba Wars of the nineteenth century. It is in fact surprising that while so much has been made of the accounts of the journeys of Clapperton and Lander through western Yoruba, so little attention has been paid to this account of a journey through the central part in 1821–22' (Ajayi, 1967:291). Professor Ajayi would be less surprised if he recognized that history is in large part the selective biography of nations, not an 'objective' interpretation of *all* documents. Certainly colonial history as taught in African schools and universities had a primary purpose: to legitimate the European colonial rule of Africa.

Inter-Tribal Feuds.   Ideological distortions also exist in the characterization of political life in pre-colonial Africa. 'Tribe against tribe' is the common theme in colonial accounts of African struggles. 'Inter-tribal', rather than 'intra-tribal', struggles are given the accent in interpretations of African political strife. It is only recently that African historians like Ajayi (Ajayi and Smith, 1964) and Dike (1956) have pointed to the scope and even the significance of 'intra-tribal' struggles in Africa. By carefully emphasizing 'inter-tribal' disharmonies in pre-colonial Africa, European colonial administrators had two things to gain at once. First, the principle of *divide et impera* was effectively employed to create disharmony between groups in the colonial situation, a strategy especially apparent in the declining days of colonialism in virtually every African nation; second, it gave the colonial administrators the image of benevolent interveners, who came to Africa *because* they wanted to establish order.

Benefits of European Colonial Rule.   The argument that European rule brought benefits is the common justification for the presence of Europeans in Africa, from the Portuguese rape of Angola to the godfather image of the French in the Ivory Coast. But it is significant that little is ever said in the same context about the disadvantages of European colonial and missionary activities in Africa. There are indeed benefits deriving from colonial rule. But it may well be the case that in the long run the crushing psychological and social implications of colonialism have disadvantages that far outweigh the heralded advantages. (It is often unnoticed, for instance, that the only non-Western nations to have successfully modernized—Japan and China—are those that have not been colonized. Is it an accident that all Asian and African nations formerly colonized by Europeans have a uniform history of failure in attempts to modernize?)

The Administrative Cost of Colonization to Europeans.   One of the most pronounced examples of double-talk in colonization (and one suspects here that what was involved was a deliberate lie rather than an unconscious ideological misrepresentation of truth) is with respect to the accounting of the cost, financial and otherwise, of colonization. While the cost was de-emphasized to the 'imperial factor' (i.e., the government) and the taxpayers in the colonizers" home countries, it was clearly exaggerated in the colonial situation. The financial benefits that the colonized nations derived from the colonizing nations were shown to outweigh the wealth that might have been taken out of the colonies. Indeed, colonial accounts were always presented in ways that showed that goods and produce in the colonies were 'bought' at good prices, when in fact the colonial market was monopolistic. On the whole the colonized were led to believe that they gained a great deal, and that they gave very little in return, in the colonial arrangement. As I shall emphasize later, when interpreted in the idiom of this essay, this posture amounts to an undue emphasis on rights and an undue de-emphasis on duties. Indeed, this ideological distortion invariably led to an exaggeration of the riches in Europe in the view of many Africans.

Native vs. Westernized. Standing somewhat apart from the rest, but central to the ideological promotion of the legitimacy of the colonizers in Africa, is the pervasive emphasis on the distinction between 'natives' (that is Africans who have no Western education) and Western educated Africans. Most colonized Africans had the perception of the European as a man blessed with much, who did nothing much more than acquire literary education to earn such luxury. To become a Western educated African in the colonial situation was for many an avenue for escaping hard work. Hard work was meant for the 'natives'. At least it was believed that the European, having acquired an adequate education, could not work with his hands. To send one's son to school was to hope that he would escape the boredom of hard work (cf. Jahoda, 1961:78).

Many of these perceptions of Europeans and of Western education were encouraged by the European colonial administrators and missionaries themselves. They were in part promoted to preserve the aura of charisma which formed the basis of legitimacy for European rule. A supreme strategy of colonial administrators was to separate 'native' from Western institutions and define the 'native' in terms of what is low (cf. Arendt, 1951:131). This condescending distinction between Westernized and 'native' sectors gained maximum expression of course in the doctrine of indirect rule. But the Western educated African did not completely escape the 'native' sector. Indeed his greatest difficulty was, and remains, the simultaneous adaptation to two mentally contraposing orders. One solution to this problem formulated by the educated African is to define one of these orders in *moral* terms and the other in *amoral* terms. The native sector has become a primordial reservoir of *moral* obligations, a public entity which one works to preserve and benefit. The Westernized sector has become an *amoral* civic public from which one seeks to gain, if possible in order to benefit the *moral* primordial public.

African Bourgeois Ideologies of Legitimation

The colonial ideologies have had a major impact on Africans. The absence of a strong traditional ethos, for instance in the form of a pan-African religion, made Africans easy targets of these ideologies. But there was considerable variation in the spread of their effects on Africans. The Western educated African was a greater victim of their intensity than the non-literate African. The acceptance of the colonial ideologies in many ways led to the creation by the African bourgeois class of its own ideologies. The purpose behind the colonial ideologies, wrought by colonial administrators and missionaries, was to legitimate an alien domination of Africans; African bourgeois ideologies were formed to achieve two interrelated goals. First, they were intended to serve as weapons to be used by the African bourgeois class for *replacing* the colonial rulers; second, they were intended to serve as mechanisms for legitimating their hold on their own people. Both types of ideologies were largely directed at the African masses. However, in terms of timing, the first set was used during colonialism and was an attack on alien rulers. I shall call this set *anti-colonial ideologies*. The second set of ideologies is more directly related to the issue of legitimation and is involved in post-colonial politics in Africa. Its appearance coincided with the departure of the alien colonial rulers. I shall call these *post-colonial ideologies of legitimation.*

(1) *Anti-colonial Ideologies*. What I call anti-colonial ideologies here refer to the interest-begotten reasons and strategies of the Western educated African bourgeoisie who sought to *replace* the colonial rulers. Anti-colonialism did not in fact mean opposition to the perceived ideals and principles of Western institutions. On the contrary, a great deal of anti-colonialism was predicated on the manifest acceptance of these ideals and principles, accompanied by the insistence that conformity with them indicated a level of achievement that ought to earn the new educated Africans the right to the leadership of their country. Ultimately, the source of legitimacy for the new African leadership has become alien. Anti-colonialism was against alien colonial personnel but glaringly *pro* foreign ideals and principles.

I shall now discuss some of the ideologies used to justify this form of anti-colonialism:

African High Standards.   In every post-colonial African nation, Western educated Africans, that is the African bourgeoisie, have bent over backwards to show that their standards of education and administration are as good *as* those of their former colonizers. The point of reference in such demonstrations is to prove that they are the 'equals', but never the betters, of their former rulers. At least if they judge their standards of education and administration not to be as high as those prevailing in the capitals of the former colonizing nations, they rue the fact of their 'low' standards and make attempts to raise them. Nowhere does one come across the statement that the prevailing standards, say, in England are not high enough or too high for the problems in, say, Nigeria. These 'high' standards are invariably defined in terms of the prevailing, that is ordinary, standards in the former colonizing nations.

This ideology of African high standards had its origin in the fight for independence. Most African leaders in the fight for independence boasted to their followers that they were as qualified *as* the English or the French colonizers; that their rule could be as 'democratic' *as* that in England or France; that Africans could attain as high a degree of efficiency in bureaucracy *as* that in Britain or France, etc. In his manner of speaking the English language and of pronouncing English words, the Nigerian 'been-to',[7] for instance, wants to demonstrate to the common man that he is as good *as* an Englishman in the use of the English language.

There is logic to these over-zealous attempts by the African bourgeois class to prove the equal, but never the better, of the former colonizers. They are a message addressed to the masses that educated Africans have attained the level of the colonizers and therefore can replace them permanently. It is not required to prove oneself the better of the former colonizers to do so, since their behaviors represented the very best in the view of Africans.

Anyone who has studied in a leading university—at Berkeley, Harvard, or Oxford—will have noticed that very little is ever said about high standards. It is the less distinguished institutions that want to appear to be as good *as* Berkeley, Stanford, or the Sorbonne. The same is true of the African bourgeois class. In many ways they are at a considerable disadvantage in attempting to do things *as* Englishmen in what Englishmen do best: speaking the English language. To take the example of the most successful non-Westerners in history, the Japanese do not strive to speak English or French as well *as* an Englishman and an American or *as* a Frenchman. They see themselves as *different* from them. The African bourgeois, born out of the colonial experience, is very uncomfortable with the idea of being *different* from his former colonizers in matters regarding education, administration, or technology. One suspects that he is unconsciously afraid that he may not be qualified to be an effective replacer of the former colonizers. If he does reject an English model, he wants to take an American model; but the point is still that he wants to validate his replacement of the colonizers by accepting the standards of the Americans who were after all potential colonizers in Africa.

Independence Strategies.   The notion, promoted by the African bourgeois class, that Africans had high standards and that educated Africans were as qualified to rule as the former colonizers constituted the principal basis of the claim of the African bourgeois class to gain independence from the alien rulers and thus to rule its own people. The 'fight' for independence was thus a struggle for power between the two bourgeois classes involved in the colonization of Africa. The intellectual poverty of the independence movement in Africa flows from this fact, that what was involved was not the issue of differences of ideas regarding moral principles but rather the issue of *which* bourgeois class should rule Africans. The colonizers did resist a great deal by discrediting the African bourgeois class and by creating divisions within it. In the long run, however, it is the African bourgeois class which had the advantage in the struggle by persuading the lay African that it had finally acquired the charismatic qualities with which Western education endowed its recipients.

The struggle entailed a necessary but destructive strategy: sabotage of the administrative efforts of the colonizers. A great deal of the anti-colonial activities by the African bourgeoisie consisted of encouragement to their followers to be late to work, to go on strikes for a variety of reasons,[8] etc. The African who evaded his tax was a hero; the African laborer who beat up his white employer was given extensive coverage in newspapers. In general, the African bourgeois class, in and out of politics, encouraged the common man to shirk his duties to the government or else to define them as burdens; in the same breath he was encouraged to demand his rights. Such strategy, one must repeat, was a necessary sabotage against alien personnel whom the African bourgeois class wanted to replace.

The irony of it all, however, is that the ordinary African took the principles involved in such activities quite seriously. There is clearly a transfer effect from colonialism to post-colonial politics. As should be apparent to anyone who is acquainted with the history of peasants and the ordinary man in other parts of the world, the line of distinction between allegiance to alien rulers and to the new African bourgeois rulers was a thin one in the mind of the lay African. Given the historical context of colonialism in Africa, it is the case that the African bourgeoisie had no basis of legitimacy independent of colonialism. In a sense then, they contributed directly, although unwittingly, to undermining their own legitimacy by encouraging the abrogation of duties and obligations to the colonial government and the demand for rights in excess of the resources available to meet them.

The Promise of Independence.   A related strategy in the fight for independence was to raise the hopes and expectations of the ordinary citizen in two different directions. First, and rather forthrightly, the ordinary man was promised increased benefits, benefits that were characterized with extravagance. Second, and less forthrightly but not less impressive in the mind of the ordinary man, was the promise to lower the 'colonial burden' which when translated into other terms means the duties of the common man, taxation for sure. Again it should be pointed out that such promises were generalized to mean that in the colonizing nations—in England, in France—the rights of the ordinary man were abundant while his duties were meager. These promises may have been honestly made in some cases because of the limited experiences of the African bourgeois class; but in many other instances they were made to discredit the alien colonizer, and to win the allegiance of the ordinary man.

(2) *Post-colonial Ideologies of Legitimation.* The African bourgeois class has a precarious foundation. It fought alien rulers on the basis of criteria introduced by them. Moreover, the alien rulers were seasoned fighters, at least judging by the success of the bourgeoisie in Europe, and they were always prepared to use that ancient weapon of 'divide and rule'. In the waning days of colonialism in many African nations two sorts of divisions were created or at least encouraged by the colonizers. The first was deliberately encouraged to undermine the African bourgeois class by reviving tradition as the basis of legitimacy, i.e., by restoring the defeated chiefs and kings to power. At best this was a delaying tactic on the part of the colonizers; the traditional rulers were much too enfeebled from the pre-colonial and colonial days to survive a struggle with the emergent African bourgeois class. In any case, the colonizers had implanted a new concept of legitimacy in matters relating to the civic public. Traditional kingship and chieftaincy has always been defined in moral terms, and the new attempt by the colonizers to drag it into the muddle of amoral civic public politics was bound to fail. A more serious division was suggested by the colonizers to the African bourgeois class, and it remains the red thread that runs through the whole of post-colonial African politics. It is a division within the bourgeois class along primordial ethnic lines. Both divisions—between the bourgeois and the traditional chiefs and within the bourgeois class itself—have led to two sets of ideologies promoted by the African bourgeois class to legitimate its threatened status in post-colonial politics. They are as follows:

Education as Guarantee of Success.   Education is at least as much needed in Africa as anywhere else. But this need has been subverted by the African bourgeois class in a curious way. In many human societies, attaining an educational standard is treated as an *avenue* to success. But in post-colonial Africa, attaining the requisite educational standard, usually phrased in terms of high-sounding university degrees, is now deemed a *guarantee* of success. There is an important difference here. To say that education is an avenue to success is to invite the benefactor of the educational system to *earn* his success by treating his educational achievement as a baseline for advancement. To treat education as a guarantee of success is to invite the benefactor of the educational system to *demand* advancement once he has successfully achieved the requisite standards in education. This latter definition of what education is intended for with respect to the individual recipient is, I suspect, an ideological invention of the Western educated bourgeois class to legitimate its rule, based on colonial education, vis-à-vis the legitimacy of the traditional chiefs. The 'first-come-first-promoted' logic in public service and in university professorial politics is a direct consequence of this ideology.

Ethnic Domain-Partition Ideology.   A fact of life in post-colonial Africa is the emergence of strong primordial ethnic groups in politics. What is interesting about them is that objectively they gained their significance only within the context of the various African nations in which they are implicated. In fact many of them have been created by modern politics. But almost everywhere separate sections of the African bourgeois class have backhandedly attempted to justify them as primordial entities that not only antedate the African nations in which they are implicated but in fact as corporate groups that have always existed. It is in this sphere that the ideology-creating achievements of the emergent African bourgeoisie approach their intellectual heights. While successfully demoting tradition as a basis of legitimacy in the new Africa and insisting that Western education provides that legitimacy, the African bourgeois class has at the same time divided Africa into domains of influence along traditional lines.

The dimensions of this problem can most profitably be illustrated in the context of Nigerian politics. As we know them today, Nigerian ethnic groups developed their boundaries and even their character only within the context of Nigerian politics. But ideologies and myths do have reality-creating functions, and the corporate character now attributed to the various ethnic groups is the reality that flowed from the ideologies and myths invented by the bourgeoisie to consolidate their parcels of influence in the new Nigeria. No ethnic group existed before Nigeria as a corporate entity with the boundaries now claimed for them and the loyalties now directed at them. What existed before Nigeria were amorphous polities: many were organized around city-states, others in kingdoms, and quasi-kingdoms, and yet others with the narrowness of villages with no conceptions of wider political entities within which they were implicated. Even the languages by which some claim to identify the ethnic groups in modern Nigeria (cf. Awolowo, 1966) are to a large extent a product of this domain-partition ideology.

Perhaps we will benefit from our discussions of this domain-partition ideology by referring directly to the two ethnic groups in Nigeria whose political and intellectual leaders are most adept at promoting this ideology. Beginning with the ranks of the 'officers' of the Ibo State Union and Egbe Omo Oduduwa to Ibo and Yoruba professors in Nigerian universities, many resources have been expended in order to *prove* that their ethnic groups have always been identifiable corporate ethnic groups. It was such an ideological assertion by Professor Biobaku (on behalf of the Yoruba bourgeois class) that led the British historian Hodgkin (1957:42) to remark, 'Everyone recognizes that the notion of "being a Nigerian" is a new kind of conception. But it would seem that the notion of "being a Yoruba" is not very much older.' The ideology of corporate Ibo ethnicity has been pushed even more vigorously by the Ibo bourgeois class. B. O. N. Eluwa, for many years the 'General Secretary' of the Ibo Federal (State) Union, told Abernethy (1969:110) that he, apparently among other Ibo bourgeois leaders, toured 'Iboland' from 1947 to 1951 to convince 'Ibo' villagers that they were in fact Ibos. In Eluwa's own words these villagers 'couldn't even imagine all Ibos'. Abernethy adds:

> In the 1930's many Aro and Onitsha Ibos consciously rejected identification as Ibos, preferring to think of themselves as separate, superior groups. The very term 'Yoruba' was popularized by Church Missionary Society leaders during the nineteenth century who were anxious to produce a Bible in a uniform language for several city-states that were warring against each other at the time (Abernethy, 1969:110n).

The Structure of the Two Publics

Taken by itself, each of these sets of ideologies of legitimation may amount to little. But taken together, they point up a major characteristic of African politics: the existence of two publics. The structure of modern post-colonial politics in Africa owes a great deal to these two publics that exist side by side and that tend to grow together. I shall now develop the implications of these ideologies further by examining the structure of politics in Africa and by doing so in the idiom of the concept of citizenship. As I shall use it here, its meaning takes as a point of departure T. H. Marshall's (1949) incisive analysis of citizenship in England and Bendix's (1964) subsequent generalization and elaboration of T. H. Marshall's and de Tocqueville's conceptions of citizenship. To put the matter rather directly, these various sources suggest that there are two distinct elements in the concept of citizenship. The individual as a member of a political community has certain *rights* and privileges which he may claim from it. Similarly he has certain *duties* and obligations which he has to perform in the interest of the political community.

The political problems of the age as well as the historical context of politics determine to a large extent the aspects and issues of citizenship that are sorted out for emphasis in a given society. It is thus the case that the conception of citizenship in the West has led to a rich analysis of rights (cf. T. H. Marshall, 1949; Bendix, 1964), whereas scant attention is paid to the analysis of duties. This is because the historical context of politics in the West led to a situation where rights and their resulting egalitarian ideals were problematic issues in the conception of citizenship, while duties were for the most part assumed as given. Similarly, it may be noted that one eminent attribute of citizenship in the West is that the two elements of citizenship are closely associated. That is, rights and duties are conceived in a transactional manner: the demand for rights implies some willingness to perform the concomitant duties, and vice versa.

The historical context of African politics, especially as it emerged from colonialism, has given a different character to African conceptions of citizenship from this Western model. In effect citizenship has acquired a variety of meanings, which depend on whether it is conceived in terms of the primordial public or the civic public.

The primordial public in Africa may indeed be fruitfully seen in terms of the elements of citizenship. The individual sees his duties as *moral* obligations to benefit and sustain a primordial public of which he is a member. While for the most part informal sanctions may exist that compel such obligations from individuals, duties to the primordial public have a moral side to them. The foci of such duties may of course vary from one setting to another, but in most of Africa they tend to be emergent ethnic groups. Informal taxation in the form of 'voluntary' contributions to ethnic associations and different other types of obligations to help out with ethnically-owned community programs are a prominent feature of modern Africa.

But what is the obverse side of the duties to the primordial public? What are the rights that the African expects from the primordial public in return for his duties to it? It is here that one must be cautious and not assign economic equations to the operation of the primordial public. Although the African gives *materially* as part of his duties to the primordial public, what he gains back is not material. He gains back intangible, immaterial benefits in the form of identity or psychological security. The pressure of modern life takes its toll in intangible ways. The cost of the rapid advance in urbanization and the sudden emergence of several individuals from a rural, non-literate background to as high as the leadership of prestigious departments in the universities and the civil service may not be measured in tangible economic terms. In all of post-colonial Africa, new men with non-literate parents and brothers and sisters—from non-chiefly families ungrounded in the ethics and weight of authority—are emerging to occupy high places. Behind the serenity and elegance of deportment that come with education and high office lie waves of psychic turbulence—not least of which are widespread and growing beliefs in supernatural magical powers. The primordial public is fed from this turbulence. For it is in the primordial public, whether it be narrowly defined as limited to an extended family of some two hundred individuals or, far more likely, to a whole emergent ethnic group ranging from half a million to some ten million people, that gives security to many first-generation educated Africans. The material manifestation of the duties of the educated African to his primordial public may or may not be balanced by the psychic benefits of security, benefits that flow from close association with the primordial public. But the point is, like most moral spheres, the relationship between the individual and his primordial public cannot be exhausted by economic equations. There is more to all moral duties than the material worth of the duties themselves.

The citizenship structure of the civic public is different. Because it is amoral, there is a great deal of emphasis on its economic value. While many Africans bend over backwards to benefit and sustain their primordial publics, they seek to gain from the civic public. Moreover, the individual's relationship with the civic public is measured in material terms—but with a bias. While the individual seeks to gain from the civic public, there is no moral urge on him to give back to the civic public in return for his benefits. Duties, that is, are de-emphasized while rights are squeezed out of the civic public with the amorality of an artful dodger.

These differing stances toward the primordial public and the civic public make sense in the historical perspective of colonialism. The ideologies of legitimation invented alike by the alien colonial rulers of Africa and their African successors have given credence to the myth among the ordinary African that the civic public can never be impoverished. On the other hand, the primordial public is pictured as needful of care—in fact from the civic public.

The Dialectics of the Two Publics

Most educated Africans are citizens of two publics in the same society. On the one hand, they belong to a civic public from which they gain materially but to which they give only grudgingly. On the other hand they belong to a primordial public from which they derive little or no material benefits but to which they are expected to give generously and do give materially. To make matters more complicated, their relationship to the primordial public is moral, while that to the civic public is amoral.[9] The dialectical tensions and confrontations between these two publics constitute the uniqueness of modern African politics.

A *good* citizen of the primordial public gives out and asks for nothing in return; a *lucky* citizen of the civic public gains from the civic public but enjoys escaping giving anything in return whenever he can. But such a lucky man would not be a good man were he to channel all his lucky gains to his private purse. He will only continue to be a good man if he channels part of the largesse from the civic public to the primordial public. That is the logic of the dialectics. The unwritten law of the dialectics is that it is legitimate to rob the civic public in order to strengthen the primordial public.

The issues which the inevitable confrontation between the two publics foments are varied.[10] I shall limit myself to three areas here:

Tribalism

Tribalism is a term used in most of post-colonial Africa to denote animosities between members of different ethnic groups. By its very nature, tribalism is a de-radicalized construct. That is, it is a term that has lost its root. Tribalism emerges only in situations where tribes and tribesmen are vanishing. Tribalism is robust in Lagos, where there are no tribes or tribesmen; it is absent in the most hinterland villages in Nigeria. Tribalism flourishes among professors and students in Nigerian universities (cf. van den Berghe, 1971, 1973), many of whom rarely visit their villages of birth in the interior; it is minimal in the secondary schools in the backwoods of Nigeria. The truth of the matter is that the degree and scope of tribalism in Africa are negatively correlated with the predominance of 'tribal' life.

Needless to say, this is because tribalism emerged from the colonial situation. It is the direct result of the dialectical confrontation between the two publics. Tribalism arises where there is conflict between segments of the African bourgeoisie regarding the proportionate share of the resources of the civic public to differentiated primordial publics. The leaders of the primordial public (who should not be confused with traditional ethnic leadership) want to channel as great a share of these resources from the civic public to individuals who are in the same primordial public as they are—in part, one suspects, because a significant proportion of them will eventually find their way into the coffers of the primordial public.

A fuller meaning of tribalism will emerge from the discussion of a concrete case. It is now commonplace knowledge that tribalism is *the* perennial and undying problem in our universities. Van den Berghe (1971, 1973) is perhaps a unique spokesman in setting forth his observation of this phenomenon, but he is by no means the only foreign visitor to our universities to be struck by it. What is so remarkable here is that tribalism is more prominent in the Federal universities in Nigeria than in the state and regional universities. This is clearly because the civic public is most operative in the Federal universities and comes into most violent confrontation with the primordial public in them. To concentrate on one example: in our Nigerian Universities confrontations continually occur between professors and lecturers from different ethnic groups in matters regarding especially appointments of new members and the promotion of old ones. But there is logic to these conflicts. They are mostly promoted by mediocre Nigerianization[11] professors who seem to feel insecure. Insecurity is in fact the stuff of which tribalism is made. That it involves and indeed hurts more efficient Nigerians is only part of the consequences of tribalism. But eventually it is the civic public that is hurt most deeply: efficiency and quality are sacrificed for expediency and, what is perhaps worse in the long-run, the amorality of the civic public deepens. Such is the source of the plight and restlessness in our universities in Nigeria today. Behind the show-case suavity of professorial pretensions lies the deep havoc wrought by the dialectical tensions between the civic public and the primordial public.

Voluntary Associations

If tribalism is an amorphous ism, ethnic 'voluntary' associations are its visible operational arm. Again, voluntary associations emerge in the big urban centers and are nourished in our universities. Like tribalism, they have developed with the civic public and in fact feed on it. That these 'voluntary' associations grow out of urbanization, that they attract well-educated Africans, that indeed they are the invention of the African bourgeois class: these are facts that have been well documented. What has not been fully emphasized, however, is that these associations do not belong to the private realm in the same sense as political sociologists conceive of voluntary associations in the West. They are an integral part of the primordial public. As such they do not complement the civic public; they subtract from it.

The tenacity of voluntary associations in the face of attempts to regulate and even ban them (as was attempted in Nigeria) indicates that they have underlying dynamics. So long as the primordial public survives—and it survives on the insecurity of the African bourgeoisie thrust into unwonted places of authority—so long will voluntary associations retain their strength. In spite of outward appearances the emergent African bourgeoisie lacks 'introspective' strength. Voluntary associations, tied to the primordial public, give a sense of security to those who have not achieved maximum differentiation from societal constraints—those, that is, who have not experienced the 'introspective revolution' that was a feature of the modern age in the West (cf. Weinstein and Platt, 1969).

Corruption

The acme of the dialectics is corruption. It arises directly from the amorality of the civic public and the legitimation of the need to seize largesse from the civic public in order to benefit the primordial public. There are two forms of corruption that are associated with the dialectics. The first is what is regarded as embezzlement of funds from the civic public, from the government, to be more specific. The second is the solicitation and acceptance of bribes from individuals seeking services provided by the civic public by those who administer these services. Both carry little moral sanction and may well receive great moral approbation from members of one's primordial public. But contrariwise, these forms of corruption are completely absent in the primordial public. Strange is the Nigerian who demands bribes from individuals or who engages in embezzlement in the performance of his duties to his primordial public. On the other hand, he may risk serious sanctions from members of his own primordial public if he seeks to extend the honesty and integrity with which he performs his duties in the primordial public to his duties in the civic public by employing universalistic criteria of impartiality.

Thanks to the de Tocquevellian skill of one English sojourner in Nigeria who has discussed this issue with limpid richness, we can look at this matter for a moment through the eyes of a foreigner. Wraith contrasts the integrity with which Nigerians handled matters of primordial ethnic character with 'the dragging footsteps and exiguous achievements of the local [government] authorities'. He notes that, while the local government authorities, with their civic structure, have 'a sad record of muddle, corruption and strife', the 'ethnic unions are handling sums of money comparable to those of many local authorities; that they are spending it constructively, *and that they are handling it honestly*' (italics in orginal). As Wraith rightly emphasizes, 'To put your fingers in the till of the local authority will not unduly burden your conscience, and people may well think you are a smart fellow and envy you your opportunities. To steal the funds of the union would offend the public conscience and ostracise you from society' (Wraith and Simpkins, 1963:50).

This differentiated attitude extends to African habits of work. Africans are extremely hard-working in the primordial public, as anyone familiar with the operation of ethnic associations will testify to. The man-hours spent in the service of the primordial public are enormous—but it would be profane to count and emphasize them, such is their moral character. On the other hand, Africans are not hard-working in matters connected with the civic public. At least one does not feel guilty if one wastes one's time in the service of the civic public. The same individual would be terribly embarrassed were he to waste time or make claims for work he has not done in the primordial public. It is not unknown that some individuals treat their duties in the civic public as an opportunity for rest in preparation for their tougher assignments in the primordial realm.

Conclusion

Modern comparative politics partially emerged with the widening interest of American and European social scientists in modern, especially post-colonial, Africa. The tools of comparative politics inhere in the traditional conception of politics in the West. That by itself seems appropriate. But the tools sometimes appear dull from overuse and cry out for sharpening. Certainly, if we are to capture the spirit of African politics we must seek what is unique in them. I am persuaded that the colonial experience provides that uniqueness. Our post-colonial present has been fashioned by our colonial past. It is that colonial past that has defined for us the spheres of morality that have come to dominate our politics.

Our problems may be partially understood and hopefully solved by the realization that the civic public and the primordial public are rivals, that in fact the civic public is starved of badly needed morality. Of course, 'morality' has an old-fashioned ring about it; but any politics without morality is destructive. And the destructive results of African politics in the post-colonial era owes something to the amorality of the civic public.

Notes

1. This distinction borrows from a parent distinction between 'civil' and 'primordial' realms in individual behavior, introduced into sociological analysis by Shils (1957) and popularized and strengthened by Geertz (1963). Ultimately of course, it dates back to Töennies" classic distinction between association-type *Gesellschaft* and community-type *Gemeinschaft*.

2. Cf. Ekeh (1972:93): 'Colonialism is to Africa what feudalism is to Europe. They form the historical background from which Africa and Europe advance to modernity. As such, they have determined the peculiar characteristics of modernity in each of these areas.'

3. Needless to say, the bourgeois influence varied a great deal from nation to nation in internal European politics. It was more significant in France and England than in Germany and Portugal (cf., e.g., Moore, 1966). There is a possibility that the different colonial policies in Africa—e.g., as between the Germans and the Portuguese on the one hand and the British and the French on the other—reflected the varied domestic influence of the bourgeois class in European national politics. My characterization of the bourgeois class seems truer of the English and French cases than of the Portuguese and German bourgeoisie.

4. Such imperial ideologies include the moral appeal to Europeans in terms of 'the white man's burden' and the fanciful flattery to Europeans that there were 'noble savages' somewhere in the non-European world that could imitate them. For good sources of such imperial ideologies see Arendt (1951) and Curtin (1964). European nineteenth- and early twentieth-century literature is suffused with im-

perial ideologies. In English, the works of Rudyard Kipling and Rider Haggard are especially effective in upholding the moral superiority of Europeans, especially Englishmen, and the evangelical call for imperial expansion. In the academic sphere, Mannoni's *Prospero and Caliban,* depicting Africans as naturally dependent and Europeans as naturally dominant, remains one of the most subtle examples of these imperial ideologies dressed up in academic 'objectivity'.

5. For a dramatic case history of Christian missionary involvement in colonization see Padmore's (1949:70–73) discussion of the religious wars between the *Ba-Ingleza* (English) and the *Ba-Fransa* (French) parties in Uganda. For a well-argued sympathetic interpretation of the role of Christian missionaries see Neill (1966).

6. It is not an insignificant matter that French colonized Africans knew nothing of these British explorers and that British colonized Africans were unaware of the French 'explorers'.

7. 'Been-to' is a Nigerian term used to refer to those who have *been* overseas, usually to England, Europe, and the U.S.A. or Canada, and who overdo their imitation of Western manners. Also cf. Fanon's (1967:17–40) discussion of this issue with respect to French-speaking Africans and West Indians.

8. Thus the Nigerian trade union leader Michael Imoudu became a hero in colonial Nigeria for encouraging strikes against the British, a practice that earned him strong resentment from his former collaborators, now in government, when he repeated it against his own independent nation, with the British gone.

9. The amoral conception of the duties of the government was decried by Okoi Arikpo (1967:112–13) as follows: 'Everybody expects the government to provide modern social amenities—[but]—Few expect the government to provide sound moral leadership.'

10. For an attempt to explain the Nigerian civil war in these terms see Ekeh (1972).

11. It was a deliberate policy at one time in our Federal Universities to 'Nigerianize' top positions by replacing foreigners with Nigerians. Such windfall promotions brought some competent Nigerians into top positions, but they also dragged up some very incompetent Nigerians into key positions.

Suggestions for Further Reading

Abernethy, David B. (1969) *The Political Dilemma of Popular Education. An African Case.* Stanford: Stanford University Press.

Ajayi, J. F. Ade (1967) 'Samuel Ajayi Crowther of Oyo' in Philip D. Curtin, ed., *Africa Remembered.* Madison: The University of Wisconsin Press.

Ajayi, J. F. Ade and R. S. Smith (1964) *Yoruba Warfare in the Nineteenth Century.* Cambridge, England: Cambridge University Press.

Arendt, Hannah (1951) *The Origins of Totalitarianism.* New York: Harcourt, Brace & World.

Arikpo, Okoi (1967) *The Development of Modern Nigeria.* Baltimore: Penguin Books.

Awolowo, Obafemi (1966) *Thoughts on Nigerian Constitution.* Ibadan: Oxford University Press.

Banfield, Edward C. (1958) *The Moral Basis of A Backward Society.* New York: The Free Press.

Bendix, Reinhard (1964) *Nation-Building and Citizenship.* New York: Wiley & Sons.

Curtin, Philip D. (1964) *The Image of Africa: British Ideas and Action, 1780–1850.* Madison: The University of Wisconsin Press.

_____(1968) (ed.) *Africa Remembered: Narratives by West Africans from the Era of the Slave Trade.* Madison: The University of Wisconsin Press.

Dike, Kenneth O. (1956) *Trade and Politics in the Niger Delta.* London: Oxford University Press.

Ekeh, Peter P. (1972) 'Citizenship and Political Conflict: A Sociological Interpretation of the Nigerian Crisis' in Joseph Okpaku, ed., *Nigeria: Dilemma of Nationhood, An African Anaiysis of the Biafran Conflict.* Westport, Conn.: Greenwood Press.

Fanon, Frantz (1967) *Black Skin, White Masks.* New York: Grove Press.

Geertz, Clifford (1963) 'The Integrative Revolution' in Clifford Geertz, ed., *Old Societies and New States.* New York: The Free Press.

Hobson, J. A. (1902) *Imperialism: A Study.* London: George Allen & Unwin.

Hodgkin, T. (1956) 'The African Middle Class'. *Corona,* 8:85–8.

_____(1957) 'Letter to Dr. Biobaku'. *Odu,* No. 4.

Jahoda, Gustav (1961) *White Man: A Study of the Attitudes of Africans to Europeans in Ghana Before Independence.* London: Oxford University Press.

Mannoni, O. (1964) *Prospero and Caliban.* New York: Frederick A. Praeger.

Marshall, T. H. (1949) 'Citizenship and Social Class'. Reprinted in T. H. Marshall, *Class, Citizenship, and Social Development.* New York: Doubleday & Company, 1964.

Moore, Barrington (1966) *Social Origins of Dictatorship and Democracy: Lord and Peasant in the Making of the Modern World.* Boston: Beacon Press.

Neill, Stephen (1966) *Colonialism and Christian Missionaries.* New York: McGraw-Hill Book Company.

Padmore, George (1949) *Africa: Britain's Third Empire.* Westport, Conn.: Negro Universities Press, 1969.

Shils, Edward (1957) 'Primordial, Personal, Sacred and Civil Ties'. *The British Journal of Sociology* 8:130–45.

Stark, Werner (1958) *The Sociology of Knowledge: An Essay in Aid of a Deeper Understanding of the History of Ideas.* New York: The Free Press.

Van den Berghe, Pierre (1971) 'Pluralism in a Nigerian University: A Case Study'. *Race,* 12:429–41.

_____(1973) *Power and Privilege in an African University.* Cambridge, Mass.: Sehenkman.

Weinstein, Fred and Gerald M. Platt (1969) *The Wish To Be Free: Society, Psyche, and Value Change.* Berkeley and Los Angeles: The University of California Press.

Wolin, Sheldon (1960) *Politics and Vision: Continuity and Innovation in Western Political Thought.* Boston: Little, Brown & Co.

Wraith, Ronald and Edgar Simpkins (1963) *Corruption in Developing Countries.* London: George Allen & Unwin Ltd.

5

Disengagement from the State in Africa: Reflections on the Experience of Ghana and Guinea

Victor Azarya and Naomi Chazan

The Issue of Disengagement from the State

Few questions have galvanized the attention of observers of African affairs in recent years as forcefully as the performance of the state on the continent. The debate on the nature of the state—its capabilities, weaknesses, external and societal connections, and impact—has come to occupy center stage in the field of African political studies. This overriding preoccupation emanates from the underlying assumption that the state constitutes a superior means for the fulfillment of economic and social aspirations; participation in its activities is deemed beneficial, and various sectors of society strive to associate with its institutions and gain access to its resources. Some recent works have cast doubt on this assumption,[1] however, and the trend in the literature has been shifting towards an emphasis on the diminishing role of the state in African social life. However, even in these new studies the focus has been primarily on the state itself, its difficulties, incapacities, and failures, rather than on societal response to its actions.

Reprinted with the permission of Cambridge University Press from *Comparative Studies in Society and History* 29 (1987): 106–131. © 1987 Cambridge University Press.

A view of the state as primary vehicle for integration and consolidation was derived from the state-centered approach that developed during the early years of independence in Africa as one country after another broke away from colonial rule. Concerned with the molding of a new civil society around the state, scholars traced the processes of participation, institutionalization, and nation building that were expected to follow decolonization. From their perspective the main question of contemporary African politics rotated around the construction of viable political entities responsive to their social and economic environments. These scholars highlighted, therefore, the study of participatory networks as mechanisms for the establishment of political order.

When the initial euphoria of independence gave way to a realization that the process of state building did not always proceed along a smooth, unilinear path, emphasis shifted to the study of political crises and instability. The state came to be seen as the arena of conflict, different groups vying for control over its apparatus. Some observers underlined the possible contradictions between institutionalization and participation[2] and accentuated the vulnerability of state institutions to participatory demands. Pluralists emphasized those pressures rooted in primordial, mostly ethnic sources. Marxists defined conflict in class terms and sought to link political upheavals to the skewed class composition of state officials. Their preoccupation with the emergence of state capitalism, the administrative bourgeoisie, and the "overdeveloped" nature of the state indicated the importance they attributed to what occurred within the state nexus.[3] Dependency theorists, by contrast, externalized the source of pressure on state institutions and focused on the state's precarious position in the global economy.[4] But for them, too, the state remained the principal target of study as the main link between the core of the world system and the African periphery.

Regardless of important internal differences, early modernization theorists, pluralists, Marxists, and adherents of dependency theories have all assumed that state-centered operations provide the key to uncovering societal trends in postcolonial Africa. We might say that they all share an *engagement paradigm* that has dominated African political studies. They focus on the political center and examine postcolonial development in terms of the differential participation of various groups and their influence on state performance.[5] The engagement paradigm may have an integrative connotation, stressing nation building, institution building, the creation of larger bases of solidarity and collective action around the new center embodied by the state. It may also have a connotation of conflict stressing the tension and struggle between groups aspiring to control the center. In both cases the focus remains the same: the engagement, or participation, of various sectors of the society in determining the structure and impact of the political center. What this paradigm neglects, however, is the possibility that engagement in state-related operations may not always be worthwhile: that in some cases the risks of vulnerability attendant upon exposure and overdependence on the state may outweigh the spoils of participation. Under certain circumstances participation might carry little reward (except, perhaps, for the very top echelons), and might lead to political and physical insecurity, to economic hardship due to overdependence on the cash nexus, and to cultural stifling that derives from a forced and empty façade of conformity.

The equivocal experiences of the first decades of independence have fostered a growing recognition that many, perhaps most, African states are unable to fulfil the expectations attendant upon participation. Some countries unendowed with the most minimal prerequisites for growth succeeded only in creating weak centers (Mali, Niger, Burkina Faso). In other countries, such as Nigeria and Zaïre, which possessed the potential means for consolidation (size, population, resources), severe internal conflict inhibited the development of cohesive centers. Even states that seemingly got off to an impressive start, such as Ghana and Uganda, have experienced a severe reduction in performance. The resource base of many African states is shrinking palpably, and their responsive capability is curtailed. They are unable to command, in many instances, even a modicum of legitimacy. These processes cut across ideological differences, colonial boundaries, and cultural variations. They raise serious doubts about the utility of close association with the state.[6]

Awareness of these conditions requires a reassessment of the assumptions that guided the initial crop of political research on Africa. It is today as crucial to analyze modes of disengagement from the state as it is to examine efforts at engagement in the state nexus. The purpose of this article is to investigate how individuals and groups in two African countries, Ghana and Guinea, have attempted to cope with the state by distancing themselves from it as a hedge against its instability and declining performance. Specifically, we address three interrelated facets of the process of disengagement. First, what are the circumstances underlying the enfeeblement of the state and the reasons for initiating steps aimed at detachment from its activities? Second, what forms does disengagement from the state take? Third, what are the general implications of disengagement on state-society relations?[7]

The Circumstances of Disengagement

The frontiers of Ghana and Guinea, like those of other African countries, were determined by the colonial powers and encompassed diverse groups that drew on distinctive precolonial legacies. Guinea had a long history of relations with the great empires of the western Sudan and gave rise to the state of Futa Jallon, the first state to emerge from a string of Islamic revolutions in the eighteenth and nineteenth centuries. It also, under the leadership of Samori Touré, sustained one of the most tenacious resistance movements to colonial conquest.[8] The Gold Coast, lying in the area of present-day Ghana, nurtured the Asante state whose expansion coincided with the growth of the slave trade. This region was also actively involved in thwarting the colonial expansion into the hinterland.[9] In the colonial period Guinea was a backwater of French West Africa. It had no important export crop and started to experience rapid socioeconomic change only a few years before independence. In the Gold Coast, under British rule, Western education was much more widespread than in Guinea and urban migration grew rapidly. The introduction of cocoa production altered the shape of the economy and rearranged domestic priorities.[10] Despite the different pace of change, however, both areas experienced the basic duality inherent in colonial rule, i.e., the existence of a European administrative polity, only partly opened to a small indigenous elite, and a heterogeneous society still organized around various traditional structures and maintaining tenuous ties with alien central political institutions.[11] The colonial state in these two areas was therefore a prototype of the minimal state; it touched only intermittently the lives of those within its boundaries.

Processes of decolonization in Ghana and Guinea have much in common. The two countries stood at the forefront of anticolonial struggle in sub-Saharan Africa and were the first of the Anglophone and Francophone countries to reach independence. In both countries opposition to colonialism was accompanied by the coalescence of new social forces antagonistic to traditional structures. Independence was perceived as a precondition for effecting a thoroughgoing reform of the social order. Decolonization in both countries led to mass mobilization and ideological innovation. There were also, however, some important differences. In Ghana the anticolonial movement started much earlier. By the time the Guinean anticolonial struggle took momentum in the 1950s, Kwame Nkrumah and his party, the Convention People's Party (CPP), had come to power in the Gold Coast. Despite the appearance of militancy so carefully nurtured by the CPP, the attainment of independence in Ghana, in stark contrast to Guinea, was a product of several years of dyarchy with the colonial administration. In Guinea, the ideological fervor of Sékou Touré and the Parti Démocratique de Guinée (PDG) was not diluted by the need to share power with colonial authorities. The country achieved independence merely two years after the PDG won its first general elections to the Territorial Assembly. Guinean independence was achieved in total defiance of the colonial power's wishes and led to an abrupt break-

down of ties between the two countries (with dire economic consequences for the new state).

Despite some internal differences, there is no doubt that Guinea and
Ghana, more than many other African countries, did experience grassroots mobilization and large-scale political participation in the years preceding independence, with considerable spillover to the first years of independence. Hence, unlike most other African countries, these two
definitely inspire the question of what has remained of that initial engagement. The issue confronting Guinean and Ghanaian citizens is not
one of continued lack of association with the state but rather one of coping with a state that, so promising at first, has visibly fallen apart during
their lifetimes.[12] One may also ask whether or not disengagement from
the state is ingrained in the very process of postcolonial political development in Africa. As Aristide Zolberg has suggested, the basic premise in
studying postcolonial African states should perhaps be the lack of authority rather than its excess.[13] Beyond weaknesses common to all African
states, however, disengagement is more accentuated in some states than
in others and should not be explained away by long-range historical
causes. Even though common roots or predispositions may exist throughout Africa, disengagement arises in response to specific political or economic difficulties that have occurred since independence. The turnabout
in the fortunes of the state in Ghana and Guinea is therefore symptomatic
of conditions in some but *not all* postcolonial African countries.

In Ghana and Guinea independence was achieved in a state of euphoria and great popular support for the ruling elite who had brought the anticolonial struggle to its successful conclusion. But the dualism embedded
in colonial rule was not eradicated. State structures maintained the artifi-
ciality and remoteness that had been their trademark during the years of
British and French rule. Nor did independence change the economic reliance on external market forces unamenable to control by the new state
managers. The state faced increased pressure from the elevated level of
popular aspiration without a concomitant strengthening of its resource
base or authority structure. In Guinea, the abrupt termination of the
French presence created a further burden on new rulers unprepared to
find themselves, suddenly and effectively, alone in the center.

Sékou Touré and Kwame Nkrumah set out to bolster the machinery of
the state and to enhance its capabilities. They both opted for the continued mass mobilization that had served them so well prior to independence and for greater politicization of economic decision making. The
vehicle for mobilization was the single party, already entrenched
throughout each country, which was expected to supplant or take over
the more remote civil service and create stronger links between state and
society. Politicization of economic decision making enhanced the impres-

sion that the state was in control, that the society was being molded according to its plans and directions.

With socialism as the guiding ideology and the CPP and PDG the instruments for its fulfillment, Nkrumah and Sékou Touré proceeded to establish an extremely centralized and politicized mobilization system in which a greatly expanded state—and party—bureaucracy penetrated into spheres heretofore immune from central intervention. They attempted to draw larger and larger segments of the population into the state domain. In Guinea shortly after independence, the government carried out sweeping nationalizations in the economic field and started large-scale "human investment" programs in public works. Cooperative farms were set up and ambitious health, social welfare, and educational programs launched. Private schools were nationalized and radical reforms introduced into the curriculum. Youth movements, trade unions, and other voluntary associations all became integrated within the party. Every citizen had to be a party member, and every village, neighborhood, factory, and office had its party committee.[14] In Ghana, although mixed enterprise became the password, the CPP established a myriad of state corporations, ranging from the Ghana Industrial Holding Corporation to the State Farm network. Heavy investments in education were supplemented by the creation of the Young Pioneers and the Workers Brigade. A monolithic Trade Union Congress was created, and the CPP established women's and students' wings in an attempt to permeate all facets of life.[15]

The ability to highlight the centrality of the state and to weave together the heterogeneous components of the population was not, however, matched by a capacity to underwrite the smooth operation of the growing state network. Mobilization did not bring efficiency nor did ideology augment control. On the contrary, politicization of economic decision making curtailed performance because it reduced the influence of experts. As for mobilization, not only did it consume valuable resources, constituting a further burden on the state apparatus, but it also led to discontent among the population, whose unfulfilled aspirations were now compounded by a loss of autonomy.

In the economic field, the performance of Ghana and Guinea has been close to abysmal, partly because of factors beyond the state's control (falling world prices for cocoa, for example), but in large part as a result of the states' own economic policies. In Guinea, independence was followed by extensive radicalization in economic policy. Banks, insurance companies, diamond mines, French-owned banana plantations, and most foreign trade companies were nationalized. The country withdrew from the franc zone, and state-owned commercial organizations monopolized most of the wholesale trade. As the state printed money to meet its needs, it produced runaway inflation that it tried to combat by establishing price controls. In

1975 private trade was abolished altogether and markets were closed, except for the sale of raw foodstuffs, which resulted in great shortages.[16] In 1978 the government adopted a more liberal policy, reopening markets and again legalizing private trade. As a result of the shift of policy, basic commodities have become more readily available. Hitherto closed frontiers with neighboring countries have also been opened for trade and travel, and further economic liberalization followed the military coup carried out a few days after Sékou Touré's death in March 1984.[17]

In Ghana, economic policy shifted drastically as regime followed regime, and desperate efforts were made to halt the backward slide of the economy. Nkrumah set out, much like Sékou Touré, to transform the structure of the colonial economy. He curtailed private concerns and aggressively pursued a policy of *étatisme*. New central economic institutions were created under the guise of socialism in an effort to make the state the hub of production, distribution, and capital accumulation. The Nkrumaist economic edifice, however, was inefficient and corrupt. It drained the substantial reserves of the country and stunted the economic initiative of its population. Under the circumstances, it is hardly surprising that Nkrumah's civilian successor, Kofi Busia, chose to move away from state centrism and advocated a greater role for local and foreign enterprise. But Busia was no more adept than Nkrumah at controlling the practices of his subordinates. I. K. Acheampong's brand of self-reliance plunged Ghana into an economic tailspin. When Jerry Rawlings came upon the scene with a philosophy of populism, the economy was barely extant. Even he has had to submit to International Monetary Fund guidelines in order to acquire the foreign backing necessary to keep the economy afloat.[18]

The economic deterioration experienced by Ghana and Guinea was manifested in severe declines in agricultural production and export due to the shrinking profit from marketing surplus goods under government control. After independence both countries lost their self-sufficiency in food and had to import large amounts of rice.[19] Industrial production also declined in both countries, and most factories have operated far below capacity because of lack of raw material or spare parts. With the dwindling of domestic supplies came an increased dependence on imports and a rising debt burden. Unemployment assumed alarming proportions and shortages in even the most basic commodities necessitated introduction of austere rationing methods.[20] Needless to say, the economic uncertainty was accompanied by widespread corruption and by sharply declining standards of living.

In Guinea, total economic breakdown was averted, however, by the rapid growth of bauxite extraction, which turned the country into a major mineral exporter. By 1975 bauxite and alumina's share in the country's export earnings had risen to 95 percent. It is not surprising that the mining sector was less affected than other sectors by nationalization and the political intervention of the state. The two companies that ushered in extensive mining operations in the country (at Fria and Boké) functioned as mixed companies, the government holding 49 percent of the shares and 65 percent of the profits. Foreign companies thus continued to hold the majority of shares and were responsible for the operation of the facilities.[21] The emerging paradox is that, with its large bauxite reserves (the country may possess as much as two thirds of the entire world's reserves) and extensive resources in diamonds and iron ore whose exploitation is only starting, Guinea is potentially one of the richest countries in Africa, but in reality it remains one of the world's poorest twenty-five, with a standard of living declining since independence.[22] Moreover, for a country priding itself on its anticolonial stand, it is overwhelmingly dependent on international capitalist economic activities.

The gold mines in Ghana have been under foreign control as well. But the low levels of production have not made them as central as bauxite in Guinea. Hydroelectric power has aided the growth of the Volta Aluminum Company aluminum smelter, but profits went to foreign concerns until 1984, when a new agreement was reached with the second Rawlings government.[23]

Politically, state deterioration has been marked by numerous upheavals. Ghanaians have experienced eight different regimes since independence. Kwame Nkrumah, whose longevity in office remains unrivaled by any of his successors, was ousted by a military coup d'état in 1966. The National Liberation Council returned power to the civilian leaders of the Second Republic in 1969. Kofi Busia's premiership lasted only into early 1972, when I. K. Acheampong overthrew the government and started a six-year phase of erratic military rule. A 1978 *putsch* forced Acheampong's resignation. Fred Akuffo, who replaced him, was himself put out of office in a populist uprising led by Flight Lieutenant Jerry Rawlings on the eve of elections to return Ghana once again to civilian rule. Hilla Limann, president of the Third Republic, barely succeeded in finding his bearings before Rawlings reappeared on the political scene at the head of the Provisional National Defense Council (PNDC) in December 1981.[24] Ghana has thus been engulfed in political turmoil since Nkrumah's days. Regimes guided by diametrically opposed precepts have succeeded each other at an increasingly rapid pace. The frequent changes in government have sowed confusion, fomented discord, and nurtured political disorientation among growing segments of the population.

On the surface, Sékou Touré's political resilience in Guinea stands in stark contrast to the bewildering fluctuations on the Ghanaian political scene. But internal mutations, realignments, and purges have generated a record of political flux similar to that prevalent in Ghana. As early as April 1960, Sékou Touré announced the discovery of a French-backed conspiracy to topple his government. Similar accusations were voiced in November 1961 and again in 1965, 1969, 1970–71, 1976, 1977, and 1980.[25] These were only the more serious of the convulsions that have beset Guinea since independence. Sékou Touré himself, in January 1970, characterized the situation in Guinea as one of perennial plot.[26] A climax of sorts was reached in 1970–71; The November 1970 attempted invasion by Guinean exiles, assisted by the Portuguese, permitted a massive crackdown on real or suspected political opponents. In 1976 a plot allegedly conducted by people of Fula origin led to the incarceration and subsequent death of Diallo Telli, the first secretary-general of the Organization for African Unity. Market women were not deterred, however, from openly demonstrating against the government in 1977, asking for liberalization of trade and the release of political prisoners.[27] The regime was clearly shaken by this incident which no doubt had some influence on the following year's more liberal shift in policy. In the 1980s accusations of plots declined somewhat, and some political prisoners were released. Still, the repression of opposition continued as did occasional violent acts against the regime. Finally the military took over in March 1984, after Sékou Touré's death, and pledged to end political repression.

During Sékou Touré's rule, Guinean political leadership functioned in a continuing siege mentality, creating fear and suspicion on all sides. With every alleged plot, real or imaginary, and the purges that followed, fewer people were left at positions of power and trust. The frightened ruling group, steadily contracting around Sékou Touré and aware of its narrowing base of support, reacted by further closing itself to the outside and purging itself inside. Of those remaining in the ruling circle many were Sékou Touré's relatives.[28] The inherent weakness and isolation of the ruling group, and its total dependence on the person of the head of state became apparent in the ease with which the coup was carried out only days after Sékou Touré's death.

The political paths of Ghana and Guinea have not always converged. Besides the longevity of Sékou Touré's rule (compared with the rapid succession of his Ghanaian counterparts), the style of political life in the two countries has varied widely. Despite Ghana's checkered political history its citizens have sustained a vibrant democratic ethos. Guinea, on the other hand, evolved into a police state where official political violence became the norm. In Ghana political debate continues, whereas Guinea was subjected to enforced unanimity. These significant differences do not, however, lessen the essential similarity in the processes of state deterioration in the two areas. Both have undergone a cycle that commenced with the circumscription of the opposition and the limitation of channels of political communication, proceeded to problems of legitimacy and the withholding of popular support, and culminated in the shrinking of the political arena. This recessionary spiral has perforce reduced access to the state, diminished commitment to its collective goals, curtailed allegiance to its institutions, and minimized its role in society. It is in this setting that processes of disengagement have evolved in both countries.

The Forms of Disengagement

Four major mechanisms of disengagement from the state, containing different combinations of social, economic, religious, political, and cultural elements, may be discerned in Ghana and Guinea. They are all attempts to adjust to an environment of diminishing opportunities and increasing vulnerability. This does *not* mean, however, that all the specific activities to be discussed here are related exclusively to disengagement. Under different circumstances, some of these phenomena, such as black markets, informal sectors, or sectarian religious cults, may also occur in connection with contrary trends, such as rising expectations from the political center and a rush toward incorporation that the state cannot totally absorb. But when taken together, these various activities do form a special pattern of disengagement clearly distinguishable from contrary patterns of participation and incorporation.

Suffer-Manage

The first mechanism of adjustment to a deteriorating state performance may be termed the suffer-manage syndrome. It encompasses an array of activities aimed at reconciliation to a declining standard of living and learning to manage in these circumstances. The most salient mechanisms of the suffer-manage strategy surfaced in the economic realm and involve finding ways of coping with shortages. People in Ghana and Guinea have become accustomed to the periodic absence of razor blades, batteries, detergent, gasoline, soap, and light bulbs. They have had to devise ways of coming to grips with the irregularity and scarcity of food supplies, altering their diets and adjusting consumption habits to accord with existing goods. The deterioration has also led to changes in the use of time. Many hours are devoted to the search for basic commodities, following tips received from friends. Worker output has diminished and absenteeism has increased, putting an even greater strain on the already precarious economies of these countries. Less time is devoted to leisure activities and cultural creativity. Transportation expenses have grown as people travel farther in quest of food and other supplies.[29] Many urban dwellers have begun to cultivate vegetable gardens for home consumption. Housewives and children, formerly outside the labor circle, have found ways to make some money to contribute to family coffers. Home crafts have been converted into cottage industries, and moonlighting, always prevalent, has increased considerably. Barter techniques and shared use of vital goods such as water and candles have developed. The acute shortage of medicine has increasingly sent people to traditional healers.

The sociocultural manifestations of the suffer-manage syndrome derive from its economic underpinnings. In both Ghana and Guinea, cynicism and alienation are widespread. Disaffection with existing conditions and with prospects for amelioration has become commonplace, breeding a studied aloofness from affairs of government and a skepticism vis-à-vis the machinations of its leaders. These perceptions have sometimes fostered a fatalism interwoven with an awareness of the shortcomings of state managers.[30] In Ghana, this reaction found expression in the proclivity to voice dissatisfaction, to engage in vocal and multiple debate on the root causes of the present condition. The verbalization of decay has become, in the Ghanaian context, an important means of handling the breakdown of the state. In Sékou Touré's Guinea, however, complaint was not tolerated. Suffering occurred in silence and criticism was muted. These variations are not only an outcome of the distinct political cultures of these states; they are also an indication of the kinds of possibilities available in the two countries. In Ghana, with all its history of turmoil, the value placed on civil rights has endured. In Guinea, the consolidation of a police state effectively restrained the ability and the desire to develop an oral culture of discontent.

The suffer-manage form of disengagement in both countries is largely an urban phenomenon. It has been adopted by residents of cities and towns who depend on a fixed income and who are therefore most severely affected by fluctuations in the state economy. This portion of the population has felt most concretely the adverse effects of inflation and dwindling purchasing power. It is also the group with the fewest alternatives to participation in the official channels of the economy. In rural areas the farming population has more direct access to food production and can revert to subsistence cropping to protect itself from the deterioration of the center.

The suffer-manage syndrome reflects the reaction of those who are unable to extricate themselves from the arena of the malfunctioning state (and thus should perhaps not be characterized as disengagement proper). It also constitutes a barometer of the patience level of Ghanaian and Guinean citizens. The essential passivity intrinsic to this approach serves as an indicator of both the extent to which people are willing to reconcile themselves to diminishing circumstances and the degree to which other possibilities are foreclosed.

Escape

The second major reaction to the deterioration of the state forms the opposite pole to the suffer-manage technique. While sufferers and managers still remain dependent on state channels, those opting for escape remove themselves not only from the state but from the country as a whole. Motivations for emigration vary: They may stem from declining economic opportunities and standards of living at home, or they may derive from restrictions on personal freedoms, from harassment and persecution by political authorities. The emigrant may feel personally in danger or may be unwilling to comply with coercive unanimity, but whatever the specific motivation, the escape device has depleted Ghana and Guinea of some of their best citizens.

Escape is prevalent among the better educated elements and causes a serious brain drain. In Guinea the exodus of trained personnel is endemic and has nullified government attempts to form a corps of well-educated officials. Those sent for study overseas have chosen not to return to the precarious environment of Conakry. Members of the diplomatic staff have left their posts or have chosen to defect at the end of their turns of service.[31] Faculties of the universities of Paris and Dakar were full of Guinean professors in the 1970s, while the Polytechnique of Conakry was in a state of suspended animation because it lacked qualified teaching personnel. In Ghana, a country that justly boasts of the high educational level of its population, the drain of skilled manpower has reached alarming proportions. The free professions have been most affected by this trend. Medical practitioners have streamed out of the country in recent years; of the approximately 1,500 doctors trained in Ghana since independence, barely 350 were on the government payroll in 1982. There are more Ghanaian physicians in West Germany today than in Ghana itself,[32] and more Ghanaian academics lecture in Nigeria than in their own country. Secondary schools have lost personnel to such an extent that many institutions are currently manned by undertrained replacements. What is apparent in these areas is true also of law, engineering, and the natural sciences.

A second kind of outward migration has been of unskilled and semiskilled labor. The unemployed, particularly in the younger age brackets, have left Ghana and Guinea in droves for frequently menial jobs with paltry salaries in the service sector or in agriculture. The flow of Ghanaians to Nigeria in the late 1970s increased so drastically that the Ghanaian colony in the Lagos area became a source of major tension there,[33] and the Guinean diaspora in Senegal assumed similar characteristics. The seasonal migration of Guineans to neighboring countries as agricultural laborers (*navétanes*) or as traders dates back to well before independence, but its proportions have risen greatly since the 1960s and the migration has become more permanent than before. In 1959 Guineans living outside the country were estimated at about 100,000, most of them seasonal workers. By the 1970s their number had risen to more than two million,[34] which is an extraordinary figure, considering that the entire Guinean population is six million people. After the liberal change of policy in 1978,

Guinea's frontiers with neighboring countries were opened and travel restrictions were eased. Some have heeded the government appeal to come home, but many more have taken advantage of the new freedom and have left the country legally.[35]

A third type of emigrant is the political exile. In reality it is difficult to distinguish this form of emigration from the brain drain because so many of the well-educated emigrants are also vocal in their opposition to their country's regime and would not feel safe returning home. This was especially true in Sékou Touré's Guinea. The implicit link between higher education abroad and opposition to the regime was highlighted by the government itself when, following the alleged Fula plot of 1976, it announced that in the future no Fula would be sent to study abroad at government expense.[36] Political emigration from Guinea started with the disturbances of the early 1960s and rose rapidly in the 1970s. Exile groups, organized in various political movements and mostly living in Senegal, the Ivory Coast, and France, staged numerous antigovernment activities. In 1970 some Guinean exiles took part in the ill-fated invasion attempt of Conakry, and in 1980 an exile group claimed responsibility for a hand-grenade attack on Sékou Touré.[37]

In Ghana, only a trickle of political refugees fled during the first decade of independence. Since then the number has swollen. Political groups may be found not only in the neighboring countries of West Africa but also increasingly in England (the Campaign for Democracy in Ghana headed by Boakye Djan is just one such example). Today centers of opposition proliferate throughout the world, and the phenomenon of Ghanaian political exiles is reaching the proportions previously seen in Guinea.

All told, it is possible that more than 10 percent of Ghana's population of about twelve million was resident outside the country in the early part of the present decade. Fully one third of Guinea's population has exited the country since independence. The targets of these migrations have been mainly other, more economically viable states on the West African littoral. About half of the Guinean emigrants live in Senegal and the Ivory Coast, but sizeable communities are found also in Sierra Leone, Liberia, Gambia, and Mali.[38] Ghanaians have been drawn first and foremost to the supposedly greener pastures of oil-rich Nigeria. Others have drifted to the Ivory Coast and even to parts of East Africa. Those Ghanaians and Guineans who have been able to secure suitable positions in Europe and North America have established congregations in key Western capitals. It should be pointed out that while Guinea has known outward migration since the colonial period, Ghana was itself a target of migration in the 1960s, and in the 1980s it still absorbs migrants from the drought-ridden Sahel. It is striking that in 1969 it was Ghana that expelled more than a hundred thousand aliens, mostly Nigerians, while in 1983 and again in

April 1985, it was the turn of more than a million Ghanaians to be expelled from Nigeria.[39] There can hardly be a more vivid illustration of the decline in fortunes of the Ghanaian state in the intervening years.

Unlike the suffer-manage technique undertaken mostly by urban dwellers, the escape from the country has affected both urban and rural groups. It has wreaked havoc in the standards of the service sectors, curtailed agricultural and industrial production, and limited the development of human resources. Educational investment by the states has been wasted as many beneficiaries chose not to use their skills in their own countries. Politically, the exodus has hampered the growth of opposition within the country and has reduced the chances of political change. Ghanaians and Guineans living abroad have been subject to abuse, discrimination, displays of xenophobia, and at times physical violence by local populations. Their mere presence and oppositionary activities have strained the relations between their governments and those of the host countries. More generally, they have added to the growing problem of refugees on the continental level. The transnational character of class formation that is a by-product of the growing utilization of escape mechanisms has important ramifications for the reordering of social stratification throughout West Africa. The escape mechanism thus highlights some of the external dimensions of state decline in Ghana and Guinea.

Parallel Systems

Not all groups in Ghana and Guinea have been in a position to detach themselves physically from the country. Many of those who have remained have engaged in a third form of disengagement: the creation of systems parallel to those of the state. Parallel systems are alternative outlets for needs that remain unfulfilled by official channels, and they reduce dependence on those channels. Typical examples include black markets, smuggling, corruption, and the use of alternative methods of justice. The parallel networks may or may not utilize the state apparatus or draw upon its resources, but basically they override its purposes and skirt its laws: They are attempts to beat the system. By reconciling itself to their existence, the state may insure some modicum of order and continue to provide the most essential services, but in the process the official legal-normative framework is further discredited and its resources diminished. The alternative system that comes into being shadows the state structure, yet undermines its vitality and potential.

The economic manifestations of this strategy are the most readily apparent. They cover such a wide range of activities that in Ghana a special term, *kalabule*, has been coined to refer to all the economic malpractices that are associated with this form of disengagement. A major aspect of this technique is smuggling. The overvalued official exchange rates, trade restrictions, and scarcities in most of the basic commodities have given farmers and traders very powerful incentives to sell their products in neighboring countries, where more consumer goods and more desirable currencies can be obtained. In both countries the illegal flow of products across the borders has expanded greatly and smuggling has become a well-organized, self-sustaining occupation. In the early 1970s it was estimated that 150,000 people working 150 days a year were needed to bring out the amount of cocoa that illegally traversed Ghana's frontiers. In 1970–71 more than a half million tons of Ghanaian cocoa found their way into the export figures of Togo and the Ivory Coast—the main beneficiaries of the cocoa operation. A decade later fully two thirds of Ghana's cocoa crop was leaving the country illegally. As for Guinea, it was estimated in 1972 that one third of its coffee crop was illegally transferred to markets in Sierra Leone, Liberia, and the Ivory Coast and contributed to the precipitous fall in official coffee export figures.[40]

Rice, root crops, fruits, and vegetables, as well as minerals and manufactured products, have similarly been smuggled in great quantities. As Thomas Morrison and Jerome Wolgin report on Ghana, "a farmer can buy a bag of fertilizer at the official rate, smuggle it across the border to, say, Upper Volta, sell the fertilizer, return with the empty bag, and sell the bag in Ghana for more than he paid for the bag and the fertilizer in the first place."[41] About 15 percent of the gold and diamonds mined in Ghana annually crosses the borders illegally. Some Ghanaian manufactured goods, like canned fruit juices, are unavailable in Ghana but can easily be purchased elsewhere. In Guinea, gold and diamond mining was forbidden in the 1960s and early 1970s in an attempt to prevent smuggling to Mali, the Ivory Coast, and Liberia. The renewed diamond and gold mining operations, since 1978, have accompanied the general opening of borders with neighboring countries.[42]

The illegal export of cattle from Guinea has reached dimensions such that the once very rich cattle stock of Futa Jallon has been devastated. This has resulted, to a large extent, from the Guinean government's imposition of cattle sales quotas (about 10 percent of the registered animals) at fixed prices in order to reduce the meat shortage in the country.[43] Being forced to sell their cattle at unprofitable prices or submit to confiscation by the government, many cattle owners have preferred to sell their herds to smugglers, and, if too hard-pressed by government investigators, they have followed their herds across the border. In both countries, smuggling coincides with the routes of illegal migration. Actively sustained by emigrant communities who live along the smuggling routes across the border, it also makes use of traditional trade routes and networks that have existed since precolonial times.

Smuggling is a two-way traffic. Imported goods covertly brought into Ghana and Guinea include food, manufactured goods, luxury items, and foreign currency. Smuggling techniques have developed into a veritable art, and rarely does a Ghanaian or Guinean traveller return from abroad without exhibiting his skills in this sphere.

Smuggling is closely connected with hoarding and black marketeering. The former occurs when stringent price controls make it unprofitable to market goods; the latter flourishes when supplies of hoarded goods diminish, thus enabling their sale at prices much higher than the ones set by the state. In Ghana and Guinea both practices have proliferated. Commodities exchanged at exhorbitant prices include locally produced items, goods stolen or diverted from government stores, products purchased abroad and imported or smuggled into the country to bolster the local market. Sometimes they are sold only a few yards away from the empty counters of the big stores. As reported in Conakry, "a few blocks from the [revolutionary] slogan, shoppers in the state-owned Printania or Nayfay general stores idle between counters whose display spaces are two-thirds empty. Around the corner from the revolutionary exhortation, however, a hole-in-the-corner black market offers the goods—imported cloth, transistor radios, bicycle tires, canned foods—that long ago disappeared from the big shops."[44]

In both states, black markets are the stronghold of petty traders, mostly market women who have devised elaborate methods of controlling the availability and price of essential commodities. They have been joined by Hausa and northern traders in Ghana and by Dyula traders in Guinea. The governments' reactions to black markets have fluctuated between periods of stringent control (accompanied by conflicts with petty traders, increased smuggling, and shortages) and periods of accommodation, of looking the other way (usually in return for some share of the profits), to prevent the total collapse of economic distribution.[45]

The parallel-system structures could not be sustained without some measure of formal collusion. Indeed, another element of the beat-the-system strategy involves corruption, embezzlement, fraud, skimming, and official theft. Ghanaian and Guinean officials have fed the shadow system and raised their incomes by tacit association with the second economy. Bureaucrats have supplied goods to the black market and have assisted in determining when such goods would be available. Thus, it is not unusual to find food aid, bearing the original labels, being sold in the black markets of Accra and Conakry. In Guinea, state-run cooperatives fairly openly smuggled their products across the borders. The misuse of import licenses, state support for shady enterprises, violations of foreign currency controls and, of course, abuse of bureaucratic procedures were commonplace in both countries. In Ghana, scores of commissions of inquiry, and lately public tribunals, have investigated the extent and intricacies of these practices. In Guinea, periodic purges of the state bureaucracy, reaching as high as cabinet ministers, have been justified by the proclaimed need to eliminate bureaucratic misdoing.[46]

The parallel system has also involved the evolution of criminal networks concerned with its support. In Ghana, organized crime styled along Mafia lines has flourished in recent years, and there has been an increase in armed burglaries, highway robberies, muggings and, at times, economically motivated murders. In Guinea, the death penalty was instituted for theft in 1976 in an attempt to stem widespread petty stealing as well as embezzlement and fraud in state enterprises. Speaking on Conakry radio the president complained that "everything is stolen, headlights from cars broken down in the streets, goods from the wharves of Conakry, mail from the Post Office, luggage at the airport, cattle from the countryside and even food for the prisoners in the gaols."[47]

The cumulative effect of these parallel-system mechanisms has been an overriding cynicism toward official structures and a widespread noncompliance with the laws. In Guinea under Sékou Touré laws and decrees were heeded only as long as they were being mentioned on the radio. They were easily promulgated and as easily forgotten with the changing needs of the government or the mood of the president. But they were not rescinded. If a particular decree was in the interest of a certain government official, it was enforced and those unaware of it paid dearly. The population lived in constant uncertainty as to what laws might be used against them and under what circumstances.[48] The collapse of the legal system was aggravated by the politicization of the courts. Judges were political appointees and received their directives from the party. At times, as in the aftermath of the 1970 attempted invasion by the exiles, the existing courts were dispensed with altogether, and popular courts were formed and given extraordinary powers. It is not surprising that the population increasingly turned away from the state's judicial system to traditional forms of litigation to settle differences. The result has been a resurgence in the status and influence of traditional authority, which despite the formal abolition of chieftaincy in 1957 never really ceased functioning.

In Ghana, the judicial system was able to survive the Nkrumah, Busia, and Acheampong eras virtually intact despite the efforts of these three to by-pass its rulings. In 1982, however, Rawlings substituted citizen's vetting committees that were intended to side-step the legal process. In August 1982 three Supreme Court judges were murdered and charges of official collusion were rife. But despite this frontal assault on the judiciary, it has persisted, and even the PNDC has increasingly been compelled to use it. Many people, however, find the judicial establishment irrelevant to their daily lives and continue to resort to traditional arbitration practices.[49]

In Ghana, more than in Guinea, parallel systems have been manifested also on the cultural plane, in the form of removal from state-backed religious systems and the existence of a vibrant popular counterculture. Established churches have been abandoned in favor of fundamentalist sects, magical cults, and a quest for new spiritual communities. Old orthodoxies are being shed, and new heterodoxies are springing up in a manner reminiscent of the colonial period, when responses to the uncertainty and ambivalence accompanying foreign intrusion were frequently expressed in a proliferation of cults, independent churches, and millenarian movements. The spiritual search is aimed either at designing a religious framework for coping with the normative frailties of the established order or at escaping reality through millenarian devices.[50]

No such increases in cult activities have been reported in Guinea. In the first years of independence the government conducted a strong campaign against syncretistic cults and pagan practices, which it accused of mystifying the world. At the same time, the established Christian and Muslim religious leadership also came under attack. Marabouts were accused of obscurantism and forbidden to go on tours to solicit alms. Missionary schools were closed, and church officials expelled or arrested. Although the regime later rehabilitated Christianity and Islam and permitted their organized religious and educational activities to resume, it maintained its attack on fetishism.[51] Since the late 1970s the regime has displayed fervent support for Islam in an obvious attempt to integrate it into the belief system of the establishment.[52]

The increasing distance between officially backed mores and personally preferred lifestyles is also noticeable in the development of a popular culture with antiestablishment overtones drawing on both traditional and Western sources. It is expressed in song and dance, in poetry and the theater, in prose and the arts, in publicist tracts and market literature. In Ghana, complete paraphernalia of such a counterculture have been in place for some time, from blaring discotheques and blue jeans to the novels of Ayi Kwei Armah, and from an underground press to the bittersweet frames of "Love Brewed in an African Pot."[53] In Guinea, by contrast, the repressive nature of the regime prevented such a counterculture from emerging. From the outset, the Guinean regime recognized the importance of popular culture as a means of control over the population. There is a curious difference, however, between the paucity of the literary field and the richness of musical activities. Hardly any books were published in Guinea except for the multiple volumes of Sékou Touré's speeches and declarations. No newspapers or magazines existed except for the party's official organ, *Horoya,* which appeared irregularly. On the other hand, music, dance, and spectacle flourished with the encouragement of the party and reached a climax in the biannual music festivals of Conakry, in which artistic groups from all regions of the country participated. Sport was also given attention and closely organized by the state.[54] The difference in treatment may be due to the fact that it is easier to officially orchestrate enthusiasm and unanimity in expressive fields such as music, dance, and sports than in the more cognitive activities of literature. In any case, by organizing some kinds of popular culture events and strictly banning others, the state seems to have succeeded in curtailing formation of a popular counterculture.

The parallel-system form of disengagement may be located in both urban and rural areas, and it often straddles the dividing line between the two. Those engaged in the parallel system have sprung up at the points of exchange between the subsistence and cash economy, between the local and the national levels, between traditional institutions and state structures. Fortification of the techniques inherent in this mechanism has depended, to a large extent, on the capacity of its purveyors to cover the same ground as the state channels while at the same time proferring additional opportunities unavailable at the state level. Because of their ability to operate at the confluence of formal and nonformal sectors, traders have been the first to adopt practices associated with parallel systems.[55] Perhaps the initiators of the parallel economy should be distinguished from its consumers. Whereas the latter could come from a wide variety of sectors, the initiative is generally traced back to those engaged in trade. However, the circle of those partaking in parallel-system activities has grown in direct relationship to the degree of disarray in the formal system. Farmers and manual laborers, professionals and government employees, students and clerks have all joined in. The net effect of the expansion has been to make virtually everyone into a speculator, cheat, corruptor, or lawbreaker. By-passing the rule of law has become a form of survival and has institutionalized a dual system. The formal economy is shadowed by a nonformal one in which official mores and structures have their unofficial and binding counterparts. Beneath the surface, another contiguous, interweaving, and frequently overlapping network persists.

Self-Enclosure

Disengagement can also be manifested in attempts to insulate oneself from the state, thereby gaining protection from its uncertainties. This kind of withdrawal entails a reduced use of state channels but, unlike the formation of parallel systems, it does not involve deviance from state regulations. However, when insulation is considered inherently illegitimate, as in Guinea, attempts at self-enclosure tend to merge with parallel systems.

Examples of self-enclosure include moving back from export to subsistence crops and from urban to rural habitation, as well as renouncing public service and any positions of high visibility that would increase one's exposure to state pressures. Self-enclosure may also involve a retreat to traditional forms or to narrower bases of solidarity (regional, ethnic, kinship).[56] Traditional or primordial structures are protected bases to which one returns when more autarchic and familiar settings are sought against uncontrollable fluctuations in employment, cost of living, or arbitrary political rule. Common to these attempts is a retraction within one's own shell as a hedge against the state's instability.

As state-generated activities have crumbled in Ghana, a reversion to subsistence techniques and a process of ruralization have begun to appear. Professionals, technocrats, soldiers, and entrepreneurs have bought land near their home villages as an extra precaution against future hardship. Some have left the cities entirely and established residence in their local communities. When Ghanaian emigrants returned in early 1983, they were reabsorbed mostly in the countryside.[57] There has also been a perceptible shift from cash to subsistence production as a response to falling cash-crop prices and increasing shortages in basic consumer goods. Farmers have curtailed cocoa and coconut production for export, choosing instead to increase the output of foodstuffs. As cooking oil cannot be procured in the city, people have resumed the collection of shea-butter nut. Throughout the forest regions poultry production has been on the rise, although fewer chickens and eggs can be obtained in the markets. In Guinea, farmers have similarly tended to withdraw from the market in favor of secret local barter systems.[58] Local self-reliance efforts have defied government attempts to dictate production items, rates, and objectives. The state-owned Mamou canned-food factory, for example, could not operate its meat section for lack of beef, and its fruit and vegetable section functioned only with great difficulty because of irregular supply of raw materials, which could, however, be readily bought for consumption in the black market.[59] In this case, self-enclosure merged with and reinforced the parallel system.

These local withdrawal techniques have all flourished on an agricultural foundation. For urban residents with no access to land the options have been more limited. Nevertheless, some indications of a quest for autonomy from the state have surfaced in Ghana also in urban settings through the flow of skilled personnel from the public sector to the private. Government employees have abandoned public service in favor of private occupations: Doctors have struck out on their own, and engineers have extricated themselves from government contracts and established their own firms. These mechanisms of withdrawal show that disengagement from the state does not lead necessarily to disengagement from the center. The highly educated professionals who moved from the public to the private sector loosened their ties with the state as a means of self-protection, but they did not relinquish their ties with the center in the economic or cultural spheres. In Guinea, by contrast, the severe restrictions laid on private enterprise prevented such movement from public to private sectors. No real withdrawal from the state could occur without withdrawal from the center because of the state's omnipresence at the center.

Self-enclosure has had important implications beyond the economic sphere. In rural areas traditional modes of stratification have been revived and adjusted. Proximity to the state and its power apparatus has lost some of its influence on social status. Power and authority have been detached, leading to increasing status incongruence. More struggles for power have concentrated on the local community or on voluntary associations, as people have increasingly shunned participation in state politics. A side effect of the narrower focus of social ties that derives from self-enclosure is that class pales in significance as compared to community.[60]

These moves have been accompanied by cultural adjustments as well. The significance of the local community has been underlined through the revival of historical ties and their endowment with new meaning. The impact of popular subcultures in Ghana has been particularly pronounced since the return of Jerry Rawlings, who embodies the paradox of populist rulers who, ushered into power on a wave of antiestablishment sentiment, must nevertheless attempt to control the formal institutional network.[61]

The outcome of self-enclosure indicates how conditional allegiance to the state apparatus really is. Self-enclosure mechanisms withhold resources from the state; they exacerbate difficulties in its operation and further the loss of control over society. Self-enclosure breeds diversity and fragmentation into subsectors. It generates semiautonomous units that vary in location, economic base, symbolic orientation, and historical grounding. The resultant entities combine traditional roots with modern additions. Under certain circumstances they may form innovative organisms capable of achieving self-sufficiency and generating new experiments at communal definition.

The effects of this withdrawal strategy underline the possibilities of preserving the standards of living of Ghanaians and Guineans, while at the same time depleting state capacities and redefining communal boundaries. The trend toward self-enclosure contains the seed of a more massive realignment of power relations predicated on the dispersion of state functions to vibrant enclaves operated by members of the collectivities that the state claims to represent. These internal enclaves are distinguished from the foreign enclaves that may replace the uncooperative citizenry as the major resource supplier of the state.

Implications of Disengagement

Citizens of Ghana and Guinea have employed four major ways of dealing with the political uncertainty, economic impoverishment, and social malaise that emanate from the state core. They have also tried to maximize their options by engaging in several patterns simultaneously. Suffering and managing have been combined with utilization of parallel systems, which in turn have been linked with self-enclosure and episodes of physical escape. The forms of disengagement encountered in Ghana and Guinea do not cover the full range of responses theoretically possible and actually found in Africa. They do not include, for example, movements of secession, regional irredentism, or civil war (as in Uganda, Chad, or Ethiopia). In Ghana and Guinea, the state, whatever its other weaknesses, still controls the society's organized means of coercion. Indeed, the particular forms of disengagement encountered in Ghana and Guinea account for the fact that, with the exception of attempted coups (which are themselves a sign of participation rather than disengagement), the state's monopoly of force has not been effectively challenged.

One could question, however, whether the state is really the critical referent in the activities here discussed. In some cases, such as emigration, the disengagement is from the society as a whole. In others, such as reduced production, it is a response to a changing economic situation. Why then call it disengagement from the state? Our contention is that, in most instances, these activities are construed in the eyes of the actors as responses to government policies and not to general economic, social, or physical forces (for example, responses to drought). They have as their critical referent the central public domain that ordinary people identify with the state and that manifests itself in a network of public officials, rules, regulations, and sanctions. Moreover, in some instances, as in the move from public to private professional practice, the disengagement is from this public domain but not from the society's cultural center or from the modern economy as a whole.

Whatever the focus, processes of disengagement in Ghana and Guinea have whittled away at the already fragile state apparatus. They have further undermined the ability of the state to control resources, to exert authority, and to garner legitimacy. The effect of disengagement has been greater disjunction between center and periphery and between polity and society, with a concomitant loss of the state's relevance to maintaining social order. States therefore usually attempt to combat such tendencies, cutting off outlets of disengagement, if necessary by coercive means. However, these attempts do not reduce disengagement so much as push it into more radical forms. If withdrawal is impossible legally, it will be undertaken by by-passing or defying the law; should that course of action become too dangerous, physical escape from the country is the next option. Campaigns of mobilization are costly and can not be sustained for long; the state is thus forced into some sort of accommodation with a recalcitrant periphery in order to ensure that the most essential societal functions will be performed. Accordingly, state-issued orders and laws continue to lose credibility. As one prominent black marketeer is executed in a public square or disappears behind prison walls, thousands of others continue to practice with the tacit consent of government officials.

One should not assume, however, that the state would always try to combat disengagement. Alternatively, it could reconcile itself to reduced control over a withdrawn periphery and even arrange for those in ruling positions to reap some profit from the situation. The state might concede limitations on the scope of its activities and control, but it would also reduce the services offered to the periphery. As ruling groups shrink and their interests narrow, even a limited state resource base might suffice. Such a reaction would aim at reducing state responsibility without relinquishing the benefits of state power. The narrow resource base that the state still controls and through which it maintains its clientage network and coercive apparatus might derive from external sources, possibly from foreign aid or foreign enclaves established in the country and tapping some of its natural resources, in striking similarity to the colonial structure that the present state replaced.

Ghana and Guinea have undergone similar processes of state decline and detachment since achieving independence in the late 1950s. Various sectors of society have disengaged from the state in response to the paucity and instability of state channels, which in turn caused further impoverishment of the state. The emerging picture of state-society relations is that of a weak political center, coalesced around the person of the head of state and having little and declining control over societal resources. But the decline of the state does not necessarily mean its total collapse. On the contrary, the state's resilience is remarkable, and it still has greater influence on society than any other institutional framework. Indeed, by focusing on societal responses to state decline, we have reasserted the importance of the state in understanding social processes in present-day Africa. Where we have deviated from established modes of analysis is in the shift of focus from the state itself to societal responses to it. Most political studies of contemporary Africa center on state building or on the reasons for the weakening of state organs. The processes of disengagement discussed in this article show, however, that the state is just one of many poles for social and economic exchange. In certain cases, social groups and communities devise protective mechanisms to shield themselves from the state's vagaries. Disengagement in some spheres (most notably the economic) is also accompanied by continued dependence in other areas, such as social services. When the state network proves inefficient or arbitrary, withdrawal to pre-existing or alternative settings is attempted; conversely, when the state appeals to specific social groups, they ally themselves with its policies and act according to its direction. The desirability of participation in the state can thus no longer be taken for granted. In analyzing these developments, the emphasis needs to shift from state to society. Societal reactions to the state should occupy a more central stage in scholarly work.

Notes

1. See, for example, Robert H. Jackson and Carl G. Rosberg, "Why Africa's Weak States Persist: The Empirical and the Juridical in Statehood," *World Politics*, 27 (October 1982), 1–29; and Nelson Kasfir, ed., *State and Class in Africa* (London: Frank Cass, 1985).

2. Samuel P. Huntington, "Political Development and Political Decay," *World Politics*, 17 (April 1965), 386–430.

3. John Saul, *The State and Revolution in Eastern Africa* New York: Monthly Review Press, 1979); John Lonsdale, "States and Social Processes in Africa: A Historiographical Survey," *African Studies Review*, 24:2–3 (June–September 1981), 139–225.

4. Claude Ake, *A Political Economy of Africa* (London: Longman, 1981). Also see Samir Amin's work, including *Neo-colonialism in West Africa* (Harmondsworth: Penguin, 1976).

5. The paradigm may also be formulated in negative terms, as departicipation, or the shrinking of the political arena that denotes difficulties faced in political access and loss of political opportunities. See Nelson Kasfir, *The Shrinking Political Arena* (Berkeley: University of California Press, 1976).

6. Following this point, Jackson and Rosberg claim, for example, that many African states would hardly qualify as such if one were to adopt an empirical definition of the state based on its ability to control the population within its territory. What maintains them as states, according to Jackson and Rosberg, is a more juridical definition that identifies them as the recognized territorial units of the international community. In other words, in this view, some states may be more relevant in the international arena than they are within their own territorial boundaries. See Jackson and Rosberg, "Why Africa's Weak States Persist," 1–24.

7. Disengagement is similar to the concept of "exit" put forward by Albert Hirschman as a possible response to declining performance in economic and political organizations. It indicates a withdrawal from the organization (ceasing to buy the firm's products or use the organization's services), as opposed to the "voice" option, which raises vocal dissatisfaction and opposition to the organization in an effort to modify its performance. Hirschman believes that the voice option would be a more likely response to such basic social organizations as the family, the church, and the state in which the exit outlet is less available, whereas exit would be a more likely response to corporations and voluntary organizations. Our focus on disengagement from the state attempts to show that the reverse might also be true, i.e., that exit may be the residual option when voice is unavailable or ineffective and

that it can be a very likely option even in the relation to the state. See Albert O. Hirschman, *Exit, Voice, and Loyalty: Responses to Decline in Firms, Organizations, and States* (Cambridge: Harvard University Press, 1970), esp. 33.

8. Victor Azarya, *State Intervention in Economic Enterprise in Pre-Colonial Africa* (Los Angeles: University of California, African Studies Center, 1981), 17–23; Yves Person, "The Atlantic Coast and the Southern Savannahs, 1800–1880," in *History of West Africa*, J. F. A. Ajayi and M. Crowder, eds., 2 vols. (London: Longman, 1974) II:262–307.

9. John Fage, *Ghana: A Historical Interpretation* (Madison: University of Wisconsin Press, 1956); Ivor Wilks, *Asante in the Nineteenth Century* (London: Cambridge University Press, 1975).

10. On colonial Ghana and Guinea, see David Kimble, *A Political History of Ghana, 1850–1928* (Oxford: Clarendon Press, 1963); Jean Suret-Canale, *La République de Guinée* (Paris: Editions sociales, 1970), ch. 2.

11. On colonial duality, see Victor Azarya, *Aristocrats Facing Change: The Fulbe in Guinea, Nigeria, and Cameroon* (Chicago: University of Chicago Press, 1978), 59–64.

12. Dennis Austin, "Things Fall Apart?" *Orbis*, 25:4 (Winter 1982), 925–48.

13. Aristide R. Zolberg, *Creating Political Order* (Chicago: Rand McNally, 1966), 133–34.

14. R. W. Johnson, "Guinea," in *West African States: Failure and Promise*, John Dunn, ed. (London: Cambridge University Press, 1978), 38, 48.

15. Richard Crook, "Bureaucracy and Politics in Ghana: A Comparative Perspective," in *Transfer and Transformation: Political Institutions in the New Commonwealth*, R. Lyon and J. Manor, eds. (Leicester: Leicester University Press, 1983), 185–213.

16. Johnson, "Guinea," 49, 56; Azarya, *Aristocrats Facing Change*, 148–49.

17. *Africa Research Bulletin* (Economic, Financial, and Technical series), vols. 15–20 (1978–83); Lansine Kaba, "Guinea: Myth and Reality of Change," *Africa Report*, 26:3 (1981), 55; *Africa Confidential*, 22:4 (11 February 1981), 6–7; Mark Doyle, "Enter the Liberals," *West Africa*, no. 3478 (16 April 1984), 804–5.

18. Tony Killick, *Development Economics in Action: A Study of Economic Policies in Ghana* (London: Heinemann, 1978); Richard Jeffries, "Rawlings and the Political Economy of Underdevelopment in Ghana," *African Affairs*, 81:324 (1982), 307–17.

19. Thomas K. Morrison and Jerome N. Wolgin, "Prospects for Economic Stabilization in Ghana" (Paper presented at the Twenty-third Annual Meeting of the African Studies Association, Philadelphia, October 1980); Claude Rivière, *Guinea: The Mobilization of a People* (Ithaca: Cornell University Press, 1977), 190–206; R. Hecht, "A Long Wait for Guinea's Farmers," *West Africa*, no. 3322 (30 March 1981), 678–81.

20. Naomi Chazan, *An Anatomy of Ghanaian Politics: Managing Political Recession, 1969–1982* (Boulder, Colo.: Westview, 1983); Deborah Pellow, "Coping Responses to Revolution in Ghana," *Cultures et développement*, 15:1 (1983), 11–36; Rivière, *Guinea*, 204, 209; *New African*, no. 136 (December 1978), 11.

21. Johnson, "Guinea," 48; Rivière, *Guinea*, 184–87. Other bauxite deposits, at Kindia, were exploited by a joint Guinean-Soviet state enterprise. See *Africa Research Bulletin* (Economic), 13:9 (October 1976), 4030–32, and 15:10 (November 1978), 4883–84; *New African*, no. 136 (December 1978), 16.

22. *Africa Research Bulletin* (Economic), 15:10 (November 1978), 4883–84.

23. Ann W. Seidman, *Ghana's Development Experience* (Nairobi: East African Publishing House, 1978).

24. Chazan, *Anatomy of Ghanaian Politics:* Dennis Austin and Robin Luckham, eds., *Politicians and Soldiers in Ghana, 1966–1972* (London: Frank Cass, 1975); Kwame Ninsin, "Ghana, the Failure of a Petty-Bourgeois Experiment," *Africa Development,* 7:3 (1982), 37–67.

25. Rivière, *Guinea,* 127–35, 226–27; Johnson, "Guinea," 43, 46; Ladipo Adamolekun, "L'agression du 22 Novembre 1970: Faits et commentaires," *Revue française des etudes politiques africaines,* no. 114 (June 1975), 92–102; Jean F. Bayart, "L'aveu sous les tropiques," *Politique africaine,* 2:7 (September 1982), 14–16.

26. Adamolekun, "L'agression," 103.

27. Hamza Kaïdi, "Qui etait derrière les manifestations du mois d'Août?" *Jeune Afrique,* no. 877 (28 October 1977), 72–73.

28. Johnson, "Guinea," 57–58; *Africa Confidential,* 22:16 (4 August 1982), 7–8.

29. Carl K. Eicher, "Facing up to Africa's Food Crisis," *Foreign Affairs,* 60:1 (1982), 153–74; K. Ewusi and S. J. Matey, "Expenditure Patterns of Middle and Upper Income Groups in Ghana: A Case Study of the Consumption Patterns of Senior Members of the University of Ghana" (Legon: Institute of Statistical, Social, and Economic Research, 1972), 72.

30. This is noticeable in films and literature in Ghana. See Deborah Pellow and Naomi Chazan, *Ghana: Coping with Uncertainty* (Boulder, Colo.: Westview Press, 1986), ch. 3.

31. Kaba, "Guinea: Myth and Reality," 56; *Jeune Afrique,* no. 875 (14 October 1977), 54.

32. Private communication from Merrick Posnansky, April 1984.

33. Roger Gravil, "The Nigerian Aliens Expulsion Order of 1983," *African Affairs,* 84:337 (1985), 523–38; Lynne Brydon, "Ghanaian Responses to the Nigerian Expulsions of 1983," *African Affairs,* 84:337 (1985), 561–86.

34. Julien Conde, "La situation démographique en République de Guinée," *Revue française d' etudes politiques africaines,* no. 123 (March 1976), 122. See also Azarya, *Aristocrats Facing Change,* 93, 193; *Jeune Afrique,* no. 875 (14 October 1977), 54. Sékou Touré himself acknowledged 1.5 million immigrants in 1972 (see Conde, "La situation démographique," 123).

35. Kaba, "Guinea: Myth and Reality," 55–57; *New African,* no. 136 (December 1978), 13; *Africa Research Bulletin* (Political), 14:7 (August 1977), 4510.

36. *West Africa,* no. 3087 (30 August 1976), 1269.

37. For the different organizations and activities of Guinean exiles, see *Africa Research Bulletin* (Political), 19:9 (October 1982), 6596; *Africa Confidential,* 19:22 (3 November 1978), 4–5.

38. Conde, "La situation démographique," 122; *Jeune Afrique,* no. 875 (14 October 1977), 54; *Africa Confidential,* 20:7 (28 March 1979), 1.

39. Margaret Peil, "The Expulsion of West African Aliens," *Journal of Modern African Studies,* 9:2 (1971), 205–29.

40. Ashok Kumar, "Smuggling in Ghana: Its Magnitude and Economic Effects," *Universitas,* 11:3 (1973), 285–305; Michael O'Connor, "Guinea and the Ivory Coast—Contrasts in Economic Development," *Journal of Modern African Studies,* 10:3 (1972), 425; Johnson, "Guinea," 48.

41. Morrison and Wolgin, "Project for Economic Stabilization," 15.

42. Kaba, "Guinea: Myth and Reality," 55–56; *Africa Confidential*, 22:4 (11 February 1981), 6; *Africa Research Bulletin* (Economic), vols. 16–20 (1979–83).

43. Azarya, *Aristocrats Facing Change*, 190; Bernard Charles, *La République de Guinée* (Pairs: Berger Levrault, 1972), 11.

44. Quoted from *The New York Times*, 16 December 1968, in O'Connor, "Guinea and the Ivory Coast," 423.

45. Keith Hart, "Informal Income Opportunities and Urban Employment in Ghana," *Journal of Modern African Studies*, 11:1 (1973), 61–91; Johnson, "Guinea," 48–49; Kaïdi. "Qui etait derrière les Manifestations," 72.

46. Victor T. Le Vine, *Political Corruption: The Ghana Case* (Stanford: Hoover Institution Press, 1975); "Ghana's Holy War: Letter from Accra," *Africa Report*, 27:3 (1982), 12–16; Rivière, *Guinea*, 130–33; *West Africa*, no. 3007 (10 February 1975), 176; *Africa Confidential*, vols. 22–23 (1981–82).

47. *West Africa*, no. 3092 (4 October 1976), 1469.

48. See Johnson, "Guinea," 49, 55–57; *Africa Research Bulletin* (Political), 14:6 (July 1977), 4465.

49. E. Gyimah-Boadi and Donald Rothchild, "Rawlings, Populism, and the Civil Liberties Tradition in Ghana," *Issue*, 12:3–4 (Winter 1982), 64–69.

50. Pellow, "Coping Responses."

51. Rivière, *Guinea*, 232–35; *idem*, "Guinée: Une église étouffée par l'état," *Cultures et développement*, 8:2 (1976), 219–41; *West Africa*, no. 3099 (22 November 1976), 1781.

52. Lansine Kaba, "Rhetoric and Reality in Conakry," *Africa Report*, 23:3 (1978), 43.

53. Ayi Kwei Armah, *The Beautiful Ones Are Not Yet Born* (London: Heinemann, 1971); Pellow and Chazan, *Ghana: Coping with Uncertainty*, ch. 3.

54. Jacques Vignes, "La double lecture," *Jeune Afrique*, no. 875 (14 October 1977), 41; Lansine Kaba, "Freedom of Expression in Guinea," *Journal of Modern African Studies*, 14:2 (1976), 203–8.

55. Keith Hart, "Swindler or Public Benefactor: The Entrepreneur in His Community," in *The Social Structure of Ghana*, Jack Goody, ed. (London: Oxford University Press, 1975), 1–35; Robert Price, "Politics and Culture in Contemporary Ghana: The Big-Man Small-Boy Syndrome," *Journal of African Studies*, 1:2 (1974), 173–204.

56. On the rise of ethnicity in Ghana, see Naomi Chazan, "Ethnicity and Politics in Ghana," *Political Science Quarterly*, 97:3 (1982), 461–85.

57. "Human Tide Sweeps West Africa," *Africa Economic Digest* (4 February 1983), 2–3; "Evacuation from Nigeria," *UNICEF Information*, 10 February 1983.

58. Merrick Posnansky, "How Ghana's Crisis Affects a Village," *West Africa*, no. 3306 (1 December 1980), 2418–20; David Brown, "The Political Response to Immiseration: A Case Study of Rural Ghana," *Geneva-Africa*, 18:1 (1980), 56–74; Kaba, "Rhetoric and Reality," 46.

59. Azarya, *Aristocrats Facing Change*, 192; Rivière, *Guinea*, 190.

60. Chazan, *Anatomy of Ghanaian Politics*, ch. 4; Azarya, *Aristocrats Facing Change*, 179–80, 184–85.

61. See Richard Jeffries, "Ghana: Jerry Rawlings ou un populisme à deux coups," *Politique africaine*, 2:8 (1982), 8–20.

6

Political Transition
and the Dilemma of
Civil Society in Africa

Peter Lewis

A wave of political change has recently swept sub-Saharan Africa.[1] In the wake of the European revolutions of 1989, at least two dozen African regimes, confronted by diverse opposition forces, have been pressured to open their political systems or accede to multiparty electoral rule. Many have instituted substantive reforms, ranging from token liberalization to wholesale adoption of democratic institutions.[2] The collapse of authoritarian governments across the continent has been accompanied by a vocal popular repudiation of personal rule, elitist domination and official corruption.

These developments signal remarkable shifts in the African political landscape, yet they also raise enormous challenges for African political development. The advent of political liberalization, constitutional change and competitive electoral regimes, however salutary, do not ensure transition to sustainable democratic rule on the continent. Democracy will stand or fall on the creation of new political communities and the quality of participation in liberalizing polities.[3]

The recent political ferment has focused attention on a newly invigorated "civil society" in Africa: Observers of African affairs point to the rich associational life that has emerged in Africa during the past 30 years amid weak state institutions and feeble market structures.[4] This proliferation of autonomous associations and social networks has been regarded as a dynamic catalyst for the advent of democracy and a crucial bulwark for the

Published by permission of the *Journal of International Affairs* and the Trustees of Columbia University in the City of New York from the *Journal of International Affairs* 46, no. 1 (Summer 1992): 31–54.

maintenance of democratic governance. Consequently, many have interpreted the decline and collapse of the *ancien regime* as an opening for the assertion of civil society in Africa. Civil society, in turn, is seen as the crucial
agency for creating public accountability and participatory government.[5]

However, this is a misleading image of political change in many
African settings. The African drama should be distinguished from recent
political changes in East Central Europe, Latin America or East Asia,
where the demise of authoritarianism has given way to the reassertion or
invigoration of civil societies. In Africa, by contrast, the decline of weak
predatory states and autocratic rule has opened opportunities for the *formation* of civil society. For most African countries, basic issues of state authority, national identity and social cohesion have not been resolved in
the decades since independence. The emergence of civil society in Africa
is still a nascent historical process.

The encouraging boldness of political opposition in Africa should not
lead us to impute unlimited democratic potential to the societal realm.[6]
Throughout much of sub-Saharan Africa, the nature of domestic social
formations and the character of state-society relations provide a weak basis for the emergence of a civil society. By virtue of their relations with
elites, disengagement from the polity and internal fragmentation, private
interests in Africa have not acted as constituent parts of a common civic
realm or public sphere. Moreover, the central institutions of civil society
are quiescent and fragmented in most African countries. The democratic
project in Africa entails basic changes in popular participation and the associational arena.

These themes will be elaborated through a discussion of civil society in
theoretical and historical perspective, focusing upon the liberal model of
civil society and its relationship to the democratic process. We will then
trace the ways in which African realities diverge from the historical model
of civil society as it has been realized elsewhere. This is followed by a cap-
sule history of state-society relations in sub-Saharan Africa, illustrating two
potential historic "moments" of civil society in Africa. The second moment
leads to an analysis of state-society relations in the current situation, with
an emphasis on patterns of political participation. I conclude with some final reflections on prospects and policy implications.

Civil Society in Africa: Concepts and Questions

In recent years state-centric approaches to African politics have been
complemented by a renewed focus on societal factors. Numerous analysts have augmented the traditional concerns with political elites and
central institutions by focusing on politics and participation at the grassroots.[7] Given the weakness and shallow penetrative capabilities of most

African state structures and the tenuous legitimacy of regimes through-out the continent, it is apparent that considerable disposition of authority and resources occur outside state purview (though not necessarily unen-cumbered by state actors).[8]

The concentration on societal dynamics has renewed interest in the concept of civil society. A rich and heterogenous associational life thrives in most of sub-Saharan Africa, encompassing diverse functional, commu-nal and affective groupings.[9] Labor unions, churches, women's and stu-dent organizations, professional and trade associations, business groups, ethnic and community associations, clan affiliations, secret societies, cul-tural groups and various economic networks have all flourished through-out the colonial and postindependence eras. Associational life often thrives in spite of, or in response to, severe economic privation and politi-cal authoritarianism. Indeed, the vitality of these independent organiza-tions can be viewed as a coping mechanism amidst weak states and tenu-ous market frameworks.[10]

There is little question that the vigorous associational realm in Africa satisfies many essential social and economic needs and implies limits to state power and authority. The advent of political reform, however, raises an array of new questions regarding state-society relations: Does the asso-ciational arena in Africa constitute an autonomous civil society? To what extent can the domain of associations, non-governmental organizations and economic and social affiliations serve the ends of a democratic agenda? Will the self-conscious organization of private interests help to institutionalize limits to state power and equally guarantee the represen-tation of autonomous societal groups? Would the emergence of a civil so-ciety in Africa imply a pluralist or a corporatist political future?

The elements of civil society, by articulating their own interests and contending with the state, may serve as vital agents for democratization. Nonetheless, the presence of an independent societal realm cannot be taken *a priori* as indication of a civil society. Civil society is not automati-cally engendered by autonomous associations and existing private inter-ests: *Society* (considered simply as activity external to the state) is not syn-onymous with *civil society* in its modern meaning. The forms of organization and the substance of political participation are integral to the consolidation of civil society and the construction of a democratic po-litical space.

Defining Civil Society

While notions of civil society may be traced back to classical political the-ory, the contemporary distinction between the state and civil society was elaborated theoretically between the mid-eighteenth and late nineteenth centuries.[11] Numerous observers, responding to the processes of European state building, the development of constitutional government and the spread of industrial capitalism, sought to clarify the distinction between public and private interests. Civil society was delineated as the arena of private and particular concerns within a given polity, institutionally separate and autonomous from the formally constituted public authority of the state.

Among the many writers who explicated theories of civil society, G.W.F. Hegel and Alexis de Tocqueville represent a central dimension of debate. Hegel discussed the idea of civil society as a distinct private realm of commerce, class interest, religion and other individual (and group) prerogatives, distinguished from and juxtaposed to the universal and encompassing power of the state.[12] The Hegelian perspective elaborated a state-centric view of civil society, emphasizing the expansion and entrenchment of state power as the realization of an immanent historical ideal. Alternatively, Tocqueville adopted a society-centered view of civil society.[13] For Tocqueville, the notion of a free and diverse civil society permitted the delimitation of government prerogatives and created a context for constraining arbitrary or intrusive state power.[14]

These divergent views on state and society proceeded from a common point of departure—the advent of national political communities, governed by institutionally articulated states that exercise sovereignty over a comparatively inclusive citizenry. Moreover, the notion of civil society reflected an expansion of participation, as myriad private interests organized around their common concerns and frequently sought direct political influence. Civil society, then, was a historically novel paradigm, referring to political and socio-economic contexts characterized by certain levels of state formation and societal cohesion.

The extensive debates over the concept of civil society have highlighted two essential tensions that help to clarify this elusive concept. First, civil society is at once both *particular* and *corporate.* By definition, civil society encompasses an array of separate and discretionary interests, including individuals, voluntary associations (such as churches, intellectual circles and the professions) and market relations (such as business or economic classes). The constituent elements of civil society freely associate, affiliate or disengage on the basis of perceived interest and preference. Consequently, civil society is neither homogenous nor cohesive; the particularities within the private realm provide considerable basis for conflict and division.[15]

At the same time these disparate, sometimes antithetical concerns are bound by common interests and behaviors, such as the principles of production and exchange, the recognition of family and organizational boundaries, the general desire for stability and antipathy toward the imposition of arbitrary external authority. A minimum of tacit, circumstantial cohesion unifies civil society. Moreover, the self-conscious organization within civil society provides a basis for aggregating interests, linking functional groups and building larger units of political affiliation.[16]

The solidarity of civil society and its separation from the state imply a second tension: Civil society is simultaneously arrayed against the state and engaged with the state in setting the boundaries of public power and guarding its own prerogatives. While civil society intrinsically resists state encroachment, the various interests within civil society also seek to influence the state in the exercise of public policy and the allocation of valued resources. This engagement may be either cordial or antagonistic, but it does reflect a common recognition of state sovereignty and (at least implicit) legitimacy.[17] State and civil society are engaged in a dialogue at arm's-length.

The theoretical construction of civil society, then, encompasses a wide array of state-society relations: The concept may apply to either plural or homogenous societies, and it may include consensual or conflictual relations between governing structures and constituent populations. At the same time, this perspective embodies a notion of corporate interest and engagement. Civil society presupposes a viable political community, in which participants recognize certain boundaries of common destiny and interest.[18] There are limits beyond which societal fragmentation and political distance render the concept inapplicable.

The state-civil society distinction was rooted in a particular historical context comprising an array of interrelated changes in the state, the economy and forms of social organization. The conceptualization of civil society was largely a response to the emergence of the modern legal-rational state, based upon territorial sovereignty, a professional bureaucracy and the rule of law.[19] In this respect, civil society was a relative construct: The idea of an autonomous private realm was defined mainly in contrast to the encompassing power of the state, incorporating society in an expansive web of public authority. The inescapable and impersonal character of state sovereignty created a corresponding imperative for the assertion of a private realm of human affairs.[20] The consolidation of state power constituted a basis not only for administrative domination of society but also for the potential guarantee of personal rights.

Second, civil society was engendered by the development of the capitalist economy.[21] The spread of market relations and commodity production fostered extensive societal integration and gave rise to the articulation of a complex division of labor. Economic change also encouraged broad functional interdependence among economic groups.[22] New forms of industrial organization accentuated both social differentiation and class consciousness. The emergence of a substantial bourgeoisie possessing autonomous sources of wealth constituted a social stratum intrinsically concerned with the limitation of state prerogatives.[23] The dynamics of the market not only accelerated forms of social cohesion but equally fostered the "atomization" of society as an arena of self-interested individuals. Market-driven processes of social stratification impelled the separation of state and society and the differentiation of state and private elites. The market economy simultaneously engendered new interests within civil society and new bases of societal affiliation.

Finally, civil society developed from changes in social organization, some of which were linked to economic transformation. The emergence of class societies reflected the predominance of horizontal social stratification based upon non-ascriptive characteristics.[24] The ascendance of bourgeois society engendered relations of status and power independent of the state.[25] Class divisions accentuated both interdependence and conflict within the "private" realm.[26] The processes of class formation coincided during the nineteenth century with ongoing social transformations, including the accentuation of individualism, the breakdown of religious hierarchies and alterations in the role of the family. These diverse changes gave further impetus to the plural and associative elements of society and encouraged the articulation of private and particular interests. The diminution of affective and corporate ties was a necessary condition for the accentuation of functional interests.

Democracy and Civil Society

From the standpoint of democratic theory, the delineation of boundaries between the state and civil society creates a context for the emergence of a public sphere or civic space, in which state and private actors seek to influence the forms and content of the polity.[27] A flourishing public sphere is engendered by a political community based upon associative relationships and regulated by clearly defined institutional and legal boundaries. In democratic regimes, this entails fairly stringent limits to official prerogatives and basic guarantees to liberty and participation. Paradoxically, the presence of an open arena of contention, debate and consensus between governments and citizens is fundamentally guaranteed by an authoritative state.[28] The coexistence of association, liberty and authority reveals a basic tension in contemporary liberal regimes.[29]

Two additional aspects of the state-civil society relationship have been especially salient for the development of democratic regimes. First, the struggle for inclusive and effective citizenship was central to mediating the relationship between the state and civil society in democratic regimes.[30] By conferring fixed rights and obligations upon members of the polity, citizenship gave substance to the notion of a delimited private realm. The extension of citizenship not only augmented the political community, but it also set explicit limits to the exercise of public authority.

A second important dimension of democratic public life was the emergence of political society, the stratum of political professionals and organizations comprising the core of the representative process.[31] The actors in political society play strategic roles in negotiating, articulating and fostering the interests in civil society, and they hold an equally crucial function in sustaining democratic rules and procedures. A relatively stable and accountable political society is integral to the relationship between civil society and the democratic state.

State and Society in Africa

The preceding discussion is not intended as a rigid historical or institutional template to be imposed on aspiring democratic societies. The challenging processes of democratic experimentation will yield different paths of transition, diverse institutional arrangements and distinctive political cultures in different regions of the world. It is useful to emphasize, however, that the structural continuities evident from the course of European development have subsequently been reflected in the experience of democratizing countries in other areas. The growth of state power and inclusive citizenship, the expansion of commodity production and formal markets, the increasing salience of class-based political participation and the assertion of bourgeois interests have all been important elements in the global political transformations of the past decade.[32]

From a comparative perspective, recent discussions of state-society relations in Africa have emphasized three concepts that serve the purposes of cross-regional analysis. First, the degree of state *hegemony,* denoting the scope of sovereignty and legitimacy, provides a framework for assessing the cohesion and stability of the political system.[33] Second, political *inclusion* denotes the extent of societal access to the formal political process, and consequently indicates the potential arena of participation.[34] Third, the concept of *engagement* suggests the degree of societal involvement or commitment to the public realm.[35]

In contrast to the newly democratizing regimes of Latin America, East Asia and East Central Europe, most African polities are distinguished by limited degrees of effective state hegemony, a narrow range of political inclusion and highly tenuous engagement with autonomous societal groups. This is evident from the structure of state-society relations in Africa and the trends of political and social change during the postindependence era.

In most of sub-Saharan Africa, the establishment of sovereign bureaucratic states was an outcome of colonialism. While it is evident that colonial rule abjured representation and repressed participation, it must also be stressed that colonial development engendered few underpinnings for the emergence of a viable civil society. Colonial domination fostered societal division and political exclusion. European administrators arbitrarily encompassed diverse socio-cultural groups in their territories. The colonial bureaucracy was alien in both its ideology and personnel and authoritarian in its governance.[36] Colonial states, possessing limited penetrative and administrative capacities, were typically distant from their subject populations. Colonial government did not engender state consolidation or effective hegemony, and intermittent patterns of social and economic change thwarted the emergence of a strong and coherent societal realm.[37]

These contours of state-society relations persisted beyond the colonial era. The modal structures of Africa's postindependence states, economies and societies have impeded the formation of a distinct civic space. African states have been distinguished by their comparative weakness and fragmentation. The contemporary state in Africa typically exercises partial and intermittent domination over its society and reflects minimal internal cohesion. State legitimacy is obviated, as claims to represent a universal public function are undermined by authoritarianism and institutional weakness.[38]

Independent African regimes have typically relied upon patrimonial forms of state consolidation and governance. In many countries, highly centralized patrimonial systems are sustained by individual rulers controlling access to sinecures, favors and state revenues.[39] In more decentralized or "prebendal" patterns, public resources are ubiquitously appropriated by a diffuse political-commercial elite.[40] The imperatives of patrimonial rule pose inherent dilemmas for the construction of a democratic civil society.

At its essence, patrimonialism effaces the distinction between public and private interests and roles. Pervasive corruption, favoritism and cronyism have undermined the very substance and neutrality of public power.[41] The prevalence and "embeddedness" of patrimonialism in sub-Saharan Africa hinders the articulation of interests distinct from, and in opposition to, state tutelage.[42] The elitist character of patrimonial rule and the prevalence of clientalism as a mode of allegiance and cohesion hamper the extension of citizenship.[43] Members of the political system appear as clients or subjects, or they are simply marginalized. Clientalism is often commingled with disengagement, as the recourse to individual patrons diverts overt pressure from the state and discourages formal participation.

Like their predecessors, postcolonial African states have typically remained distant from their societies. The autocratic cast of governance and the failure to penetrate or "capture" significant portions of society limit the potential scope of political community.[44] The weak administrative capabilities of African states and the personalization of authority also inhibit the exercise of the rule of law. Patrimonial authority is arbitrary and capricious, offering few guarantees to property, civil rights or public expression. The essential institutional and legal safeguards permitting citizens to defend the private realm are largely absent. In sum, the character of state power in Africa has obscured the boundaries of the public realm and has engendered disengagement from a central political community.

African economies have provided scant basis for the aggregation of private interests or the attenuation of state authority. The tenuous spread of market relations and commodity production throughout much of the continent has given rise to widespread societal fragmentation and marginality. Many African economies are still comprised largely of self-provisioning peasant households with substantial capacity to remain aloof from the formal economy. Markets for capital, labor and commodities are regionally or ethnically segmented and often localized. Society is weakly incorporated in national exchange and authority relations, giving rise to inchoate class identities and uncertain functional linkages.[45]

The marginality and disengagement of many economic sectors in Africa is mirrored by the symbiosis of state elites and the (mainly urban) formal sector. The indigenous private sector in African countries is heavily oriented toward rent seeking and so-called "directly unproductive, profit-seeking" (DUP) activities, entailing the appropriation of politically generated returns from non-productive economic enterprise.[46]

The prevalence of *rentier* activities fosters an intimate interdependence among state and private-sector elites, blurring public-private boundaries and impeding the formation of autonomous means of accumulation outside of state fiat.

The statist character of development strategy and the proliferation of the public sector in most African countries have focused the arena of class formation and private attainment on the state.[47] The combination of economic statism and patrimonial governance has engendered cooptation and dependence on the part of indigenous entrepreneurs. Consequently, there is little social base for contesting state prerogatives or advocating institutional neutrality.[48] Paradoxically, *rentier* activities rely not only on collaboration with state officials, but also evasion of state regulation, taxation and oversight. *Rentiers* are dependent upon the state yet also partially disengaged from public authority.

Alongside the ambiguities of *rentier* groups, there exists an extensive zone of economic activity that is not incorporated in the state domain and is internally fragmented. Large parallel economies have placed enormous resources and networks outside the reach of the central state, save for the depredations of individual officials or freelance security forces.[49] In sum, two distinct tendencies in state-society relations are rooted in the economic structure: first, an ambivalent dependence upon the state, and second, a parochial disengagement from the state. Neither of these tendencies are consonant with the assertion of corporate, private interests or the articulation of an open public sphere.

The dearth of broad solidarities among autonomous social groups in Africa and the inability of private interests to confront the state within a common civic domain constitute the greatest hindrances to the consolidation of civil society.[50] Most African societies are heterogenous and vertically segmented. Primary and corporate group ties have undermined the development of functional or class linkages. Kinship, local and ethnic affinities typically cut across or subsume other social divisions, and consequently class identities have remained weak or embryonic. The ambivalent expressions of class or interest-group politics in Africa, even in nominal corporatist regimes, have limited the strength and programmatic content of participation and association.[51]

Ethnic pluralism is not necessarily antithetical to the formation of inclusive political community and a generalized public sphere. However, the prevalence of invidious communal politics in Africa has engendered societal fragmentation rather than integration. Since the late colonial period, political mobilization in Africa has typically coincided with the accentuation of communal or factional allegiances.[52] The exercise of authority by ethnic patrons, often according to traditional or status criteria, isolates individuals and small groups from wider arenas of association. Indeed, the parochial basis of associational life in much of sub-Saharan Africa, while understandable as a coping mechanism, impedes the processes of inclusion and engagement.

In sum, the historical path of African development has reflected considerable contrast with the patterns found in Europe, Latin America and much of Asia and the Middle East. Low levels of state formation have impeded the articulation of public authority and limited the inclusion of societal groups. African economies have engendered parochialism and self-reliance rather than interdependence and engagement. The fragmentation of African societies, the scant basis of national political community and the commingling of state elites and strategic social groups all hinder the assertion of institutionalized private interests. The typical dispositions of African social groups are partial, clientalist engagement with the state or total alienation from the public sphere.

Historical Trends in Africa

The creation of civil society must be regarded as a historical process, not simply a static structural condition. Since the end of the Second World War, there have appeared in Africa two essential "moments" of civil society: junctures when high levels of popular participation, engagement and commonly articulated interests have coincided with the weakening of established state structures and the redefinition of political regimes. These circumstances have opened opportunities for the establishment of new political communities and the consolidation of an autonomous private realm. The first moment can be dated from the late 1950s through the early 1960s, that is, the late colonial period through the early years of independence. The second moment may be traced to 1989.

The year 1960 stands as the pivotal date of independence in Africa and the culmination of the nationalist movements that appeared after the Second World War. The era of nationalism witnessed a broad popular mobilization against colonial domination. Emergent local elites, spurred by the dislocations and intellectual ferment of the war, pressed for an end to foreign rule. The political space opened by liberalizing colonial regimes facilitated an outpouring of mass participation, while the ensuing negotiations and struggles over independence created an arena for debate over the future of the polity.[53]

A diverse array of organizations, from labor unions to village societies, youth groups, professional associations and syncretist churches, were drawn into the nationalist movement.[54] These myriad elements, representing both traditional interests and new social groups, were typically merged under the umbrella of plural, "congress"-type party organizations. The basis of unity among the disparate participants in nationalist politics was neither deep nor enduring, but the apparent pluralism and enthusiasm of their activities engendered optimism about political change throughout the continent.[55] Though motivated chiefly by a negative goal—the end of foreign rule—their solidarity against colonial domination was often viewed as the nucleus of a new national community.

The postwar movement for independence, then, represented the first possibility for the emergence of civil society, i.e., a flourishing associational arena mobilized for the pursuit of broad popular goals. However, this initial moment quickly subsided with the achievement of independence. The newly independent regimes, dominated by narrow elites, rapidly asserted centralized, authoritarian control over the political system and preempted or suppressed the arena of autonomous association.[56] The democratic constitutions and parliamentary forms hastily transplanted by colonial rulers were rapidly supplanted by a variety of personalistic, single-party or military regimes. While these rulers exhibited a wide range of governing styles—from relatively benign personal rule to corporatist domination to predatory assaults against society—they commonly fashioned systems of governance based upon the exclusion of popular groups from the public realm.

Under these constraints, autonomous association and engagement soon gave way to passive de-participation, repression or empty forms of controlled participation.[57] The common societal response was a retreat into the solidarity and resources of communities and primary groups and an abdication from the public sphere. In the most extreme instances, this was manifest as a virtual "exit" from the state and the economy, an effort to disengage altogether.[58] Alternatively, many groups and individuals adapted to the exigencies of patrimonial rule, utilizing clientalist ties with state elites or appealing as supplicants for special considerations or dispensations from the ruler, whether an individual patron, a ruling junta or a dominant party.

Owing to the weakness and ideological ambivalence of the new regimes, efforts to subordinate the private realm were rarely successful.[59] In the decades after independence, episodes of spontaneous participation and societal resistance appeared regularly on the African landscape. Yet the sporadic initiatives of disparate social groups failed to engender a legally independent arena of associational activity in most countries. While participation and association persisted throughout this period, such activities were often marginal, oblique and dispersed. Private associations rarely entered an open public sphere, and disengagement was far more prevalent than incorporation or inclusion. State domination and societal quiescence contravened the engagement of an autonomous societal realm.

The 1970s witnessed a flurry of political innovation and a spreading pall of economic decline in Africa. Neither of these developments proved salutary for the invigoration of civil societies. Following the 1974 Portuguese coup and the military revolt in Ethiopia, Marxist-Leninist regimes were established in several African countries. A number of established military governments followed the example of the former Portuguese colonies and the Ethiopian junta. While some of these governments displayed impressive attempts at popular inclusion, the centralized model of mobilization of the Leninist party was utterly inimical to the assertion of autonomous societal interests.[60] The ideological and institutional deficiencies of these party-states, aggravated in several instances by the dislocations of war, famine and poverty, engendered a further popular retreat into the private sphere.

By the end of the decade, most of sub-Saharan Africa was in the grips of a sustained economic downturn, reflecting the combined effects of global price shocks, profligate state spending, inappropriate macroeconomic policies and ubiquitous corruption. Economic crises eroded both the extractive and distributive capabilities of many states, fostering a defensive regeneration of associational life. For the next several years, amidst the scarcities resulting from economic decline and the privations entailed by structural adjustment, communities and groups sought recourse to collective coping strategies. Once again, these responses were largely parochial and private—that is, within the realm of *society* rather than civil society—but they did constitute an important new stratum of organization, and in some instances they provided the foundations for an incipient civic realm.[61]

We are currently witnessing the second moment of civil society in Africa, which may be dated from 1989. Throughout the continent, independent political and social forces have emerged to challenge moribund, authoritarian-patrimonial regimes of many varieties.[62] Churches and organized labor, lawyers and students, market women, academics, physicians, journalists, business elites and a host of other interests may be identified among the growing realm of associational participation. Many of these groups were initially provoked by narrow economic or professional concerns, but in country after country their grievances quickly accumulated and became politicized.[63] The result has been a succession of movements pressing for fundamental political change.

In such personalized single-party states as Cote d'Ivoire, Kenya and Zambia, broad-based opposition campaigns have induced leaders, however reluctantly and half-heartedly, to liberalize political life. In the Zambian case, President Kaunda acquiesced to a full-fledged transition to multiparty electoral rule at the end of last year. In an array of Francophone countries including Benin, Togo, Niger and Congo, long-standing military regimes have acceded to popular demands for "national conferences" bringing together opposition groups and government officials to engineer transitions to competitive politics and civilian rule. Military rulers in Nigeria, Guinea and Ghana have initiated planned transitions to civilian electoral government, and the Marxist regimes in the former Portuguese colonies have both muted their ideological identities and committed themselves to democratic reforms.

The recent drive for political transformation may be distinguished from earlier experiences of popular participation. First, the contemporary opposition movements draw upon a greater depth and diversity of associational life. The survival mechanisms necessitated by three decades of weak authoritarian rule and economic stagnation have given rise to a resilient and resourceful associational arena, often bolstered by international linkages and transnational nongovernmental organizations (NGOS).[64] Recent events suggest that the leaders of these organizations are less willing to be compromised or shunted aside by state elites, and the rank and file membership is not easily marginalized.[65]

Second, there appears to be a new ideological climate with regard to participation and governance. The failures of the past three decades have dampened illusions about a sudden political or economic renaissance. Many activists in Africa today evince an appreciation for the travails of evolutionary change, as well as greater skepticism regarding the centralization of power. Moreover, among certain movements and countries

there is a palpable normative commitment to democratic values and procedures.[66] It would be premature to evaluate the depth and resolve of
these attitudes, but they do signal an erosion of the prevailing charismatic
and millenarian premises of political leadership and an abandonment of
the obsolete nostrums of single-party rule. This would suggest greater
ideological tolerance for an autonomous associational realm.

Recent political changes in Africa have also reflected a new international
context. Without neglecting the domestic sources of reform, it is clear that
pressures for democratization in sub-Saharan Africa have been impelled by
the diffusion effects of democratic transitions in other regions, as well as by
changing geopolitical conditions and trends in the global political economy. The current external environment is more hospitable to the assertion
of an autonomous private realm in Africa. Influential models of political
change in Europe and Latin America reflect an important role for interest-
group activity and independent associations. Moreover, external patrons
may actively foster the associational realm, by promoting liberalization as a
condition for aid, and through direct assistance to NGOs.

The course of political struggle and reform in Africa since 1989 suggests a variety of possible outcomes, ranging from the survival of authoritarian rulers to a protracted cycle of liberalization and repression to the
successful consolidation of democratic government.[67] These consequences will be determined not only by the disposition of state actors, but
also by the institutional strength and political cohesion of the opposition
movement and its relation to the broader associational realm. Civil society is not synonymous with political opposition, and the disposition of
activists and incumbents toward an independent arena of private interests will be crucial to the future of the polity.

The possibilities for a limited public sphere and the emergence of a
"core" of civil society are more propitious in some areas than others. We
may discern the origins of a public sphere in such countries as Zambia,
Kenya, Nigeria and possibly Ghana, fostered by a mobilized associational
arena. In each of these countries, there exist durable organizations that
may serve to assert the autonomy of private interests and the integrity of
open political engagement. Labor in Zambia, churches and lawyers in
Kenya, Nigeria's lively independent press and vigorous professional
groups and a proliferation of local and functional associations in Ghana
could potentially foster a substantial civic realm in each of these countries. On the other hand, the fragmentation and weakness of associations
in such countries as Zaire, Cameroon, Mozambique or Gabon suggest
that the assertion of private interests may be less certain and the orientations of the opposition more ambiguous. Moreover, the capacities and inclination of the state apparatus to guarantee participatory space are less
substantial in the latter instances.

The Struggle for Democracy

Analysts of democratic change are agreed upon one point: The global democratic transitions of the past decade represent an open-ended, contingent and uncertain process.[68] However, we can identify certain dimensions of change that foster the consolidation of competitive, participatory regimes in Africa. The emergence of a genuine civil society is an integral part of this process. The character of participation and the forms of associational activity are essential areas to consider.

In this context, several key issues and problems are prominent. First, is the question of institutional consolidation. In Latin America, East Central Europe and East Asia, we can readily identify the key institutions and leaders of civil society. These include the church, organized labor, intellectual circles, student organizations and business associations. These organizations and groups are not always in the vanguard of the democratic opposition, but they are the leading elements in delimiting and defending the autonomy of private interests against the hegemony of an authoritarian state. In most African countries, these institutions are fragmented, weak, coopted or disaffected. The consolidation of institutions *within* civil society is the primary task in the construction of a public sphere.

The political orientations of societal institutions must also be addressed. The ubiquitous parochial and acquisitive influences found within African states are no less pervasive within the associational realm. There is a critical need to assert and define civic orientations in most African countries: a concern with broad questions of public policy, institutional design and issues of national consequence. It is also important to promote habits of conciliation and compromise. Civic orientations must contend directly with the array of sectional, factional and communal particularisms that currently dominate most politics in sub-Saharan Africa.[69] The segmentation of independent associations and the splintering of opposition movements in many countries suggest that the task of constituting a civic space among societal groups is among the most pressing tasks in the quest for democracy.

The reform of political behavior will entail crucial changes in the style of political leadership; this is a third key issue in the creation of civil society. Accountability has typically been lacking in most African institutions, whether at the state or societal levels. The leading institutions of civil society must themselves operate democratically. If accountability and democratic leadership do not prevail, the likely outcome is a reassertion of ethnic entrepreneurs, machine politicians, traditional patrons and notables. Under these circumstances, the process of inclusion may extend no further than a narrow circulation of elites, and the realization of civil society may again be preempted.

There is in the present moment no coherent or inexorable movement toward the creation of a public sphere in Africa. There are certainly dramatic and hopeful movements toward a core of civil society in some countries, as well as the opportunity for an institutionalized private realm. For example, the recent electoral upset in Zambia resulted from struggle by a fairly unified opposition (in which labor leaders played a key role) to protect the associational arena and open the public sphere. The spate of national conferences in West and Central Africa also reflect impressive steps toward political inclusion, and they create a format for assertion of civic participation.[70] The traditional tolerance of diverse interest groups in Nigeria and the profusion of associations under the structural adjustment program in Ghana also provide harbingers of a public sphere.

Alongside these encouraging developments, there exist in most African countries large segments of alienated, inchoate and fragmented groups, whose inclusion and engagement are tenuous at best. Economic decline and stultifying political repression have badly fractured the societal realm in many states. Previous experience suggests that the window of opportunity for the associational realm may be only five years; if a strategic nucleus of civil society can consolidate its position quickly, prospects for the establishment of a public sphere will be enhanced. Moreover, in several states the emergence of a vital associational realm is largely precluded by war and civil strife. Bitter conflicts in Liberia and Somalia call into question the viability of these states as coherent entities, and the legacy of civil war in Mozambique, Angola, Chad and Ethiopia severely impedes the formation of effective linkages among societal groups.

The Prospects for Civil Society

How do we assess the possibilities for the creation of civil societies in Africa and the establishment of democratic political community? Several broad structural changes are implied by the foregoing analysis. Some of these transitions can be addressed by short-term policies, while others entail more comprehensive and protracted alterations. The ongoing challenge of reforming African state structures is essential to the creation of new political community. Democratic institutions and societal autonomy can be guaranteed only by an effective state. There has been widespread recognition that the scope of state intervention in Africa should generally be reduced. However, many existing institutions must also be strengthened (notably the judiciary) or reorganized (notably the security apparatus). Guarantees to personal rights, respect for legal convention and the extension of effective citizenship are all political conditions residing with the state. These conditions are a *sine qua non* for the emergence of a vibrant civil society.

The process of economic reform is also relevant to political change. The reduction of rent-seeking opportunities and the expansion of independent bases of wealth and social mobility will help to engender economic conditions and social groups compatible with a vigorous realm of private interest. In this respect, the implementation of structural-adjustment initiatives and the trend toward privatization may provide openings for the reordering of property rights and the emergence of self-conscious entrepreneurial groups.

With regard to social organization, it is clear that class societies are unlikely to coalesce in most of sub-Saharan Africa in the short term. To a significant extent, communal and factional cleavages will continue to structure the political and associational realm. However, the assertion of civic orientations, undergirded by societal pressures for an expanded public sphere, will tend to bolster the democratic movement. The reciprocal interaction of state elites and autonomous associations is the only context in which sustainable democratic governance can be achieved.

Finally, it is important to note the current absence of a viable political society in much of sub-Saharan Africa. This is perhaps the most essential missing link in the democratic equation. A stratum of intellectuals, entrepreneurs, organizers and legislators who can mediate popular interests, link societal groups with the state and sustain new forms of political procedure will be essential to the democratic project in Africa. An accountable and responsible political stratum can engender both societal autonomy and state regeneration; a prebendal, self-interested and elitist political class may equally scuttle the reform project and prompt further disengagement from the public sphere.

Conclusion

The renaissance of popular opposition to a distant and authoritarian state evokes renewed possibilities for the constitution of civil society in Africa. Prospects for the construction of civil society reside in the nature of associational activity and the behavior of state elites. Associations must forge common ground both organizationally and programmatically around a series of civic demands, including guarantees for political freedoms, institutional safeguards for individual rights and effective participatory structures and processes. These include specific calls for the protection of civil rights, the strengthening of an independent judiciary, the ability to affiliate or interact with political parties and the maintenance of a transparent and legitimate electoral system.

A leadership committed to civic perspectives and willing to attenuate parochial, clientelist or communal modes of politics may also play a pivotal role in fostering broader inclusion and engagement. State elites must respect equally political and civil rights, protect the integrity of democratic institutions and engage in civic politics, thus bolstering the universality and legitimacy of the state. The assertion of civil society in Africa is a multifaceted process, entailing basic changes in the associational arena, the role of an emergent political society and the reconstruction of the state.

Finally, guarantees to property and the consolidation of an efficacious realm of private accumulation will be essential to the construction of civil interests and social differentiation. Political development in sub-Saharan Africa is no more amenable to quick fixes than the intractable problems of economic underdevelopment, the dilemmas of state weakness or the challenges of communal division. A long process of restructuring state-society relations is involved. While policy measures and institutional reforms can help these changes, they do not ensure them.

Notes

1. The author gratefully acknowledges the comments of Nicolas van de Walle and Donald Rothchild in the preparation of this article.

2. For a general profile of these dramatic changes, see Michael Bratton and Nicolas van de Walle, "Toward Governance in Africa: Popular Demands and State Responses," in Goran Hyden and Michael Bratton, eds., *Governance and Politics in Africa* (Boulder, CO: Lynne Rienner Publishers, 1991); and Jon Kraus, "Building Democracy in Africa," *Current History* (May 1991).

3. The emphasis here on political requisites for democratic change does not obviate other important factors (for example, economic performance) that may crucially affect the democratic prospect.

4. The evolving interest in civil society is elaborated by Michael Bratton, "Beyond the State: Civil Society and Associational Life in Africa," *World Politics*, 41, no. 3, 1989; and Naomi Chazan, "Patterns of State-Society Incorporation and Disengagement in Africa," in Donald Rothchild and Naomi Chazan, eds., *The Precarious Balance: State and Society in Africa* (Boulder, CO: Westview Press, 1988).

5. See, for example, Robert Fatton, "Democracy and Civil Society in Africa," *Mediterranean Quarterly* (Fall 1991); Dwayne Woods provides a critical assessment of this image in "Civil Society in Europe and Africa: Limiting State Power Through a Public Sphere," paper presented at the Annual Meeting of the African Studies Association, Baltimore, 1990.

6. Claude Ake, "Rethinking African Democracy," *Journal of Democracy*, 2, no. 1 (Winter 1991) p. 37.

7. The state-centric bias toward "high politics" is contrasted with the "deep politics" revealed by societal perspectives in Naomi Chazan, Robert Mortimer, John Ravenhill and Donald Rothchild, *Politics and Society in Contemporary Africa* (Boulder, CO: Lynne Rienner, 1988); see also Victor Azarya, "Reordering State-Society Relations: Incorporation and Disengagement," in Rothchild and Chazan.

8. Woods, p. 1.

9. Bratton, p. 411.

10. See, for example, Goran Hyden, *No Shortcuts to Progress* (Berkeley: University of California Press, 1983); and Naomi Chazan, "The New Politics of Participation in Tropical Africa," *Comparative Politics*, 14, no. 2 (January 1982).

11. For an incisive perspective on the evolving conceptions of civil society, see John Keane, "Despotism and Democracy: The Origins and Development of the Distinction Between Civil Society and the State, 1750–1850," in John Keane, ed.; *Civil Society and the State* (London: Verso, 1988).

12. Keane, "Despotism and Democracy," p. 50.

13. John Keane, "Remembering the Dead: Civil Society and the State from Hobbes to Marx and Beyond," in John Keane, *Democracy and Civil Society* (London: Verso, 1988). See also Adebayo Olukoshi, "Associational Life During the Nigerian Transition to Civilian Rule," presented at the Conference on Democratic Transition and Structural Adjustment in Nigeria, Hoover Institution, Stanford University, 26–29 August 1990, p. 10.

14. Keane, pp. 50–1.

15. Jean-François Bayart, "Civil Society in Africa," in Patrick Chabal, ed., *Political Domination in Africa* (Cambridge, UK: Cambridge University Press, 1986) p. 112; see also Olukoshi, p. 5.

16. Bayart emphasizes the salience of an "organizational principle" in the consolidation of civil society and observes the weakness of such cohering principles in Africa, pp. 118–9.

17. State legitimacy may be distinguished from the popularity of a given regime; see Giuseppe di Palma, "Legitimation from the Top to Civil Society," *World Politics*, 44, no. 1 (October 1991) p. 55.

18. Reinhard Bendix, *Nation-Building and Citizenship* (Berkeley: University of California Press, 1977) p. 23. See also Edward Shils, "The Virtue of Civil Society," *Government and Opposition*, 26, no. 1 (Winter 1991) p. 7.

19. See Michael Mann, "The Autonomous Power of the State: Its Origins, Mechanisms and Results" in John A. Hall, ed., *States in History* (Oxford: Basil Blackwell, 1986) p. 112. The classic treatment derives from Max Weber, *Economy and Society* (Berkeley: University of California Press, 1978) p. 56.

20. As noted below, this was also prompted by the ascendance of the bourgeoisie; see Shlomo Avineri, *Hegel's Theory of the Modern State* (Cambridge, UK: Cambridge University Press, 1972) p. 51.

21. See Keane, "Remembering the Dead," p. 32; and Shils, "The Virtue of Civil Society," p. 9.

22. Avineri, p. 146.

23. Gianfranco Poggi, *The Development of the Modern State* (Stanford, CA: Stanford University Press, 1978) pp. 79–80.

24. On the distinction between "status" and "class" societies, see Kenneth Jowitt, *The Leninist Response to National Dependency* (Berkeley: Institute of International Studies, 1979) pp. 7–8.

25. Bendix, pp. 64–5; and Keane, "Remembering the Dead," p. 58.

26. Shils, p. 6.

27. Diverse writers have advanced the notion of commonly recognized civic space as the core of participatory political community. See, for example, Jürgen Habermas, "The Public Sphere," in Steven Seidman, ed., *Habermas on Society and*

Politics (New York: Beacon Press, 1989); Samuel Huntington, *Political Order in Changing Societies* (New Haven, CT: Yale University Press, 1968) p. 31; Peter Ekeh, "Colonialism and the Two Publics in Africa: A Theoretical Statement," in *Comparative Studies in Society and History*, 17, no. 1 (January 1975); and Poggi, p. 84.

28. Keane, "Despotism and Democracy," p. 43; Shils, p. 16.

29. Thomas Callaghy, "Politics and Vision in Africa: the Interplay of Domination, Equality and Liberty," in Chabal, p. 48.

30. Gianfranco Poggi, *Images of Society* (Stanford, CA: Stanford University Press, 1972) p. 35.

31. *Ibid.*, p. 31; see also Alfred Stepan, *Rethinking Military Politics* (Princeton: Princeton University Press, 1989). Stepan focuses especially on politicians and political parties.

32. These diverse factors do not necessarily constitute a "package"; different elements have been decisive in distinct circumstances.

33. Crawford Young, "The African Colonial State and its Political Legacy," in Rothchild and Chazan, p. 26.

34. Different forms of political inclusion are discussed by Donald Rothchild and Michael Foley, "African States and the Politics of Inclusive Coalitions," in Rothchild and Chazan, pp. 234–8.

35. Azarya, pp. 6–7. I am modifying Azarya's terminology here; the term "engagement" is synonymous with Azarya's notion of "incorporation."

36. See Young.

37. Larry Diamond, "Roots of Failure, Seeds of Hope," in Larry Diamond, Juan Linz and Seymour Martin Lipset, eds., *Democracy in Developing Countries: Africa* (Boulder, CO: Lynne Rienner, 1988) pp. 6–7.

38. Thomas Callaghy, *The State-Society Struggle: Zaire in Comparative Perspective* (New York: Columbia University Press, 1984) pp. 34–5; Joel Migdal, *Strong Societies, Weak States: Power and Accommodation* (Princeton: Princeton University Press, 1988).

39. Robert Jackson and Carl Rosberg, *Personal Rule in Black Africa* (Berkeley: University of California Press, 1982) p. 42.

40. The concept of prebendalism as a variant of patrimonial rule has been elaborated by Richard Joseph in *Democracy and Prebendal Politics in Nigeria* (Cambridge, UK: Cambridge University Press, 1987) pp. 63–8.

41. *Ibid.*, p. 68; and Ekeh.

42. The concept of embeddedness is elaborated by Mark Granovetter in "Economic Action and Social Structure: The Problem of Embeddedness," *American Journal of Sociology*, 91, no. 3 (November 1985).

43. Otwin Marenin, "The Managerial State in Africa: A Conflict Coalition Perspective," in Zaki Ergas, ed., *The African State in Transition* (London: Macmillan, 1987). See also John A.A. Ayoade, "States Without Citizens: An Emerging African Phenomenon," in Rothchild and Chazan, pp. 112–3.

44. Hyden, pp. 18–22.

45. See Thomas Callaghy, "The State and the Development of Capitalism in Africa: Theoretical, Historical and Comparative Reflections," in Rothchild and Chazan, pp. 78–9.

46. On the phenomenon of rent-seeking, see Catherine Boone, "The Making of a Rentier Class: Wealth Accumulation and Political Control in Senegal," *Journal of*

Development Studies (1989). The acronym DUP was coined by Jagdish Bhagwati; see "Directly Unproductive, Profit-Seeking (DUP) Activities," *Journal of Political Economy,* 90, no. 5 (1982).

47. Larry Diamond, "Class Formation in the Swollen African State," *Journal of Modern African Studies,* 25, no. 4 (1987).

48. Boone, p. 444. See also Paul Kennedy, *African Capitalism: The Struggle for Ascendancy* (Cambridge, UK: Cambridge University Press, 1988) pp. 75–6.

49. For an examination of these dynamics in Zaire, see Michael Schatzberg, *The Dialectics of Oppression in Zaire* (Bloomington: Indiana University Press, 1988) p. 57; and Janet MacGaffey, "Initiatives from Below: Zaire's Other Path to Social and Economic Restructuring," in Goran Hyden and Michael Bratton, eds., *Governance and Politics in Africa* (Boulder, CO: Lynne Rienner, 1992).

50. Bayart, pp. 119–20.

51. See for example John Dunn, "The Politics of Representation and Good Government in Post-Colonial Africa," in Chabal, p. 168.

52. Zolberg, p. 22.

53. *Ibid.,* pp. 19–21.

54. Immanuel Wallerstein, "Voluntary Associations," in James Coleman and Carl Rosberg, eds., *Political Parties and National Integration in Tropical Africa* (Berkeley: University of California Press, 1964) p. 336.

55. Zolberg voiced early skepticism about the depth of the unifying tendency, pp. 34–5.

56. Young, pp. 56–7.

57. Ayoade, p. 114; Callaghy, "Politics and Vision in Africa," pp. 32–4.

58. The "exit" of rural producers is examined by Goran Hyden in *Beyond Ujamaa in Tanzania: Underdevelopment and an Uncaptured Peasantry* (Berkeley: University of California Press, 1980). Naomi Chazan, while emphasizing a broad spectrum of state-society relations, elaborates modes of exit and disengagement in "Patterns of State-Society Incorporation and Disengagement in Africa" in Rothchild and Chazan.

59. Chazan, "The New Politics of Participation," p. 181.

60. Moreover, it is evident that in several instances, the political practice of African Marxist regimes departed from their Leninist ideological mantle. See Edmond J. Keller, "Afro-Marxist Regimes," in Edmond J. Keller and Donald Rothchild, eds., *Afro-Marxist Regimes* (Boulder, CO: Lynne Rienner, 1987).

61. Naomi Chazan has argued that popular associations in Ghana experienced a transformation through the course of the 1980s, from a diffuse and atomized realm of survival to a burgeoning arena of "civil" community; see "The Political Transformation of Ghana under the PDNC," in Donald Rothchild, ed., *Ghana: The Political Economy of Recovery* (Boulder, CO: Lynne Rienner, 1991).

62. The diverse array of political opposition in Africa, and the equally disparate responses of incumbent regimes, has been detailed recently by Richard Joseph, "Africa: The Rebirth of Political Freedom," *Journal of Democracy,* 2, no. 4 (Fall 1991).

63. These processes are analyzed by Bratton and Van de Walle.

64. As in Ghana, for example; see Chazan, "The Political Transformation of Ghana under the PNDC," p. 32.

65. Bratton and Van de Walle, pp. 49–50.

66. Kraus, p. 211.

67. See for example Carol Lancaster, "Democracy in Africa," *Foreign Policy*, no. 85 (Winter 1991) pp. 157–8.

68. Guillermo O'Donnell and Phillippe Schmitter, *Transitions to Democracy: Tentative Conclusions About Uncertain Democracies* (Baltimore, MD: Johns Hopkins University Press, 1986).

69. The distinction between "civic" and "ethnic" political orientations has been emphasized by Kenneth Jowitt; see *New World Disorder: The Leninist Extinction* (Berkeley: University of California Press, 1992) pp. 320–1.

70. See Joseph.

Suggestions for Further Reading

Bratton, Michael. "Beyond the State: Civil Society and Associational Life in Africa." *World Politics* 41, no. 3 (1989).

Chabal, Patrick, ed. *Political Domination in Africa.* London: Cambridge University Press, 1986.

Chazan, Naomi. "The New Politics of Participation in Tropical Africa." *Comparative Politics* 14, no. 2 (1982).

Huntington, Samuel P. *Political Order in Changing Societies.* New Haven: Yale University Press, 1968.

Hyden, Goran. *Beyond Ujamaa in Tanzania: Underdevelopment and an Uncaptured Peasantry.* London: Heinemann, 1980.

_____. *No Shortcuts to Progress.* Berkeley and Los Angeles: University of California Press, 1983.

Kasfir, Nelson. *The Shrinking Political Arena.* Berkeley and Los Angeles: University of California Press, 1976.

Keller, Edmond J, and Donald Rothchild, eds. *Afro-Marxist Regimes.* Boulder: Lynne Rienner Publishers, 1987.

Lonsdale, John. "States and Social Processes in Africa: A Historiographical Survey." *African Studies Review* 24, no. 2/3 (1981).

Migdal, Joel. *Strong Societies and Weak States: State-Society Relations and State Capabilities in the Third World.* Princeton: Princeton University Press, 1988.

Rothchild, Donald, and Naomi Chazan, eds. *The Precarious Balance: State and Society in Africa.* Boulder: Westview Press, 1988.

Scott, James C. *The Moral Economy of the Peasant: Rebellion and Subsistence in Southeast Asia.* New Haven: Yale University Press, 1977.

Part Three

Class, Ethnicity, and Gender

Understanding the major social inequalities and the relationships among different groups or sectors is integral to grasping the dynamics of African development. Social divisions form an important basis for political alignments and conflicts. Studies of the region have traditionally focused on class distinctions and ethnic cleavages, but more recently greater attention has been focused on the role of gender inequalities in politics and society. All three forms of stratification have patterned the contours of participation, competition, and change in African countries.

The conventional view of class relations focuses on social hierarchies defined by income and occupational categories. In many regions, the horizontal inequalities among class groups are frequently manifest in participation in different interest-based organizations. In many Latin American and Asian countries, for instance, business groups, labor organizations, or peasant movements play important roles in political life. In most African settings, however, we are confronted with a more ambiguous picture, as economic disparities have not always given rise to strong class identities, and politics have rarely been defined by class-oriented parties or associations. In part, this can be attributed to the comparatively low levels of industrialization and economic diversification in most African economies. Political participation is also influenced by other cleavages and the strategies of ruling groups.

Ethnicity has been a more potent source of mobilization in African politics. Ethnic groups usually form around common identification on the basis of language, culture, locality, religion, race, or other attributes. Ethnicity is often an ascribed identity, passed on through kinship and community, although it is also a subjective affiliation, based upon the feelings of individual group members. While ethnic distinctions may have great durability and force, it would be misleading to assume a fixed, essential identity peculiar to each group of people. Ethnic allegiances are often shaped by political and economic circumstances, including competitive challenges or threats from others. To an important degree ethnicity is defined by contemporary situations, rather than age-old cultural determinants.

The patterns of ethnic association in Africa have been formed by the historical contours of state formation as well as the initiatives of contemporary leaders. Group identity was often formed or strengthened by the definition of territorial boundaries under colonial rule. The arbitrary merger of peoples within the colonial state created new competition for resources and influence. Such tensions were accentuated by the discriminatory policies of colonial authorities along with general processes of economic modernization. Nationalist leaders and politicians in the postindependence era frequently encouraged ethnic allegiance as a means of building constituencies. Moreover, the inequitable treatment of groups and regions by many governments has accentuated contemporary tensions, as witnessed in countries as diverse as Nigeria, Kenya, Congo, and Rwanda.

Analysts have been slower to recognize the importance of gender inequalities in African societies. In addition to the burdens of class and ethnic disparities, African women experience the hardships of gender discrimination. Women provide the greater proportion of rural labor in most of Africa, while also shouldering domestic responsibilities and other economic roles within the household. Political mobilization along gender lines has been relatively limited in the region, and issues of interest to women are often slighted in national politics. In consequence, the site of struggle over gender issues has commonly been at the community and household levels. In many instances women are most strongly organized in local associations and community-based networks. Although these sectors can exert considerable influence on certain issues, women's organizations continue to push for acceptance within "mainstream" politics.

The following readings explore the nature of social inequalities in Africa and the effects of societal division on political activity. The first two articles address complementary aspects of class relations. Richard Sklar observes that class domination in Africa has typically been constructed on political rather than economic foundations. Elite status and social hierarchies have arisen not so much through control over assets or production, as access to state power. Conversely, as Catherine Boone points out in her study of Senegal, the economic underpinnings of class position are commonly sustained through special access to resources controlled by government. Rent-seeking behavior, in which economic opportunities are afforded through selective entry to state-regulated markets, has been the basis of private accumulation in most countries of the region.

Turning to the ethnic dimension, Donald Rothchild, in an essay published here for the first time, provides a concise account of evolving state strategies toward ethnicity, extending from the colonial period to the present. Noting the shift from authoritarian hegemony toward more reciprocal interactions between states and social groups, Rothchild considers the implications of political liberalization for ethnic relations and identifies some alternative political arrangements available to reforming countries. He evaluates the possibility that different institutional arrangements can foster greater ethnic accord in Africa's potentially fractious states.

Aili Mari Tripp begins with the theme of ethnicity and then shifts our focus to the crosscutting influence of gender on political association. Her article details the forms of organization among women's groups in two East African countries, offering an illustration of the political and economic strategies of this traditionally subordinated sector. The study provides insight into the role of gender divisions in shaping political participation, and it suggests some important implications of organization in the informal sector for the contours of a nascent civil society.

7

The Nature of
Class Domination in Africa

Richard L. Sklar

In the newly developing countries, major aspects of economic organisation are subject to foreign control. The citizens and governments of such countries learn to live with the effects of pervasive economic dependence upon the industrial powers. Foreign governments and businessmen often determine the rate and scope of local capital investment, the development and use of economic resources, the composition and direction of external trade.

Given this condition, it is widely believed that privileged groups and those who conduct the business of government in non-industrial countries are, knowingly or not, local agents of foreign domination. The Marxist conception of class fosters that belief. Marxist theory posits an economic basis of class determination: classes in society are determined by the mode of economic production; they emerge when people who occupy similar positions in the economic structure of society become aware of their common interests. A dominant class is then defined as one whose members own and control the means of economic production. Where the economy of a country is subject to foreign control, the very existence of a truly dominant indigenous class is called into question by this doctrine. Those who may appear to constitute a dominant class are alleged, by many analysts of this persuasion, to subserve a foreign class that is *really* dominant.[1]

The idea of foreign domination by proxy, through the medium of a clientele or puppetised upper class, is controverted by a large body of evidence. In many post-colonial and newly developing countries, governments, businessmen, and leaders of thought regularly defy the demands and frustrate the desires of their counterparts in the industrial countries.

Reprinted with the permission of Cambridge University Press from the *Journal of Modern African Studies* 17, no. 4 (1979): 531–552. © 1979 Cambridge University Press.

The diplomatic independence of states that are formally non-aligned in the conflict of superpowers is a leading feature of contemporary international relations. In the economic sphere, it is now commonplace for countries that welcome foreign investment to nationalise, or 'indigenise', foreign-owned enterprises, in whole or in part. Furthermore, the evidence of sustained industrial growth in agrarian countries that have adopted capitalist strategies of economic development is unmistakable.[2]

Nationalisation and industrial growth undermine traditional forms of foreign economic domination; but they do not necessarily abolish the condition of fundamental economic dependence. Indeed, the processes of economic modernisation often result in new and more stable forms of class-based exploitation. Nor does the exercise of political authority by a nationalistic state refute the idea of domination by a foreign capitalist class. Marxist political theory specifically allows for a limited or 'relative' autonomy on the part of any state that acts 'in behalf' of a dominant class.[3] At issue for those who adopt a class analytic approach to the study of development is the origin and social basis of the dominant class in question. Is it indigenous to the newly developing country itself, or is it based in an alien society?

To date, social theorists have dimly and doubtfully perceived the reality of indigenous class domination in newly developing countries. In Marxist thought, the presumed economic basis of class determination is a major obstacle to the comprehension of class structures that may appear to have been reared, largely, upon non-economic foundations. However, a revisionist tendency in Marxian sociology does envisage a much broader basis of class determination. Stanislaw Ossowski, for one, has argued that the orthodox Marxian determinants of class—ownership of the means of production and the employment of hired labour—are, by themselves, poor points of departure for realistic class analyses of modern industrial societies.[4] In his opinion, corporate capitalism and bureaucratic socialism, alike, give rise to class structures that imply the presence of two additional determinants; control over both the 'means of consumption' and, remarkably for a Marxist approach, the 'means of compulsion'.[5] Surely, these 'political' determinants of class position are also relevant to class analyses of the non-industrial countries, where class domination on an economic basis, primarily, is not a credible idea.[6]

A theory of class structure, grounded, as Ossowski appears to suggest, in a broad conception of social control, might illuminate a new horizon for development studies. It would clarify the relationship of political organisation to social structure, and reveal the basis of autonomous action by dominant classes that are indigenous to newly developing countries. Although the elements of class analysis for non-industrial societies cannot, as yet, be specified with the confidence that is born of wide acceptance, various studies indicate several topics that would be fruitful to explore, including class formation, consolidation, identification, and action.

Class Formation

Social scientists have been relatively slow to recognise the appearance of dominant classes in modern African societies. During the 1950s, a few scholars did identify the African 'middle class' as the primary source of nationalist assertion.[7] My own study of Nigerian political parties during the final decade of British rule described an 'emergent or new and rising class', one that was 'engaged in class action and characterized by a growing sense of class consciousness'. The composition of this incipiently dominant class was indicated by four objective criteria:

> high-status occupation (notably professionals, educators, substantial business-men, and senior functionaries in the public service and in public or private enterprise), high income, superior education (especially in the cases of professionals, civil servants, and teachers), and the ownership or control of business enterprise.[8]

Political parties in Nigeria, before and immediately after the attainment of independence in 1960, were conspicuous agents of class formation. They created elaborate systems of administrative and commercial patronage, involving 'the liberal use of public funds to promote indigenous private enterprise, while many of their leading members entered upon a comparatively grand manner of life in parliamentary office'. The major parties, and those governmental agencies that were subject to their control, exercised power derived from the emergent class and the existing communal foundations of society. In cases of conflict between newly dominant class-interest groups and communal-interest groups, the former would normally prevail.[9]

By far the most populous country in Africa, containing between 16 and 20 per cent of the continental population, Nigeria is noted for its cultural, linguistic, and social diversity. The contrast between dominant-class formation in the communities of southern Nigeria, where class-like forms of social stratification are not traditional, and similar social processes in the theocratic Muslim Emirates of the North, is especially striking.[10] In southern Nigeria, the dominant class is a virtually exclusive product of the major forces of modern social change—western education, modern methods of communication, urbanisation, and the growth of commerce.[11] In the northern Emirates, by contrast, modern class formation occurs within the firm context of a traditional order structured by the feudal principles of aristocratic birth and sociopolitical rank. Dominant-class formation in this region involves the social and political coalescence of traditional rulers, administrative functionaries of both aristocratic and humble origins, and business-men. The persistence of traditional authority in northern Nigeria exempli-fies the complexity of class formation in many parts of modern Africa.[12]

So too in Ethiopia has a modern ruling class arisen within the frame-work of a feudal-type traditional order. Nurtured in urban centres and small towns, the core of this class is an educated administrative élite, re-cruited from the families of landowners, merchants, and officials.[13] John Markakis, who has described the formation of this class, estimated its size in 1970 to be 'a few tens of thousands' in a society of some 25 million[14] Prior to the revolution of 1974 and the subsequent abolition of private property in land, members of this class were closely associated with land-lordism. In addition to their inherited holdings, they were avidly engaged in the acquisition of both rural and urban land for commercial purposes. The revolution has now blocked this avenue of enrichment, but the main forces of class formation—modern education and public employment—are likely to sustain the vitality of Ethiopia's ruling class whatever may become of the practice of landownership.

In eastern and central Africa, economic opportunities during the colonial era were largely monopolised by immigrant races—European and Asian in that order. Africans were subjugated by means of their exclusion from the exercise of political rights and the denial of access to educational opportu-nities above primary-school grades. Since the attainment of national inde-pendence by numerous states in this region from 1960 onwards, dominant classes have arisen with remarkable rapidity. This process has been studied by social scientists in most of the countries concerned, notably in Kenya, where the right to acquire productive property is upheld in the name of 'African' as opposed to alien conceptions of 'socialism'.[15]

As a result of this policy, a large and racially diversified landowning sector coexists with the most affluent and vigorous business community in eastern Africa. By 1974, African proprietors owned more than one-third of the few thousand farming estates that were exclusively held by Euro-peans 20 years earlier. Although industry and finance are still largely con-trolled by foreign interests, African (and to a lesser extent Asian) busi-nessmen control the means of internal distribution and transportation.[16] The frequently competing interests of economic groups in Kenya are co-ordinated by officials who relate positively to the goals and values of for-eign and domestic businessmen.

In Zambia, a badly deprived African population of some 4 million emerged from colonial domination in 1964 with a tiny educated élite of but 109 university graduates (including one engineer and four doctors) and about 1,200 secondary-school 'graduates'. Since then, Zambia has experi-enced a breathtaking organisational revolution effectuated from above. Thousands of graduates from post-secondary institutions in Zambia and abroad have entered the senior divisions of the civil service and even more lucrative positions in the burgeoning public enterprise or 'parastatal' agencies. Despite the egalitarian precepts of a national doctrine propagated by the political leaders of a one-party state, the immediate beneficiaries of Zambia's educational and organisational revolutions, in the aggregate, exhibit élitist patterns of behaviour and acquisitive tendencies that mark the process of class formation. With genuine dismay, President Kaunda has deplored the appearance of 'this new class', nurtured by reforms that were intended to foster egalitarian democracy.[17] By contrast with Kenya, the Zambian Government does not overtly encourage large-scale farming. However, members of the new class have rushed to purchase farmland formerly held by white settlers, often obtaining loans secured by their regular salaries or by political influence.[18] Their incomes from such holdings will scarcely be affected by the formal conversion, in 1975, of freehold tenure into long-term (100-year) leaseholdings for ideological reasons.

These cases serve to identify a few intellectual issues that arise in recent studies of dominant-class formation. First, what are the precipitants of this process and the principal agencies that cause it to occur? In every case, the exertion of political power in the form of state action appears to overtake and outweigh more gradual processes of economic and social change. In reality these forces are not entirely separable; nor are they easily isolable for analytical purposes. For example, special interest groups, including property owners and traditional rulers, have often supported political action to create economic opportunities, institute modern education, and indigenise both public and private bureaucratic organisations. However, the beneficiaries of these innovations have sometimes used the logic of modern nationalism to destroy their patron saints of yesteryear, as in the case of Ethiopia. In other cases, as in northern Nigeria, propertied and traditional interest groups have rushed to the head of events, thereby creating an overall impression of social continuity rather than change. In all cases, dominant-class formation is a consequence of the exercise of power by those who control various and diverse social organisations.[19]

It is important to add that the 'political' basis of class formation is not limited in meaning to the political control of economic resources. The latter idea is probably not inconsistent with doctrines that posit a strictly economic basis of class determination. Here I wish to advance a more controversial proposition: that class relations, at bottom, are determined by relations of power, not production.

A second, yet related issue for students of dominant-class formation in Africa involves the rôle of both traditional ruling classes and indigenous, primarily rural, capitalists. This issue is ably analysed by Irving Leonard Markovitz in his synoptic overview of class action in Africa.[20] The matter is clarified by his perceptive distinction between 'chiefs' acting in concert as a 'pressure group', in which case their group is but 'one among many others', and such persons 'as ongoing elements of the ruling class'. With particular reference to northern Nigeria, Markovitz identifies the contribution of traditional rulers to modern class formation thus:

> As members of [the ruling class today], the chiefs might not exist as chiefs, for ruling might very well necessitate radical changes of appearance and expertise. What matters are not so much the formal instruments of power, but the relative position of dominance vis-à-vis other social strata.[21]

This perception reveals a further fundamental distinction: that between traditionalism and conservatism. Chiefs united as a pressure group thereby assert the values of tradition, whatever else they may intend to accomplish. As members of a modern ruling class, however, traditional rulers are more profoundly conservative, as they seek 'to maintain their social, political, and economic power'. From this perspective, Markovitz observes, 'change need not necessarily be viewed as a threat; it may even be welcomed as a means of consolidating power'.[22]

A third, purely abstract, issue relates to the way in which the process of class formation is conceptualised. This account draws attention to the 'fusion of élites' as a critical process in dominant-class formation.[23] It identifies diverse élites—wealthy businessmen, senior administrators of both private and public-sector organisations, leading politicians, members of learned professions, and prominent traditional authorities—that represent various kinds and sources of power. Yet they identify with one another more firmly and in more ways than they do with their respective institutional bases or organisational activities. They appear to unite and act in concert—consciously so—on the basis of their common interest in social control, and this may be identified as the wellspring of class formation.

Class Consolidation

Whereas class formation, as Marx believed, is consummated by the political consciousness of a class acting for itself *(für sich)*,[24] class consolidation is an idea about social organisation, including the economic and specifically political foundations of power. In order to consolidate—protect and extend—their positions of power, the leaders of newly dominant classes quickly reconstruct the existing organisation of authority in accordance with their perceived needs. Class action of this kind is divisible for analytical purposes into economic and political components.

Economic Consolidation

Class interests are likely to prevail when they are promoted in the name of national aspirations. Economic independence is a broadly accepted nationalist ideal; a patriotic national leadership will always seek to indigenise economic power.[25] In all but a few African countries, this endeavour takes two principal forms: support for indigenous enterprise, including the transfer of foreign assets to local owners; and nationalisation or state participation in the ownership of productive property and natural resources. The relatively few exceptions to this dual approach are those countries with strictly socialist régimes—Guinea, Guinea-Bissau, Congo People's Republic, Angola, Mozambique, Tanzania, Somalia, and Ethiopia—that actively discourage or prohibit many, if not all, forms of private enterprise. Elsewhere indigenisation spells economic consolidation of the dominant class.

The techniques of this consolidation process are displayed on a massive scale in Nigeria, where public programmes in support of indigenous private enterprise have existed since 1949. They were used imaginatively to promote nationalist goals and more dubious partisan political aims during the decade prior to independence and the succeeding era of regionalist rivalry from 1960 to 1966. Since the civil war of 1967–70, indigenisation has been a cornerstone of economic policy; its meaning has been summarised thus:

> Indigenization in the private sector is a policy of extending Nigerian ownership and control by government fiat or pressure. Government leverage is employed either to exclude or to evict foreign concerns from certain fields of economic activity or to require direct sale of partial or complete ownership of existing foreign firms.[26]

Successive versions of the Nigerian Enterprises Promotion Decree have specified nearly 100 categories of enterprises for either 100 or 60 per cent Nigerian ownership. All unspecified categories are required to have a 40 per cent Nigerian shareholding. By 1979, assets valued at more than $700 million had been transferred from foreign to Nigerian owners. Public and private lending agencies facilitated the purchase by Nigerians of high-yielding shares at transfer prices that were set at enticingly low levels (and would quickly appreciate in value) by an official commission. As Sayre P. Schatz remarks, 'Indigenization provided a windfall for a sprinkling of fortunate Nigerians.'[27]

Indigenisation under military auspices in Nigeria coincided with the great petroleum boom during the decade of the 1970s that permitted generous wage and salary increases, authorised, at first, by the Government for public-sector employees in 1974, and adopted by private enterprise in 1975. The specified salary hikes of 30 to 100 per cent for individuals who were already relatively well paid were characterised by some Nigerian critics with biting realism as a 'bribe' to privileged elements so that they would accede to the continuation of military rule. Whatever the motivation, 'The surge in oil wealth and the resultant ... wage increases unleashed a veritable frenzy of acquisition'.[28] Furthermore, nationalised banks, including Barclays and Standard (now 60 per cent owned by the Government), provided low-interest loans to many thousands of Nigerians who wished to invest in foreign firms.[29]

While the indigenisation of capitalist enterprise in Nigeria is a leading nationalist goal, capitalist development as such is undeniably dependent upon public and foreign investment. Under the Third (1975–80) National Development Plan, foreign investors continue to provide the lion's share of private investment. Increasingly, they undertake to form partnerships with local private investors and governmental agencies. In the oil sector, the Nigerian National Petroleum Corporation soon acquired 55 per cent ownership of the producing companies and 60 per cent of the companies that market oil in Nigeria. The current policy for economic development is succinctly characterised by Schatz as follows: 'nurture-capitalism with state capitalist, welfare and accelerated-development tendencies.'[30]

There are ample grounds for scepticism about the 'welfare' component of Nigerian economic policy and reason to doubt (as does Schatz) the probability that public-sector investment will soon develop 'state capitalism' as the dominant force in Nigeria. What cannot be gainsaid, however, is the consolidation of a dominant class committed to capitalist development. More elaborate by far than other such examples in Africa, each of which has its own distinctive features, the Nigerian situation is striking and by no means atypical.

Political Consolidation

The most common political device for dominant-class consolidation in Africa has been authoritarian government.[31] Authoritarian régimes infringe liberty by disallowing the right of citizens freely to form political associations that may compete for control of the state. When the political leadership of a dominant class is unable to organise state power effectively, military intervention becomes probable. This kind of organisational revolution, or drastic change in the structure of authority, does not normally produce a change in the class content of power. As José Nun has commented with reference to 'the middle-class military coup' in Latin America, military régimes usually 'represent' the dominant class 'and compensate for its inability to establish itself as a well-integrated hegemonic group'.[32]

Similarly, an embattled class may seek salvation in military rule, although the social cost of this resort cannot be reckoned in advance. Thus, in Uganda, the régime of Milton Obote threatened the interests of closely-knit privileged elements—businessmen, professionals, civil servants, and landowners—in the southern, wealthier part of the country. As his redistributionist programme was sabotaged by antagonistic civil servants, Obote relied upon an aggrandised military establishment to uphold his authority. In an explanation of the Uganda *coup d'état*, Michael F. Lofchie shows why Obote's position was virtually untenable.

> the Uganda army was one of the most highly paid military organizations in all of Anglophone Africa, especially at its rank and file levels, and its commander, Idi Amin, was, in all likelihood, one of the most highly paid soldiers in all of the English-speaking African countries . . . The salary scale of the army was directly comparable to that for the civil service with commissioned officers enjoying levels of income that were at least the equivalent of those of the country's highest level bureaucrats. Moreover, soldiers enjoyed a host of additional material benefits not available to any other Uganda citizens, including free clothing, food and housing, free educational and medical benefits, burial grants and family allowances. If it is taken into account that the average per capita income for Africans in Uganda during the mid-1960s was only about £12 or $30 per year, then military incomes [e.g. £510 or $1,275 per year for sergeants] appear truly astronomic by comparison with those of the vast majority of the population, the peasant and subsistence farmers . . . soldiers of all ranks had become a self-consciously privileged stratum, deeply aware of their materially favored status and determined to protect it at all costs . . . [The coup of 1971] made it possible for soldiers to continue an ongoing process of personal accumulation.[33]

In brief, the army shared the values of the dominant class and seized its leadership with ruthless abandon.

At the time of writing, only three of the 50 sovereign states in Africa, namely Botswana, Gambia, and Mauritius—each with a population of just over a million or less—have constitutional, as distinct from authoritarian, governments. But the cause of constitutional, or limited, government has been revived in several other countries, notably Nigeria and Ghana, where the oppressive features of authoritarian rule are manifestly incompatible with the liberal values of dominant classes.

Following the conclusion of the Nigerian civil war, in 1970, the military Government of General Yakubu Gowon unveiled a programme for the restoration of civilian rule in 1976. Gowon's repudiation of that pledge in 1974 was a major factor in his removal as Head of State the following year. His successor, General Murtala Muhammed, appointed an all-civilian, 50-member constitution drafting committee, representing all sections of the country and a broad spectrum of opinion, tilted towards the learned professions and university faculties. The committee produced a draft constitution, firmly grounded in the precepts of liberal democracy,[34] that was approved with minor alterations, in 1978, by an elected constituent assembly. The constitution provides for a federal form of government, separation of powers at the centre, a bicameral legislature with equal representation of the states in a co-ordinate upper chamber, and democratic representation in the federal and state legislatures by means of electoral competition between political parties that would be free to form on a national (as opposed to a sectional) basis.

This example appears to have influenced the course of events in Ghana, where educational development and dominant-class formation is proportionate to that in Nigeria. In 1977, university students and members of all professional bodies in the country united to demand the resignation of a faltering military régime. In the face of threats by the bar association, the medical association, and other professional groups to withhold services to the state, General I. K. Acheampong declared that civilian and constitutional government would be restored.

Limited government implies a commitment to political freedom. Its reappearance on a grand scale in West Africa also betokens the existence of dominant social classes, whose members are confident of their ability to manage the affairs of society. Liberal governments are far more stable and less susceptible to revolutionary upheaval than dictatorships that serve the interests of privileged classes in an oppressive and demeaning manner.

Class Identification

The methodology of class analysis includes both subjective and objective identification. Subjective identification, or consciousness of class, is the expression for what people think about their own class position (self-identification) and the positions of others. This subject has not been studied widely or comprehensively enough in Africa to justify general conclusions. However, evidence relating to the attitudes of university students does indicate a strong identification with class privilege on their part. Having analysed a large sample survey of university students in Ghana, Tanzania, and Uganda, Joel D. Barkan reports findings that attest to their socially conservative consciousness of class:

> Most African university students conceive of themselves as future members of a technocratic upper-middle class of organization men rather than as members of a presumptive ruling elite ... Most students regard the elite/mass gap as inevitable, and justify its existence on the grounds that the technocratic class makes a significant contribution to national development ... Consistent with their desire to become technocrats in the bureaucracies of their countries' governments, most African university students are relatively apolitical. Though they subscribe to a technocratic conception of authority and perceive the political elite in pejorative terms, students are unlikely to challenge the political elite so long as it solicits their expertise and guarantees them the life style of the upper-middle class they covet. As a result, it

would seem that a tacit bargain of mutual non-interference has been reached between the new organization men of Africa and the political elites which they will soon serve.[35]

In the absence of systematically acquired data on this subject, similar to that presented by Barkan (survey research data may be indispensable for this purpose), the class consciousness of large groups of people can only be inferred from their actions. This need not be an entirely impressionistic method, since astute and knowledgeable observers can draw reasonable inferences from observations of events and discussions with participants. However, class action, itself, is an inference from behaviour that can be observed and described, specifically individual or group action. As a concept, then, class action has analytical and explanatory rather than descriptive significance. Hence, alleged examples of class consciousness that are not directly derived from individuals themselves by scientific survey methods are twice removed from reality.

Classes may be identified objectively for analytical purposes on the basis of either criteria or group actions that can be described. A list of objective criteria for the composition of newly-dominant classes in non-industrial countries would include the four that I have specified above in relation to class formation—high-status occupation, high income, superior education, and the ownership or control of business enterprise—in addition to a specific measure of power, such as the ability to control the means of consumption and compulsion, as suggested by Ossowski.[36] When the dominant class has been identified on this basis, it must shed its anonymity as the fledgling 'new class' and receive a name that is appropriate to its nature. The problems of naming are not without substantive significance.

The Nomenclature of Class Analysis

Engels defined the term 'bourgeoisie' to mean 'the class of modern capitalists, owners of the means of social production and employers of wage-labour'.[37] Recently, the term has been used by Marxists and others to identify dominant classes in societies that maintain market economies and allow capitalist accumulation as a consequence of private property in the means of production. Thus broadly conceived, the generic term may be variously qualified for analytical purposes. Such qualification would correspond to stages in bourgeois class development and variations of social composition. Several different qualifiers have been systematically applied by students of bourgeois class domination in Africa, among them 'bureaucratic', 'state', 'auxiliary', 'managerial', and 'organisational'.

The conception of a 'bureaucratic bourgeoisie' as the new ruling class has been adopted in several works, notably the influential studies of Ian

Clegg in Algeria and Issa G. Shivji in Tanzania.[38] Many others have used this popular term as a merely felicitous expression without particular reference to class analysis. A related term, 'administrative bourgeoisie', corresponds to the phrase 'bourgeoisie of the civil service', used with opprobrious intent by René Dumont and Frantz Fanon.[39] To my mind, all such terms are too narrowly conceived to comprehend the dominant class of a developing country that has a significant entrepreneurial sector in addition to a large and growing number of persons in professional occupations. Theoretically, a functional élite, such as the civil and military bureaucratic élite, by itself could form an élite-class. But this limiting case does not exist anywhere to my knowledge. In all societies, the functionary element is part of a social class, not its sole constituent.[40]

A few scholars have preferred the closely related term 'state bourgeoisie'. Thus, for Samir Amin, the state bourgeoisie grows out of an administrative bureaucracy when the state takes over large portions of the foreign-owned sector of the economy. Then, in his view, the state bourgeoisie or 'upper strata of the bureaucracy' may merge with the 'landed oligarchy' to form a 'new bourgeoisie of the comprador type'.[41] Evidently, Amin does not use the term 'state bourgeoisie' to identify the entire new class, which is, in his view, dominated by an alien bourgeoisie, based in the industrial capitalist countries.

With specific reference to Zaïre, J. Ph. Peemans describes the 'state bourgeoisie' as 'essentially a political group, which exercises an overall control over the economic resources of the country'. Most of the new recruits to this class are 'sons of the petty bourgeoisie', many of whom have received post-secondary education:

> Through its control of the State . . . [this new class] is able, as a group, to control the capital accumulation process in Zaïre, and is responsible for the conditions of its relation to the international system; the use of State power is likewise the means by which individual members of the emerging class can insert themselves into the structures of capital ownership, not only as administrators of State and 'mixed economy' enterprises, but also through savings on high salaries, various earnings and sideline incomes channelled by the exercise of public authority. Savings can be invested in trade, transport and real estate, or converted into land. The State bourgeoisie can acquire a more secure economic position, and can join the upper ranks of the commercial bourgeoisie.[42]

Here again, the identity of socially dominant 'bourgeois' elements as a single class is left open to question.

In his work on Kenya, Colin Leys—unlike Shivji, Amin, or Peemans—distinguishes between all sections of the 'bourgeoisie' and the 'higher bureaucracy'.[43] He refers to the highest stratum as an 'auxiliary bourgeoisie' in 'firm alliance' with foreign capital. The 'higher bureaucracy', he notes, emulates the earning power of management in the private sector and promotes the interest of foreign capital.[44] These formulations support a finding of neo-colonialist domination in Kenya, but they do not result in the conception of a single dominant class.

An attempt to represent the dominant class of a non-industrial and non-socialist country comprehensively, and as an incarnation of the bourgeoisie, appears in my study of the impact of multinational mining companies in Zambia:

> [The] term or category should reflect the coexistence of a newly developing and dependent private enterprise sector with a preponderant yet protective public sector. In this circumstance, which is widespread in the 'Third World', businessmen, bureaucrats, leading politicians, and members of the learned professions constitute a new ruling class. I suggest the term 'managerial bourgeoisie' to designate this class. Inasmuch as this term clearly refers to the private business elite as well as the managers of public enterprises and high governmental officials, it may be preferred to either 'bureaucratic' or 'state' bourgeoisie. Moreover, this term, in contrast with the term 'entrepreneurial bourgeoisie', reflects the apparent disposition of bourgeois elements in newly developing countries to manage the production and distribution of wealth rather than to create new wealth-producing enterprises.[45]

Since the managerial bourgeoisie, as here described, arises during a period of economic reconstruction, its composition is protean and its capacity for adaptation to change is considerable. In directly productive economic spheres, its members include managers of foreign firms, managers of domestic firms, local—i.e. national—entrepreneurs, and state bureaucrats. Although this mixture, as an equilibrated composition of diverse elements, is likely to persist for a long time in many countries, it is, none the less, characteristic of a transitional economic phase. Should a given economy foster public, at the expense of private, enterprise, state bureaucrats would displace other elements, and the dominant class as a whole would then become increasingly state-centred. Conversely, the development of private enterprise as the predominant mode of production would transform the 'managerial' bourgeoisie into a 'corporate' or 'entrepreneurial' bourgeoisie depending upon the form of capitalist economic organisation.

In his wide-ranging examination of 'power and class in Africa', Markovitz introduces the term 'organizational bourgeoisie'.

> I use the term *organizational bourgeoisie* to refer to a combined ruling group consisting of the top political leaders and bureaucrats, the traditional rulers and their descendants, and the leading members of the liberal professions and the rising business bourgeoisie. Top members of the military and police

forces are also part of this bureaucratic bourgeoisie. Over time, leading elements in this coalition change. Although the bureaucratic and political components have dominated until now, they have had to seek a social base. Increasingly in West African countries, as in independent countries everywhere on the continent, a developing commercial and business class provides that base.[46]

Like my 'managerial bourgeoisie', and by contrast with the previous expressions that have been discussed, Markovitz's conception is meant to comprehend the dominant class as a whole.[47] This cannot be done by using conceptions that identify classes with specific occupational groups, functional élites, or eclectic mixtures of groups and élites that are not chosen in accordance with a theoretical principle.[48] It is difficult to see how such conceptions can be reconciled with the requirements of class analysis.

Class Action

Class analysis attributes social solidarity to social inequality and domination. Collective action may be interpreted as class action if the effect is to increase or reduce social inequality and domination, or to strengthen or weaken the means whereby the domination of a privileged stratum is maintained. Each of these effects is subject to confirmation by empirical means.

Thus it can be demonstrated that collaboration between regional power groups in Nigeria between 1962 and 1965 served to intensify class domination. Political regionalism was a conservative strategy that facilitated the use of ethnic and sectional prejudice by dominant class elements as a political weapon against challengers from below. However, the regional power system 'was undermined by an acute contradiction between the constitutional allocation of power and the real distribution of power in society'.[49] Since one Region—the North—had a numerical majority, the party that monopolised power there virtually dominated the entire Federation. But the three southern Regions were far more advanced in the development of their educational and technological capacities. Anti-regionalism, emanating mainly from the South, merged with radical opposition to class privilege. Consequently, conservative southerners allied with aristocratic northerners to suppress opposition to the regional power system. Repression breeds revolution; hence the upsurge of widespread agitation against the régime in deeply aggrieved Yorubaland, culminating in the popular, Ibo-led, *coup d'état* of January 1966.

In the absence of a political organisation to represent the interests of lower classes in an effective manner, a disorganised dominant class may easily regroup and make the most of an opportunity to reorganise itself.

Thus were the inept regionalist politicians in Nigeria displaced by a more progressive alignment of military officers and civil servants. The tragic blunders of this group, culminating in civil war, were largely attributable to their deeply ingrained technocratic sentiments. They tried to impose a new political structure upon the country without consultation and public approval, but lacked the power to do so. During the civil war of 1967–70, dominant-class interests were never threatened; indeed, they were energetically served by the military régime.[50] Post-war policies, as previously described, have been clearly designed to consolidate the power of Nigeria's dominant class.

It cannot be emphasised too strongly that class action is an interpretive conception, without descriptive significance, inferred from empirical evidence of group action. This interpretation is most likely to appeal to scholars who wish to investigate the causes and consequences of social inequality. Hence the seizure of power by the Ugandan army in 1971, an action that initially served to protect a threatened system of class privilege, was provocatively interpreted by Lofchie as 'class action by the military'.[51] Similarly, the statist and essentially authoritarian political system of Kenya has been interpreted by M. Tamarkin as a consequence of dominant-class action rather than 'tribalist' politics or neo-colonialist manipulation.[52] And, in an especially well-informed account of 'state-building' in Algeria, Jean Leca finds that 'the army is nothing but a part of the state bureaucracy with the same organizational values and the same goals as those of its civilian counterparts'.[53] From this perspective, populist manipulation of the citizenry by the Algerian military-controlled Government could be interpreted as a form of defensive action by the dominant class.

Class action may be analysed into various forms; these include class formation, consolidation, collaboration, and struggle. Many commentators in Africa appear to be preoccupied with class struggle, although the other forms affect many more people at the present time. Class collaboration is especially important as an explanation of continued bourgeois rule. Evidence has been adduced to support a hypothesis to this effect: that under the auspices of a populist, bourgeois-dominated régime, the bourgeoisie will collaborate with the peasantry at the expense of the relatively small and immature proletariat.[54] The marks of bourgeois-peasant collaboration include these: a rising level of agricultural subsidies, the shift of public-service expenditures from urban to rural areas, the elimination of trade-union autonomy, severe restriction of the right to strike, and an insistence upon wage restraint while the salary scales for executive, senior administrative, and other white-collar employee elements are allowed to rise. Bourgeois collaboration with a narrowly based proletariat at the expense of a populous peasantry would be unlikely to persist for long without effective methods to control and repress the peasantry. Finally, collaboration between the proletariat and the peasantry at the expense of the bourgeoisie is the classic formula for social revolution in non-industrial countries. These schematic ideas have not as yet attracted much attention in African studies. Their utility remains to be established by comparative class analyses of representative social orders.

Yet another, highly significant, form of class action may be inferred from the economic behaviour of members of the 'managerial bourgeoisie' in many non-industrial countries. Such persons often pursue their interests by means of economic 'partnership' or collaboration with foreign investors. Increasingly, such partnerships take the form of joint ownership agreements in which the host state, itself, participates. Whenever foreign managers are present within the host country, the managerial bourgeoisie includes a foreign or corporate international wing. In such cases, the managerial bourgeoisie is a transnational class.[55]

The domestic, or local, section of the managerial bourgeoisie is, in effect, the dominant stratum of a national bourgeoisie that is normally far larger than the managerial bourgeoisie itself. Yet the latter has a distinctive class (or sub-class) identity that 'is manifest behaviorally in the collective actions and attributes of its members'. Specifically, the managerial bourgeoisie has a pronounced 'tendency to coalesce with bourgeois elements at comparable levels of control in foreign countries'.[56] Coalescence of the managerial bourgeoisie (domestic section) with the corporate international bourgeoisie means that class action has taken the historically significant form of transnational class formation.

Conclusion

In colonial Africa, the imperial powers favoured and facilitated the emergence of a collaborative bourgeoisie. Yet, the ongoing formation and consolidation of this class since independence has not been attributable to foreign domination of the African economies. At bottom, class relations are determined by relations of power. Class formation is a consequence of determinants that are specifically political as well as economic. However 'dependent' or 'extraverted' the economy of an underdeveloped country may be, the autonomy of its bourgeoisie may yet be firmly established upon a foundation of indigenous political organisation.[57]

For lack of an adequate theory of class determination, the study of class domination in non-industrial countries has often fallen into the populistic trap of a dogmatic belief in foreign domination by proxy. Despite the professed intentions of those who propagate this idea, its practical political effect is likely to be conservative. Disparagement of the indigenous bourgeoisie as a 'comprador', 'clientele', or 'neo-colonial puppet' class betrays a serious lack of appreciation for the nature and strength of dominant-class formation in the non-industrial countries. Those who wear such intellectual blinkers invariably misconstrue as subservience to the dominant classes of industrial-capitalist countries actions that stem from the self-motivated desires of an emergent bourgeoisie to collaborate with bourgeois elements abroad. What is more, they fail to comprehend the mutation of simple forms of transnational class collaboration between an indigenous bourgeoisie and sectors of the corporate international bourgeoisie into more lasting forms of transnational class coalescence. In typically populist fashion, they foster cultural and national antagonism instead of serious criticism of class domination.[58]

If, as the proponents of this doctrine allege, persons who hold positions of authority in non-industrial countries lack real power, it would follow that they are not really responsible for their actions. It then becomes logical, in a superficial way, to attribute both economic mismanagement and political oppression by such persons to their presumed foreign masters. By implication, the denial of national political responsibility minimises the significance of local organisations and institutions since these do not seem to be a matter of great moment. Hence, the 'neo-colonial puppet' doctrine helps to create a frame of mind that lacks concern for the values of liberty; conversely, it fosters attitudes that are compatible with various justifications for authoritarian government.

In newly developing countries, as elsewhere, the foundations of class domination include political factors that are basic to the structure of society. Of them, the most important is the presence or absence of liberty—meaning, at the very least, freedom of speech, freedom of political association, and limited government. In the absence of liberty, democracy will collapse upon an insubstantial foundation, and attempts to build socialism will be retarded, if not foiled, by dominant-class practices. This conclusion is supported by the decline of socialist thought and practice under various authoritarian régimes that were, at first, dedicated to the elimination of class privilege and the prevention of bourgeois rule. Régimes that fit this description in post-colonial Africa include Nkrumah's Ghana, Sékou Touré's Guinea, Keita's Mali, Nyerere's Tanzania, Kaunda's Zambia, Siyad Barre's Somalia, Algeria, Congo People's Republic, and the revolutionary régimes of Guinea-Bissau, Cape Verde, Mozambique, and Angola. Nearly all of them, however, are judged to have produced bourgeois domination of one kind or another—bureaucratic, state, or managerial—by critics who are themselves sympathetic to socialism.[59] The logical conclusion for socialists to draw from this experience would be to the effect that there should be a working (or subject) class struggle for liberty as well as equality in Africa.

Normally, authoritarian régimes operate to consolidate the power of dominant classes. However, their oppressive features are widely resented, and they do not, as a rule, provide for orderly changes in governmental organisation and personnel. On the contrary, authoritarian rule virtually guarantees that political change will be eruptive and costly to privileged classes. This liability renders it distasteful and expendable to dominant classes that are able to maintain themselves in power by other means. Unremitting demands for the introduction or restoration of liberal and limited government in many African countries appear to reflect the rejection of authoritarianism by bourgeois classes that are steadily consolidating their power.

Socialists would be ill-advised to scorn liberal constitutions that guarantee freedom of political association as the basis of democratic representation. The fact that such constitutions may be introduced at the urging and under the auspices of bourgeois elements for their own reasons, as in Nigeria, does not detract from their value to socialist movements. Liberty is a universal interest; its emblem has been inscribed upon the banner of socially creative classes and progressive movements in every age, everywhere. A socialist movement that could not gain and hold power where constitutional government has been established would lose the spirit of freedom and become socialist in name only under the aegis of an authoritarian régime.

Notes

1. For an exposition of this thesis, see Samir Amin, *Unequal Development*, translated by Brian Pearce (New York, 1976).

2. See the seminal article, documenting this process from a Marxist perspective, by Bill Warren, 'Imperialism and Capitalist Industrialization', in *New Left Review* (London), 81, September–October 1973, pp. 3–44.

3. Ralph Miliband, *Marxism and Politics* (Oxford, 1977), ch. V.

4. Stanislaw Ossowski, *Class Structure in the Social Consciousness*, translated by Sheila Patterson (New York, 1963), pp. 33 and 157.

5. Ibid. pp. 185–6.

6. For a similar view, see James A. Bill, 'Class Analysis and the Dialectics of Modernization in the Middle East', in *International Journal of Middle East Studies* (New York), 111, October 1972, pp. 417–34, at p. 420.

7. Martin L. Kilson, 'Nationalism and Social Classes in British West Africa', in *The Journal of Politics* (Gainesville, Fla.), XX, 2, May 1958, pp. 368–87. A symposium sponsored by the International Institute of Differing Civilizations reached this conclusion: 'the driving force in nearly all the nationalist movements has come from the middle class'; *Development of a Middle Class in Tropical and Sub-Tropical Countries* (Brussels, 1956), p. 453. See also Thomas Hodgkin, *African Political Parties* (Harmondsworth, 1961), pp. 27–9; and the survey by Immanuel Wallerstein, 'Class, Tribe, and Party in West African Politics', in Seymour M. Lipset and Stein Rokkan (eds.), *Party Systems and Voter Alignments* (New York, 1967), pp. 497–518.

8. Richard L. Sklar, *Nigerian Political Parties* (Princeton, 1963), pp. 480–1.

9. Ibid. pp. 481–2 and 501–2.

10. Richard L. Sklar and C. S. Whitaker, Jr., 'Nigeria', in James S. Coleman and Carl G. Rosberg, Jr. (eds.), *Political Parties and National Integration in Tropical Africa* (Berkeley and Los Angeles, 1964), pp. 612–19.

11. The indispensable study of these processes in colonial Nigeria is James S. Coleman, *Nigeria: background to nationalism* (Berkeley and Los Angeles, 1958).

12. The classic study of political change in northern Nigeria is C. S. Whitaker, Jr., *The Politics of Tradition* (Princeton, 1970).

13. John Markakis, *Ethiopia: anatomy of a traditional polity* (Oxford, 1974).

14. Ibid. p. 182.

15. Republic of Kenya, *African Socialism and Its Application to Planning in Kenya* (Nairobi, 1965), Sessional Paper No. 10.

16. The evidence adduced in numerous studies has been summarised by Kipkorir Aly Azad Rana, 'Class Formation and Social Conflict: a case study of Kenya', in *Ufahamu* (Los Angeles), VII, 3, 1977, pp. 17–72.

17. Kenneth D. Kaunda, *Humanism in Zambia and a Guide to Its Implementation*, Part II (Lusaka, 1974), pp. 110–11; see also William Tordoff (ed.), *Politics in Zambia* (Berkeley and Los Angeles, 1974), pp. 385–401.

18. Maud Shimwaayi Muntemba, 'Rural Underdevelopment in Zambia: Kabwe Rural District, 1850–1970', Ph.D. dissertation, University of California, Los Angeles, 1977, p. 338.

19. This idea differs from the traditional Marxist conception of class formation as an outcome of relationships to the means of production primarily. Cf. Szymon Chodak, 'Social Stratification in Sub-Saharan Africa', in *Canadian Journal of African Studies* (Montreal), VII, 3, 1973, pp. 401–17. Chodak's thoughtful discussion of class formation from a Marxist perspective barely conceptualises the formation of a dominant class in Africa.

20. Irving Leonard Markovitz, *Power and Class in Africa: an introduction to change and conflict in African politics* (Englewood Cliffs, 1977). On class formation, see especially pp. 153–72 and 280–1, where Markovitz cites the 'path-breaking' work of Polly Hill on 'rural capitalism' in West Africa.

21. Ibid. p. 158.

22. Ibid. p. 171.

23. Sklar, op. cit. p. 482.

24. Marx used this phrase in *The Poverty of Philosophy* (1847). His theory of class is succinctly presented with relevant quotations in Reinhard Bendix and Seymour Martin Lipset, 'Karl Marx's Theory of Social Class', in Bendix and Lipset (eds.), *Class, Status, and Power: a reader in social stratification* (New York, 1966, 2nd edn.), pp. 6–11.

25. The tensions created by conservative economic policies in the Ivory Coast that perpetuate foreign ownership and control of most industrial enterprises are discussed by Bonnie Campbell, 'Ivory Coast', in John Dunn (ed.), *West African States: failure and promise* (Cambridge, 1978), pp. 98–100 and 105–16.

26. Sayre P. Schatz, *Nigerian Capitalism* (Berkeley and Los Angeles, 1977), p. 58.

27. Ibid. p. 60.

28. Ibid. p. 55.

29. See Richard A. Joseph, 'Affluence and Underdevelopment: the Nigerian experience', in *The Journal of Modern African Studies* (Cambridge), XVI, 2, June 1978, pp. 227–33.

30. Schatz, op. cit. p. 46.

31. See Martin Kilson, 'Authoritarian and Single-Party Tendencies in African Politics', in *World Politics* (Princeton), XV, 1963, pp. 262–94; also Christopher Allen, 'Sierra Leone', in Dunn (ed.), op.cit. pp. 196–200, where authoritarianism is identified as the political strategy of a 'dependent bourgeoisie'.

32. José Nun, 'The Middle-Class Military Coup', in Claudio Veliz (ed.), *The Politics of Conformity in Latin America* (London, 1967), p. 112.

33. Michael F. Lofchie, 'The Political Origins of the Uganda Coup', in *Journal of African Studies* (Los Angeles), 1, 4, Winter 1974, pp. 489–92.

34. Federal Republic of Nigeria, *Report of the Constitution Drafting Committee,* Vols I and II (Lagos, 1976).

35. Joel D. Barkan, *An African Dilemma: university students, development and politics in Ghana, Tanzania and Uganda* (Nairobi and London, 1975), pp. 187–9. A similar finding, derived from a sample survey of university students in Nigeria, is reported by Paul Beckett and James O'Connell, *Education and Power in Nigeria* (London, 1977), pp. 168–9.

36. See Ossowski, op.cit. pp. 185–6. For a similar enumeration of 'objective class concepts', including power, defined 'as the ability to affect the life chances of others, or conversely as the amount of freedom from control by others', see Seymour Martin Lipset, 'Issues in Social Class Analysis', in *Revolution and Counterrevolution* (Garden City, 1970, revised edn.), pp. 191–2.

37. Karl Marx and Friedrich Engels, *Manifesto of the Communist Party* (1848), English edn. edited by Engels (1888).

38. Ian Clegg, *Workers' Self-Management in Algeria* (New York and London, 1971); and Issa G. Shivji, *Class Struggles in Tanzania* (New York and London, 1976).

39. René Dumont, *False Start in Africa,* translated by Phyllis Nauts Ott (New York, 1969, 2nd revised edn.), p. 81; and Frantz Fanon, *The Wretched of the Earth,* translated by Constance Farrington (New York, 1968 edn.), p. 179.

40. Shivji's identification of the 'bureaucratic bourgeoisie' as a class is guarded but unmistakable; op.cit. pp. 85–94. Defining the bourgeoisie as a class in functional terms, he writes of a 'class struggle' between the 'bureaucratic bourgeoisie' (originally a section of the 'petty bourgeoisie') and the 'commercial bourgeoisie'; ibid. pp. 67–77 and 94.

41. Samir Amin, *Accumulation on a World Scale,* Vols. I and II, translated by Brian Pearce (New York, 1974), pp. 374–5 and 384.

42. J. Ph. Peemans, 'The Social and Economic Development of Zaire since Independence: an historical outline', in *African Affairs* (London), LXXIV, 295, April 1975, p. 163.

43. Colin Leys, *Underdevelopment in Kenya: the political economy of neo-colonialism, 1964–1971* (Berkeley and Los Angeles, 1974), pp. 193–8.

44. Ibid. pp. 119, 147, 169, 196, and 257.

45. Richard L. Sklar, *Corporate Power in an African State: the political impact of multinational mining companies in Zambia* (Berkeley and Los Angeles, 1975), pp. 198–9. For an earlier use of the term 'managerial bourgeoisie' as a synonym for the dominant 'managerial élite', see Arthur Tuden and Leonard Plotnicov, 'Introduction', in Tuden and Plotnicov (eds.), *Social Stratification in Africa* (New York, 1970), p. 21.

46. Markovitz, op.cit. pp. 208–9.

47. Markovitz suggests that my conception of the 'managerial bourgeoisie' underestimates the entrepreneurial capacity of 'ascending' classes in Africa; ibid. p. 210. I do not think that he has correctly interpreted the passage in my book quoted above. Since I do not see any significant substantive difference between his 'organisational' and my 'managerial' bourgeoisie (although I would question the inclusion of 'traditional rulers and their descendants' in all but a relatively few carefully selected instances), it matters little to me which term is used. I like the term 'managerial' because it is specifically reminiscent of the business tradition. For a similar conceptualisation of the dominant class in Middle Eastern societies, see Bill, loc. cit. pp. 427–34, although he does not adopt the term 'bourgeoisie'.

48. For an example of this occupational-functional bind, see Bonnie Campbell's rebuttal of Michael A. Cohen's contention in *Urban Policy and Political Conflict in Africa* (Chicago and London, 1974), p. 41, that a 'politico-administrative class' has become dominant in the Ivory Coast. Following Samir Amin, Campbell identifies the 'planter bourgeoisie' as the dominant class; loc. cit. pp. 73, 89, and 229, fn. 6.

49. Richard L. Sklar, 'Nigerian Politics in Perspective', in Robert Melson and Howard Wolpe (eds.), *Nigeria: modernization and the politics of communalism* (East Lansing, 1971), p. 46, and also 'Contradictions in the Nigerian Political System', in *The Journal of Modern African Studies*, 111, 2, August 1965, pp. 201–13.

50. See Ruth First, *The Barrel of a Gun: political power in Africa and the coup d'état* (London, 1970), pp. 255–7.

51. Michael F. Lofchie, 'The Uganda Coup—Class Action by the Military', in *The Journal of Modern African Studies*, X, 1, May 1972, pp. 19–35. For an interesting debate on this question, see the comments by John D. Chick and Irving Gershenberg, in ibid. X, 4, December 1972, pp. 634–9; and Lofchie's response, 'The Political Origins of the Uganda Coup', loc. cit.

52. M. Tamarkin, 'The Roots of Political Stability in Kenya', in *African Affairs*, LXXVII, 308, July 1978, pp. 297–320.

53. Jean Leca, 'Algerian Socialism: nationalism, industrialization, and state-building', in Helen Desfosses and Jacques Levesque (eds.), *Socialism in the Third World* (New York, 1975), p. 141.

54. Sklar, op. cit. pp. 211–12.

55. Ibid. pp. 201, 207, and 209.

56. Richard L. Sklar, 'Postimperialism: a class analysis of multinational corporate expansion', in *Comparative Politics* (New York), IX, 1, October 1976, pp. 75–92.

57. The political basis of class formation in Africa has been emphasised by Robin Cohen, 'Class in Africa: analytical problems and perspectives', in Ralph Miliband and John Saville (eds.), *The Socialist Register, 1972* (London, 1972), pp. 231–55. However, Cohen appears to underestimate the resourcefulness and potential strength of emerging dominant classes, which could be a consequence of the distinction that he draws between the ruling 'political class' and the 'intendant class' of 'state functionaries, middle-level bureaucrats and supervisory personnel'; ibid. pp. 247–50.

58. Samir Amin may deserve pride of place for his exposition of this viewpoint; see his *Unequal Development* and *Accumulation on a World Scale*. The influence of André Gunder Frank should also be noted; see, for example, his *Lumpenbour-*

geoisie, Lumpendevelopment: dependence, class, and politics in Latin America, translated by Marion Davis Berdecio (New York and London, 1972).

59. For a socialist analysis of bourgeois tendencies in non-industrial countries under avowedly revolutionary leadership, see Gérard Chaliand, *Revolution in the Third World: myths and prospects,* translated by Diana Johnstone (Harmondsworth, 1978 edn.). The degradation of socialist thought and practice under a tyrannical dictatorship in Guinea has been described with brilliant clarity by Lansiné Kaba, 'The Cultural Revolution, Artistic Creativity, and Freedom of Expression in Guinea', in *The Journal of Modern African Studies,* XIV, 2, June 1976, pp. 201–18, and 'Guinean Politics: a critical overview', in ibid. XV, 1, March 1977, pp. 25–45. See also Claude Rivière, *Guinea: the mobilization of a people* (Ithaca, 1977), and R. W. Johnson, 'Guinea', in Dunn (ed.), op.cit. pp. 36–65.

8

The Making of a Rentier Class: Wealth Accumulation and Political Control in Senegal

Catherine Boone

Efforts to understand the sources, extent, and social locus of indigenous capital accumulation are central to analyses of capitalism in post-colonial Africa. In the 1980s, underdevelopment theory's stark formulations about "blockages" and structural constraints on indigenous capitalism have given way to more nuanced arguments about the scope and nature of local accumulation. Yet one of the central issues raised by underdevelopment theorists continues to attract interest because it frames so concisely critical questions about class formation and the progressive development of African economies. This issue concerns the "political class," defined as the dominant social stratum which derives its economic and political power from direct access to the state itself. The question is: will Africa's political classes use their power to expand the scope of local capital accumulation, especially by supporting and facilitating local private investment in industry? Arguments to the effect that these social strata are invariably comprador in character can no longer be accepted. There is too much empirical evidence to suggest that in some places, at some times, and under certain circumstances, the political class is able and willing to use state power to promote local capital accumulation in general, and local investment in industry in particular, be it in partnership with, or at the expense of, foreign capital.[1] In light of this, it now seems more fruitful (and the thrust of new research demonstrates that this is so) to begin inquiry into the economic activities of political classes by considering seri-

Reprinted by permission from the *Journal of Development Sudies* 26, no. 3 (1990): 425–449, published by Frank Cass & Company, Ilford, Essex iG2 7HH, England. © Frank Cass & Co Ltd.

ously the hypothesis that members of the political class will accumulate capital and with the help of the state, invest in productive activities.

This, however, is a hypothetical scenario of great contingency. It is contingent on the emergence of a class or part of a class committed to a bourgeois project, the consolidation and effective exercise of its political power, and the existence of a state with the institutional and political capacities needed to promote effectively the interests of nascent indigenous capitalist strata. Questions about state capacities, the emergence of class consciousness, and domestic political struggles are immediately placed at the centre of the stage. These are internal processes and forces that are conditioned, but not determined, by external factors. They are as political in nature as economic. If such forces are critical in explaining why capitalist classes-in-the-making are appearing in some parts of sub-Saharan Africa, then they are also critical in explaining why indigenous capitalist classes may not be emerging in many, perhaps most, countries.

In much of post-colonial Africa, no significant stratum or fraction of the wealth-accumulating political class invests in productive activities (that is activities that create surplus value through the on-going combination of capital and wage labour, such as industry or capitalist agriculture). In these situations, political classes are predominantly "rentier" in nature. This paper is concerned with the relationship between clientelist strategies of political control and the rise and persistence of rentierism. It suggests that the clientelist strategies of political control which promote rentierism reduce the likelihood that fractions of the political class backing "nurture capitalism" or "dependent development" strategies will emerge and prevail. It also suggests that clientelist strategies of political control may erode the capacity of the state to maintain conditions propitious for the expansion of capital in general.[2] A study of the rise of a dominant rentier class in Senegal illustrates this case.

The possibility that capitalist classes-in-the-making are emerging in some African countries, such as Kenya and Nigeria, justifies a closer look at the internal political forces which condition the economic activities, potential, and agendas of political classes.[3] Within constraints imposed by history and the world economy, African ruling classes have shown considerable capacity to "innovate in their own interests".[4] While the economic project of indigenising the locus of capital accumulation may be central to the interests of *some* political classes, the political project of consolidating internal political dominance and retaining control over the state apparatus is central in all cases. I argue that the political project should be viewed as analytically distinct from the economic one, thus permitting the theoretical possibility that in some situations, political strategies employed in the effort to consolidate power may involve efforts to curb the development of indigenous capitalist strata. This line of argument implies an analysis of the specifically political mechanisms and dynamics of ruling class consolidation and cohesion. Hence the focus here on clientelism as a means of asserting and maintaining a form of political control over diverse fractions of political classes.

In Senegal, clientelist strategies of political control fostered the rise of a rentier political class within the framework of a relatively stable and highly structured regime. The emergence of this rentier class strengthened the regime's hold on power as new social strata were co-opted into a national system of machine politics organised around the distribution of state-controlled resources. State-sponsored rentierism (which some have called "parasitic capitalism"), therefore, is not necessarily associated with the kind of dramatic and widespread political decay that has been observed, for example, in Zaire.[5] Meanwhile, rentierism in Senegal appears to have contributed to forms of economic decline that resemble those found in Zaire and elsewhere on the continent. Analysis of the Senegalese case may thus contribute to more systematic and broadly comparative discussions of how struggles to consolidate post-colonial state power and ruling coalitions have conditioned patterns of capitalist development at the national level.

I. Rentier Activities: A Definition

My definition of rentier activities is based upon particular notions of "rent". Rent is classically defined as fixed income derived from property holding that is not invested in the expansion of productive activities (for example, feudal landlords). Economists now use the term rent to refer to "unearned" profits which derive from disequilibrium prices. Disequilibrium prices prevail when the market's price setting mechanisms—supply and demand—have been distorted by non-market forces (for example, producers' cartels which restrict supply to drive up prices). The specific notion of rent that is used here builds on these definitions. First, it adopts the idea of income or profit generated in "non-productive" activity (that is, income or profit which does not represent surplus value created through the on-going combination of capital and wage labour). The definition therefore rests on the nature of the accumulation process, not on a sectoral designation of economic activity. Second, the definition of rent employed here gives the notion of "non-market forces" a specific meaning. The non-market force is direct government intervention in markets.[6] Thus, rentier activities are defined as *politically mediated* opportunities for *obtaining wealth* through *non-productive* economic activity. Patterns of rentier activity reflect patterns of access to politically mediated resources. By this definition, then, rentierism is an activity open to the political class.

Rentiers accumulate wealth through the privatisation of state resources, grants from the state (loans, property, subsidies, cash transfers), and the appropriation of rents generated by state intervention in markets (trading in state-controlled markets, business activity carried out under state-created monopolies, obtaining government contracts awarded on a non-competitive basis, bribes and kickbacks). They channel their wealth into consumption and into other state-mediated non-productive activities (purchase of real estate, commercial activities which generate rents). This definition and description of rentier activities should be plausible to anyone familiar with the ways in which business and politics often intersect in African countries. Specifying the phenomenon at hand only clears the way for posing a more interesting question: will rentier activity give rise to a politically cohesive and politically influential stratum of would-be capitalists, ready and able to mobilise state power behind efforts to invest this wealth productively?

II. The State and Local Private Accumulation

In post-colonial Africa as in other parts of the late developing world, the state has played a central role in shaping patterns of local private accumulation. State power is used not only to channel economic resources into the hands of members of the dominant class, but also to structure opportunities for the use of this wealth. In this sense, the role of the state in shaping patterns and forms of local accumulation is two-sided. State power and state resources are used to *create* private wealth. Meanwhile, patterns of state intervention in the domestic economy shape individual decisions about how to *deploy* this wealth (that is, nature and extent of consumption, possibilities for investment, possibilities for rent-seeking, possibilities for expatriation of funds, etc.). Most analysts have focused on the wealth-acquisition side of this equation, showing that over the course of the post-colonial period, political and bureaucratic power has been wielded to promote the enrichment of the political class. Analysis of the deployment side of the equation has been less systematic.

Explaining the emergence or non-emergence of production-oriented, indigenous capitalist strata requires analysis of both aspects of the role of the state in shaping the accumulation process. In analysing how state power promotes the enrichment of the political class, the use of state power cannot be seen as unstructured, unconstrained, or guided only by the individual or corporate interests of state agents in material gain. On both sides of the accumulation equation, domestic political struggles and interests condition and shape the role of the state. While patterns of state intervention in domestic economies and the distribution of state resources have enriched political classes by design and by default, they have simultaneously served other political purposes. State allocation of resources has worked to promote the consolidation of weak and loosely-integrated regimes, create social bases of support for those regimes, penalise and marginalise opponents of the status quo, and give regimes some claim to legitimacy. In this sense, the patrimonial allocation of state resources, as well as state actions which affect the deployment of private wealth, are inseparable from and shaped by broader strategies of domestic political consolidation and control.

Robert Bates draws attention to this aspect of state patronage. He argues that scarcity rents generated by state intervention in domestic markets and other politically-mediated opportunities for private accumulation are allocated in ways that "are designed to secure advantages for particular interests, to appease powerful political forces, and to enhance the capacity of political regimes to remain in power" [Bates, 1981: 5]. This can mean, and in practice obviously does mean, that those who control the levers of bureaucratic and political power are the best placed to take advantage of opportunities for private accumulation mediated by the state. The point, however, is that state patronage can be an important component of a *system of political control* as well as a means of enrichment for the politically powerful.

III. Clientelism, Political Control, and Rentier Classes

Class-based analyses of clientelism provide the theoretical basis for developing this point and linking it to the study of local private accumulation. Peter Flynn provides such an analysis. He sees clientelism as a system of political control based on patronage and coercion. Flynn describes clientelism as "a deliberately fostered system of political integration and control exercised from above which reinforces class control in the system as a whole" [1974: 149–50].[7] Patron-client networks regulate and narrow access to the state and state resources. They are mechanisms which distribute state-controlled resources strategically, working either to marginalise key individuals and groups or to win their political support (or acquiescence). Clientelist systems are distinctive in that benefits and sanctions in the system are distributed to individuals, rather than social groups, via the particularistic and discretionary exercise of state prerogative. As a system of political control, clientelism requires and creates clients who are dependent on, and therefore tend to respond to, inducements and sanctions meted out by state agents.

Flynn maintains that the most striking feature of clientelistic systems of political control is "the degree to which vertical clientelistic chains and the dyadic links of personal interdependence cut through and weaken efforts toward class and other category group organization" [1974: 148]. By particularising demands on the state, clientelism preempts the mobilisation of broad-based political demands and collective political consciousness. In this way, according to Flynn, the system works to maintain and reinforce the economic and political dominance of the ruling class.

The logic of this argument, minus its functionalist bent, can be extended to power relations *within* the ruling class. As the history of military *coups d'état* and succession crises suggests, the ruling class in much of post-colonial Africa is not as cohesive and united as Flynn's model might suggest. State agents are themselves tied into a clientelist system of political control when they secure access to state-mediated avenues of private accumulation through patronage networks. They are targets as well as the prime beneficiaries of the system. When the political class is viewed from this perspective, possible constraints on its emergence as a capitalist class can be identified.

Impediments to the formation of a domestic capitalist class may be inherent in clientelistic strategies which are aimed at curbing or preempting the autonomy of fractions of the political class. Those in control of the post-colonial state may not be interested in using state power to underwrite the emergence of capitalist class strata which would, by dint of independent control over significant productive assets, enjoy some autonomy *vis-à-vis* the state and thus, some power to constrain state action. At the same time, clientelistic structures of control can impede the political mobilisation of factions within the political class around the "nurture capitalism" agenda.

The possibility that internal power struggles may give regimes vested political interests in fettering the rise of indigenous capitalist classes has not been articulated in a general way in the literature on capitalist-oriented regimes in sub-Saharan Africa. The point was made about regimes that embraced "scientific" or "African" socialism in the 1960s. Many of these, however, are now viewed as state capitalist regimes which display few signs of commitment to socialism other than the rapid extension of direct state control over various sectors of the economy.[8] To the extent that this observation is valid, the distinction between capitalist-oriented regimes and the "socialist" regimes of the 1960s is blurred. Thus, it may be possible to look beyond ideological distinctions and identify a more general stance *vis-à-vis* the possible emergence of indigenous capitalist strata that is characteristic of many sub-Saharan regimes. Consider the following cases.

John Iliffe writes that one of three models of capitalist-politician relations that has emerged in post-colonial Africa is one in which the regime

has sought to prevent the emergence of private African capitalism in any form. One example of this approach was Nkrumah's Ghana . . . [Nkrumah] feared, according to a senior advisor, "that if he permits African business to grow, it will grow to the extent of becoming a rival power to his and the party's prestige." Moreover, within the Convention People's Party were many men anxious to use state power to channel the economy's surplus in their own direction. . . . [Nkrumah] deliberately confined local capitalism to small-scale operations . . . [1983: 77]

C. de Miras, after reviewing the Ivoirian government's efforts to promote a local capitalist class in the 1970s, writes that the way in which the "Ivoirisation" process unfolded

suggests a new proposition about the policy of promoting local private accumulation in Côte d'Ivoire: the policy was actually the reverse. The state does not appear to be the motor force pushing the development of an indigenous private sector. Rather, the state appears to be more of a regulator which, through a moderate and controlled Ivoirisation, has been able to maintain within its orbit a *milieu aux ambitions economiques* which only the state could satisfy, without permitting a social class independent from the State to emerge. . . . [n]o social faction has been able to detach itself from the State to emerge as a counterpower to the State itself [1982: 228–29].[9]

Thomas Callaghy argues that "Mobutu does not want an autonomous bourgeoisie and has worked to stunt the growth of one" [1987: 116]. In developing this point, he cites another observer who claimed that "the intention of the president is to prevent the development of a bourgeoisie with an economic base which could escape his control" [1987: 101].[10] Analysts of Senegalese politics have echoed this argument. Rita Cruise O'Brien argued that the Senghor regime feared that a true national bourgeoisie would constitute a serious alternative force in politics, likely to ally with the ever-problematic intelligentsia [1979: 108].

A common theme runs through these case studies. In the struggle to retain hegemony within the post-colonial state and to enforce the political status quo, dominant social actors may work to impede the rise of indigenous capitalist class strata. In this situation, politicised accumulation may be deliberately structured, on both the acquisition side and the deployment side, along the lines of rentier activities. Access to rentier activities is gained on the particularistic and *ad hoc* basis of clientelistic relations. Rentiers are clients of the state, co-opted and controlled. Because the source of their wealth is not self-sustaining and self-reproducing, they are dependent on the discretionary exercise of state power. As economic actors, rentiers remain vulnerable to changes in their own political fortunes and that of their patrons. As Flynn argues, this form of dependency and political control inhibits the emergence of political coalitions organised around corporate interests and programmatic goals. Pervasive clientelism and rentierism may work together to inhibit the emergence of cohesive frac-

tions within the political class committed to advancing a "nurture capitalism" agenda.

A self-reinforcing dynamic can also be identified from a micro-economic
perspective. In principle, members of the political class can channel their
wealth into productive activities with or without direct state support. In
practice, however, pervasive clientelism and rentierism can create an economic climate which is not propitious for long-term projects involving
risk and fixed investment. Where patterns of state regulation of economic
activity are extensive and, from an economic point of view, often arbitrary, basic parameters affecting the profitability of investment (such as *de
facto* tax rates, conditions and cost of access to raw materials and inputs,
bureaucratic transactions costs) may be unpredictable. The success of an
entrepreneur is sensitive to the political climate and the political strategies of those with direct control over the economic prerogatives of the
state. In this context, businessmen (and women) who specialise in rentier
activities may be displaying sound and rational business sense. Pervasive
clientelism and rentierism tend to perpetuate the same.

This line of reasoning suggests that clientelistic structures which work
to weld together a fissiparous political class, and thereby enhance the
ability of regimes to remain in power, can also reduce the likelihood that
fractions of the political class will sink roots in the production process.
The argument may apply generally to cases where the indigenous capitalist stratum was very weak as an economic, political, and social force at
the time of regime consolidation in the 1960s. This criterion may differentiate most African states from the much discussed Kenya case. Colin Leys
highlights the political and economic significance of this initial condition
when he argues: "In noting the important role of the [Kenyan] state in facilitating this movement of African capital out of circulation and into production [after 1963], we must avoid the mistake of attributing to it an independent role. Its initiatives reflected the *existing* class power of the
indigenous bourgeoisie, based on the accumulation of capital they had *already* achieved" [1978: 251]. In much of Africa, colonialism did not foster
the emergence of capitalist classes-in-the-making. Yet the case of Ghana
suggests that *even where* nascent capitalist strata were forged under colonialism, class power already achieved was not always sufficient to guarantee that state power would be used to facilitate the move of African
capital into production. In Ghana, big planter-traders constituted a powerful social stratum in the 1950s, yet they were defeated in the struggle
over the post-colonial state. Once in power, the Nkrumah regime promoted the rise of a rentier political class, largely at the expense of producers and independent traders in the cocoa sector [Beckman, 1976]. This
rentier class persisted as such after Nkrumah's fall.

These cases provide grounds for venturing a more general argument.
Persistent rentierism is likely to emerge as a dominant mode of local

wealth accumulation where, as in much of sub-Saharan Africa, social strata based on the accumulation of capital did not establish decisive positions of power within the post-colonial state. In these cases, persistent rentierism reflects, at least in part, a strategy of political control aimed at weakening or fettering the emergence of a particular class fraction which, by dint of roots in the production process, could exercise some autonomy *vis-à-vis* the state.

The study of Senegal presented here provides support for this argument and thus contributes to the more systematic analysis of the rise of dominant rentier classes. The study shows how a system of local private wealth accumulation organised along the lines of rentier activities gradually became a dominant and apparently self-reinforcing feature of the Senegalese economic system. Because a powerful rentier class developed incrementally within the framework of a fairly stable regime, the recurrent patterns of political choice and strategy that fostered its rise are particularly clear in this case. The study draws attention not only to the forces that tend to perpetuate rentier activity on the part of the political class, but also to the economic and political limits, or contradictions, of rentierism and clientelism.

IV. Politics and the Rise of a Rentier Class in Senegal

Previous studies of the Senegalese political economy provide generally consistent analyses of contextual factors that are of critical importance here.[11] These factors are: the marginal position of local private capital in the Senegalese economy at the time of independence from France; the archetypical neo-colonial development strategy pursued by the Senegalese government in the 1960s; and the strategy of repression and "spoils-oriented" clientelism that the Senghor regime relied upon in the 1960s to demobilise reform-oriented and nationalistic political factions both within and outside the regime and to consolidate its hold over the state apparatus.[12] Previous analyses of Senegalese politics have not viewed clientelism *per se* as a force shaping the class formation process [for example, Schumacher, 1975; D. Cruise O'Brien, 1975; Jackson and Rosberg, 1982].[13] Those who focus on domestic social classes tend to attribute the weakness of the local bourgeoisie during the post-colonial period to "the exigences of foreign investment" [R. Cruise O'Brien, 1979: 18].

The argument presented here differs from previous work by treating clientelism as central to explaining the continuing weakness of local capital in Senegal. The case study traces the specific ways in which the Senghor regime used state control over commercial activity and the state-controlled financial sector to create space for politically-mediated forms of wealth accumulation within the structures of the neo-colonial economy.[14] Economic niches open to state-sponsored rent-seeking widened and deepened over time as the regime sought to tap new reservoirs of state patronage. This process, propelled forward by the regime's efforts to consolidate and reconsolidate power in the face of internal challenge, constrained the emergence of an indigenous bourgeois stratum. At the same time, it promoted the rise of a rentier class. The interests and activities of this rentier class, and the state policies which fostered its rise, increasingly impinged upon and compromised the interests of foreign capital established in Senegal's commercial and light industrial sectors. Incrementally, the rise of the rentier class worked to erode, rather than sustain, the profitability of neo-colonial foreign enterprises operating in Senegal. It also compromised the ability of the state to create and sustain local conditions conducive to the expansion of capital in general.

The analysis below focuses on how state power was used to structure, constrain, and politicise local wealth accumulation in the post-colonial economy. Government initiatives taken at two historical junctures were decisive. First, in the early 1960s, the government opted to assert state control over commercial niches vacated by colonial trading companies, thus pre-empting the market as chief arbiter of the fortunes of local traders interested in expanding their businesses in these areas. Second, in the early 1970s, the government moved to canalise the ambitions of a frustrated local private-sector by creating broader avenues for state-mediated rent-seeking in the commercial sector and in the state-controlled banking sector. Over the course of the 1960–85 period, state power was used to (1) create local business opportunities that were subject to continuing, discretionary state control, (2) determine who gained access to these opportunities, and (3) ensure that the growing Senegalese business community was tied to the party-bureaucratic political machine and, as a consequence, that it did not emerge as an independent political force. These parameters conditioned patterns of class formation in Senegal, blurring the distinction between the local private sector and the political class and channelling local private accumulation into rentier activities. By the late-1970s, a social stratum of state agents and their political clients that Senegalese refer to as *"hommes d'affaires sénégalais"* had emerged as a critical force shaping the local economy.

The 1960s: Parameters Are Established

Colonialism did not create a powerful indigenous merchant class or a rural bourgeoisie in Senegal. At the time of political independence in 1960, French firms owned over 95 per cent of Senegal's modest industrial sector which consisted of groundnut processing firms and light manufacturing firms serving the local market [R. Cruise O'Brien, 1979: 109]. French corporations owned all the banks, French commercial houses monopolised the import-export trade at the wholesale level, and immigrant French and Lebanese businessmen controlled retail trade in the urban and rural areas. Meanwhile, peasants eked out a living growing Senegal's sole export crop, groundnuts, while French export houses and the colonial administration appropriated most of the surplus they produced. The Senegalese business sector that formed at the margins of the colonial economy was small and weak, both economically and politically. Within what can be called the modern economy, the local private sector comprised about 300 "medium-scale" *commerçants* in semi-wholesale trade and perhaps several thousand small-scale transporters and traders working in the interstices of a commercial sector dominated from above by the French [Diop, 1972; Amin, 1969]. Most were connected to the groundnut trade as sub-contractors, agents, or middlemen in circuits monopolised by French trading houses. The politically-disenfranchised immigrant Lebanese entrepreneurs controlled a broad array of small-scale, competitive activities in the service sector, such as laundries, hotels, restaurants, travel agencies, movie theatres, and real estate agencies.

As others have shown, the Senegalese government pursued macroeconomic strategies which were decidely neo-colonial. Government policy clearly worked to favour the interests of French investors in local industry and the interests of Senegal's powerful Islamic leaders, the *marabouts*, who controlled the peasantry and the land in the groundnut-producing areas. The position of established foreign-owned industries was guaranteed when the government renewed production monopolies and other investment incentives granted by the colonial administration. State support for new investors (subsidies, import protection, tax breaks, new production monopolies) was targeted at foreign firms. In the groundnut sector, the government did not impinge on *marabouts'* prerogatives and pursued rural development policies which reinforced the rural order established under colonial rule. Groundnut production expanded as the Islamic leaders received land grants from the government to expand their groundnut estates, as they had during the colonial period. Their religious followers cultivated these estates for a fixed period of time and then received land of their own for groundnut cultivation. Post-colonial rural development policies allowed the *marabouts* to retain and strengthen their positions as intermediaries between the government and the market, on one hand, and the peasants on the other [D. Cruise O'Brien, 1975].

Repression, the creation of a one-party state, and centralisation of power in President Senghor's office suppressed debate over the regime's macroeconomic strategy. The Senghor regime assumed the task of welding a politically and ideologically factionalised elite into ruling coalition supportive of the status quo. A pervasive system of patronage politics, backed up by the occasional use of force, worked to coopt and control the labour leaders, intellectuals, urban professionals, and political leaders who opposed the Senghor-led political party in the late 1950s and early 1960s, or who challenged Senghor himself. The same system rewarded and disciplined Senghor loyalists and backers. The development of spoils-oriented, patron-client networks within the post-colonial regime was predicated on party-cum-bureaucratic control over an ever-expanding reservoir of patronage resources. The political machine distributed jobs, allocated government expenditures, and governed access to health care, government housing, and educational opportunities. The primary beneficiaries of government-allocated resources were politicians, political appointees, bureaucrats, and other state employees [Schumacher, 1975]. Business opportunities open to Senegalese were defined and distributed under the same system and according to the same logic.

In the mid- to late 1950s, French trading companies operating in Senegal responded to rising overhead costs and the slump in world commodity prices by moving out of urban and rural retail trade. As they began to consolidate their operations at the wholesale level in Dakar, Senegalese traders and transporters expanded their operations in the rural areas. The consolidation of the French companies was accelerated in 1960 when the government of Senegal placed the export of groundnuts under state monopoly. The French commercial houses withdrew abruptly from the rural areas and continued to scale down their retail operations in the cities. From the perspective of Senegalese transporters and traders, this process cleared the way for expansion into commercial domains long closed to them by the presence of French commercial oligopolies. Businessmen aspired, first and foremost, to take over middleman positions between groundnut producers and the Port of Dakar. Access to importation, the most profitable segment of the commercial sector, was also a priority. Most of them, however, needed capital.

The government moved at this critical juncture. It defined the rural economy as a "commercial vacuum" and laid out a strategy to assure that the "Africanisation" of commerce would be carried out in an "organised and orderly" way.[15] In the early 1960s, the government created new bureaucratic structures to oversee, manage, and finance what it called "the insertion" of local *commerçants* into trading niches vacated by the French companies. At the same time, the existing and extensive bureaucratic apparatus for regulating the import trade allowed the regime to define the scope and nature of activities open to Senegalese in this domain. State control over the partial reorganisation of the commercial sector gave members of the political class direct access to the most promising avenues for private accumulation which opened to Senegalese in the 1960s. The process of Africanisation also tied established private traders to the regime through relations of patronage and clientelism.

Government policy ensured that the commercial opportunities open to local businessmen were located downstream from Senegal's large-scale importers, the French trading companies. Mechanisms for licensing importers and allocating import quotas were inherited from the colonial administration. An elaborate system of import taxes, bans, and quotas allowed the government to play a large role in defining the volume, price, and quality of imported goods sold on the local market, and thus to determine the value of the licenses and quotas it distributed to private traders and firms. These controls protected light industry in Dakar from competition and generated tax revenues for the government. In the 1960s, the government used them as the colonial administration had to protect import monopolies that French trading companies had enjoyed for decades. Licensing and the distribution of quotas made it possible for large French commercial houses to retain unrivalled control over the importation of staple manufactured goods, such as basic textiles and hardware, which otherwise could have been imported by a multitude of smaller firms. Licensing combined with the enormous financial resources of these firms allowed them to continue to monopolise the importation of consumer durables and machinery.

The government selectively "inserted" Senegalese businessmen, state agents, and the relatives and clients of state agents into segments of the commercial sector which were open to local private traders: the wholesale trade, the retail trade, and positions within the state-controlled commodities trade. This was done through licensing, the distribution of loans, and the creation of new, government-sponsored retail distribution networks.

In the early 1960s, the licensing system was extended to regulate entry into intermediate stages in the commercial circuit. Wholesalers and semi-wholesalers were required to obtain yearly authorisation from the Ministry of Commerce. Licences were distributed through the party-cum-bureaucratic machine. At the same time, the government organised about 1,000 of these licensed individuals into two retail trading consortia. Some of these individuals were established traders, others were members of what the Minister of Commerce called "a new class of *techniciens-commerçants*".[16] Under terms negotiated by the government, the large French trading companies provided credit to consortium members for the purchase of imported consumer goods. These arrangements provided businessmen selected by the regime with access to working funds and imported consumer goods. The consortia fell apart in the early 1960s when the French companies claimed that Senegalese traders were defaulting on their loans. Consortia members argued that the French companies used their control over credit and importation as a stranglehold over local *commerçants*.

The government then devised a formula that increased its control over the distribution circuit and the Senegalese traders that operated within it.

The consortia were restructured into one state-run company, the *Société Nationale de Distribution* (SONADIS).[17] The government itself purchased manufactured goods and food staples from the French importers. These goods were sold either by the government itself (through SONADIS stores) or on credit to Senegalese businessmen operating independent outlets. As SONADIS became the largest retail distributor of consumer goods in the rural areas in the 1960s, hundreds of Senegalese traders became either SONADIS employees or indebted to it.

For a better-placed stratum of Senegalese traders and would-be traders, more attractive opportunities opened up in the 1960s. The state-controlled commodities trade generated immediate profits for individuals who obtained contracts to operate in this domain. In 1960, the newly-created *Office de la Commercialization Agricole* (OCA) assumed control over the purchase of the groundnut crop from producers. This initiative was not well received by private traders and small-scale entrepreneurs pushing to expand their rural operations. Because the official bureaucratic structures for crop collection and purchase were not in place until 1968, between 1960 and 1967 the OCA licensed 1,000 individuals each year to handle this activity. Many of those who obtained licences were political influentials and *"bons militants"* at local levels of the ruling party, the *Union Progressiste Sénégalaise* (the UPS) [Schumacher, 1975: 136–7]. Commercial margins set by the marketing board allowed the most favoured individuals to accumulate millions of CFA francs in gross profits during the transition period. The OCA also controlled the importation of Senegal's staple food, rice. The government imported rice and sold it on credit to 20 leading Dakar businessmen and other bigwigs, 50 "large-scale" traders, and 200 "medium-scale" traders. These individuals distributed about 120,000 tons in the mid-1960s at profit margins fixed by the government. Rice quotas generated substantial profits for the individuals that obtained them [Amin, 1969: Diop, 1972: 151]. The system was a tremendous boost to the development of a wealthy stratum of politicians and local businessmen with political connections.

State control over commerce guided the post-colonial expansion of the local business sector along lines defined by the regime, and according to terms defined by the regime. Licences, contracts, and credit were allocated through the UPS and politico-administrative machines to bureaucrats, politicians, local-level government administrators, leading Senegalese traders, and traders and transporters who had been linked to Senghoriste political factions since the 1950s. When government price-fixing, quotas, and loans allowed individuals with licences (which were granted for fixed periods of time) to buy cheap and sell dear, often on an *ad hoc* basis, state-mediated rent-taking occurred. When government-sponsored loans were extended to individuals and then not serviced or reimbursed, rent-taking also occurred. The system created additional rent-taking opportunities for political intermediaries who helped those without the necessary political connections to gain access to licences and credit.

By about 1970, "observers of various origins agree[d] that the local private sector [was] responsible for 10–15 per cent of all business activity [total *chiffre d'affaires*] in Senegal" [Rocheteau, 1982: 90–1]. Yet over the course of the 1960s, a elite group of dynamic and wealthy Senegalese businessmen had emerged. Majhemout Diop estimated in 1968 that about 250 of them had achieved *"une certaine importance"* on the national level [1972:151]. A few amassed large fortunes. Politics and politically mediated commercial opportunities were firmly established as the main avenues of private wealth accumulation. How would this wealth be deployed? The regime's responses to political challenges which erupted at the end of the first decade of independence played a critical role in expanding and entrenching the political system which worked to canalise local accumulation along the lines of rentier activities.

The 1970s: The System Expands

At the end of the 1960s, the fragility and shallowness of Senegal's clientelist system of political control were exposed. Economic recession, followed by government austerity measures affecting students, civil servants, and unionised workers, ignited smouldering frustration with the political status quo [Martens, 1983]. Several simultaneous and mutually reinforcing currents of opposition erupted in 1968 and 1969 in a broad, urban-based attack on the Senghor–UPS political monopoly and on the neo-colonial economic strategy pursued by the regime. At the vanguard were two movements that the regime had failed to absorb or completely control in the 1960s: student groups and labour unions. Industry-level strikes expanded into general strikes which included civil servants. Criticism of excessive centralization of power in the hands of Senghor arose within the regime [Gellar, 1982: 35–6].

The government used force to restore a semblance of political order. Yet the challenge was profound enough to force the government to move on several fronts, making concessions to disaffected groups, creating new corporatist structures to co-opt and divide the opposition, decentralising power within the state apparatus, and accommodating restive elements within the regime. The 1968–70 political crisis and the changes that followed in its wake represent the second critical juncture in the development of a rentier class in Senegal.

In the midst of the broader crisis, 2,600 small-scale traders, transporters, and small business owners formed the *Union des Groupements*

Economiques du Sénégal (UNIGES).[18] Many of these transporters and traders had been pushed out of intermediary positions in the state-controlled groundnut economy when the government assumed direct control over the purchase of the crop in 1968. The largest Senegalese traders and commercial firms, meanwhile, were conspicuously absent from the UNIGES membership list. The organisation denounced Senegal's "neo-colonial" economic policies which forced the local private sector "to vegetate in marginal sectors of the economy.... After 10 years of independence, this situation is not acceptable" [UNIGES, 1968]. Foreign monopolies in the import trade and French banks' stranglehold over private credit came under sharp attack. UNIGES blamed the government for economic stagnation, declared that the regime was "incapable of implementing a coherent policy promoting the national interest", and perhaps most significantly, called for the privatisation of the groundnut and rice trades [ibid.]. It demanded that the government promote local private participation in the industrial sector and ban foreign capital from 30 branches of economic activity including butcheries, bakeries, fishing, garment-making, and printing.

The government countered this current of protest with the same strategy it used in 1968 and 1969 to divide and co-opt the student and labour movements. A second organisation emerged under the wing of the ruling party to represent what the regime called "moderate and responsible" private sector interests. The new business group, *Confédération des Groupements Economiques du Sénégal* (COFEGES), was inaugurated in the company of government and party dignitaries just two months after UNIGES' first congress. The 200 members of this organisation included the largest Senegalese business operations and wealthiest private traders, all with close ties to the ruling party.[19] COFEGES stressed its full support of Senghor, its loyalty to the UPS, and its favorable view of the role of French capital in the Senegalese economy. In a "pro-government fashion", members expressed interest in participating in joint venture arrangements with foreign investors and in increased access to bank credit [Van Chi Bonnardel, 1978: 823–6, 845–6].

The government then proclaimed that it would vigorously assist the local private sector. This commitment was backed up with the creation of two new lending facilities, the *Société Nationale de Guarantie* (SONAGA), which began to provide commercial loans to licensed Senegalese businessmen, and the *Société Nationale des Etudes et de Promotion Industrielle* (SONEPI). In the wake of these initiatives, UNIGES and COFEGES were fused in 1970 at Senghor's request. The fusion created a new, thoroughly domesticated local business organisation which affirmed its solidarity with the ruling party and vowed to work "within the framework of options defined by the government".[20] The elimination of UNIGES as a political force put an end to attacks on foreign capital, the state monopoly over the groundnut trade, and the regime.

The government's "framework of options" expanded the regime's reservoir of patronage resources, enhancing its ability to deal with the broad political crisis of 1968–70. These options offered new and interesting opportunities for the accumulation of wealth on the part of businessmen, politicians, and state agents. They did little to support or induce the movement of local wealth into productive activities, either alongside, in partnership with, or at the expense of French and Lebanese capital. The government did not create "reserved sectors" for local private capital or facilitate local purchases of shares in established foreign-owned companies. It did, however, create a series of new lending facilities that channelled funds into the hands of well-connected individuals and local businessmen. At the same time, the government made it possible for Senegalese with financing and connections to engage in lucrative import operations. The net result in the 1970s was the rise of a better-financed and wealthier Senegalese business sector, more intimately intertwined with the political class and entrenched in *ad hoc*, politically mediated rent taking activities.

In official statements, support for "small- and medium-scale industry" was the central goal of government efforts to promote local business in the 1970s. Official efforts in this domain, however, were marginal and confined to marginal activities. In 1972, SONEPI began lending funds for private investment in priority activities targeted by the government: village-based cottage industries (pottery, weaving); artisanal activities (handicrafts, tailoring); small-scale service activities (small hotels, mechanical work-shops); and activities based on agriculture and fishing (fish drying, market gardening). By the late 1970s, about 50 enterprises had received financial assistance under the programme.[21] The largest of these were Dakar-based firms created to fill government service and supply contracts. According to SONEPI personnel in the mid-1980s, most of the firms aided by SONEPI in the 1970s declared bankruptcy when, after a six-year grace period, their loans to the government fell due.[22] Even in terms of the programme's modest, officially-stated goals, its concrete achievements were minimal.

SONEPI did distribute government-controlled funds, however, and in this sense it performed the same function as other lending institutions created during the same period: SONAGA and the *Société Financière Sénégalaise pour le Développement de l'Industrie et le Tourisme* (SOFISEDIT, created in 1974). SONAGA's short-term loans provided liquidity for many individuals engaged in commerce and non-business activities. SOFISEDIT granted the largest loans to local private parties. It provided medium- and long-term credit for the creation of "medium-scale" enterprises and for the purchase of shares in new foreign ventures, especially in the tourism industry. By 1977, SOFISEDIT had financed 19 investment projects which were "controlled by Senegalese" through shareholding and nine wholly Senegalese-owned projects.[23] Like SONEPI, which financed mostly artisanal-scale ventures, SOFISEDIT was more effective in allocating government-controlled funds than in providing seed capital for viable projects. By the early 1980s, its loan portfolio was in shambles. Most of the ventures it financed had declared bankruptcy. SOFISEDIT's original capital of seven million US dollars was lost, some of it without a trace.

Government efforts to increase local access to bank credit were amplified by reforms of central bank rediscount operations. In 1974, the central bank made more capital available through the rediscount mechanism to the state treasury, to the *Banque National du Développement du Sénégal* (BNDS), and to other state controlled banks [Robson, 1983: 154–5]. The reforms allowed the government to provide loans to local private parties *via* the public banks.

There is wide agreement amongst inside and outside observers that government lending to local private parties in the 1970s followed political, rather than economic or developmental criteria. Political connections rather than the creditworthiness of borrowers or the viability of investment projects guided much of the lending carried out by SOFISEDIT, SONAGA, and the BNDS. Many of the loans drawn from these institutions were never recorded, serviced, or reimbursed.[24] Free-wheeling lending eroded the credibility of the BNDS in the eyes of Senegal's commercial banks and foreign creditors. In 1985, the central bank of the West African Monetary Union (the BCEAO) observed that in Senegal, financial reforms of the 1970s "seem to have given rise to a marked increase in lending to private parties without consideration of how this credit is to be used or the creditworthiness of borrowers. The portfolios of the government banks have deteriorated considerably . . . The new discretion of the banks has led to an ill-considered distribution of credit to the detriment of the classic rules of banking orthodoxy."[25] The government's liberal lending practices did fuel a construction boom in Dakar. State loans financed the building of private residences as well as the construction of villas which were rented to the government itself. Government loans provided funds for the construction of apartment buildings in downtown Dakar which yielded returns on investment of 25–50 per cent a year in the mid-1970s [Colvin, 1980]. Some of the money fed foreign bank accounts.

While the government allocated funds to *hommes d'affaires sénégalais*, it also created new avenues for the use of this capital in the commercial sector. Breaking with the practices of the 1960s, the government began the "rapid insertion" of Senegalese businessmen and women into a domain long dominated by French trading companies: the importation of consumer goods in product categories which were subject to heavy state regulation. By 1978, the number of import licences allocated by the Ministry of Commerce each year reached about 3,000, three times the number authorised in 1965. The number of licensed textile importers increased tenfold over the same period.[26] At the same time, the Ministry of Commerce began to allocate import quotas to a select group of *hommes d'affaires sénégalais* chosen for priority treatment. The sale of quotaed goods on the local market, the single most lucrative niche of the import trade, had been completely "Senegalised" by 1980.

State efforts to create space for Senegalese *hommes d'affaires* within the trading circuit were far-reaching and touched virtually every aspect of state-regulated commerce. In 1978, Prime Minister Abdou Diouf announced that the problem of Senegalisation of the economy had been solved. (*"C'est un problème dépassé."*)[27] Yet by the end of the decade, little had been done to respond to the most fundamental demands made by the local private sector in 1968–70. Industry, private commercial banking, and formal sector service activities remained strongholds of French and Lebanese capital. After more than 15 years of political independence, local private capital in the industrial sector accounted for three per cent of the total.[28] As Sheldon Gellar wrote in 1982, "because of their heavy dependence upon the government for contracts and credit, Senegalese businessmen have not yet been able to act as an autonomous power center strong enough to force the government to make major shifts in favor of the Senegalese private sector" [1982: 34].

Official promotion of the local private sector in the 1960s and 1970s created a stratum of Senegalese businessmen, including many very wealthy individuals, planted firmly in real estate and state-regulated commercial activities, and tied to the political machine. The factors which combined to give wealth accumulation on the part of the political class (and its clients) a rentier character—the dependence of businessmen on licencing and on *ad hoc* commercial transactions mediated by the government, the tendency of borrowers not to invest loans (or to invest in activities which could not generate income without on-going state support), and borrowers' tendency not to repay loans from the state—made private fortunes insecure, dependent on the continual renewal of political privilege, and not self-reproducing. Reforms of the commercial and financial sectors did generate patronage resources in an ailing economy and opened politically mediated rent-taking opportunities to a new generation of politicians, state employees, restive elements within the business community, and an heterogeneous stratum of other state clients. The regime solidified its social base and provided more to the political class, contingent on political favour. The regime also tightened its hold on what might otherwise have emerged as a private sector capable of representing an alternative force, or even an independent force, in the political arena.

Limits and Contradictions

The kinds of government policies that have nurtured indigenous capitalism elsewhere in the post-colonial world were not pursued in Senegal. Instead, state action structured local private wealth accumulation in Senegal along the lines of rentier activities. While clientelism and rentierism enhanced the ability of the regime to remain in power, the limits and contradictions of this system became increasingly apparent by the late 1970s. Particularistic, rent-seeking interests operating within the regime privatised state resources at an impressive rate and captured the bureaucratic levers of economic policy implementation. As a bureaucratic organisation, the state became more responsive to the rent-seeking interests of its agents than to managerial directives aimed at promoting the regime's basic economic policies. One result was the growing incapacity of the regime to circumscribe and limit the scope of rentier activity. From the perspective of peasant producers in the groundnut sector and foreign owners of local manufacturing industry, patterns of state intervention in the economy became less coherent, more unpredictable and contradictory, and more predatory in nature. The use of state power to promote rentierism began to undercut the coherence of legal structures, long-established market structures, and government programmes designed to sustain industrial and agricultural production. In short, the capacity of the state to maintain the conditions that sustained existing patterns of investment and production eroded.

These changes were reflected in the deepening and intractability of the process of decline in Senegal's agricultural and industrial sectors which became marked in the mid-1970s. Productivity, output, and new investment were declining in both sectors when the economy was hit by recession precipitated by droughts, severe balance of payments disequilibrium, and the demands of external creditors. By the 1980s, Senegal was in the midst of profound economic crisis marked by financial bankruptcy of the state, declining groundnut production, and crisis in the industrial sector. The weakness of productive sectors of the economy and the weakness of the state itself deepened the crisis and rendered it more intractable. Pervasive clientelism and rentierism compromised the ability of the government to respond to the recession with coherent initiatives aimed at stemming the decline of the export-oriented agricultural sector and the industrial sector.

Previous analyses of the demise of the groundnut economy in Senegal provide support for this argument [D. Cruise O'Brien, 1984: Caswell,

1984]. State institutions charged with encouraging groundnut production (Ministry of Rural Development) and with appropriating agricultural surpluses on behalf of the state (ONCAD, the groundnut marketing board) ceased to do either in the mid- to late 1970s.[29] Corruption,
fraud, and inefficiency diverted resources away from groundnut producers and the state treasury and into the hands of state agents and the
regime's rural clients. These informal mechanisms of surplus extraction
compounded already-high taxation rates imposed on groundnut producers. Peasants responded to these conditions by withdrawing from
official marketing circuits and reducing their dependence on groundnut
cultivation. In efforts to reverse this trend, the state increased producer
prices. These measures produced meagre results and did not weaken
the informal mechanisms of rent extraction which had become institu-
tionalised in the structures and operations of ONCAD. Meanwhile, the
privatisation of groundnut revenues sapped the state treasury. The
government-controlled daily newspaper, *Le Soleil*, declared in 1980 that
ONCAD had become "an obese parasite, serving the interests of its own
agents at the expense of the state and the peasantry".[30] Over the course of
the 1960s and 1970s, clientelism and rentierism intensified the pressures
which drove peasant producers out of the formal sector of the economy
and weakened the revenue base of the state.

Analogous processes were underway in the commercial and industrial
sectors. The use of state power to create and distribute rent-seeking opportunities for state agents and their clients in the commercial sector gave
rise to widespread fraud in the import business. One of the ways in which
state agents in the Ministry of Commerce, the Ministry of Finance, and
the customs service created and collected rents was by arranging import
transactions which breached commercial laws. Non-payment of import
taxes, importation in excess of quantitative restrictions, and trafficking in
import licenses became widespread. Large-scale fraudulent importation
was blatant in the 1980s, reflecting the unwillingness of government
agencies with direct control over importation to try to suppress it.[31] As a
consequence, the restrictive system of import control which delivered
captive markets to import-substitution industries eroded.

Long-established, uncompetitive French import-substitution industries
(shoes, textiles, enamel cookware, and cosmetic products) faced competition for the first time in the mid-1970s when illegally-imported goods began to supply a large segment of the domestic market. The loss of captive
markets was reflected in production cut-backs, falling rates of profit, layoffs, and wage reductions in the industrial sector. The textile industry, the
largest and best-integrated segment of local manufacturing, was hit the
hardest. Bankruptcies and firm closures reduced the industry's total
workforce by 40 per cent over the course of the 1978–84 period. Govern-

ment analysts described the situation in the textile industry in 1977 as cat-astrophic and alarming.[32] In 1980, the government estimated that 70 per cent of all textile goods available on the Senegalese market in 1978 were imported illegally and argued that "rapid measures must be undertaken to stop illegal importation if the textile industry in Senegal is to sur-vive."[33] This state of affairs provided the French owners of the industry with a rationale for not servicing loans they received from the govern-ment, not investing in the modernisation of their factories, not paying state utilities companies, and breaking union contracts.

The government raised import taxes, banned the importation of a wide array of textile goods, and made textile import quotas more restrictive. Yet it took no visible action to enforce these restrictions. In 1985, govern-ment officials estimated that the volume of illegally-imported textile goods available on the domestic market had grown since 1978, when the decay of the textile industry was proclaimed "a national crisis".[34] In the interim, the French owners of Senegal's three largest textile firms (ac-counting for 70 per cent of total local textile production and employing 1,700 workers) called it quits. In 1981, government-controlled banks fi-nanced the transfer of ownership of these firms to two of Senegal's largest textile importers, a team with business and family ties to President Ab-dou Diouf.[35] Like the French industrialists before them, in the early 1980s the new owners of the industry did not service their loans from the gov-ernment on a regular basis and resisted government pressure to invest in the modernisation of antiquated capital stock. In the mid-1980s, *ad hoc* state subsidies and direct grants from the President's office kept the tex-tile firms operating. Responding rationally to the economic risks and po-litical incentives they confront in the local environment, the new owners of the Dakar textile industry remained rentiers: they channelled the new financial resources transferred to them by the government into lucrative commercial activities conducted under government-granted monopoly.[36]

The expansion of state-sponsored rentier activity over the course of two decades created the basis for the growth and enrichment of the political class. Patronage resources enhanced the ability of the regime to co-opt restive individuals and to channel the economic ambitions of various ele-ments embraced within the ruling coalition along the lines of rentier ac-tivities. While this process deflected and undercut pressure on the gov-ernment to Senegalise control over industry and service sector activities, it also reinforced and exacerbated general economic and political condi-tions which were most unpropitious for investment in productive activ-ity. In Senegal in the 1980s, there appears to be no social agent to provide the impetus for re-establishing or creating economic and legal conditions conducive to private investment in production. The power of the state to structure economic activity is deployed to sustain and expand clientelist networks cemented together by the distribution of politically-generated rents. At a more fundamental level, there is no sign of a coherent class stratum committed to creating the conditions that would promote local private investment, let alone confident that state power could be employed to realise this project.

V. Conclusion

In principle, rentierism can generate wealth which is transformed into capital *via* investment in productive forms of private enterprise. Yet the possibility that a capitalist social stratum will emerge from the ranks of a given political class is inseparable from and dependent upon political forces which are not determined at the level of "capital logic". These political forces condition regimes' willingness to tolerate and support the emergence of indigenous social strata which, by dint of possession of sources of wealth and profit independent of direct state control, could exercise growing autonomy and initiative in the political sphere. Simultaneously, internal political forces condition the ability of regimes to create and sustain broad political and economic conditions which foster productive private investment.

One of the legacies of colonial rule in much of sub-Saharan Africa was the weakness of indigenous capitalist classes. This weakness was mirrored in the political dominance of social strata which were not rooted in the production process. While neo-colonial economic strategies served the interests of foreign capital, they also worked to perpetuate internal balances of political power which were weighted overwhelmingly in favour of those with direct control over the state apparatus. Dominant social fractions devised strategies of governance designed to undercut internal challenges to this status quo and to minimise internal constraints, including class based constraints, on state power. Repression and the rise of authoritarian forms of rule, coupled with clientelism and rentierism, promoted the extension of state power into new domains while demobilising and fragmenting organised social forces and excluding other social groups from narrow political arenas defined from above. This political process shaped patterns of indigenous accumulation.

Political classes appropriated the lion's share of economic surpluses not drained overseas. The ways in which members of this social group deploy these resources have been influenced by prevailing mechanisms and strategies of political control. Where clientelism emerges as a strategy for consolidating political classes and where state-nurtured rentierism provides a material base for the cohesion of this class, the political process works to channel private wealth into *ad hoc* economic activities which are not self-sustaining and which do not involve investment in productive assets or activities. If they can, rentiers remain rentiers, and thus dependent upon, and responsive to, the discretionary exercise of political prerogative from above. Clientelism and rentierism have not always been effective in consolidating regimes and maintaining the political cohesion of ruling classes. Yet the strategy itself has reduced the likelihood that fractions of political classes will have an interest in, or be capable of, using state power to nurture the movement of private wealth into productive investment. Meanwhile the economy narrows and contracts, further undercutting incentives and opportunities for productive investment. Political processes which make rentierism a dominant mode of local accumulation do not create conditions propitious for the expansion of capital in general. In particular, they do not creation conditions likely to foster the rise of capitalist strata from the ranks of sub-Saharan Africa's politically- and economically-dominant social classes. As Colin Leys [1987] and Robert Brenner [1977] have suggested, exceptions to these general tendencies require analyses which specify the economic, social, and political forces or conditions which combine to impel and "require" holders of wealth to invest in productive activities, for the "capital logic" which drives the development of local productive forces does not always prevail.

Notes

1. See Leys [1978], Swainson [1980], Beckman [1982], and Biersteker [1987].

2. My argument thus qualifies the case, advanced by Bjorn Beckman for example, that the post-colonial state can be understood as an organ promoting the development of local productive forces and representing the interests of capital in general. [Beckman, 1980; Beckman, 1982]. In an analysis of the Nigerian case, Beckman argues that "contemporary forms of imperialism need domestically rooted bourgeois class forces in order to establish the appropriate material and political conditions for its profits" [1982: 48]. Beckman argues that indigenous bourgoisies, as they consolidate their own power and bourgeois class rule in the context of a world-market-oriented accumulation process, are not in fundamental conflict with foreign capital, although sectional rivalries may exist. The state mediates rivalries which may emerge between these two "fractions" of capital and promotes the interests of capital as a whole. Beckman points out that "(i)t is important to note the extent to which the bourgeoisie is constituted from above, in and through the state, rather than emerging through class struggle from below. This reflects the manner in which the state is determined at the level of international accumulation and as such embodies a higher level of development of productive forces" [ibid.: 49–50]. In contrast to Beckman, I stress the fact that the relationship between the needs of capital and the political imperatives of the post-colonial situation (as perceived by those in control of state power, and as reflected in the way they use state power) may be contradictory.

3. See Leys [1978], Swainson [1980], Beckman [1982], and Biersteker [1987].

4. The phrase "innovate in their own interests" is used by Markovitz [1987: 8].

5. See MacGaffey [1987] and Sandbrook [1985]. The term "parasitic capitalism" is used by Iliffe [1983: 80].

6. Bates uses the term "rent" in this sense when he speaks of an "administratively generated rent", that is, value in excess of market value which has been created by an administratively generated fixity in the supply of a commodity [Bates, 1981: 99].

7. In a study of Senegal, Robert Fatton [1987: 92–107] makes a similar argument and offers a critique of writers who believe that class analysis is not relevant to understanding political systems structured by patron-client relations.

8. Rosberg and Callaghy [1979: 5–6], in an overview of the "first wave" of African socialism, indicate the grounds upon which such arguments are advanced. See also Sandbrook [1985: 10–11].

9. My translation.

10. See also MacGaffey [1987: 203, 213].

11. See in particular Amin [1969]; Donal Cruise O'Brien [1975]; Schumacher [1975]; and Rita Cruise O'Brien [1979].

12. In discussing Senegal, Donal Cruise O'Brien [1975] uses the term "spoils-oriented" to describe a system of machine politics organised around the distribution of jobs and material rewards.

13. Fatton's work is, in part, an exception. Fatton argues that patron-client relationships in Senegal "represent the internal mode of capital appropriation and political control of the weak . . . " [1987: 106]. In contrast to the argument presented here, Fatton does not argue that cllentelistic modes of appropriation and control have shaped the nature of the ruling class itself (except insofar as such relations provide mechanisms for unifying a factionalised elite), or its possibilities for sustaining or promoting the expanded accumulation of capital in Senegal. Fatton believes that in the 1970s, the penetration of international economic forces and institutions "required" the remolding and rationalisation of patron-client relationships. Means of rationalisation "had to be devised" since they were necessary to support effectively the on-going integration of the Senegalese economy into the world system [108]. This logic is sound; it is consistent with the arguments presented by Beckman [1980, 1982]. Fatton proceeds to argue that these "requirements" did in fact produce "a rationalisation of the state "[1987: 108, 109] and suggests that this process may have strengthened the position of the local bourgeoisie [111]. I would argue that evidence that a such rationalisation is under way is weak indeed, and that the existence of a powerful rentier class in Senegal (forged through state patronage and clientelistic mechanisms of control) helps to explain why the "necessary" remolding of the state has not occurred. See Brenner [1977].

14. This analysis of the role of the state in promoting the rise of a rentier class in Senegal is based on a study of Senegal's commercial and industrial sectors over the course of the 1930–84 period [Boone, 1987]. Research for the larger study was carried out in 1984–86. It involved archival work in Dakar and France, analysis of governmental and non-governmental publications and reports, and interviews with industrialists, Senegalese government officials, importers, and bankers in Dakar and Paris.

15. *Marchés Tropicaux et Méditerranés,* 30 Sept. 1961: 2385; 4 Nov. 1961: 2625–27; 28 April 1962, p. 950.

16. Ibid.

17. On the creation and organization of SONADIS, see Amin [1969: 60–63] and Diop [1972].

18. For discussions of the emergence and significance of UNIGES, see Diop [1972: 167]; Gellar [1982] and Van Chi Bonnardel [1978: 923–26].

19. COFEGES presidents were the owners of the two largest Senegalese trading companies (Ousmane Diagne of SOCECI and Ousmane Seydi of CSSE, als deputé au Parliament). See Ediafric [1970: 273–4] and R. Van Chi Bonnardel [1978: 823–6, 845–6].

20. *Jeune Afrique*, No. 494, 23 June 1970: 50; *Marchés Tropicaux*, 7 Feb. 1970: 306. See also Senghor's "Message to the Nation" of 3 April 1970, reported by *Le Bulletin de l'Afrique Noire*, No. 595, 15 April 1970.

21. *Le Point Economique* (Dakar), No. 13, 1978, pp. 7–8.

22. Information gathered through interviews in Dakar, Nov. 1984.

23. *Le Point Economique* (Dakar), No. 13, 1978, pp. 10–12.

24. This argument appeared in internal bank reports [Banque Centrale des Etats de l'Afrique de l'Ouest (BCEAO), 1985].

25. Ibid.

26. The 1965 figures come from Republique Française, Ministère de la Coopération [1965:4]. The 1978 figures come from: Gouvernement du Sénégal: SONED [1978].

27. *Le Soleil*, interview with Abdou Diouf, 28 March 1978.

28. *L'Economie Sénégalaise* (4th ed., Paris, 1977) cited in Fieldhouse [1986:224].

29. Office National de Coopération et d'Assistance au Développement (ONCAD).

30. *Le Soleil*, 25 août 1980, cited by Caswell [1984: 65].

31. For local commentary on this, see *Liberté*, "L'industrie textile: la morte en fraude", 1 March 1985, p. 20; *Promotion* 2, "La Fraude: du scandale du Touba à l'incompétence des ministres", 21, 7 mars 1985; *Le Soleil*, "Un marché Dakarois: Sandaga", 1 and 2 Oct 1983, pp. 12–13.

32. The government of Senegal issued a very informative and comprehensive study of the textile sector in 1978. See Gouvernement du Sénégal: SONED [1978].

33. This statement is cited from: Gouvernement du Sénégal, Ministère du Développement Industriel et de l'Artisanat [1981: 24].

34. Senegal's Ministries of Industry and Commerce undertook a "Recensement du marché" in 1984. Findings of this study were reported verbally to the author in Dakar by an ex-Ministry of Commerce official in April 1985.

35. The government was the sole or the majority shareholder in each of the 3 banks that financed this business transaction: BNDS, the USB, and the BSK. Changes in the Dakar textile industry after 1980 are described in more detail in Boone [1987].

36. With the growing pool of financial resources at their disposal, the new owners of the basic textile industry imported finished textile goods under state licence, imported Japanese cars under an exclusive importer licence, and imported duty-free luxury foods.

References

Amin, Samir, 1969, *Le Monde des Affaires Sénégalais*, Paris: Editions de Minuit.

Banque Centrale des Etats de l'Afrique de l'Ouest (BCEAO), Direction Centrale du Crédit, 1985, "Seminaire sur les regles d'intervention et de distribution du crédit dans l'UMOA; Les instruments de la politique sélective du crédit dans l'UMOA", Dakar, 11–15 March.

Bates, Robert, 1981, *Markets and States in Tropical Africa*, Los Angeles, CA: University of California Press.

Beckman, Bjorn, 1976, *Organizing the Farmers: Cocoa Politics and National Development in Ghana*, Uppsala: Scandinavian Institue of African Studies.

Beckman, Bjorn, 1980, "Imperialism and Capitalist Transformation: A Critique of a Kenyan Debate", *Review of African Political Economy*, No. 19, pp. 37–51.

Beckman, Bjorn, 1982, "Whose State? State and Capitalist Development in Nigeria", *Review of African Political Economy*, No. 23, pp. 37–51.

Biersteker, Thomas, 1987, *Multinationals, the State, and Control of the Nigerian Economy*, Princeton NJ: Princeton University Press.

Boone, Catherine, 1987, "State Power and Private Interests: Politics, Markets, and the Textile Industry in Senegal", Ph.D. dissertation, Massachusetts Institute of Technology, Department of Political Science.

Brenner, Robert, 1977, "The Origins of Capitalist Development: A Critique of Neo-Smithian Marxism", *New Left Review*, No. 104, pp. 25–92.

Callaghy, Thomas M., 1987, "Absolutism, Bonapartism, and the Formation of Ruling Classes: Zaire in Comparative Perspective", in I.L. Markovitz (ed.), *Studies in Power and Class in Africa*, Oxford: Oxford University Press, pp. 94–117.

Caswell, Nim, 1984, "Autopsie de l'ONCAD, La politique arachidière du Sénégal, 1966–1980", *Politique Africaine*, No. 14, pp. 38–73.

Colvin, Lucy, 1980, "Private Initiatives in the Senegalese Economy", unpublished consultant report for USAID mission to Dakar, 9 June–25 July.

Cruise O'Brien, Donal, 1975, *Saints and Politicans: Essays on the Organization of a Senegalese Peasant Society*, Cambridge: Cambridge University Press.

Cruise O'Brien, Donal, 1984, "Les bienfaits de l'égalité", *Politique Africaine* No. 14.

Cruise O'Brien, Rita, 1979, "Introduction", in Rita Cruise O'Brien (ed.), *The Political Economy of Underdevelopment: Dependence in Senegal*, London: Sage Publications, pp. 13–37.

Diop, Majemout, 1972, *Histoire des Classes Sociales dans L'Afrique de L'Ouest, Tome II: Le Sénégal*, Paris: François Maspero.

Ediafric, 1970, *La Politique Africaine en 1969*, Paris: La Documentation Africaine.

Fatton, Robert, 1987, *The Making of a Liberal Democracy: Senegal's Passive Revolution, 1975–1985*, Boulder: Lynne Rienner Publishers.

Fieldhouse, D.K., 1986, *Black Africa 1945–1980* London: Allen & Unwin.

Flynn, Peter, 1974, "Class, Clientelism, and Dependency: Some Mechanisms of Internal Dependency and Control", *Journal of Commonwealth and Comparative Politics*, Vol. 12, No. 2, pp. 133–56.

Gellar, Sheldon, 1982, *Senegal: An African Nation Between East and West*, Boulder, CO: Westview.

Gouvernement du Sénégal (GOS), SONED, 1978, "Le Textile au Sénégal", Dakar: GOS.

Gouvernement du Sénégal (GOS), Ministère du Developpement Industriel et de l'Artisanat, 1981, "Rapport du Groupe de Travail Textile", unpublished report, Dakar: GOS, 25 Sept.

Iliffe, John, 1983, *The Emergence of African Capitalism*, Minneapolis: University of Minnesota Press.

Jackson, Robert H. and Carl G. Rosberg, 1982, *Personal Rule in Black Africa: Prince, Autocrat, Prophet, Tyrant*, Los Angeles, CA: University of California Press.

Leys, Colin, 1978, "Capital Accumulation, Class Formation, and Dependency— the Significance of the Kenyan Case", *The Socialist Register*.

MacGaffey, Janet, 1987, *Entrepreneurs and Parasites: The Struggle for Indigenous Capitalism in Zaire*, Cambridge: Cambridge University Press.

Markovitz, Irving Leonard, 1987, "Introduction", in I.L. Markovitz (ed.), *Studies in Power and Class in Africa*, Oxford: Oxford University Press, pp. 3–19.

Martens, George, 1983, "Révolution ou participation: syndicats et partis politiques au Sénégal (4ème partie)", *Le Mois en Afrique*, Nos. 213–14, pp. 63–80, 97–109.

Miras, C. de, 1982, "L'entrepreneur ivoirian ou une bourgeoisie privée de son état", in Y.-A. Fauré and J.-F. Médard (eds.), *Etat et Bourgeoisie en Côte d'Ivoire*, Paris: Karthala, pp. 181–229.

Republique Française, Ministère de la Coopération, 1965, Le Secteur Textile au Sénégal, Dakar: GOS.

Robson, Peter, 1983, *Integration, Development and Equity: Economic Integration in West Africa*, Boston, MA: Allen & Unwin.

Rocheteau, Guy, 1982, *Pouvoir Financière et Indépendence Economique: Le cas du Sénégal*, Paris: Karthala-ORSTROM.

Rosberg, Carl G. and Thomas M. Callaghy, 1979, "Introduction", in Rosberg and Callaghy (eds.), *Socialism in Sub-Saharan Africa: A New Assessment*, Berkeley: Institute of International Studies, University of California, Berkeley.

Sandbrook, Richard, 1985, *The Politics of Africa's Economic Stagnation*, Cambridge: Cambridge University Press.

Schumacher, Edward J., 1975, *Politics, Bureaucracy, and Rural Development in Senegal*, Los Angeles, CA: University of California Press.

Swainson, Nicola, 1980, *The Development of Corporate Capitalism in Kenya: 1918–1977*, Los Angeles, CA: University of California Press.

UNIGES, 1968, "Rapport du Premier Congrès", unpublished paper released in Dakar, 1 June.

Van Chi Bonnardel, Regine Nguyen, 1978, *La Vie de Relations au Sénégal: La Circulation des Biens*, Dakar: IFAN.

9

Reconfiguring State-Ethnic Relations in Africa: Liberalization and the Search for New Routines of Interaction

Donald Rothchild

Africa's current economic liberalization and democratization carries with it broad opportunities for choice that could be either creative or destructive. The removal of the old authoritarian structures in the 1990s is likely to alter the boundaries between individuals and groups and to shift the rules of encounter between the state and various social forces. In more destructive situations, a collapse of the social contract is likely to bring with it incivility, where connections disintegrate among elites and across the society at large. The loss of a prevailing sense of common purpose weakens the interdependencies between state and society, allowing the triumph of parochialism over community-wide trust and responsibility. In the most fatal of these scenarios, the results can assume grievous proportions, taking on such forms as forced assimilation, displacement, "ethnic cleansing," and genocide.[1] In less grim circumstances, which, fortunately, are more commonplace, a tacit (or, in some cases, explicit) recognition of social contract can establish a context in which liberalization will result in a flourishing of multiple identities and shared political and economic participation. Although the state may accept the need to decentralize some responsibilities, it may also gain in legitimacy if it can effectively perform the functions that remain under its control.

Under what conditions can the reconfigured state be expected to promote constructive—that is, life-affirming—patterns of reciprocity and political exchange? Recognizing the dangers implicit in political and economic transitions, how is it possible to structure political regimes so as to reduce the risks of overpoliticization and restrain the determination of

political leaders to use whatever means are necessary to ensure a preferred share of scarce resources for themselves and their group? To answer these questions, I will examine the shifting dynamics of state-ethnic
relations in three contexts: the colonial, the immediate postcolonial, and
the current period of political and economic liberalization. Although intertwined and overlapping, these different regime patterns nonetheless
organize interactions in different ways, leading variously to constructive
and destructive outcomes. In the conclusion, I will identify several alternative regime patterns that might provide incentives for creative pluralism, even when societal linkages are weak and there is little consensus
about national goals or common purpose.

Stage 1: Colonial Hegemonic Regimes and the Independence Bargain

The African colonial state's authoritarian nature reflected both the coer-
civeness of its establishment and the logic of its means of control. Intrud-
ers from Western Europe thrust their institutions, procedures, and values
upon the various peoples in a given area, who were in no position to offer
effective resistance to this externally projected power. As these new institutions were put in place, European officials, largely unaccountable to the
local populace, came to exercise wide discretionary authority to structure
the relations between state and society and among the groups making up
the society. The very arbitrariness of the colonial relationship enabled European administrators to override local opposition, facilitating the
processes of institutional transfer and state building. Extensive political
centralization kept the costs of decisionmaking low and limited the expenditures on administration and development. By making low investments in political and administrative infrastructure, however, hegemony
lost much of its fleeting opportunity to overcome fissiparous forces and to
create national identities, establish acceptable authority systems, and enhance territory-wide development.

The colonial state's latitude in organizing its relations with society was
enhanced by the fluidity and variability of local ethnic group identities. In
a number of territories, ethnic self-consciousness lacked deep historical
roots, being a relatively recent phenomenon that emerged in response to
the modernist forces unleashed during the colonial era. In territories
where cultural identities had crystallized, relations between ethnic
groups ranged from peaceful contact to antagonism. The impact of colonial hegemony on these complex and variegated interactions was considerable. The institutionalization of European authority systems brought
group self-awareness to the fore as various ethnic groups competed with
one another for favorable state treatment—in recruitment for military and

civil service positions, district and regional development allocations, scholarships, industrial locations, and so forth. This competition for preferred treatment resulted in more pronounced cleavages between groups, which have given rise to lasting patterns of tension in postcolonial times. In the economic sphere, differential rates of modernization intensified tensions between ethnoregions that were advantaged by close contact with Western education, infrastructural improvement, and agricultural and industrial development and those in the hinterland that remained neglected. In the political sphere, the creation of administrative units and boundaries at the local and regional levels emphasized cleavages between ethnic groups, intensifying the competition between them for the scarce goods of modernity. Larry Diamond has described this process in Nigeria, where the three-region structure, a "colonial construction" established by British authorities, "produced the peculiar coincidence of region and ethnicity observed during the final decade [the 1950s]—one that reified the tripartite ethnic division, forged a volatile contradiction between the political power of the one and the socioeconomic pre-eminence of the other two, and fostered deep, reciprocal distrust and insecurity not only between the three major groups but between these and the numerous minority groups as well."[2] In a similar way, the separate administration of the Southern Sudan and the general disregard for its economic modernization created a dualism between North and South that had grave disintegrative implications in the postindependence period.

With the approach of self-government and independence, colonial authorities began the shift from hegemony to a regime based on political exchange and shared power. In a rather hasty and improvised way, they presided over a process of internal negotiation that succeeded in most (but not all) cases in hammering out constitutions linking institutional continuity with public participation. In this bargain between the colonial government and the nationalist local elite, the transfer of power was conditioned upon the latter's acceptance of extensive limitations on central control. This coercive negotiating process was intended to ensure political stability following decolonization, reassuring ethnic and racial minorities that state power would be dispersed among a number of political authorities. The new constitutions built up institutions of efficient government control, such as the bureaucracy, military, and police, while also setting up a series of checks on the arbitrary exercise of state or party power: multiparty elections, second chambers, federalism, regional autonomy, rigid amendment clauses, protected judiciaries, and bills of rights. Such constitutional engineering, mediated by colonial interests and ideas, frequently proved most controversial and unsatisfactory. Instrumental and pragmatic in nature, this colonially mediated bargaining was unable to frame a normative consensus in the years to follow.

Stage 2: Postcolonial Hegemonies
and the Flawed Bargain

Following the transfer of power in the 1960s, the postcolonial elite in many African countries accepted the basic framework for a transitional period defined in the independence bargain. For the time being at least, there was an uncertain continuity in political principles and practices. In the early 1960s, a number of the dominant political elites managed to maintain political routines that contributed to reasonably stable state-society interactions, lending an air of political normality to some of these initial postindependence regimes.

Despite such appearances of continuity, the new leaders were intent upon reshaping their societies along centralized, welfare capitalist, even socialist lines. They were openly hostile to politicized ethnicity in its various expressions and were determined to consolidate power at the political center. Africa's new rulers, anxious to overcome the inheritance of colonial indifference and dependency, looked upon the centralized state as a solution to the many economic and social problems confronting them. This view facilitated the growth of institutions of control, such as the executive, civil service, military, police, and governing party, and inhibited others that might limit the elite's capacity for action, such as federalism, multiparty elections, complex franchise formulas, and various constitutional protections. With public expectations soaring to new heights, the state elite responded through the only channel that appeared readily available—the state and its parastatal organizations. The consequence of this choice was an enormous growth of state institutions and state administrative and economic responsibilities. In turn, this enlargement of the state heightened the competition between ethnic spokespersons for a preferred share of state-controlled resources. In the late Claude Ake's terms, social life became "overpoliticized," gravely weakening the state at the very moment that it strove to incorporate civil society and bring economic activities within its embrace.[3] The colonial bargain was crumbling and, as I will show, the efforts made to renegotiate its terms were cautious and elitist.

The interval from 1966 to 1989 was marked by a weakening of state-society connections. Despite an evident decline in economic performance, ethnic and other interest groups competed more intensely than ever for scarce public resources. The state became greatly overextended, unable to regulate its society effectively or to implement its ambitious development program. "The inability of the state to [meet public expectations]," writes John A. A. Ayoade, "has created a credibility gap, which has necessitated the delinkage of the people from the state."[4] The state came to appear alien and aloof, lacking the legitimacy it had secured from the earlier struggle for independence.

As state legitimacy decreased, ruling elites at the political center frequently sought to compensate for their diminished authority with forceful and repressive approaches. The dominant political elite, which in many instances was also identified with a principal ethnic group, made use of the institutional resources at the state's command to favor its class interests while requiring compliance from the community at large. All too often, "officeholders compete[d] for the acquisition of material benefits," creating an air of resignation and cynicism—or what Ghana's head of state Jerry Rawlings described as "a culture of silence."[5] In the more abusive cases, where the state employed the military or the "special branch" to contain opposition or to oppress dissident sections of the community, resistance took the form of insurgent action or disengagement from the formal economy. Social groups became fully aware of the state's limitations, and, disdainful of its claims and pretensions, withdrew for some purposes from the formal economy. As a consequence, corrupt practices spread, and such activities as hoarding, illegal currency exchange, and smuggling became commonplace. Unable to extract the necessary resources for energetic leadership or to mediate effectively among various interest groups, the weakened African state inclined all too readily to authoritarian and self-serving forms of class action. Although for a time such efforts did succeed in stifling the outward manifestations of opposition, the hegemonic postcolonial regime was unable to firmly establish political legitmacy and inevitably encountered conflict, either within its ruling coalition or between that coalition and an ethnic or class-based counterelite.

With the breakdown of the colonially mediated bargain, communal elite representatives in a one- or no-party system faced three basic options: acquiescence, cooptation, or resistance. Many ethnic leaders recognized that, for all its shortcomings, the modern African state was a critically important source of resources at a time of deepening scarcity and remained central to the continued well-being of their client groups. These communal brokers perceived the state as a provider of financial support for security, welfare, infrastructural development, education, marketing, and other services, a valued dispenser of scarce resources and well worth fastening onto. As a result, intense competition ensued among ethnic and other group leaders for preferred positions in the cabinet and ruling party and for a favored share of executive and civil service positions and public allocations.

Much of the competition among elite representatives in the hegemonic postcolonial state followed well-understood rules of the game. The resulting "hegemonic exchange" regime represented a new, albeit flawed bargain that linked state/party control with the limited participation of elite notables in the decisionmaking process. Hegemonic exchange was a transitionary regime form that characterized the untidy but expedient political process of the early years following independence. As such, it represented a type of state-facilitated coordination in which a somewhat autonomous central state actor and a number of considerably less autonomous ethnoregional interests engaged, on the basis of commonly accepted procedural norms, rules, or understandings, in a process of mutual accommodation.[6] It brought together some elements of control, such as the one- or no-party system and centralized decisionmaking, with some elements of political exchange, such as elite coalitions at the political center, which allow for quiet, behind-the-scenes negotiations by state and societal elites over the distribution of tangible resources.

Within the circle of the favored elite cartel, such a framework for elite bargaining did facilitate the management of conflict over a transitionary period. In Kenya, Côte d'Ivoire, and Cameroon, authoritarian leaders included the genuine leaders of the main ethnoregional groupings in an informal and pragmatic bargaining process at the political center. These state and ethnic representatives at the top of the hierarchy formed dyadic or broadly coalitional exchange relationships, thereby promoting cooperative relations in a variety of arenas, such as an ethnic balance in cabinet appointments, proportional civil service recruitment patterns, and relatively equitable resource allocation formulas. In some cases, such as Uganda and Zambia, the political representation of ethnic groups was regarded as illegitimate; even so, their leaders—Milton Obote in Uganda and Kenneth Kaunda in Zambia—proved masters of balancing the competing claims of ethnic interests. Thus the postcolonial hegemonic regime could in many instances make up for a weak state and adjust to a persistent ethnic clientelism. What these regimes crafted was an inclusive elite cartel that formed informal exchange relationships based on well-understood procedural rules. The result was considerable stability for an interim period. In the long term, however, such arrangements were circumscribed, confined to a transitory period by the elitist and highly instrumental nature of the social compact. Moreover, as the erratic and coercive nature of personalistic rule became increasingly apparent in many of these countries, the practices of inclusion and proportionality slipped from view, revealing the harsh and unpredictable side of authoritarian rule for all to see.

At times, the methods of the repressive state left little or no scope for exchange relationships. "Oligarchic regimes replaced popularly elected ones," writes P. Anyang' Nyong'o, "and, in certain cases, this change was accompanied by violence, the assassination of popular political figures and the imposition on society of repressive military regimes."[7] As the state became abusive and intolerant of opposition, ethnic strongmen and others sometimes rejected cooperation as intolerable, opting instead for open resistance. As the rules of relationship became more brittle, these leaders took advantage of the state's apparent softness to assert their autonomy from the political center.

This assertion of political autonomy took on both internalist (autonomy within the state) and externalist (autonomy outside the state—i.e. separation or secession and independence) dimensions. In a conscious attempt to reconcile ethnic pluralism with national purposes, the state in Nigeria, Ghana, Kenya, Cameroon, and Côte d'Ivoire willingly adapted to the claims of ethnoregional interests, allowing regional authorities a measure of administrative autonomy. In other cases, however, the state was not prepared to "accommodat[e] tensions within a common frame."[8] Where the state continued to press zealously for an extreme form of concentrated power at the political center, the local community sometimes resisted forcefully, resulting in certain instances in a kind of de facto autonomy. During the late 1980s and early 1990s, while the Sudan People's Liberation Army was in control of much of the South, its commander, Col. John Garang de Mabior, could speak accurately of his people's insulation from the reach of the Khartoum government.[9] As indicated by events during the 1970s and 1980s—including the confrontation between the Eritrean, Tigrayan, and Oromo-based national movements and the Mengistu government in Ethiopia and the struggle for political power led by Jonas Savimbi's National Union for the Total Independence of Angola (UNITA)—these insurgent movements were capable of creating their own autonomous administrative structures, providing inhabitants of the areas under their control with basic health, educational, and economic services.[10]

Since the identities of a number of these ethnically pluralistic states are still in a process of formation, it is not surprising that some ethnic and nationality leaders, uncomfortable over the past uses and abuses of state power and disappointed over the failure to develop, have gone further by asserting the autonomy of their region apart from the whole. The result has been a demand for political self-determination beyond the state structure, a claim that has often generated various forms of external involvement—including recognition, economic and military assistance, and third-party mediation. In Nigeria, the Biafran leader, Lt. Col. Chukwuemeka Odumegwu Ojukwu, asserted in 1967 that the people of Eastern Nigeria could "no longer be protected in [their] lives and in [their] property by any Government based outside Eastern Nigeria" and declared that henceforth the territory would be an independent sovereign state.[11] State leaders responded to this challenge in a firm manner, achieving a decisive military victory on the ground. Similar externalist confrontations have taken place in the Congo—Leopoldville, the Sudan, and Western Sahara, with equally disappointing results for the insurgents. Only in the case of Eritrea, where the Eritrean People's Liberation Front fought successfully for the territory's self-determination and subsequently pursued a concerted policy of isolating itself from Ethiopian affairs, was external recognition accorded by the international community following a successful referendum in 1993.

Stage 3: Reconfiguring the State-Society Compact: A New Bargain Based on an Implied Consensus?

By the 1990s, the cold war had come to an end and a number of the old, authoritarian leaders had lost their external patrons. Fatigued by the dominance and unresponsiveness of the authoritarian state and encouraged by democratic trends outside the continent, leaders of many African civil associations and other organizations developed a national consensus around the goals of political and economic reform and liberalization. In an effort to find a new basis for political legitimacy, they championed an emergent national understanding that would reconnect state and society. Clearly, sustained economic growth and development required coherent strategies to ensure regularized state-society interactions. Without these, the state would remain perilously isolated from society, unable to secure reliable information or to extract sufficient resources to achieve its tasks. In the worst cases, such as Somalia and Liberia, the fall of the autocratic ruler was accompanied by the collapse of civil society itself, initiating a kind of factionalized civil war that brought new levels of immiseration. Thus, unless norms and practices could emerge that buttressed values like participation, inclusiveness, and civility, reform efforts seemed likely to suffer from what the Organization for Economic Cooperation and Development calls "policy incoherence."[12]

With the urban protests of the late 1980s and early 1990s and increasing exogenous pressures for political liberalization, the leaders of various political, economic, and social associations escalated their demands to replace the heavy-handed authoritarian regimes of the past with new, more accountable systems of governance. Associational activity increased markedly in range and intensity, as trade unions, professional organizations, students, communal spokespersons, and disaffected political leaders, among others, expressed their disapproval of the repression, corruption, and inefficiency of the old order. Although the opposition was often fragmented and poorly coordinated, coalitions were established in some countries. In Zambia, for example, an alliance of workers, entrepreneurs, and church leaders and members was brought together under the banner of the Movement for Multiparty Democracy.[13] The impact of this internally generated protest was enormous. As the ruling elites responded, often quite grudgingly, to the calls for democratization and change, they allowed national conventions and constitutional deliberations to go forward. What materialized from these initiatives has been described as the "second wave of liberation in Africa," a process resulting in the holding or scheduling of national elections in well over two-thirds of the African countries in the early 1990s.[14] Some of these elections seemed to be stage managed and marred by "serious irregularities,"[15] but when the leadership was more prepared to entertain the possibility of defeat, elections allowed for an open choice among party representatives. Given the opportunity for choice, a number of African publics expressed themselves in no uncertain terms, replacing one set of rulers with another in countries such as Benin, Zambia, Cape Verde, and São Tomé and Principe.

Although multiparty elections allow for a definitive change in ruling elites, it hardly presages an end to the ethnic or national question in Africa. In Zambia, where the incoming president, Frederick Chiluba, appointed a significant number of Bemba from the Copperbelt to his cabinet, the Lozi were quick to charge that he was favoring their ethnoregional rivals.[16] The Ghana elections, which enabled Rawlings to hold on to high office, brought sharp protests in Kumasi from the Ashanti opposition. In Cameroon, President Paul Biya's election and subsequent cabinet appointments engendered criticism from the Anglophones, fearful of their marginalization in the newly emerging political order of the country.[17] Clearly, elections are consciousness-raising experiences. Ethnic patrons view them as an important political juncture, offering opportunities for either a beneficial inclusion or a highly disadvantageous exclusion. The struggle for state resources is as ubiquitous as ever and structural adjustment programs continue to exacerbate interregional tensions by constricting the state's role, possibly undercutting the implementation of balanced recruitment policies in the public sector, and reversing the rural-urban terms of trade.[18] Thus it is not surprising that elections in the current period point up the continuing saliency of ethnic consciousness and conflict in contemporary African political life.

If elections and economic reforms have brought a number of rivalries to the surface, political liberalization has also created hopes that a new spirit of conciliation and compromise will emerge, leading to the advent of regularized patterns of relationships between state and ethnic leaders. There are signs of a new sensitivity and willingness on the part of state elites to accommodate ethnic identity issues, largely in order to achieve their objectives of political stability and economic reform.[19] Rather than cavalierly dismissing ethnic ties as "false consciousness," African statesmen and academics are now more inclined to recognize that ethnic politics cannot be written off as a premodern phenomenon but instead represents competition by modern group representatives for the goods and opportunities of contemporary life.[20]

Thus, in his opening address to a conference at the African Centre for Applied Research and Training in Social Development in Tripoli, Adebayo Adedeji, the former UN undersecretary general and executive secretary of the Economic Commission for Africa, described this as an opportune time to develop positive strategies for coping with ethnic issues. Criticizing the tendency of African state leaders "to ignore the fact of ethnicity," Adedeji stressed the importance of "devising ways and means of avoiding ethnic tensions and the marginalization of ethnic groups and of transforming ethnic loyalties and values from being perceived as a threat to national cohesion to being utilized as an engine of development and positive social change."[21] Ethnicity has been gradually coming out of the closet, recognized as a legitimate force to be dealt with in an open manner. The Nigerian leadership has been most keenly aware of the need to recognize the legitimacy of ethnic claims and to provide for the inclusion of ethnic groups on a roughly proportional basis, perhaps reflecting their grim experiences with civil war and a recognition of the costs of further conflicts of this sort. Thus Nigeria's constitutional provisions on "federal character" can be viewed as an earnest expression of their intention to ensure broad ranging participation of group interests in the affairs of state.

With political liberalization gaining momentum and, in certain quarters at least, ethnicity gaining a grudging acceptability, the 1990s has come to represent an opportune time to explore the possibilities of a new national consensus on reconfiguring state-society relations. It is not possible for me to examine all the current alternatives as fully as I would want to in this context, but I will point to some of the general directions of this search for desperately needed confidence-building measures. I will focus upon four overlapping choices under active consideration on the African scene today.

Constitutional Guidelines on Ethnic Proportionality

Perceiving a connection between authoritarian tendencies and zero-sum civil conflict, some African regimes have sought to promote conciliatory behavior through political liberalization and the use of formulas of proportionality when allocating scarce public resources. Although mildly authoritarian regimes have made use of the proportionality principle to encourage intergroup cooperation (as in the "hegemonic exchange" practices of the 1960s–1980s), pacted democracies and polyarchical regimes have tended to be more systematic about formulas for sharing government positions and developmental distributions. Cognizant of the social costs of mutually damaging ethnic conflicts in their societies, ruling coalitions in such regimes may be more inclined to accept some form of "intergroup equity as the major decision rule for the political system, su-

perseding such alternative criteria as individual ability or social efficiency."[22] Given the potentially volatile feelings surrounding the issue of
resource allocation, governing elites in polyarchical countries, such as
Botswana, are attracted to a proportionality principle because it is relatively neutral and easy to administer under Africa's soft state conditions.
Provided that ethnic demands continue to be reasonable in nature and
that there is some room for adjustment in proportionality arrangements
to take account of demographic and other changes, it remains possible for
African leaders to work within the political system to meet the guidelines
of fairness. The effect of utilizing such guidelines is to compensate ethnic
minority interests and thereby encourage their confidence. For example,
in Nigeria, data from the late 1970s indicate an increasing tendency to apply the proportionality principle in budgetary allocations among the
states. In the roads, health, and education programs from 1975/1976 to
1979/1980, the index of variation in that country decreased from 1.18 to
0.48, .96 to .88, and from .70 to .51 respectively.[23] And in Ghana, the short-
lived polyarchical regimes of Dr. Kofi Busia and Dr. Hilla Limann made
concerted efforts to channel resources from the urban centers to the rural
areas. Although in both cases their plans were cut short by military interventions, some reallocation did take place as a consequence of changed
budgetary priorities. Clearly redistributive policies can themselves
"cause intense controversy," as Edmond Keller notes.[24] Even more certain, however, is the likelihood that perceptions of discriminatory allocative policies will contribute to bitter ethnoregional antagonism, as the
case of Isaak rebellion and separatism in northern Somalia illustrates only
too clearly.[25]

Electoral Arrangements to Ensure
Broad Minority Participation

In an effort to reassure ethnic minority groups about their place in the
newly reconfigured societies of Africa, constitutional engineers have begun to experiment with a variety of mechanisms intended to promote a
sense of inclusion. The possibility of being represented in the ruling coalition at the political center, it is assumed, will encourage ethnic leaders
and their constituents to act with moderation. If their representatives are
a part of the ruling coalition, ethnic memberships are likely to feel that
they have access to those in authority and that the power elite will be responsive to their demands. As a consequence, the ethnic leaders will have
more incentive to direct their constituents along positive channels.

Two very different examples of electoral efforts to facilitate a sense of
inclusion indicate the possibilities for experimentation in this respect. In
an attempt to ensure that the president has the support of a broad-based

constituency in Nigeria, the 1993 Constitution stipulates that to win a national election, a candidate must secure a simple majority of the total number of votes cast, as well as one-third of the votes cast in each of at least two-thirds of the states. If no candidate meets this requirement, then an electoral college consisting of all the members of the national and state assemblies, sitting in their respective houses and voting on the same day, will elect a president on the basis of a simple majority of those present and voting.[26] Such provisions work to structure institutions that will break down narrow parochialism and build confidence on the part of smaller ethnic groups.[27]

Although the background and goals are rather different in South Africa, the preparedness of the major parties to adopt a system of proportional representation reflects their determination to reassure minority groups regarding their participation in the new ruling coalition. Recognizing that a first-past-the-post electoral system tends to polarize the society into winners and losers (as was the case with Angola's presidential election in 1992), participants at the inaugural meeting of the Convention for a Democratic South Africa in December 1991 issued a Declaration of Intent that proposed a proportional representation (PR) strategy. Commenting on the African National Congress's preparedness to opt for PR, Timothy Sisk notes: "The ANC has been sensitive to a crucial aspect of electoral system choice: the need to consider not only what is desirable [clearcut parliamentary leadership], but also what is *possible* given the preferences of others."[28]

As the experience of Namibia indicates, PR creates an incentive for minority interests to act in a conciliatory manner, because they see in it an opportunity to exert influence from within the ruling coalition. The chance of electoral victory encourages them to present party lists that contain representatives from all major communities, increasing their likelihood of inclusion in the dominant, centrist coalition at the political center. The effect is to promote conciliatory behavior and to reduce the possibility that appeals from militant parties on the flanks will outbid moderate leaders. In South Africa's case, PR will be based upon the country's ten developmental regions, which are ethnically heterogeneous in character. Even so, the tendency of some ethnic peoples to concentrate in certain areas gives a partial ethnic dimension to South Africa's PR arrangement.

Elite Power Sharing at the Political Center

When the leaders and allies of a single ethnic group appear to have captured control of state institutions and have then proceeded to exclude the representatives of other groups from the centers of power, the costs in terms of intense interethnic conflict have invariably proven high (as in South Africa, Ethiopia, and Burundi). In this respect, Daniel arap Moi's underrepresentation of the Kikuyu and Luo in the Kenyan cabinet following the 1992 election and his suspension of Parliament in January 1993, which thereby denied the Opposition an effective voice, may have done more to heighten ethnic tensions than his manipulation of the rules in the preelection period.[29] Ethnic leaders on the periphery feel barred from effective participation and often conclude, rightly or wrongly, that state policies threaten the political interests, even the security, of their group.

An alternative to the dominance of a single group is an intentional strategy of representing major ethnic and other interests in the ruling coalition. When the leaders of major ethnic and national groups are assured of participation in the governmental process—whether by formal political rules (Mauritius's "best loser" formula; South Africa's agreement to include major parties in the government under the interim constitution; Nigeria's constitutional provisions on "federal character") or by informal rules (elite power-sharing arrangements at different stages in Zambia, Kenya, Côte d'Ivoire, and Cameroon)—group conflict is more likely to be channeled along collaborative lines. To be sure, there is a risk that members of the ruling elite will use their positions to exacerbate tensions by mobilizing their supporters at the grassroots level to political action along communal lines. Even allowing for such risks, however, inclusive coalitions seem likely to involve the various elite groups in learning about one another's concerns, thereby promoting empathy and conciliatory behavior. To the extent that regimes do operate according to widely understood, formal or informal norms for involving major groups and their representatives on a proportional basis, as increasingly appears to be the case, a confidence-building mechanism will be in place that seems likely to facilitate predictable rules of social relations, which are critical to the effective management of conflict.

Decentralization and Federalism

In situations where ethnic groups are concentrated in specific areas of a country, it is possible to give expression to institutional pluralism through mechanisms such as devolution, decentralization, regional autonomy, and federalism.[30] These various arrangements differ significantly in the powers they assign to the central and regional governments as well as local authorities, but they share in common the objective of reducing conflict by separating groups into distinct political units, each of which is responsible for certain functions. In the past, African leaders such as Kwame Nkrumah and Sekou Touré, determined to concentrate political and economic power at the center, have looked suspiciously at such autonomous arrangements, which appeared to create pockets of power that were likely to hinder their transformationalist objectives. Early semifederal experiments in Uganda, Kenya, Ghana, and the Congo (Zaire) were scuttled, largely out of fear that political autonomy would create intergroup tensions, weaken central control and, in the worst cases, lead to secessionist movements. Also, the autonomy granted to the Southern Region of the Sudan under the 1972 Addis Ababa agreement was gradually undercut, as President Gaafar el-Nimeiry shifted his position to increase his support within the northern-dominated state coalition.[31]

In recent times, however, some African leaders have become more accepting of geopolitical expressions of ethnic identity. In Senegal, Zambia, and Ghana, for example, measures of decentralization have been implemented that offer new scope for participation and influence in local politics and administration. Displaying increasing pragmatism regarding the symbolic role that traditional authorities will henceforth be permitted to play in the life of their country, the ruling elite in formerly Afro-Marxist Mozambique agreed in the 1992 peace accords "to respect and not antagonize the traditional structures and authorities where they are currently de facto exercising such authority."[32] A 1993 conference on democratic governance and decentralization in Kampala went further and broached the subject of giving traditional authorities a political role by reserving seats for them on local councils.[33]

Even federalism, one of the fullest expressions of horizontally based stratification arrangements, has won acceptance in Nigeria and in certain circles in Ethiopia and South Africa. Recommending that Nigeria should continue with a federal form for governance, the Political Bureau described one alternative, "confederalism," as "the first dangerous step toward the disintegration of Nigeria," and another, "unitarism," as failing to take adequate account of "the centrifugal forces of the country's ethnic, social, linguistic, and religious pluralities and the historic experiences of uneven development among the various nationalities and geographical sections of the country which could . . . seriously undermine the growth of the Nigerian nation-state if they are not adequately contained in a political framework which is generally acceptable to all sections of the country."[34] Federalism, then, was perceived by then President Ibrahim Babangida and key members of the Nigerian elite as a political necessity,[35] for by dispersing limited powers to the states, it provided a minimally acceptable political formula in which the main interests would exercise at least some power and therefore have an incentive to cooperate with others. As Donald Horowitz notes, federalism "proliferate[s] the points of power and so make[s] control of the center less vital and pressing." By spreading state authority among an array of key actors, federalism encourages cooperation in the exercise of functions whose jurisdiction is assigned to central authorities.[36]

In Ethiopia and South Africa, movement toward some form of federal relationship has been evident, but it remains to be seen whether a consensus over this form of governance will emerge. Since the downfall of Mengistu Haile Mariam's regime, the new ruling Ethiopian Peoples' Revolutionary Democratic Front has also come to look more favorably on federalism as a useful confidence-building mechanism. Noting that "previous [repressive and centralizing] attempts to [unify Ethiopia] have led to wars, to fueling nationalistic tendencies," President Meles Zenawi argues that federal government is necessary to adjust to the realities of his country's pluralistic character.[37] As a result, he has issued a series of proclamations declaring the right of "nations" to "administer [their] own affairs within [their] defined territory" and giving regional administrations legislative, executive, and judicial powers over all internal matters within their jurisdictions, except for central responsibilities in such spheres as defense, foreign affairs, economic policy, and so forth.[38] However, the boundaries the EPLF set for the new regions favored Tigray and the Afars, at the expense of the Amhara and the Somali Issaks in the Awash Valleyland, fuelling suspicions that might be the source of future problems.[39]

In July 1993 in South Africa, the ANC and the South African Communist Party (SACP) made major concessions on regional power to the government, the Inkatha Freedom Party, and the Conservative Party to gain their support for the draft constitution. As a result, the autonomous powers of the regions were increased, and ANC negotiators—recognizing federalism as an inducement for cooperative behavior—indicated that they were prepared to negotiate over additional powers as well as extra representation in the central legislature. For SACP negotiator Joe Slovo, there was no reason to be afraid of increasing regional representation in the National Assembly: "This will cement a new South Africa rather than fragmenting it," he declared.[40] In both Ethiopia and South Africa, then, reconfiguring institutions along federal lines has had some appeal as an incentive to assure amicable relations. Nevertheless, for all their disclaimers, the new governments in both cases did seem to fear the divisive effects of ethnically inspired federalism and to prefer strong central leadership. The dependence of the regions upon central government transfers casts further doubts upon the likelihood of creating genuine federalism in these countries at this juncture.[41]

Conclusion

Ethnic consciousness and a history of ethnic conflict create a context in which contemporary elite competition comes to the fore, in Africa and elsewhere. Old identities, some long dormant or suppressed, have become more assertive in recent years, and new identities are emerging, contesting the distributions made by the state. The source of intergroup conflict is not ethnic pluralism as such, but competition between ethnic and other spokespersons for favorable state allocations. Because clientelism survives and adapts to the new political reality of contemporary Africa, and because ethnicity has a dynamic quality that is likely to remain responsive to people's psychological and economic needs in the 1990s and beyond, there is no reason to expect that ethnic identities and attachments or the competition among political elites based on these ties will disappear any time soon. Rather, politicized ethnicity can properly be regarded as an aspect of the modernization process, one that can be expected to adapt to the forces of change in the world today.

If ethnic consciousness and competition is unlikely to go away, the problem that confronts us is how to reconfigure state and society to accommodate the ethnic experience in a constructive manner. To start with, it is necessary to recognize that ethnic group spokesmen act much as do the spokesmen of other economic and social interests when making demands on the state for a preferred share of allocations. Viewed in this light, the challenge is to structure relations in such a way that ethnic groups have an incentive for cooperative behavior. As we have seen, the end of authoritarian rule and the opening to political liberalization in many African countries have created new possibilities for choice in four key issue areas: constitutional guidelines to promote proportionality, electoral arrangements organized to facilitate minority representation, elite power sharing at the political center, and decentralization and federalism. If the current opportunity for change leads to a new acceptance of the legitimacy of political pluralism, and if state-society relations can be reconfigured to create new, positive routines of encounter, then it will be possible to create the enabling environment so indispensable for genuine development.

Notes

1. On charges that the Sudanese government has been engaging in "ethnic cleansing," relocating tens of thousands of Nuba people from Kordofan Province, see "Senate Resolution 94—Relative to the Sudan," 103rd Cong., *Congressional Record,* 139, 46 (April 3, 1993): S4508. For similar charges in Kenya, see Republic of Kenya, The National Assembly, *Report of the Parliamentary Select Committee to Investigate Ethnic Clashes in Western and Other Parts of Kenya 1992* (Nairobi: Government Printer, 1992).

2. Larry Diamond, *Class, Ethnicity, and Democracy in Nigeria* (New York: Syracuse University Press, 1988), p. 59.

3. Claude Ake, quoted in *West Africa,* May 25, 1981, pp. 1162–1163.

4. John A. A. Ayoade, "States Without Citizens: An Emerging African Phenomenon," in *The Precarious Balance: State and Society in Africa,* ed. Donald Rothchild and Naomi Chazan (Boulder: Westview, 1988), p. 115.

5. René Lemarchand, "The State, the Parallel Economy, and the Changing Structure of Patronage Systems," in *The Precarious Balance*, ed. Donald Rothchild and Naomi Chazan (Boulder: Westview Press, 1988), p. 153.

6. For a more detailed discussion of the hegemonic exchange regime, see Donald Rothchild, "Hegemonial Exchange: An Alternative Model for Managing Conflict in Middle Africa," in *Ethnicity, Politics and Development*, ed. Dennis L. Thompson and Dov Ronen (Boulder: Lynne Rienner Publishers, 1986), pp. 65–109.

7. P. Anyang' Nyong'o, "Democratization Processes in Africa," *CODESRIA Bulletin*, no. 2 (1991): 2.

8. Comment by Todd Gitlin in a roundtable on "Nationalism and Ethnic Particularism," *Tikkun* 7, 6 (November/December 1992): 53.

9. Dr. John Garang de Mabior, *Statement to the Sudanese People on the Current Situation in the Sudan* (General Headquarters: Sudan People's Liberation Movement, August 10, 1989), p. 2. (Mimeo.)

10. James Firebrace, *Never Kneel Down: Drought, Development, and Liberation in Eritrea* (Trenton: Red Sea Press, 1985), pp. 35–38; Linda M. Heywood, "Unita and Ethnic Nationalism in Angola," *Journal of Modern African Studies* 27, 1 (March 1989): 60.

11. A. H. M. Kirk-Greene, *Crisis and Conflict in Nigeria*, vol. I (London: Oxford University Press, 1971), pp. 451–452.

12. Alexander R. Love, *Development Co-operation* (Paris: OECD, 1992), p. 43.

13. Michael Bratton and Nicolas van de Walle, "Toward Governance in Africa: Popular Demands and State Responses," in *Governance and Politics in Africa*, ed. Goran Hyden and Michael Bratton (Boulder: Lynne Rienner, 1992), pp. 50–51.

14. Sahr John Kpundeh, ed., *Democratization in Africa: African Views, African Voices* (Washington, D. C.: National Academy Press, 1992), p. 3; *Africa News* 37, 5 (November 23–December 6, 1992).

15. *Report of the Carter Center Ghana Election Mission*, November 6, 1992, p. 1.

16. L. Gray Cowan, "Zambia Tests Democracy," *CSIS Africa Notes*, no. 141 (October 1992): 5.

17. Tikum Mbah Azonga, "Biya Shuffles Cabinet," *West Africa* December 7–13, 1992, p. 2099.

18. Thomas Callaghy, "Lost Between State and Market: The Politics of Economic Adjustment in Ghana, Zambia, and Nigeria," in *The Politics of Economic Adjustment in Developing Nations*, ed. Joan Nelson (Princeton: Princeton University Press, 1990), pp. 257–319.

19. See Donald Rothchild, "The Internationalization of Africa's Ethnic and Racial Conflicts," in *Africa Contemporary Record 1988–1989*, ed. Marion E. Doro (New York: Africana Publishing Co., 1992), pp. A102–A103.

20. Hussein M. Adam, "Somalia: Militarism, Warlordism, or Democracy?" *Review of African Political Economy*, no. 54 (1992): 13.

21. Obinna Anyadike, "Tribe to Citizen," *West Africa*, August 28–September 3, 1989, pp. 1417–1419.

22. Milton J. Esman, "The Management of Communal Conflict," *Public Policy* 21 (Winter 1973): 62.

23. This data is presented in Donald Rothchild, "Middle Africa: Hegemonial Exchange and Resource Allocation," in *Comparative Resource Allocation*, ed.

Alexander J. Groth and Larry L. Wade (Beverly Hills, Calif.: Sage, 1984), pp. 167–176.

24. Edmond J. Keller, "The State, Public Policy, and the Mediation of Ethnic Conflict in Africa," in *State Versus Ethnic Claims*, ed. Donald Rothchild and Victor A. Olorunsola (Boulder: Westview Press, 1983), p. 263.

25. Adam, "Somalia: Militarism, Warlordism, or Democracy?" p. 18; Rakiya Omaar, "Somalia: At War with Itself," *Current History* 91, 565 (May 1992): 233.

26. Federal Republic of Nigeria, *Official Gazette* 76, 29 (May 3, 1989), sects. 131, 132.

27. By contrast, Kenya's election rules in 1992, which provided that the president would have to obtain 25 percent of the vote in five out of eight provinces, were not an attempt to promote a sense of ethnic inclusiveness. Rather they represented an effort on the part of President Daniel arap Moi to keep himself in power.

28. Timothy D. Sisk, "South Africa Seeks New Ground Rules," *Journal of Democracy* 4, 1 (January 1993): 87.

29. Moi's new cabinet, reports the International Republican Institute, was "a disheartening mix of defeated ministers and KANU loyalists, not at all representative of Kenya's ethnic majorities. Cabinet ministers include five Kalenjin, four Luhya, four Kamba, two Maasai, two Kisii, two Meru, one Somali, one Embu, one Mijikenda, one Taita, one Kikuyu, and one Luo. The only Kikuyu and Luo nominated were two defeated ministers from Moi's previous government." IRI, *Kenya: The December 29, 1992 Elections* (Washington, D.C.: IRI, 1993), p. 53; also see Joel D. Barkan, "Kenya: Lessons from a Flawed Election," *Journal of Democracy* 4, 3 (July 1993): 91–99.

30. William Safran, "Ethnicity and Pluralism: Comparative and Theoretical Perspectives," *Canadian Review of Studies in Nationalism* 18, 1–2 (1981): 8.

31. See Donald Rothchild and Caroline Hartzell, "The Peace Process in the Sudan, 1971–72," in *Stopping The Killing*, ed. Roy Licklider (New York: New York University Press, 1993), pp. 63–93.

32. See Republic of Mozambique, *General Peace Agreement of Mozambique, 1992*, p. 54.

33. See the chapters by Irea Baptista Lundin and Donald Rothchild in *Strengthening Local Initiative: Local Self-Governance, Decentralization, and Accountability*, ed. Donald Rothchild (Hamburg: Institute for African Affairs, 1994).

34. Federal Republic of Nigeria, *Report of the Political Bureau* (Lagos: Federal Government Printer, 1987), p. 80.

35. Babangida told a conference on intergovernmental relations in Abuja that federalism "provided a unique medium for coping with certain problems in the country's association as ethnic groups which formed a new political community." *The Republic* (Lagos), January 19, 1993, p. 1.

36. Donald L. Horowitz, *A Democratic South Africa?* (Berkeley: University of California Press, 1991), p. 221.

37. Cameron McWhirter and Gur Melamede, "Ethiopia: The Ethnicity Factor," *Africa Report* 37, 5 (September/October 1992): 33.

38. "Transitional Period Charter of Ethiopia, No. 1," *Negarit Gazeta, Peaceful and Democratic Transitional Conference of Ethiopia* (Addis Ababa: July 22, 1991): 2; "National/Regional Self-Governments Establishments Proclamation No. 7/1992," *Ne-*

garit Gazeta of the Transitional Government of Ethiopia, No. 2 (Addis Ababa: January 14, 1992): 10.

39. Marina Ottaway, "Nationalism Unbound: The Horn of Africa Revisited," *SAIS Review* 12, 2 (Summer/Fall 1992): 123.

40. Billy Paddock, "Constitution to Be Redrafted: Bid to Break Deadlock on Regional Plan," *Business Day* (Johannesburg), July 29, 1993, p. 1.

41. By one estimate, some 88 percent of the money for provincial administrations in South Africa comes in the form of central government transfers. Tim Cohen, "Regions May Still Be Tied to Central Govt's Purse Strings," *Business Day,* August 2, 1993, p. 4.

10

Gender, Political Participation, and the Transformation of Associational Life in Uganda and Tanzania

Aili Mari Tripp

Uganda and Tanzania are two of many African countries with diverse post-colonial experiences that have taken steps towards political liberalization in the 1990s.[1] In both countries, the continued pursuit of political liberalization is threatened by sectarianism. Any consideration of Uganda's political future immediately raises questions of how to resolve the seemingly intractable religious, regional and ethnic differences that have had devastating consequences in its recent history. Concerns voiced by non-Baganda over the recent upsurge in monarchism in Buganda and the resented perceived political advantage of individuals from western Uganda in positions of power are but two examples of the ever present issue of ethnicity in Uganda.[2] Tanzania, which has had a less volatile recent past, was by the early 1990s seeing manifestations of religious sectarianism and undercurrents of ethnic tensions, including tensions between Muslim and Christian communities[3] and between the African and Asian business communities,[4] that were being expressed more openly than at any other time in its post-colonial history.

Rather than explore the new manifestations of sectarianism in Tanzania and Uganda, which remains an important task, this essay asks what are the countervailing forces within society that challenge these new or revived sectarian tendencies? Are there concurrent developments that provide bases for institutional change that might serve as alternatives to a political, economic and social order based on sectarianism? While there

Reprinted with permission from *African Studies Review* 37, no. 1 (April 1994): 107–131.

are no simple answers to these questions, research on the informal economy in Tanzania and its related organizations (1987–88) and currently on women's associations in Uganda (1992 to the present) suggests one arena where one finds such cross-cutting tendencies: in the emergence of new women's urban associations in the late 1980s. There are two main reasons why women's groups, in particular, serve this purpose. One has to do with the fact that women of diverse backgrounds have found themselves sharing common interests in fighting for greater inclusiveness in the current process of political liberalization, having historically been left out of formal politics. The second reason has to do with the deepening economic crisis that has placed greater pressures on women to become key providers within the household, necessitating new organizational strategies. Economic survival and the belief that one's own survival is contingent on the survival of others are the bases of women's associations, rather than an ascriptive affiliation. To cope with unprecedented hardship, women have joined to form groups to facilitate income-generating activities, savings and the provision of social services such as daycare.

What is especially striking, as this essay will show, is how consistently these groups are *not* based on ethnicity or religion in the urban context, even when possibilities exist for organization based along such lines. Women do participate in ethnically based cultural and burial groups and ethnically based urban associations that are concerned with the development of a rural hometown or home region, but the membership of these groups tends to be both men and women, not exclusively women. Because the new non-sectarian based groups cannot fall back on traditional kinship obligations or other patterns of establishing trust that work within ascriptively based groups, many groups are struggling to establish new mechanisms to ensure accountability. The push for greater inclusiveness and accountability continues to be a painful learning experience for many groups, but there are some small and important changes taking place. This is not to minimize the difficulties that persist, but rather to acknowledge what changes have occurred and recognize that they may form a potential basis for institutional reform that would stress greater accountability, pluralizing society and instituting more democratic procedures.

A second purpose of this essay is to reexamine the utility of the concept of "civil society" in non-Western contexts—a concept that has gained currency among donors, scholars and participants in social movements. Uganda and Tanzania are undergoing major transformations in associational life and some of the most dramatic changes have occurred in women's organizations. The remarkable new visibility of women in formal and informal unregistered groups provides an opportunity to explore the meanings of changing associational life in relation to political liberalization.

This article draws primarily on interviews with leaders of key women's associations and female political leaders and case studies of eight women's organizations involved primarily in local gender-based conflicts (e.g., to establish a health center, to reclaim market space). The article is also based on interviews with women involved in over 150 formal and informal women's associations in Kampala and Jinja. The research was ongoing at the time of writing and was carried out from May to July 1992 and January through July 1993.[5] The article focuses primarily on Uganda because the research in that country dealt specifically with the political impact of women's organizations. References to Tanzania, which are not as extensive as the references to Uganda, are nevertheless important from a comparative point of view because of the many noticeable similarities. They are based on fieldwork conducted in Tanzania between 1987 and 1988 that focused on the informal economy but also looked at its organizational dimensions. In addition to conducting several hundred interviews with small scale entrepreneurs (a snowball survey of 51 mostly middle income women entrepreneurs), I also carried out a cluster survey of 287 residents (145 men and 142 women) in two parts of Dar es Salaam (Buguruni and Manzese).[6] In particular, the survey vividly demonstrated the link between the informal economy and women's informal savings associations. The study also included interviews with national leaders of women's associations like the Women's Union (UWT) and its small projects branch (SUWATA), the Young Women's Christian Association (YWCA) and other such formal groups.

Uganda and Tanzania Cases Contrasted

In many ways this is a heuristic essay because it is an attempt to recast some of the questions being asked by others working on problems of institutional weakness in Africa (see, for example, Brett 1991, Hyden 1983, Wunsch and Olowu 1991) and explore the existing resources within society that might shed light on new bases of organization and possibilities for institutional reform. Both countries are in a process of rapid social transformation, the outcome of which is not self-evident.

An examination of women's formal and informal organizations in urban Uganda and Tanzania can usefully serve as a basis for a study of institutional reform because in both countries women's organizations are among the fastest growing types of new associations. In Tanzania, for example, the emergence of informal savings societies, which are primarily women's groups, coincides with women's new involvement in income-generating activities. Most women interviewed had joined a savings group shortly after they began their income-generating projects, which was after 1985 for 80 percent of the women interviewed in 1988. Similarly, formal women's organizations have proliferated. For example, the Tanzania Women Lawyers Association was formed in 1988, the Tanzania Media Women's Association in 1987, the Association of Businesswomen in Tanzania in 1990 and a Dar es Salaam handicraft cooperative of retired women, Getting Old is to Grow, was established in 1991. By 1993, the number of formal groups had increased to the point that women were forming networks such as the Tanzania Gender Networking Programme to coordinate activities and share information.

In Uganda the recent proliferation of women's groups, both at the local and national level, occurred after 1986 when the current regime led by Yoweri Museveni came into power. Notable exceptions include the Young Women's Christian Association formed in 1952, the Mothers Union formed in 1908, the Uganda Catholic Women's Guild started in 1963 and the Uganda Muslim Women's Association established in 1949. But a significantly large number of prominent groups came into existence after 1986, including the Uganda Women Entrepreneurs Association formed in 1987, the Uganda Women's Effort to Save Orphans in 1986, Action for Development (ACFODE) in 1985, Akiika Embuga Women's Self Help Association in 1989 and the Uganda Global Network on Reproductive Rights in 1988. The growth of women's organizations parallels that of nongovernmental organizations in general, which had increased to the point that a Development Network of Indigenous Voluntary Associations (DENIVA) was formed in 1988 (Musheshe 1990, 4). Even though this paper focuses on urban associations, similar patterns were evident in rural areas. For instance, one woman who had grown up in Kamuli district said that in the past in her home village there had been only emergency-based self-help groups and religious and welfare associations. Since 1989 women had become involved in savings, income-generating, market, farming and animal husbandry groups, which formed, as she explained, because "the economic situation forced women to think about their needs, to raise money and to take matters into their own hands."[7]

Unlike Tanzania, which has enjoyed relative stability, Uganda plunged into years of civil war, internal conflict and institutionalized violence beginning with Idi Amin's takeover in 1971 and lasting roughly until 1986 when the National Resistance Movement (NRM) led by Museveni came to power after waging a prolonged guerrilla war, bringing relative stability to the country. Fifteen years of conflict left over 800,000 people dead, 200,000 exiled and millions displaced within the country (Watson 1988, 14). Tanzania, in spite of its many ethnic nationalities, troublesome union with Zanzibar and strong religious affinities, has not been plagued by the kinds of conflicts Uganda has faced due to sharp ethnic and religious divisions.[8] Tanzania has had a single ruling party since independence but in 1992 took steps towards establishing a multiparty system. Uganda has had a no-party system since 1986 and has been led by the broad-based NRM. Opposition parties operate openly and unofficially and are constituted primarily along religious and ethnic lines, with the Uganda Peoples Congress (of the former President Obote) made up mainly of non-Baganda Protestants and the Democratic Party comprised mainly of Catholics.[9] In April 1993 a group of Muslims formed a Uganda Islamic Revolutionary Party.[10] In spite of widely different experiences with governmental leadership, Tanzania and Uganda share the experience of state decline and economic crisis that became especially severe in the late 1970s. Out of these crises, new spaces for associational life emerged in both countries, bearing a strong resemblance to one another.

The examples of Tanzania and Uganda are illustrative because both countries have taken unprecedented steps towards political liberalization as a result of pressures from above and below. Yet, in many ways, they embody characteristics that are generally considered antithetical to liberalization and democratization, including a small middle class, weakness of the official private sector, the lack of a democratic tradition and severe economic crisis in the past decade. Similar trends in associational life are emerging in both countries even though they have faced considerably different conditions.

Economic Pressures and Changing Associational Life

An important factor contributing to the increase in women's associations in both countries has been the economic crisis that began in the late 1970s, which put particular pressures on women to expand their income-generating activities and consequently to seek collective means of coping with new economic pressures. In Tanzania real wages fell by 83 percent from 1974 to 1988 (Bureau of Statistics 1989). Uganda's real minimum wages fell by a staggering 26.4 percent annually between 1980 and 1983 alone (Mamdani 1990, 438). Women's economic strategies became especially prominent in the 1980s because of women's key role in sustaining the household. The increased burden has been felt especially in urban areas which were hit hard by dramatic declines in real wage incomes, by civil service and factory layoffs, cutbacks in social and welfare services and the imposition of austerity measures as part of economic reform programs. Urban women in both countries have been primarily responsible for providing food and clothing for the household and for paying school and health fees. Women have subsequently expanded their involvement in urban farming and small businesses through self-employment or joint ventures. This has necessitated an array of various collective coping strategies, giving rise to new women's associations and networks.

Women's role in informal and private enterprises has been in large measure determined by the fact that women have been less tied to the formal economy than men and have not had access to jobs in the formal wage sector due to lack of education and discriminatory hiring practices. This has meant that as formal incomes have declined, there have been increasing pressures on women to seek informal and alternate sources to sustain the household. In both countries this shift from reliance on formal incomes to reliance on informal and private incomes occurred in the 1980s.

In many rural areas, women have also pursued these kinds of economic activities because of increasing land pressures and customary land inheritance and ownership patterns which discriminate against women holding land of their own. In Uganda only 7 percent of the land is owned by women in a country where the majority of the population obtains their sustenance from agriculture and where women grow 90 percent of all food crops and 60 percent of all cash crops (Tamale 1992; Watson 1988).[11] Single, divorced and widowed women and women who want independent sources of livelihood have often entered into trade or small-scale production or crafts without options to own and reap benefits of smallholder land tenure.

While most urban women have been involved in small businesses, ranging from hairdressing to making and selling pastries and other foodstuffs, running vegetable and fruit stalls, and making and selling beer, there is also a growing class of large-scale entrepreneurial women. Some (in Uganda popularly known as the "Dubai traders") are engaged in trade with the Gulf States, others trade with neighboring countries and still others set up large factories, such as bakeries or textile mills. As women, they generally have not had access to patronage and personalistic networks tied to the state and instead are part of the emerging bourgeoisie in Africa that is not based on extracting and diverting state resources.

In Uganda the women best known for these activities are the women running the retail trade, which was largely taken over by female entrepreneurs after the expulsion of Asians from Uganda in 1972 by Idi Amin. In rural areas, women—especially those living in coastal or border areas—are major traders. Take, for example, one of the most important commodities traded by women: smoked and salted fish from the Albert Nile. Not only is trade in this fish extensive, but it is also very profitable. The fish are obtained from Panyimur, Wanseko and Rhino Camps on the Albert Nile, Pawar and Jinja and are transported as far as Zaire in the west, Yei in Sudan in the north and Juba in the east (Meagher 1990).

In Tanzania professional and middle-income women would frequently leave their salaried positions to go into business or were involved in sideline enterprises. They had established large tailoring businesses, dry cleaning companies, flour mills, secretarial service companies, hair salons, export and import businesses, bakeries and other small manufacturing and service industries. The pervasiveness of such businesses among women was unprecedented, representing a phenomenon which began to emerge in a significant way only in the mid-1980s.

The emergence of this new business class whose wealth was not primarily based on the diversion of resources from the state is a phenomenon that has been described most extensively by Janet MacGaffey in the context of Zaire, where women also appear to have been especially prominent in such activities. MacGaffey calls this class of business owners "an indigenous local capitalist class," which invests in enterprises that produce for the internal and external markets. Their wealth is not based on holding political office nor is it drawn from activities based on fraud or extortion, rather it is based on business (MacGaffey 1986, 162–63). As in Uganda and Tanzania, women in Zaire have less access to formal institutions than men and therefore have tended to remain within the second economy in which economic activities are unregulated and unlicensed.

Linked to this private sector and informal economic activity in Tanzania and Uganda are a growing number of organizations of varying nature. For instance, women are increasingly joining small groups set up specifically to assist in generating income. In Uganda and Tanzania these groups are varied and are involved in farming, animal husbandry, tailoring, fishing, trade of small household items, making and selling of foodstuffs and alcohol, and services such as hairdressing. Even the older, formal women's associations such as the Mother's Union, YWCA and Catholic Women's Association are today providing training and other assistance in starting income-generating projects.[12] Yet these associations were formed prior to independence primarily to socialize women into traditional roles, provide educational opportunities, serve welfare functions and promote religious concerns.

Most women's organizations remain small and informal. Take, for example, the savings associations that have become especially popular in Tanzanian, Ugandan and other African urban centers. These associations serve as a means of saving money to reinvest in businesses, to get businesses started or to save profits which are later used for major purchases, school fees, building houses or medical expenses. In Uganda these savings clubs are frequently the basis for organizing other kinds of cooperative ventures. Some are formed within but separate from formal associations; in other words, women attending a women's church group might use this organization as a forum for organizing themselves into smaller savings clubs. In both Tanzania and Uganda these savings clubs were generally made up of women, although it was becoming increasingly common to find men also organized into such societies.

Close to half of all self-employed and employed women interviewed in the 1987–88 survey of Dar es Salaam reported belonging to associations called *upato*. Women who participated in *upato* societies made on average 26 percent more than other self-employed women, which suggests that their businesses were more stable. The societies averaged around 12 participants with each participant putting 20–100 Tsh in a kitty each day and then, after 5 days, a designated participant would claim the entire kitty. Each participant had her turn to receive the kitty. Other societies regularly pooled money every 3, 4, 7, 10, 14, or 30 days, depending on the arrangement. The amount of money set aside by individual women added up to roughly 20 to 30 percent of their average monthly income. Women who participated in *upato* societies belonged to the 35–50 year age bracket, while self-employed women generally fell into the 20–35 year range. This can probably be explained by the greater financial demands placed on women with small children who were not in as good a position to save. Finally, women involved in the *upato* societies (61 percent) were more likely than self-employed women in general (49 percent) to have some education.

Thus, the proliferation of women's associations is tied to the new financial responsibilities that have fallen on women and the fact that women have used these new pressures to advance themselves economically and politically.

The Politics of Exclusion, the Struggle for Inclusion

The struggle for greater inclusiveness is not a new one. In fact, one of the reasons that women's groups have the potential to bridge sectarian affiliations has to do with women's common fight for inclusion in the political process and within public life. From the early 1960s up to the mid-1980s, Tanzania's ruling party, known as the Tanganyika African National Union and after 1977 as *Chama Cha Mapinduzi*, increasingly curtailed opportunities for independent organizations, especially economic ones, and attempted to bring all formal associational activity under state control while discouraging the formation of new organizations. Local women's activities were to come under the direction of the party's mass organization, *Umoja wa Wanawake wa Tanzania* (Union of Tanzanian Women). This meant that while some well-established associations like the Young Women's Christian Association (YWCA) continued in the face of various proscriptions, most independent women's organizations were confined to being small and informal in character.

Similarly, in Uganda Idi Amin passed a decree in 1978 forming a National Council of Women. The decree declared that "no women's or girls' voluntary organizations shall continue to exist or be formed except in accordance with the provisions of this decree" (Tadria 1987). This decree pushed many professional and religious-based women's groups underground, where they functioned quietly with their activities significantly curtailed.[13] Moreover, it prevented the formation of new organizations. After Amin's overthrow, many women's organizations felt that their autonomy continued to be jeopardized under the second regime of Milton Obote, whose party, the Uganda Peoples Congress, used its women's wing to exert political control over independent women's associations through the then parastatal body, the National Council of Women.[14]

It should be added that the years of internal warfare in Uganda had profound effects on women's self-perceptions and men's perceptions of women in ways not experienced in Tanzania. It unwittingly thrust women into new roles and situations which fundamentally transformed their consciousness. Rural women found themselves talking to, harboring and feeding Tanzanian soldiers and hiding weapons in their homes during the war in which Tanzania helped oust Amin. Amin's troops did not suspect them because they were women. Women later joined the NRM and fought side by side with men. The sight of women carrying both guns and babies on their backs left an indelible impression on many. Women were involved in spying and in smuggling guns into the bush. In the cities, husbands taught their wives to drive and run their businesses in the event that they might have to disappear into the bush.[15] While the fighting did not directly have an impact on women's associations, it affected women's overall perception of their capabilities (Ankrah 1987; Watson 1988).

National women's organization leaders point to the 1985 Decade of Women conference in Nairobi as a turning point in the history of Ugandan women's associations. Women activists in nongovernmental organizations, many of whom had attended on their own, independent of the official delegation, returned from the conference with a new sense of urgency to begin revitalizing and creating autonomous women's associations as part of an active women's movement. It was not possible to begin realizing this goal until the NRM came to power the following year. The NRM responded favorably to direct pressures from women's groups to place women in key leadership positions in the government. The state had been significantly weakened by the years of conflict but also by economic decline as in Tanzania. It was in no position to restrict private social and economic initiatives when it could no longer provide comparable services or ensure economic well-being. Thus, the state's position was a key determinant of the possibilities for autonomous association and women's associations in both countries.

As in the period prior to independence, voluntary associations have had an impact on the broader political arena (White 1973), serving as fora to exchange ideas and develop opinions.[16] Take the example of Uganda where some of these influences on national politics have been among the most dramatic in Africa. As a result of pressure from women's organizations, the Museveni government has been compelled to address women's issues at a national level in a way not addressed by previous governments. In 1988 the Ministry of Women in Development was established, and it was merged with the Ministry of Youth and Culture in 1991. The ministry's objectives included seeking equal rights for women through changes in the law and in institutional arrangements, integrating women's concerns in the national and district development programs, fostering women's income-generating activities and enterprises and engendering full participation in decision making within the political and development process.

In 1991 Uganda's Ministry of Women in Development coordinated a nationwide discussion of women at the local level to discuss a new constitution. Out of these discussions, a memorandum was drawn up and sent to the constitutional commission, which made an open invitation to any group or section of the population to submit memoranda. The WID memorandum addressed issues of national concern (e.g., national language), but also particular concerns of women, including the elimination of discrimination on the basis of sex, which would involve the repeal of marriage, divorce, inheritance and property laws and employment regulations that are discriminatory against women.

Although women's representation in national bodies is still numerically small, it is considerably more than five years ago as a result of direct pressure from women's groups. There were four women cabinet ministers in 1992 and a woman held the key position of minister of agriculture. Women are now represented on national commissions and parastatal boards. For example, there are 2 women out of 21 representatives on Uganda's constitutional commission that drafted the new constitution (Matembe 1991). At independence there was a 2:88 female:male ratio in parliament; in 1967 there were no female members of parliament. By 1980 there was still only 1 female out of 142 members of parliament, but after the NRM takeover the numbers significantly increased to 39 women out of 263 members, or 15 percent of the parliament.

Political representation in the Resistance Council (RC) system is more controversial.[17] Women frequently mention that they take encouragement from the fact that the NRM established the RC system to include one guaranteed position for women at each of the levels. In addition, one seat was reserved for women for each district in the National Resistance Council (parliament) (Kasfir 1991, 272). Some have pointed out, however, that since both men and women vote for the women's secretary, men tend to vote for a woman who is submissive, quiet and "has a pretty face," as one woman put it. Some women activists have noted and wondered why at the NRC level the women who are elected rarely come out of the leadership of popular women's associations even though many have later become spokeswomen for women's issues (the outspoken Miria Matembe is an important exception).[18] Others have argued that women are increasingly making use of the RC system as they become more politically astute. In the first RC elections in 1987, women stood for only the post of women's secretary, and there were a few cases in which men stood for the position of women's secretary because no woman would run. But by the 1992 elections, women were running for the positions of chairman, vice chairman and finance secretary of the RCs, and there were many new women running who had never contested before.[19] The visibility of women running for positions in the October 1993 constituent assembly elections has also not gone unnoticed.[20]

Women's organizations like ACFODE and the Women Lawyers Association have been active not only in pressing for greater female leadership, but also in other areas as well. Because Uganda has the highest number of people who are HIV positive in Africa, according to World Health Organization figures, and women are the fastest growing group affected, women's groups and leaders have become vocal around issues of sexual harassment, rape, wife beating and child abuse for the first time. Uganda's women parliamentarians were instrumental in passing amendments to the penal code in 1990 that made rape a capital offense and punished hotel owners for allowing prostitution on their premises, and they have been raising the issue of teachers who sexually harass female students.

Women's groups helped draw up a domestic law bill which would give women more rights in divorce, marriage and other personal relations in which women face discrimination due to customary practices around inheritance and property rights. In the area of education, women's groups got the admissions standards lowered for women entering university in 1991 and initiated the formation of a women's studies program. Finally, ACFODE has helped the Ministry of Education introduce sex education into the curriculum for teenagers attending the upper primary school (junior high level) to address issues such as the AIDS epidemic and its relation to women's position in society.

Inclusiveness Within Women's Groups

While women have pressed for greater inclusiveness within the public sphere, they have also sought greater inclusiveness within women's groups, often with noticeable success. During Amin's rule, the executive committee of the Muslim Women's Association was made up almost entirely of Nubians. Today the same body includes Batoro, Nubian, Banyoro, Banyankole and Baganda women.[21] Unlike political parties, many women's associations are explicit about their rejection of the politics of sectarianism. In recent years, women in many parts of the country have deliberately loosened or severed their ties to organizations based on religion (such as local chapters of the Protestant Mothers Union) in order to join with women of other religions. For other women's groups the struggle has been an internal one to stem accusations of favoritism based on ethnicity. One leaflet supporting a candidate as chair for the prominent women's group ACFODE appealed for unity in the face of such rumors:

> Friend, if you find yourself dividing up the ACFODE membership into subgroupings like: . . . 'Westerners,' 'Easterners,' etc. stop and think because you are then killing the ACFODE spirit of singlemindedness and substituting it for cleavages, cliques and faction—the hallmarks of anarchism and disintegration. We in ACFODE have always maturely worked together, side by side, without bothering to find out one another's nationalities or other sectional tags. All genuine lovers of ACFODE should by all means wish to uphold the original non-sectarian spirit.[22]

Most of the new urban women's associations, even small informal and neighborhood associations, are not formed along sectarian lines. Because their primary motive for organizing is economic betterment rather than solidifying a primary affiliation, one's ethnic or religious background is rarely considered in forming an association such as a savings club.[23] Savings clubs are sometimes established at the workplace, be it a factory floor, office or market place. They can be formed by friends and friends of friends, neighbors, or within a larger association that has already brought women together like a church. In both Kampala and Dar es Salaam, this meant that the savings clubs connected people of various backgrounds. Of 150 women's groups whose members were interviewed in Kampala, less than a handful were formed strictly around ethnicity. The cultural organizations that are based on ethnicity usually involve both men and women. It is extremely rare to find an all-women's group of only one ethnicity. Even in rural areas, savings clubs incorporated women of different ethnicities. To take one example, within a formal rural nongovernmental organization in Busoga, Masese Low Cost Housing Women's Cooperative Group, informal savings clubs combined Basoga, Baganda, Banyankole and other ethnic groups.

Apart from the common economic goals that bring women together, another reason for these nonsectarian tendencies is that urban areas by definition have brought together people of different ethnic groups, clans and religious affiliations. Intermarriage between couples of different ethnic groups has become much more common. New associations are thus formed in the workplace and in neighborhoods, creating new bases for community beyond particularistic interests and primary affiliations.

Yet another reason women's groups cut across particularistic ties is that married women from patrilineal societies tend to find it easier than men to form associations that cut across ethnic, clan and kinship ties. This is because once she is married a woman effectively cuts herself off from her blood kin because she is expected to join her husband's clan, but yet she is never entirely accepted into the clan of her husband and is always considered an outsider. Wives are restricted from membership of clan and kin associations. Unlike men, who are more likely to be involved in clan or kinship associations, women from such societies find it easier to associate with people outside of their primary affiliations and can extend what anthropologists call "fictive kinship" ties to other women who are not blood relations. It is the kind of societal arrangement which forces women to establish closer ties to non-kin.[24]

When confronted with ethnic and linguistic differences, women's groups have sought ways to work around potential problems that may arise from such diversity. The example of one savings club in Kampala illustrates this phenomenon. But first by way of background, 13 woman formed the club in one complex of 24 government-owned apartments. The women came from several ethnic groups and included both Christians and Muslims. The women represented a wide range of occupations and wage levels. They included a nurse, secretary, university professor, waitress and several housewives. All the women had additional primary sources of income, most of which were informal (untaxed and unlicensed). They had individual businesses selling beer, beans, soap, second-hand clothes and books. As is common for women retailers in Kampala, one rented a few square meters of a bookstore to sell her books. Another was a consultant for foreign donor agencies and nongovernmental organizations, gave private French lessons and did French-English translations for extra money. One had a poultry shed, another ran a canteen and yet another owned a private clinic.

The group formed when one woman in the housing complex lost her husband as the result of an accident. As is the Kiganda custom, the husband's family laid claim to her children and pressured her to marry her husband's brother to finish compensating for the bridewealth payment. The neighbor women got together and found her a job as a waitress. They also helped her start a business selling second-hand clothes, called *kunkumura* in Luganda (which literally translates into "shake and see"). The woman rented a meter in a shop from which she sells the clothes. The group's joint efforts thus enabled the woman to maintain her financial independence and related individual autonomy. When a second woman in the group lost her husband to AIDS, the group intervened and convinced the housing authorities to let her keep her apartment for an additional six months until she could relocate. They also helped her with transport. She eventually had to leave, but she is still part of the group. When this second woman was widowed, the women realized how precarious their own positions were and solidified their organizational structure in a savings club.

Clearly, the main organizing principle was economic survival and mutual support rather than a primary affinity. As one member put it: The main purpose of the group is to share contacts, exchange business and other ideas, provide financial assistance for income-generating activities and give financial and other assistance in emergencies. The women save money to pay for school and health fees, emergencies and for reinvesting in businesses. One woman used the money to complete a house that she was going to rent out.

Because the women had different religious affiliations, they went to great lengths to accommodate these differences. The group had two funds, one they contributed to regularly and another emergency fund, which they built up by catering food to the local RC and other organizations holding social functions. They consciously chose to cater on non-religious holidays like New Year so that their activities would not interfere with the various religious holidays of different group members. If they had to meet on Friday, the Christian members would consult with the Muslim members to make sure it was alright to meet without them. Because the women are of different ethnic affiliations they hold meetings in English and translate into Luganda for the women who do not speak English. Similar translating arrangements were reported by other savings clubs in Kampala where English is spoken among educated classes.

More generally, among women interviewed in Kampala, issues of religion and ethnicity were not seen as problematic. While women reported problems with raising funds, attending meetings, collecting dues, managing funds, dealing with age and education differences and dealing with husbands who objected to their participation, virtually all denied that religion and ethnicity/language had given rise to problems in their groups.

Women are so vehement in insisting that their groups are based primarily on economic concerns and not on ethnicity or religion that even groups which are active politically in advocating women's rights deny that their groups are political because of the way in which politics has been equated with sectarianism in Uganda's past. When asked whether such an organization could be a basis for broader political activity, one member explained:

We do not want these organizations to become terribly political. It would hurt too much. There would be too much pain, too much tension that we do not need right now. Everything has been so politicized along tribal, religious and party lines. Women through these organizations are rejecting that. We know the divisions exist among us, but it is more important right now to survive and to help each other out. We do not want to go back to the way it was, back to the repression, back to having to escape to the bush for fear of one's life. These organizations are non-denominational, non-tribal, non-partisan. They do not exclude anyone. The reason they are generally organized around sex is because of the gender division in our culture.[25]

This is an interesting position, especially coming from a woman who is in the leadership of a women's rights organization. This kind of position was reiterated by other women leaders as well. When asked whether multiparty politics would help or hinder an organization like ACFODE, which has been especially active in promoting female leadership in government and in promoting women's rights, its general secretary, Margaret Kikamphikaho, was quick to reply: "We don't talk about things like that. We are not into politics." As far as she was concerned, party affiliations, along with their related ethnic and religious affiliations, were seen as too divisive to raise in her organization. Clearly, even though women may be intensely involved in public activities, they define politics as a divisive activity that women do not engage in because it is associated with parties which in Uganda are organized along religious and regional lines.

It would be a serious distortion to suggest by this that ethnic, religious and other kinds of politics based on particularistic ties fall along gender lines. But the sentiments of the women cited here do suggest that many women, through their new associational activity, are pursuing a kind of politics that is more inclusive in its orientation and see economic necessity and survival strategies as bases for organizing along more inclusive lines.

Ensuring Accountability

One of the consequences of the fact that groups are not based on affective ties—familial, clan, ethnic or other close ties—as in many rural areas is that forms of accountability have had to be developed. While it may be a long struggle to institutionalize ways to ensure accountability, it is worth considering what various women's groups have accomplished in this regard. The National Organization for Women's Associations of Uganda (formerly the National Council of Women) has reported a significant rise in the number of women's groups seeking assistance from them in drafting constitutions, suggesting a greater need for establishing structures to guarantee accountability.[26] Even the most informal savings clubs studied in both Kampala and Dar es Salaam had created mechanisms, including drawing up constitutions, to strengthen accountability. This was the case regardless of how much the members emphasized the importance of trust, and irrespective of the size of the club. One Kampala club with only

13 members, each of whom contributed 1,500 Ush ($1.50) a month, had a chairperson, deputy chairperson, treasurer, secretary and deputy assistant who comprised the executive committee. They needed at least two present from the executive committee in order to make a decision and at least four members of the executive committee present to approve the application of a new member, which had to be made in writing. Similar kinds of arrangements were found in Dar es Salaam, where even among illiterate women a secretary-treasurer (*kijumbe*) would be appointed to collect the money and redistribute it. Sometimes she herself could not belong to the society. In larger societies, participants provided the names of next of kin who were responsible for making payments if the participants failed to do so.

Take another example of a fairly typical informal (unregistered) group, Namasuba Pinda Zone Women's Club in Kampala, which is made up of 16 members representing several ethnic groups, Protestants, Catholics and Muslims. The women vary in their levels of education, with occupations ranging from secretaries to housewives, traders to teachers. The group, which is involved in drama and singing, handicrafts, and farming and animal husbandry, was formed in 1986 by a woman who, according to its members, thought women should be self-sustaining and develop independently. The group has a chairperson, general secretary, information secretary, secretary for mobilization, sports secretary, head of the weaving section, project manager and treasurer. Elections are conducted annually by lining up behind the person one prefers. In spite of the organization's informality, it is governed by several bylaws, which one member elaborated:

> Number one, a member must be trustworthy. Number two, well, if there is anything to be done and it involves large sums of money, we don't let an individual handle it alone. We choose three members to assist in carrying out the task. It is hard then for one person to waste the money. We keep our money with the treasurer and she banks it. There are four members who sign on the check if the money is to be released by the bank. Third, there is the discipline law, a woman must behave like a woman [not commit adultery, drink a lot, etc.]. If you are not behaving well, then you face the disciplinary committee for punishment. The final bylaw concerns dress: women must dress decently in our club.

These fit patterns of proceduralism found in other parts of Africa in associations such as student groups, women's organizations and self-help groups that hold elections, operate according to constitutional guidelines and have clear-cut mechanisms for changes in administration (Chazan 1982; Little 1973).

Thus the struggle to pluralize associations is intricately linked to the need for greater accountability so that associations do not fall prey to the same kind of ethnically based favoritism that pervades government and public institutions, especially in the way appointments are made. This has had consequences beyond the issue of ascriptive ties. For example, in the 1980s many organizations of physically disabled people were monopolized by individuals who used them to enhance their own positions. Today, members are demanding greater accountability and throwing out corrupt leaders while others have formed new groups because the old ones did not serve their purposes. One woman, for example, left a physically handicapped women's group and joined the Disabled Women's Association of Mukono because, as she put it, "the leader was unfair and gained a lot from us. She took all the foreign trips and offered herself the aid meant for us."

Another aspect of the inclusiveness of many groups is the way in which they combine different educational and income levels. Professional and middle class women's associations have formed explicitly with the intention of involving low-income women in their organizations and of providing services to rural or low-income women. In Uganda, ACFODE works primarily with rural women, carrying out seminars and helping women initiate efforts around a variety of issues, ranging from health, family planning, legal rights and politics to income-generating projects. The Legal Aid Clinic of the Uganda Association of Women Lawyers carries out education around marriage, divorce, succession, affiliation, land, commercial and constitutional laws which affect women. In 1988 they opened a legal aid clinic to provide low-income women with free legal counseling and litigation. The Uganda Women's Credit and Finance Trust also works with low-income women to provide them with credit and technical and training assistance in starting and sustaining micro-businesses. Even organizations like the Tanzania Businesswomen's Association, which was initiated by wealthier businesswomen, included as part of its constituency poor women involved in income-generating activities and wanted to form with them a strong business community of women.

Certainly, not all the women's service organizations are formed with purely altruistic motives. In fact, the government temporarily froze the establishment of new orphanages in 1992 because it was brought to the authorities' attention (by women leaders) that some of these orphanages were nothing more than money-making schemes with the interests of children of peripheral concern to the women who started the institutions.

Problematizing Civil Society

The existence of these new women's organizations poses numerous challenges to emerging concepts of civil society. In Western political thought, civil society has been variously described as a relational concept: civil society connects state and society and at the same time acts independently outside of the state. Similarly, many have characterized civil society in the African context as the part of society that interacts with the state to influence its conduct and yet is simultaneously autonomous from it (Chazan 1991). Some have characterized civil society as an oppositional force to the state (Bayart 1986; Chabal 1986). Others such as Michael Bratton have adopted Alfred Stepan's distinction between political society, which includes political parties, elections and legislatures, and civil society, which encompasses neighborhood associations, women's groups, and religious groups (Bratton 1989, 417–18). And for still others, the defining characteristic is the location of civil society, between the family and the state (Barkan 1991).

Thus, most definitions of civil society appear to revolve around the part of society that interacts with the state. As Walzer puts it, the state "both frames civil society and occupies space within it. It fixes the boundary conditions and the basic rules of all associational activity (including political activity)" (1991, 302). A focus on this particular relationship is problematic because, while it may capture some of the many changes occurring in African politics, it may also overlook the complexity of some of the more fundamental political, economic and social transformations taking place that do not fall easily into the state-society dualism that civil society implies.

The experience of associational life in Uganda and Tanzania raises the question of whether these fundamental disjunctures between state and society can be resolved by invoking the concept of civil society that comes out of a very different Western configuration of state-society relations. In other words, how applicable is the notion of civil society in the African context where the state was a colonial implant, did not emerge from social structures within society itself and the post-colonial state did not fundamentally renegotiate the bases of state-society interactions? Is it a useful concept where state-society interactions are often characterized by the use of patronage networks to extract cheap/free state resources, services or to acquire jobs? What does it mean in countries where the state is weak and barely autonomous from society and is infused by personalistic rule and patrimonial politics that cater to ethnic, religious and other particularistic interests? Women's groups and other associations have often situated themselves outside this sphere of state influence precisely because it does not serve their interests and at times has undermined those same interests.

The view that the state determines the basic rules of associational activity cannot be taken for granted in societies where those very rules are in dispute and are being contested, often through noncompliance. As Migdal has argued, noncompliance in such instances is not simply per-

sonal deviance, criminality or corruption, but involves a fundamental
conflict over which organizations in society should make the rules and
what the rules should be (Migdal 1988). The battle over which institutions
should hold sway in allocating authority may be quite explicit at times: In
some localities in Uganda and Tanzania, the church is clearly the dominant institution. In Buganda, monarchism has been revived with a force-
fulness not seen in Uganda since the death of the exiled Buganda King
Mutesa in 1969. Where women's groups have replaced state efforts in the
provision of social services the state's centrality is diminished. At the
same time, the idea that the state frames the rules of associational life can
be questioned in contexts in which patronage and corruption increasingly
dominate state institutions while many (not all) autonomous associations
are struggling to create new rules that would enhance accountability.

In other instances the conflict over who makes the rules manifests itself
in nonengagement of the state. With the drying up of state resources due
to economic crisis and the imposition of economic liberalization, often
under pressure from international financial institutions and donors, it has
become increasingly common to find the creation of economic and political spaces outside of the state. In some situations it involves nonengagement of the state, simply because the state has become financially and organizationally too weak to provide basic social, welfare and public
services that it once provided. It also includes the creation of wealth by
independent entrepreneurs, wealth that is not derived from state coffers
directly or indirectly, legally or illegally. Nonengagement in some contexts does not preclude that the same individuals or groups might not engage the state in other situations given the multidimensional nature of
people's lives. It simply suggests that people, and women in particular,
have had to rely more heavily on their own individual and collective resources for health, education and other social services. Even personal security is provided by local citizens' groups throughout both Uganda and
Tanzania.

There are many new and important national women's organizations in
both Tanzania and Uganda that engage the state by lobbying for women's
political leadership and for changes in laws that discriminate against
women. By the same token, there are many local women's groups that do
not engage the state, yet are vital to the welfare of their communities precisely because the state has so little impact in making these provisions. It
would therefore seem necessary to look at the whole spectrum of institutional changes occurring in Africa today and not simply at those organizations that engage the state in a particular way.

The concept of civil society tends to revive modernization preoccupations with linear and evolutionary political development. It lends itself to
analyses that push nonformal associations, regardless of how recently

constituted, into the category of *traditional,* only to fall outside of civil society, which itself comes to mean modern institutions that espouse liberal democratic values. An analysis of the organizational changes in Uganda and Tanzania suggests that it is not possible to *a priori* categorize organizations without looking at the role they in fact play. So-called modern, registered, middle class associations may be infused with particularistic interests, while small, informal organizations that do not interact with the state may be horizontally structured to include heterogeneous memberships operating along strict guidelines to ensure accountability. Where opportunities exist, small local women's groups in urban areas are every bit as likely to form along multiethnic lines as any group of middle class, highly educated women.

At the minimum, the idea of a civil society-state dichotomy is or ought to be problematic for theorists of liberalization and democratization in a continent such as Africa. Some have cautioned against transferring abstract concepts derived from particular conditions in the West to other contexts without considering the complex ways in which they have evolved in the West and the varying meanings and reality of civil society in the West (Taylor 1990). Others have taken the critique even further and argued that one should not take concepts developed out of the particularities of Western society and claim that they are universal when they are nothing more than a particular form of a more universal concept (Chatterjee 1990). Surprisingly, most of the new debate around civil society in developing countries has sidestepped the most trenchant critiques of the use of the concept that have emerged out of feminist political theory. Most of these critiques have shown how Western political theorists have treated civil society as undifferentiated, while in fact defining citizenship, the public domain and individual rights as male privilege (Elshtain 1981; Pateman 1983; Phillips 1991; Okin 1990; Yeatman 1984).

The issue here is not that concepts that have relevance in the West are not applicable elsewhere or vice versa. Nevertheless, it is important to pay attention to the particular historical contexts that give rise to concepts like civil society that have now gained currency in the worldwide discussion of democratization. Moreover, dualities like civil society/state that fall into public-private conceptualizations are problematic even in the West when they have been used to define public activity in a way that excludes certain categories of people (Elshtain 1981).

Certainly it would be simpler and theoretically more satisfying to describe developments in Africa in ways that afford greater cross-national comparability and in terms that correspond to the popular terminology of social transformations occurring elsewhere in the world, given the apparent similarity in trends. But this does not change the fact that notions such as "civil society" do not comfortably describe the changes in associational life, capital formation and state-society interactions being experienced in many parts of Africa today. In Uganda and Tanzania these changes are so dramatic as to constitute a major social transformation. These circumstances suggest that we need new conceptual tools and frameworks with which to understand these changes.

Conclusions

Although there are many useful critiques of the concept of civil society that are not addressed in this paper (e.g., the feminist theorists' insights into the gendered interpretations of civil society), this paper adopts the line of argument that civil society is not a universal concept, but rather is a construct that has evolved out of the specific Western historical context and is, as Chatterjee suggests, a particular form of a more universal concept (1990). While the meanings of civil society have many parallels with associational life in non-Western contexts, they cannot automatically be transposed without looking at the particular ways in which state, society and capital have evolved in relation to one another. To do so obscures more than it reveals.

The notion that the state frames civil society and the emphasis on accountability in formal modern institutions are examples of perspectives embedded in the concept of civil society that are unable to account for many important features of changing associational life in Africa today. For example, women's informal and formal associations have proliferated in part due to new opportunities afforded by liberalizing states, which have significantly less resources at their disposal and have therefore been forced to allow more political and economic space to nongovernmental actors. But the increase in women's organizations is also affected by the economic crisis that has placed greater pressures on women to meet household needs through various individual and collective strategies. Because women have particular responsibilities around caring for the old, the children, the sick and covering health and school expenses, they have been more likely to involve themselves in organizations providing social and welfare services and economically based associations. It has been in these contexts equally important to consider women's nonengagement of the state and reliance on their own resources as it has been to look at their associational interaction and dependence on the state.

Because the basis of women's associations tends to be survival and economic advantage, urban women tend to organize themselves in both formal and informal, large and small associations that cut across ethnic, religious and other particularistic lines. Ironically, even though women may belong to organizations that lobby for women's rights and are politically active in a conventional sense, they themselves frequently identify formal politics in their countries as being the pursuit of particularistic interests that should be avoided at all costs because of the divisive nature of activities based along such lines. Thus, the public spiritedness, active participatory involvement and inclusiveness of many of these associations are characteristics that could be drawn on in thinking about institutional reform. Similarly, some of the mechanisms of accountability found even in small informal associations need to be examined in carrying out institutional development.

The other issue that this paper addresses is whether small and informal associations that are formed to meet everyday needs can have broader political impact and whether they could, for example, fundamentally affect the position of women. This paper argues that by organizing to meet their everyday needs, women in self-help groups, voluntary associations, savings associations and other such groups are responding to the fact that they have been excluded not only from formal economies but also from formal politics. They are ultimately redefining politics by seeking tangible solutions to problems caused by the vagaries of the market and the failure, negligence or outright repression of the state. It is important to see the practically oriented organizations as forming a part of a broader web of associations that as a whole can effect more basic change. But more to the point, even the economically oriented organizations have brought about transformations in the political consciousness of women which have in fact led to political change.

It is thus possible, without romanticizing such organizations or exaggerating their transformative capacity, to discern bases for institutional reform that would make political participation more participatory, public spirited and inclusive and make leadership more accountable. Women in these new and often unassuming organizations have attempted to reclaim the necessary space to define their own needs, formulate their own organizational strategies and rely on their own abilities, and this has brought about a change in consciousness. One Kampala women entrepreneurs' group captured the essence of this particular moment in Uganda's associational history when they named themselves *"Togaya kye zinze,"* which literally translates into "do not discard a rolled up piece of paper," understood to mean "do not dismiss what appears to be insignificant."

Notes

1. This article is based on a paper presented at the annual meeting of the American Political Science Association, Chicago, Illinois, 3–6 September 1992. I would like to thank Michael Schatzberg, James C. Scott, Ron Kassimir, Susan Dicklich and Juliet Kiguli for helpful comments on this paper.

2. The coronation of *Ssabataka* (Prince) Ronald Mutebi in July 1993 and the government's promise to return the Baganda cultural sites known as *ebyaffe* (our things) are part of a renewal of monarchism not seen since the country's first president Milton Obote abolished Uganda's kingdoms in 1966 as undemocratic and unconstitutional.

3. One manifestation of the souring of Christian-Muslim relations occurred in April 1993 when Muslim fundamentalists went on a rampage smashing shops that sold pork (*New Vision* 30 April 1993).

4. This sentiment was reflected, for example, in an 18 April 1993 BBC interview with Tanzanian businessmen Allan Sykes who came out openly called for the expulsion of Asians from Tanzania.

5. The study in Uganda also involved a stratified random survey of 1200 households in four urban centers (80 percent women, 20 percent men) on associational participation and political participation. The results of this survey had not been analyzed at the time of this writing.

6. The response rate for the cluster survey was 99 percent. For survey questionnaire, see Appendix B of Aili Mari Tripp, "The Urban Informal Economy and the State in Tanzania," Ph.D. Dissertation, Northwestern University, 1990.

7. Lucia Kiwale, interview conducted by author, June 1992.

8. Approximately 50 percent of Uganda's population is Catholic, 26 percent Anglican (Church of Uganda), and 7 percent Muslim.

9. In the 1987 elections, the DP reported winning 84 percent of the RC5 seats, while the UPC and NRM won 7 percent each (Kasfir 1991, 255). Democratic Party leaders have been brought into top positions in the government.

10. *New Vision* 1 May 1993.

11. Legally any Ugandan, male or female, can purchase or acquire title to land according to the Land Reform Decree, No. 3 of 1975.

12. Florence Nekyon, interview conducted by author, 21 May 1993; J. B. Kwesiga, interview conducted by author, 30 May 1993.

13. These included organizations like the Catholic Women's Association, Mothers Union, YWCA, Muslim Mother's Association, Muslim Women's Association, Uganda Midwives and Nurses.

14. Lucia Kiwale, interview conducted by author, June 1992.

15. Ruth Kisubika, interview conducted by author, 8 June 1992.

16. Historically, voluntary associations have had an impact on the broader political scene. During the colonial period, the authorities placed restrictions on formal organized activity, leaving it up to more informal voluntary associations and primary groups to serve as the bases from which the nationalists mobilized support for independence. In Tanzania, for example, groups ranging in diversity from the *beni* dance societies, burial societies and ethnically based hometown associations and football clubs, and African Association which drew together middle class professionals and civil servants served as precursors to the Tanganyika Africa Nationalist Union. In other parts of Africa, the voluntary associations were often the precursors of the nationalist movement, providing forums for advancing anticolonial ideas (Chazan 1982, 172; Wallerstein 1964, 331).

17. The Resistance Council system is a hierarchical one in which all adults belong to their village RC and elect nine members to the executive committee at this

first level of RC1. All RC1 executive committees in a parish form RC2. RC3 is formed similarly out of the RC2s at the subcounty level, and the RC3s form RC5 at the district level, skipping the county level (Nsibambi 1991, 279). The National Resistance Council, the highest governing body or parliament, includes 38 original NRC members who had been core NRM cadre during the guerrilla war and 20 members appointed by the President. The NRA Council, which is the highest decision making body in the army, selects another 10 members. Thus one quarter of the seats are selected by the NRM leaders, while the remainder of the 284 seats are selected by RC3s (Kasfir 1991).

18. Discussion, Olivia Mutibwa, 5 June 1992.

19. Irene Wekiya, NRC women's representative, interview conducted by author, Jinja, 30 March 1993.

20. Samuel Muwanguzi, "Will the Women Beat Men?" *Weekly Topic,* 4 June 1993, 22.

21. Hajati Nantongo, acting Chairman of the Uganda Muslim Women's Association, interview conducted by author, 27 March 1993.

22. Letter by Dr. R. G. Mukama in support of Joy Kwesiga as Chairperson of ACFODE in 1993 election.

23. In Uganda savings clubs go by various names: *kilab* (club) in Lusoga, cash round, *munno mukabi* (mutual aid, wealth, investment) in Luganda; *kalulu* (throw lots) or *emigabo* (shares) in Ankole. In Tanzania, where Kiswahili is widely spoken, the savings clubs are known simply as *upato* (something obtained), *upatu, kisahani* (small dish) or *mchezo* (game).

24. Discussion with Harriet Birungi 26 June 1992.

25. Edith Natakunda, interview conducted by author, 2 June 1992.

26. Florence Nekyon, interview conducted by author, 21 May 1993.

References

Ankrah, M. 1987. "The Role of Women in Conflict Resolution." Paper presented at International Seminar on Internal Conflict sponsored by International Alert (London), Makerere Institute for Social Research (MISR), International Peace Research Institute, United Nations University.

Barkan, J. D. 1991. "The Rise and Fall of a Govenance Realm in Kenya." In *Governance and Politics in Africa,* edited by G. Hyden and M. Bratton, 167–92. Boulder & London: Lynne Rienner Publishers.

Bayart, J.-F. 1986. "Civil Society in Africa." In *Political Domination in Africa,* edited by P. Chabal, 109–25. New York: Cambridge University Press.

Bratton, M. 1989. "Beyond the State: Civil Society and Associational Life in Africa." *World Politics* 41/3: 407–40.

Brett, E. A. 1991. "Rebuilding Survival Structures for the Poor: Organizational Options for Reconstruction in the 1990s." In *Changing Uganda: The Dilemmas of Structural Adjustment and Revolutionary Change,* edited by H. B. Hansen and M. Twaddle, 297–310. Athens: Ohio University Press.

Chabal, P. ed. 1986. *Political Domination in Africa: Reflections on the Limits of Power.* New York: Cambridge University Press.

Chatterjee, P. 1990. "A Response to Taylor's 'Modes of Civil Society'." *Public Culture* 3/1: 119–32.

Chazan, N. 1982. "The New Politics of Participation in Tropical Africa." *Comparative Politics*, 14/2: 169–89.

_____. 1991. "Africa's Democratic Challenge." *World Policy Journal*, 9/2: 279–307.

Elshtain, J. B. 1981. *Public Man, Private Woman: Women in Social and Political Thought.* Princeton NJ: Princeton University Press.

Hyden, G. 1983. *No Shortcuts to Progress: African Development Management in Perspective.* Berkeley and Los Angeles: University of California Press.

Kasfir, N. 1991. "The Ugandan Elections of 1989: Power, Populism and Democratization." In *Changing Uganda: The Dilemmas of Structural Adjustment and Revolutionary Change,* edited by H. B. Hansen and M. Twaddle, 247–78. Athens: Ohio University Press.

Little, K. (1973). *African Women in Towns: An Aspect of Africa's Social Revolution.* London: Cambridge University Press.

MacGaffey, J. 1986. "Women and Class Formation in a Dependent Economy: Kisangani Entrepreneuers." In *Women and Class in Africa,* edited by C. Robertson and I. Berger, 161–77. New York: Africana Publishing Company.

Mamdani, M. 1990. "Uganda: Contradictions of the IMF Programme and Perspective." *Development and Change,* 21: 427–67.

Matembe, M. R. K. 1991. "How Far Have the Women of Uganda Gone in Realising their Rights." Unpublished paper.

Meagher, K. 1990. "The Hidden Economy: Informal and Parallel Trade in Northwestern Uganda." *Review of Political Economy* 47: 64–83.

Migdal, J. S. 1988. *Strong Societies and Weak States.* Princeton NJ: Princeton University Press.

Musheshe, Mwalimu J. 1990. "Preface." In *A Directory of Non-Governmental Organisations in Uganda,* edited by DENIVA. Kampala.

Nsibambi, A. R. 1991. "Resistance Councils and Committees: A Case Study from Makerere." In *Changing Uganda: The Dilemmas of Structural Adjustment and Revolutionary Change,* edited by H. B. Hansen and M. Twaddle, 279–96. Athens, Ohio: Ohio University Press.

Okin, S. M. 1990. "Gender, the Public and the Private." In *Political Theory Today,* edited by D. Held, 67–90. Cambridge: Polity Press.

Pateman, C. 1983. "Feminist Critiques of the Public-Private Dichotomy." In *Conceptions of the Public and Private in Social Life,* edited by S. I. Benn and G. F. Gauss. London: Croom Helm.

Phillips, A. 1991. *Engendering Democracy.* University Park: Pennsylvania State University Press.

Tadria, H. M. K. 1987. "Changes and Continuities in the Position of Women in Uganda." In *Beyond Crisis: Development Issues in Uganda,* edited by P. D. Wiebe and C. P. Dodge, 79–90. Kampala: Makerere Institute of Social Research.

Tamale, S. 1992. "The Women's Movement in the USA: Lessons to be Drawn by African Women Movements." Paper presented at the Third American Studies Colloquium, Entebbe, Uganda, 1992.

Taylor, C. 1990. "Modes of Civil Society." *Public Culture* 3/1: 95–132.

Wallerstein, I. 1964. "Voluntary Associations." In *Political Parties and National Integration in Tropical Africa,* edited by J. Coleman and C. Rosberg, 318–39. Berkeley: University of California Press.

Walzer, M. 1991. "The Idea of Civil Society: A Path to Social Reconstruction." *Dissent* (Spring): 293–304.

Watson, C. 1988. "Uganda's Women: A Ray of Hope." *Africa Report* (July–August): 29–32.

———. "Ending the Rule of the Gun." *Africa Report* (January–February), 14–17.

White, Carolyn Day. 1973. "The Role of Women as an Interest Group in the Uganda Political System." M.A. dissertation, Makerere University.

Wunsch, J. S. and D. Olowu, ed. 1991. *The Failure of the Centralized State: Institutions and Self-Governance in Africa.* Boulder: Westview Press.

Yeatman, A. 1984. "Despotism and Civil Society." In *Women's View of the Political World of Men,* edited by J. H. Stiehm. New York: Transnational.

Suggestions for Further Reading

Allen, Chris, and Gavin Williams, eds. *Sociology of "Developing Countries": Sub-Saharan Africa.* New York: Monthly Review Press, 1982.

Berry, Sara. *Fathers Work for Their Sons: Accumulation, Mobility, and Class Formation in an Extended Yoruba Community.* Berkeley and Los Angeles: University of California Press, 1985.

Kuper, Leo, and M. G. Smith, eds. *Pluralism in Africa.* Berkeley and Los Angeles: University of California Press, 1971.

Lemarchand, Rene. "Political Clientelism and Ethnicity in Tropical Africa." *American Political Science Review* 64, no. 1 (1972), 68–90.

Markovitz, Irving L. *Power and Class in Africa.* Englewood Cliffs, N.J.: Prentice-Hall, 1977.

Parpart, Jane, and Kathleen Staudt, eds. *Women and the State in Africa.* Boulder: Lynne Rienner Publishers, 1989.

Rothchild, Donald, and Victor A. Olorunsola, eds. *State Versus Ethnic Claims: African Policy Dilemmas.* Boulder: Westview Press, 1983.

Sandbrook, Richard, and Robin Cohen, eds. *The Development of an African Working Class.* Buffalo, N.Y.: University of Toronto Press, 1975.

Scott, James C. *The Moral Economy of the Peasant: Rebellion and Subsistence in Southeast Asia.* New Haven: Yale University Press, 1977.

Young, Crawford. *The Politics of Cultural Pluralism.* Madison: University of Wisconsin Press, 1976.

Part Four

Democracy and Political Transition

Democratization is an important frontier in contemporary African development. The broad sweep of political liberalization throughout the region has produced a new climate for participation and governance. In the late 1980s, nearly all the countries in sub-Saharan African were ruled by military regimes or restrictive single-party states. By the mid-1990s, fourteen new democracies could be counted across the continent, while more than two dozen other countries had shifted to some form of competitive, multi-party system. Only a handful of military governments remained in the region, and many of these were beset by internal dissent and global censure.

The speed and scope of political reform in Africa has been truly impressive. The intensification of domestic opposition combined with sundry international influences to produce a spate of regime changes after 1990. Economic degeneration and political repression steadily eroded the legitimacy of authoritarian governments, and by the late 1980s a variety of restive groups had mobilized to challenge the established order. The collapse of communist regimes in Eastern Europe and the abatement of Cold War rivalries also removed vital sources of patronage for many autocrats in the region. The demonstration effects of the Eastern European transitions and liberalization in South Africa encouraged the trend toward political opening. Few of the incumbent regimes in Africa were able to fully resist pressures for political reform, and many fell by the wayside. The degree of political renaissance has been ardently debated, yet it is clear that politics in the region has been fundamentally altered.

Africa's wave of political change raises two urgent questions: First, how democratic are these transitions? The fall of an authoritarian regime does not automatically yield a democratic successor, as evidenced in such countries as Liberia, Rwanda, and Ethiopia. Moreover, the establishment of competitive political institutions hardly guarantees accountable representative government or an effective voice for popular sectors. In settings as diverse as Zambia, Madagascar, Ghana, and Benin, the introduction of democratic practices has prompted a longer struggle for acceptable rules of political competition and a quest for effective leadership. In short, regime change is the beginning of a process of democratic development, rather than its resolution.

A second question arises: How sustainable are these transitions? African democratization has emerged in a challenging environment, as most countries in the region do not reflect the attributes associated with strong democracies elsewhere. The region's low per capita incomes, limited urbanization, weak educational base, and limited experience with democratic practices would seem to create an inhospitable setting for sustainable, legitimate competitive rule. It is possible, however, that elite accommodation, popular participation, and a changed international setting can reinforce the region's emerging democracies. Rather than witnessing a decisive "second independence," we see a more open-ended process of trial, testing, and negotiation toward new political formulas in the region.

The following four selections address distinctive phases and challenges of political reform in Africa. Larry Diamond chronicles the scope and diversity of regional change and describes the central causes of breakdown among Africa's established autocratic governments. He also points to the central catalysts of democratization in the region. Michael Bratton and Nicolas van de Walle place Africa's political transitions in comparative perspective, observing the distinctive problems of change within neopatrimonial systems. Neopatrimonialism is the distinctive blend of personal, clientelist rule and formal administration evident in African political systems. The authors note the different institutional settings for change in such countries and the relatively unique patterns of democratization in neopatrimonial regimes.

Pearl Robinson takes up an important, and often neglected aspect of political transformation—the cultural context of power and representation. The author situates cultural approaches to politics in relation to other theories of democratization and political change. Robinson departs from conventional discussions of political culture by stressing the dynamic nature of norms and expectations. Focusing on the process of political learning, she argues for the possibility of transforming the common premises of political life and underscores the importance of popular engagement in democratic change.

In the final selection, Crawford Young provides a general assessment of African democratization at the close of the transitional "wave" of the early 1990s. He explores the varying results of regime change, the obstacles confronting Africa's new democracies, and the signs of success or failure in the first few years after the transitional elections of the region. He offers a guardedly optimistic prognosis for the persistence of democratic governments and other catalysts for democratization in the region.

11

Africa:
The Second Wind
of Change

Larry Diamond

Since the beginning of 1990, and thirty years after the British Prime Minister Harold Macmillan made his historic pronouncement in Cape Town, a new "wind of change" is blowing through the continent of Africa. This process of change, and pressure for change, has been called a "second African independence" or "second liberation" for the promise it carries of freeing African peoples from the tyranny, oppression, corruption and gross misgovernance that have characterized the political experience of most African states since decolonization in the 1960s. Just last month, this promise was expressed anew when the people of Malawi voted for multi-party democracy in a referendum that overwhelmingly rejected the repressive thirty-year dictatorship of President Kamuzu Banda.

The pace and spread of political change in Africa since 1989 have been breathtaking. The programme on African Governance at the Carter Center, in the United States, which has been tracking democratic trends on the continent, estimates that more than half of all African states are now largely democratic or show a moderate to strong commitment to democratic change. Last year, an observer judged that "nearly three-fourths of the 47 countries south of the Sahara are in various stages of political liberalization."

At the end of 1989, just before the start of the rapid transformations of regime, Freedom House rated thirty-four of the fifty-two African states (almost two-thirds) as not free, fifteen as partly free, and only three as free, or in essence democratic. Moreover, forty of the fifty-two African states—about three-quarters—were clustered in the four "most authori-

Reprinted with permission from *Times Literary Supplement*, July 2, 1993: 43–4

tarian" categories on a thirteen-point scale of political rights and civil liberties. This pattern was in striking contrast to that for the world overall, which, by 1989, was a decade and a half into what Samuel Huntington has called the "Third Wave" of global democratization, with more than a third of the total number of states classified as "free".

In just two years, the picture changed quite significantly. By the end of 1991, eight (or 15.4 per cent of) African states—Benin, Botswana, Cape Verde, Gambia, Mauritius, Namibia, São Tomé and Principe, and Zambia—were rated as free, and twenty-three (44.2 per cent) as partly free. Mali joined the ranks of these democracies in the first half of 1992. Particularly striking was the decline in highly authoritarian, or "not free" states, from thirty-four in 1989 to twenty-one in 1991, and down to seventeen by the end of 1992.

Not all the change has been positive, however. During 1991, political freedom and civil liberties deteriorated in the Arab North African states of Morocco, Tunisia and Egypt, and by mid-1992 there had also been a reversion to harsh dictatorship in Algeria. Progress towards democracy in Angola fell apart with the refusal of Jonas Savimbi's UNITA to accept its defeat at the polls in September 1992; Liberia remained mired in a brutal civil war; and—most disturbingly for the future of Africa's overall trend towards democracy—Nigeria's military dictator, General Ibrahim Babangida, cancelled the country's transition to democracy last month when the candidate he apparently favoured was soundly defeated in the presidential elections. Thus, the movement towards democracy in Africa must be seen as tentative, partial, and in many cases fragile and ambiguous.

In Zaïre, hopes for democratization have foundered again on the stubborn resistance of its long-established patrimonial dictator, Mobutu Sese Seko, to any notion of yielding power; as the opposition to him fragments, and the dictator hunkers down in his floating bunker on the river, Zaïre draws nearer to Somali-like disintegration than to Beninois-style democratization (as described below). In Algeria, a ruthless crackdown by the regime on the Islamic Salvation Front (FIS) early in 1992 has effectively derailed movement towards democracy, and the options have tragically polarized into a dictatorship of the status quo or a totalitarianism of the now wholly radicalized Islamic fundamentalists.

Even where democracy has come into being, governments face daunting challenges. The newly elected presidents of Benin, Zambia and Mali have inherited bankrupt economies that will take many years of painful adjustment and sacrifice to put right. The need to create stable political institutions and more equitable social arrangements must be confronted before these and other new and emerging democracies can begin to be considered viable.

Africa's "second liberation" may be traced to two crucial events that took place in February 1990: a national conference in Benin, turning into a civilian coup, that stripped President Mathieu Kérékou of effective power, established a transitional government and prepared the way for multi-party elections; and the release of Nelson Mandela from almost three decades of imprisonment and the "unbanning" of the African National Congress by the white minority government in South Africa. It is noteworthy that these two events followed, in rapid fashion, the collapse of Communist power in Eastern Europe, in late 1989. Whatever the effect of the comprehensive discrediting of socialist doctrines that this collapse signalled, it is clear that as a direct result of what happened in Benin and South Africa, pressures for democratic change accelerated dramatically across the continent. A number of countries—including Togo, Niger, Madagascar, Zaïre and the Republic of Congo—deliberately followed the Beninois model of the national conference (though so far without much success, except in Niger).

Of the interim factors that have contributed to the movement for democratic change in Africa, probably the most important has been the widespread failure throughout the continent of every type of authoritarian regime. These failures may be seen to have several dimensions. The economic dimension has been widely documented. The average annual growth rate of per capita GNP for sub-Saharan Africa in the past decade has been *negative* (-1.1 per cent), compared with 2.9 per cent for South Asia, 6.3 for East Asia and the Pacific, 0.5 for Latin America and the Caribbean, and 1.5 for all low and middle-income countries. By 1989, total external debt for sub-Saharan Africa stood at $147 billion, 99 per cent of its annual gross domestic product, almost four times annual export earnings, and twice the level of just seven years previously. Debt service obligations, equivalent to 46 per cent of export earnings on average, impose crushing burdens on financially strapped African economies: On virtually every measure of economic and human development, African countries are among the poorest and materially most miserable in the world. For example, on the "Human Development Index" developed by the United Nations Development Programme (UNDP)—a broadly based development indicator that includes measures of literacy and life expectancy as well as income—twenty-five of the thirty bottom-ranking countries are African. Despite an annual inflow of $15 billion of aid, standards of life have declined since independence (not surprisingly, a good many older Africans confess to a longing for the days of colonial rule). And numbers do not begin to tell the whole story of the pervasive decay and breakdown of public services and economic life. In Benin, before the fall of Kérékou according to one observer, "Civil servants went unpaid for months; the police could not even write up crime reports for lack of carbon paper." Throughout the continent, the physical infrastructure created in the late colonial and early post-colonial periods was breaking down. Clinics were without drugs, schools without books, paper, ink, or chalk. With governments lacking the foreign exchange to purchase spare parts, public transportation has been crumbling to the point where people have been trekking hours each day to and from work.

A second dimension of failure, heavily underlying the first, has been the absence of social justice. In virtually all the authoritarian regimes there has been a complete lack of accountability, with ruling élites ("kleptocracies", as Stanislav Andreski called them) brazenly appropriating public resources to themselves, their extended families and kinship networks, as well as to their business, political and "ethnic" cronies and clients. This political and bureaucratic corruption has been so institutionalized that it has become the main avenue of class formation and personal wealth accumulation in Africa, with political or bureaucratic office being sought and distributed as essentially a licence or "prebend" for personal and group enrichment. The problem not only massively afflicted "capitalist" states like Nigeria, Kenya and the Ivory Coast, which made few ideological gestures in the direction of socialism and equality, but also those states, such as Tanzania and Zimbabwe, which in their ruling ideologies drew heavily on socialist rhetoric and ideas. The shortage of foreign exchange due to corrupt transactions at high level is believed to be a major reason why Zimbabwe has not been able to import the spare parts needed to keep its public transport operating. Even before the demise of Communism in Eastern Europe and the Soviet Union, the idealism, self-conviction, and revolutionary élan of socialist and Afro-Marxist regimes were almost totally exhausted.

Beyond the huge personal accumulation accruing from office, African ruling parties and élites have used the state as a means of patronage to maintain themselves in power, burdening the economy with levels of public employment that were utterly unsustainable (consuming by 1989 throughout Africa 60–80 per cent of national budgets). This may have been justified in terms of a distributionist programme, but its effect was to saddle the economy with bloated and unproductive state sectors, and to provide another avenue for corruption. A further inequality resulted from the gross urban biases, aimed at maintaining political support, in the pricing of foodstuffs and the spread of services. When policies for structural adjustment began to be demanded by international donors during the 1980s, in order to reverse these inequalities and restore economic rationality and production incentives, African regimes were further weakened politically by the intensification of opposition from articulate urban groups whom they had tried to subdue with these subsidies and pay-offs.

The third dimension of the failure of authoritarian regimes in Africa has been the treatment of individual rights. Perhaps this goes without saying, as violations of rights are intrinsic to the nature of authoritarian rule. But most African dictatorships have been particularly arbitrary and abusive, and the lack of freedom and due process has been especially offensive to urban "counter-élites"—students, journalists, intellectuals, professionals, trade unionists, opposition politicians—groups with the ideas, energy, and sometimes resources to organize in opposition to the regime. These real and potential dissident forces were heavily victimized, but not exclusively so. People in the rural areas with little education also felt the heavy hand of the authoritarian, patrimonial state, which extracted resources while returning little in the way of development, punishing all forms of protest and resistance, and offering none of the mechanisms for recourse to elementary justice that existed, in varying degrees, in many of Africa's traditional systems of rule. As a consequence of this pervasive victimization and predation, ordinary Africans became alienated from the state and increasingly withdrew from it into alternative, informal channels of production and exchange.

The fourth dimension of failure, which followed in many respects from the third, was the systematic violation and abuse of group rights, as élites of certain ethnic groups captured state power and barricaded themselves behind it. In some cases, this produced regimes—such as Eyadema's in Togo, Bongo's in Gabon, and Moi's in Kenya—with extremely narrow ethnic bases, which increased the insecurity of their rule and hence their own tendency to resort to repression in order to maintain their grip. While some African authoritarian rulers managed to distribute enough patronage across ethnic groups to sustain their rule with some order, others—like Obote in Uganda, Doe in Liberia, and Siad Barre in Somalia—plunged their countries into devastating civil wars. Most other instances of ruinous civil conflict, notably in Ethiopia, Angola and the Sudan, also owe much to the failure of narrowly based authoritarian regimes to respect and accommodate group rights within some kind of pluralist framework for sharing power and resources.

It should be noted that the failure of authoritarian regimes in Africa has not been the result of "diffusion effects" from one country to another. Independently of each other, in some fifty African states authoritarian regimes of widely different structures, ideologies and leaderships have produced broadly similar consequences with respect to economic development, social justice and accountability, and individual and group rights. While there has been some variation—more economic growth (for a time) in Kenya and the Ivory Coast, higher literacy in Tanzania—not a single authoritarian regime in Africa can be counted a success. All types of authoritarian regime have failed: patrimonial, neo-traditional, one-party, military, Marxist, populist, autocratic, and every stripe in between.

The remarkably consistent record of all these experiments with authoritarian rule over the past three decades has given rise to an important development. Intellectuals and young élites in particular, but to a surprising degree, ordinary people as well, have drawn the broad conclusion that, at bottom, the problem has not been with corrupt leaders, flawed ideologies (right or left), the wrong institutional framework, or the wrong historical moment; and increasingly, the crutch of blaming the world system is being discarded as well. Africans are recognizing that the problem is systemic, having to do with the nature of authoritarian rule and its interaction with the economic and cultural circumstances of Africa. There is a generic problem common to all of this, and it is the lack of democracy. The absence of political competition, freedom and pluralism is now seen as the logical and inevitable precursor to abuse of power and lack of accountability. The absence of constitutionalism and power-sharing now appears as the source of the wholesale violations of individual and group rights. Only with democracy, it is realized, will it be possible to combat the corruption, stagnation, injustice and tyranny that have destroyed the promise of the first African liberation.

In this reaction against the failures of authoritarianism lies another important cause of the democratic revolution in Africa. There has been an important shift in intellectual thinking and political culture over the past decade or so, which has rapidly accelerated. As in Latin America, left and progressive forces have become committed to political democracy, not just for instrumental but for intrinsic reasons, as they realize that social justice and economic advancement cannot be achieved without political liberty and multi-party competition. At the mass level, this shift has manifested itself mainly as anti-authoritarianism and anti-statism, rather than as a sophisticated and positive appreciation of democracy as encompassing the need for tolerance, bargaining, accommodation, compromise and restraint. Because the political culture of mobilized groups in civil society has featured resistance to the encroachments of an overbearing state, those aspects of citizenship that entail support for the state and constructive engagement with it have had little opportunity for cultivation. This has serious implications for the challenges of democratic consolidation that lie ahead. Nevertheless, the questioning of authority, resistance to abuse, demand for accountability, and active (if largely informal) participation that have increasingly come to characterize the political cultures of contemporary Africa, provide a major impetus for democratization.

Other domestic factors helped to make African countries ripe for change in the wake of the anti-Communist revolutions of 1989 and of the two key triggers—in Benin and South Africa—of African democratization in February 1990. One of these factors was demographic. Populations exploded in the post-colonial era, doubling in twenty-five to thirty years. In some countries, such as Kenya, Zambia and the Ivory Coast, the rate of growth exceeded 3 per cent annually. Such rapidly expanding populations are extremely *young* populations, and the young of course are typically more restless, idealistic, excitable and prone to risk-taking. Urbanization facilitated protest and resistance, by breaking traditional bonds of clientage, creating new, more functional and market-oriented ethnic identities, and concentrating people into denser areas, where they became more available for political mobilization. The spread of education also increased political awareness and the readiness to participate and organize. Further, it interacted with rapid urbanization and huge population growth to produce veritable powder-kegs of protest against nonperforming and abusive regimes: large concentrations of young, unemployed or underemployed people, with high aspirations and dim economic prospects.

The spread of mass communications also heightened consciousness. Although in most African countries the state monopolized the electronic media and controlled or censored most or all of the print media as well, alternative sources of information emerged to challenge the regimes and spread news of democratic developments in other parts of the world. The alternative press played a particularly important role in raising political awareness and facilitating mobilization against the regime in South Africa, and privately owned publications also had an impact, in countries like Nigeria and Kenya. Throughout Africa, word of mouth, the "radio of the streets", spread news of corruption and political abuse, and those with access to short-wave radios (a large proportion of many African populations) learned from the BBC and the Voice of America about the global democratic revolution.

The growth of alternative media was part of a larger process that undermined authoritarianism: the development of civil society, the realm of organized social life independent of the state and concerned with public or collective (as opposed to private) goals and needs: this involves groups, media, and networks of various kinds that seek to relate to the state—to pressure it, influence it, check it and hold it accountable—but not to conquer it. In Africa during the 1970s and especially the 80s, there emerged a vigorous array of associations, movements and networks, formal and informal, that challenged the state or organized to evade its predatory grasp. Despite catastrophic economic decline, and in many cases because of it, these groups managed to grow in aggressiveness, resources, size of membership and organizational savvy.

During the past ten years of military rule in Nigeria, the Nigerian Bar Association, the Nigerian Medical Association, the Academic Staff Union of Universities, the National Association of Students and several young and effective human rights groups have taken leading roles in resisting oppressive rule and pushing forward the transition to democracy. Critical leadership for the pro-democracy movement in Kenya, which eventually coalesced into the Forum for the Restoration for Democracy (FORD), has come from the Law Society of Kenya, the Federation of Women Lawyers, and small networks of human-rights lawyers, non-governmental publications like the *Nairobi Law Monthly,* and intellectuals. Organized forces in civil society have played a major role in national conferences (on the Benin model) for democratic change. And the dramatic transition to electoral democracy in Zambia was spearheaded by a resilient civil society—led by the powerful and broadly based Zambia Congress of Trade Unions (ZCTU)—that successfully resisted the efforts of the one-party state to incorporate or eliminate it. With the ZCTU and its chairman, Frederick Chiluba, in the lead, a coalition of trade unionists, students, businessmen and dissident politicians catalysed the pro-democracy movement in Zambia that eventually took shape (and ultimately won power) as the Movement for Multiparty Democracy. A similarly broad coalition of forces in civil society is now beginning to press for democratic reform in Zimbabwe. Again, the chief trade union federation, the Zimbabwe Congress of Trade Unions, led by Morgan Tsvangirai, is in the forefront, as are the recently formed Zimbabwe Human Rights Association (Zimrights) and the Forum for Democratic Reform, led by the widely respected former Chief Justice, Enock Dumbuchena.

In a number of African countries, religious organizations have come forward to denounce authoritarian rule and to provide both legitimacy and sanctuary to vulnerable opponents of it. Roman Catholic prelates presided over the national conferences in both Benin and Congo. In several countries, including Madagascar and Zambia, church leaders have served as intermediaries between the regime and its opponents. When governments have become intransigent, religious organizations have kept up the pressure with well-publicized sermons and pastoral letters. Here the contemporary democratic movement is following the trail blazed during the anti-apartheid struggle by religious leaders such as the Revd Beyers Naudé and the Anglican Archbishop Desmond Tutu.

In Zimbabwe, the Catholic, Anglican and other Protestant churches have all stoutly criticized the growing corruption and blemished human rights record of the Mugabe government, and have joined with the legal community to launch Zimrights. Even in long-quiescent Malawi, the widespread circulation of a courageous letter by seven Catholic bishops attacking the government for human rights abuses helped to inspire the popular pressure for democratization that now seems likely to bring down the Banda dictatorship.

Another factor that has contributed to the demise of African authoritarian regimes has been the collapse of their resource bases. To a considerable extent, this has followed from their gross economic mismanagement, which has plunged into bankruptcy such mineral-rich states as Zaïre, Zambia, Sierra Leone, Angola and even Nigeria. When the ruling coalition is preserved largely through the patrimonial distribution of material resources, the drying up of these resources means the collapse of the regime. This exhaustion of resources owes much to the decisions of major international aid donors to cease subsidizing the theft and oppression of African dictators.

The turnabout of France has been particularly striking: its refusal to keep subsidizing Kérékou's bankrupt regime in Benin was the trigger that forced him to call a national conference that was his undoing. French pressure has also helped to persuade one-party dictators in the Ivory Coast, Cameroon, Gabon and elsewhere to open up their regimes to public criticism and multi-party competition. In each of these cases, however, France has more recently appeared willing to content itself with a façade of multi-party competition, behind which corrupt presidents have rigged themselves back into power in the face of widespread (and in the case of Cameroon, massive) popular opposition. Where international aid donors have presented a united front, making aid conditional on democratic reforms, the results have been more dramatic, as in Kenya and most recently Malawi.

The sensitivity of African regimes to international pressures was shown in July 1990 when the Organization of African Unity (OAU) adopted a statement on the need for recognizing human rights, political accountability, and the rule of law. Significantly, that statement was entitled, "The Political and Socio-Economic Situation in Africa and the Fundamental Changes Taking Place in the World". Africans have been acutely aware of the democratic revolution in Eastern Europe and in other parts of the world. As Nigeria's UN ambassador, Ibrahim Gambari (also an astute political scientist), observed, Africans "listen to the BBC, the Voice of America, Radio Moscow, sometimes in their local language. They're fully aware [of events in Eastern Europe] and they ask, 'Why not here?'" Reflecting on the revolutionary changes then engulfing Eastern Europe, Zambia's Frederick Chiluba launched the opening refrain in the campaign for multi-party democracy when he asked at the end of 1989, "If the owners of socialism have withdrawn from the one-party system, who are the Africans to continue with it?" Even one of the architects of the African one-party state, Tanzania's Julius Nyerere, conceded that his country could learn a "lesson or two" from Eastern Europe.

"Demonstration effects" have also been evident from within Africa. The example of Benin's national conference asserting its sovereignty and seizing power from a seventeen-year-long dictatorship had electrifying effects in other countries, especially with the creation of a fully fledged electoral democracy and the defeat of the dictator at the polls a year later.

The changes in South Africa may have had almost as great an effect as those in Eastern Europe. Developments there exposed the contrast between what African political leaders were demanding for that country and what they were willing to tolerate and condone in the rest of the continent. By the end of the decade, Africans themselves were exposing the hypocrisy of demanding political liberties in South Africa that were routinely trampled on elsewhere in Black Africa. Roger Chongwe, Chairman of the African Bar Association, declared, "All Africa demands: if South Africa is to have one man, one vote, why not us?" African leaders themselves finally began to concede, as they put it in their July 1990 OAU statement, that they would need "to democratize further our societies and consolidate democratic institutions".

With the collapse of the Communist model, the main ideological rival to political and economic liberalism disappeared from the African scene. It was not only because of the drying up of Soviet aid that the Marxist regimes in Angola and Mozambique (and to a lesser extent Ethiopia) "undertook ideological somersaults" and began adopting the capitalist and pluralist development models they had so long denounced. These regimes had lost faith (or whatever faith remained) in the viability of Marxism-Leninism. This has left only the Islamic fundamentalist state as an ideological rival to liberal, multi-party democracy in Africa.

It is uncertain how many of Africa's new attempts at democratization will succeed. However, what Africa most cries out for is good governance. If new democratic leaders govern well—with restraint, accommodation, accountability, respect for individual and group rights, and some real commitment to the public good—African publics will remain steadfast in their commitment to democracy. Slowly, and with some international sympathy and support, democracy could then sink enduring roots on the African continent, and demonstrate to those peoples still burdened with dictatorship the real promise of this "second liberation".

12

Neopatrimonial Regimes and Political Transitions in Africa

Michael Bratton and Nicolas van de Walle

Introduction: Comparing Political Transitions

The current wave of scholarly studies of democratization and political transition is not fully comparative. Conceptually, these studies employ models of political change that are useful in explaining the demise of bureaucratic forms of authoritarianism but cannot account for transitions from more personalistic types of rule. Empirically, entire regions of the world are excluded. Whereas most studies of democratization have focused on Latin America and Southern Europe and latterly on Eastern Europe, Africa has received much less attention. In this article, we examine recent patterns of political change in Africa and on that basis propose revisions to the theory of political transitions.

Africa is not immune from the global challenge to authoritarianism. Between 1990 and 1993 more than half of Africa's fifty-two governments responded to domestic and international pressures by holding competitive presidential or legislative elections. The dynamics and outcomes of these transitions have been highly variable: in some cases, a competitive election has led to an alternation of political leaders and the emergence of a fragile democratic regime; more often the transition has been flawed (with the incumbent stealing the election), blocked (with the incumbents and opposition deadlocked over the rules of the political game), or pre-

Reprinted with permission from *World Politics* 46, no. 4 (July 1994): 453–489. © 1994 The Johns Hopkins University Press.

cluded (by widespread civil unrest).[1] While democratization is clearly incomplete in Africa, it has already discredited military and one-party regimes, few of which are likely to survive intact. And recent African experience poses interesting general questions: Why do some regimes undergo transitions from authoritarian rule while others do not? Are there different paths of transition? Why do some transitions occasionally result in democracy but others fall short? Why, in Africa, are transitions to democracy generally problematic?

In this article, we argue that the nature of the preexisting regime shapes the dynamics and outcomes of political transitions. Our thesis is as follows: contemporary political changes are conditioned by mechanisms of rule embedded in the ancien régime. Authoritarian leaders in power for long periods of time establish rules about who may participate in public decisions and the amount of political competition allowed. Taken together, these rules constitute a political regime. Regime type in turn influences both the likelihood that an opposition challenge will arise and the flexibility with which incumbents can respond. It also determines whether elites and masses can arrive at new rules of political interaction through negotiation, accommodation, and election, that is, whether any transition will be democratic.

We cast the argument comparatively in order to highlight differences among political regimes, initially between Africa and the rest of the world and subsequently among African countries themselves. First, we compare African transitions with those in Latin America and Southern Europe and find that transition dynamics in Africa have been distinctive. We attribute this to the neopatrimonial nature of African authoritarian regimes, which we contrast to the corporatist regimes that democratized in Southern Europe in the mid–1970s and in Latin America in the mid-1980s. Thereafter, we compare transitions within Africa. Based on the degree of political participation and contestation tolerated under the ancien régime, we distinguish several regime variants under the general rubric of neopatrimonialism and show that here, too, regime characteristics can help explain transition processes. The argument, though driven by African examples, can be generalized to neopatrimonial regimes elsewhere.

Especially for Africa, the scholarly study of political transitions has vacillated between ideographic case studies (with detailed description of events and actors) and abstract ruminations about principles of democracy supported by little systematic evidence. This article makes a modest effort to bridge the gap between these two extremes. We emphasize political institutions in a bid to develop midlevel generalizations and to help make the study of regime transitions more comparative.

The article is divided into four sections. The first section argues that the literature on political transitions has focused excessively on the contingent interactions of key political actors and underestimated the formative impact of political institutions. A second section defines neopatrimonialism as a regime type and describes its characteristic features in Africa. Third, we discuss how the features of neopatrimonialism are likely to mold transitions in patterns quite different from those observed in transitions from other regime types. A fourth section distinguishes variants of the neopatrimonial regime, which we use to explain transition dynamics and outcomes observed recently in sub-Saharan Africa. A conclusion extends the argument about the distinctiveness of transitions from neopatrimonial rule and discusses its implications.

Regime Type and Political Transition

Are there relationships between regime type and the likelihood, nature, and extent of political transition? Scholars have so far only scratched the surface in understanding political transitions in terms of the structure of the preceding regime. Karen Remmer argues that once one recognizes the "enormous range of variation concealed within the authoritarian (and democratic) categor(ies)," political outcomes vary systematically with regime type.[2] From recent Latin American experience she proposes that inclusionary democracies tend to collapse as a result of intrigue among the political elite, whereas exclusionary democracies are more likely to succumb to pressure from below. Moreover, once inclusionary regimes have held power, the reimposition of an exclusionary regime requires heavy doses of state coercion.[3] It is unclear, however, whether Remmer's generalizations apply to the demise of autocracies as well as to the breakdown of democratic rule.

Huntington's analysis of "third wave" democratic transitions in thirty-five countries finds little overall relationship between the nature of the incumbent authoritarian regime and the pattern of political transition.[4] He contends that whereas political transitions are most likely to be initiated from the top down, such dynamics are equally likely in one-party military or personalistic regimes. Nevertheless, leaders of one-party and military regimes are somewhat more likely than personal dictators to engage the opposition in a negotiated transfer of power. Indeed, personalistic regimes are more susceptible than other regime types to collapse in the face of a popular protest. Huntington notes that dictatorial leaders usually refuse to give up power voluntarily and try to stay in office as long as they can.[5]

The notion of an underlying structure to regime transitions runs counter to the most penetrating and influential contemporary work on this subject. Guillermo O'Donnell and Philippe Schmitter eschew the possibility of systematic causality and instead advance what can be termed a contingent approach to transitions. They argue that transitions are abnormal periods of "undetermined" political change in which "there are insufficient structural or behavioral parameters to guide and predict the outcome."[6] Compared with the orderliness of authoritarian rule, transitions are marked by unruly and chaotic struggles and by uncertainty about the nature of resultant regimes. Analysts cannot assume that the transition process is shaped by preexisting constellations of macroeconomic conditions, social classes, or political institutions. Instead, formerly cohesive social classes and political organizations tend to splinter in the heat of political combat, making it impossible to deduce alignments and actions of any protagonist. Political outcomes are driven by the short-term calculations and the immediate reactions of strategic actors to unfolding events.

There is much merit in this contingent approach, which captures well the chaotic nature of regime transitions, but we remain dissatisfied with the open-ended implication that any one transition process or outcome is just as likely as any other. The excessive voluntarism of O'Donnell and Schmitter's framework has been criticized by other commentators. Nancy Bermeo notes that "the authors' emphasis on individual actors . . . constitutes a most significant challenge to the structuralist perspectives that have dominated . . . (comparative) political science scholarship."[7] Terry Lynn Karl makes a case for what she calls structured contingency, an approach "that seeks explicitly to relate structural constraints to the shaping of contingent choice."[8] In her words:

> Even in the midst of tremendous uncertainty provoked by a regime transition, where constraints appear to be most relaxed and where a wide range of outcomes appears to be possible, the decisions made by various actors respond to and are conditioned by the types of socioeconomic structures and political institutions already present.[9]

We agree that there are potentially fruitful avenues for research at a "meso" level between individual choice and structural determinism.[10] To date, most propositions in the transitions literature concern the effects of deep socioeconomic structures. For example, Bermeo posits that "authoritarian regimes do not seem to collapse during periods of relative prosperity";[11] Karl suggests that democratic consolidation depends on "the absence of a strong landowner elite engaged in labor-repressive agriculture."[12] Important as the condition of the economy and the formation of classes may be, we feel that these propositions focus on structures that are *too* deep. There are more proximate, political institutions—which together constitute a political regime—that are likely to have a direct bearing on transitions.

The argument that the political institutions of the preceding regime condition historical transitions is of course not novel; it runs through the historiographic literature, notably on revolutions.[13] But the recent transitions literature has not grappled with regime types, in part because the universe of relevant country cases has displayed a relatively uniform set of dominant political institutions.[14] It has tended to assume the presence of the corporatist institutions that predominated in the bureaucratic authoritarian regimes of Southern Europe and Latin America.[15] In Africa, however, political institutions have on the whole evolved within neopatrimonial rather than corporatist regimes, forcing us to assess the impact of regime type.

Neopatrimonial Regimes

In the main, African political regimes are distinctly noncorporatist. Leaders of postcolonial African countries may have pursued a corporatist strategy to the extent that they promoted an organic ideology of national unity and attempted to direct political mobilization along controlled channels. But African leaders have rarely used bureaucratic formulas to construct authoritative institutions or granted subsidiary spheres of influence to occupational interest groups within civil society. Contemporary African regimes do not display the formal governing coalitions between organized state and social interests or the collective bargaining over core public policies that characterize corporatism. At best, African efforts to install corporatist regimes have been a "policy output" of an ambitious political elite rather than a reflection of organized class interests within domestic society.

Rather, the distinctive institutional hallmark of African regimes is neopatrimonialism. In neopatrimonial regimes, the chief executive maintains authority through personal patronage, rather than through ideology or law. As with classic patrimonialism, the right to rule is ascribed to a person rather than an office.[16] In contemporary neopatrimonialism, relationships of loyalty and dependence pervade a formal political and administrative system[17] and leaders occupy bureaucratic offices less to perform public service than to acquire personal wealth and status. The distinction between private and public interests is purposely blurred. The essence of neopatrimonialism is the award by public officials of personal favors, both within the state (notably public sector jobs) and in society (for instance, licenses, contracts, and projects). In return for material rewards, clients mobilize political support and refer all decisions upward as a mark of deference to patrons.[18]

Insofar as personalized exchanges and political scandals are common in all regimes, theorists have suggested that neopatrimonialism is a master concept for comparative politics. Theobold argues that "some of the new states are, properly speaking, not states at all; rather, they are virtually the private instruments of those powerful enough to rule."[19] And Clapham maintains that neopatrimonialism is "the most salient type (of authority)" in the Third World because it "corresponds to the normal forms of social organization in precolonial societies."[20]

We draw a finer distinction, namely, that while neopatrimonial practice can be found in all polities, it is the *core* feature of politics in Africa and in a small number of other states, including Haiti, the Philippines, and Indonesia. Thus, personal relationships are a factor at the margins of all bureaucratic systems, but in Africa they constitute the foundation and superstructure of political institutions. The interaction between the "big man" and his extended retinue *defines* African politics, from the highest reaches of the presidential palace to the humblest village assembly. As such, analysts of African politics have embraced the neopatrimonial model.[21]

Neopatrimonialism has important implications for the analysis of political transitions. On the one hand, one would expect transitions from neopatrimonial rule to be distinctive, for example, centering on struggles over the legitimacy of the discretionary decision making by dominant, personalistic leaders. On the other hand, one would also expect the dynamics of political change to be highly variable, unpredictably reflecting idiosyncratic patterns of rule devised by strongmen. Hence the need to emphasize both the commonalities *and* variations in transition dynamics and outcomes. Bearing this in mind, let us now turn to our central questions: how does neopatrimonialism influence whether transitions ever begin, how they unfold, and how they turn out?

Comparing Regimes and Transitions

The recent literature on democratization in Europe and Latin America[22] converges on a modal path of political transition. The transition begins when a moderate faction within the state elite recognizes that social peace and economic development alone cannot legitimate an authoritarian regime. These soft-liners promote a political opening by providing improved guarantees of civil and political rights and later conceding the convocation of free and fair elections. The greatest threat to democratic transition comes from a backlash by elements of a hard-line faction, most commonly when the military executes a reactionary coup. To forestall hard-liners and complete the transition, government and opposition leaders meet behind the scenes to forge a compromise "pact" to guarantee the vital interests of major elite players.

We propose that political transitions in neopatrimonial regimes depart from this modal path in the following major respects:

1. *Political transitions from neopatrimonial regimes originate in social protest.* As is well known, the practices of neopatrimonialism cause chronic fiscal

crisis and make economic growth highly problematic.[23] In addition, neopatrimonial leaders construct particularistic networks of personal loyalty that grant undue favor to selected kinship, ethnic, or regional groupings. Taken together, shrinking economic opportunities and exclusionary patterns of reward are a recipe for social unrest. Mass popular protest is likely to break out, usually over the issue of declining living standards, and to escalate to calls for the removal of incumbent leaders. Unlike corporatist rulers, personal rulers cannot point to a record of stability and prosperity to legitimate their rule.

Endemic fiscal crisis also undercuts the capacity of rulers to manage the process of political change. When public resources dwindle to the point where the incumbent government can no longer pay civil servants, the latter join the antiregime protesters in the streets.[24] Shorn of the ability to maintain political stability through the distribution of material rewards, neopatrimonial leaders resort erratically to coercion which, in turn, further undermines the regime's legitimacy. The showdown occurs when the government is unable to pay the military.

Przeworski has argued that the stability of any regime depends not so much on the legitimacy of a particular system of domination as on the presence of a preferred opposition alternative.[25] It may be true that a powerful autocrat can coerce unwilling popular compliance over very long periods of time if he retains control over the executive and military bureaucracies. But regimes built on personal loyalty rather than bureaucratic authority are susceptible to institutional collapse when patronage resources run out. In these cases, a crisis of legitimacy may be a sufficient condition to undermine or topple a regime, and there need not yet be an organized opposition offering a programmatic alternative.

As a result of twin political and economic crises, political transitions are more likely to originate in society than in the corridors of elite power. The existing literature is inconsistent on this point. O'Donnell and Schmitter assert that "there is no transition whose beginning is not the consequence—direct or indirect—of important divisions within the authoritarian regime itself."[26] Yet the same authors note that authoritarian rulers usually miss opportunities to open up when the regime is riding a wave of economic success and that instead they "attempt liberalization only when they are already going through some serious crisis."[27] We read this as implying that political liberalization is an elite *response* rather than an elite initiative. It also begs the question of how leaders apprehend the existence of a "crisis"; presumably, elites are awakened to the necessity of reform by an outpouring of popular protest.[28]

The well-known distinctions between top-down, bottom-up, and negotiated transitions are helpful here.[29] One might be tempted to predict that neopatrimonial regimes would undergo elite-initiated transitions, since personal rulers concentrate so much decision-making power in their own hands.[30] But in an earlier analysis, we found instead that transitions in Africa seem to be occurring more commonly from below. Of twenty-one cases of transition in sub-Saharan Africa between November 1989 and May 1991, the initiative to undertake political reform was taken by opposition protesters in sixteen cases and by incumbent state leaders in only five cases.[31] In general, neopatrimonial rulers are driven by calculations of personal political survival: they resist political openings for as long as possible and seek to manage the process of transition only after it has been forced upon them.[32]

The structure of political incentives in neopatrimonial regimes helps to explain why state elites rarely initiate political transitions. When rule is built on personal loyalty, supreme leaders often lose touch with popular perceptions of regime legitimacy. They lack institutional ties to corporate groups in society that could alert them to the strength of their popular support. Instead, they surround themselves with sycophantic lieutenants who protect their own positions by telling the leader what he wants to hear and by shielding him from dissonant facts. Thus, even skillful personalistic leaders lack a flow of reliable information on which to base sound judgments about the need for, and timing of, political liberalization. Instead, they react to popular discontent by falling back on tried-and-true methods of selective reward and political repression. To make themselves heard—to penetrate the conspiracy of silence surrounding the supremo—ordinary citizens therefore have little choice but to persist with protest and raise the volume of their demands.

Ironically, neopatrimonial rule also undercuts civil society, thus weakening the foundation for antisystemic change. Because personal rulers are sensitive to threats to their authority, they set about weakening all independent centers of power. Migdal shows how fear of rivals drives dictators to emasculate the very state institutions that could institutionalize their rule.[33] The same irrational logic of political survival informs the attitudes of personal rulers toward the institutions of civil society. Most African leaders have demobilized voters and eradicated popular associations except those headed by hand-picked loyalists. Therefore, when political protest does erupt in neopatrimonial regimes, it is usually spontaneous, sporadic, disorganized, and unsustained. Because civil society is underdeveloped, the completion of the transition and the consolidation of any subsequent democratic regime are problematic.

2. *Neopatrimonial elites fracture over access to patronage.* By arguing for popular agency, we are not stating that elite factionalism is unimportant in African political transitions. But we side with the view that "political struggle . . . begins as the result of the emergence of a new elite that arouses a depressed and previously leaderless social group into concerted

action"[34] rather than with "a move by some group within the ruling bloc to obtain support from forces external to it."[35] At issue is whether the leadership of the reform coalition comes from inside or outside the incumbent group. We favor the latter interpretation.

At face value, one would expect elite cohesion to be particularly problematic in governing coalitions built on the quicksand of clientelism. But the dimensions of elite factionalism are distinctive in personalistic regimes.[36] The conventional distinction between hard-liners and soft-liners does not capture the essential fault line within a neopatrimonial elite.[37] Instead of fracturing ideologically over whether or not to liberalize, neopatrimonial elites are more likely to take sides on pragmatic grounds in struggles over spoils. Their political positions come to be defined according to whether they are insiders or outsiders in relation to the patronage system.

Fragmentation occurs as follows. Neopatrimonial regimes are characterized by rapid turnover of political personnel. To regulate and control rent seeking, to prevent rivals from developing their own power base, and to demonstrate their own power, rulers regularly rotate officeholders.[38] Moreover, few rulers tolerate dissent; they typically expel potential opponents from government jobs, from approved institutions like ruling parties, or even from the country itself. Even if most individuals can expect eventually to be forgiven and brought back into the fold, such practices establish a zero-sum, nonaccommodative pattern of politics. Whereas insiders enjoy preferential access to state offices and associated spoils, outsiders are left to languish in the wilderness. The more complete their exclusion from economic opportunity and political expression, the more strongly outsiders are motivated to oppose the incumbent regime. Outsiders take refuge from official institutions in civil society, the parallel economy, or international exile. From these locations, they mount a campaign against the incumbent regime that attributes economic decline to the personal failings of the supreme ruler and his coterie. These opponents grasp for control of popular protest movements, usually by promoting symbols (such as multiparty democracy) that can convert economic grievances into demands for regime change.

Meanwhile, the insiders in a patrimonial ruling coalition are unlikely to promote political reform. Stultified by years of obeisance to the official party line, they have exhausted their own capacity for innovation. Recruited and sustained with material inducements, lacking an independent political base, and thoroughly compromised by corruption, they are dependent on the survival of the incumbent regime. Insiders typically have risen through the ranks of political service and, apart from top leaders who may have invested in private capital holdings, derive their livelihood from state or party offices. Because they face the prospect of losing all visible means of support in a political transition, they have little option but to cling to the regime and to sink or swim with it.

Even if the state elite does begin to fragment over the pace of political reform, such splits are governed more by considerations of self-interest than of ideology. As patronage resources dwindle, incumbent leaders try to tighten their grip on revenues (especially export returns and foreign aid) in order to reward the loyalty of remaining insiders and to attempt to buy back the outsiders.[39] At some point during the transition, waverers may calculate that their access to rents and prebends is best served by crossing over to the opposition.

Thus, the operations of neopatrimonialism tend to create simultaneously a defensively cohesive state elite and a potential pool of alternative leaders outside of the state. The neopatrimonial practice of expelling rather than accommodating dissenters is a primary cause of the emergence of organized opposition. For this reason we stress the cleavage between insiders and outsiders rather than the divide within the ruling clique between hard-liners and soft-liners. Given the weakness of civic associations and the repression of opposition organizations, it is striking how commonly opposition in Africa today is led by former insiders who have fallen out of official favor.

3. *Elite political pacts are unlikely in neopatrimonial regimes.* Pacts are "more or less enduring compromises . . . (in which) no social or political group is sufficiently dominant to impose its ideal project, and what typically emerges is a second-best solution."[40] They figure prominently in the literature because of their role in the transitions of countries like Spain,[41] Brazil,[42] and Venezuela.[43]

Some conditions conducive to pact making, such as the inability of any single political actor to impose a preferred outcome, are present in the late stages of neopatrimonial rule. But other conditions are absent. First, incumbent and opposition leaders are usually so polarized as a result of winner-take-all power struggles that there is slim possibility that moderate factions from either side can negotiate an agreement. Instead, transitions unfold along a path of escalating confrontations until one side or other loses decisively. To the extent that transitions occur without setting a precedent for compromise, the chances are reduced that any resultant democratic regime can be sustained and consolidated.

In addition, the likelihood of pacts is a function of the degree of formal political institutionalization in a regime. In corporatist regimes the parties to a political pact are the acknowledged leaders of major interest blocs within state and society; by carrying their supporters along, they can make agreements stick. In neopatrimonial regimes political leaders may represent no more than a tiny coterie of clients and may be unable to build a political consensus around any intraelite agreement. The emerging political parties and civic organizations typically lack traditions, experience, and funds, and find it difficult to escape factionalism.[44] As a result, contending opposition leaders within a pluralistic social movement do not usually have the authenticity and legitimacy to strike a deal on behalf of all dissident factions. Pacts are only likely where well-developed institutions—for example, the military on the government side or political parties on the opposition side—present cohesive bargaining positions and demonstrate credible political clout. In other words, pacts tend to form after leaders build institutions that replace the shifting alliances of convenience that characterize neopatrimonial regimes.

Under neopatrimonialism, the prospect of political compromise depends more on the personality, management skills, and governing institutions of the incumbent ruler. A leader who has attempted to legitimate a personalistic regime with populistic rhetoric—for example, of "peoples'" democracy or "African" socialism—is more likely to respond positively to demands for political liberalization than is a leader who has ruled on the basis of claims of traditional paternalism or revolutionary purity. A leader who has allowed political rivals to live freely within the country is more likely to strike a deal on the rules of transition than is a leader who has systematically eliminated opponents. But we contend that neopatrimonial practice reduces the possibility of the "grand" compromise of power sharing. Rather, a common condition of political transition is that the strongman and his entourage have to go.

4. *In neopatrimonial regimes, political transitions are struggles to establish legal rules.* As struggles over the rules of the political game, political transitions determine the future constellation of winners and losers in the socioeconomic realm. Here, too, regime type shapes the status of rules and the nature of rule-making conflicts. Corporatist regimes elsewhere in the world may have been installed by extraconstitutional means and may have suspended constitutional rights. But to the extent that corporatist rule is bureaucratic, it is rule governed and elites and masses are acculturated to an orderly rule of law.

But because personalistic leaders enjoy sweeping discretion in making public decisions, political transitions in neopatrimonial regimes are concerned fundamentally with whether rules even matter.[45] The opposition leadership, which commonly includes lawyers within its ranks,[46] calls for a rule of law. Indeed, the law, in its different national and international manifestations, is one of the more potent weapons the opposition has at its disposal. In an effort to establish the primacy of legal rules, it challenges the regime to lift emergency regulations, allow registration of opposition parties, hold a sovereign national conference, limit the constitutional powers of the executive, or hold competitive elections. At some moment in the struggle, the contents of the constitution and the electoral laws become key points of contention. In other words, the opposition attempts to reintroduce rule-governed behavior after a prolonged period in which such niceties have been suspended.

Part of the opposition's objective in establishing legal rules is to gain access to resources monopolized by the ruling clique. In the context of a democratic transition, the opposition is most immediately interested in the regime's control of the media and other electoral campaign assets. In the longer run, business interests in the opposition may be keen to alter the rules of government intervention in the economy permanently. At this point, internal conflicts may emerge within the opposition over the extent of regime transition, with old-guard politicians seeking to limit rule changes and thereby ensure that they can benefit from state patronage once they capture state power. Thus, the struggle over political rules is often a pretext or a prelude to even more fundamental economic struggles that are laid bare in efforts to strip neopatrimonial rulers of their power.

5. *During transitions from neopatrimonial regimes, middle-class elements align with the opposition.* Struggles over the status of property rights reveal the deeper structure of a regime's social base. The relationship between state and capital in Latin America and Southern Europe is very different from that in African countries. Corporatist regimes promote accumulation through "triple alliances" with foreign and national private capital, and they draw domestic political support from the expanding entrepreneurial middle classes.[47] This structure of political support has maintained or deepened great inequalities of wealth and income, which in turn limit the options for transition. Under capitalism, democracies can be installed gradually only if the distribution of assets is not to be disrupted; if they occur by a popular upsurge, a rapid transition, and the introduction of redistributive policies, right-wing forces may be prompted to intervene to reverse the transition. Some analysts argue that in order to achieve a stable democracy, the Right must do well in a founding election and the Left must accept the inviolability of the bourgeoisie's property rights.[48]

Because neopatrimonial regimes are embedded in precapitalist societies, one would expect a different transition scenario in Africa. The pervasiveness of clientelism means that the state has actively undermined capitalist forms of accumulation. Property rights are imperfectly respected and there are powerful disincentives against private entrepreneurship and long-term productive investments. Unlike in Latin America, governing alliances between military rulers and national bourgeoisies are uncommon. Instead, the weak national bourgeoisies of Africa are frustrated by state ownership, overregulation, and official corruption. Rather than regarding the incumbent regime as the protector of property rights, private capital opposes the use of the state machinery by a bureaucratic bourgeoisie to appropriate property for itself. Thus, instead of demanding that property rights be ruled out of bounds, would-be capitalists want to use a transition from neopatrimonialism as an opportunity to include them in the new rules of the political game.

This explains the tendency of emergent middle classes in Africa to side with the democratic opposition rather than to uphold the incumbent government. Businessmen and professionals often take on political leadership roles in the opposition, drawing in other middle-class groups, like public servants, whose downward economic mobility is a powerful impetus to forge an alternative ruling coalition. These elements are unlikely to pose a threat to the acceptance of a new government established by a founding election, not only because any new government is likely to be more economically liberal than its predecessor but also because bourgeois elements are unlikely to turn to military officers in a quest to reverse democratization. In transitions from neopatrimonial rule, the threat of backlash comes mainly from the military acting alone, with the emergent middle classes being the strongest and most articulate advocates of civilian politics.

Variations in Neopatrimonial Transitions in Africa

The unifying theme of this paper is the concept of neopatrimonial rule. So far, we have defined the concept and explored its general implications for the dynamics of political transitions. Yet the variety of transition trajectories—occasionally democratic but more commonly blocked or flawed—that unfolded in Africa between 1989 and 1993 demands further explanation. Hence, recognizing that not all African leaders govern in identical ways, we now explore variations on the theme of neopatrimonial rule. Meaningful variants exist within the general type of African regime. These differences are due in part to the proclivities of individual leaders but, more importantly, to institutional structures that have evolved historically in response to political crises and needs.

First, regime variation can be traced to the political dynamics of the immediate postindependence years.[49] The circumstances in which different leaders consolidated power partly determines the degree of pluralism that came to characterize the existing regime. When a dominant party emerged early during the period of competitive party politics at independence, that party was typically able to integrate, co-opt, or eliminate other political parties and to install stable civilian single-party rule, at least until the first leader retired.[50] In the absence of a dominant party, ensuing regimes have been characterized by instability and a greater reliance on coercion, notably through military intervention.[51]

Partly overlapping this first set of factors, distinct variants of neopatrimonial regimes emerged as a result of specific historical attempts to overcome tensions created by ethnic, linguistic, and regional heterogeneity. Very few regimes in Africa adopted a discourse of exclusivity;[52] the preference instead was to expend resources to promote cultural assimilation and a sense of nationhood.[53] Some leaders extended material inducements and social concessions to promote stability through various kinds of intraelite accommodation, arrangements that have resulted in relatively high levels of elite participation.[54] Governments have agreed to ethnic, communal, or regional quotas for official positions and rent-seeking opportunities, and traditional chiefs have been allowed to retain at least limited authority over their domains. Other regimes have pursued approaches that rely more extensively on a mixture of ideology, coercion, and strong limits to pluralism to maintain national unity and political stability. This has often been the case for radical military regimes, such as Ethiopia under Mengistu or Burkina Faso under Sankara, where state leaders have sought to rely less on material inducements or to place strict limits on beneficiaries.[55]

Various typologies of African regimes have been advanced in the recent literature to capture such institutional differences.[56] Following Dahl's classic formulation,[57] we find it is useful to distinguish the neopatrimonial regimes in sub-Saharan Africa according to two distinct dimensions: the extent of competition (or contestation) and the degree of political participation (or inclusion).

First, African regimes have varied in the extent to which members of the political system are allowed to compete over elected positions or public policy. Even when state elites have worked to eliminate, control, or co-opt opposition parties, they have sometimes tolerated pluralism within the single party or lobbying activities of nonstate associations. At one extreme, opposition parties have formed and even been allowed into the legislature in a small number of countries. At the other extreme, some regimes have banned any contestation of the policies formulated by an inner group of politicians. In between, islands of contestation have been tolerated, either independently of the state or formally under the authority of the ruling party.

Second, African regimes have varied in the degree of political participation allowed, most obviously, through the timing and frequency of legislative and executive elections. Postcolonial African regimes that have held elections have rarely limited the franchise. In contrast to the historical record in Europe or Latin America, women in Africa have generally enjoyed the same formal political rights as men. Nor have African states instituted literacy, property, or income requirements for the right to vote. Nonetheless, decision making in public affairs in African regimes is typically restricted to elites with a narrow social base. Only rarely is the population at large consulted in policy-making, and then through a single party or approved membership associations such as farmer cooperatives or trade unions.

Competition and participation may vary independently of each other. We use these two dimensions to construct a schema of political regimes in Africa. The axes of the figure depict the extent to which a regime is competitive (along a scale from authoritarianism to democracy) and participatory (along a scale from exclusiveness to inclusiveness). By using the Dahlian dimensions, we endeavor to ensure consistency with existing theoretical literature and comparability across world regions. At the four corners of the table lie four ideal regime categories, for which we adopt Remmer's conceptual terminology: exclusionary authoritarianism, inclusionary authoritarianism, exclusionary democracy, and inclusionary democracy.[58]

Actual regimes occupy real-world locations within the space bounded by the idealized extremes. The specific coordinates of actual regimes derive from the extent to which they are more or less competitive and participatory. While transition from exclusionary authoritarianism involves changes along both dimensions, democratization is essentially a process of securing increased opportunities for political competition. Hence we draw finer distinctions along this dimension. We thus derive six regime variants for Africa.

Four of these regime variants are consistent with personal rule and can be regarded as varieties of neopatrimonialism: personal dictatorship, military oligarchy, and plebiscitary and competitive one-party systems.[59] They are distinguished by whether the strongman's following is broadly or narrowly mobilized (participation) and by the plurality of political association within governing institutions (competition). When the supremo "subcontracts" executive functions to subordinate barons, power is divided and decisions are made only after some degree of competition and bargaining has occurred among the powerful. But because these barons recruit clients and operate state agencies as personal fiefdoms, they tend to reproduce varieties of neopatrimonialism rather than another genus of regime. Although party and military organizations may have been built to buttress a regime, these structures have not been institutionalized to the extent that they inhibit a strong leader from taking personal control of decision making.

We wish to stress that the proposed regime variants are neither rigid nor immutable. Actual African regimes reflect their own peculiar histories, which even during the postcolonial period may encompass shifts from one regime variant to another. In part as a result of these changes, actual regimes may display characteristics of more than one variant, with combinations of personal dictatorship with military or single-party structures being quite common. In fact, this possibility is inherent in the logic of our framework, which proposes neopatrimonial rule as a master concept that embraces a variety of subsidiary regime variants. But even if a given regime at a particular time is not a perfect exemplar of one of the variants in our model, it can usually be categorized roughly for analytic purposes.

The remaining regime variants found in Africa are settler oligarchy and multiparty polyarchy. Since they are not neopatrimonial regimes, we limit our discussion to a few comments.

Multiparty polyarchies display relatively high levels of both participation and competition and have already completed a democratic political transition.[60] A plurality of political parties contest open elections and voters enjoy guarantees of a universal franchise and equality before the law. African regimes that have sustained this type of regime for at least a decade include Botswana, Gambia, Mauritius, Senegal, and Zimbabwe. Each of these regimes could be further democratized by curtailing intimidation of opposition supporters (Zimbabwe), guaranteeing the neutrality of electoral officials (Senegal), or strengthening opposition parties to enable an electoral change of government (Gambia, Botswana). While these regimes are imperfectly democratic, personal power is significantly checked by formal-legal rules, leadership turnover, and a measure of objectivity in decision making.

Settler oligarchies approximate exclusionary democracy. This form of bureaucratic regime is found in places in Latin America and Africa where European settlers gained independent control of the state.[61] We consider the settler variable to be just as formative of the institutional structure of postcolonial politics as the culture of the colonizer. In these regimes the dominant racial group uses the instruments of law to deny political rights to ethnic majorities, usually through a restrictive franchise and emergency legislation. At the same time, however, because settlers permit a good degree of political competition within their own ranks, settler oligarchy, while exclusionary, is also competitive.[62] The classic contemporary case in Africa is, of course, South Africa, but at least half a dozen other African countries, mostly in the eastern and southern subcontinent, have a settler colonial heritage. Comments on the transition prospects of this regime type can be found in the conclusion.

We now examine in greater detail the characteristics of the four main neopatrimonial regime variants and predict the distinct dynamics of political transition in each case.

Personal Dictatorship

This regime variant is the quintessence of neopatrimonialism. It is highly exclusionary because the strongman rules by decree; institutions of participation exist in name only and cannot check the absolute powers of the chief executive. The regime disallows even a semblance of political competition, for example, by physically eliminating or indefinitely incarcerating opponents. The strongman may even preempt his own removal from office by declaring himself "president for life."

A personal dictator can emerge from either the army or a dominant political party but then consolidates power by weakening these formal political structures or by asserting total control over them.[63] He rules personally by controlling the flow of public revenues and selectively disbursing rewards to a narrow entourage of familial, ethnic, or factional clients. He takes exclusive charge of policy-making (rather than relying on technocratic planning) and implements instructions through personal emissaries (rather than formal institutions). In recent times, the archetypal personal dictators in Africa have been Idi Amin of Uganda, Bokassa of Central African Republic, and Macias Nguema of Equatorial Guinea. Of those still in power and currently confronting demands for political transition, we refer below to Mobutu Sese Seko in Zaïre and Hastings Banda of Malawi.

The personalization of power in these regimes has several implications for the dynamics of political transition. First, transitions are likely to be driven almost completely by forces outside of the state, either in domestic society or from the international arena. Personal rulers are unlikely to initiate political liberalization from above or relinquish power without a struggle; they have to be forced out.[64] Self-generated reform is problematic because the regime has no mechanism of competition or participation to bring alternative ideas to the surface. Power is so concentrated that the disposition of the regime is synonymous with the personal fate of the supreme ruler. Real political change is unlikely as long as the ruler remains, since he has made all the rules. Likewise, opportunity for regime change occurs only with the death, deposition, or flight of the strongman, which becomes the primary objective of the opposition throughout the transition.

For his part, the supreme leader tends to identify the sustainability of the regime with his own political survival and is likely to make major efforts to ride the wave of protest. This confusion between self and national interest is not unique to personal dictatorships, but it has more serious implications there, given the institutional realities of these regimes. Leaders in other regimes might believe themselves to be essential, but they are rudely reminded of the need to compromise by other institutions, for example, when the military and judiciary refuse to repress protest. Because personal dictators can deploy public revenues (however limited these may be) in support of personal survival, they can avoid accountability to the state's own institutions.[65]

The willingness of personal dictators to step down often depends on whether they fear prosecution for their egregious abuse of state powers and privileges. They tend to cling desperately to power. Even when friendly powers promise protection from extradition demands as an inducement to accept retirement, leaders with a poor human rights record and a history of state violence may hesitate to give up the protection of office. They believe the opposition's promises to prosecute them and, recalling the ignominious exile of Marcos of the Philippines or the Shah of Iran, fear they can never be safe.

As a result, the demise of personal dictators is usually protracted and painful, with incumbents tenaciously attempting to control the transition. President Mobutu of Zaïre provides perhaps the best example of this process. Although officially acceding to popular and Western pressures to democratize, he has exercised considerable guile to manipulate events and maintain effective power. He has flouted his own reforms, subverted the constitution, manipulated the electoral process, and tried to bribe, intimidate, and co-opt the opposition; he has been willing even to destroy his nation's economic and political structures.[66] Over time, the state's authority over territory and the very existence of the state as an organized body may become a fiction. The leader shrinks to little more than a local warlord who survives by controlling residual resources and retaining the loyalty of a segment of the old coercive apparatus.

Transitions in personal dictatorships are also conditioned by the weaknesses of political institutions. In the absence of institutional mechanisms for political competition, the protagonists find difficulty in reaching a compromise formula to end the regime. Because it provides few institutional channels for negotiation over rules and power sharing, personalistic rule instead gives rise to all-or-nothing power struggles. As far as participation is concerned, personal dictatorships are characterized by an absence of civic associations. Even if the crisis has generated an outpouring of social protest against the regime, there are few mass organizations capable of effectively contesting the regime. True, opposition parties, human rights organizations, and trade unions mushroom as soon as the regime's repressive capabilities weaken, but they are fragmented, impoverished, and themselves lacking traditions of participatory politics. In this context, the emergence of the church as a primary actor in the transitions reflects, as much as its own prestige and power, the scarcity of credible secular candidates to lead the opposition.[67] The absence of institutions and habits of competition and participation combine virtually to eliminate the chances that a transition from personal dictatorship will end in the consolidation of a democratic order.

Plebiscitary One-Party System

This is a more inclusionary form of authoritarian regime in which a personal ruler orchestrates political rituals of mass endorsement for himself, his officeholders, and his policies. Voters are mobilized and controlled through the mechanism of one-party "plebiscites."[68] Electoral turnout rates and affirmative votes for the president typically exceed 90 percent, results that cannot be achieved by electoral fraud alone. Between elections, the regime employs a party machine to distribute patronage to a wider array of economic and regional interests than is customary in personal dictatorships. While more inclusive, plebiscitary one-party systems are nevertheless decidedly undemocratic because they preclude genuine political competition.[69] Opposition political parties are proscribed and only one candidate from the official party appears on the ballot. As rituals of ratification, plebiscites can postpone but not eradicate a legitimacy crisis.

One-party plebiscitary systems in Africa are usually headed by first-generation leaders, whether civilian or military. If civilian, the leader is usually the "grand old man" of nationalist politics who won independence in the early 1960s; if military, he commonly came to power in the first round of coups in the late 1960s or early 1970s. This latter group of leaders typically tries to civilianize and legitimize the regime by abandoning military rank and uniform and attempting to construct mass mobilizing political parties. Examples include Presidents Eyadema in Togo and Bongo in Gabon.

In these regimes, national conferences are the distinctive institution and watershed event of the transition. Patterned on both traditional village assemblies and the Estates General of the French Revolution, national conferences bring together national elites to address the country's political problems and attempt to formulate new constitutional rules. National conferences have been held in over half a dozen West and Central African states, resulting in governmental changes in Benin, Congo, and Niger, and the exertion of intense political pressure on incumbent rulers in Zaïre and Togo.[70]

We argue that the characteristics of the plebiscitary one-party regime make the national conference appealing to both opposition and ruling elite. These regimes have a tradition of participation, notably within the single party, but much less real effective political competition. The regime has sustained a modicum of legitimacy through ritualistic plebiscitary elections that, while seriously flawed as democratic instruments, nonetheless provide the citizenry with a limited political voice.[71] The regime is attached to these rituals, which it considers politically useful. When the crisis of legitimacy erupts, it is predisposed to holding a national conference—an institution that harks back to familiar forms of direct democracy but poses little real threat to the regime. Such a forum will allow the regime to make minimal concessions, let off steam, and perhaps even end up with a show of support. Rulers believe that they can turn such events to their advantage, just as they have always done.[72]

But the plebiscitary tradition has created enough political space for the emergence of a nascent opposition, to whom the national conference also appeals for several different reasons. First, the existing rules of the political game provide considerable built-in advantages to the regime, and the opposition quickly understands that reform of those rules is a prerequisite for political change. The opposition conceives of the national conference as an impartial public forum in which to refashion more advantageous ground rules that for the first time will include provisions for genuine political competition. Second, participatory structures are strong enough that the regime is incapable of completely disregarding or repressing calls for a national conference. Unlike more competitive systems, however, they are too weak for the transition to advance without a forum such as the national conference; the opposition is too divided and inexperienced to contest elections successfully, particularly if they are carried out by the administration under the current rules. The opposition is typically composed of several dozen parties, few of which have a national appeal or program; furthermore, they are poorly organized outside of a few urban areas. As in Ivory Coast and Gabon, when the regime organized quick elections, opposition leaders know they are likely to lose an electoral contest in which the regime holds all the cards. The national conference appeals to the opposition for strategic reasons, therefore, because it is perceived as a forum that will less expose its weaknesses.

Leaders and oppositions thus proceed toward a national conference with very different expectations. The former see it as a harmless participatory ritual that will provide the regime with a much needed boost, whereas the latter see it as the first step in a democratic takeover. Such a misunderstanding cannot last long, and the critical point comes when the national conference demands full sovereign power. The regime resists, recognizing that real political competition would pose grave dangers to its hold on power. The ultimate outcome, which for these transitions is hard to predict, then depends on the relative strengths of the parties: strong leaders like Biya or Eyadema were able to avoid the conference or limit its impact; more desperate leaders like Kérékou and Sassou-Nguesso gave in, convincing themselves it had become the best alternative.

Although the national conference is a logical extension of the institutional configuration of plebiscitary regimes, it is important to note that contingent forces do influence whether or not they occur. In particular, specific leaders have learned from the transition experiences in neighboring countries. Initially, leaders in Benin and Congo quickly agreed to national conferences in the belief that their regime would survive largely unscathed. In each case, however, the conference turned into a devastating public inquisition into patrimonial malfeasance and incompetence: it ultimately stripped the leaders of executive powers. Other leaders learned the lesson that there was little to be gained from agreeing to a conference, and they have steadfastly resisted opposition demands. Plebiscitary forms continue to appeal to these leaders, but they now seek them elsewhere, for example, in organized mass marches on behalf of the regime.

Military Oligarchy

Military oligarchies are exclusionary regimes in the sense that elections (even mock elections) are suspended and all decisions are made by a narrow elite behind closed doors. Although there is a visible personal leader, power is not concentrated exclusively in his hands. Rather, decisions are made collectively by a junta, committee, or cabinet that may include civilian advisers and technocrats in addition to military officers. There is a degree of debate within the elite, and objective criteria may be brought to bear in assessing policy options. A relatively professional civil or military hierarchy implements policy, and executive institutions are maintained in at least a token state.[73]

Military oligarchies in Africa tend to be led by a younger generation of junior military officers that came to power in a second, third, or later round of coups during the late 1970s and the 1980s. Political participation is severely circumscribed because there are no elections of any kind, especially in the early years of military rule. Existing political parties and many civic associations are banned, although in self-professed radical regimes such as Ethiopia or Congo, the military has usually established "people's committees" or a vanguard party to disseminate its message.[74] Even when military oligarchs espouse a populist ideology, however, their methods of rule do not include genuine participation, at least not until these leaders begin to make good on promises to return to civilian rule— as Huntington noted, most militaries harbor a deep distrust of politics.[75] Yet, even when they would like to, military elites lack the organizational capability to develop grassroots support.[76] This variant of neopatrimonial regime is exemplified by the governments of Jerry Rawlings in Ghana and Ibrahim Babangida in Nigeria.

Managed transitions from above are most likely in a military oligarchy. Because leaders come to power by force and govern with force, these regimes commonly encounter a crisis of legitimacy, which also results from their inability to deliver the economic growth they had promised during the takeover, the population's democratic aspirations, and the military's own promises of an eventual return to civilian rule. Yet the eventuality of a political transition is inherent to the logic of most military regimes: military oligarchs can respond to the crisis by renewing promises of a managed transition and agreeing to a more precise and perhaps shorter timetable. Thus, in Guinea and Ghana popular discontent in 1990 and 1991 compelled the regimes to speed up a managed transition that had been allowed to lapse. Military regimes as varied as Burundi, CAR, Guinea, Ghana, Lesotho, Nigeria, and Uganda have all been undergoing managed transitions since 1991. On the other hand, the annulment of the May 1993 Nigerian elections by General Babangida indicates dramatically that many of these promises to hand back power may be less than genuine.[77] And the reactionary coups that followed elections in both Nigeria and Burundi emphasize that military forces are loath to abdicate power and may easily reverse democratic gains.

The degree of military penetration of polity and society is a key regime variable in determining the prospects for regime transition. Where the military is not immersed in governmental affairs, it can easily adopt a hands-off attitude; but where it has led or participated in the governing coalition, it necessarily plays a more directive role. The latter is true of the regimes we classify as military oligarchies, in which small networks of military men dominate decision making with a shallow stratum of senior civil servants, and participatory politics is severely limited. In contrast to Latin America, however, African military rulers are more reticent about handing power back to civilians, and they initiate managed transitions either without great sincerity or in response to popular protest and pressures.[78] In this sense, among others, transitions from military oligarchies remain typical of the general neopatrimonial pattern.[79]

A managed transition appeals to the military for several reasons. First, it flatters the military's idealized view of itself as a rational, orderly, and organized force trying to impose order on a discordant civilian political process. For military oligarchs, the biggest challenge is the gradual introduction of political participation. The efforts of Babangida and Rawlings to engineer the transition process, specifying rules about the formation of voluntary associations, political parties, and phasing in elections, are revealing in this respect. Second, the military's near monopoly on the means of coercion significantly enhances its control over the dynamics and outcomes of the transition. Maintaining popular support and legitimacy during the transition is less crucial for military governments, which can resort to force and repression more systematically than can civilian regimes.[80]

Moreover, because military oligarchs have repressed participatory politics, the transition unfolds with little or no organized opposition powerful enough to contest the regime's timetable. Military oligarchies have, for example, typically imposed a ban on party activity. In more pluralistic systems, political leaders may want to manage the transition unilaterally, but their plans are overturned by civic organizations strong enough to push their disagreements with the regime. In military oligarchies, by contrast, these organizations are weak and have no choice but to accept the government's plans. Moreover, whatever defects the managed transition may have, it does have the advantage of reducing uncertainty and imposing on the state a kind of accountability that weak social actors may find advantageous.[81] For its part, the regime finds the reduction in political uncertainty appealing; it can promote political compromises that bring outsiders back in, protect the position of the military as an institution, limit the possibilities of getting punished for its role in various abuses of power, and slow down or halt the transition if it begins to evolve in an unfavorable direction.[82]

Competitive One-Party System

This variant of the one-party system is as inclusive as the plebiscitary variant but also (as the label suggests) somewhat more competitive. This regime is distinguished from the military oligarchy by the locus of limited competition at the mass level. Elections in these systems allow for two or more candidates in party primaries or parliamentary elections. Voters possess a restricted electoral choice among candidates from a single official party with an established policy platform. They seem sufficiently attracted by the available choices to sustain turnout figures at relatively high, though declining, levels.[83] Such regimes have also been relatively stable, resisting military intervention.

As an aspect of institutional longevity, competitive one-party regimes are often headed by nationalist founding fathers like Kaunda of Zambia and Houphouët-Boigny of Ivory Coast.[84] In some cases, the original ruler has previously engineered a smooth but nondemocratic leadership transition to a hand-picked successor (such as Moi of Kenya or Mwinyi in Tanzania). In these regimes, long-serving leaders have consolidated and institutionalized support in ruling parties and are, or consider themselves, politically secure.[85] They tolerate a degree of pluralism, which allows for significant opposition to the government on the fringes of the single party, in the press, and in various civic associations, which are strong by African standards.

These regimes are vulnerable to collapse when economic crisis and donor-mandated economic policy reform programs cut the resources available to the ruler for managing the political game. The rotation of the political personnel becomes more frenzied, with the ranks of outsiders swelling and security declining for insiders. This paves the way for discontent and recriminations. The political transition is sparked by an upsurge of popular sentiment against the regime, which then causes stress in the elite coalition. The first casualty of political crisis tends to be the sustainability of the integrative formulas that cemented national unity and ensured political stability. The pluralistic mechanisms that promoted elite accommodation and compromise now hasten the transition and at the same time channel it.

Although the rules of the political game favor the regime, the opposition is confident enough to move directly to an election without first convening a national conference. They calculate that there are adequate opportunities to win a multiparty election under existing institutional arrangements. They demand only minor adjustments to the rules of participation and competition to ensure that elections are free and fair.[86]

Incumbents respond according to whether they are first- or second-generation leaders. Old-guard nationalists like Houphouët or Kaunda calculate on the basis of their past electoral record that they still enjoy personal political legitimacy and that their parties have the organizational strength to win a competitive election. As a result, they are willing to accept the opposition's call for elections.[87] That regular elections are held distinguishes these regimes from others in Africa. Rulers see them as a mechanism for retaining power, confident not only that they retain substantial support within the population but also that official control over the press and the electoral machinery, plus the availability of public funds to finance the ruling party, will ensure a comfortable electoral victory.

The situation is more troubling for second-generation civilian leaders who lack the historical legitimacy of their predecessors. Without a well-established personal political base, they are less willing to risk multiparty elections; instead, they prevaricate and delay. Mwinyi has stretched out the transition in Tanzania for more than half a decade. When, by 1992, Moi could no longer avoid elections, he tried to restrict debate about political reform, amended the electoral code to his own advantage, and pumped up the national money supply for a massive vote-buying campaign.[88] The likelihood of ethnic tensions increases sharply in these regimes if the transition does not proceed smoothly. Leaders who lack confidence about their popular base may attempt to develop one through ethnic demagoguery once the old integrative formulas no longer appear capable of assuring political stability.

Despite these very real obstacles, the prospects for a democratic process are greater for transitions from competitive one-party regimes than from other forms of neopatrimonial regime. The reason lies in the structure of political institutions in which competitive one-party elections laid a foundation for both political participation and contestation. While incumbent and opposition forces in a transition distrust each other deeply and squabble over constitutional and electoral regulations until the eleventh hour, they also are in sufficient agreement on the rules of the political game to allow an election to take place, with each side betting it has a chance to win. Even if the losers of a transition election complain about malfeasance, they will often eventually and reluctantly accept its results and begin to organize to win the next one.[89]

Conclusions and Implications

In this essay, we have argued against the prevalent view that political transitions are driven contingently and unpredictably by the initiatives and responses of key actors. We have also contended that a search for democratic prerequisites that focuses on deep structures of economic and social modernity overlooks important proximate political influences. Instead, we think that the institutional characteristics of the preexisting political regime impart structure to the dynamics, and to a lesser extent the outcomes, of political transitions. Regime type provides the context in which contingent factors play themselves out. If this claim is true for the weakly institutionalized neopatrimonial regimes in Africa, then it challenges political scientists to reveal the structures underlying regime transitions from more bureaucratized forms of authoritarianism in other world regions.

Our main point is that political transitions from neopatrimonial rule display distinctive features. These intervals of dramatic political change are likely to be driven from below rather than initiated by elites; they tend to be marked by factional struggles over patronage rather than by divisions of political ideology; and they are usually backed rather than resisted by emerging middle classes. Evidence for these arguments is found in the dynamics of current transitions in sub-Saharan Africa, in which the relations between state and society are shaped by personal authority, the absence of stable property rights and opportunities for capitalist accumulation, and the weakness of civic associations and political organizations. These characteristics impinge decisively on the way that political transitions unfold. Even if transitions are characterized by considerable uncertainty and some serendipity, the outcome of political struggles hinges on the way that power had been exercised by personalistic rulers.

When subjecting Africa to comparative analysis, we have tried to avoid reducing a complex continent to a single, undifferentiated category. Instead, we draw attention to variants of political regime. In the second half of this essay we have compared African neopatrimonial regimes, based on regime dimensions with proved analytic utility, and related the comparison to the continent's recent history of political turmoil. On the basis of this schema, we argue that the dynamics of political transition and the likelihood of a peaceful transition to democracy are shaped by the amount of formal political participation and competition allowed by the ancien régime.

We contend that our approach has greatest utility for analyzing transition dynamics, that is, the way political transitions unfold, rather than how they turn out. Within Africa we perceive several distinctive tendencies. Typically, transitions from personal dictatorships are driven by spontaneous street protests, focus on the fate of the ruler, and, in the absence of effective political institutions to channel political participation and contestation, tend to dissolve into chaotic conflict. Military oligarchs aim at more orderly dynamics. They seek to regulate and graduate the pace at which civilian political participation is reintroduced. To this end, they initiate and attempt to manage the process of political reform, albeit sometimes without any real intention of forfeiting power. By contrast, transitions from plebiscitary one-party regimes hinge on the issue of political competition and tend to come to a head when a national conference asserts rules that challenge the long-standing political monopolies enjoyed by incumbents. Finally, in transitions from competitive one-party regimes, the dynamics of political struggle center on whether elections, to which all parties ultimately agree, are free and fair.

Do any of these processes lead to democracy? Because political transitions in Africa are ongoing at the time of writing, we insist that it is too early to make definitive judgments. But there are beginning to emerge a few tentative trends that can serve as hypotheses for further research.

First, a consolidated democracy is much less likely to eventuate from the abrupt collapse of a personal dictatorship than from the gradual reform of a competitive one-party system. For these regime variants, levels of participation and competition are mutually reinforcing: participation and competition exist at at least moderate levels for the competitive one-party systems, yet both are extremely low for the personal dictatorships. Thus the constellation of institutional attributes (or lack of attributes) is particularly clear for these regimes, and it is somewhat easier to predict transition trajectories. Democracy is possible only in the presence of a set of political institutions that allows protagonists to propose, negotiate, and win popular acceptance for political accommodations; even then, it is never guaranteed.

Second, the messy outcomes of transitions from military oligarchies and plebiscitary regimes currently defy prediction. Transitions from these regimes invariably end imperfectly, incompletely, or ambiguously. These transitions are racked by cross-pressures deriving from a mixed institutional heritage, which promotes either limited competition without participation (military oligarchies) or symbolic participation without competition (plebiscitary systems). In military regimes the efforts of soldiers to manage participation are likely to foster artificial political institutions that lack genuine popular legitimacy. In plebiscitary regimes incumbents and opposition disagree so fundamentally about whether the rules of the game should allow political competition that repression, stalemate, or open conflict are likely to result. Although our model allows us to note tendencies in transition dynamics in these cases (that is, by a managed handover to civilians or a confrontational national conference), we cannot presently foresee outcomes.

Third, we note the particularly vexatious nature of transitions from dictatorial and plebiscitary regimes, both of which generate unregulated political conflict. This is because in both regime variants, political contestation is outlawed rather than channeled through political institutions. This suggests the general proposition that political competition is essential for a transition to democracy. While personalistic rulers may sometimes promote inclusive coalitions of support or rituals of mass participation, they cannot tolerate independent centers of political opinion and power. They would rather permit open political conflict and the decay of political institutions than share or abdicate power. Thus, getting to democracy is easier from a regime where competition is tolerated and where the main challenge is to broaden political participation; getting to democracy is much more difficult from a regime that has no tradition of political competition, however inclusive and participatory it may be.

Finally, if our logic is correct, the prospects for democracy are better in transitions from regime types other than neopatrimonial ones. This is so because greater progress has been made in other regimes in routinizing participation and (especially) competition in formal political institutions. We do not know enough about political transitions outside Africa to assess the effects of various bureaucratic authoritarian regime structures there. But our model suggests, perhaps counterintuitively, that within Africa the prospects for democracy are better in transitions from settler oligarchies than from all variants of neopatrimonial regime. Recall that settler regimes established traditions of pluralistic politics, competitive elections, and loyal opposition but that their fatal flaw was the restriction of political participation to a racial elite. Transition in these regimes is less a struggle over the right of political actors to hold diverse political beliefs than over the extension of the franchise to previously excluded sections of the population. In South Africa—in contrast to the neopatrimonial pattern outlined here, and following other bureaucratic authoritarian regimes in Latin America and Southern Europe—political transition is occurring by pact between the moderate leaders of corporate factions in the government and opposition. One might even assert that settler oligarchies stand a better chance than most other African regimes of consolidating democratic institutions. There is already evidence that former settler colonies tend to become somewhat more democratic regimes than do nonsettler colonies: for example, Zimbabwe and Namibia became multiparty competitive polyarchies after independence; and Zambia and Kenya adopted competitive, rather than plebiscitary, forms of one-party rule. These observations suggest that although political transition in

South Africa may be protracted and punctuated by violence, it may well ultimately occur by negotiation. And the long-term prospects for democratic consolidation may be better there than in other parts of contemporary Africa.[90]

One might object that an argument linking the institutional makeup of the ancien régime to the process of transition is trivial or circular. Are we simply suggesting that the more pluralistic the regime the likelier the transition will produce a pluralist democracy, surely not a very interesting theoretical claim? In fact, our argument links institutional characteristics only tangentially to the outcomes of transitions but directly to their internal dynamics, so this criticism is at best only partly on the mark. The criticism is nonetheless worth addressing in order to bring out the implications and limits of the thesis.

That history moves in incremental steps is not an earth-shattering proposition, although the current emphasis in the transitions literature on individual agency perhaps makes it a useful one. Indeed, we have tried to show that the prospects for democracy in African regimes depend on prior traditions of political pluralism. It is theoretically useful to investigate the reasons for this correlation. Bermeo has emphasized the importance of learning in the process of democratization in which changing attitudes and norms lead actors to accept new modes of political behavior.[91] Our argument suggests that organizations both within and outside the state, and the interaction between them, provide critical arenas for this learning. It will be difficult, that is, to institute new rules of accountability, tolerance, and participation if political parties or trade unions are missing or underdeveloped and if judicial and legislative bodies have no tradition of independence from the executive.

This article also stresses the formal status of institutions. For example, if civil society is weakly and informally organized, the incumbent government will probably be able to ride out any pro-democracy protests. Opportunities may exist for the fall of the regime, but in the absence of formal organizations to engineer the transition, the regime may well survive. Chazan and others have argued forcefully that, as African states repressed formal participatory structures, people shifted their efforts into informal organizations, which flourished.[92] These structures—such as market women's associations, ethnic associations, and credit clubs—have directly improved peoples' welfare and by sapping the government's legitimacy may even have laid the groundwork for political liberalization. But, in the final analysis, only formal institutions—such as trade unions, human rights organizations, and, especially, political parties—can force recalcitrant governments into amending constitutions and calling elections, and appear to populations as plausible alternatives to the government in power.

Last, we emphasize that the relationship between regime type and transition is not mechanistic. Especially in relation to political outcomes, the structure of the preceding regime provides only a template that predisposes, but does not fully determine, particular results. The remainder of the explanation of political change must be derived from other factors. We consider that the effectiveness of contending state and societal organizations at achieving preferred outcomes is largely a function of the political and economic resources at their disposal during the transition. Within every regime there is a wide band of potential differences in the levels of these resources. For example, the strength of state organizations depends on the ability of leaders to maintain a flow of discretionary spoils and to sustain prebendal networks of support. Within the opposition, the strength of unions and parties depends on achieving a significant funding and membership base independent of the state and an organizational network that extends outside of the capital and into the countryside. It is these differences in resources that explain the dissimilar outcomes in, say, Benin and Togo. The tremendous fiscal crisis of Benin forced Kérékou to compromise, whereas Eyadema's intransigence has been buttressed by his continued access to international and domestic resources.[93] Unfortunately, there is currently little systematic information on the resource attributes of state and opposition organizations in Africa, and this remains a priority for future research.

Notes

1. Of the 18 presidential elections held in Africa between 1990 and March 1993, 9 were vouchsafed as "free and fair" by international observers, and 8 resulted in the peaceful replacement of the incumbent ruler. In all cases where the incumbent survived, the opposition charged electoral fraud. See Michael Bratton, "Political Liberalization in Africa in the 1990s: Advances and Setbacks" (Paper presented at a donors conference on Economic Reform in Africa's New Era of Political Liberalization, Carnegie Endowment for International Peace, Washington, D.C., April 14–15, 1993).

2. Remmer, "Exclusionary Democracy," *Studies in Comparative International Development* 20, no. 4 (1986), 64–68.

3. Ibid., 77–78.

4. Samuel Huntington, *The Third Wave: Democratization in the Late Twentieth Century* (Norman: University of Oklahoma Press, 1991). Huntington classifies transitions into three main types: transformation, replacement, and transplacement. These labels are unnecessarily jargonistic; we prefer to speak of three routes—top-down, bottom-up, and negotiated political change—distinguished according to whether state elites, opposition forces, or both take the lead in pressing transition forward. On this theme, see Dankwart A. Rustow, "The Surging Tide of Democracy," *Journal of Democracy* 3, no. 1 (1992), 119–22.

5. Huntington (fn. 4), 588.

6. O'Donnell and Schmitter, *Transitions from Authoritarian Rule: Tentative Conclusions about Uncertain Democracies* (Baltimore: Johns Hopkins University Press, 1986), 3. See also Guiseppe Di Palma, *To Craft Democracies: An Essay on Democratic Transitions* (Berkeley: University of California Press, 1990).

7. Bermeo, "Rethinking Regime Change," *Comparative Politics* 22 (April 1990), 361.

8. Karl, "Dilemmas of Democratization in Latin America," *Comparative Politics* 5 (October 1990).

9. Ibid., 6; emphasis added.

10. For general theoretical discussions of this point, see Anthony Giddens, *The Constitution of Society: An Outline of the Theory of Structuration* (Cambridge, Mass.: Polity Press, 1984); and Michael Taylor, "Structure, Culture and Action in the Explanation of Social Change," *Politics and Society* 17, no. 2 (1989).

11. Bermeo (fn. 7), 366–67.

12. Karl (fn. 8), 6–7.

13. This central point is made in relation to the French Revolution by Alexis de Tocqueville, *The Old Regime and the French Revolution* (Garden City, N.Y.: Doubleday, 1955); and in a comparison of the Russian and German revolutions by Barrington Moore, *Injustice: The Social Bases of Obedience and Revolt* (New York: M. E. Sharpe, 1978), 357–75, where differences in outcomes are linked to differences in the strength of political institutions.

14. Interestingly, two recent comparative studies of regime change are based on the analysis of political institutions. Ruth Berins Collier and David Collier, *Shaping the Political Arena: Critical Junctures, the Labor Movement, and Regime Dynamics in Latin America* (Princeton: Princeton University Press, 1992); and Dietrich Rueschemeyer, Evelyne Huber Stephens, and John D. Stephens, *Capitalist Development and Democracy* (Chicago: University of Chicago Press, 1992).

15. Not all extant analyses assume corporatist institutions and ignore regime variations. See Robert M. Fishman, "Rethinking State and Regime: Southern Europe's Transition to Democracy," *World Politics* 42 (April 1990); and Terry Lynn Karl and Philippe Schmitter, "Modes of Transition in Latin America, Southern and Eastern Europe," *International Social Science Journal* 128 (May 1991). See also the interesting analyses of the role of political parties as an explanatory factor in Brazil's transition in Scott Mainwaring, "Political Parties and Democratization in Brazil and the Southern Cone," *Comparative Politics* 21 (October 1988); and idem, "Brazilian Party Underdevelopment in Comparative Perspective," *Political Science Quarterly* 107 (Winter 1992).

16. Max Weber, *Economy and Society* (New York: Bedminster Press, 1968). See also Robin Theobald, "Patrimonialism," *World Politics* 34 (July 1982).

17. Shmuel N. Eisenstadt, *Traditional Patrimonialism and Modern Neopatrimonialism* (London: Sage, 1972); Christopher Clapham, ed., *Private Patronage and Public Power* (London: Frances Pinter, 1985); and Richard Snyder, "Explaining Transitions from Neopatrimonial Dictatorships," *Comparative Politics* 24, no. 4 (1992).

18. See Richard Joseph, *Democracy and Prebendal Politics in Nigeria: The Rise and Fall of the Second Republic* (New York: Cambridge University Press, 1987), esp. chap. 5. On the recent evolution of these phenomena, see the excellent analysis in René Lemarchand, "The State, the Parallel Economy, and the Changing Structure

of Patronage Systems," in Donald Rothchild and Naomi Chazan, eds., *The Precarious Balance: State and Society in Africa* (Boulder, Colo.: Westview Press, 1988).

19. Theobald (fn. 16), 549.

20. Christopher Clapham, *Third World Politics: An Introduction* (Madison: University of Wisconsin Press, 1985), 49.

21. John Waterbury, "Endemic and Planned Corruption in a Monarchical Regime," *World Politics* 25 (July 1973); Robert H. Jackson and Carl G. Rosberg, *Personal Rule in Black Africa* (Berkeley: University of California Press, 1982); Thomas Callaghy, *The State-Society Struggle: Zaire in Comparative Perspective* (New York: Columbia University Press, 1984); Richard Sandbrook, *The Politics of African Economic Stagnation* (New York: Cambridge University Press, 1986); Joseph (fn. 18); Jean François Bayart, *L'Etat au Cameroun* (Paris: Presses de la Fondation Nationale de Sciences Politiques, 1985); and idem, *L'Etat en Afrique* (Paris: Fayard, 1989).

22. In addition to works already cited, see Enrique A. Baloyra, ed., *Comparing New Democracies: Transitions and Consolidation in Mediterranean Europe and the Southern Cone* (Boulder, Colo.: Westview Press, 1987); James M. Malloy and Mitchell A. Seligson, eds., *Authoritarians and Democrats: Regime Transitions in Latin America* (Pittsburgh, Pa.: University of Pittsburgh Press, 1987); Robert A. Pastor, ed., *Democracy in the Americas: Stopping the Pendulum* (New York: Holmes and Meier, 1989); Karen L. Remmer, "New Wine or Old Bottlenecks? The Study of Latin American Democracy," *Comparative Politics* 23 (July 1991).

23. See Sandbrook (fn. 21); and Callaghy (fn. 21).

24. Thus, Allen argues that "in failing to pay salaries [the Kérékou regime in Benin] . . . signed the death warrant it had drafted by its own gross corruption, for it led to the actions of 1989 that in turn caused the regime's collapse." See Christopher Allen, "Restructuring an Authoritarian State: Democratic Renewal in Benin," *Review of African Political Economy* 54 (July 1992), 46.

25. Adam Przeworski, "Some Problems in the Study of the Transition to Democracy," in Guillermo O'Donnell, Philippe Schmitter, and Laurence Whitehead, eds., *Transitions from Authoritarian Rule: Comparative Perspectives* (Baltimore: Johns Hopkins University Press, 1986), 51.

26. O'Donnell and Schmitter (fn. 6), 19.

27. Ibid., 17.

28. Elsewhere, O'Donnell and Schmitter (fn. 6) concede that ordinary citizens commonly take a leading role in transitions: whereas "political democracies are usually brought down by conspiracies involving a few actors . . . the democratization of authoritarian regimes . . . involves . . . a crucial component of the mobilization and organization of large numbers of individuals" (p. 18).

29. Juan Linz, "Crisis, Breakdown and Reequilibration," in Juan Linz and Alfred Stepan, eds., *The Breakdown of Democratic Regimes* (Baltimore: Johns Hopkins University Press, 1978); Samuel Huntington, "How Countries Democratize," *Political Science Quarterly* 106, no. 4 (1992); René Lemarchand, "African Transitions to Democracy: An Interim (and Mostly Pessimistic) Assessment" (Revised version of a paper presented at a seminar on Democracy and Economic Development, Oslo, February 1992).

30. Samuel Huntington finds only six cases of transitions by "replacement," that is, from below; see Huntington (fn. 29).

31. See Michael Bratton and Nicolas van de Walle, "Popular Protest and Political Reform in Africa," *Comparative Politics* 24 (July 1992). The five exceptions were Cape Verde, Guinea Bissau, Madagascar, São Tomé, and Tanzania. Of these, only Cape Verde and São Tomé have completed a protest-free full transition. See also M. Cahen, "Vent des Iles: La victoire de l'opposition aux Iles du Cap Vert et à São Tomé e Príncipe," *Politique Africaine* 43 (October 1991). In Madagascar massive protests erupted in mid-1991, when it became clear that President Ratsiraka's reforms were only window dressing. The elections of February 1993, which brought the opposition to power, were clearly the result of popular pressures. See "Madagascar: Hanging on in the Face of Change," *Africa Confidential,* September 1991, p. 7. Finally, in Tanzania and Guinea Bissau, political liberalization has fallen well short of a full transition.

32. African states with particularly acute fiscal crises were also vulnerable to donor pressures to engage in political liberalization. See Bratton and van de Walle (fn. 31) for a discussion of the relative role of domestic and international factors in recent African transitions.

33. Joel S. Migdal, *Strong Societies and Weak States* (Princeton: Princeton University Press, 1988), chap. 6.

34. Dankwart Rustow, "Transitions to Democracy: Toward a Dynamic Model," *Comparative Politics* 2 (April 1970), 352.

35. Przeworski (fn. 25), 56.

36. A large literature analyzes factional conflict within the African state elite; see, for example, Sandbrook (fn. 21); and Bayart (fn. 21).

37. In Huntington's work (fn. 29), for example, the success of democratization hinges largely on the ability of "liberal reformers" within the government to outmaneuver the standpatters.

38. As Waterbury (fn. 21) argues with respect to the monarchy in Morocco, "The king's degree of political control varies directly with the level of fragmentation and factionalization within the system. . . . The king must always maintain the initiative through the systematic inculcation of an atmosphere of unpredictability and provisionality among all elites and the maximization of their vulnerability relative to his mastery" (p. 552).

39. Nicolas van de Walle, "Neopatrimonialism and Democracy in Africa, with an Illustration from Cameroon," in Jennifer Widner, ed., *Economic Change and Political Liberalization in Sub-Saharan Africa* (Baltimore: Johns Hopkins University Press, 1994).

40. O'Donnell and Schmitter (fn. 6), 38.

41. Raymond Carr and Juan Pablo Fusi Aizpurua, *Spain: Dictatorship to Democracy* (London: Allen and Unwin, 1979).

42. Frances Hagopian, "Democracy by Undemocratic Means? Elites, Political Pacts and Regime Transition in Brazil," *Comparative Political Studies* 23, no. 2 (1990).

43. Terry Lynn Karl, *Petroleum and Political Pacts: The Transition to Democracy in Venezuela,* Latin America no. 107 (Washington, D.C.: Wilson Center, 1981).

44. Thus, by 1991, some 76 parties had been officially recognized in Cameroon, 42 in Guinea, 27 in Gabon, and allegedly over 200 in Zaïre. In these countries, as well as in the Ivory Coast, the opposition's credibility and strength has been under-

mined by internal divisions, ethnic rivalries, and personal disputes. See Yves A. Fauré, "Nouvelle donne en Côte d'Ivoire," *Politique Africaine* 20 (December 1985).

45. Confronted by a journalist on national television with evidence that the government had disregarded its own laws in the manipulation of voter lists on the eve of the legislative elections of March 1992, the Cameroonian minister of territorial administration explained that "laws are made by men, and are no more than reference points." Cited in Célestin Monga, "La recomposition du marché politique au Cameroun (1991–1992)" (Unpublished paper, GERDES, Cameroon, 1992), 10.

46. The national bar associations played leading opposition roles in Cameroon, Mali, the Central African Republic, and Togo. See Paul John Marc Tedga, *Ouverture démocratique en Afrique Noire?* (Paris: L'Harmattan, 1991), 64–72.

47. Peter Evans, *Dependent Development: The Alliance of Multinational, State and Local Capital in Brazil* (Princeton: Princeton University Press, 1979); David Collier, ed., *The New Authoritarianism in Latin America* (Princeton: Princeton University Press, 1979).

48. O'Donnell and Schmitter (fn. 6), 62, 69. For a critique of these arguments, see Daniel H. Levine, "Paradigm Lost: Dependence to Democracy," *World Politics* 40 (April 1988).

49. Ruth Berins Collier, *Regimes in Tropical Africa* (Berkeley: University of California Press, 1982).

50. Numerous studies have chronicled and analyzed this process. The locus classicus remains Aristide Zolberg, *Creating Political Order: The Party States of West Africa* (Chicago: University of Chicago Press, 1966). But see also Henry Bienen, *Tanzania: Party Transformation and Economic Development* (Princeton: Princeton University Press, 1967); and William Foltz, "Political Opposition in Single-Party States of Tropical Africa," in Robert Dahl, ed., *Regimes and Opposition* (New Haven: Yale University Press, 1973).

51. Henry Bienen, *Armies and Parties in Africa* (New York: Africana Publishing, 1979); Samuel Decalo, "The Morphology of Military Rule in Africa," in John Markakis and Michael Waller, eds., *Military Marxist Regimes in Africa* (London: Frank Cass, 1976); and idem, *Coups and Army Rule in Africa* (New Haven: Yale University Press, 1976).

52. The exceptions include South Africa, of course, but also arguably present-day Sudan and Mauritania, where Arab/Islamic regimes are increasingly excluding non-Arab/non-Muslim segments of the population.

53. See, for example, Crawford Young, *The Politics of Cultural Pluralism* (Madison: University of Wisconsin Press, 1976), esp. chap. 3.

54. Bayart (fn. 21, 1989). See also Donald Rothchild and Victor Olorunsola, eds., *State versus Ethnic Claims: African Policy Dilemmas* (Boulder, Colo.: Westview Press, 1983).

55. On Ethiopia, see Christopher Clapham, "State, Society and Political Institutions in Revolutionary Ethiopia," in James Manor, ed., *Rethinking Third World Politics* (New York: Longman, 1991). On Burkina Faso, see René Otayek, "The Revolutionary Process in Burkina Faso," in Markakis and Waller (fn. 51), 95–96.

56. For a proposal of seven regime types based loosely on seven diverse criteria, see Naomi Chazan et al., *Politics and Society in Contemporary Africa* (Boulder,

Colo.: Lynne Rienner, 1988). For competing typologies, see also Crawford Young, *Ideology and Development in Africa* (New Haven: Yale University Press, 1982); Roger Charlton, "Dehomogenizing the Study of African Politics: The Case of Interstate Influence on Regime Formation and Change," *Plural Societies* 14, no. 1–2 (1983); and Dirk Berg-Schlosser, "African Political Systems: Typology and Performance," *Comparative Political Studies* 17, no. 1 (1984).

57. Robert A. Dahl, *Polyarchy: Participation and Opposition* (New Haven: Yale University Press, 1971).

58. Remmer (fn. 2).

59. These categories and labels build on existing typologies. Ruth Collier distinguishes military, multiparty, and two types of one-party regime: plebiscitary and competitive. Huntington identifies four regime types: personal, one-party, and military regimes, plus the special category of racial oligarchy for South Africa.

60. Dahl (fn. 57) labeled regimes that had been "highly popularized and liberalized" as polyarchies rather than democracies because, he argued, no large system in the real world is fully democratized (p. 8).

61. See Michael Bratton, "Patterns of Development and Underdevelopment: Toward a Comparison," *International Studies Quarterly* 26, no. 3 (1982); and Remmer (fn. 2), 71–76.

62. Remmer (fn. 2) even holds that "it is possible for exclusion to be achieved even more effectively under competitive political arrangements than under authoritarian ones. Exclusionary democracy not only makes it possible to secure regime support from dominant social groups in a highly stratified society, it obviates the costs of coercion and problems of regime legitimacy that are associated with exclusionary authoritarianism" (p. 74).

63. Writing about Mobutu's consolidation of power, Callaghy (fn. 21) speaks of the systematic "dismantlement of inherited structures, especially departicipation and depoliticization," including the emasculation of parliament, the elimination of the position of prime minister, the banning of all parties and youth organizations, and the centralization of state power away from the provinces to Kinshasa (p. 171).

64. For a similar argument, see Snyder (fn. 17).

65. News reports in mid-1992 indicated that Zaïre's national currency, printed in Germany, was being flown directly to Mobutu's luxury yacht on the Zaïre River, for use as he saw fit (*Africa News,* May 24, 1992). Amidst a crumbling economy, in which the average civil servant had not been paid in months, Mobutu was still personally ensuring the support of key followers, including elements of the armed forces charged with protecting him. See also "Mobutu's Monetary Mutiny," *Africa Confidential,* February 5, 1993; and "Zaïre, a Country Sliding into Chaos," *Guardian Weekly,* August 8, 1993.

66. René Lemarchand, "Mobutu and the National Conference: The Arts of Political Survival" (Manuscript, University of Florida, 1992).

67. See Tedga (fn. 46).

68. Collier (fn. 49), 104–8.

69. For country examples of these practices, see Bayart (fn. 21) on the Ahidjo regime in Cameroon (pp. 141–84); and Comi M. Toulabor, *Le Togo sous Eyadema* (Paris: Karthala, 1986), on Togo.

70. See Lemarchand (fn. 29); Pearl T. Robinson, "The National Conference Phenomenon in Francophone Africa" (Paper presented at the colloquium on the Economics of Political Liberalization in Africa, Harvard University, March 6–7, 1992); and Fabien Eboussi-Boulaga, *Les conférences nationales en Afrique Noire: Une affaire à suivre* (Paris: Karthala, 1993).

71. Collier (fn. 49), 119–24. See also Aristide Zolberg, "The Structure of Political Conflict in the New States of Tropical Africa," *American Political Science Review* 62, no. 2 (1968).

72. As Allen (fn. 24) argues in relation to the national conference in Benin: "It was conceived originally by the government as a means of discussing mainly the political and economic problems of the time . . . and of co-opting the opposition into a joint solution in which the government would retain the leading role" (p. 48).

73. Bienen (fn. 51), 122–45; Decalo (fn. 51, *Coups and Army Rule in Africa*), 231–54.

74. Even then, the military has sought to limit the power and autonomy of the party, despite Leninist principles regarding the supremacy of the party over all other political institutions. See Decalo (fn. 51, "Morphology of Military Rule in Africa"), 134–35.

75. Samuel Huntington writes: "The problem is military opposition to politics. Military leaders can easily envision themselves in a guardian role; they can also picture themselves as the far seeing impartial promoters of social and economic reform in their societies. But with rare exceptions, they shrink from assuming the role of political organizer. In particular, they condemn political parties." See Huntington, *Political Order in Changing Societies* (New Haven: Yale University Press, 1968), 243.

76. Henry Bienen, "Military Rule and Political Processes: Nigerian Examples," *Comparative Politics* 10 (January 1978).

77. On these events, see "Nigerian Military Rulers Annul Election," *New York Times*, June 24, 1993; and "Nigeria: About Turn!" *Africa Confidential*, July 30, 1993.

78. Christopher Clapham and George Philip, "The Political Dilemmas of Military Regimes," in Clapham and Philip, eds., *The Political Dilemmas of Military Regimes* (London: Croom Helm, 1985).

79. For a discussion of this point, see Claude Welch, "Cincinnatus in Africa: The Possibility of Military Withdrawal from Politics," in Michael F. Lofchie, ed., *The State of the Nations: Constraints on Development in Independent Africa* (Berkeley: University of California Press, 1971).

80. Nonetheless, the military coup by junior officers that toppled the Traoré regime in Mali in March 1991 shows that there are limits to the extent to which even a military regime can rely on force to maintain its power. See Jane Turrittin, "Mali: People Topple Traoré," *Review of African Political Economy* 52 (November 1991).

81. As Lemarchand (fn. 29) argues: "Transitions from above are the more promising in terms of their ability to 'deliver' democracy in that they tend to be rather specific about the time frame, procedural steps and overall strategy of transition. Unlike what often happens with transitions from below, the net result is to reduce uncertainty" (p. 10).

82. In addition to the aborted transition in Nigeria, one might note events in Ghana, where Rawlings lifted the ban on political parties in May 1992 in preparation for pluralist elections in November, while simultaneously having the constitution rewritten to protect members of the ruling Provisional National Defense Council (PNDC) from prosecution by future governments. Rawlings won the elections of November 1992, in a contest widely perceived to have been marred by extensive fraud; see David Abdulai, "Rawlings 'Wins' Ghana's Presidential Elections," *Africa Today* 39 (Fall 1992), 66–71. In Uganda, President Museveni slowed down his country's managed transition in order to give himself time to build a new political party with a broad ethnoregional base; see *Africa Confidential*, April 17, 1992.

83. These trends can be attributed to elite efforts at demobilization of formerly active participants and the co-optation or elimination of opposition power centers. They are well covered by Nelson Kasfir, *The Shrinking Political Arena: Participation and Ethnicity in African Politics with a Case Study of Uganda* (Berkeley: University of California Press, 1976). On the characteristics of single-party elections in Africa, see the following: D. G. Lavroff, ed., *Aux urnes l'Afrique! Elections et pouvoirs en Afrique Noire* (Paris: Pedone, 1978); Naomi Chazan, "African Voters at the Polls: A Re-Examination of the Role of Elections in Africa Politics," *Journal of Commonwealth and Comparative Politics* 17 (July 1979); and Fred M. Hayward, *Elections in Independent Africa* (Boulder, Colo.: Westview Press, 1987). On competitive single-party elections in Tanzania and Kenya, see Goran Hyden and Colin Leys, "Elections and Politics in Single-Party Systems: The Case of Kenya and Tanzania," *British Journal of Political Science* 2 (April 1972); and Jankees Van Donge and Athumani Liviga, "The 1985 Tanzanian Parliamentary Elections: A Conservative Election," *African Affairs* 88 (January 1989).

84. Ivory Coast moved progressively to competitive primaries within the single party after 1980. See Tessi Bakary, "Côte d'Ivoire: Une décentralisation politique centralisé," *Géopolitique Africaine* 2 (June 1986).

85. Henry Bienen and Nicolas van de Walle, "Of Time and Power in Africa," *American Political Science Review* 83 (March 1989).

86. The 1991 transition in Zambia was "a struggle over the rules of the political game and the resources by which it is played (in which) . . . the ruling party employ(ed) all its strength to tilt the rules of political competition in its own favor." See Michael Bratton, "Zambia Starts Over," *Journal of Democracy* 3, no. 2 (1992), 82. Even so, the opposition successfully forced incumbent president Kaunda to forgo a referendum on multiparty politics and move directly to elections. They also felt confident enough to contest the October 1991 election under a less-than-perfect voter register and constitution.

87. In the case of Ivory Coast at least, this calculation proved to be sound. Thus, regarding Ivory Coast, Fauré (fn. 44) argues that the victory of the ex-single party was due to the fact that "the government, thanks to its effective and very loyal territorial administration, and to the PDCI apparatus, present all over the country down to the most isolated hamlet, controlled electoral operations throughout . . . and all official information sources" (p. 37).

88. Joel Barkan, "Kenya: Lessons from a Flawed Election," *Journal of Democracy* 4 (July 1993); Bard-Anders Andraesson, Gisela Geisler, and Arne Tostensen, *A*

Hobbled Democracy: The Kenya General Elections, 1992 (Bergen, Norway: Chr. Michelson Institute, 1993).

89. On the Ivory Coast, for example, see the sanguine assessment of the recent progress being made toward a stable pluralist system in Yves A. Fauré, "L'Economie politique d'une démocratisation: Éléments d'analyse à propos de l'experience récente de la Côte d'Ivoire," *Politique Africaine* 43 (October 1991), 46–47. And however flawed the December 1992 election in Kenya, the transition led to democratic gains. True, the opposition did not win the election, but nowhere do we claim that this is a requirement for a democratic transition. Instead, the opposition has de facto accepted the results of the election by taking its seats in parliament; see Barkan fn. 88. Moreover, there is a new plural division of power in Kenya and a functioning opposition in parliament. These are positive factors for democratic consolidation that even paradigmatic African cases of democratic transition like Zambia do not yet enjoy. On the importance of opposition for democratic consolidation, see Stephanie Lawson, "Conceptual Issues in the Comparative Study of Regime Change and Democratization," *Comparative Politics* 25, no. 2 (1993).

90. Analysts are divided regarding the prospects for democracy in South Africa. On the one hand, South Africa's lack of national homogeneity, of broad-based economic development, and of unambiguous defeat of the old order predispose the country to continued conflict. The posttransition government may also be tempted to use the formidable apparatus of repression inherited from the current government for its own ends. See Herman Giliomee and Jannie Gagiano, eds., *The Elusive Search for Peace: South Africa, Israel and Northern Ireland* (London: Oxford University Press, 1990); and Herman Giliomee, "Democratization in South Africa" (Paper presented at the congress of the American Sociological Association, Miami, Fla., August 1993). On the other hand, some commentators see "an individually-based liberal democracy" as a viable option for permanently settling conflict in the country. See Sammy Smooha and Theodor Hanf, "The Diverse Modes of Conflict-Regulation in Deeply Divided Societies," *International Journal of Comparative Sociology* 33 (January–April 1992), 41; and F. van zyl Slabbert, *The Quest for Democracy: South Africa in Transition* (Johannesburg: Penguin Forum Series, 1992). Our claim is comparative: we do not say that consolidated democracy is easy, imminent, or preordained in South Africa but only that it is more likely than in those African neopatrimonial regimes where political competition has been outlawed. For a similar argument, see Samuel Huntington, "Will More Countries Become Democratic?" *Political Science Quarterly* 99 (Summer 1984); and idem (fn. 4), 111–12.

91. Nancy Bermeo, "Democracy and the Lessons of Dictatorship," *Comparative Politics* 24, no. 3 (1992).

92. Naomi Chazan, "The New Politics of Participation in Tropical Africa," *Comparative Politics* 14 (January 1982); Jean François Bayart, Achille Mbembe, and C. Toulabor, *La Politique par le Bas en Afrique* (Paris: Karthala, 1991).

93. Marc Pilon, "La transition togolaise dans l'impasse," *Politique Africaine* 49 (March 1993), 136–40; John R. Heilbrunn, "Social Origins of National Conferences in Benin and Togo," in *Journal of Modern African Studies* 31, no. 2 (1993).

13

Democratization: Understanding the Relationship Between Regime Change and the Culture of Politics

Pearl T. Robinson

The comparative literature on regime change offers a range of plausible explanations for the democratic ferment that began spreading across Africa in 1989 (Joseph 1991; Bratton and van de Walle 1992a). Theorists of democratization in general focus on three areas of conceptual concern: structural and contingent factors that precipitate openings in authoritarian rule (Moore 1967; O'Donnell et al. 1986),[1] the relative importance of elite behavior versus mass mobilization strategies of reform (O'Donnell and Schmitter 1986; Karl 1986, 1990; Rueschemeyer et al. 1992),[2] and diffusionist explanations of change (Huntington 1991). Within these broad rubrics, regional variations come into play. While many analysts readily assert that *glasnost* in the Soviet Union and the collapse of dictatorships in Eastern Europe influenced the rise of pro-democracy movements in Africa, leading theorists of democratic transitions have downplayed the relevance of external factors and the international context to political liberalization in Latin America during the 1980s (O'Donnell and Schmitter 1986; Whitehead 1986; Lowenthal 1991).[3] What this variance suggests is that theories of regime change must be historicized and contextualized in order to incorporate local conditions and circumstances.

Historian Achille Mbembe cautions against overemphasizing the specificity of Africa (1990)—but my point is different. Indeed, inasmuch as key

Reprinted with permission from *African Studies Review* 37, no. 1 (April 1994): 39–67.

theoretical propositions derived from the Latin American, Southern and Eastern European experiences have oriented a great deal of the recent conceptual and empirical work on democratization in Africa, the cultural dynamics of transitions bear closer scrutiny. The argument to be advanced here is that the efficacy of theories of democratic transition for analyzing political processes in any region of the world is hampered by a failure to problematize the relationship between regime change and the culture of politics.

As used here, the term "culture of politics" refers to political practice that is culturally legitimated and societally validated by local knowledge.[4] Rooted in a community's habits, customs and symbols regarding power, authority, participation and representation, its mores are readily accessible to elites and ordinary people alike. Moreover (and this is a critically important point), a given culture of politics may be altered over time through a process of political learning. A culture of politics is thus the product of a polity's distant and its more proximate political past.

What I am proposing is a construct that builds on the more familiar concept of political culture but is distinguishable in several important ways. Broadly defined, political culture is "the orientation people have to the political process" (Almond and Verba 1965, 498). Modeled after holistic definitions of culture, it is made operational by aggregating individual attitudes and values towards political behavior and the polity to arrive at a snapshot of a particular society's cultural norms. Sameness, not difference, is its analytical focus. By contrast, the notion of a culture of politics assumes a sense of mutuality that is far less hegemonic. De-centered, historicized and contextualized, it accommodates contested meanings, acknowledges asymmetrical power relations, and encompasses marginal as well as modal political practices (O'Hanlon 1988; Said 1986). Many of the leading analysts of political culture place a premium on emulating the scientific method with survey research techniques, insights from psychology, and a commitment to developing reliable measures for prediction. Indeed, methodological refinements of this sort have been extraordinarily consequential for advancing the *science* of politics. But when explication, not prediction, is the goal, "blurred genres" that capture a broad range of contextual variables are more suited to explaining the complex interactions of politics and culture (Geertz 1979–80).

In this regard, it is important to recall that a political regime is not a value neutral environment. Regimes are the formal rules that link the main political institutions of the state. They define the political nature of the ties between citizens and rulers (Cardoso 1979) and over time shape the social construction of values. It is therefore reasonable to expect some degree of correlation between the ideational configuration of a culture of politics and the hegemonic ambitions of its political regime. But the precise nature of that relationship is variable and should be treated as an empirical question. Moreover, during periods of transition there is an inevitable disjuncture between regime change (at the level of the *state*), a shift in values (at the level of the *individual*), and changes in the culture of politics (at the level of *society*).

The goal of this essay is threefold: first, to characterize the major streams of the contemporary literature on democratization and democratic consolidation in Africa; second, to introduce a discussion of practice theory as a way of understanding the relationship between regime change and a culture of politics; and finally to underscore the need for political analysts to ask questions about the changing meaning of politics and the cultural and social patterns that shape and reshape the basic character of political life (Geertz 1973).

Conceptualizing the Process of Democratization

There has been a virtual explosion of literature on democratization in Africa since the publication of *Popular Struggles for Democracy in Africa*, edited by Peter Anyang' Nyong'o (1987). This book was the outgrowth of a United Nations University project on Transnationalization or Nation-Building in Africa coordinated by Samir Amin. The project involved a network of African scholars who explored the impact of the international economic crisis on the political, economic and cultural situation prevailing in Africa during the early 1980s; their resulting essays detail the emergence of democratic movements and the revolt of the popular classes.

One year later Larry Diamond, Juan Linz and Seymour Martin Lipset published *Democracy in Developing Countries: Africa* (1988). These African case studies form part of a four-volume compendium that covers developments in Latin America and Asia as well. By incorporating Africa into a broadly comparative analysis of democratization in a global context, Diamond and his collaborators wrote the continent into a trans-regional story of democratic emergence and renewal.

Taken together, these two projects mark a major turning point in the intellectual and research agendas guiding students of African politics.[5] Taken individually, they set the stage for a range of perspectives and methodological orientations running through the literature on democratizing processes in Africa. What follows is a brief overview of the dominant paradigms of the early 1990s. The discussion focuses first on approaches to democratic transitions and secondly on the requisites for democratic consolidation. Just as there is considerable overlap in the real-world muddle of transition politics, these approaches should not be thought of as mutually exclusive.

Comparative Historical Analysis

Diamond, Linz and Lipset's *Democracy* employs a framework of comparative historical analysis. Building on the premise that how the process of democratization is triggered affects the prospects for its durability, the editors invited contributors to make "an exhaustive examination of all the historical, cultural, social, economic, political, and international factors" that "fostered or obstructed the emergence, instauration, and consolidation of democratic government around the world" (Diamond et al. 1988, xiii). Examining 26 countries, this project is boldly expansive and ambitious in its scope. Particular attention is paid to each country's cultural traditions (loosely construed), colonial heritage, and post-independence history "in order to explain the over-all path of a country's political development" (Diamond et al. 1988, xiv).

Robert Dahl's concept of *polyarchy*—defined as a system that combines regularized competition for the essential positions of government power, broad-based participation and guarantees of civil and political liberties—frames the discussion of democracy (Dahl 1971). Writing in 1988, Diamond acknowledged that all six of the African country studies fell short of the project's operational definition of democracy.[6] Yet he justified their selection on the basis of certain shared characteristics: non-socialist economic systems, vigorous informal economies, expanding networks of voluntary associations and decaying state bureaucracies pruned by structural adjustment programs. These factors, dubbed "seeds of hope," were considered positive indicators of the prospects for democratization (Diamond 1988a, 25–27).

In his introductory essay Diamond identifies a range of factors—including ethnicity, political culture, leadership, political institutions, civil society and the external environment—as possible explanations for the prevalence of "democratic decay" in Africa. Drawing from the work of Gabriel Almond and Sydney Verba on the civic culture (1963), he associates democracy with institutionalized habits of tolerance and fair play. Contrasting case studies drive home this point. On the one hand the essay on Botswana (Holm 1988) argues that traditional Tswana culture, which values "moderation, nonviolence," and "obedience to the law," promotes public discussion of issues through an indigenous forum called the *kygotla*. The regime's interpretive embrace of these values closely approximates the ideal of the civic culture and is thus considered key to the longevity of Botswana's stable multiparty system.[7] On the other hand in Nigeria, where the values of "freedom and public accountability" are purportedly "entrenched in associational life" (Diamond 1988b), and in Ghana, where "consultation, autonomy, participation, and supervision of authority" are touted as deeply held values rooted in the indigenous culture (Chazan 1988), we find that multipartyism has been repeatedly dislodged by single-party or military regimes in wanton violation of these sociocultural values. In these two cases the *volatility* of a civic culture of tolerance and fair play is advanced to explain, at least in part, the cycles of democratic breakdown and renewal as well as the failure of authoritarian alternatives to endure.

However suggestive these accounts may be, they are undertheorized. Indeed, the modalities of the relationship between political culture and democratization remain to be clarified. We shall return to this issue later in the discussion.

Phased Transitions

Inspired by Dankwart Rustow's 1970 *Comparative Politics* article, "Transitions to Democracy," this literature conceptualizes the process of democratization as a sequence of tasks, "each with its own logic" and the "ingredients" of which are "assembled one at a time." Rustow delineated four phases: background conditions, the preparatory phase, the decision phase and the habituation phase—and developed a series of propositions to characterize the internal dynamics of each. Analysts who take a phased approach to democratic theory are less interested in the conditions that make stable democracy possible and more concerned with "the genetic question of how democracy comes into being in the first place" (Rustow 1970, 340).

Richard Joseph has adapted Rustow's model to construct a conceptual road map as a guide for his work with former President Jimmy Carter and the Carter Center's Governance in Africa Program (1991). Joseph enumerates eight phases in a transition to democracy: decay, mobilization, decision, formulation, electoral contestation, handover, legitimation and consolidation. He has further amplified this basic grid with a "mach II" framework that identifies seven transition paths from the point of decision to the consolidation phase of democratization.[8] Finally, in an effort to capture the quality and content of democratic practice in any given country at a particular time, Joseph has built a Quality of Democracy Index (QDI) composed of 10 indicators.[9] This expanded framework serves as an instrument for categorizing regime types and monitoring the status of democratic transitions in Africa over time.

Several important assumptions underlie the transitions to democracy paradigm. Although consensus on fundamentals is considered an implausible precondition, certain ingredients are deemed essential to the genesis of democracy. In this regard, Rustow's most important contribution to democratic theory may well be his insight that "the factors which keep a democracy stable [e.g., a civic culture] may not be the ones that brought it into existence" in the first place (1970, 346).

Civil Society and Democratization

After more than a decade of trying to understand and explain the break-down of democratic regimes in Latin America and Southern Europe, the field of transition studies took a major shift in 1986 with the publication of Guillermo O'Donnell, Philippe Schmitter and Laurence Whitehead's four-part series *Transitions from Authoritarian Rule*. In the concluding volume, O'Donnell and Schmitter (1986) devote an entire chapter to a discussion of resurrecting civil society. Although they refer to these theoretical specula-tions as "tentative conclusions," many readers have embraced the text as a how-to primer on democratization. In fact, the book's step-by-step rendi-tion of the critical role played by groups and individuals in civil society during democratic openings is frequently cited by analysts of popular protest and political reform in Africa (Bratton and van de Walle 1992a).

The appeal of civil society as an organizing concept is not puzzling. In-deed, there is widespread agreement across a range of theoretical per-spectives that political accountability is an essential condition for democ-racy, and that the degree of accountability depends upon the capacity of a robust, autonomous civil society to curb the hegemony of the state. Dur-ing the 1950s and early 1960s, when Africa's new states were emerging on the world scene, studies of voluntary associations were a central feature of the literature on the nationalist movements. But by the late 1960s, many of these associations had lost their autonomy and were incorpo-rated into single-party regimes under the control of personal rulers. For most scholars of African politics, interest in civil society waned with the rise of the party-state. Naomi Chazan was one of the notable exceptions.

Chazan took an interest in the modalities of political participation under autocratic rule. Writing in the early 1980s, she remarked that the informal channels of political access provided by voluntary associations in Africa were more efficacious than many of the formal political institutions sanc-tioned by authoritarian regimes (Chazan 1982). Explaining how interest ar-ticulation was negotiated through groups in civil society, she raised the specter that a return to more formalized modes of political representation such as party politics and elections might have the perverse effect of dimin-ishing political participation among the population as a whole.[10]

By the end of the decade, however, observers began to once again associ-ate civil society with the prospects for limiting state power (Woods 1992). As noted earlier, Anyang' Nyong'o and his co-authors focused attention on the emergence of "popular democratic struggles" aimed at smashing "the neocolonialist state" (1987, 24). Similarly, Robert Fatton, Jr. characterized civil society as a potentially subversive space in which dissidents grounded in private routes to power and wealth may, under certain conditions, force an autocratic regime to accept a democratic pact (1992).

Michael Bratton has been more sanguine about the potential for mutually beneficial state-society relations. His work on civil society in Africa (Bratton 1989a, 1989b) stresses the dependence of civic associations and nongovernmental organizations (NGOs) on the state for the basic conditions of their existence. Offering a series of hypotheses about the conditions under which conflict or congruence might occur, Bratton acknowledges that conflict and political struggles may arise, but insists that such contingencies should be treated as empirical variables ranging "from mutual disengagement . . . to direct confrontation . . . [to] close collaboration" (1989a, 430). In this framework actors based in civil society advance democracy not by tearing down the state, but rather, by engaging the state as interest groups for the purpose of influencing public policy. Bratton further contends that weak authoritarian states may become more effective and more legitimate "by permitting a measure of pluralism in associational life" (1989a, 428–29).

What these divergent orientations share is their treatment of state-society relations as a variable, and their concern with what happens as the parameters of such relations shift. Consequently, analyses of civil society and democratization give rise to considerations of political openings, political opportunity structures, power asymmetries, contested meanings and marginal as well as modal political practices. These are the channels through which a culture of politics is reconstituted.

The New Institutionalism

According to James March and Johan Olsen, the new institutionalism expresses a belief in the relative autonomy of political institutions and insists that "meanings develop in politics, as in the rest of life, through a combination of education, indoctrination, and experience" (1984, 739). Within this framework both community-generated institutions and the wider institutional environment shape the context in which individual choices are made and have a determining effect on the way community-owned resources are managed. As a paradigm with a growing number of adherents, institutional analysis is generating an ever larger corpus of studies focused on African organizational factors in political life and their critical role in affecting markets and political processes.

Robert Bates' pioneering contribution to the development of an institutionally focused form of political economy relies heavily on African case materials to demonstrate how institutions—especially public agencies, bureaucracies and electoral systems—affect markets and government capabilities (1989). For analysts interested in political democracy, the design of political institutions has become an explicit topic of concern. Thus research examining critical flaws in the institutional arrangements of

African states is being directed toward revealing how such structures have given rise to practices that are politically repressive and/or inimical to economic growth. *The Failure of the Centralized State*, edited by James Wunsch and Dele Olowu (1990), is the collaborative result of one such effort. This collection of essays systematically applies institutional analysis to issues of democratic self-governance in Africa.

Guided by the analytical framework of the Workshop in Political Theory and Political Analysis at the University of Indiana, the contributors to this volume maintain that Africa's institutional environment has been shaped by an over-centralized state. They trace the origins of these political and administrative hierarchies back to colonial rule and contend that the concentration of power in the hands of a very few people has fostered instability, hindered economic development, and reduced "civic capacity." Given these institutional constraints, decentralization alone is judged an insufficient condition for democratic reform. What is called for, rather, is self-governance—a two-track approach which consists of dismantling the apparatus of authoritarian rule, while strengthening those institutions that expand the individual's capacity "to engage in collective choice and action at every level" of the polity (Wunsch and Olowu 1990, 294).

The new institutionalism offers one possible solution to ongoing debates about the relative importance of structural factors versus the role of human agency in political regime change (Kitschelt 1990; Mahoney and Snyder 1993). Terry Lynn Karl deploys the phrase "structured contingency" to press the point that this method of analysis gets around the "excessively deterministic conclusions" of an exclusively structural approach and the "overly voluntaristic interpretations" of models that privilege human agency (1990, 7–8). Economist Douglass North brings in an historical dimension by suggesting that institutions established in the past constrain present choices by setting a "path-dependent" developmental course that is reinforced through organizational learning and subjective modeling (1990). One can then follow the evolution of structural changes as they become embedded in institutions, which in turn shape the preferences and capacities of political actors in ways that affect transition trajectories and are thus conducive to (or obstructive of) political democracy.

Regime Change Theory

The collaborative work of Michael Bratton and Nicolas van de Walle on regime change seeks to integrate African-based knowledge into theories concerned with the breakdown and replacement of governance structures. They began this project by updating the typology of African regimes elaborated by Ruth Berins Collier (1982); they then set out to associate distinctive patterns of transition dynamics with particular regime types. Their ultimate goal is to contribute to democratic theory and theories of regime change on the basis of empirical evidence from Africa (Bratton and van de Walle 1992b).

Bratton and van de Walle have drawn on a body of literature that details the patrimonial nature of political relations in Africa to make the case for a distinctive style of regional politics. As good comparativists, they proceed to examine the prospects for democratization in Africa with concepts and frameworks developed in studies of transitions from authoritarian rule in Latin America, Southern and Eastern Europe. Dahl's typology of democratizing regimes (1971, 12–13) is the theoretical thread that links most of these studies, and Bratton and van de Walle follow suit. They next construct a funnel of causality to associate the likelihood of a democratic transition with the structural features of four variants of neopatrimonialism. Any deviations from transition trajectories as predicted by regime type are then accounted for by institutional factors or by the strength and cohesion of societal actors.

A thumbnail sketch cannot possibly do justice to the complexity of Bratton and van de Walle's contribution to an understanding of the processes of regime change in Africa. Their project promotes broad theory-building based on the quantification of variables, predictors of probabilistic outcomes and explanations of causation. Though emphasizing the formal political order and privileging structuralist over voluntaristic explanations of transition, they nevertheless incorporate social interactions and cultural norms into their model. However, the model's causal logic relies on sweeping generalizations about the neopatrimonial nature of African regimes—so much so that the explanatory power of the analysis is weakened by its essentialist treatment of culture.

Human Rights and Democratization

Recalling Rustow's observation that the factors sustaining democracy may not be the same as those that caused it to come into existence in the first place, we turn now to a consideration of factors more centrally related to democratic consolidation. At issue is not how transitions occur but, rather, how they are sustained over time.

Africa's human rights advocates argue that the consolidation of democracy requires the institutionalization of procedures designed to guarantee human dignity, protect individual liberty and assure public contestation. Indeed, there is a growing body of literature—produced by lawyers, social scientists and political activists—that links support for human rights with democratization.[11] This work generally focuses on the specifics of present-day struggles to restore the institutions of liberal democracy, multipartyism and the rule of law in Africa.

Rather than taking the long historical view, much of the human rights literature is either highly contemporary or diachronic in its timeframe. For instance, Rhoda Howard's *Human Rights in Commonwealth Africa* (1986), a comparative political sociology of authoritarian rule, is a book firmly anchored in the here and now, while Abdullahi Ahmed An-Na'im and Francis Deng's edited volume *Human Rights in Africa: A Cross-Cultural Perspective* (1990) reveals the present-day disjuncture with a more humane past.[12] The scholarly writings of human rights lawyers such as Gibson Kamau Kuria (1991), Makau wa Mutua (1992) and David Giles (1992) generally treat more immediate issues of political oppression and abuse of power. Parenthetically, it should be noted that the logic of human rights advocacy invites external intervention in the domestic affairs of sovereign states for the purpose of protecting individual liberty and promoting democracy.

In sum, the literature on human rights and democracy in Africa is largely the product of scholar-activists or policy advocates concerned with calling attention to violations and correcting abuses perpetrated by incumbent political regimes. Therefore many of its conclusions are prescriptive—emphasizing the need to foster a propertied, entrepreneurial middle class to serve as the custodians of democracy, or espousing constitutional reforms such as a bill of rights and other guarantees to affirm civil liberties and protect individuals from the state. In view of the dominant role played by Western countries in the initial attempts to formulate international standards of human rights, there is an ongoing debate about the viability of these norms when applied in cultures that are not grounded in the traditions of Western liberalism.

African Research Networks

Africa's intellectuals are key players in the spread of support for democracy on the continent. Moreover, their influence is being institutionalized via the proliferation of research networks on democratic processes. Sometimes these arrangements are short-lived or task oriented, as, for instance, the University of Nairobi group whose workshop resulted in the publication of *Democratic Theory and Practice in Africa* (Oyugi, Odhiambo, Chege and Gitonga 1985). Others emerge as special projects of pan-African professional associations. Thus in 1991 the African Association of Political Science established a research network on "Democratization Processes in Africa" and dedicated a major portion of its 1993 meeting in Dar es Salaam to the question, "What is the place of democracy/good governance in the promotion of peace, security and development in the post cold war period?" Similarly, the Council for the Development of Social Science Research in Africa (CODESRIA) held a 1992 conference in Zimbabwe on the theme "Democracy and Human Rights." This event brought together a mix of African scholars, political activists, politicians and human rights advocates in a forum that provided opportunities for "rethinking democracy not merely as a phenomenon for analysis and prognosis but also as an urgent necessity that has to be acquired" (Ibrahim 1992, 1).

For two decades CODESRIA has consistently endeavored to build intellectual support structures for African scholars while encouraging research with practical applications. Its project on social movements and democracy, initiated in 1985, underscored a commitment to the desirability of political liberalization. Since that time a number of national and multinational research networks have been launched to facilitate contact among scholars from different parts of Africa around work on themes that address the possibilities for political openings. Networks on legal succession and political transition, peasant organizations, and the military and militarism in Africa are now fully functioning.

These research networks also provide safe space for nurturing diversity of opinion and giving voice to dissent. Indeed, the "Debates, Ideas, Viewpoints" section of the *CODESRIA Bulletin* is a wellspring of ideological pluralism and at times a harbinger of generational change. Take for example Jibrin Ibrahim's trenchant critique of the "icons of the African left" that appeared in the *Bulletin*'s 20th anniversary issue. Jibrin, a young Nigerian political scientist, accused some of Africa's most brilliant senior scholars of having "spent too much of their intellectual careers abolishing liberalism, [and] too little time learning or practicing democracy" (1993, 17). Such statements are not only tolerated but encouraged in the institutional space carved out by CODESRIA.

Taken as a whole, the collaborative networks of CODESRIA and similar research consortia form the centerpiece of a strategy to spur the development of a democratic culture of politics, create a protected space for intellectual freedom, and contribute to ongoing debates about democracy and its requisite conditions in Africa.

Democracy Engendered

A lack of attention to gender analysis is a frequent complaint raised in disciplinary and paradigm critiques of African studies. When CODESRIA convened a Workshop on Gender Analysis and African Social Science, its executive secretary Thandika Mkandawire was initially skeptical and even doubted the existence of a body of gender-oriented methods, approaches and empirical studies waiting to be "appropriated" by Africa's social science community.[13] But at the end of the four-day session, Mkandawire publicly recanted and became an enthusiastic advocate of "gendering" social science in Africa.

A consideration of gender and democratization begins with the recognition that political liberalization will not *a priori* install gender equity as one of the rules of the political game. Several of the workshop papers explored the nature of women's involvement in pro-democracy movements and reported that new types of political struggles were emerging—including a reluctance to recognize or grant political representation to explicitly female interests; interjection of the politics of "tradition" and women's place into new arenas in the public sphere; and the promotion of "state feminism," defined as "state-controlled women's organizations and institutions which only address women's issues in a non-threatening way and often act against the interests of women" (Sisulu et al. 1991, 9).[14]

Recurring controversies over the political status of women expose a disquieting undercurrent of sexism running through this recent wave of transition politics. Gender bias is evident in laws, decrees and constitutional provisions that prohibit political parties based on sex, and women are decidedly underrepresented in the councils charged with preparing the ground rules for political liberalization (Mba 1990; Robinson, forthcoming).[15] And women who protest their exclusion from such bodies are likely to find themselves criticized by male reformers instead of being encouraged in their struggles to broaden the base of participation. In some contexts we are seeing women who are politically assertive or independent subjected to harassment or violence that is justified by an ideology of domesticity (Stamp 1991; Ampofo 1993). To shed light on this development, Adame Ba-Konaré (1991) has called for more studies that historicize the complexities of female subordination in order to reveal how societies construct ideologies to rationalize the control of women by men.

Recent work by Patricia Stamp (1991) on the politics of gender and ethnicity is particularly germane, for it builds on the theoretical point developed by Nicos Poulantzas (1976, 1978) that "the state is not a monolithic entity but a contradictory, disunified set of structures, processes and discourses, the different parts of which often act at cross purposes." Stamp reasons that keeping women in their place is part and parcel of the suppression of dissent. When a political opening occurs and a regime begins to liberalize, contradictory orientations within the state do not suddenly vanish. On the contrary, continued struggles over the definition and control of gender relations in the state are likely to persist throughout the starts and stops of democratic consolidation.

Since a goal of feminist epistemology is to uncover the ways in which women attempt to circumvent the control of gender relations (or in Stamp's terms, "to render visible the agency of women in politics," p. 485), it follows that concepts, theories and methods from feminist scholarship offer a framework to begin exploring the politics of nonelites. As a corrective to conventional approaches that treat women as passive victims of oppression and discrimination, feminist researchers have favored qualitative methods, oral histories and participatory research techniques that amplify "formerly suppressed voices and experiences" by generating and validating new knowledge from different types of sources (Sisulu et al. 1991, 5). Such methods are well-suited to probing contested meanings, shifting power relations and the dialectics of domination and dissent. They raise the salience of suppressed voices and force consideration of whether there can be effective governance without gender equity in the realm of political life.

Governance

The World Bank study *Sub-Saharan Africa: From Crisis to Sustainable Growth* (1989) identifies a crisis of governance as one of the major causes of Africa's poor economic performance. Generalizing about the continent as a whole, the report blames the prevalence of personalized politics, unaccountable government, human rights abuses, arbitrary rule and the concomitant loss of political legitimacy for a systemic failure that has created an environment incapable of supporting a dynamic economy. Governance, defined as "the exercise of political power to manage a nation's affairs," is judged to be more bad than good in Africa (pp. 60–61).

While the most exacting analysts of governance take pains to distinguish between democracy and good governance, the two notions are often conflated—especially in measures established by aid donors to monitor political conditionality. This blurring of the boundaries is evident in a paper prepared by the Bank's Dunstan Wai for a conference at Oxford. After taking pains to delineate the core characteristics of good governance in terms of the accountability of government officials, transparency of government procedures, predictability of government behavior, openness in government transactions and observance of the rule of law, Wai insists that an economic order controlled by a leader who wields arbitrary power is perforce undemocratic (1991).

The publication of *Governance and Politics in Africa* (Hyden and Bratton 1992) marks a move to endow the concept of governance with the explanatory power of a new paradigm. As explained by Goran Hyden, this theory-driven approach to governance assumes "that human beings make their own history but not in circumstances of their own choice, and that political culture is an independent and superordinate factor in the study of development" (Hyden 1992, 8). Stressing the empirical dimensions of governance, Hyden's operational definition focuses on citizen influence and oversight, responsive and responsible leadership, and social reciprocities. This formulation makes it possible to locate the quality of governance under different regime types along a spectrum of efficient-to-inefficient management of the public realm, and allows for systematic examination of claims that equate democracy and "good" governance. Thus while acknowledging that the prospects for good governance tend to be greater under liberal democracy, Hyden is able to argue that his notion of governance is not tied to any particular form of the polity.

What Hyden does venture to do, however, is offer generalizations about the characteristic attributes of political systems by geographic region, and then locate each region in a property space delineating regime types.[16] Four commonalities of political culture are highlighted for sub-Saharan Africa: the prevalence of personal rule, frequent violations of human rights, over-centralized authority and the tendency for individuals to withdraw from politics (Hyden 1992, 23; Jackson and Rosberg 1982; Callaghy 1984; Joseph 1987). Similar attributes are emphasized by Bratton and van de Walle in their work on regime change, which points to neopatrimonialism as the core feature of politics in Africa (1992).[17] These characteristics of the political culture are taken to be implicated in the prevalence of "bad" governance in Africa.

Reflecting on current trends in the study of political liberalization in Africa, Edmond Keller echoes Hyden's contention that a research focus on democracy is misplaced, but he is equally skeptical about the suitability of governance as a replacement (1991). When looked at critically, Hyden's conceptualization of "good" governance is virtually indistinguishable from liberal democracy. Keller's retort: that focusing on factors which seem to explain the nature and the timing of transitions from authoritarian regimes is a more promising route to understanding politics in present-day Africa. Now we have come full circle—back to the discussion of regime change.

Although the approaches presented thus far all acknowledge the relevance of culture to political life, none builds in the assumptions of dynamic, nuanced cultural phenomena. Therefore for the remainder of this essay the effort will be to establish how practice theory and ideas about political learning can both broaden and deepen our understanding of the relationship between regime change and the culture of politics.

Regime Change and Practice Theory

We shift now to a discussion of practice theory—a theoretical strategy that gained currency in anthropology during the 1980s (Ortner 1984). As explained by Sherry Ortner, practice theory is "a theory about the relationship between the structures of society and culture on the one hand, and the nature of human action on the other. . . . Practice emerges from structure, it reproduces structures, and it has the capacity to transform structure" (1989, 11–12). The classic statement is found in Pierre Bourdieu's *Outline of a Theory of Practice* (1977).

Bourdieu formulates a dynamic approach to structure that seems well-suited to the methodological challenges of rapidly changing transition periods. The pivotal concept is his notion of *habitus,* defined as "a system of dispositions." *Habitus* connotes structure that is practiced, lived in and enacted. Insisting on the necessity of abandoning "all theories which explicitly or implicitly treat practice as a mechanical reaction, directly determined by . . . antecedent conditions," Bourdieu proposes instead an analytical focus directed toward discovering the generative principles that structure the disposition to act (1977, 73). He theorizes that practices produced by the *habitus* become strategy-generating principles "enabling agents to cope with unforseen and everchanging situations" (1977, 72). Once the structuring principle is known, the behavior of individual actors becomes intelligible.

The concept of a *cultural schema* represents the operation of this structuring principle in the cultural realm. Defined as a "configuration of cultural forms, social relations, and historical processes that move people to act in [certain] ways," it is based on the premise that historical events may be structured in much the same way as social behavior (Ortner 1989, 12). The idea of culturally constituted practice implies that preorganized schemes of action can serve as models on which individuals or groups draw in the course of social action (Ortner 1989; Geertz 1980; Sahlins 1981). These cultural scripts are located in the stories, myths, legends, songs or pivotal historical events of a people. And at times they may take on an ordering function, or become generalized and transferred across a wide range of social situations. Precisely how a given cultural schema becomes operational is an empirical question that cannot be separated from the particular historical context. But the central point is that this shared store of cultural knowledge structures an orientation toward the world that is familiar to members of a common cultural heritage—whatever their social position and interests.

In yet another contribution to practice theory, Ortner combines political economy and ethnographic history to argue that external political and economic forces impinging on a society's culture and history may, under special circumstances, motivate various "social beings" with diverse motivations and intentions to attempt to change the world in which they live (1989). To appreciate the theoretical bridge-building entailed, it is necessary to recognize that political economy and ethnographic history were long considered as disparate poles of anthropology. The one draws attention to external forces such as colonial legacies and international economic linkages; the other is concerned with the structures of a society and culture over the long span of history. But by focusing on the conjuncture, Ortner targets the analysis on the mediation of external forces by internally generated social structural arrangements and cultural patterns. She shows how people can be pushed by these external forces, or actively appropriate them, or both, "to transform their historical situations" at a given point in time (p. 195).

Thus, unlike path-dependent analysis, which emphasizes history-as-constraint, practice theory privileges a creative and inventive theory of history. Studies of practice present individuals as "competent actors" (Feierman 1990) capable of shaping events and responding to changes in their environment through "regulated improvisation" (Bourdieu) or "rule-governed creativity" (Giddens 1979). Steven Feierman's compelling treatment of peasant intellectuals is a good example. Feierman relies on practice theory to frame an analysis of how the Shambaa in northeastern Tanzania have used culturally patterned politics over the past 150 years to create an alternative discourse that challenges the basic structure of political control. The success of his historical account rests on "a method and a form of ethnographic description" which portrays "the cultural categories as both continuous and in transformation, and the actors as both creating new language and speaking inherited words, all at the same time" (Feierman 1990, 13).

We learn that variability, not sameness, is an outcome of culturally constituted practice. A culture includes many streams of discourse, and the whole of a society never shares a single body of practice (Feierman 1990, 33). From this perspective the analytical stance advocated by practice theory opens up questions about the diverse forms of political consciousness, and challenges the basic assumption of regime change theorists that only elite competition, behavior and values are of critical import to the dynamics of transitions. Sidney Tarrow's work on the recent wave of mobilization and political opportunity structures in Eastern Europe is equally instructive in this regard.

Tarrow finds the failure of social scientists to anticipate these events "particularly glaring" in light of the vast amount of research and theorizing undertaken in Western Europe and the United States since the 1960s. Stressing the importance of exploring opportunities for political action wherever they can be found, he reaches beyond the formal political institutions to collect leaflets, manifestos, speeches, the minutes of meetings, along with oral accounts of leaders and ordinary citizens alike. These data on the "ephemera of popular politics" yield some of the best evidence of the "evolving repertoire of collective action" and provide insight into "the diverse forms of meaning" that animated the mass public (Tarrow 1991, 17). They constitute a good first step toward developing an ethnography of transitions with "thick description."

In sum, two hypotheses derived from practice theory merit emphasis: First, cultural schemas are dynamic, generative structures which function as strategy-generating principles. Second, culturally constituted practice may transform the contextual situation in ways that create new possibilities or expand options for some (but not all) actors. The notion of structure-as-constraint is thus turned on its head. Ortner maintains that, in certain circumstances, dynamic structural forces may actually change people's lives by "giving them new interests," and making certain actions "materially feasible, or politically practical, or morally powerful, or personally exciting—or all of these at once" (p. 195). The analytical challenge is to identify the key actors, describe the structural dynamics and clarify the special circumstances.

For an application of practice theory to explain one of the streams of liberalizing transitions that began in 1989, we look now at the national conference phenomenon in francophone Africa.

Sovereign National Conferences in Francophone Africa

On 19 February 1990, a National Conference opened in Benin at the Hotel PLM-Aledjo in Cotonou. Organized by prominent professionals and trade union leaders, this gathering included representatives of the ruling People's Revolutionary Party, nascent political parties, labor activists, voluntary associations, civil servants, students, religious leaders, a few rural producers, military personnel, the former heads of state, as well as Beninese living and working abroad (Heilbrunn 1993). Members of the diplomatic corps and officials from the international financial institutions were also in attendance. The conferees claimed to represent the nation in its entirety—*toutes les forces vives de la nation, quoi que soient leurs affinitées.* In reality, they were drawn from the political class and the educated elites of civil society. President Mathieu Kérékou opened the conference with a call for political renewal and a pledge to implement the IMF's structural adjustment program. He focused on the country's severe economic crisis and called on the delegates to draw up a list of the problems to be addressed.

General Kérékou was a reluctant reformer. Forced to convene the conference by the threat of a general strike, the reality of empty state coffers (government salaries had not been paid for nearly six months), and a push from French President Mitterrand, he had accepted the inevitability of political and economic liberalization as the price for holding onto power. He was unprepared for what was to follow.

Benin's National Conference lasted 10 days. The delegates' first official act was to declare the conference sovereign. When the deliberations ended, they had suspended the constitution; dissolved the National Assembly; adopted plans for multiparty elections; and chosen Nicéphore Soglo, a former World Bank official, as interim prime minister. Although Kérékou remained in office as head of state until the elections, he was stripped of most of his powers and executive authority. A year later when Benin held its first openly competitive elections in 17 years, Kérékou came in second to Soglo in a three-way race.

The Benin story became an instant media event throughout francophone Africa. It was carried live on Benin radio, rebroadcast on national television, given prominent international coverage on Radio France International (RFI), reported and analyzed by the government media as well as the independent press in every francophone African country, and held up as a model of political reform by *Jeune Afrique,* a Paris-based journal with worldwide circulation. The text of this political drama was preserved by the Benin government news agency, which produced a two-hour video tape of conference highlights. Over 400 copies of the video had been sold by the end of 1991, and untold numbers of pirated copies began to circulate.

The lessons of Benin's National Conference were not lost. Between March of 1990 and August 1991, the rulers of Gabon, Congo, Mali, Togo, Niger and Zaïre faced the demands of pro-democracy forces and convened national conferences. During this same period, opposition groups in the Central African Republic (CAR), Cameroon, Madagascar, Burkina Faso, Mauritania and Chad began mobilization campaigns to press their demands for national conferences. Outcomes have varied. In some cases the incumbents retained control by manipulating the conference proceedings, or by rigging multiparty elections. In other cases the opposition prevailed—at least in the short run. For as long as possible, however, besieged autocrats resisted convening national conferences because, in essence, they knew the script. Momar Coumba Diop and Mamadou Diouf of CODESRIA are clear on this point: "Viewed as an institution, [the] national conference has . . . been instrumental . . . in the transition towards democracy." And an essential part of that transition is "political reforms that might make it possible for certain leaders to hand over power in an orderly transition" (1991, 8).

Although the innovational impetus rests squarely with the Beninese,[18] the notion of a sovereign national conference as an instrument for regime change is grounded in Jean Jacques Rousseau's ideas about popular sovereignty and the people's right to renegotiate the social contract. Rousseau's theory became practice in the Estates-General of 1789—an historical referent that stands as one of the master narratives in the political heritage of French republicanism. And only in francophone Africa have such conferences been central to the process of regime change. Indeed it should be noted that in Zaïre, a former Belgian colony, President Mobutu Sese Seko was able to ignore the conferees' declaration of sovereignty with impunity while deliberations spanned nearly two years before finally ending in a stalemate with two prime ministers—one elected by the national conference and the other appointed by Mobutu. Thus the structural relationship with France, backed up by the possibility of French military intervention, has proved critical to the success of the national conferences in francophone Africa. Still, what practice theory can help to explain is why, at this particular historical juncture, certain African political actors perceived the utility of the national conference as a strategy for regime change; what motivated them to pursue that strategy; and how it came to pass that the French government was willing—though only for a short while—to support the process.

The argument is as follows: External factors played a decisive role in creating an enabling environment for political reform throughout Africa. The spread of liberalizing tendencies in the Eastern bloc coincided with the bicentennial of the French Revolution. And the historic precedent of the Estates-General, transformed into a structural schema, became a strategy-generating principle for regime change in francophone Africa.

By 1988 a number of developments on the world scene were threatening the sustainability of Africa's authoritarian regimes. The Soviet Union's fateful experimentation with *glasnost* was ratcheting down of the Cold War; human rights advocates were escalating the pressure for politically conditioned aid; funding agencies sought to strengthen civil society by supporting the nongovernmental sector in lieu of the state; and the ILO and Western-based trade union organizations were aggressively promoting trade union autonomy. Price liberalization and layoffs mandated by structural adjustment programs strengthened the position of investors considered essential to economic recovery, but they also stepped up the pace of domestic political dissent (Diop 1991). And as the introduction of fax machines and electronic mail began to revolutionize communications, the media of the air waves (BBC, RFI, the VOA, and CNN television) increased their Africa coverage thereby undercutting the ability of the state to limit access to news.

Although African countries absorbed the force of these liberalizing trends differentially, momentum toward more pluralistic political structures began to sweep across the continent. The tide of reform rose to a crescendo in 1989, when the world celebrated the bicentennial of the French Revolution in July, and found even more to cheer about in November with the opening of the Berlin Wall. During the next 12 months no less than 21 African governments—11 in francophone Africa—initiated some semblance of democratic reform (Bratton and van de Walle 1992a).

This was also a period of dramatic developments on the African scene: in February 1989, Algerians approved a constitutional referendum guaranteeing civil liberties and the right to form political parties; the African Charter for Popular Participation in Development and Transformation was adopted by delegates at an Arusha conference held the following

February; and the Government of South Africa released Nelson Mandela from prison while the Arusha conference was still in session. News of these events was celebrated in the media and absorbed into the consciousness of politically aware citizens in every African country.

The cumulative impact of these developments reconfigured political opportunity structures in the domestic politics of African states. Suddenly, would-be reformers could reasonably believe that the time was ripe to mobilize for change. And in francophone Africa, the national conference emerged as the method of choice for regime change.

The bicentennial of the French Revolution worked as a catalyst. Because 1989 was also the bicentennial of the Declaration of the Rights of Man and of the Citizen, human rights issues held center stage. As the African heads of state prepared to join Mitterrand for the July 1989 Bastille Day ceremonies in Paris, their pro-democracy opponents seized the opportunity to publicize the denial of political liberty and claim basic democratic freedoms as a universal human right. For a brief interlude, the salience of the French revolutionary narrative made the link between a national conference and popular sovereignty at once conceptually compelling and politically viable—among francophones in the metropole as well as overseas.

One year later, as Mitterrand prepared to host the 16th Franco-African summit at La Baule in June of 1990, domestic political pressures mounted for him to take a more principled stand in favor of the rising democratic ferment in Africa (Bayart 1991). Africans resident in France were becoming a more vocal constituency on the Left. At the same time, human rights groups went on the offensive. Amnesty International–France prepared a dossier detailing cases of arbitrary arrests and detentions, summary executions, torture, and the denial of political rights in francophone African countries. Similarly, media professionals belonging to the group *Raporteurs sans frontières* produced a report on the dismal status of press freedom in Africa. Both groups timed the release of their reports to coincide with the arrival of the heads of state for the summit.

Meanwhile the growing number of corruption scandals involving members of Mitterrand's Socialist Party left the president vulnerable to charges of soft-pedaling human rights in exchange for financial contributions from African dictators. Mitterrand's sagging popularity, and the general disillusionment with his party, raised the domestic political stakes for La Baule. Ultimately, the summit was used as a backdrop to announce that France would start linking aid to progress on democratization. The summit's final communique proclaimed the new norms: Henceforth aid would be calibrated to reflect progress toward democratic reform—as evidenced by free and fair elections, press freedom, an independent judiciary, multipartyism and less censorship. In line with this directive, the Socialists established a study group to work on a strategy for reform. Several emissaries traveled to Africa to meet with local leaders and extend material assistance.

What was significant about these gestures was not the fact of involvement per se but rather, their implied support for political reform. In fact, France has never ceased to be an active participant in the affairs of her former African colonies. These states continue to belong to the franc zone and share a common currency, the CFA franc, which is controlled by the French treasury. Bilateral accords provide for budget subsidies; furnish technical, administrative and cultural assistance; and buttress security arrangements. Thus France has the ability to affect the political options of rulers in francophone Africa simply by regulating the resources available to the state. This form of external governance is an especially powerful lever when a debt crisis and budget deficits, aggravated by corruption, leave empty state coffers. Such was the situation in 1989.

Writing about the French Revolution, historian Simon Schama observed that the "monarchy collapsed when the price of its financial rescue was measured . . . in political concessions" (1989, 228). Similarly, each of the national conferences in francophone Africa was preceded by the escalation of public demonstrations and strikes, which wrested political concessions—such as press freedom, recognition of the right to strike, legalization of opposition parties and rhetorical acceptance of the rule of law—from reluctant regimes.

In pre-revolutionary France, the demise of the *ancien régime* was hastened by politicization of the money crisis. Given the extent to which the prologue to the national conferences replicated this pattern, it is useful to recap the schematic structure.[19]

The story line begins in the immediate aftermath of the American War for Independence, when France faced a soaring debt burden. Excessive borrowing to finance participation in the war, followed by a peacetime spending spree paid for by additional borrowing, precipitated a debt crisis and eventual exclusion from international financial markets. Faced with insolvency and the threat of bankruptcy, Louis XVI bowed to pressure to convoke the Estates-General. The Swiss banker Jacques Necker was called in to take charge of the finance ministry, and Necker insisted on political reforms to consolidate the support needed for new taxes. Political liberalization ushered in freedom of the press, expression and political association. Elections for deputies to the Estates-General triggered the preparation of grievance lists. The formula for representation to the Estates-General was contested, but after a struggle, the regime agreed to quotas that put control of electoral outcomes in the hands of its opponents. When the Estates-General convened, the Third Estate declared itself sovereign, changed its name to the National Assembly, and was joined by splinter elements from the clergy and the nobility. After trying unsuccessfully to shut down the proceedings, the king submitted to the will of the delegates, and the locus of sovereignty shifted to the new National Assembly.

Thus French support for the national conference process was facilitated by the fact that they knew the script. In effect, each of the national conferences can be seen as an improvisation on this basic theme. Their schematic structure is part of the store of cultural knowledge shared by the French and the African elites who invented the strategy and provided the organizational leadership to bring it to fruition. For these reasons, the sovereign national conference appeared as a mutually viable solution to the problem of regime change for the pro-democracy activists as well as their allies in France. At the macro level, the Estates-General as schematic structure could be understood and manipulated by all of the key players—both politically and symbolically.

The philosopher Fabien Eboussi Boulaga's interpretation of national conferences moves the analysis from political economy to ethnography. He identifies five African cultural archetypes as the sources for the behavior of the conference participants: the fête, the game, therapy, the palaver and the initiation rite (1993). These activities are said to represent different ways of simultaneously giving value to society and to the individual. As Eboussi Boulaga contemplates the cultural subconscious that undergirds participation in a sovereign national conference, he suggests that the norms and general orientation of a political ethos are transmitted and expressed in the language of the imagination and in these cultural archetypes. Repeated over and over through ritualization, dramatization and theatricalization, they can purportedly serve to root and validate an ethical political code in a society. Because the national conference is itself a dramatized cultural schema, it can draw on these archetypal sources to justify, orient and motivate. In other words, Eboussi Boulaga's approach locates regime change in the culture of politics. We turn finally to consider the implications of transitions for political learning.

Regime Change and Political Learning

Defined operationally, political learning involves the cognitive changes brought on by changes in one's political environment (Bermeo 1990, 372). Much of the early literature on political transitions in Latin America assumed that the prolonged experience of authoritarian rule engenders a normative commitment to democratic values. But in a recent review article Frances Hagopian argues that protracted dictatorship might, as well, result in value changes that weaken the prospects for democratic consolidation. Insisting on the need to study politics "after regime change"—

that is, during the consolidation phase—she probes the extent to which "the programs and policies of authoritarian regimes" have left their mark on "the informal networks and formal institutions of political representation" (1993, 446). The recognition that the influence of authoritarianism on values and beliefs is uncertain suggests that political learning is important enough to warrant closer attention.

Nancy Bermeo has done significant work to advance the concept of political learning and explore its implications for empirical democratic theory (1990, 1992). Parting with scholars like Verba (1965) and Moore (1967) who emphasize the cultural continuities across time, she is interested in the *discontinuities* of values and beliefs (Bermeo 1992, 281). In this regard, political learning provides answers to two perplexing questions: "[I]t helps explain why a new regime becomes democratic in the first place; [and] it helps explain why . . . a dictatorship . . . is replaced by a democracy rather than another dictatorial regime" (1992, 273).

The concept of political learning is based on the premise that the relationship between authoritarianism and value change is a variable and can be affected by political events. Noting that the forces of the center-right "fare better in the aftermath of authoritarianism than we might expect," Bermeo hypothesizes that "the trauma of dictatorship can cause critical changes in the way people view politics" (1990, 372). In many instances, moreover, the policies pursued by authoritarian regimes actually shape the organization and mediation of political interests (Hagopian 1993, 488).

There is compelling testimony in the Africanist literature to support the proposition that political learning by "those at the bottom" of society may pose problems for the current wave of liberalization. Bayart (1992), for example, has called attention to the profound ambivalence toward power-holders evident among subordinate groups and considers this one of the legacies of authoritarian rule. He notes that such groups may at times prefer to live with an established structure of domination that they have learned to accommodate, rather than opt for a new political structure that is less intelligible or predictable and has no obvious interests for them.

A substantial body of empirical work by Africanists interested in this dilemma has appeared in the Paris-based journal *Politique Africaine*. Combining a paradigm based on popular modes of political action with an interest in the symbols and idioms that constitute the concept of democracy, Bayart, Mbembe and Comi Toulabor have been examining political participation in Africa as experienced *par le bas* (Bayart, Mbembe and Toulabor 1992). They have concentrated on the mediating sites in which marginalized actors may occasionally challenge the prevailing hegemony and assert the right to reorient their political behavior. Paradoxically, Bayart has found a perverse effect apparent since the rise of pro-democracy movements in 1989: People at the bottom are intervening "against democracy" in small ways with counter-demonstrations, riots, pillaging, killings, delinquency and dismantling of the state on a daily basis (1992, 17).

Quite possibly we could be witnessing in these reactions a cathartic reversal of what Claude Ake has termed "the criminalization of political dissent" practiced by authoritarian regimes (1991, 33). That is to say, marginalized groups or individuals who find themselves alienated from the formal institutions of the new pluralism may be resorting to the criminalization of participation as a means of signaling their disaffection. Whatever the case, there is clearly a need for political analysts to develop conceptual frameworks capable of explaining the waves of violence that are accompanying Africa's liberalizing transitions.[20]

It is in this context that we must confront the elite/mass divide and ask whether the beliefs, attitudes and values of subordinate groups matter for the outcomes of political transitions. Regime change theory is about elite competition. It brackets community norms, customs and symbols of power and considers such factors irrelevant to transition outcomes. Studies of culture, local knowledge and their impact on participation are generally not presented in the context of regime change. While regime change theory recognizes that mass mobilization can bring down a government and is therefore important in the first phase of democratization, in the consolidation phase critical elites are considered to be the only actors who matter. I submit that it is time to reconsider this conventional wisdom in light of the post-1989 African experience. Without minimizing the importance of elite values and behavior, my insistence is on the need to revisit the political relevance of non-elites and subordinate groups to the success of democratic consolidation in Africa.

Transitions create memory and feed into the process of political learning across all strata of society. As such, the politics of transitions are fought out on constantly shifting and contested terrain. It may well be time to come to grips with Ake's contention that in the minds of many Africans, the democratic principles of broad-based participation, consent of the governed and political accountability often exist as political values with deep cultural roots—but are neither uniquely nor solely associated with the institutions and procedures of parliamentary democracy (1991, 34). If this is indeed the case, then the relationship between regime change and the culture of politics is best understood as an ongoing problematic that is shaped and reshaped as new alternatives become visible, or as actors/citizens gain the power to bring them into being.

Notes

1. The divide is between those who stress structural relations of power within society (Moore 1966), and those who emphasize process and the strategic deci-

sions of leaders (O'Donnell et al. 1986; Gunther and Higley 1992). Structuralists insist upon the limitations of institutional constraints, while those who prefer process-driven theories assume that social actors have the capacity to break through those constraints.

2. Much of the transitions literature emphasizes elite behavior and attitudes at critical junctures and treats popular mobilization as a matter of secondary importance. O'Donnell and Schmitter's framework assumes that the capacity of regime "soft-liners" to come to terms with leaders of the pro-democracy opposition is the critical factor shaping outcomes (1986, 15–28). Karl (1986, 1990) focuses on the role of elite pacts in transitions to democracy. However, Rueschemeyer et al. (1992) depart from this course to argue that the bourgeoisie is frequently an impediment to democracy, and that working-class mobilization drives democratic transitions.

3. For O'Donnell and Schmitter, even the military fiasco of Argentina's Malvinas/Falklands war, which is generally credited with ushering in a transition to democracy, is more accurately seen as the desperate act of an internally stalemated regime rather than the cause of the regime having reached such an predicament.

4. The phrase "culture of politics" was suggested to me by Arjun Appadurai as a way of signaling a departure from the conventional treatment of political culture.

5. The African Studies Association, USA, has also been an important forum for debates about new directions in scholarship. Richard Sklar's presidential address to the ASA (1983) called Africa a "workshop of democracy" and offered a typology as the basis of a research agenda on evolving democratic experiments. Nzongola-Ntalaja's presidential address (1989) focused more explicitly on the politics of regime change.

6. The African case studies are Nigeria, Ghana, Senegal, Uganda, Zimbabwe and Botswana.

7. Botswana's party system has remained stable since the country achieved independence in 1966.

8. Joseph (1991) derives these transition paths from the African experiences of the past decade. They include 1) the National Conference, 2) government change via democratic elections, 3) co-opted transitions, 4) guided democratization, 5) recalcitrance and piecemeal reforms, 6) armed insurrections culminating in elections, and 7) conditional transitions.

9. The indicators comprising the QDI are access of social groups, autonomy of civic associations, constitutionalism and the rule of law, electoral process, freedom of assembly and association, freedom of conscience and expression, human rights, judiciary, media and military; each variable is scaled. A regularly updated classification of regime types appears in *Africa Demos*.

10. Chazan (1982) warns that "In most instances, the utilization of the political party gives undue advantage to the government-backed party or to previously outlawed parties that reform with alacrity when the ban on formal activity is lifted" (p. 183).

11. Initially the literature emphasized the link between human rights and development (Welch and Meltzer 1984; Shepherd and Anikpo 1989). Later the focus shifted to human rights and democratization.

12. See especially, Francis Deng, "A Cultural Approach to Human Rights among the Dinka;" Kwasi Wiredu, "An Akan Perspective on Human Rights;" and

James Silk, "Traditional Culture and the Prospect for Human Rights in Africa," in An-Na'im and M. Deng, eds. 1990.

13. My discussion of the Workshop on Gender Analysis and African Social Science is based on the report that appears in the *CODESRIA Bulletin* (1991).

14. It was noted that the wives of African heads of state invariably play a dominant role in state-feminist institutions. In this respect, the "first-lady syndrome" should be recognized as a structural problem rather than a personality issue.

15. For a gender analysis of events leading up to the sovereign national conference in Niger, see Pearl T. Robinson (forthcoming). A review of the controversies surrounding women's representation during the transition to Nigeria's Second Republic is provided by Nina Mba (1990).

16. Hyden identifies four regime types: communitarian, libertarian, corporatist and statist. The regions depicted are sub-Saharan Africa, southeast Asia, the (former) Soviet Union, Latin America, Western Europe, the United States and Middle East Kingdoms.

17. Bratton and van de Walle highlight the extreme personalization of power; the pervasiveness of clientelism, prebendalism and rent-seeking behavior; and the underdeveloped nature of civil society.

18. Herschelle Challenor reminded me that the Beninese have been politically innovative in the past, as when they created a 3-person rotating presidency to allow for equity in geographical representation.

19. This summary of events is based on the accounts presented by William Doyle (1989) and Georges Lefebvre (1957).

20. Franz Fanon (1963) needs to be re-read in the context of Africa's so-called second independence movement of the 1990s.

References

African Governance Program. 1990. "Transitions to Democracy: Toward a Dynamic Model." *Africa Demos* 1/1 (November). The Carter Center of Emory University.

Ake, C. 1991. "Rethinking African Democracy." *Journal of Democracy* 2/1 (Winter): 33–44.

Almond, G. and S. Verba. 1963. *The Civic Culture*. Princeton: Princeton University Press.

Ampofo, A. A. 1993. "Controlling and Punishing Women in Ghana." *Review of African Political Economy* 56 (March): 102–11.

An-Na'im, A.A. and F. M. Deng eds. 1990. *Human Rights in Africa: Cross-Cultural Perspectives*. Washington DC: The Brookings Institution.

Anyang' Nyong'o, P. ed. 1987. *Popular Struggles for Democracy in Africa*. London and New Jersey: The United Nations University and Zed Books Ltd.

Ba-Konaré, A. 1991. "Rôle et image de la femme dans l'histoire politique du Mali (1960–91): Perspectives pour une meilleure participation de la femme au processus démocratique." Paper presented at the CODESRIA Workshop on Gender Analysis and African Social Science, Dakar, 16–21 September.

Bates, R. 1989. *Beyond the Miracle of the Market: The Political Economy of Agrarian Development in Kenya*. Cambridge: Cambridge University Press.

Bayart, J-F. 1991. "La problématique de la démocratie en Afrique noire: La Baule, et puis après?" *Politique Africaine* 43 (Octobre): 5–20.

_____. 1992. "Introduction." In *La politique par le bas en Afrique noire,* edited by J-F. Bayart, A. Mbembe, and C. Toulabor, 9–23. Paris: Éditions Karthala.

Bayart, J-F, A. Mbembe, and C. Toulabor. 1992. *La politique par le bas en Afrique noire: Contributions à une problématique de la démocratie.* Paris: Éditions Karthala.

Bermeo, N. 1990. "Rethinking Regime Change." *Comparative Politics* 22/3 (April): 359–77.

_____. 1992. "Democracy and the Lessons of Dictatorship." *Comparative Politics* 24/3 (April): 273–91.

Bourdieu, P. 1977. *Outline of a Theory of Practice,* translated by Richard Nice. Cambridge: Cambridge University Press.

Bratton, M. 1989a. "Beyond the State: Civil Society and Associational Life in Africa." *World Politics* 41/3 (April): 407–30.

_____. 1989b. "The Politics of Government-NGO Relations in Africa." *World Development* 17/4 (April): 569–87.

Bratton, M. and N. van de Walle. 1992a. "Popular Protest and Political Transition in Africa." *Comparative Politics* 24/4 (July): 419–42.

_____. 1992b. "Regime Type and Political Transition in Africa." Paper presented at the American Political Science Association, Chicago, 3–6 September.

Callaghy, T. 1984. *The State-Society Struggle: Zaïre in Comparative Perspective.* New York: Columbia University Press.

Cardoso, F. H. 1979. "On the Characterization of Authoritarianism in Latin America." In *The New Authoritarianism in Latin America,* edited by D. Collier, 33–57. Princeton: Princeton University Press.

Chazan, N. 1982. "The New Politics of Participation in Tropical Africa." *Comparative Politics* 14/2 (January): 169–89.

Chazan, N. 1988. "Ghana: Problems of Governance and the Emergence of Civil Society." In *Democracy: Africa,* edited by Diamond et al., 93–139. Boulder: Lynne Rienner Publishers.

Collier, R. B. 1982. *Regimes in Tropical Africa.* Berkeley: University of California Press.

Dahl, R. 1971. *Polyarchy: Participation and Opposition.* New Haven: Yale University Press.

Diamond, L., J. Linz, and S. M. Lipset, eds. 1988. *Democracy in Developing Countries: Africa.* Volume 2. Boulder: Lynne Rienner Publishers. The other books in the series are Volume 1, *Persistence, Failure, and Renewal;* Volume 3, *Asia,* and Volume 4, *Latin America.*

Diamond, L. 1988a. "Introduction: Roots of Failure, Seeds of Hope." In *Democracy: Africa,* edited by Diamond et al., 25–27. Boulder: Lynne Rienner Publishers.

_____. 1988b. "Nigeria: Pluralism, Statism, and the Struggle for Democracy." In *Democracy: Africa,* edited by Diamond et al. 33–91. Boulder: Lynne Rienner Publishers.

Deng, F. 1990. "A Cultural Approach to Human Rights among the Dinka." In *Human Rights in Africa: Cross-Cultural Perspectives,* edited by A.A. An-Na'im and F.M. Deng. Washington DC: The Brookings Institution.

Diop, M. C. 1991. "The Politics of Structural Adjustment Programmes in Africa." *CODESRIA Bulletin,* 3: 2–7.

Diop, M. C. and M. Diouf. 1991. "Statutory Political Successions: An Afterword." *CODESRIA Bulletin*, 3.

Doyle, W. 1989. *The Oxford History of the French Revolution.* Oxford: Clarendon Press.

Eboussi Boulaga, F. 1993. *Les conférences nationales en Afrique noire: Une affaire à suivre.* Paris: Éditions Karthala.

Fanon, F. 1963. *The Wretched of the Earth,* translated by Constance Farrington. New York: Grove Press.

Fatton, Jr. R. 1992. *The State and Civil Society in Africa.* Boulder. Lynne Rienner Publishers.

Feierman, S. 1990. *Peasant Intellectuals: Anthropology and History in Tanzania.* Madison: University of Wisconsin Press.

Geertz, C. 1973. "The Politics of Meaning." In *The Interpretation of Culture,* edited by C. Geertz, 311–26. New York: Basic Books.

_____. 1979–80. "Blurred Genres: The Reconfiguration of Social Thought." *American Scholar* 49: 165–79.

_____. 1980. *Negara: The Theatre-State in Nineteenth Century Bali.* Princeton: Princeton University Press.

Giddens, A. 1979. *Central Problems in Social Theory: Action, Structure and Contradictions in Social Analysis.* Berkeley and Los Angeles: University of California Press.

Gilles, D. and M. Mutua. 1992. *A Long Road to Uhuru: Human Rights and Political Participation in Kenya.* Montreal: International Center for Human Rights and Democratic Development.

Girard, P. 1989. "Bicentenaire: Que la fête commence!" *Jeune Afrique* (19 Juillet): 4–11.

Gunther, R. and L. Higley. 1992. *Elites and Democratic Consolidation: Latin America and Southern Europe.* Cambridge: Cambridge University Press.

Hagopian, F. 1993. "After Regime Change: Authoritarian Legacies, Political Representation, and the Democratic Future of South America." *World Politics* 45/3 (April): 464–500.

Heilbrunn, J. R. 1993. "Social Origins of National Conferences in Benin and Togo." *Journal of Modern African Studies* 31/2: 277–99.

Holm, J. 1988. "Botswana: A Paternalistic Democracy." In *Democracy: Africa,* edited by Diamond et al., 179–215. Boulder: Lynne Rienner Publishers.

Howard, R. 1986. *Human Rights in Commonwealth Africa.* Totowa: Rowman & Littlefield.

Human Rights Internet. 1991. *HRI Reporter* 14 (Summer/Autumn): 103.

Huntington, S. 1991. *The Third Wave: Democratization in the Late Twentieth Century.* Norman: University of Oklahoma Press.

Hyden, G. 1992. "Governance and the Study of Politics." In *Governance and Politics in Africa,* edited by G. Hyden and M. Bratton, 1–26. Boulder: Lynne Rienner Publications.

Ibrahim, J. 1992. "Democracy and Human Rights in Africa: The Internal and External Contexts," report of a conference held in Harare, Zimbabwe, 11–14 May 1992." *CODESRIA Bulletin* 4: 1–8.

_____. 1993. "History as Iconoclast: Left Stardom and the Debate on Democracy." *CODESRIA Bulletin* 1: 17–18.

Jackson, R. and C. Rosberg. 1983. *Personal Rule in Black Africa.* Berkeley: University of California Press.

Joseph, R. 1987. *Democracy and Prebendal Politics in Nigeria.* New York: Cambridge University Press.

_____. 1991. "Africa: The Rebirth of Political Freedom." *Journal of Democracy* (Fall): 10–24.

Karl, T. L. 1987. "Petroleum and Political Pacts: The Transition to Democracy in Venezuela." *Latin American Research Review* 22/1: 63–94.

_____. 1990. "Dilemmas of Democratization in Latin America." *Comparative Politics* 23/1 (October): 1–21.

Keller, E. J. 1991. "Political Change and Political Research in Africa: Agenda for the 1990s." *Issue* 20/1 (Winter): 50–53.

Kitschelt, H. 1992. "Political Regime Change: Structure and Process-Driven Explanations?" *American Political Science Review* 86/4 (December): 1028–34.

Kuria, G. K. 1991. "Human Rights and Democracy in Africa." *The Fletcher Forum* 15/1 (Winter): 23–36.

Lefebvre, F. 1957. *The Coming of the French Revolution 1789,* transl. by R. R. Palmer. New York: Vintage Books.

Le Monde, "Le seizième sommet franco-africain de La Baule." 20 Juin 1990: 5.

Le Monde Diplomatique, "Droits de l'homme. . . ." Juillet 1990: 4.

Lowenthal, A. 1991. *Exporting Democracy: The United States and Latin America.* Baltimore. Johns Hopkins University Press.

Mahoney, J. and R. Synder. 1993. "Rethinking Agency and Structure in the Study of Regime Transitions." Paper presented at the annual meeting of the American Political Science Association, Washington DC, September 1–5.

March, J. G. and J. P. Olsen. 1984. "The New Institutionalism: Organizational Factors in Political Life." *American Political Science Review* 78/3 (September): 734–49.

Mba, N. 1990. "Kaba and Khaki: Women and the Militarized State in Nigeria." In *Women and the State in Africa,* edited by J. L. Papart and K. A. Staudt, 69–90. Boulder: Lynne Rienner Publishers.

Mbembe, A. 1990. "Democratization and Social Movements in Africa." *Africa Demos* 1/1 (November): 4.

Mkandawire, T. 1991. "Gendering Social Science." *CODESRIA Bulletin* 4: 1.

Moore, B. 1967. *The Social Origins of Dictatorship and Democracy: Lord and Peasant in the Making of the Modern World.* Boston: Beacon Press.

Mutua, M. 1992. "Democracy in Africa: No Easy Walk to Freedom." *Reconstruction* 2/1: 39–42.

North, D. 1990. *Institutions, Institutional Change and Economic Performance.* Cambridge: Cambridge University Press.

Nzongola-Ntalaja. 1989. "The African Crisis: The Way Out." *African Studies Review* 32/1 (April): 115–28.

O'Donnell, G. and P. Schmitter. 1986. *Transitions from Authoritarian Rule: Tentative Conclusions about Uncertain Democracies.* Baltimore: Johns Hopkins University Press.

O'Donnell, G., P. Schmitter, and L. Whitehead, eds. 1986. *Transitions from Authoritarian Rule: Prospects for Democracy.* Baltimore and London: Johns Hopkins University Press.

O'Hanlon, R. 1988. "Recovering the Subject: Subaltern Studies and Histories of Resistance in Colonial South Asia." *Modern Asian Studies* 22/1, 189–224.

Ortner, S. B. 1984. "Theory in Anthropology since the Sixties." *Comparative Studies in Society and History* 26/1: 126–66.

_____. 1989. *High Religion: A Cultural and Political History of Sherpa Buddhism.* Princeton: Princeton University Press.

Oyugi, W.O., A. Odhiambo, M. Chege, and A. K. Gitonga, eds. 1988. *Democratic Theory & Practice in Africa.* Portsmouth: Heinemann.

Poulantzas, N. 1976. *The Crisis of Dictatorships.* London: New Left Books.

_____. 1978. *State, Power, Socialism.* London: New Left Books.

Robinson, P. T. Forthcoming. "The National Conference Phenomenon in Francophone Africa."

Rueschemeyer, D., E. H. Stephens, and J. D. Stephens. 1992. *Capitalist Development and Democracy.* Chicago: University of Chicago Press.

Rustow, D. A. 1970. "Transitions to Democracy: Toward a Dynamic Model." *Comparative Politics* 2/3 (April): 337–63.

Said, E. 1986. "Orientalism Reconsidered." In *Literature, Politics and Theory: Papers from the Essex Conference,* edited by F. Baker et al., 210–29. London: Methuen.

Schama, S. 1989. *Citizens: A Chronicle of the French Revolution.* New York: Vintage Books.

Shepherd, Jr., G. and M. O. C. Anikpo, eds. 1989. *Emerging Human Rights: The African Political Economy Context.* New York: Greenwood Press.

Silk, J. 1990. "Traditional Culture and the Prospect for Human Rights in Africa." In *Human Rights in Africa: Cross-Cultural Perspectives,* edited by A.A. An-Na'im and F. Deng, 290–328. Washington DC: The Brookings Institution.

Sisulu, E. with A. Imam and M. Diouf. 1991. "Report on the Workshop on Gender Analysis and African Social Science, held in Dakar, 16–21 September 1991." *CODESRIA Bulletin* Number 4: 2–14.

Sklar, R. 1983. "Democracy in Africa." *African Studies Review* 26/3–4 (September-December): 11–24.

Stamp, P. 1991. "Burying Otieno: Politics of Gender and Ethnicity in Kenya." *Signs* 16/4 (Summer): 808–45.

Tarrow, S. 1991. "Aiming at a Moving Target: Social Science and the Recent Rebellions in Eastern Europe." *PS* 24/1 (March): 12–20.

Verba, S. 1965. "Comparative Political Culture." In *Political Culture and Political Development,* edited by L. Pye and S. Verba. Princeton: Princeton University Press.

Wai, D. 1991. "Governance, Economic Development and the Role of External Actors." Paper delivered at the Conference on Governance and Economic Development in Sub-Saharan Africa, Queen Elizabeth House, Oxford University, 2–4 May.

Wauthier, C. "'Démocratie' 'développement', ces mots pièges." *Le Monde Diplomatique,* Juillet 1990: 4.

Welch, Jr., C. E. and R. I. Meltzer, eds. 1984. *Human Rights and Development in Africa.* Albany: State University Press of New York.

Whitehead, L. 1986. "International Aspects of Democratization." In *Transitions from Authoritarian Rule: Prospects for Democracy,* edited by G. O'Donnell, P.

Schmitter, and L. Whitehead, 3–46. Baltimore and London: The Johns Hopkins University Press.

Wiredu, K. 1990. "An Akan Perspective on Human Rights." In *Human Rights in Africa: A Cross-Cultural Perspective,* edited by A. A. An-Na'im and F. Deng, 243–60. Washington DC: The Brookings Institution.

Woods. D. 1992. "Civil Society in Europe and Africa: Limiting State Power through a Public Sphere." *African Studies Review* 35/2 (September): 77–100.

World Bank. 1989. *Sub-Saharan Africa: From Crisis to Sustainable Growth.* Washington DC: The World Bank.

Wunsch, J. S. and D. Olowu. 1990. *The Failure of the Centralized State: Institutions and Self-Governance in Africa.* Boulder: Westview Press.

14

Africa:
An Interim Balance Sheet

Crawford Young

When the global "third wave" of democratization began to lap the shores of Africa in 1989, even the most sanguine observers expected that transitions from the continent's dominant mode of governance—patrimonial autocracy—would be rife with contradictions.[1] Recent events have proved them right: astonishingly high participation in Algerian presidential elections despite violence and threats from some Islamist extremists; a show of elections, with minimal participation, put on by the integralist military autocracy in Sudan; the promulgation of yet another constitution for military-ruled Nigeria, with further prolongation of that country's "permanent transition"; a political impasse leading to a coup in Niger, followed by promises that democracy would be restored within months; the return, via the ballot box, of former strongman Mathieu Kérékou to the presidency of Benin, birthplace of the national conference; elections in Sierra Leone held amid such widespread insecurity that voting was impossible in many regions; elections in the island republic of Mauritius in which (for the second time in 13 years) the ruling coalition stepped down after losing every one of the 60 seats at stake. The crosscurrents evident in these strikingly divergent events, occurring within months of each other, showed both the vitality and the fragility of the liberalization process.

A preliminary inventory of outcomes shows that only Libya and Sudan have held out resolutely against the third wave, with even the latter eventually feeling compelled to make a token gesture in the form of the above-mentioned nonparty elections. The other holdout, Colonel Muammar Qadhafi's contrarian regime in Libya, has used defiance of conventional norms as a source of legitimacy for nearly three decades. Elsewhere in

Reprinted with permission from the *Journal of Democracy* 7, no. 3 (July 1996): 53–68. © 1996 The Johns Hopkins University Press.

Africa, the tides of political opening have almost always brought changes. Transitions have ranged from the abortive (Nigeria) or denatured (Cameroon, Zaïre) to the profound (South Africa). But even where incumbents have manipulated democratization to preserve their power, some of the parameters of politics have changed.

Most of the early scholarship on liberalization in Africa centered on the dynamics of transition.[2] Now, as many countries begin to undergo their second set of postliberalization elections, it is time to shift focus and begin evaluating the breadth and depth of democratic consolidation in various countries and the sustainability of the new practices.[3]

Independence and Its Aftermath

Borrowing Samuel P. Huntington's imagery, one might say that Africa has experienced its own three waves of democratization. The first consisted of constitutional changes, following models provided by the outgoing colonial powers, that laid down the ground rules for decolonization in the late 1950s and early 1960s. The second wave, feeble and short-lived, affected scattered locales in the late 1970s and early 1980s.

Powerful international and domestic forces propelled both these earlier waves. As anticolonialism intensified both in colonies and in the world at large following World War II, beleaguered metropolitan powers began to open once-exclusionary institutions of rule to indigenous participation as part of an apprenticeship in democratic self-government. Giving the colonies constitutional structures modeled on those of the metropole became a key step in the dignified retreat from empire. Local nationalists cooperated because they saw elections as a means of hastening independence and boosting their own claim to rule. Communist and Third World dictatorships supported democratization as part of the fight against imperialism. The West, meanwhile, viewed democratization as the natural endpoint of the transition to self-rule.

As soon as independence was won, however, support for democratic governance largely ceased. The doctrine of the mass single party as the vanguard of African progress soon took root, planted by the most charismatic leaders of the independence generation (Habib Bourguiba of Tunisia, Kwame Nkrumah of Ghana, Sékou Touré of Guinea, Julius Nyerere of Tanzania), and nurtured by persuasive academic commentators.[4] There was little public resistance to the destruction of the fragile constitutional structures created as part of the decolonization process, nor, a little later, to the epidemic of military coups.

African leaders' overriding goals became rapid development and the liberation of their economies from neocolonial control. Democracy, argued the new leaders, was a luxury that poor countries could not afford.

Political competition and debate would divert energies from the urgent task of mounting a united assault on underdevelopment. Pluralism would allow fissiparous tendencies to emerge, threatening the consolidation of nationhood. The concentration of authority, not its dispersion, would be best for development and economic sovereignty.

At the time, the Soviet bloc and Maoist China seemed to offer the most impressive examples of swift economic transformation. Few Western observers were questioning Soviet claims of double-digit growth, and China's "great leap forward" of 1958–60 was viewed by many as a stunning achievement. Only years later did many realize that there were fatal contradictions in the Soviet economic model, and that the "great leap forward" was a catastrophe that had cost the lives of as many as 30 million people. Although the advent of full-fledged Afro-Marxism was years away, the late 1950s and early 1960s saw many an African leader adopt a Soviet-style emphasis on central planning, the capacity of the state to organize and direct development, the urgency of industrialization, large state-run enterprises, and so on.

Neither state socialism nor radical Third World nationalism saw much of value in postindependence constitutional democracy, and vocal defenders of democracy for Africa were scarce in the West as well. Development economists were sympathetic to state-led development, and dominant "modernization" theories readily acknowledged that economic development came first with democratization expected to follow later, a perspective that could easily rationalize military rule.[5] Former colonial powers were less interested in democracy than in preserving their economic advantages and privileged connections in their former colonies. Global strategists wanted reliable clients in the great game of the Cold War. The human rights movement was still weak and scattered, and gave scant attention to Africa. International backing for democracy in Africa vanished almost as soon as the independence celebrations ended. Indigenous nationalists had seen democracy primarily as a weapon in their struggle for independence; once that was won, democratic arrangements introduced under late colonialism seemed superfluous.

Africa's Second Wave

The second wave, when it came in the 1970s, was no *tsunami* but a discernible stirring, though apparent mainly in retrospect. The single-party regimes and military dictatorships that had dominated the continent since the morrow of independence were visibly fraying and had few intellectual defenders left. Three of the bloodiest and most notorious tyrants—Idi Amin of Uganda, Jean-Bédel Bokassa of the Central African Republic, and Francisco Macias Nguema of Equatorial Guinea—were overthrown in 1979. The destruction of the public realm by unchecked personal tyranny in each country bore witness to the perils of what Richard Sklar calls "developmental dictatorship."[6] Several single-party regimes sought renewed legitimation by copying the Tanzanian practice of allowing competitive contests for parliamentary seats within the ruling party. These elections invariably led to the displacement of roughly half the incumbents and provided some outlet for public discontent.

Other significant democratic openings included Senegal's 1976 decision to begin phasing out the single-party model. By 1983, the country had multipartism, albeit with dominant-party control. Burkina Faso in the late 1970s experienced a period of competitive democracy. Gambia and Botswana remained throughout moderately democratic, though without political alternation. Mauritius in the Indian Ocean, which is perhaps only ambiguously an African state, was the sole example in the second wave where greater political opening produced a change of rulers. In the 1982 elections, the ruling party lost all 60 directly elected seats in the National Assembly.

The second wave's two defining cases were Ghana and Nigeria; their simultaneous political openings in 1979 were the high-water mark, and with their failure the tide of liberalization receded. After taking over Ghana in 1972 and indulging in a brief initial period of reformism, the military regime of General Ignatius Acheampong had descended into unrestrained corruption, much of it involving cocoa, the country's leading export. By 1979, pressures for transition were becoming irresistible. After failing to win support for a military-civilian diarchy, the military agreed to full democratization.

Nigeria's was the single most important transition in the second wave. It began in earnest in 1975 with the coup that brought General Murtala Muhammad to power. Murtala was assassinated within a few months, but not before he had set up the transition that would be faithfully executed by his successor, General Olusegun Obasanjo. As with the first Nigerian transition in the 1950s, the process unfolded amid exceptionally favorable economic circumstances thanks to soaring world oil prices.

Although its results proved ephemeral, the extensive and broad-based process of public reflection and debate that produced the Second Nigerian Republic stands out as an innovative exercise in constitutional engineering. It showed groundbreaking candor by proposing institutions that explicitly took into account the country's cultural diversity, abandoning illusory notions that it could be coercively contained, marginalized by "national integration," or dissipated by "modernization."

In the event, it was not cultural pluralism but colossal financial and political corruption, culminating in the rigging of the 1983 elections, that destroyed the legitimacy of the Second Republic. The popular welcome that greeted the Nigerian military intervention of late 1983 marked the end of the second wave. Across most of Africa, democracy faded into the background for the time being.

On the whole, the global conjuncture remained unfavorable to democratization. The Soviet strategy of promoting a "socialist orientation" in Africa crested in the late 1970s with the emergence of seven states professing a Marxist-Leninist doctrinal commitment and the radicalization of populist-socialist regimes in Algeria and Tanzania. In response, Western powers bestowed more favors upon governments willing to resist this trend. For the most part, aside from the cases of Ghana and Nigeria, the political openings of the second wave liberalized autocratic formulas, rather than introducing fully democratic regimes.

The Crisis of the Autocratic State

Yet even as Africa's second wave was petering out, the worldwide third wave of democratization was gathering force, especially in Latin America. In Asia as well, entrenched autocracies in South Korea, Taiwan, Pakistan, and the Philippines gave way to more polyarchic regimes. African patrimonial autocracy began to seem outside the Third World mainstream.

At about the same time came a radical change in the terms under which African states engaged the international community. It began in the area of economic policy. The 1970s had been a time of aggressively asserted economic nationalism, a decade peppered with nationalizations and sweeping indigenization programs. In dramatic contrast, the beginning of the 1980s found Africa at a developmental impasse. In 1981, the World Bank offered a blistering critique of African development performance.[7] A widespread debt crisis became evident at the same time, and African states found themselves facing a phalanx of public and private international creditors. The World Bank ventured into "policy-based lending" for the first time, teaming up with the International Monetary Fund and Western donor countries to propose rigorous economic liberalization programs as the ransom for debt rescheduling and further development aid. "Neoliberalism" and "structural adjustment" entered the lexicon of political economy.

Meanwhile, the alternative of recourse to the "camp of socialism," so valuable to African states as a source of political leverage and room for international maneuver, progressively vanished. By the 1980s, the Soviet Union was reassessing its commitments and cutting its financial obligations in the Third World. The turning points for Africa were Moscow's 1981 rejection of Mozambique's attempt to join COMECON, and its 1982 rebuff of a Ghanaian delegation seeking support for a radical approach to the economic crisis. In the mid-1980s, a pattern of Soviet disengagement from Africa was becoming clear; by the end of the decade, the USSR would be in full retreat.

In the West, Keynesian economics and the social democratic ethos, which had colored much of the thinking about development in the 1960s and 1970s, came under fierce attack from doctrinaire advocates of free-market policies. At this time there arose the "Washington consensus" on development policy, which favored making external assistance conditional on economic liberalization. The progressive discrediting of state socialism during the 1980s, well before the fall of the Berlin Wall, made "economic reform" the only game in town. Africa had little choice but to accept at least the discourse of reform.

The failure of structural adjustment programs to bring about early recovery (their sponsors had predicted positive results within three to five years) intensified the mood of crisis. Influential voices both inside and outside Africa began to argue that political reform was a necessary concomitant of economic liberalization. The African state itself, as historical agent of development, came under challenge.[8] The argument ran that the thorough prebendalization of the public realm had created a state incapable of effective macroeconomic management.[9] Without a remoralization of public institutions, plus minimal accountability, economic liberalization could never endure.

Along with economic buffeting, dwindling state legitimacy was also helping to create a favorable climate for political change. For the citizens of many lands, the state had become a predator. Silent disengagement from the state became increasingly evident. Obstacles mounted to the patrimonial management of power. The resources needed to oil the gears of clientelism were drying up and becoming subject to tighter monitoring by international financial institutions intent upon structural adjustment. The stage was set for the third wave of African democratization. The 1988 Algerian riots were an early sign, shredding the three-decade-old revolutionary mystique of the National Liberation Front (FLN) and opening the way to political competition. The army aborted the transition in 1992, when it seemed that elections would bring the Islamic Salvation Front (FIS) to power, but the FLN's 1989 abandonment of its claim to political monopoly resonated.

Also in that year, longtime Beninese ruler Mathieu Kérékou, one of the deans of Afro-Marxism, found himself at bay. His government could not meet the state payroll or obtain external credits; he was abandoned by his former clientele and faced rising street protests as well as a barrage of denunciations from intellectuals, teachers, civil servants, unions, and students. There seemed no way out except to accede to their demand for a "national conference" of the so-called *forces vives* of the nation. Once assembled, the conference declared itself sovereign, and proceeded to create transitional institutions; Kérékou, isolated, could not resist this seizure of power by "civil society." The contagion soon spread throughout French-speaking Africa, whose people saw in Benin's national conference, as one admirer put it, "the beauty of something unique, incomparable."[10] National conferences drove incumbents from power in Mali, Niger, Congo, and Madagascar; they failed to do so in Gabon, Zaire, and Togo, but still changed the "rules of the game."

In Zambia, the support system sustaining the three-decade-long political monopoly of the United National Independence Party collapsed. Possibly overconfident of his capacity to survive multiparty competition, President Kenneth Kaunda permitted an honest election in 1991 and was swept from power. Even more potent in their continental impact were events in South Africa, where the unexpected release from prison of Nelson Mandela and the legalization of the African National Congress set in motion a process that led to the end of apartheid and then to genuine majority rule in 1994. In 1990, Nigeria—Africa's most populous polity—was in the midst of what looked like a credible, if slow, transition back to constitutional rule. Thus currents of change seemed to run strongly throughout the continent; democratization appeared to be mantled in the same cloak of inevitability that had clad the independence movements of the 1950s.

Equally important was the international conjuncture. The completely unexpected demolition of the Berlin Wall, and then the collapse of state socialism and of the Soviet Union itself, echoed powerfully throughout the world. By 1990, U.S. policy was aggressively promoting democratization, aided by the efforts of unusually outspoken ambassadors in Cameroon, the Central African Republic, Zaïre, and Kenya. Even France—long indulgent toward its African partners—warned that the *pré carré* was not exempt from democratization. Within the World Bank, influential voices called for political reform as a necessary companion to economic liberalization.[11] "Governance"—including such polyarchic features as citizen influence and oversight, responsible and responsive leadership, and meaningful accountability and transparency—became a regular theme in the discourse of structural adjustment.[12] Political conditionality was far less systematic than the economic variety, but nonetheless was in the air.

Yet another factor driving democratization was the need for elections as part of accords settling longstanding crises. In Angola and Mozambique, some mechanism for gauging the relative constituencies of the internationally recognized regimes and their insurgent challengers was indispensable. In Namibia, recognition from the Organization of African Unity (OAU) was not enough to install the South West African People's Organization (SWAPO) in power; the sanction of an internationally supervised election was crucial. In war-torn Sierra Leone and Liberia, elections—however problematic—seem essential to any settlement pact.

These last two instances, along with Somalia and Rwanda, suggest another conjunctural factor of increasing, even frightening, weight: the collapsed state, an outcome as unanticipated as the disappearance of socialism. Before Charles Taylor and his insurgents sparked a chain reaction of disintegration in Liberia in 1989, and before factional combat following the ouster of President Mohamed Siad Barre triggered a similar process in Somalia two years later, analysts of African politics had never considered state collapse a likely prospect. Although the weakness and declining authority of African states was widely acknowledged, the international system was expected to sustain at least the shell of what Robert H. Jackson has termed the "quasi-state" by shoring up sovereignty through a variety of external means. Yet the "collapsed state" goes beyond the "quasi-state," for the international system is not easily capable of bringing the former back to life.[13]

Uneven Progress

Africa's third wave of democratization is now well into its second half-decade. However uneven its progress, democracy now sets the terms of political discourse in Africa; in this sense, the third wave has already proved more durable than the first two. Yet the euphoria that accompanied the arrival of the third wave in Africa has long since evaporated; even the most optimistic advocates of democratization would join Larry Diamond in cautioning that democratization is "bound to be gradual, messy, fitful, and slow, with many imperfections along the way."[14]

In no other region of the world has the global third wave encountered such a hostile economic and political environment. African economic difficulties are far more debilitating than those found elsewhere. Prolonged state decline and attendant corrosion of the effectiveness and legitimacy of the public realm have exacerbated cleavages of ethnicity, religion, and race. Not even in the post-Soviet world—the closest parallel, where wrenching economic adjustment, scarce social capital, and unsupportive political cultures impede the consolidation of democratic regimes—does the path seem so thorny.

Despite all this, many countries have made it beyond the initial phase of transition and are now wrestling with the more complex problems of consolidation and institutionalization. In some other cases, initially promising transitions have become sidetracked, without necessarily being entirely compromised or abandoned. In other countries, such as Nigeria and Zaïre, incumbents have strung out and manipulated the transition process so much that democratization has lost its initial credibility and degenerated into a permanent charade.

In only a handful of instances can one speak with reasonable confidence of a beginning of consolidation, as measured by at least a second set of reasonably fair, open, and competitive elections (Benin, Cape Verde, Mauritius, Botswana, and Namibia are plausible candidates, although the latter two have yet to see any alternation in power). In a number of countries, longtime incumbents were evicted in the first transitional elections (Central African Republic, Congo, Madagascar, Malawi, São Tomé and Príncipe, South Africa, and Zambia). The journal *Africa Demos* provides the most extensive classification of degrees of democratization.[15] Its 1995 findings list just three states as irretrievably authoritarian: Libya, Nigeria, and Sudan; after the shameful fiasco of the 1996 elections, many would add Equatorial Guinea. Seven others were unclassifiable because sovereignty was contested (Algeria, Angola, Burundi, Liberia, Rwanda, Sierra Leone, and Somalia). Each of the 42 remaining countries had some form of partial or substantial democracy.

In a significant number of cases, incumbents won elections, often by encouraging the proliferation of opposition parties, exploiting control over regional administrations, and wringing out whatever political mileage remained in the old ruling party. Some observers conclude that such outcomes reveal a deep flaw in the entire third wave. Claude Ake writes of "the crude simplicity of multiparty elections," which allows "some of the world's most notorious autocrats . . . to parade democratic credentials without reforming their repressive regimes." This observation leads Ake to a broader dismissal of the whole process as a form of democracy "whose relevance to Africa is problematic at best and at worst prone to engender contradictions that tend to derail or trivialize democratization in Africa."[16]

Elections like Kenya's in 1992 have shown how determined autocratic cliques are to cling to power, at considerable cost to the polity. Intent on discrediting the very notion of political competition, key individuals in President Daniel arap Moi's inner circle fomented ethnic clashes in the Rift Valley that drove 350,000 from their homes and killed 1,500. It also came to light that Moi and his clique had illicitly acquired almost $400 million in campaign-related funds.[17] Despite all this, however, Kenyan civil society is breathing easier after partial liberalization, and the political climate is less fear-ridden and closed than it was in the late 1980s.

Chicanery by incumbents can backfire, for denatured elections lose much of their legitimating value. Opposition protests and boycotts, whether of tainted elections themselves or of the institutions that result from them, can make an impact. Cases that might fit this pattern include Burkina Faso, Cameroon, Egypt, Ethiopia, Equatorial Guinea, Gabon, Ghana, Guinea, Guinea-Bissau, Côte d'Ivoire, Kenya, Mauritania, Togo, Tunisia, and Zimbabwe. Opposition protest was most vehement in Cameroon and Kenya. At the other end of the spectrum, complaints about the electoral process were relatively muted in Burkina Faso, Ghana, Tunisia, and Zimbabwe.

The occupants of Africa's presidential palaces have learned from experience in the half-decade since political liberalization began affecting the parameters of politics in their various countries. Such adaptive behavior is not new. After the epidemic of military coups in 1965–66, autocrats began constructing protective devices that helped to keep a number of them in power for three decades: scrambled command lines, ethnic-security maps, presidential-guard forces staffed by foreign mercenaries, multiple security forces. Tunisia's Zine al-Abidine Ben Ali, Gabon's Omar Bongo, Zimbabwe's Robert Mugabe, and Egypt's Hosni Mubarak are still in power because they have been agile enough to retain the initiative under changed rules.

The global conjuncture has changed significantly since the early 1990s. The international community today is less united and compelling in its pressures. And in Africa, since political liberalization has not produced the "second independence" initially imagined, citizen skepticism concerning the process is several shades deeper. Internationally, the competing imperatives of neorealism and what one recent commentator stigmatized as "Mother Teresa" diplomacy have become more evident.[18] Within a year, France had retreated from the commitment to African democratization that it made at the 1990 La Baule meeting with French-speaking African heads of state. Britain and Japan were never enthusiastic partisans of a high priority for political liberalization. In the case of the United States, contradictions soon became apparent. Pressure for democratization has not been applied in situations (such as those of Egypt and Algeria) where security and strategic—or Huntingtonian "clash of civilizations"—preoccupations have ranked high.[19] States like Uganda and Ghana, which receive high marks for economic liberalization, feel less pressure for democratization. The talk about "governance" that comes out of the international financial institutions is confined to the institutional requisites for "sound macroeconomic management" and an "enabling environment" for freer markets.

The Politics of Identity

Skeptics have advanced two main arguments challenging the therapeutic value of democratization for African states. First, they charge that competitive multipartism and open elections necessarily bring regional, ethnic, religious, and racial identities into play, intensifying disintegrative pressures on fragile states without contributing to either stability or legitimacy. Second, pointing to what Thomas M. Callaghy calls the "high historical correlation in the contemporary era between authoritarian rule and the ability to engage in major economic restructuring in the Third World," the skeptics note the severity of Africa's economic crisis, and claim that the intrinsic difficulty of convincing electorates of the need for painful austerity measures renders recovery impossible, and ensures another turn of the downward spiral.[20]

Few would deny that electoral competition readily flows along societal fault lines of ethnicity, religion, or race, in the world at large as well as Africa. Such identities serve as tempting vote banks for party organizers. With the perhaps momentary eclipse of ideological divisions, in an epoch where all forms of socialism remain blighted by the stigma of the failed Soviet version, political challengers have great difficulty in defining an alternative vision of society. Electoral discourse is thus limited to vague slogans expressing desire for change and opposition to incumbents. One finds few cases (Senegal is one) where political alignments are not significantly affected by communal solidarities.

Of the many transitions now in process, however, only four have seen escalating communal violence: Rwanda, Burundi, Algeria, and Congo. The endemic intercommunal strife in Sudan and Somalia has nothing to do with democratization, which on the contrary appears necessary if there is to be any hope for peace. Of the four cases, only in Congo did the ethnic violence involve armed factions directly issuing from electoral politics. The violence unleashed by the ethnic youth militias that terrorized Brazzaville for several months in 1993 and provoked large-scale ethnic cleansing of the capital's neighborhoods finally subsided at the end of that year when the party leaders who had fomented it reverted to more civil forms of rivalry under prodding from the OAU. The militias, however, are still at large, and Congo remains a cautionary tale in the drama of political liberalization.

In Algeria, the violence broke out when the military intervened to suspend an election process that would have produced a victory for the FIS. It cannot be known whether the FIS would have followed the Iranian path of political exclusion of those not sharing its vision of the Islamic state. What is certain is that an armed uprising by FIS elements, and later by far more extreme factions of the Groupe Islamique Armé, began soon after, and brought the country to the brink of civil war. Also clear is that the successful political opening begun by President Liamine Zéroual with the November 1995 elections created new opportunities for isolating the extremists and reincorporating most of the religious currents within civil society into the political process.

In Burundi, after the searing experiences of ethnic massacres in 1965, 1972, and 1988, the Tutsi-dominated military regime of Pierre Buyoya took meaningful steps toward national reconciliation. Buyoya expected his Union pour le Progrès National to reap electoral victory from this, and indeed, its main challenger, the Hutu-dominated Front Démocratique Burundais (FRODEBU), won only 60 percent of the vote even though the country was 85 percent Hutu. Buyoya accepted defeat graciously, and

ceded power to the FRODEBU presidential candidate, Melchior Ndadaye. There was hope for ethnic accommodation through power-sharing
and liberalization. The fatal flaw in the transitional arrangements was
Tutsi control over the security forces. Tutsi officers assassinated Ndadaye
and several other FRODEBU leaders in October 1993, unleashing ethnic
violence that has brought Burundi to the brink of a genocidal dissolution
of state and society.[21]

As for the holocaust in neighboring Rwanda, which horrified the world
in the spring of 1994, the evidence is even clearer that only some formula
for power-sharing accompanied by political opening could have averted
armageddon. Power had long been in the hands of a Hutu ethnarchy that
later recast itself as a single-party military autocracy under Juvenal Habyarimana, who seized power in 1973. For more than a decade, the regime enjoyed a reasonable quotient of legitimacy with the Hutu majority, bolstered
by a moderately competent development record and substantial external
assistance. By the late 1980s, however, decline had set in amid increasing
venality, growing regional favoritism, and decreasing governmental effectiveness. In 1990 came the invasion by the Rwandan Patriotic Front (FPR),
an insurgent group consisting mostly of Tutsi exiles long resident in
Uganda. Although contained with French, Belgian, and Zaïrian military assistance, the insurgency triggered a political crisis that led to the abandonment of single-party rule in 1991. Multipartism did not completely cure the
deepening disaffection of civil society, but at least offered hope for political
compromise and the containment of ethnic and regional tensions.

Hope vanished when the April 1994 assassination of Habyarimana became the occasion for genocidal massacres instigated and executed by ex-
tremist Hutu bands linked to the former ruling party. At least half a million people (mostly Tutsis) were killed, and two million Hutus later
became refugees in neighboring countries. (Rwanda's total population
before the massacres had been about eight million.) The FPR successor
regime is unlikely to enjoy peace or stability until the country can come to
terms with its past through a negotiated settlement that provides security
to all citizens. Given the depth of the trauma, democracy will probably be
off the national agenda for a long time.

Democratic responses to the problem of ethnicity can take many institutional forms. Consider the Ethiopian and Ugandan cases. In Ethiopia,
the Shoan Amharic hegemony that lay at the core of both the imperial
regime and its Afro-Marxist successor provoked a spate of rebellions
around the ethnic and regional periphery. The 1991 military defeat of the
Afro-Marxist regime at the hands of the Eritrean People's Liberation
Front and the Tigrean People's Liberation Front (TPLF) compelled a far-
reaching redefinition of the polity. Eritrea became independent, and ethnicity became the basis for a redrawing of Ethiopia's provincial bound-

aries. The new Ethiopian constitution goes farther than any other existing in the world today toward enshrining the principle of ethnic self-determination, up to and including the right to secession.

The actual exercise of ethnic self-determination, however, is constrained by the residue of Leninism that still affects the ruling Ethiopian People's Revolutionary Democratic Front (EPRDF), which is essentially a creature of the TPLF. So far, the EPRDF leadership has handled the ethnic question by creating client parties in the various regions; full acceptance of the new political order by major ethnic groups such as the Oromo or Somali—to say nothing of the once-dominant Amhara—has yet to be demonstrated. Still, many Ethiopians regard the present limited political opening as an improvement upon the authoritarian regimes of the past.

In Uganda, President Yoweri Museveni is maneuvering to preserve the rule of his National Resistance Movement (NRM) under the ostensible constitutional sanction of a no-party democratic order. Large sectors of Ugandan opinion view this arrangement with an acquiescence that is at best temporary and uneasy. Yet the remarkable recovery that Uganda has enjoyed under his leadership has earned Museveni substantial room for maneuver. Enthusiasm for a return to political parties is tempered by the prospect of a return to prominence of the Uganda People's Congress and the Democratic Party, whose intense and partly religion-based rivalry dating to the 1960s is blamed for many of the misfortunes that followed. But the 1994 Constitution provided only a five-year delay for introduction of party politics, not a permanent mandate for NRM rule under the disguise of a no-party system.

The evidence to date does not permit the conclusion that identity politics offers an insuperable obstacle to political liberalization. The saliency of cultural diversity in most African states, however, poses clear challenges to sustainable democratization. There is need for thoughtful statecraft to devise constitutional formulas that can accommodate ethnic, religious, or racial differences. Evidence from around the world suggests that cultural pluralism should be acknowledged rather than ignored, through arrangements that induce inclusionary politics and create structural incentives for intercommunal cooperation.[22]

Economic Performance

Less clear is the critical issue of whether a politically liberalized state can sustain the rigorous macroeconomic management that is needed to restore economic health. The evidence on African economic performance since 1960 shows beyond doubt that patrimonial autocracy has failed. There is no need to review the dismal statistics through the 1980s; it suffices to note that while Ghanaian per-capita income comfortably exceeded that of South Korea in 1957, by 1993 per-capita income in South Korea was nearly 18 times what it was in Ghana.[23]

However strong the general case that can be made for the sequencing of reform on the East Asian model, with political opening coming after economic development, the applicability of this model to Africa is doubtful. Only Tunisia, with its highly effective and cohesive state apparatus, remotely resembles East Asia's "little tigers," yet Tunisian per-capita income grew by an average of only 1.2 percent a year from 1980 to 1993.[24] The logic of sequencing operates in reverse in Africa: partial or substantial *political* transitions or liberalizations have occurred in most states, and the present international environment is hostile to overt authoritarian restoration. Although large states such as Nigeria and Sudan, or a maverick rentier state like Libya, can withstand external pressures, smaller and weaker African states are far more vulnerable. One may recollect the speed with which forcible coups have been reversed in the last three years in São Tomé and Príncipe, Lesotho, and Comoros; the authors of the January 1996 coup in Niger, though they could point to a debilitating institutional impasse and poorly designed "national conference" constitution to justify their actions, were soon compelled to agree to new elections (now slated for September 1996).

Relatively effective economic liberalization can earn some breathing space. Ghana and Uganda experienced far less international pressure for further political liberalization than did Kenya and Cameroon. But the conscious construction of a regime modeled on the Taiwan or South Korea of the 1960s and 1970s is impossible to imagine, even if internal societal and political circumstances permitted.

It is also worth noting that the two most impressive sustained economic-development records among Africa's 53 states belong to a pair of continuously democratic polities, Botswana and Mauritius. Botswana enjoyed average annual growth of 14.5 percent from 1970 to 1980, and 9.6 percent from 1980 to 1993. Over the same quarter-century, Mauritius maintained a steady growth rate of over 6 percent. Mauritius, little more than a huge sugar plantation at the time of its independence in 1968, has since the mid-1980s doubled its per-capita GDP to more than $3,000 per year. Its now-diversified economy has an unemployment rate of only 2 percent. And yet, in 1982 and again in 1995, fairly conducted elections resulted in ruling parties' losing all the contested seats, with peaceful turnover of power ensuing in both instances. Some special factors operate in both cases, but the indisputable success of Botswana and Mauritius is not just luck. Effective, cohesive bureaucracies, relatively high levels of public integrity, and careful economic management have played a large role. An expanding economy has in turn doubtless made democratic governance more sustainable.

Thus the question of the relationship between regime type and economic performance in Africa remains open. World Bank figures and other country-level statistical indicators yield no definitive answers. Indeed, it would be naive to expect causal pathways to stand out with much clarity when there are so many intervening variables involved. Stephan Haggard and Robert R. Kaufman, in their study of the political economy of democratic transitions in Latin America and Asia (but not Africa), conclude that the challenge of building state capacity in the poorer developing countries is forbidding, especially given the enormous debts and acute economic distress that many suffer. Winning political support for economic reform is hard at best, and becomes harder when its gains are intangible to constituents.[25] Electoral imperatives can spur profligate spending by incumbents: the Tanzanian government borrowed 33 billion Tanzanian shillings before the flawed 1995 elections.

The interim balance sheet on democratization in Africa is mixed but mildly positive. Not all experiments will survive, yet many countries have experienced important changes beyond the most visible one of multiparty elections: a freer and more vocal press, better respect for human rights, some headway toward achieving the rule of law. The more visionary forms of integral populist democracy are unlikely to be attained. The democratizing reforms that have occurred so far fall far short of consolidated democracy by any reasonably rigorous criteria, such as those proposed in a recent seminal article by Juan J. Linz and Alfred Stepan.[26] Nevertheless, slow, halting, uneven, yet continuing movement toward polyarchy is possible. There is no plausible and preferable alternative on the horizon.

Notes

1. Samuel P. Huntington, *The Third Wave: Democratization in the Late Twentieth Century* (Norman: University of Oklahoma Press, 1991).

2. For example, Jennifer A. Widner, ed., *Economic Change and Political Liberalization in Sub-Saharan Africa* (Baltimore: Johns Hopkins University Press, 1994); Goran Hyden and Michael Bratton, eds., *Governance and Politics in Africa* (Boulder, Colo.: Lynne Rienner, 1992); John W. Harbeson, Donald Rothchild, and Naomi Chazan, eds., *Civil Society and the State in Africa* (Boulder, Colo.: Lynne Rienner, 1994); Larry Diamond, Juan J. Linz, and Seymour Martin Lipset, *Democracy in Developing Countries: Africa* (Boulder, Colo.: Lynne Rienner, 1988).

3. By liberalization, I mean such measures as acceptance of freer media, particularly the press, more respect for human rights, the ending of politically motivated incarceration, and the widening of freedom of association, as well as formally democratic measures such as competitive elections. Thus liberalization moves the polity toward a democratic opening, and as such is closely akin to democratization.

4. See, for example, the well-reasoned arguments in Government of Tanzania, *Report of the Presidential Commission on the Establishment of a Democratic One-Party*

State (Dar-es-Salaam: Government Printer, 1965). For influential academic briefs for the single party, see Ruth Schachter Morganthau, *Political Parties in French-Speaking West Africa* (Oxford: Clarendon, 1964); Immanuel Wallerstein, *Africa: The Politics of Independence* (New York: Vintage, 1961); Thomas Hodgkin, *African Political Parties: An Introductory Guide* (Harmondsworth: Penguin, 1961).

5. One may recollect the (in retrospect) surprisingly indulgent appraisals of the military as equipped with the integrity, nation-building commitment, and discipline to direct the early stages of development, in such influential works as Morris Janowitz, *The Military in the Political Development of New Nations: An Essay in Comparative Analysis* (Chicago: University of Chicago Press, 1964) and John J. Johnson, ed., *The Role of the Military in Underdeveloped Countries* (Princeton: Princeton University Press, 1962).

6. Richard Sklar, "Democracy in Africa," in Patrick Chabal, ed., *Political Domination in Africa: Reflections on the Limits of Power* (Cambridge: Cambridge University Press, 1986), 17–29.

7. *Accelerated Development in Sub-Saharan Africa: An Agenda for Action* (Washington, D.C.: World Bank, 1981).

8. See Richard Sandbrook, *The Politics of Africa's Economic Stagnation* (Cambridge: Cambridge University Press, 1985); Donald Rothchild and Naomi Chazan, *The Precarious Balance: State and Society in Africa* (Boulder, Colo.: Westview, 1988); John Ravenhill, ed., *Africa in Economic Crisis* (New York: Columbia University Press, 1986).

9. Richard Joseph, *Democracy and Prebendal Politics in Nigeria* (Cambridge: Cambridge University Press, 1987).

10. F. Eboussi Boulaga, *Les conférences nationales en Afrique Noire: Une affaire à suivre* (Paris: Karthala, 1993).

11. See, for example, the article by World Bank official Pierre Landell-Mills, "Governance, Cultural Change, and Empowerment," *Journal of Modern African Studies* 30 (December 1992): 543–67.

12. Goran Hyden has most systematically advanced and defended this concept; see his "Governance and the Study of Politics," in Hyden and Michael Bratton, *Governance and Politics in Africa* (Boulder, Colo.: Lynne Rienner, 1992), 1–26.

13. I. William Zartman, ed., *Collapsed States: The Disintegration and Restoration of Legitimate Authority* (Boulder, Colo.: Lynne Rienner, 1995); Robert H. Jackson, *Quasi-States: Sovereignty, International Relations, and the Third World* (Cambridge: Cambridge University Press, 1990).

14. *West Africa* (London), 4–10 March 1996, 328.

15. *Africa Demos* (Atlanta), 3 (March 1995): 35.

16. Claude Ake, *Democracy and Development in Africa* (Washington, D.C.: Brookings Institution, 1996), 130–31. To replace the "impoverished liberal democracy which prevails in the industrial countries" (p. 129), Ake proposes a resolutely utopian, integral-populist version.

17. *Africa Confidential*, 2 December 1994, 4–5.

18. Michael Mandelbaum, "Foreign Policy as Social Work," *Foreign Affairs* 75 (January–February 1996): 16–32.

19. Samuel P. Huntington, "The Clash of Civilizations?" *Foreign Affairs* 72 (Summer 1993): 22–49.

20. Thomas M. Callaghy and John Ravenhill, eds., *Hemmed In: Responses to Africa's Economic Decline* (New York: Columbia University Press, 1993), 467. See also the more pessimistic reading in Callaghy, "Africa: Back to the Future?" *Journal of Democracy* 5 (October 1994): 133–45. In these two arguments, we may note, one encounters a reprise of the brief for the single-party regime, circa 1960: the overriding urgency of nation-building, and the imperative of centralized, unchallenged state developmental authority.

21. For illuminating background, see René Lemarchand, *Burundi: Ethnocide as Discourse and Practice* (Washington, D.C.: Woodrow Wilson Center Press, 1994); Filip Reyntjens, "The Proof of the Pudding Is in the Eating: The June 1993 Elections in Burundi," *Journal of Modern African Studies* 31 (December 1993): 563–84.

22. I agree with Donald L. Horowitz on the primacy of incentives for cooperation; see his *A Democratic South Africa? Constitutional Engineering in a Divided Society* (Berkeley: University of California Press, 1991). Cf. Arend Lijphart, *Power-Sharing in South Africa* (Berkeley: Institute of International Studies, University of California–Berkeley, 1985), and *Democracy in Plural Societies* (Berkeley: University of California Press, 1977).

23. World Bank, *Workers in an Integrating World: World Development Report 1995* (New York: Oxford University Press, 1995), 162–63.

24. Ibid., 162.

25. Stephan Haggard and Robert R. Kaufman, *The Political Economy of Democratic Transitions* (Princeton: Princeton University Press, 1995), 377–79.

26. Juan J. Linz and Alfred Stepan, "Toward Consolidated Democracies," *Journal of Democracy* 7 (April 1996): 14–32.

Suggestions for Further Reading

Ake, Claude. *Democracy and Development in Africa.* Washington, D.C.: Brookings Institution, 1996.

Anyang' Nyong'o, Peter, ed. *Popular Struggles for Democracy in Africa.* Atlantic Highlands. N.J.: Zed Books, 1987.

Bratton, Michael, and Nicolas van de Walle. *Democratic Experiments in Africa.* Cambridge: Cambridge University Press, 1997.

Diamond, Larry, Juan Linz, and Seymour M. Lipset, eds. *Democracy in Developing Countries: Africa.* Boulder: Lynne Rienner Publishers, 1988.

_____. *Politics in Developing Countries.* 2d ed. Boulder: Lynne Rienner Publishers, 1995.

Hayward, Fred M., ed. *Elections in Independent Africa.* Boulder: Westview Press, 1986.

Huntington, Samuel. *The Third Wave: Democratization in the Late 20th Century.* Norman: University of Oklahoma Press, 1991.

Sandbrook, Richard. *The Politics of Africa's Economic Recovery.* Cambridge: Cambridge University Press, 1993.

Wiseman, John A. *Democracy in Black Africa.* New York: Paragon House Publishers, 1990.

Wiseman, John A., ed. *Democracy and Political Change in Sub-Saharan Africa.* New York: Routledge, 1995.

Part Five

Political Economy: Crisis and Reform

As a whole, independent Africa has confronted a distinct set of challenges in economic development. Each country of the region emerged from colonial rule with a different endowment of resources, investment, and human capital, yet they all share a similar array of structural problems. African economies are predominantly rural, and the mass of their populations are extremely poor. They often lack the capital, technology, and expertise to diversify output and achieve higher productivity. The patterns of trade inherited from colonialism have created acute burdens of external dependence for most countries, as they rely on a narrow range of primary commodities for export income and require a broad range of imported manufactures. In the decades since independence, development efforts throughout the region have been animated by the pursuit of autonomy and the flight from poverty.

Until the mid-1980s, it was possible to identify development strategies by their different ideological and policy orientations.[1] Populist strategies, evident in countries such as Tanzania, Ghana, and Guinea, emphasized extensive government ownership and regulation of the economy, aligned with policies to reduce inequality and enhance popular welfare. Capitalist strategies—pursued, for instance, in Kenya and the Ivory Coast—stressed growth-oriented policies allowing wider roles for private investment, commerce, and trade. These governments also showed greater tolerance for domestic income disparities. In the 1970s, the emergence of several Marxist states, including Ethiopia and Mozambique, engendered policies oriented toward central planning, collective ownership, and pervasive state control of domestic economic activity. Their commitments to doctrines of class struggle were distinctive in the region.

359

In certain respects, there were important similarities among these disparate approaches to development. Regardless of formal ideology, economic policy was highly nationalist, as local enterprise and self-reliance were given priority over foreign investment or global economic interactions. Most governments also reflected a statist preference for direct political controls on resources, rather than permitting open market forces to determine allocations. More specifically, many regimes emphasized strategies of import-substitution industrialization, typically aided by large state-owned enterprise sectors. These policies were commonly linked to regulations on trade, investment, and finance. Moreover, there was a recurrent bias against the rural economy, as governments sought to extract resources from agriculture and subsidized important urban constituencies.

These policies and economic structures gave rise to a typical cluster of problems; slower growth, lagging investment, fiscal and trade deficits, chronic poverty, and persistent inequalities beset most African countries by the 1970s. The oil price hikes of 1973 worsened regional balance of payments problems and escalated foreign borrowing. A second price shock in 1979 brought these problems to a head, as terms of trade turned sharply against African economies, debt obligations began to accumulate rapidly, and traditional sources of external financing dried up. In the early 1980s, dozens of African countries reflected crises of production, public finance, and popular welfare.

Throughout the region, a remarkably consistent predicament appeared as growth rates became flat or negative, numerous economies reflected food shortfalls and industrial decline, and trade and investment shrank while external payments soared. These discouraging trends were joined by a serious decay of infrastructure and social services, as deepening immiserization affected broad segments of society. The degeneration of the formal economy led to a rise in parallel markets, heightened dependence on foreign aid, and recurrent signs of political instability. These patterns were evident in traditionally populist and Marxist economies as well as capitalist states; the main differences were in the degree of crisis.

Pressed by acute fiscal problems, dozens of African governments turned to the international "lenders of last resort," the International Monetary Fund and the World Bank. These multilateral financial institutions were instrumental in advancing a series of market-oriented reforms for African economies. Encouraged by the conditional lending of external donors, many countries adopted stabilization and structural adjustment programs. These measures were generally designed to reduce state intervention and enhance the role of private economic activity. They stressed fiscal and monetary restraint, more open trade and investment regimes, freer prices, and privatization. In the 1980s, the donors exercised new leverage over African economic policies and significantly altered the regional development agenda.

External influence, though significant, was neither uniform nor absolute. African states responded in various ways to the challenges of reform. Economic liberalization entailed a number of political risks for African regimes, as cutbacks in state intervention reduced their patronage resources and threatened their traditional constituencies. In practice, many governments were highly selective in the pursuit of reform, heeding a few conspicuous features of policy conditionality while evading other important elements. A contentious relationship developed between African governments and the international financial institutions, as each group sought advantage in the trade-off of resources for policy change. In consequence, the pattern of reform was uneven and inconsistent.

These circumstances have produced an ambiguous record of change throughout the region. There is little question that recovery has been sluggish and tentative for most countries, but the reasons for this have been hotly contested. Critics of structural adjustment insist that conventional reforms do little to promote economic growth but undermine production and hurt the poor. They view the policies of the international financial institutions as a scheme for collecting debts and compelling African economies to open up to exploitive foreign capital. Proponents argue with equal vigor that the orthodox package is painful but necessary medicine for restructuring African economies and putting them on a better footing for sustained growth. Pointing to the manifest failure of statist policies across the continent, they contend that private investment and international trade are the crucial engines of recovery in the region.

Africa's intractable economic malaise has been a dominant regional challenge since the early 1980s. The issue of recovery continues to provide the setting for debates over development and change. The readings in this section consider alternative theories of economic development while recounting Africa's economic evolution and describing the regional context of reform. The first selection, by Tony Killick, provides a concise overview of development policy debates at the beginning of the 1980s. The contention between dependency theory and neoclassical views of economic development has remained an important theme in the evolving controversies over policy reform and economic restructuring, even as new perspectives have been introduced into mainstream discussions.

The articles by Thomas Callaghy and John Ravenhill complement each other. Callaghy reviews the genesis of the African debt crisis and the global context of economic reform. He explains the distinctive roles of the IMF, the World Bank, and the leading creditors' cartels, observing the political issues that surround adjustment along with conventional policy concerns. Ravenhill gives an extended assessment of the debates surrounding economic reform in the 1980s. He explores the achievements and limitations of the structural adjustment agenda and the changing international setting for African recovery. A central part of this story is the evolution of policy approaches by the multilateral financial institutions.

In the final selection, Jeffrey Herbst focuses on the political challenges of economic restructuring. As noted above, a fairly consistent set of policies and practices have contributed to the regional economic crisis. These patterns are linked to state structures and political interests evident in a wide variety of countries. Economic adjustment inevitably challenges the traditional interests of governing elites and other important constituencies, producing a series of political hazards in the course of reform. Herbst notes the consequences of neglecting the political dimensions of adjustment, a traditional weakness in the approach of international donors.

Notes

1. This is elaborated by Crawford Young in *Ideology and Development in Africa* (New Haven: Yale University Press, 1982).

15

Trends in Development Economics and Their Relevance to Africa

Tony Killick

Important changes have been occurring in the ill-defined area of study called development economics. The purpose of this article is to identify and describe what are judged to have been the most important changes in development economics during the last decade, and thereafter to evaluate their relevance to the circumstances of the economies of Africa.

Recent Changes in Development Economics

The Broadening of Development Economics

If we define development economics broadly as the application of economic principles and methods to conditions in the so-called "less-developed countries" (L.D.C.s), there is a real sense in which the subject has come of age during the last decade. Once "development" became accepted as a respectable subject for study by economists it was generally taught—in both industrial and developing countries—as another specialism, alongside money and banking, or agricultural economics, or international trade. This, no doubt, was (and is) a sensible way of tackling the subject in the universities of the industrial world. It was far less satisfactory in developing countries, where it is surely preferable that *all* aspects

Reprinted with the permission of Cambridge University Press from the *Journal of Modern African Studies* 18, no. 3 (1980): 367–386. © 1980 Cambridge University Press.

of economics be taught from an orientation based on national conditions and concerns.

One of the least remarked but most important changes now under way is the publication of an increasing volume of writings designed to promote this reorientation of the teaching of economics in L.D.C.s. Although there remain many gaps and many teachers frustrated from doing what they want because they lack suitable materials, there has nevertheless been a burgeoning of textbooks on specialised subjects written specifically to meet L.D.C. needs. As well as introductory texts, there are now solid treatments of such specialisms as agricultural, industrial, and monetary economics, as well as economic policy and econometrics. No doubt some of these succeed better than others, but that is scarcely unique to the developing world.

The Breakdown of the Old Consensus[1]

During the 1950s and into the 1960s a good deal of agreement grew up among economists concerning the nature of underdevelopment and how it could be conquered. A substantial (but not necessarily identical) majority of economists working on development could have been mustered in the early 1960s in support of each of the following propositions:

1. Economic development is a discontinuous process of structural transformation.
2. National poverty is self-perpetuating, with low-income countries caught in a vicious circle of poverty. But, with the savings ratio as a rising function of income, growth tends to become self-sustaining above a certain critical level of income *per capita.*
3. A "big push" or "critical minimum effort" is required to break out of the "low-level equilibrium trap" and achieve self-sustaining growth. This will entail the use of development planning.
4. While the "big push" requires many inputs, its single most important ingredient is a massive increase in the ratio of investment to national income.
5. Development entails industrialisation which, by choice or necessity, will concentrate on satisfying the home market for manufactures by substituting for imports.

This broad consensus had a further feature of note: although it was chiefly generated by the work of "conventional" economists based in the universities of the industrial West, it was none the less strongly congruent with Marxian writings on development, and with the views of nationalist leaders in Africa and elsewhere. The latter groups were particularly attracted by the notions of the "big push", of planning, of a rapid "take-off" into self-sustaining growth, and of accelerated industrialisation.

With the probable exception of item (1), not one of these propositions would today command general assent among western-based or trained economists. The evidence has refuted the ideas of a "poverty trap" and that high incomes automatically ensure sustained growth. Faith in the efficacy of a big push engineered by development planners and fuelled by massive investments in fixed capital has similarly faded. Both planning and import-substituting industrialisation are now regarded as having failed to deliver the benefits they seemed to offer.[2]

The erosion of the consensus of the 1950s and 1960s has had great significance for the evolution of development economics in recent years, especially as there is now widespread recognition that no single theory could possibly fit all the countries conventionally classified as "developing"—from Bhutan to Brazil, from India to Saudi Arabia. Outside the diplomatic conveniences of international agencies and other aid donors, there is a real sense in which the Third World no longer exists. Its more advanced members have a good deal less in common with most African states than with the industrialised North; and the burdens thrust upon a majority of L.D.C.s by the monopolistic actions of the minority which exports petroleum provides only the most obvious example of differences of interest within the Third World. It is now necessary to differentiate between countries on the basis of various socio-economic criteria, and we now have categories such as the "N.I.C.s" (newly industrialising countries), the oil-exporting, "middle-income", "least developed", and "most seriously affected" L.D.C.s. Partly for reasons of this kind, the old style of grand theorising has been virtually abandoned (except by some neo-Marxian writers), and future progress in development economics seems to lie with the identification and analysis of reasonably homogeneous sub-groups of developing countries.[3] Greater appreciation of the complexities of different situations has also contributed to the near-demise of single-problem-single-solution approaches to development.

Redefining "Development"

Implicit in the old consensus was a tendency to view development and economic growth as synonymous, with trends in income *per capita* taken as the chief indicator of the rate of progress. It was left mainly to Marxian writers to draw attention to the existence of large inequalities within L.D.C.s, and to warn that the benefits of growth may be captured by a privileged few at the expense of the many. It is not necessary to elaborate much on the proposition that the situation today is very different. Beginning about ten years ago, economists began increasingly to question whether the benefits of increased production were generally percolating through to all socio-economic strata of L.D.C. populations. Evidence of large, perhaps widening, income inequalities, and of a growing employment problem, suggested that the simple average statistic provided by G.N.P. *per capita* was a drastically deficient indicator of development.

Increasingly, therefore, writers insisted that considerations of social justice and human satisfaction were essential components of any adequate definition of development. Thus Michael Todaro asserts, in a popular introductory text of economics for L.D.C.s, that development in all societies must have *at least* the following objectives:

> to increase the availability and widen the distribution of basic life-sustaining goods such as food, shelter, health and protection to all members of society;
>
> to raise levels of living, including, in addition to higher incomes, the provision of more jobs, better education and more attention to cultural and humanistic values. These all serve not only to enhance material well-being but also to generate greater individual and national self-esteem;
>
> to expand the range of economic and social choice to individuals and nations by freeing them from servitude and dependence not only in relation to other people and nation-states but also to the forces of ignorance and human misery.[4]

The strongly moralistic flavour of this illustrates one of the sharpest points of contrast with conventional "western" economic theory: namely, the normative nature of much of development economics, as contrasted with the positivist tradition which would deny that it is a task of economists to specify policy objectives. On the other hand, the concern now being expressed about the incidence of inequality and associated evils in L.D.C.s is entirely in the tradition of earlier writers on development. A desire to alleviate income disparities has always been a special regard of development economists, but their attention in the 1950s and 1960s was largely focused on the problem of inequality between nation-states.

While the broader definitions of development carry the danger of reducing its utility by making it too all-embracing, they certainly serve to emphasise the truth that the study of development cannot fruitfully be limited to the confines of economics.[5] The broad view has also been associated with an enormous upsurge of research into inequality, unemployment, basic needs, and related features of developing countries, to which we return shortly. And underlying the reference in Todaro's definition to freeing individuals and nations from "servitude and dependence" is another recent and influential body of writings about what is now known as "dependency theory".

Dependency Theories of Underdevelopment[6]

It may in this context be useful to distinguish "dependency worriers" from "dependency theorists". The former may be described as those concerned about the possibly adverse effects on development of various aspects of dependency, and about ways of preventing these, while the latter go further by building dependency into a general theory of underdevelopment. Such an analysis is concerned with the manner in which the advanced capitalist economies ("the centre") impinge upon the domestic structures and socio-economic progress of developing countries ("the periphery"), whose interests are perceived as being opposed to one another: "What is decisive is that economic development in the underdeveloped countries is profoundly inimical to the dominant interests in the advanced capitalist countries".[7]

There are, in fact, a number of competing theories of dependency, and this makes it difficult to present an adequate summary. Nevertheless, most would include the following as among the factors that create a relationship of dependency of the periphery upon the centre:

1. There is a heavy penetration of foreign capital, mainly in the form of direct investments by multinational corporations (M.N.C.s) in the mineral, plantation, and light manufacturing sectors, but also as Euro-dollar loans by international banks. These are highly profitable to the investors, and result in a large return flow of income to the centre.
2. There is unbalanced reliance upon the export of a few primary products (some writers add labour-intensive manufactures as another type of lop-sided export structure).
3. Centre-periphery trade is characterised by "unequal exchange". Among non-Marxian writers, this mainly refers to unfavourable trends in the terms of trade for commodities, but also to other aspects of unequal bargaining strength in trade, investment, and taxation. In Marxian terminology, unequal exchange has a rather different connotation, referring to a situation in which the L.D.C.s are forced to exchange commodities that embody a great deal of socially necessary labour time for products from the industrialised countries that embody a lesser quantity.
4. The technology employed in the industrial and other modern sectors is inappropriate to the needs of the developing economies, having been imported unchanged from the industrial countries, chiefly through the medium of M.N.C. investments. This technology fails to meet the consumption and employment needs of the masses; it creates and perpetuates a skewed distribution of income.
5. The consumption patterns of L.D.C.s are largely determined by standards set in industrial countries. Local élites have a symbiotic relationship with external investors, and thus perceive their own interests as congruent with those of the foreigners, rather than with the mass of the population.

6. The relationships just described give rise to large and increasing inequalities in the functional and inter-personal distributions of income.
7. Economic penetration spills over into influence over culture, social organisation, education, and politics. In consequence, policies and development plans are "influenced and even determined by foreign private interests and governments".[8]

All members of this school agree that the relationship just described has a severely adverse effect on the economies of the periphery, but some go further than others. Some assert that it leads to stagnation,[9] or even to immiserisation;[10] others concede the possibility of limited development, but of a subservient or marginalised type;[11] and some prefer to remain vague, claiming merely that dependence prevents "balanced" development.[12]

The policy inferences drawn from the facts of dependence differ as between the theorists and the worriers. The latter urge the introduction of reforms to minimise the various adverse effects of dependency: tougher policies towards M.N.C.s, heavy industrialisation, diversification of the export structure, a new international economic order, and so on. Most dependency theorists, however, deny the possibility of piecemeal reforms, because such changes would be against the interests of the ruling élites of the periphery, and would also be opposed by the centre. In their view it is impossible to develop within the capitalist system, and no half-way house between capitalism and socialism is available. The only alternative to continued dependence is revolution and socialism.

It could be argued that there is nothing new about dependency theory, and that it belongs to the stagnationist school mentioned in the earlier description of the post-war consensus. After all, Paul Baran's seminal contribution dates back to 1957.[13] This is true, but it is also the case that his original formulations have since undergone many refinements, chiefly during the 1970s. Moreover, dependency theory as such has only come to exert much influence on academic and political opinion during the last few years.

Basic Needs and Redistribution Through Growth

Along with the greater concern with issues of social equity, noted earlier, has emerged a growing awareness that the distribution of income and the creation of employment opportunities are not topics that can be approached separately from the achievement of economic growth. Improvements in our understanding of the relationships between these objectives are among the most important changes in development economics during the 1970s. The growth path followed by an economy necessarily has a strong influence on employment and income disparities, and it is now widely agreed that a strategy of "grow now, redistribute later" is neither feasible nor desirable.[14]

The tasks of reducing inequalities and unemployment thus devolve upon the choice of a series of measures that will achieve these objectives without sacrificing continued growth. Such a strategy has become known as "redistribution through growth",[15] the basic elements of which are as follows:

1. *Sectoral priorities* which favour the development of small-holder agriculture, as well as "informal" small-scale, non-farm activities of all kinds. These sectors are favoured because they are thought to contain a high proportion of the poor, as well as being labour-intensive. Modern industry and large-scale plantation-style farming receive lower priorities, especially by comparison with the policies favoured in the period of the post-war consensus.
2. *Rural development* is a related aspect of this strategy, but goes beyond the raising of agricultural output and productivities by seeking to improve social services and amenities simultaneously with the expansion of incomes. These aspects are often associated with proposals for the decentralisation of planning and, in some countries, for land reforms. A basic goal is to reduce disparities in urban-rural living standards.
3. *Factoral priorities* which favour labour-intensity and economise on the use of capital and foreign exchange. Employment creation is seen as crucial to improving the well-being of the landless, the urban unemployed, and the multitude of the underemployed.
4. The adoption of more *appropriate technologies* is regarded as crucial to both the employment-creating and redistributive aspects of the strategy. These can be described, for L.D.C. conditions, as technologies which are labour-intensive; suitable for application in small-scale production; versatile but also adapted to prevailing ecological conditions; simple; and utilising local, rather than imported, raw materials. Edwin Mansfield's distinction between embodied and disembodied technological change has also been fruitful in this context, with the latter less likely to be biased towards capital-intensity.[16] Modern theories of the diffusion of technological change have also yielded important insights into the spread of new techniques and their likely distributional consequences.[17]
5. Policies of *population restraint* are seen as another important aspect in countries with rapidly expanding populations (and most African countries fall under this heading), because of the connections between family size and the incidence of poverty, and between the growth of population and of unemployment.

6. This strategy is intended to focus especially on the needs of defined *poverty groups*. This requires breaking "the poor" down into functionally useful sub-groups, each of which are likely to have various links with the wider socio-economic systems, and to be affected differently by particular policy measures.
7. As already implied, the strategy emphasises improved *access* of poverty groups and neglected regions to the goods, services, and capital assets provided by the state. Special emphasis is placed here on educational, health, and infrastructural services.

Considered separately, most of these policy recommendations can scarcely be described as new. The chief innovation has been to bring all the components together into a comprehensive and internally reinforcing development strategy, which consciously seeks to reconcile the goals of equity and economic growth. The so-called "basic needs" approach, if not the same animal dressed up in different language, is a very close relative. The differences between the "redistribution through growth" and "basic needs" approaches mainly concern the connoisseur of such matters and need not detain us here, except to note that "basic needs" writers place a characteristic stress on the measurement of human wants and the setting of quantified targets for their satisfaction.[18]

The Neo-Classical Renaissance

A final important change in development economics to be noted here is the renaissance in the application of neo-classical analysis to development problems that occurred with the breakdown of the former concensus, where "neo-classical" is used loosely to refer to analyses that stress the efficacy of product and factor markets in the allocation of resources. The attitude of writers in this tradition is nicely summarised by a quotation attributed to C. P. Timmer: "Getting prices right is not the end of development; but getting them wrong often is".

This renaissance has resulted in a number of important applications. The "human capital" approach to education and training, originating in the Chicago school of dread repute, is a case in point.[19] This treats the acquisition of useful knowledge as analogous to inanimate capital formation, i.e. the foregoing of short-run consumption in order to increase future productivities and output. Investments in formal education and other types of training yield rates of return which are—in principle—measurable, and thus comparable with returns from other investments. From the national point of view, the planning task is to allocate investible resources so as to equalise social returns at the margin. On this view, spending on education has to compete with alternative investments by yielding higher (or not lower) social rates of return. In fact, and especially in primary education, social rates of return from education are probably low in many L.D.C.s, and neo-classical writers increasingly warn against the uncritical acceptance of educational spending as self-evidently deserving high priority.

Related work which seeks to provide an economic rationale for the large-scale rural-urban migration typical of L.D.C.s provides another example of the fruitful application of marginalist principles and human capital theory. The strongest influence here has been Todaro's well-known model based on the premise that individuals conform to the view of economic man as a maximiser. To over-simplify, this explains migration as a function of expected real income differentials, i.e. as a function of the urban real wage (Wu), *times* the expected probability of finding a job in the urban formal sector (Pu), *minus* real income in the rural economy (Wr). If (WuPu) > Wr, then migration is rational (assuming Pr = 1) and can be expected to continue.[20] Reduced migration—and the urban unemployment with which it is associated—is thus seen as necessitating narrower urban-rural real income differentials.

The precept of "getting prices right" has led also to increased attention to the importance of agricultural pricing decisions, to the misallocative effects of "excessive" industrial protection, and to other ways in which price "distortions" move the internal terms of trade against rural dwellers and agriculture.[21] Artificially low prices for capital and high formal-sector wages are also blamed for the capital-intensive development that has characterised many L.D.C.s; and more economists are now willing to believe that the elasticity of substitution between labour and capital is large enough for significant new employment opportunities to result from measures that increase the price of capital relative to labour.

Important recent studies of the effects of alternative instruments of balance-of-payments management on the course of economic development have, I believe, shifted the debate strongly against the use of direct controls in favour of an active exchange-rate policy.[22] A combination of controls and an over-valued currency has been shown to lead to economic distortions which hamper development, and a good deal of evidence has accumulated which suggests that currency depreciations are a more effective instrument of policy than has often been supposed. Here again, we see an assertion of the static and dynamic efficacy of price (the price of foreign exchange) in the allocation of resources.

• • •

This concludes our sketch of the most important changes in development economics in recent years, and we must now consider the extent to which they may be able to contribute to an understanding of Africa's economic problems.

Relevance to African Economic Conditions

By comparison with other major developing regions, the African continent is marked by the special problems of early-stage development. The average size of the economy, as measured by total G.N.P., is quite small; average incomes are below the L.D.C. average; a majority of all the countries classified by the United Nations as the "least developed" are African; the annual growth of income *per capita,* at 2.0 per cent during 1966–78, is only two-thirds the L.D.C. average; domestic savings are also low, which implies that Africa is heavily reliant on inflows of foreign capital in order to sustain investment; there is a special degree of dependence on international trade, on primary product exports, and on agricultural production; life expectancy is short; calorific intake and literacy are well below the L.D.C. norm. To this list could be added another problem which cannot be reduced to statistics: that to an especially marked extent there is a low level of governmental effectiveness in Africa, implying a large discrepancy between what is stated as policy or as the law, and what actually happens on the ground.

It is immediately necessary to add, however, that these generalisations are subject to many specific exceptions, and that a wide variety of economic conditions exists within the continent—differences in resources, living standards, economic performance, and so on. Indeed, grouping countries by geography, rather than by more economically significant criteria, is not very helpful for analytical purposes. It could well be argued that the economic differences among African countries are more important than the similarities and, therefore, that it is not very meaningful to enquire about the relevance of progress in development economics to Africa, as if "Africa" defined some homogeneous grouping.

Subject to this caveat, it does none the less seem justified to offer the general description of Africa as at an early stage of development, by the standards of many other low-income countries. If this is accepted, we can pose the following question: To what extent do the recent changes in development economics relate to the special problems of early-stage developers?

Instead of going through the full list of the changes summarised earlier, I shall concentrate on the relevance of the re-examination of the concept of development and the associated "redistribution through growth" strategy, on the contribution of dependency theory, and on the neo-classical renaissance.

The Increased Concern with Equity Considerations

From the fact of Africa's early stage of development and also from some features of African socio-economic systems, we can hypothesise that there is a lesser degree of income inequality than in other developing regions, although the lack of reliable data prevents us from testing this. There *is* evidence of a rather systematic relationship between inequality and stage of development, with relatively less skewed distributions in the early years, rising rather sharply as the next stage proceeds, and then falling again at advanced levels of development.[23] This is quite compatible with the obvious fact of widespread poverty in Africa and—because skewness is measured in relative terms—of large visible inequalities.

The presence of poverty, various forms of unemployment, and inequalities, and *the prospect that the latter are liable to increase,* give particular relevance to writings which stress the necessity to look beyond mere statistics of average incomes towards the desirability of attempting the difficult task of building anti-poverty egalitarian measures into development strategies. A glance at the components of the "redistribution through growth" strategy summarised above is surely sufficient to demonstrate its relevance. This appreciation does, however, need to be tempered by an awareness of some weaknesses:

1. While not wanting to argue that economics should or could be value-free, there are nevertheless dangers in the extent to which economists have adopted the rôle of moralisers in redefining "development". As a result, the profession has less to offer to societies which do not share this view of development. And it may be misled into assuming that the objectives it is proposing are actually accepted because régimes pay lip-service to them, while actually pursuing different goals or priorities. It is not at all clear that many African governments are deeply concerned to reduce inequalities, whatever their development plans may say.

2. It also seems that reaction against the growth objective has gone too far (note the subsidiary rôle it plays in Todaro's definition on page 366). Rapid economic growth may not be a sufficient condition for a successful attack on absolute poverty and unemployment in Africa, but it is certainly a necessary condition. To lose sight of that basic truth would be a costly error.

3. It has yet to be established whether the strategy of redistribution through growth can be made internally consistent. The literature is agreed (*a*) that there are potential trade-offs between the distributional and growth objectives (chiefly due to possible negative effects of egalitarian measures on the quantity and productivity of investment), and (*b*) that appropriate policies can in principle minimise, even eliminate, these trade-offs.[24] But the feasibility and practical effect of these resolutions remain to be demonstrated.

4. There remain additional doubts about whether the proposals of the strategy are sufficiently robust to cope with the problems to

which they are addressed. To a worrying extent, the strategy depends on the development and widespread adoption of more appropriate technologies. But R and D is a difficult area for governments to work in, and few developing countries have yet adopted sufficiently radical departures from past research efforts to convince that they will be able to develop the technologies on which the strategy depends. There are similar doubts about the potential of policies to promote the development of the informal sector. One can also question whether the strategy can alleviate poverty, inequality, and unemployment *fast enough* to satisfy the frustrations being expressed in some countries.

5. Finally, there is the related question of whether the strategy can be successfully implemented on a continent which has hitherto had scant success with its attempts to plan development.[25] The strategy is best thought of as a mutually reinforcing package containing many policy specifics. Weak public administrations preoccupied with the rudimentary tasks of maintaining law and order may not have the executive capacity to carry such a package into effect.

These comments are not intended to debunk the strategy, which in many ways is an example of development economics at its best, but rather to caution against a naïve acceptance of it as a panacea.

The Relevance of Dependency Theory

At first sight, dependency theory seems to be of particular relevance to Africa, even though it has largely been developed for application to Latin America. In varying degrees, virtually all African economies possess the characteristics listed on pp. 367–368 as comprising a relationship of dependence. In warning of the dangers of an unwary approach to M.N.C. investments, or of excessive reliance on a small number of primary-product exports, or of large self-perpetuating inequalities, writers of this school are drawing attention to real problems. But it is doubtful whether efforts to produce a general theory of underdevelopment from these ingredients have added a useful contribution.

The theory can, in fact, be criticised on logical, evidential, and practical grounds. Thus, Lall's sympathetic review of the literature concludes that the theory fails because dependency "is impossible to define and cannot be shown to be causally related to a continuance of underdevelopment. It is usually given an arbitrarily selective definition which picks up certain features of a much broader phenomenon of international capitalist development."[26] Viewing the theory from an explicitly Marxian standpoint, Gabriel Palma is similarly critical of the authors of most dependency models because "they are unable to explain with precision the mechanisms of social reproduction and modes of social transformation of dependent societies. This leads them to use vague and imprecise concepts"[27] Many, including the authors of the 1980 Brandt Report, would also dispute the premise that the interests of the centre are invariably opposed to the development of the periphery.[28]

It is at least arguable that growth and development in L.D.C.s benefits the industrial world, not only by ensuring supplies of the (increasingly diversified) range of goods imported from L.D.C.s, but also by providing growing markets for the outputs of their own high-technology industries. Certainly, the rapid expansion in world trade during the past two decades (an expansion in which L.D.C.s shared, even though not as fully as would have been desirable), has been an important source of growth for the industrial economies of the centre. And that growth in the periphery remained relatively buoyant during the world slump of 1974–5 was a factor materially helping the industrial countries subsequently to improve their own levels of economic activity. One must also have doubts about the validity of a theory which classifies almost all L.D.C.s under the single heading of "dependent", despite their enormously disparate conditions, experiences, and relations with the outside world.

There is also the theory's distressing inability to fit the facts of L.D.C. performance, although Palma criticises those who fall into the "trap . . . of understanding dependency as a formal concept that can be made uniform and reduced to operational dimensions",[29] while Timothy Shaw and Malcolm Grieve suggest that the dependence approach "is fundamentally unsuited to the employment of . . . aggregate measures".[30] Against the predictions of those who see dependence as resulting in immiserisation or stagnation we must set the fact that total G.D.P. in developing countries taken as a whole has grown more rapidly during the past two decades than in the advanced capitalist countries. In the generality of cases the poor have benefited from this growth. It is true that the rich have often profited proportionately more, but there is evidence that at least some L.D.C.s have achieved reduced disparities in income shares.[31] Taking Africa by itself, we have also seen that both total and *per capita* incomes have risen at a rate that is significant even though unsatisfactory. Less casual empiricism confirms the failure of dependency predictions to fit the facts. Patrick J. McGowan carried out statistical tests on data for 30 black African countries and found not only an absence of association between indicators of dependence and economic performance but, perhaps even more damagingly, that the dependency indicators did not even correlate with one another.[32]

Finally, there is the question whether dependency theory has contributed important new insights into the improvement of economic policy. It might in this context be useful to distinguish those (mainly Marxian or neo-Marxian) who treat dependency as a formal theory of underdevelopment, and the larger numbers of "dependency worriers" who recognise the existence and negative effects of the various aspects of dependency listed earlier. Many of the latter have certainly been concerned to suggest policy remedies for these ills: tougher negotiating stances *vis-à-vis* M.N.C.s; more self-reliant development strategies; export diversification; redistributive measures; and that group of proposals labelled "the new international economic order".

The theorists, on the other hand, have contributed little of this kind because they see piecemeal reform as futile, and revolution as a necessary pre-condition of economic independence. The dependency theory of underdevelopment is still evolving, and may have more that is positive to offer in the future. At present, though, it appears to mark a retreat from rigorous thought and careful empirical research, whose main value is to remind us of the strength of the frustrations and injustices still felt in Africa and elsewhere.

Getting Prices Right

At the other end of the spectrum of ideas, the neo-classical renaissance has had more to offer, although again not without qualifications. An insistence on the importance of pricing decisions has important lessons for the several African governments which:

- impose exorbitant taxes on export crops, and are then surprised when production stagnates;
- hang on to grossly over-valued exchange rates, and are then surprised when smuggling flourishes, exports stagnate, and the foreign-exchange reserves dwindle;
- set high minimum wages for urban modern-sector labour and legal limits on interest rates, and are then surprised when capital-intensive techniques are introduced and unemployment increases;
- think they can allocate resources through import, price, and other administrative controls, and are then surprised by the appearance of bottlenecks and other inefficiencies;

and so on . . .

However, members of the neo-classical school are sometimes inclined to overlook the existence in Africa of deep-rooted conditions which are bound to reduce the effectiveness of the market mechanism in allocating resources and promoting development. For one thing, the efficiency of capitalism depends ultimately on the quality of the entrepreneurs responsible for production and investment decisions. But in at least some parts of Africa, for a complex of reasons which we cannot go into here, it is doubtful whether sufficient of an entrepreneurial class exists. Moreover, it is still true that most African economies exhibit strong symptoms of dualistic market structures which imply failures to equalise at the margin, resulting from imperfect markets for labour and capital, and inefficient information flows.

Markets are often far from perfect for products also, with individual manufacturing firms often wielding large monopoly powers, and an often wide spread of prices for the same item between different locations. By no means all these imperfections could be attributed to the malign influence of state interventions or would be easily rectified, and their continued existence implies that heavy reliance on the allocative functions of the price system would result in unsatisfactory results.

Many would add that the neo-classical prescriptions pay insufficient attention to the need for structural transformation in early-stage developing economies. While it is incorrect to say that market forces cannot bring structural change—how else were the economies of nineteenth-century Europe transformed?—it surely is right to suggest that a sub-optimal pattern or pace of change may result. For example, the removal of distortions in factor markets, raising the price of capital relative to labour, can be expected to lead both to the choice of more labour-intensive techniques, and the accelerated growth of more labour-intensive industries. But it would take a bold person to suggest that the manipulation of factor prices would be *sufficient* for the solution of the employment problem. Greater state participation in research, land reforms, public works programmes, family planning services, and a variety of other "structural" interventions would also be needed in order to effect a solution. And because planning has not been very effective so far, it does not follow that the whole idea should be abandoned.

Conclusions

It seems reasonable to conclude from this survey that development economics remains in vigorous health, responsive to the emergence of newly felt problems, still throwing up ideas, and still committed to an attack on poverty. If the former consensus has given way to a rather more anarchic situation, the resulting state of flux is healthy.

On the other hand, economists are still over-inclined to generalise about L.D.C.s, to put them all together into a mythological Third World. It is fairly clear that in order to maintain its relevance, development economics will increasingly need to differentiate between various categories of what have become conventionally regarded as developing countries. It would be fruitful to construct typologies of L.D.C.s, utilising at least the following overlapping criteria:

1. *Stage of development:* Income and other socio-economic indicators of human well-being and wealth could be utilised; also data of sectoral shares and other structural characteristics strongly correlated with stage of development, including indicators of the efficacy of the state.

2. *Natural resource availabilities:* Apart from the obvious variables like availability of economic minerals (especially petroleum), soil types, and climate, we could include such indicators as access to the sea (permitting us to isolate the special problems of landlocked states), and demographic characteristics (notably population density and growth).

3. *Size and openness* (or dependence?): Size is often measured by reference to area or population, but for much economic analysis total G.N.P. is probably a preferable indicator. Openness is strongly correlated with size and can be measured in terms of the magnitude of trade relative to G.D.P., and of capital flows relative to total investment and trade.

In general, it is less likely to be analytically useful to classify countries by geographical region because of the large variety of economic conditions typically found among different economies within a region. It may not be fruitful to undertake research on "the economic problems of Africa" as such, because of the great diversity of conditions. But research into the special problems of small, open, early-stage developers which are not rich in natural resources would be highly relevant to the circumstances of much of the continent.

Notes

1. See Tony Killick, *Development Economics in Action: a study of economic policies in Ghana* (London, 1978), ch. 2, for a fuller statement, and documentation, of this argument. Some writers—e.g. in David Lehmann (ed.), *Development Theory: four critical studies* (London, 1979)—offer a quite different interpretation from that presented here, viewing the 1950s and 1960s as dominated by what they see as a neo-classical orthodoxy that has since become discredited, although I do not believe that careful analysis supports such a contention.

2. Simon Kuznet's famous demolition of W. W. Rostow's theory of the stages of economic growth was influential in casting doubt on the validity of the big push and take-off ideas, as were Ian Little et al. in drawing attention to the limitations and dangers of a strategy of import-substituting industrialisation. See W. W. Rostow, *The Stages of Economic Growth* (Cambridge, 1960), S. Kuznets, "Notes on the Take-Off", in W. W. Rostow (ed.), *The Economics of Take-Off into Sustained Growth* (London, 1963), and I. Little, T. Scitovsky, and M. Scott, *Industry and Trade in Some Developing Countries: a comparative study* (London, 1970); also Tony Killick, "The

Possibilities of Development Planning", in *Oxford Economic Papers,* July 1976, pp. 161–84, for a review of the literature on planning.

3. For a statement of this point of view, see Gustav Ranis, "Development Theory at Three-Quarters Century", in Manning Nash (ed.), *Essays on Economic Development and Cultural Change in Honor of Bert F. Hoselitz* (Chicago, 1977).

4. Michael P. Todaro, *Economics for a Developing World: an introduction to principles, problems and policies for development* (London, 1977), p. 98. See Nancy Baster (ed.), *Measuring Development: the role and adequacy of development indicators* (London, 1972), for a more extensive treatment of this topic, especially the essay entitled "What Are We Trying to Measure?" by Dudley Seers, who adds a postscript to this in Lehmann (ed.), op. cit.

5. See Robert A. Flammang, "Economic Growth and Economic Development: counterparts or competitors?", in *Economic Development and Cultural Change* (Chicago), 28, 1, October 1979, pp. 47–61, for an interesting and multi-disciplinary exploration of the relationships between economic "growth" and "development", including the argument that these are different processes, complementary in the long-run albeit initially competitive.

6. The most influential statements of dependency theory include the following: Paul Baran, *The Political Economy of Growth* (New York, 1957); André Gunder Frank, *Capitalism and Underdevelopment in Latin America* (New York, 1967), and *Latin America: underdevelopment or revolution?* (New York, 1969); T. dos Santos, "The Structure of Dependence", in *American Economic Review* (Providence, R.I.), 60, 2, May 1970; and Samir Amin, *Unequal Development* (London, 1976). Valuable critical surveys are provided by Sanjaya Lall, "Is 'Dependence' a Useful Concept in Analysing Development?" in *World Development* (Oxford), 3, 11–12, November-December 1975, and Gabriel Palma, "Dependency: formal theory of underdevelopment or a methodology for the analysis of concrete situations of underdevelopment?", in ibid. 6, 7–8, July-August 1978. Timothy M. Shaw and Malcolm J. Grieve, "Dependence as an Approach to Understanding Continuing Inequalities in Africa", in *Journal of Developing Areas* (Macomb, Ill.), 13, April 1979, survey the literature as it relates to Africa.

7. Baran, op. cit. p. 28.

8. Richard Harris (ed.), *The Political Economy of Africa* (New York, 1975), p. 18.

9. Cf. dos Santos, loc. cit.

10. Cf. Frank, op. cit.

11. Cf. F. H. Cardoso, "Dependency and Development in Latin America", in *New Left Review* (London), July-August 1972, and "Associated Dependent Development", in A. Stepan (ed.), *Authoritarian Brazil* (New Haven, 1973).

12. Cf. Harris, op. cit.

13. Baran, op. cit.

14. An important example of this type of exploration of the influence of alternative development paths on distributional and other variables is provided by Hollis Chenery, *Structural Change and Development Policy* (New York, 1979).

15. See Hollis Chenery et al. (eds.), *Redistribution with Growth* (London, 1974), for an authoritative discussion of this strategy. E. O. Edwards (ed.), *Employment in Developing Countries* (New York, 1974), and Richard Jolly et al. (eds.), *Third World Employment* (London, 1973), also contain relevant materials.

16. Cf. Edwin Mansfield, *Economics of Technological Change* (New York, 1968).

17. The work of Frances Stewart, *Technology and Underdevelopment* (London, 1977), has been particularly important in exploring the relationships between technology and development. See also Mansfield, op. cit. and Austin Robinson (ed.), *Appropriate Technologies for Third World Development* (London, 1979).

18. For an influential statement of the basic-needs approach, see International Labour Office, *Employment, Growth and Basic Needs* (Geneva, 1976).

19. It is true that the initial statements of the "human capital" theory date back to the early 1960s—see T. W. Schultz, "Investment in Human Capital", in *American Economic Review*, 51, March 1961, and Gary Becker, *Human Capital: a theoretical and empirical analysis* (New York, 1964)—and this can hardly be described as recent. However, it was not until the 1970s that this theory became strongly influential in development economics.

20. See Michael P. Todaro, *Internal Migration and Economic Development* (Geneva, 1976), and *Economics for a Developing World*, ch. 14, for statements of this model.

21. Little et al. op. cit. and the associated series of country studies were particularly influential in this context and, more generally, in the reassertion of the important role of relative prices.

22. The volumes by Jagdish Bhagwati, *Anatomy and Consequences of Exchange Control Regimes* Cambridge, Mass., 1978), and Anne O. Krueger, *Liberalisation Attempts and Consequences* (Cambridge, Mass., 1978), and the country studies they draw upon, are still being digested, but seem likely to become highly influential in the future.

23. Simon Kuznets marshals evidence suggesting that on a graph measuring the degree of inequality on the vertical, and income *per capita* on the horizontal, the relationship between them is described by a curve with an inverted U-shape; see *Economic Growth and Structure* (London, 1965), and *Modern Economic Growth: rate, structure and spread* (New Haven, 1966). For more recent confirmation of this relationship, see F. Paukert, "Income Distributions at Different Levels of Development", in *International Labour Review* (Geneva), 108, 2–3, August-September 1973; Montek S. Ahluwalia, "Inequality, Poverty and Development", in *Journal of Development Economics* (Amsterdam), December 1976; Jerry Cromwell, "The Size Distribution of Income: an international comparison", in *Review of Income and Wealth* (New Haven), 23, 3, September 1977; and H. Lydall, "Income Distribution During the Process of Development", W.E.P. Working Paper, International Labour Office, Geneva, 1977.

24. Jeffrey G. Williamson, however, stresses the complexities involved in determining the extent of trade-offs; see "Inequality, Accumulation, and Technological Imbalance: a growth-equity conflict in American history?", in *Economic Development and Cultural Change*, 27, 2, January 1979.

25. Two excellent studies by T. Y. Shen come to strongly negative conclusions about the effectiveness of development planning, namely, "Sectoral Development Planning in Tropical Africa", in *Eastern Africa Economic Review* (Nairobi), June 1975, and "Macro Development Planning in Tropical Africa", in *Journal of Development Studies* (London), July 1977.

26. Lall, loc. cit. pp. 808–9.

27. Palma, loc. cit. pp. 911–12. It is worth stressing that both Lall and Palma are ideologically highly sympathetic reviewers of this body of writings. Thus, Lall,

loc. cit. pp. 800–1, agrees with Marxian analyses of imperialism, and does not dispute the existence of deeply unsatisfactory relationships between the centre and the periphery; indeed, he argues that dependency theorists make the mistake of criticising capitalism "on its least vulnerable points". Palma, loc. cit. p. 912, is concerned to advocate his own interpretation of the theory, as providing a valuable methodology for the study of "concrete situations of dependency".

28. See *North-South: a programme for survival. The Report of the Independent Commission on International Development Issues under the Chairmanship of Willy Brandt* (London, 1980).

29. Palma, loc. cit. p. 905.

30. Shaw and Grieve, loc. cit. p. 233.

31. See Ahluwalia, loc. cit. for an empirical rejection of the hypothesis that there has been a general immiserisation of the poor, and Ranis, loc. cit. for examples of L.D.C.s with reducing inequalities. See also Montek S. Ahluwalia, Nicholas G. Carter, and Hollis B. Chenery, "Growth and Poverty in Developing Countries", in *Journal of Development Economics*, 6, 3, September 1979, for evidence of declining proportions living in absolute poverty during 1960–75.

32. See Patrick J. McGowan, "Economic Dependence and Economic Performance in Black Africa", in *The Journal of Modern African Studies* (Cambridge), 14, 1, March 1976, pp. 24–40. Nadim G. Khalaf, "Country Size and Economic Growth and Development", in *Journal of Development Studies*. 16, 1, October 1979, utilising data for 30 L.D.C.s, similarly found an absence of significant correlation between growth or development and trade dependence or export concentration.

16

Between Scylla and Charybdis: The Foreign Economic Relations of Sub-Saharan African States

Thomas M. Callaghy

What all this [International Monetary Fund activity] amounts to is an increasing tendency towards a kind of international authoritarianism. Economic power is used as a substitute for gun-boats . . . in enforcing the unilateral will of the powerful. The sovereign equality of all nations is ignored, as is the future stability of the world.

—Julius Nyerere

Nigeria . . . has already fallen into "debt trap peonage." . . . And like the heroin addict, we are craving these loans, not for sound purposes, but simply to finance our spendthrift consumer habits and our ambitious maldevelopment plans. . . . Economic history shows that development happens to be one of those journeys . . . for which there are no easy paths, only more or less difficult ones.

—Chinweizu

Within the cluster of internal causes of Africa's external indebtedness, the following can be identified: . . . a policy of excessive dependence on external resources for financing development . . . poor economic management coupled with misuse of resources and wastage of public funds . . . the inability to utilise fully external finance to generate enough surpluses to enable them to repay the loans . . . the inadequacy of policies and institutions for monitoring the contracting of external debts, their utilisation and servicing (poor debt management) and . . . lack of trained personnel to administer resource policies.

—Adebayo Adedeji, Executive Secretary,
Economic Commission for Africa[1]

Reprinted by permission of Sage Publications, Inc. from *Annals of the American Academy of Political and Social Science* 489 (Jan. 1987): 148–163. © 1987 Sage Publications, Inc.

Over the last decade the foreign relations of sub-Saharan African states have focused increasingly on their severe economic and fiscal crises.[2] These foreign economic relations have involved wrestling with the burdens of debt service and the rigors of rescheduling; conducting difficult negotiations with bilateral and private creditors; bargaining over conditionality packages with the International Monetary Fund (IMF) and the World Bank or fending them off; distributing the painful costs of adjustment; coping with import strangulation; and devising new development policies and strategies. Sub-Saharan states were already highly dependent on the outside world; the intensity, stakes, and levels of conditionality of these states' economic relations with external actors have increased substantially since the middle of the 1970s.

Foreign economic relations are in many ways high foreign policy writ large. They are certainly political. There is very little that is neutral about them, impinging as they do on very central issues—sovereignty, political and social order, development, mass welfare, and class formation, consolidation, and conflict. In this sense, they are foreign economic relations with very powerful domestic roots and consequences.

The weak, predominantly primary-product-dependent, highly trade-dependent African economies were hit severely by a rapid sequence of external shocks—the oil shocks of 1973 and 1979; extensive drought; a major recession in the industrialized North, forcing a decline in both demand and price for their commodity exports not seen since the Great Depression; increasing protectionism by the Organization for Economic Cooperation and Development; generalized inflation in the world economy, which encouraged the accumulation of debt, and then disinflation in the context of relatively high levels of debt at high real interest rates; and, as new credit and direct foreign investment dried up, the tapering off of aid. In the face of these shocks, the already weak states of Africa were confronted with decreasing or negative growth rates, stagnant or falling per capita income figures, and severe balance-of-payments and debt-service problems. These difficulties were often exacerbated by inappropriate policies, unproductive investment, deteriorating infrastructure and productive capacity, lax implementation, limited administrative and technical capabilities, the rise of magendo or parallel economies, and pervasive corruption. Many of these phenomena predated the external shocks and were not caused by them, but they certainly aggravated their effects.

By the 1980s the situation had become catastrophic, for much of the continent output per head was lower than in 1960. Between 1980 and 1984, the gross domestic product of African countries declined an average of 1.4 percent a year; per capita gross national product, an average of 4.4 percent a year; export volume, 7.4 percent a year; and import volume, 5.9 percent per year.[3] There has been considerable debate about the primary causes of this multifaceted crisis between those who believe that they are predominantly exogenous and those who aver that they are largely internal. Clearly they are both, and counterfactual arguments are important.

If the external variables had been significantly more favorable, would development prospects have been strikingly better? If the internal factors had been much more propitious, would the overall outcome have been dramatically improved? The answer in both cases is probably no. Whatever the importance of the various causes, debt has been a central feature of this pervasive crisis, and, by looking at the debt problems, we can examine the major actors, processes, issues, and policies that have affected Africa's foreign economic relations over the last decade.

Size and Nature of the Debt

In 1974 the total debt of sub-Saharan Africa was about $14.8 billion, but by the end of 1984, according to World Bank figures, it had reached about $91 billion. Other estimates put the figure closer to $125 billion. Of the $91 billion, 63.5 percent was public and publicly guaranteed medium- and long-term debt, broken down as follows, as percentages of the total $91 billion: bilateral, 24.3 percent; multilateral, 16.1 percent; suppliers' credits, 2.4 percent; and private bank, 20.7 percent. The remaining 36.5 percent is as follows: private nonguaranteed medium- and long-term debt, 4 percent; short-term, 13.6 percent; IMF, 5.9 percent; and arrears, 13 percent.

By comparison to Latin American debt, which has so riveted world attention, several factors are striking. First, the total amount is not large; it is about 10 percent of total developing-country debt and less than that of either Mexico or Brazil. Second is the very low percentage of private-bank debt, which makes up by far the bulk of Latin American debt. In addition, a large percentage of Africa's private-bank debt is guaranteed by public agencies of countries of the Organization for Economic Cooperation and Development such as the U.S. Export-Import Bank. As a result, this debt is rescheduled by these countries under the auspices of the Paris Club mechanism, rather than by the banks themselves, usually referred to as the London Club. Third is the relatively high percentage of African debt that is owed to the IMF and the World Bank, 5.9 and 5.2 percent, respectively. This type of debt cannot be rescheduled. These facts reflect great differences in the level of development and nature and degree of incorporation into the world capitalist economy of the two regions.

The following countries are sub-Saharan Africa's major debtors; they are listed with their debts, in billions of U.S. dollars, as of the end of 1984: Nigeria, 19.7; Ivory Coast, 7.4; Sudan, 7.2; Zaïre, 5.0; Zambia, 4.8; Kenya, 3.8; Tanzania, 3.3; Cameroon, 2.7; Zimbabwe, 2.1; Senegal, 2.0; Ghana, 2.0; Madagascar, 2.0; Congo, 1.6; and Ethiopia, 1.5. Despite the low percentage of debt owed to private creditors, six countries owe more than two-thirds of their 1985–87 debt service to private sources—Benin, Congo, Gabon, Ivory Coast, Zimbabwe, and Nigeria. The figures for debt owed to private creditors for Nigeria and the Ivory Coast are 88.2 and 64.1 percent, respectively.

African debt has grown faster than that of any other region. The annual nominal growth rate between 1970 and 1984 was 20.4 percent, slightly higher than that of Argentina, Brazil, and Mexico; between 1975 and 1980 it was 25.2 percent. Medium- and long-term debt quadrupled between 1975 and 1983. Until 1981 borrowing from commercial sources increased more rapidly than that from official sources, but then dropped off dramatically. The terms of borrowing also worsened over time. In 1979, 54 percent of debt was on concessional terms; by 1981 it was only 35 percent. For bilateral debt, from 1974 to 1984 average interest rates rose from 3.1 to 4.6 percent, while maturities declined from 22.5 to 19.6 years, grace periods from 7.7 to 5.6 years, and grant elements from 49.2 to 36.3 percent. For commercial borrowing, interest rates went from 8.7 to 10.4 percent, while maturities declined from 9.5 to 8.0 years. In 1983 an average of 15.1 percent of the debt was at floating rates. As a result, the recent drop in interest rates will not help African states as much as others. On the other hand, that same year 47 percent of the Ivory Coast's debt was at floating rates and 62 percent of Nigeria's was. For Nigeria, of course, the dramatic fall in oil prices will greatly overshadow any benefit from falling interest rates.

Debt Management and Service

African debt use and management capabilities are on average the worst in the world. Many African countries at first had little idea how much they owed or to whom; debt service was haphazard at best; and borrowed resources were often poorly used or invested. The World Bank states its position bluntly:

> A major cause of Africa's precarious situation has been the failure of many countries to invest borrowed resources productively . . . [and] hand-in-hand with economic policy reform, African economies need to strengthen their debt-management capabilities, requiring, in some cases, changes [in] the legislative framework for foreign borrowing as well as improvements in the institutional and administrative procedures used to monitor and process information on external debt.

And, as one seasoned and sympathetic observer has noted, this "institutional infrastructure . . . appears to have deteriorated radically in many sub-Saharan states over the past few years."[4]

In short, state capability is central to much of Africa's difficulties, and, even if all the major external constraints were greatly ameliorated, significant problems would remain. One result has been the frequent use of external financial advisers—individuals, investment bank groups, and legal, public relations, accounting, and consulting firms. For example, Lazard Frères; Lehman Brothers; S. G. Warburg; Morgan Grenfel; Samuel Montague; Arthur D. Little; Elliot Berg Associates; White and Case; Peat, Marwick, Mitchell and Company; and several major money-center banks have all been involved in Africa. As one experienced observer notes, "This can lend a comic-opera character to some of the international squabbling, wherein virtually all of the local memoranda are in fact drafted by foreign advisors." External actors took more extreme action in Zaïre, where expatriate teams were placed directly in management positions in the Bank of Zaïre, the Office of Debt Management, the finance and planning ministries, and the customs office. The effectiveness of the forward and backward linkages of foreign advisers and such technocratic enclaves is questionable. As Green has stressed, "'Have a headache? Take two expatriates' has at times worked well in a technico-managerial context, but it is neither generally practicable nor desirable even in the short run, and it is inherently dangerously addictive."[5]

The size of a country's debt is not the important issue; it is, rather, the ability to use it productively and to service it. While the size of Africa's debt has increased, the ability to use it productively and service it has declined significantly. As a result, Africa's dependence on the IMF and the World Bank, with all its attendant conditionality and monitoring, has increased dramatically, as has its reliance on rescheduling. This pattern can affect a country with a large debt, such as Nigeria, or countries with quite small debts, such as Sierra Leone, with a debt of $416 million, and Togo, with a debt of $798 million.

In 1970 Africa paid $449 million in debt service; by 1984 the figure had risen to $7.4 billion—a sixteenfold increase. For most countries there will be no significant decline in debt service before the end of the century. Over the next five years Africa will be required to pay out over $6.8 billion a year in debt service. In the context of extreme foreign exchange scarcity, such burdens pose very stark choices for governments between debt service, upon which their external financial, economic, and political relations depend, and food, fuel, and other imports necessary to protect their peoples and maintain order and existing productive capacity and infrastructure.

Debt service ability is most accurately reflected in scheduled debt service ratios, that is, annual payment of principal and interest as a percentage of exports of goods and services. African states have the highest average scheduled debt service ratios in the world. The average for 1986–87 is

31.1 percent; for 1986–90 it is projected at 38.6 percent, and at 31.5 percent for 1991.[6] For about ten countries the figures are significantly higher. For example, for the Sudan they are 150.9, 128.0, and 88.5 percent, respectively; for Somalia, 97.2, 77.7, and 67.2 percent; for Zambia, 59.0, 71.2, and 71.4 percent; for Tanzania, 50.4, 60.0, and 54.8 percent; for Nigeria, 36.2, 48.6, and 38.9 percent; and for Benin, 34.9, 43.5, and 44.4 percent.

These amounts can be lowered by rescheduling, but often the relief simply postpones and even increases eventual burdens. For example, Liberia, Senegal, the Sudan, Zaïre, and Zambia have each rescheduled more than once in the 1975–85 period, and their scheduled debt service is more than three times what they paid in 1982–84. The same holds true for countries that have rescheduled only once or not at all during this period, such as Benin, Mali, Somalia, and Tanzania. Only Gabon, Lesotho, and Mauritius have projected debt service less than they paid in 1982–84. These figures include IMF repurchases, and World Bank and African Development Bank debt service, none of which can be rescheduled. When linked to the fact that African states have been drawing increasingly on the resources of these institutions, repayments to them become an increasingly large percentage of debt service. Debt service ratios can grow despite rescheduling and important adjustment progress; Ghana is an important recent example.

Actual debt service is often substantially less than what is scheduled. In 1984, Benin had a scheduled debt service ratio of 38.3 percent; it paid only 16.4 percent. The respective figures for Madagascar were 80.9 and 40.5 percent; for the Sudan, 96.4 and 25.0; for Zambia, 55.2 and 24.5; and for Senegal, 29.0 and 16.9. Arrears thus become an increasingly contentious aspect of Africa's foreign relations. In 1980, 19 countries were in arrears for a total of $4.2 billion. At the end of 1984, there were 22 countries in arrears for 13 percent of the total debt. Of the $12 billion in arrears, 70.6 percent was on short-term debt and 29.4 percent on medium- and long-term. Arrears are particularly significant because they can threaten new loans, disbursements of existing ones, prospects for reschedulings, and assistance from the IMF and World Bank. Arrears to the IMF are projected to be nearly 20 percent of the 1985–90 debt service for the most severely affected countries.

For a couple of countries arrears to the IMF have led to their being declared temporarily ineligible for IMF assistance. This means no rescheduling and probably no private credit either. Short-term trade arrears often lead to the refusal of suppliers to sell or higher import prices as suppliers hedge against payment uncertainty. The issue of arrears leads directly to a discussion of rescheduling.

Both Paris and London Club reschedulings are increasingly important in the foreign relations of African states. Repeat reschedulings are now the norm for Africa, which is by far the most rescheduled region of the world. The low capability of Africa to service its debt is reflected in the number and frequency of the reschedulings. The following data are for Paris and London Club reschedulings for the period 1975–85. Of the 42 countries that rescheduled, 19, or 45.0 percent, were from Africa. Of the 144 reschedulings, 67, or 46.5 percent, were African; 49 of the African reschedulings were with the Paris Club and 18 with the London Club.

This ratio of Paris to London Club reschedulings is not surprising given the composition of Africa's debt discussed earlier. Zaïre and Togo have each rescheduled seven times; the Sudan, Senegal, Madagascar, and Liberia, six times; Sierra Leone and Niger, four times; and Zambia, Malawi, the Ivory Coast, and the Central African Republic, three times. By the end of 1984, rescheduled debt constituted three-quarters of the total debt of both Zaïre and the Sudan. In 1975 the one Paris Club rescheduling was not African; in 1976 the only one was; in 1977 both of them were; in 1978, 1 of the 2; in 1979 all 3; in 1980 both were; in 1981 all 7; in 1982, 5 of the 6; in 1983, 9 of the 17; in 1984, 9 of the 13; and in 1985, 10 of the 19.

Because of the severity of the African situation, the Paris Club creditor countries have shown some flexibility by quietly bending a number of norms—amounts and types of debt, the period of debt service covered, the length of grace and repayment periods, and the rescheduling of interest and previously rescheduled debt.[7] This is all done, however, at or near commercial rates and on a tight leash. It is not coordinated with Consultative Group aid consortia and is done on a case-by-case basis for fear of losing leverage and setting precedents for Africa or other regions. In addition, these frequent reschedulings generate considerable uncertainty and are very consuming of scarce talent and time, with resulting high opportunity costs. Repeated pleas for multiyear and concessional reschedulings have been ignored. In short, rescheduling has rarely resulted in viable or stable financial conditions. Finally, a few African countries, such as Botswana and Rwanda, have serviced their debt and have not needed rescheduling, or, like Gabon, have rescheduled once and subsequently maintained good debt service.

Adjustment: The IMF and Conditionality

With severe debt service difficulties and limited relief from reschedulings, adjustment became necessary for many African states. Such adjustment, planned or unplanned, imposed or voluntary, is a dramatic, difficult, and unsettling phenomenon. With major foreign exchange scarcity, declining levels of aid, especially bilateral, and increasingly limited access to private capital markets, the dire need for adjustment resources has led to an increasing reliance on the IMF. The fund plays a central linchpin role. Relations with the World Bank, the Paris and London Clubs, private capital markets, and bilateral creditors are usually contingent on a viable relationship with the fund—the IMF's seal of approval. These ties to the fund have usually meant high levels of imposed conditionality, especially as its upper-tranche, or upper-level, resources—stand-by agreements and extended fund facilities (EFFs)—came into increasing use. In addition, the IMF became but the leading edge of greatly increased conditionality that has now spread to almost all forms of external assistance to Africa—multilateral, especially from the World Bank, bilateral, and even private. Over time the initial focus of conditionality on balance-of-payments adjustment to facilitate repayment shifted to a much broader structural adjustment, which entails substantial monitoring of African economies.

Structural adjustment has meant efforts to restructure African political economies in significant ways. It has been based on an increasingly pervasive dual belief that without structural adjustment any new resources would be poured down a voracious sinkhole and that African leaders will not make appropriate changes unless they are pressured. This position is based on the view that the major causes of the crisis, or at least those that anybody is able or willing to do anything about, are internal to Africa. There is, as the World Bank contends, an increasing consensus between African governments and external actors that a crisis exists and that fundamental changes must take place.

There is much less agreement on the causes of the crisis and on the specific changes, their relevance and effectiveness, and whose interests they serve. Many African rulers would agree with Nyerere when he points to "an increasing determination by donors to use their aid for ideological and foreign policy purposes . . . monies are now set aside to be allocated just to such African countries as accept an untrammelled capitalist economy."[8] Is it "policy dialogue" as the fund and World Bank contend or neocolonialism as Nyerere asserts? These are clearly two faces, two sides of the same phenomenon.

Helleiner notes that, given this perception,

> the stage is set for a decade of battles between African governments and the IMF. There will undoubtedly be mutual exasperation and fatigue—with charges of foreign interference in domestic affairs on the one hand, and countercharges of policy "slippage," "indiscipline," and failure to abide by agreements on the other.

The ultimate outcome of these efforts is clearly open to question. As Green suggests, "Strategies and their articulation can, up to a point, be imposed on desperate countries. But they are unlikely to avoid major technical flaws, to be implemented more than grudgingly and partially, or to yield the intended results of their sponsors."[9]

The ability of a state to adjust depends on three major factors: (1) political will; (2) administrative capacity; and (3) economic capacity. African countries are often weak in all three areas, which accounts in large part for the heavy reliance on the IMF. Between 1970 and 1978, African countries accounted for 3 percent of total IMF assistance from stand-bys and EFFs. Their share of the total number of IMF programs for this period was 17 percent; it rose to 55 percent in 1979. These countries have the highest number of repeat programs of any region of the world. In 1978 only two African countries had agreements with the IMF. At the end of February 1986, 15 of the 31 active programs were for Africa—14 stand-bys and 1 EFF. Between 1979 and early 1986, 28 African countries had a total of 95 programs, and 24 of those countries had more than 1 program. Seven countries had 2 programs; 2 had 3 programs; 8 had 4; 3 had 5; 3 had 6; and 1 country, Madagascar, had 7.

Due to this heavy reliance on the IMF, African countries now owe about 6 percent of their total debt to the fund. At the end of 1984, 27 of the 39 sub-Saharan countries owed money to the IMF, ranging from Zambia's $698 million, or 14.6 percent of its total debt, to Guinea's $11 million, or 0.9 percent. Nigeria, the Congo, Gabon, and Botswana did not owe the fund anything. Percentages of debt service owed to the fund are increasing rapidly. For debt service owed during 1986–87, the African average is 11.8 percent, but for low-income countries it is 20.1 percent. Some countries have significantly higher figures: Ghana, 50.9 percent; Uganda, 44.7 percent; Sierra Leone, 38.7 percent; and Zambia, 32.6 percent. Since these amounts cannot be rescheduled and must be paid on time, arrears become a very contentious issue. In early 1986 eight countries were in arrears to the fund, and the Sudan and Liberia were temporarily declared ineligible for IMF resources due to $280 million in arrears. Given the fund's linchpin role, this is a significant sanction, one that countries will go to interesting lengths to avoid. Zambia had arrears that threatened to impend the flow of fund resources. To pay them off, Zambia borrowed funds from a British bank, which presumably will be repaid with new IMF funds.[10]

The standard IMF conditionality package is heavily weighted toward demand management and includes the following basic elements: budget and money supply contraction, especially to control inflation; reduction or elimination of subsidies, especially for consumer goods and services; changes in exchange rate policy, especially large devaluations; raising nominal interest rates; liberalization of import controls, especially of licensing systems; expansion of primary product exports; reduction and rationalization of the role of the state in the economy, especially in the parastatal sector; and encouragement of the private sector through increased reliance on market and price incentives, especially in agriculture.

Disagreement about the appropriateness of this package for African conditions focuses on devaluations, import controls, market and price incentives, the size and role of the state, and reliance on primary product export-led growth.

How effective have the IMF adjustment programs been? There is considerable variance of opinion. Given the unreliable statistical capabilities of African states, it is genuinely difficult to gauge effectiveness. The overall impact, however, appears to be modest. General agreement exists that the fund has had less success in Africa than in other regions. This largely has to do with the nature and level of development and state capabilities. Based on recent fund studies, Helleiner notes that "one may infer that previous IMF proclamations of 'success' have been overstated," and he points to "the extraordinary difficulty of successful adjustment under severe economic and political constraints in a rapidly changing environment."[11]

Most commonly the country formally accepts the conditions and then evades them or waters them down in implementation because they threaten deeply rooted interests or are perceived to be a threat to political order or socioeconomic peace. Even where sufficient will exists, economic inflexibility and limited administrative capability make full implementation difficult. Unsustainability and "slippage," as the IMF refers to it, are major phenomena.

Recently, the IMF and the World Bank have, themselves, been modest in assessment. The latest of the major World Bank reports on Africa, issued in the spring of 1986, notes that while many governments have made some progress, "they still have much to do to correct the accumulated policy distortions of the past."[12] In a study of 1980–81 programs, the IMF asserts that "generally adjustment efforts of African countries remained fairly limited. . . . The implementation of programs showed mixed results. Where data are available, they show that only one fifth of the countries reached the targeted level of economic growth." The major constraint was "slippages in implementation" due primarily to "the emergence of unforseen developments, an inability to mobilize sufficient political support to implement the requisite adjustment measures, limitations in administrative infrastructure, overly optimistic targets, and delays or shortfalls in net inflows of development assistance."[13] Of the 82 programs between 1979 and 1984, 16, or 19.5 percent, were canceled for noncompliance. For the remainder, waivers were used extensively for unmet targets. For the 12- to 18-month stand-bys, which constituted 89 percent of the 82 programs, there was significant rollover of both canceled and noncanceled programs.

One method of coping with the problems generated by the short duration of stand-bys has been to use three-year EFFs instead. There have been nine of them in Africa, all but one since 1980, used by Kenya, the Sudan, Gabon, Senegal, Sierra Leone, the Ivory Coast, Zambia, Zaïre, and Malawi. Five EFFs were formally canceled for noncompliance, and one was allowed to lapse. Only two were completed, and the only current one—Malawi's—ended in September 1986. The problems that plagued the EFFs were essentially the same as for the stand-bys.[14]

In 1982 the IMF decided to rely almost exclusively on stand-bys, but to use a medium-term view of adjustment and a slightly wider set of policies to augment exports and improve monitoring and implementation. While things improved, success remained modest, leading the fund to stress its "catalytic role." Some in the fund have become quite uncomfortable with this record. They advocate pulling back in Africa, arguing that the fund is only meant to be used for situations of short-term adjustment.[15] Pulling back is not likely to occur, however.

An important psychological side effect of these foreign economic relations is that scarce talent is constantly preoccupied by negotiations with external actors about adjustment issues, while attempting to implement previous agreements. When linked to limited results, the impact can be quite damaging. As Green notes,

> In political and national terms continued stagnation makes the mobilisation of energy ever harder: confidence in the ability to succeed is increasingly eroded by repeated failures, whatever their cause. Unfortunately, both nationally and internationally there is often an unhappy mix of frenetic, ill thought out attempted action, which proves unsustainable, together with interminable debate and negotiation over secondary issues.[16]

The IMF and the World Bank have several African success stories that they tout. Amazingly, Zaïre is now one of them. A March 1986 IMF article extolled the success of reform efforts since the 1983 stand-by, especially greatly improved debt service, which accounted for 56 percent of Zaïre's 1985 budget. It compared the reform efforts to the relatively successful 1967 program. In fact, Zaïre has had six programs since 1967—in 1976, 1977, 1979, 1981, 1983, and 1985. The article did not, however, bother to mention the 1976–81 programs, the fact that they were all total failures, that in 1979 the fund took the highly unusual step of placing expatriate teams directly into several important ministries, that the 1981 EFF was canceled for noncompliance, or that it was followed by a year-long shadow program before the 1983 stand-by. In discussing the so-called success of the post-1983 reforms, the article notes that "these measures have considerably improved the image of Zaïre abroad, but the economic recovery at home has remained modest so far." About the same time a group of World Bank officials pointed out that "the existing debts, despite rescheduling, are unserviceable, and Zaïre has a long way to go before its debt problem is resolved." In a 1985 assessment of the reputed reforms, Crawford Young asserts that, "if Rip Van Winkle fell asleep again for a couple of years, chances are he [would] reawaken to a more familiar set of circumstances, and find the fourth reform cycle in its downward phase."[17]

The underlying fact is that Zaïre has not reaped the implicit quid pro quo of substantially increased donor, creditor, and investor support. As the *Financial Times* points out, "Net capital flows from donors have actually been negative for several years, despite the high donor praise for the country's reform efforts." Thus debt service is up substantially, with serious opportunity costs for imports, rehabilitation, and investment and without any new resources. Clearly the IMF article is a plea for badly needed external support. Such are the politics of so-called success. To encourage support, the World Bank announced that it will lend Zaïre an additional $550 million between 1986 and 1988, mostly via the International Development Association and the bank's new Special Facility for Sub-Saharan Africa.[18]

The IMF and Political Instability

Is IMF conditionality a major cause of political instability in Africa, as is often alleged? The answer depends on how political instability is defined. In fact, there has been surprisingly little major political instability or regime change tied directly to IMF programs. As Bienen and Gersovitz point out, "IMF programs are far more common than instances of serious instability." Clearly "there have been some violent reactions to IMF programs in the short-run, such as strikes and food riots after subsidies have been cut or currencies devalued. Governments usually have either persisted and faced down these reactions or backed off from or only partially implemented the IMF package."[19] This is not at all to deny the obvious harsh consequences for much of the population. Planned or unplanned, imposed or voluntary, adjustment must eventually come, and it will entail harsh consequences.

Since substantial political instability has always existed in Africa, linking it directly to IMF adjustment is a tricky analytic exercise. Rather than the direct causal factor, IMF adjustment is more frequently a triggering or precipitating factor. The Sudan is one of the most commonly cited cases of instability tied directly to the IMF. But, as Jackson has indicated,

IMF conditionality did not cause the coup; Nimeiri's downfall must ultimately be attributed to numerous political and economic failures that had already thrust the country into chaos and bankruptcy. But, insofar as Nimeiri's move to end subsidies for bread and other basic commodities resulted in sharp price rises, which in turn sparked the riots, the IMF program was clearly a precipitating factor.[20]

For both rulers and opposition groups, it is often useful to attribute unrest to the IMF, even when the cause clearly lies elsewhere—commonly in the political logic of struggle itself.

In fact, actual instability is less important than the fear of it, which leads to partial or slack implementation in order to continue the much-needed relationship with the IMF. Haggard points out that for "weak authoritarian regimes," so common in Africa, "the rationalization associated with adjustment and stabilization is . . . in an immediate sense, politically irrational." Rulers often make preemptive changes in adjustment programs for fear of the political consequences. The result is not regime change or major instability, but weaker adjustment. As one World Bank official has noted, "We need to avoid proposing prescriptive policy packages which are not politically feasible. We must take into account real political fears and carry out detailed analyses of implementation problems."[21]

Regime legitimacy is crucial to how important the political fallout of adjustment becomes. Jerry Rawlings, for example, has been able to pursue quite orthodox IMF adjustment in Ghana precisely because his regime is perceived to be legitimate. This was not the case in the Sudan. The new Babangida military regime in Nigeria will need all the legitimacy it has acquired from its public dialogue about IMF conditionality and the ultimate rejection of it in applying its homegrown brand of adjustment.

How is it possible to account for so little political instability directly linked to the obvious pernicious effects of even partial adjustment? At least part of the answer is that African populations, unlike most of those in Latin American countries, often have the exit options of withdrawing from the national and world economies and/or of participating in the rapidly expanding magendo or informal economies. Magendo economic activity may play an important role in reducing the tensions created by recession, austerity measures, infrastructure decline, and domestic political repression.

The World Bank and Structural Adjustment

One primary effect of Africa's current crisis, which has been greatly aggravated by the IMF's particular conditionality package, is import strangulation. This short-term adjustment strategy badly threatens medium- and long-term adjustment and growth. It has worsened existing underutilization of productive capacity, led to further infrastructure deterioration, hampered state investment, and discouraged foreign and domestic private investment. Imports per capita have been declining since 1970, and Africa's investment rate is now the lowest of any developing region. A broader and longer-term view of adjustment is needed. The World Bank has been attempting to achieve this by concentrating on structural adjustment.

The World Bank now uses a new lending instrument—the structural adjustment loan—particularly to finance badly needed imports and support policy change. By early 1986, it had nine structural adjustment loans in six African countries, with about nine more lined up. These are definitely high-conditionality facilities, and recipients usually must have a program with the IMF or be in its good graces. The World Bank also now uses sector, rehabilitation, and specific import commodity loans, all with lesser conditionality. About 80 percent of the bank's policy-based lending is now in Africa, having doubled between the late 1970s and 1984. By the end of 1984, the bank accounted for 49 percent of all multilateral lending—including the IMF—and 12.4 percent of total African debt.

How effective has this new policy-based lending been? Like the IMF, the World Bank has found it difficult to achieve its aims in Africa. Results have been quite mixed. For example, a structural adjustment loan to Senegal was canceled for noncompliance. In its 1986 special report on Africa, the bank noted that many countries are making some progress, "but they still have much to do to correct the accumulated policy distortions of the past." One example will suffice. The bank has put considerable emphasis on scaling down and rationalizing the state, especially the parastatal sector. According to the report, many governments are "trying to reduce the size of the public sector and to improve its management. However, these reforms are still at an early stage."[22] Low-income states have closed down or divested only "about 5 percent of their public enterprises during the 1980s."

Two of the World Bank's key recommendations involve scaling down budgets and levels of employment as rationalization efforts. The report notes, however, that implementation has had the diametically opposite outcome from the one desired and expected:

> Budget restraint, reflected in lower public employment, is desirable in much of Africa, but in some cases it has led to excessive cuts in financing for equipment, maintenance, operating costs, and materials. The result has been a steady deterioration in the quality of public services and further declines in the productivity of public employees. . . . This deterioration in public services is especially disruptive for programs designed to deal with the basic constraints on development.[23]

Clearly, these governments felt it was politically irrational to reform public enterprises by cutting employment. Wishing to appear compliant with the World Bank, they simply cut the budgets in other less politically sensitive areas.

This role has led to the World Bank to increase its data collection, monitoring, and analysis activities about and in Africa significantly. It now has 24 resident representatives, a large increase over previous levels and more than in any other region. The bank has also gone into the development strategy business in a big way, pushing primary product export-led growth and extolling the virtues of the private sector—what Green has called the "Bank's apparent aspiration to become SSA's [sub-Saharan Africa's] . . . planning ministry and Platonic Guardian." Considerable African skepticism remains about relying heavily on a primary product export-led development strategy, but there is also considerable confusion about what else to do. Many observers have noted the fallacy of composition inherent in the bank's development strategy recommendation; that is, if all countries follow the advice, undertake reform, and significantly increase production, they will all be worse off. Those supportive of the bank's position have noted in response that "not all countries will follow counsel to expand primary exports. So those that do will capture the markets of those that do not, regardless of their respective comparative advantages." But the bank itself points out that

> because of the region's economic structure, exports will be relatively slow to respond. They are mostly primary commodities, which have limited prospects . . . it will be very hard to achieve a rapid expansion of exports in the near term . . . exports in current prices during 1986–90 could, at best, be about 25 percent higher than in 1980–82. And this assumes substantial export-oriented policy reforms in Africa and no increase in protectionism in the industrial countries.[24]

Skepticism about the private sector also abounds.

Conclusion

What does the future hold for African countries and their creditors? Modest expectations are in order on both sides. African states cannot expect any major beneficial structural or procedural reforms in the international political economy on the part of their Western creditors. Likewise, the latter cannot expect any significant restructuring of African regimes and economies or substantial improvement in their economic and debt performance. Western actors clearly determine most of the rules of the game, shaping the parameters of action, but African regimes do have some autonomy and room for maneuver.

On the external side, the World Bank notes that

> the major structural reform efforts undertaken by many African countries to address their long-term development problems have not received adequate donor support . . . growth and equity enhancing reform programs already underway are foundering because of inadequate donor funding, which is often inappropriate in form and timing.

Despite some projected increases in resource flows from Lomé III, an enlarged International Development Association, the World Bank's new Special Facility for Sub-Saharan Africa, and the IMF's Trust Fund reflows via the new Structural Adjustment Facility, the report still projects a $3.5 billion to $5.5 billion resource gap per year for 1986–90.[25] With little new private-bank lending or direct foreign investment and the ongoing peripheralization of Africa in the world economy, these inadequate resource flows are quite alarming. Given current politics on the part of the Organization for Economic Cooperation and Development, it is not likely that this gap can be closed. For example, while the May 1986 United Nations General Assembly special session on Africa—the first ever on a regional economic problem—drew attention to Africa's plight, it produced no change in creditor-country policies or major pledges of new aid. Finally, the World Bank calls for more coherent, coordinated, and realistic donor practices. Again, it is not clear how much this situation will change.

African governments must do their part via more systematic adjustment and realistic proposals of their own about how to cope with the current crisis, as the Latin Americans have now begun to do in a serious way. Some progress was made at the 1985 Organization of African Unity summit, which focused on the economic crisis. As in the past, the governments placed considerable blame on an "unjust and inequitable" international economic system, but they also acknowledged that their policies had contributed to the crisis and need to be changed. More realistic rhetoric must now be transformed into viable action.

If Africa is to avoid both Scylla and Charybdis, its leaders and external actors will have to do their respective parts. According to a leading African official,

> a more open and constructive dialogue between Africa and the North must take place. This dialogue should include a better articulation of development strategies and policies by African countries themselves than has been the case in the past. It will also require a commitment by the North to improve its understanding of African problems, and to take the steps necessary to improve development prospects and financial strength in Africa.[26]

Notes

1. Julius K. Nyerere, "Africa and the Debt Crisis," *African Affairs,* 84(337):494 (Oct. 1985); Chinweizu, "Debt Trap Peonage," *Monthly Review,* 3(6):22, 22, 34 (Nov. 1985); Adebayo Adedeji, "Foreign Debt and Prospects for Growth in Africa during the 1980s," *Journal of Modern African Studies,* 23(1):60–61 (Mar. 1985).

2. This article concerns the 39 countries that the World Bank considers to be in sub-Saharan Africa; it does not include South Africa. Because comprehensive data

on Angola and Mozambique are usually not available to the bank, much but not all of the data presented here exclude these two countries. Whenever "Africa" is used in the text, it refers only to sub-Saharan Africa.

3. Since space precludes item-by-item citations for the bulk of the data presented in the text, please note that in addition to the sources cited later, the data are drawn directly from or recalculated from the following: World Bank, *Financing Adjustment with Growth in Sub-Saharan Africa, 1986–90* (Washington, DC: World Bank, 1986); idem, *Development and Debt Service* (Washington, DC: World Bank, 1986); idem, *World Development Report 1985* (New York: Oxford University Press, 1985); idem, *Toward Sustained Development in Sub-Saharan Africa* (Washington, DC: World Bank, 1984); Chandra Hardy, "Africa's Debt: Structural Adjustment with Stability," in *Strategies for African Development*, ed. Robert J. Berg and Jennifer Seymour Whitaker (Berkeley: University of California Press, 1986), pp. 453–75; Rupert Pennant-Rea, *The African Burden* (New York: Twentieth Century Fund/Priority Press, 1986); *IMF Survey*, 15(7):106 (31 Mar. 1986); and the following chapters from Carol Lancaster and John Williamson, eds., *African Debt and Financing* (Washington, DC: Institute for International Economics, 1986); Eduard Brau, "African Debt: Facts and Figures on the Current Situation," pp. 11–15, 30–43; John Williamson, "Prospects for the Flow of IMF Finance," pp. 134–41; Edward V. K. Jaycox et al., "The Nature of the Debt Problem in Eastern and Southern Africa," pp. 47–62.

4. World Bank, *Development and Debt Service*, p. xxvi; Reginald Herbold Green, "Reflections on the State of Knowledge and Ways Forward," in *Crisis and Recovery in Sub-Saharan Africa*, ed. Tore Rose (Paris: Organization for Economic Cooperation and Development, 1985), p. 299.

5. G. K. Helleiner, "The IMF and Africa in the 1980s," *Canadian Journal of African Studies*, 17(1):61 (1983); Green, "Reflections," p. 308; on the case of Zaïre, see Thomas M. Callaghy, "The Political Economy of African Debt: The Case of Zaïre," in *Africa in Economic Crisis*, ed. John Ravenhill (New York: Columbia University Press 1986), pp. 307–46.

6. It is important to note that these figures are based on World Bank projections of commodity prices, which often prove to be overly optimistic. These figures therefore may prove too low.

7. It might be possible to argue that interaction between countries of the Organization for Economic Cooperation and Development on African debt matters in the Paris Club and other fora in the 1970s and early 1980s laid the important case law that greatly facilitated Group of Five cooperation in coping with the Mexican debt crisis in 1982 and other major cases since then. On the international political economy of the post-1982 efforts, see Miles Kahler, "Politics and International Debt: Explaining the Crisis," *International Organization*, 39(3):357–82 (Summer 1985).

8. Nyerere, "Africa and the Debt Crisis," p. 492.

9. Helleiner, "IMF and Africa," p. 61; Green, "Reflections," p. 308.

10. Carol Lancaster, "Multilateral Development Banks and Africa" (Paper delivered at the Conference on African Debt and Financing, Institute for International Economics and Georgetown University, Washington, DC, 20–22 Feb. 1986), p. 21.

11. Gerald K. Helleiner, "The Question of Conditionality," in *African Debt and Financing*, ed. Lancaster and Williamson, p. 70.

12. World Bank, *Financing Adjustment*, p. 1.

13. Justin B. Zulu and Saleh M. Nsouli, "Adjustment Programs in Africa: The Recent Experience," IMF Occasional Paper no. 34 (International Monetary Fund, 1985), pp. 26–27.

14. See Stephan Haggard, "The Politics of Adjustment: Lessons from the IMF's Extended Fund Facility," *International Organization*, 39(3): 505–34 (Summer 1985).

15. Rattan J. Bhatia, "Adjustment Efforts in Sub-Saharan Africa, 1980–84," *Finance and Development*, 22(3):19–22 (Sept. 1985).

16. Green, "Reflections," p. 293.

17. Louis M. Goreux, "Economic Adjustment Efforts of Zaïre Require Support of External Creditors," *IMF Survey*, 15(5):72–75 (Mar. 1986); Jaycox et al., "Nature of the Debt Problem," p. 36; M. Crawford Young, "Optimism on Zaïre: Illusion or Reality?" *CSIS Africa Notes*, 50:8 (22 Nov. 1985).

18. *Financial Times*, 11 Apr. 1986.

19. Henry S. Bienen and Mark Gersovitz, "Economic Stabilization, Conditionality, and Political Instability," *International Organization*, 39(4):730, 753 (Autumn 1985).

20. Henry F. Jackson, "The African Crisis: Drought and Debt," *Foreign Affairs*, 63(5):1087 (Summer 1985).

21. Haggard, "Politics of Adjustment," p. 511; Edward V.K. Jaycox, "Africa: Development Challenges and the World Bank's Response," *Finance and Development*, 23(1):22 (Mar. 1986); on the nature of the African state and its political economy, see Thomas M. Callaghy, "The State as Lame Leviathan: The Patrimonial Administrative State in Africa," in *The African State in Transition*, ed. Zaki Ergas (New York: St. Martin's, forthcoming); idem, "The State and the Development of Capitalism in Africa: Theoretical, Historical, and Comparative Reflections," in *The Precarious Balance: State-Society Relations in Africa*, ed. Donald Rothchild and Naomi Chazan (Boulder, CO: Westview Press, 1988).

22. World Bank, *Financing Adjustment*, pp. 1, 21–22.

23. Ibid., p. 22.

24. Reginald Herbold Green and Caroline Allison, "The World Bank's Agenda for Development: Dialectics, Doubts, and Dialogues," in *Africa in Economic Crisis*, ed. Ravenhill, p. 72; Elliot Berg, "The World Bank's Strategy," in ibid., p. 54; World Bank, *Financing Adjustment*, p. 38; see also the very pessimistic analysis of Peter F. Drucker, "The Changed World Economy," *Foreign Affairs*, 64(4):768–91 (Spring 1986).

25. World Bank, *Financing Adjustment*, "Forward."

26. Philip Ndegwa, governor of the Central Bank of Kenya, quoted in *African Debt and Financing*, ed. Lancaster and Williamson, p. 9.

17

Adjustment with Growth: A Fragile Consensus

John Ravenhill

Six years of intense debate have produced a measure of agreement on a solution for Africa's malaise. This is captured by the latest catchphrase of the International Monetary Fund and the World Bank, 'Adjustment with Growth', which implicitly acknowledges past errors by African governments—or, minimally, that a continuation of previous policies is no longer tenable in a changed external environment. An emphasis on 'growth' recognises that 'adjustment' must encompass more than 'stabilisation', that the continent needs additional externally-provided financial resources on concessional terms if import strangulation is not to exacerbate the downward economic spiral in which many countries are currently trapped. This fragile consensus is facing its first serious practical test as the World Bank attempts to extend its Structural Adjustment Lending programme in Africa. Clearly, significant differences remain between the attitudes of African governments and external donors, and within the academic community, on the sources of the continent's problems and on the policy measures that are needed to counteract them.

That adjustment with growth has gained such widespread support itself represents a triumph for the World Bank, and in particular for its *Accelerated Development in Sub-Saharan Africa* (1981), the principal author of which was Elliot Berg. In retrospect, it is difficult to over-emphasise the extent to which this publication changed the nature of the debate on Africa's development problems. Although the Bank was at pains to emphasise that it did not perceive any contradiction between the Berg report and the Organisation of African Unity's *Lagos Plan of Action* (1980), this was widely disputed both by continental bureaucracies and by aca-

Reprinted with the permission of Cambridge University Press from the *Journal of Modern African Studies* 26 (June 1988): 179–210. © 1988 Cambridge University Press.

demics. *Accelerated Development* subsequently has effectively taken the *Lagos Plan* off the agenda. Although the O.A.U.'s most recent (1985) statement, *Africa's Priority Programme for Economic Recovery, 1986–90* (A.P.P.E.R.), continues to pay lip service to the *Plan*, it incorporates what are probably the two most central arguments in the Berg report.

The first is an acknowledgement, albeit grudgingly in A.P.P.E.R., that domestic policy errors have contributed to Africa's economic woes, whereas the *Lagos Plan* placed the blame exclusively on historical, structural, and external factors. This recognition is elaborated in the O.A.U.'s submission to the U. N. General Assembly's Special Session (1986) on Africa's Economic and Social Crisis:

> the programme [A.P.P.E.R.] candidly acknowledges that shortcomings in development policies have been partly responsible for the rapid and continued deterioration in the region's social and economic structures. The programme is, therefore, an unambiguous sign of full commitment on the part of the African leaders to undertake a number of policy measures that will remedy the shortcomings of past approaches.[1]

Secondly, new emphasis has been given to improving the performance of agriculture, whereas this was treated in a perfunctory manner in the *Lagos Plan*, being accorded only eight pages of exhortative and often tautological statements which lacked analysis of the problems experienced. Now the O.A.U. member-states have committed themselves to raising the share of agriculture in national public investment to between 20 and 25 per cent by 1989, and have pledged $57,400 million or 44.8 per cent of the total investment under A.P.P.E.R. to this sector.[2]

There are two principal reasons why *Accelerated Development* has dislodged the *Lagos Plan* from Africa's agenda. The first is that the depth of the crisis, particularly its manifestations in balance-of-payments deficits and debt problems, has left African governments with little practical alternative but to seek massive assistance from the World Bank and the I.M.F., and to subordinate themselves to the conditions that the Washington institutions wish to apply to such finance. Secondly, although O.A.U. member-states reiterate their 'full commitment to the principles and objectives of the *Lagos Plan of Action* and the Final Act of Lagos, which are more valid today than ever before', they admit that these 'have neither always been translated into concrete action nor reflected in national development plans'. The reasons, they conclude, lie in 'either ignorance of the requisites of the *Lagos Plan* and Final Act, or sheer inertia or lack of political will or all three in varying measures'.[3]

'Lack of political will' is not, of course, a satisfactory explanation but something which itself needs to be explained. A substantial part of the failure of political will can be attributed to the lack of faith in the prescriptions of the *Lagos Plan;* in particular, the absence of specific short- and medium-term measures to cope with Africa's crisis, as well as the commitment to establish regional integration schemes (and ultimately a continental common market) as the principal mechanism for stimulating self-reliance and industrialisation. African governments have every reason to doubt the efficacy of the latter proposal: to date, common markets have done much to hamper rather than to promote regional co-operation in Africa.[4]

To be fair to the drafters of the *Lagos Plan,* it was conceived at a time when the full dimensions of the crisis that was to afflict Africa had not become apparent. African states, however, have been unwilling to acknowledge, other than through their actions, that the *Lagos Plan* does not offer any short- to medium-term solutions to the current crisis. By accepting the conditions that the World Bank and I.M.F. have imposed on their financial assistance, African governments have relegated the *Lagos Plan* to the 'back-burner' if it has not been removed from the agenda completely. Having previously argued that the Berg report's emphasis on an export- and agriculture-based strategy fundamentally contradicted their own internally-oriented and intersector strategy, African governments would be disingenuous if they were to assert that the two approaches are compatible.

A similar transformation of the agenda is apparent in academic studies of Africa. Like the *Lagos Plan,* much of the academic work on Africa in the 1970s was rooted in dependency approaches which were the dominant paradigm in African studies in this period. Over the last five years there has been a new emphasis on how the internal characteristics of African states have limited their effectiveness,[5] and a new interest in policy analysis. By no means can this change in the academic agenda be attributed in any substantial degree to the Bank's *Accelerated Development.* Nevertheless, the economic crisis and the consequent emphasis on economic rationality has helped to 'rehabilitate' countries like Côte d'Ivoire and Malawi, references to which in the past had frequently been couched in the pejorative terms of neocolonialism.[6]

African governments may have had to move furthest in order that a consensus on 'adjustment with growth' was realised, but this has been facilitated by a modification of the Bank's stance since the publication of *Accelerated Development.* The aggressive expression of faith in its first report in what, even to sympathetic critics, appeared to be textbook neoclassical economics, has been toned down in a move towards a more conciliatory and nuanced approach.[7] The theme of 'getting the prices right', which dominated its early discussion, has been acknowledged as but one element of a solution that is inadequate unless accompanied by an overall reform package that includes increased inputs. Much greater attention has been given to the effects of exogenous factors on Africa's poor economic performance, particularly the decline in the terms of trade, which *Accelerated Development* appeared to go out of its way to deny.

Faith in the ability of agricultural exports to lead a recovery has also been tempered in the face of substantial criticisms that rested, in part, on the Bank's own pessimistic projections of future commodity prices. Accompanying this, in *Toward Sustained Development,* is an acknowledgement that high priority to greater self-sufficiency in foodstuffs may be more rational than *Accelerated Development* allowed. In its most recent report, *Financing Adjustment with Growth,* the Bank, perhaps feeling secure that the 'shock' tactics of its first report have had the desired effect, admits that 'it is important to realize that the region's performance has not been uniformly poor. The region has its success stories, some of which are better than average for the developing world'.[8] A greater element of positive reinforcement now appears to be the order of the day.

Besides agreement that priority must be given to the agricultural sector, and on the rôle of past policy mistakes in the continent's poor economic performance, the emerging consensus on 'adjustment with growth' also appears to embrace the following conclusions:

1. A necessary first step towards the creation of appropriate incentives is 'getting the prices right', including establishing realistic exchange rates. However:
2. Domestic policy reforms will not succeed unless they are supported by a massive inflow of resources on concessional terms. Many African economies are now suffering 'import strangulation' and, in the words of the former President of the World Bank, 'adjustment through further economic contraction is not a feasible alternative'.[9] In particular:
3. Africa's debt burden is now 'unmanageable', and to preclude widespread defaults, significant rescheduling will have to occur. Among non-official commentators, at least, the consensus appears to go further in asserting that a cancellation of some debts is necessary.
4. African states are over-extended, and need to establish clearer priorities for their activities. The public-sector deficit, often arising in large part from the inefficient operation of parastatals, must be significantly reduced.
5. Aid policies towards the continent have been far from optimal, with excessive emphasis having been given, in the words of the former E.E.C. Development Commissioner, Edgard Pisani, to the construction of 'cathedrals in the sand'. A change in priorities towards rehabilitation of existing infrastructure, greater financing of recurrent costs, and programme and sector aid is required. There is also a growing recognition that the proliferation of donors has cre-

ated a severe administrative burden for many African countries, and that greater coordination among donors is necessary.
6. The continent's rate of population growth will severely hamper efforts at raising standards of living, and there is now a widespread, although not universal, consensus among African governments that greater efforts must be made to curb the birth rate.

Beyond these general themes, however, there is disagreement both on instrumentalities and on how policy reforms might best be implemented. The Bank surely overstated its case when it asserted that 'the emerging consensus on policy issues dwarfs any remaining areas of dissent'.[10] Certainly, there is no general acceptance of what John Lewis has termed the 'new conventional wisdom' of the Bank.[11] Indeed, as Gerald Helleiner has pointed out, there is considerable suspicion among African governments that the Bank is pursuing a thinly-veiled long-term agenda whose objectives are significantly different from those that they seek.[12] And, it is still too early to establish how deeply many governments are committed to the new consensus, or whether it is a matter of posturing in the hope of attracting desperately-needed finance.[13] If the O.A.U.'s 'Submission' to the General Assembly is taken as an example, a commitment to encouraging the 'positive role of the private sector' appears to be a token genuflection tacked on to the end of a paragraph.[14] Temporary respite from the balance-of-payments crisis—e.g. through the windfall of higher coffee prices—may encourage some states to adopt a less compliant stance.

It has been easier to reach agreement on what measures are appropriate for the immediate future rather than on long-term principles, largely because African countries have so few policy alternatives available to them. To move beyond short-term adjustment to the encouragement of economic growth is, as Helleiner has pointed out, to become entangled in a much wider debate:

> the heart of the problem lies in the fact that the quasi-technical (though quite difficult enough) issues relating to medium-term balance-of-payments adjustment inevitably overlap in the Bank's policy-based programme lending with much more controversial and highly political issues of development strategy.[15]

A number of other factors preclude movement beyond agreement on the few general themes listed above. One is simply the current lack of knowledge of the probable impact of various policies on economies at Africa's level of development. Neither the World Bank nor the I.M.F. have any extensive experience of promoting adjustment in low-income countries, and there is now substantial evidence to suggest that their economies may behave differently from others.[16] A country's performance is subject to so many extraneous factors beyond the changes brought about by new policies that attributing causality is extremely problematic. Adjustment with growth in Africa is also of such recent origin that there is not even any significant body of case-study material available. Data problems are particularly acute in sub-Saharan Africa, nowhere more so than in the agricultural sector where most of the information on yields is little more than informed guesswork. Finally, given the structural diversity of African economies, any attempt at suggesting detailed universal solutions to their problems would seem to be profoundly misguided.

Causes of the Crisis: Do They Matter?

A great deal of discussion has been devoted to whether internal or exogenous factors were the principal cause of Africa's recent economic woes. That this should have been such a contentious issue is partly an unfortunate consequence of the attempt in *Accelerated Development* to assign exclusive blame for poor economic performance to inadequate government policies. For some observers, these ongoing arguments are rather pointless since they do not in themselves contribute towards resolution of the problems. A continued discussion of the causes of the crisis does have the danger of degenerating into mutual recriminations; it also potentially may be used as a diversionary tactic, as appeared to be the case, for instance, in the Soviet Union's behaviour in the U.N. Special Session on the Critical Economic Situation in Africa.

At the heart of the matter, however, is the question of how the burden of adjustment should be apportioned. Two of the principles underlying the establishment of the Bretton Woods institutions were, first, that countries should be provided with liquidity in sufficient volume to make it unnecessary to resort to costly adjustment because of a temporary balance-of-payments shortage, but not with excessive funds that might discourage essential change in the event of fundamental disequilibria; and, secondly, that the burden of the measures that *have* to be undertaken should be shared equitably between creditor and debtor countries. Those arguing that the causes of Africa's crisis are largely irrelevant have sometimes seized on the first of these principles: since Africa faces not a temporary but what appears to be a permanent deterioration in its terms of trade, governments must adjust their economies regardless of whether the sources of the disequilibria are beyond their control. There is certainly more than an element of truth in this assertion, but the necessity for adjustment needs to be considered in the context of the second principle: the equitable sharing of the costs of the remedial action. In addition, consideration of the causes of the crisis is necessary in order to identify those components of previous policies that need to be changed.

Intuitively, the universal downturn in performance in Africa after 1979, despite the heterogeneity of economic structures and policies, suggests that exogenous factors must have played a significant rôle. This line of analysis has been supported by econometric studies, particularly that of David Wheeler, who suggests that environmental constraints were more important than policy variables in explaining Africa's economic stagnation in the 1970s.[17] To estimate with any accuracy the relative contribution of the factors is probably beyond current econometric modelling capabilities, and would require inordinate faith in the reliability of available data. There appears, in fact, to have been a complex interaction between internal and external factors in producing the post-1979 economic crisis. For example, Kathie Krumm shows that adverse world prices turned what had been projected to be viable investment projects in Senegal into costly white elephants.[18]

There are two issues that sometimes appear to be confused in the discussion of Africa's economic crisis. The first is an explanation for the relatively poor performance of many countries during the 1970s, which surely lies in both internal and external variables; the second is whether the economic downturn in Africa since 1979 need have been so severe had adequate external financing accompanied appropriate policy reform. Helleiner found that there was a stronger negative relationship during 1960–80 between rates of growth and instability in the volume of imports rather than with whether or not an economy was export-oriented.[19] This analysis supports the assertion made by several writers that lack of import capacity played a significant rôle in preventing African governments from adjusting successfully to the second round of oil price rises and the subsequent recession in the West.[20]

African economies were set on a steep downward spiral by sudden external shocks, import strangulation, and the inexperience of governments in dealing with a crisis of this nature. The volume of resources made available to Africa after 1979 was far smaller than after the first oil shock—the I.M.F. created no equivalent to the Oil Facility or the Trust Fund, while commercial bank lending to oil importers after 1979 was of little significance. African governments have a strong case that they were not treated equitably in the creation of new international liquidity after 1979.[21] And, they were not alone in misjudging the nature of the crisis: I.M.F. staff have admitted that the Fund failed to anticipate the depth of the problems that emerged, and accordingly did not suggest the necessary policy adjustments.[22]

Lack of adequate external support, poor policy advice, and the activities of some export-credit agencies in tempting African governments into poorly-conceived projects that they lacked the technical capacity to evaluate, all suggest that the burden of adjustment to the current crisis should not rest on Africa's shoulders alone. In the absence of their acceptance by the international community, however, such arguments provide little consolation to African governments.

Agriculture

There is almost universal agreement that Africa's recovery from economic crisis will have to be led by agriculture, albeit a great deal less certainty about what can or needs to be done. As Carl Eicher has stated:

> there is little understanding of the technical and institutional requirements for agricultural change and a tendency to underestimate the gestation period required to develop human capital, managerial skills, and bio-chemistry technology—the prime movers of agricultural change.[23]

Many countries face a long-term crisis, a reflection of the exhaustion of the traditional mode of production and the absence of appropriate technological inputs. The crisis is not amenable to quick solutions.

The current unsustainable level of food imports—with horrific projections if recent trends are maintained to the end of the century[24]—underlines the logic of emphasising food self-sufficiency. Again, the aggressive stance taken in *Accelerated Development* against this strategy was unfortunate—even more so when it became translated into neglect of such governmental aspirations in the Bank's structural-adjustment lending.[25] Justifications for concentration on food production include its contribution to (i) reducing the demands on scarce foreign exchange made by current food imports; (ii) preventing long-term changes occurring in food preferences in Africa,[26] (iii) minimising dependence on uncertain supplies of imports, particularly food aid; and (iv) providing a more logical distribution of resources given opportunity costs—particularly in the context of dismal projections for the prices of most export agricultural crops. This does not imply support for food self-sufficiency at any cost—but rather that the Bank has tended to underweight the advantages of this strategy in favouring an emphasis on export agriculture.[27]

Since parallel markets are estimated to handle as much as 70 per cent of food supplies in many countries,[28] and food prices have risen more rapidly in recent years that the income of urban workers, a strategy of 'getting the prices right' appears to offer only a very partial solution to the problem of stimulating food production. Indeed, a Bank staff working paper concluded that pricing policies 'are not the most important factors explaining agricultural performance in sub-Saharan Africa', that 'the impact on aggregate production of keeping many farmgate prices low is considerably less than is generally thought', and that 'the price policy remedies suggested in the literature are too stereotyped'.[29]

Although the figures are unreliable, the best estimates suggest that the overall price elasticity of supply is low in Africa.[30] Michael Lipton points out that total output inevitably will respond only moderately to the policy changes recommended by the Bank in the absence of immediately applicable new technology.[31] A number of authors have suggested that a focus on prices alone is insufficient. First, farmers are motivated not so much by the net barter but rather the income terms of trade; Cathy Jabara found that improvements in yields for some crops in Kenya were more important in leading to increased production than were higher prices.[32] Second, it may be less costly, as Reginald Green has argued, to foster production through the provision of incentive goods—particularly health, education, and water in rural areas. Not only does this encourage people to remain on their farms but also enables their time to be used more productively.[33]

There is now a general consensus that emphasis should be given to small farmers (although disagreement on whether 'progressive' farmers or ordinary peasants should receive priority), since they are most likely to utilise scarce resources efficiently.[34] But giving pride of place to small farmers, and changing policy to favour their interests, is difficult to reconcile with what we know about political coalitions in most African countries. Robert Bates provided a masterly analysis of the political logic of anti-agricultural bias.[35] As his study predicted, evidence suggests that pricing and other policies have been most favourable towards agriculture where members of the political élite have an interest in production—e.g. Côte d'Ivoire, Kenya, and the estate sector in Malawi.[36] Africa lacks the pro-agricultural lobby that has been created within most governments in Asia.[37] One solution to this problem lies in encouraging small-holders to organise themselves into farmers groups and co-operatives, as Michael Bratton found in Zimbabwe,[38] although how outside agencies might best promote such a movement has yet to be detailed.

Another approach favoured by many writers is to foster institutional pluralism, particularly in the delivery of rural inputs and the purchasing of agricultural products. This need not, however, necessarily mean the removal of the state from the arena. As Helleiner points out, there is no logic in replacing a public with a private monopoly.[39] Nor is it assured that private institutions will always be more efficient at delivering the goods, or that producers will receive a higher farm-gate price from private purchasers compared to their state equivalents.[40]

While some improvement in agricultural output can be expected through the rectification of faulty macro-economic policies, especially over-valued exchange rates, the current production boundaries of African agriculture are rapidly being reached. In part this reflects the closing of the land frontier: according to the F.A.O., 14 countries in the continent do

not have enough land to support their present levels of population in subsistence farming.[41] While there is consensus that long-term improvements
in productivity will come only if Africa moves to a scientifically-based
agriculture, expert opinion shares the view of the World Bank that 'the
technology shelf in sub-Saharan Africa is nearly bare'.[42] This is explained,
in part, by the difficulties faced by agricultural researchers—given the
heterogeneity of the continent's climatic and soil conditions, and the dependence on unreliable precipitation—but their output has been perceived by many observers as particularly disappointing.

Lipton asserts that 20 years have been largely wasted in agricultural research in many (not all) sub-Saharan African countries. This reflects, in
part, poorly conceived priorities: the colonial emphasis on research on export crops has been maintained and food crops relatively neglected[43]—
aid donors must share the blame since they have tended to favour the former.[44] Lipton calls for greater congruence between the distribution of
research expenditures and the actual or potential contribution of crops to
the economy; particular attention should be given to Africa's three principal staple cereals—maize, millet, and sorghum.[45] Commentators are
agreed, however, that no quick fix is foreseeable: Eicher estimates that it
takes ten years to produce a new plant variety, and a further five to eight
years for it to be widely accepted by farmers.[46]

There is general agreement on the need for institution-building in the
field of agricultural research. Some of those employed in this work have
been characterised as underqualified, underproductive, and overpaid. Too
often, their findings have not been tested in on-farm conditions. The need
for more knowledgeable researchers suggests a priority item for external assistance; aid donors in the past, however, have demonstrated a preference
for financing buildings rather than the less glamorous task of training staff.
Another area neglected in agricultural research and policies in the past has
been the rôle of women, who are estimated to be responsible for as much as
70 per cent of Africa's food production. Little consideration has been given
to improving their access to land, credit, and other inputs.[47] Extension services are also judged to have performed poorly, but there appears to be little
consensual knowledge on how this record might be improved. Green reports that Tanzania restructured its extension service four times on external
expert advice, but without any evident increase in effectiveness.[48]

A record of negative achievements has provided substantial evidence
of undesirable policy options—most notably state farms, capital-intensive
irrigation projects, and tractorisation. Unfortunately, there is less knowledge of what should be done rather than what should be avoided. For the
foreseeable future, the best prospects for enhancing the performance of
African agriculture appear to lie in the increased use of fertilisers, improved rural infrastructures, and better rural storage. The rehabilitation

of existing facilities can play a significant rôle—there are widespread reports of crops rotting just because vehicles have broken down and governments lack the foreign exchange to import the necessary spare parts.[49]

Industry

In contrast to the attention given to agriculture, industry seems almost to have disappeared from the new agenda. This neglect has occurred despite the very poor record in this sector—U.N.I.D.O. reports negative rates of growth in the period 1973–81 in manufacturing value-added for 21 of 40 sub-Saharan African countries. The continent's share of global manufacturing (0.54 per cent in 1981) is unlikely to exceed 1.2 per cent by the year 2000.[50]

Almost universal agreement now exists that Africa's industrial performance has been adversely affected by the excessive protection given to the process of import-substitution, and by flawed macroeconomic policies such as over-valued exchange rates. While there is a consensus that the bias against export enterprises should be removed, there are few practical recommendations as to how this may be combined with the need to help infant industries. Their wholesale deprotection as advocated by some proponents of the virtues of market forces does not appear to be a realistic solution, and runs contrary to the findings reported in a World Bank document regarding the experience of the newly-industrialising countries (N.I.C.s).[51]

Inappropriate technology bears some responsibility for poor performance in the industrial sector. Again, this blame has to be shared between African countries and their western trading partners, who have induced various régimes to undertake inappropriate purchases through the provision of export credits.[52] Robert Berg asserts that 'donor finance tends to distort rather than reinforce government planning', and cites the example of a high official in West Africa who said that while his government 'had certain minimal criteria for accepting a project, the availability of donor financing could override all other criteria'.[53]

Privatisation has become the predominant recommendation for the industrial sector. While there is ample evidence that state-owned enterprises have performed poorly in many (although not all) African countries,[54] in part because of the various non-economic rôles that they have been expected to play, privatisation may not necessarily be the answer. Faith in a bourgeois revolution in Africa, as Hyden, for example, appears to hold,[55] makes the questionable assumption that privatisation will generate an entrepreneurial rather than a rentier-capitalist class. There is simply no guarantee that an economic system based predominantly on private enterprise in Africa will necessarily correspond to the alleged rationality of the market-place. After all, countries such as Nigeria and Kenya have long had significant private sectors, elements of which have been every bit as inefficient as state-owned enterprises. The issue here is the degree to which the state is insulated from social groups. Where there is often not merely a close relationship between local capitalists and political élites but also an identity—they are one and the same, as is true to a considerable extent throughout Africa[56]—there is a probability that state power will be employed not to promote market efficiency but to sustain oligopolistic advantages and to generate economic rents.

Privatisation—in Africa as in Britain—may generate 'one-off' benefits for the treasury, and for purchasers when assets are sold at a discount. But once enterprises are privatised their new owners may quickly request additional protection in order to ensure continuing profitability. Privatisation may be most expected to stimulate efficiency where (i) there is competition within that particular sector (usually where the costs of entry are fairly low); (ii) there are realistic prospects for exports; and (iii) the new owners of industry cannot be assured of a sympathetic hearing from the state for requests for assistance. Privatisation thus appears much more likely to succeed in generating economic efficiency in sectors such as transport and distribution, where entry costs are modest, than in most manufacturing industries.

Even the most enthusiastic proponents of the private sector acknowledge that Africa cannot expect a significant inflow of new private foreign capital in the foreseeable future.[57] Nevertheless, there is much that African states can do to enhance these prospects, in particular through guarantees on investment and on the repatriation of profits. Capitalism, whether in the form of domestic firms or foreign enterprises, above all requires certainty in its conditions of operation. It is this which has been lacking in many African states. As Thomas Callaghy has argued convincingly, many neo-patrimonial régimes have failed to provide the political and procedural predictability necessary for capitalist development.[58]

Industrial production, like agriculture, has been adversely affected by import strangulation. The greater availability of foreign exchange would assist rehabilitation and make a substantial contribution towards restoring the productivity of existing enterprises. Beyond this, however, there appear to be few prescriptions of universal applicability. Certainly, prospects for efficient production would be enhanced if industries were assured of access to enlarged markets through regional co-operation, but African governments have for the most part yet to translate their nominal support for this strategy into concrete measures. Industrialised countries might also give greater attention to facilitating contacts between African entrepreneurs and their own private sectors through institutions such as the Lomé Convention's Centre for the Development of Industry.

Exports

Similar uncertainty is evident in the discussion of what can be done to increase Africa's exports, a move which is urgently required not only to break the current foreign-exchange strangulation, but also for financing Africa's desired strategy of greater self-reliance. As Mike Faber and Reginald Green note, there are 'no easy, general answers—except wrong ones',[59] a statement aimed particularly at the enthusiasm in *Accelerated Development* for increased agricultural exports.

Earlier optimism on the part of the World Bank that growth could be led by agricultural exports appears to rest on an assumption that Africa could recapture lost market shares from other producers. This is by no means certain, particularly given the investment in agricultural export production in middle-income countries, and the prescription of export-led growth by the Bank for all developing regions.[60] Even the Bank seems now to have bowed to the logic of the 'fallacy of composition' argument. In its most recent report, it notes that 'exports will be relatively slow to respond. They are mostly primary commodities, which have limited prospects'.[61] Prices for many of Africa's exports of commodities are expected to decline still further until the mid-1990s. In 1986, the continent's terms of trade declined by 25 to 30 per cent—equivalent to a loss in some countries of 5 per cent of G.D.P.[62] The I.M.F. predicts a further 3.5 per cent deterioration in sub-Saharan Africa's terms of trade in 1987, to be followed by an additional 0.3 per cent annual fall in the years 1988–91.[63]

Studies of two countries that have been most successful in pursuing an agricultural-export growth strategy raise serious doubts regarding the long-term viability of this approach. Mathurin Gbetibouo and Christopher Delgado identify both internal and external constraints to continuing reliance on cocoa in Côte d'Ivoire: the increasing cost of agricultural labour, the rising relative value of foodstuff production, the need to promote regional equality which will entail policies that discriminate against cocoa producers, and increasing internal competition for a stagnant market.[64] In Malawi, where increased agricultural exports have been derived almost exclusively from estate production, Livingstone questions whether the present strategy of resource-based industrialisation can be maintained given the lack of purchasing power in rural areas.[65]

Faith in agricultural exports may have dissipated, but there has been little serious analysis of alternatives. Given Africa's relatively expensive labour costs and poor infrastructure, as well as the high transport costs to major overseas markets, there is little optimism that export-led industrialisation as pursued by the Asian N.I.C.s will prove to be a viable strategy.[66]

One area where Africa lags behind other L.D.C.s is in the local processing of primary products. But major moves in this direction are likely to run foul of protectionist sentiments, particularly in Africa's principal market, the European Economic Community. Lack of reciprocity is evident too often in the insistence by industrialised countries on investment guarantees in Africa without any accompanying assurance of secure market access.[67] Other ways in which, for example, the E.E.C. could assist African exporters would be through the provision of technical assistance to provide information about market and export finance, and through financing their participation in trade fairs.

Debt Problems

Debt problems have become one of the most important barriers to economic recovery. Although Africa's share of the total owed by developing countries has been estimated to be only 9 per cent, its debt and debt-service ratios have deteriorated more rapidly than those of any other geographic area. The *circa* $15,000 million owed in 1974 is now estimated to have risen to over $150,000 million, while debt-service ratios more than doubled in the period 1980–5 as a consequence of both an increase in borrowing and the dismal performance of African exports. Debt-service ratios now exceed 50 per cent on average, and are much higher for many low-income countries. In addition, the terms of repayment have become significantly harder as a result of the flexible interest rates, the larger share of privately-held debt in the total outstanding, and the higher proportion of export credits in the publicly-held debt.[68]

Large current-account deficits have depleted Africa's foreign-exchange reserves. In 1986 the continent's current-account deficit doubled to more than $16,000 million. More than two-thirds of all governments are unable to meet their scheduled repayments: arrears currently amount to over $12,000 million, or roughly 13 per cent of all debts.[69] The problems are reflected in the fact that more than two-thirds of all the rescheduling undertaken by the Paris Club since 1969 has been at the request of sub-Saharan states, notably Nigeria, the Sudan, Côte d'Ivoire, Zaïre, and Zambia.

Africa's problems are exacerbated by two factors: the bunching of amortisation payments in the next few years, and the relatively large share of debt (11.1 per cent of the total, but over 50 per cent for some least-developed countries) that is held by the I.M.F. and the World Bank. Estimates of scheduled repayments range from the latter's figure of $6,800 million annually for 29 I.D.A. countries, to Eduard Brau's $15,000 million for all sub-Saharan Africa for 1986–7, to the O.A.U.'s $14,600 million to $24,500 million per year for 1986–90. With most African governments being unable to meet their existing (lower) obligations, the projected level of debt-servicing is clearly 'unmanageable'. However, the debt owed to multilateral institutions cannot be rescheduled, and for some countries the I.M.F. will emerge as the single largest recipient of debt-service payments for the remainder of the decade.

While there is widespread agreement that the current method of debt-rescheduling is inefficient and largely ineffective, creditors have shown no willingness to move to multi-year rescheduling, and only a few official creditors have been willing to commute loans into grants or to offer debt moratoria. Annual rescheduling has tended to increase the financial burden as debts are 'rolled over' at higher rates of interest with additional servicing fees. Despite the pleas of the World Bank, the Paris Club of official creditors has refused to reduce interest rates below market levels. Chandra Hardy estimates that repeated rescheduling has increased the debt burden by $21,000 million since 1979, whereas net inflow increased by only $1,000 million annually.[70] In the absence of prospects for a significant improvement in Africa's export earnings, such rescheduling merely postpones the day of reckoning. To make matters worse, a large proportion of the scarce administrative resources of African governments are being absorbed in a process that will, at best, bring uncertain short-term relief.[71]

The prospect of obtaining additional funds from commercial banks is remote, and even if these were available, most experts believe that it would be reckless to take out any more loans on commercial terms.[72] Even continued borrowing from the I.M.F. on conventional terms is regarded as risky, given the high interest rates and the obligation for early repayment. As both Helleiner and Green have argued, African countries have little prospect of being able to restore external equilibrium in the short period of time allowed by the Fund's standby facilities.[73]

Africa desperately needs additional transfers not merely to enable it to meet its debt-servicing obligations, but also to interrupt its steep downward economic spiral. With imports in many countries down 30 per cent from their level in 1980, import strangulation threatens economic recovery. Estimates of the total finance that Africa needs to restore growth to acceptable levels are inevitably gross approximations. Even though the Bank's projection that Africa needs $35,300 million per year in foreign exchange is already $2,500 million above expected flows, many observers believe that this will be insufficient if the needs of *all* countries are to be financed. This perspective is reinforced by what appear to be overly optimistic assumptions about export earnings, because the Bank assumes that their annual rate of growth will be in excess of 10 per cent to the end of the decade. Given the projected deterioration in Africa's terms of trade, the sluggish growth rates of industrialised countries, and the apparent secular decline in demand for some primary products, the Bank's projection appears to be highly unrealistic. If export earnings grow by 'only' five per cent each year, the financing gap is doubled to more than $5,000 million annually.[74] In fact in 1986 alone, according to the Economic Commission for Africa, the collapse in commodity prices, coupled with the fall in the value of the U.S. dollar, is estimated to have cost Africa $19,000 million in foreign-exchange earnings.[75]

Some observers, consequently, are extremely sceptical of the Bank's estimates. Helleiner, for example, argues that they appear to have been based more on a projection of the total funds that might feasibly be obtained, rather than on the amount that Africa needs.[76] Others believe that the Bank intends to engage in a new form of *triage,* in which assistance will be offered only to those countries that are willing to subordinate themselves completely to its 'new conventional wisdom'.[77] Such suspicions are reinforced by statements such as that made by the U.S. Assistant Secretary of State, Chester Crocker, in justifying the Administration's fiscal-year 1987 request to Congress:

> I am not arguing for a gap-closing exercise for all of Africa. For better or for worse, this is not sustainable in the United States, or most other countries. What is needed is a combination of donor concentration of assistance on programs to produce results in those countries in Africa seriously engaged in adjustment and to provide incentives for the future to other countries that must eventually take this path.[78]

Whichever estimate of Africa's total funding needs is employed, there appears to be no avoiding what Ramgopal Agarwala has termed the 'minimax' problem: minimum resource needs exceed the maximum available flow.[79] The response of the international community to the World Bank's appeals for additional finance to support African adjustment programmes has been disappointing. Although the I.D.A. VIII replenishment totalled $12,400 million (of which 50 per cent was allocated to Africa), this only restored the nominal value of resources to the level of I.D.A. VI. According to the O.E.C.D.'s Development Assistance Committee, total net resource flows to sub-Saharan Africa show a trend *decline* of 5 per cent in real terms between 1980 and 1985. In 1986, Africa actually repaid the I.M.F. substantially more than it received in new loans—when net purchases and interest charges are taken into account, the net outflow of resources to the I.M.F. amounted to over $960 million. Some relief will be provided by the Fund's new Enhanced Structural Adjustment Facility, announced in December 1987, which will add S.D.R. 6,000 million (approximately $8,400 million) to the resources that the Fund agreed to provide as part of the 'Baker Initiative'. The annual net addition that the Enhanced Facility will make to the resource flow to the 34 low-income African countries eligible to receive assistance is estimated at $600 million.

Also in December 1987, the Bank succeeded in cajoling the major industrial countries (with the notable exception of the United States) into promising $2,900 million in co-financing funds. This will supplement the

$400 million per year the Bank will contribute from I.D.A. funds to the low-income, highly-indebted, countries that are pursuing approved economic reform programmes. Their desperate plight is revealed by the very modest aspiration of the new programme: to permit an annual increase in imports of one per cent above the rate of population growth. Even if this target is achieved, it will not be until the year 2000 that the volume of imports will be restored to the 1980 level. And although the bilateral assistance promised will largely be untied and on highly concessional terms, it will not be additional finance for the most part but the reallocation of aid already committed. The O.E.C.D. projects that bilateral and multilateral aid from its members will increase by a maximum of only two per cent a year—which translates in real terms into an additional sum of only $700 million per year.[80]

Conditionality or Policy Dialogue?

Policy dialogue has become the vogue catch-phrase in aid circles in the 1980s. To a considerable extent, this represents acceptance of the idea that the function of aid is less to provide an externally-financed 'missing link' than to induce policy reform on the part of recipient governments.[81] Aid donors argue that one reason for the ineffectiveness of some project assistance in the past has been the unfavourable macroeconomic environments in which they have had to operate. There has also been growing acceptance of the argument, made most coherently by Robert Bates, that although African governments have pursued policies that may have been politically rational, these have not promoted economic growth. Rather than having served as an instrument of development, the African state is increasingly perceived as having frequently been an obstacle to progress.[82] In the words of Robert Cassen et al.:

> The introduction of conditionality results in part from the view that, in success or failure at structural adjustment, vested interests count as much as the rationality of policy-making; the donor agency must therefore sometimes find a way to exert leverage. At times even governments intent on change may be inhibited by domestic vested interests; conditions 'imposed' from without can be helpful in combating those interests.[83]

However, 'leaning on an open door' is very different from imposing reforms from outside. Various reviews of I.M.F. and Bank conditionality have suggested that this has been most successful, as in India, when seen as helping countries along a path that they wished to pursue; in these circumstances, governments regard the reforms as their own. Imposed programmes, in contrast, may attract token compliance in order to gain an initial transfer of resources, but they are likely to fail quickly as a result of lack of official commitment.[84] The manner in which programmes are ne-gotiated is also important—Green has recorded that the confrontational and inflexible stance of the I.M.F. teams in Tanzania not only ensured that no agreement with the Government would be reached, but also weak-ened the hands of those promoting reforms and delayed desirable changes that would otherwise have been introduced.[85]

Widespread doubts exist regarding the relevance of the standard I.M.F. adjustment programme for African circumstances. As Green argues, de-valuation and deflation may have little relevance if the principal cause of Africa's contemporary balance-of-payments crisis was not domestic in-creases in the use of real resources but reductions of imports, often cou-pled with decreases in government revenues and food supplies. The large 'one-off' devaluation that the I.M.F. appears to favour is likely merely to set off an inflationary spiral in the absence of increased supplies of re-sources—this appears to have been the case in Kenya, Sierra Leone, the Sudan, and Zaïre. Deflation similarly is likely to be of dubious utility as a policy tool in economies operating at a fraction of their full capacity as a result of import strangulation.[86]

Cassen et al., although generally sympathetic to the Fund, found that its programmes on some occasions have been more severe than necessary, and that they were unduly inflexible. In the African context, many ob-servers have asserted that the Fund has paid insufficient attention to the supply side.[87] Here the danger is that stabilisation may be achieved with-out development. The problem has been succinctly summarised by Joan Nelson:

> The changes necessary to diversify and expand production cannot be in-duced by stabilization alone—by belt-tightening and changes in relative prices—but will require years of investment and institutional and human re-source development. In such nations, a shock approach can indeed 'balance' the budget and the trade account, but only by reducing consumption, gov-ernment services, production, and employment far below any level that could facilitate real adjustment—that is, changes in the composition of pro-duction and expanded productive capacity. Indeed, in such economies a dra-conian approach can seriously weaken the capacity for real adjustment.[88]

In accepting the assertion that 'in contemporary circumstances it is im-possible to draw any sharp distinction between balance-of-payments management and the design of development strategies',[89] a number of observers have suggested that the World Bank should be the lead agency in Africa, particularly given the I.M.F.'s obligations to engage primarily in short-term balance-of-payments financing.[90] But, as noted earlier, there is even less agreement among experts and governments on the broader is-sues of development strategy than there is on the measures necessary to rectify payments crises. And it is this more complex agenda that has produced one line of criticism against the conditionality imposed by the Bank: that it is simply too intrusive, embracing an excessive number and diversity of targets. Berg has argued that 'this torrent of conditionality is misguided', having produced a situation where 'fictional' and 'nonmonitorable' conditions have proliferated, thereby hampering real policy dialogue.[91] With structural adjustment loans depending on prior agreement between recipients and the Fund, countries face the risk of the double jeopardy of cross-conditionality.

Other criticisms of the Bank's implementation of structural adjustment lending in Africa include: (i) excessively optimistic estimates of commodity prices and capital flows, leading to mis-specification of targets (Kenya); (ii) excessive faith in the ability of pricing policies to induce increased output of individual crops (Kenya); (iii) over-optimistic assessment of the overall price elasticity of supply of agricultural products (Malawi); (iv) dogmatism regarding the necessity for privatisation; (v) continuing support for previous policies of dubious effectiveness (integrated rural-development projects in Malawi); (vi) underestimation of the timetable in which reform can be expected to generate results; and (vii) neglect of impoverished groups and the supply of basic social services.[92]

Professional uncertainty is again reflected in criticisms of specific elements of Bank programmes. Helleiner disputes the Bank's argument that policy reforms will make any significant difference to development, noting that econometric work suggests growth is related significantly only to two major categories of price 'distortion'—exchange rates and real wages—and that there is also a limited relationship with degree of protection of manufacturing. No association has been found between growth and the degree of taxation or protection of capital, interest rates, energy prices, or rate of inflation.[93] Bank insistence on user charges in Malawi, especially in the field of education, not only ran contrary to government policy but also to the predictions of independent experts that it would lead to an undesirable decline in both standards and enrolments.[94]

To date, neither the Fund nor the Bank have enjoyed more than modest success in promoting structural adjustment in Africa. According to the Fund's own assessment of its recent programmes, 'in many cases the performance fell short of targets', with the majority of countries failing to achieve targeted economic growth, improvement in current account position, credit expansion, external debt position, and ratio of government expenditure to G.D.P. The causes of policy failure, in estimated order of importance, were: (i) unforeseen developments, especially commodity price changes, interest rate increases, and drought; (ii) difficulties that governments faced in mobilising sufficient political support for their adjustment efforts; (iii) weaknesses in implementation due to lack of administrative capability; (iv) inappropriate targets; and (v) delays or shortfalls in expected inflows of development assistance.[95]

These findings are very much in accord with the arguments made by critics of the Fund's activities. Exogenous factors have been emphasised by several authors who have opposed the rigidity of some I.M.F. programmes. John Williamson's suggestion that 'contingency conditions' be built into Fund (and, one might add, Bank) programmes seems particularly appropriate.[96] The problem of inappropriate and mis-estimated targets reinforces doubts about the completeness of the Fund's knowledge of either the structure or the operation of African economies.[97] Lack of administrative capability suggests the need for long-term investment in institution-building and education. But perhaps the most critical factors in terms of programme design are the difficulties of mobilising support for policy reform and the (not entirely unrelated issue of) shortfalls in development assistance.

Although, as Henry Bienen and Mark Gersovitz have argued, the correlation between adoption of a Fund programme and the onset of régime instability may not be perfect,[98] there is sufficient risk that key political constituencies will be so alienated by the I.M.F.'s agenda as to make governments very reluctant to embark on suggested reforms. As Green points out, an unpalatable reform package in which 'sticks' predominate over 'carrots' will encourage governments to wait until the last possible moment before approaching the Bank or the Fund. If one accepts that governments make choices in accordance with their perceptions of political rationality, then they need to be offered some 'pay-offs' if programmes are to gain their full support. From her survey of various case-studies, Joan Nelson concludes that government scepticism regarding the possibility of benefits being generated by policy reform is often as important an obstacle to its adoption as fear of political risk.[99] External agencies are seldom given the benefit of the doubt in such calculations.

While the 'sudden shock' approach is advocated by some who emphasise the short-time horizon of governments and the limits to public tolerance of austerity measures, few commentators advocate this approach for Africa, given the already fragile state of many economies. Rather, the emerging consensus is that policy reform will have to be sold to African governments by providing more incentives, and through a gradual approach that recognises the inflexibility of African economies and the political problems faced by incumbent régimes. As a senior Bank official emphasises:

> We need to avoid proposing prescriptive policy packages which are not politically feasible. We must take into account real political fears and carry out detailed analyses of implementation problems to avoid undesirable income

distribution and power distribution effects. We must propose step-by-step implementation sequences with buttressing and buffering measures to make them less painful or dangerous.[100]

Although many observers remain sceptical, it does appear that the Bank has learnt from the errors of previous structural adjustment loans and is beginning to heed this advice from the Vice-President of its Eastern and Southern African Regional Office.[101] It is now able to point to what appear to be a number of (at least short-term) success stories for the policy package that it advocates, most notably in Ghana and Zaïre.

The question of adequate financial resources remains unresolved, however. Even with the Structural Adjustment Facility and a replenished I.D.A., it remains doubtful whether the Bank and the Fund have adequate resources themselves, or can mobilise sufficient support from bilateral donors to provide enough 'carrots' for reform-minded governments. Without the necessary external support, the credibility of the Fund, the Bank, and market-oriented reforms will be at risk.[102]

The Response from Industrialised Countries

Evaluations of the U.N. Special Session on Africa range from a 'significant success' to a 'waste of time'. The continent's problems did gain a prominent place, at least temporarily, on the international agenda, and the outcome might be perceived as a considerable rhetorical triumph for the Reagan Administration. But the failure to persuade most industrialised countries to do more than 'rededicate' themselves to working towards a solution for Africa's problems generated considerable cynicism regarding the commitment to assist and, particularly, the willingness to provide the necessary finance in support of structural adjustment. The Secretary-General of the O.A.U. commented: 'Let's be candid, we asked for a commitment and it was not forthcoming. We did not expect this to be a pledging conference, but what we have received in the way of proposals is far less concrete than what we expected'.[103] As the *Financial Times* emphasised in an editorial:

> What is at stake is the credibility of western-inspired reforms adopted by more and more African countries. A lecture in Reaganomics by the US Secretary of State, Mr. George Shultz, and a homily from Sir Geoffrey Howe are not what African states . . . either expected or deserved from two influential aid donors. The call by African countries for a major restructuring of external debt and greater support for reforms already under way deserves a more sympathetic response.[104]

On the critical issue of debt restructuring, little was forthcoming beyond partial moratoria from Canada, the Netherlands, Norway, and Sweden.

The major western creditors refused to discuss the problem outside their traditional case-by-case consideration. Also notable in this context was the reluctance of other members of the Group of 77 to agree to the proposition that the African crisis needed some kind of special remedy, a stand that undoubtedly increased the fear on the part of industrialised countries that any generalised form of debt relief would be seized upon as a precedent.

Neither were African countries successful in their efforts to gain additional measures to alleviate the problems arising from fluctuating earnings from commodity exports. In response to Adebayo Adedeji's question 'Is a global Stabex for African produce during the five years possible?',[105] the answer, to judge by the Special Session, is a firm 'No'. At a time when the terms of trade of African economies underwent a steep decline which many observers believed gave them a legitimate claim to additional low-conditionality finance, the I.M.F. actually tightened the conditions on access to its compensatory financing facility.[106] The apparent logic is that Africa's external position has deteriorated so significantly that no low-conditionality finance should be made available in case it might possibly delay the adoption of what the Fund considers to be appropriate adjustment measures.

Unfortunately, the negative response to Africa's requests at the Special Session is representative of the recent attitude of major donors. Although the United States is most closely identified with the new thrust of World Bank policies towards Africa, and hence inevitably was expected to provide leadership in financing the suggested policy adjustments, its recent record on aid has been quite lamentable. In marked contrast to the $3,000 million recommended by the proponents of a new 'compact' for African development,[107] the Administration requested a total of $1,200 million, over half of which was concentrated in nine countries—Cameroon, Kenya, Liberia, Niger, Senegal, Somalia, the Sudan, Zambia, and Zaïre. Less than 30 per cent of the Administration's request was for development assistance; food aid constituted a further 22 per cent; economic support funds, 35 per cent; and military assistance, 17 per cent. And, as Robert Berg noted, 'to an increasingly large extent, the quid pro quo for US aid is political loyalty rather than economic performance',[108] as Zimbabwe discovered to its cost in 1986. Even governments pursuing the type of economic policies that the Reagan Administration favours may find themselves cut out of the U.S. aid programme for largely extraneous reasons. Congressional doubts on the political criteria being applied by the Administration led to the blocking of its Economic Policy Initiative for Africa in 1984, the $75 million being diverted instead to the economic support funds.

The hostility displayed by the Reagan Administration towards multilateral institutions until 1985 probably affected Africa more than any other region. In particular, the refusal to fund its share of the I.D.A. VII replenishment deprived the World Bank of resources at a time when they were most desperately needed. Similarly, America's unwillingness to participate in the Bank's Special Facility for Africa led to its being considerably scaled down: even after Congress authorised a $225 million multiyear contribution, further delays by the Administration caused it to be ensnared by the Gramm-Rudman Act. Meanwhile, disputes with other donors over the funding of the International Fund for Agricultural Development, whose operations have been widely perceived as very effective, led to a 50 per cent cut in the organisation's funding level. The withdrawal of U.S.A.I.D. assistance from the U.N. Fund for Population Activities in 1986 will inevitably have a negative effect on an agency working on one of the areas most critical for Africa's long-term economic development. In December 1987, the United States was alone among the world's major industrialised countries in refusing to contribute to the I.M.F.'s new Enhanced Structural Adjustment Facility.

If the United States has failed to play a leadership rôle, no other donor has rushed to take its place. The U.N. Special Session illustrated clearly that the eastern bloc was 'more concerned with apportioning the blame for Africa's economic plight than doing anything about it'.[109] France was unusually critical of African aspirations at the Session, explicitly rejecting the O.A.U.'s estimates of the continent's financing needs and its call for a debt moratorium. Although the E.E.C., through the third Lomé Convention, increased its nominal level of development funding, this only maintained aid at the real levels of the second Convention despite the deterioration of African economies and the increase in the continent's population. However, the multi-year commitments and contractual overtones to the Convention do offer African states more security than most other aid relationships.

While the European Community can justifiably claim to be doing more for African countries through the Lomé Conventions than any other major donor, the record suggests, however, that these are an imperfect model.[110] The European Development Fund has long been criticised for its concentration on capital-intensive infrastructure, with the lion's share of both the work and the profits going to European contractors. Although the Community has committed itself to an emphasis on agriculture and other sectoral-support strategies in the new Convention, there is considerable scepticism among observers as to whether the bureaucratic and other vested interests in Europe will thwart the implementation of any changes to the existing pattern of development aid.

Japan is the one O.E.C.D. country whose balance-of-payments leaves it best placed to make a significant contribution to financing Africa's development needs. Although Tokyo has promised a substantial expansion of its foreign-assistance programme as a means of recycling its enormous trade surplus, Africa has traditionally been one of the lowest priorities for Japan's Development Co-operation Agency, receiving in recent years only 11 per cent of the total aid, a large proportion of which has been devoted to resource projects.[111] Given Japan's lack of expertise in bilateral aid to Africa, a significant increase in its contribution might best be brought about through multilateral agencies. The recent Japanese commitment to enlarge its share of the I.D.A. VIII replenishment, and the June 1987 pledge of an additional $500 million in aid to Africa over a three-year period, are welcome steps in the right direction.

Conclusion

'Adjustment with Growth' has proved to be a popular phrase for expressing the nominal commitments of the international community to provide Africa with additional financial assistance, and of African governments to implement reform programmes. Yet will these promises be translated into purposeful action, or will adjustment with growth be reduced to yet another slogan that obtains only fleeting popularity with the aid community?

The current consensus between international agencies and African governments rests on fragile foundations. Agreement exists on the need for policy change to promote agricultural recovery and more rapid economic growth. That there are few policy options available to governments in the short-term probably facilitates accord: it may diminish the impression that changes have been imposed by international agencies. But the lack of short-run viable alternatives may mask profound disagreement over the desirable development strategy for the medium and long terms. Here, the protestation of I.M.F. officials that its preferred policy choices are politically neutral is particularly disingenuous. Development strategies in Africa—and elsewhere in the world, for that matter—inevitably involve political questions of the highest order.

One thing is certain: adjustment with growth is a strategy that will be given only a limited time to produce desired results. The political costs that the typical I.M.F./World Bank package imposes on African governments will be tolerated only if the promised economic pay-offs rapidly materialise. Zambia's renunciation of its I.M.F. programme in May 1987 was an early indication of the likely unwillingness of African governments to persist with costly policies when the anticipated benefits are not forthcoming. As the World Bank has shown itself to be keenly aware, the need for a substantial increase in western aid is particularly important in assisting African governments to weather the hardships that adjustment inevitably entails—and as an inducement to adopt the desired policies. It will be not just ironic but tragic if adjustment with growth is abandoned because western governments, and the international agencies that they dominate, fail to provide the necessary financial support.

Notes

1. Organisation of African Unity, 'Africa's Submission to the Special Session of the United Nations General Assembly on Africa's Economic and Social Crisis', Addis Ababa, March 1986, OAU/ECM/2XV/Rev. 2, p. 17.

2. Ibid. p. 30. See also Organisation of African Unity, *Africa's Priority Programme for Economic Recovery, 1986–90* (Addis Ababa, F.A.O. for the O.A.U., 1985), p. 3.

3. *Africa's Priority Programme*, pp. 3, 12, and 14.

4. The failings of the *Lagos Plan* are examined in greater detail in John Ravenhill, 'Collective Self-Reliance or Collective Self-Delusion: is the Lagos Plan a viable alternative?', in Ravenhill (ed.), *Africa in Economic Crisis* (New York and London, 1986), pp. 85–107. See also Carol Lancaster, 'Multilateral Development Banks and Africa', in Lancaster and John Williamson (eds.), *African Debt and Financing* (Washington, D.C., 1986), Institute for International Economics, Special Report No. 5, pp. 124–5.

5. The best examples are Thomas M. Callaghy, *The State-Society Struggle: Zaire in comparative perspective* (New York, 1984); Goran Hyden, *No Shortcuts to Progress: African development management in perspective* (Berkeley, 1983); and Robert Jackson and Carl Rosberg, *Personal Rule in Black Africa: prince, autocrat, prophet, tyrant* (Berkeley, 1982).

6. Contrast, for instance, the favourable emphasis given to these two countries by Richard Sandbrook in *The Politics of Africa's Economic Stagnation* (Cambridge, 1985) with his earlier treatment of them in *The Politics of Basic Needs* (London, 1982).

7. For criticisms of *Accelerated Development*, see O.A.U. Council of Ministers, 38th Ordinary Session, 22 February–1 March 1982, 'Report of the Secretary-General on the World Bank Report', Addis Ababa, 1982, p. xxxviii; Philip Ndegwa, 'Accelerated Development in Sub-Saharan Africa: a review', in Ndegwa, L. P. Mureithi, and Reginald H. Green (eds.), *Development Options for Africa in the 1980s and Beyond* (Nairobi, 1985), ch. 3; *IDS Bulletin* (Brighton), 14, 1, January 1983; and Michael J. Schultheis, 'The World Bank and Accelerated Development: the internationalization of supply-side economics', in *African Studies Review* (Los Angeles), 27, 4, December 1984, pp. 9–16.

8. World Bank, *Financing Adjustment with Growth in Sub-Saharan Africa 1986–90* (Washington, D.C., 1986), p. 12.

9. A. W. Clausen, 'Foreword' to ibid. p. v.

10. World Bank, *Toward Sustained Development in Sub-Saharan Africa: a joint programme of action* (Washington, D.C., 1984), p. 3.

11. John P. Lewis (ed.), *Development Strategies: a new synthesis* (New Brunswick, 1985).

12. Gerald K. Helleiner, 'The Question of Conditionality', in Lancaster and Williamson (eds.), op. cit. pp. 72–3.

13. See, for instance, the comments of Elliot Berg, Carol Lancaster, and Tony Killick in ibid.

14. 'Africa's Submission', p. 18.

15. Gerald K. Helleiner, 'Policy-Based Programme Lending: a look at the Bank's new role', in Richard E. Feinberg et al., *Between Two Worlds: the World Bank's next decade* (New Brunswick, 1986), p. 53.

16. See the studies cited in G. K. Helleiner, 'Outward Orientation, Import Instability and African Economic Growth: an empirical investigation', in Sanjaya Lall and Frances Stewart (eds.), *Theory and Reality in Development* (London, 1986), p. 141.

17. David Wheeler, 'Sources of Stagnation in Sub-Saharan Africa', in *World Development* (Oxford), 12, 1, January 1984, pp. 1–23.

18. Kathie L. Krumm, *The External Debt of Sub-Saharan Africa: origins, magnitude, and implications for action* (Washington, D.C., 1985), World Bank Staff Working Paper No. 741, p. 11.

19. Helleiner, 'Outward Orientation'.

20. A position argued consistently and cogently by Reginald H. Green—see, for example, 'Reflections on the State of Knowledge and Ways Forward', in Tore Rose (ed.), *Crisis and Recovery in Sub-Saharan Africa* (Paris, 1985), p. 292.

21. Gerald K. Helleiner, *The IMF and Africa in the 1980s* (Princeton, 1983), Princeton University Essays in International Finance No. 152.

22. E.g. Rattan Bhatis, 'Adjustment Efforts in Sub-Saharan Africa, 1980–84', in *Finance and Development* (Washington, D.C.), 22, 3, September 1985, p. 20.

23. Carl K. Eicher, 'Strategic Issues in Combating Hunger and Poverty in Africa', in Robert J. Berg and Jennifer Seymour Whitaker (eds.), *Strategies for African Development* (Berkeley, 1986), p. 243.

24. According to 'The Critical Economic Situation in Africa: report of the Secretary-General', New York, U.N. General Assembly, 13th Special Session, 20 May 1986, p. 10, food self-sufficiency ratios dropped from 98 per cent in the 1960s to 86 per cent in 1980, while Africa's share of cereals food aid to developing countries rose from 14 per cent in 1970–1 to 61 per cent in 1984–5. If current trends continue according to F.A.O., *African Agriculture: the next 25 years* (Rome, 1986), Africa will need to import over 100 million tonnes of cereals annually by the year 2000—a figure in excess of the current yearly volume of world trade in wheat.

25. As appears to have been the case in Malawi. See Jonathan Kydd and Adrian Hewitt, 'The Effectiveness of Structural Adjustment Lending: initial evidence from Malawi', in *World Development*, 14, 3, March 1986, pp. 347–65.

26. Dunstan S. C. Spencer, 'Agricultural Research: lessons of the past, strategies for the future', in Berg and Whitaker (eds.), op. cit. p. 219.

27. But see the more moderate statement of the Bank's position in Stanley Please and K. Y. Amoako, 'OAU, ECA and the World Bank: do they really disagree?', in Ravenhill (ed.), *Africa in Economic Crisis*, pp. 132–4.

28. Benno J. Ndulu, 'Governance and Economic Management', in Berg and Whitaker (eds.), *Strategies for African Development*, p. 88.

29. Kevin M. Cleaver, *The Impact of Price and Exchange Rate Policies on Agriculture in Sub-Saharan Africa* (Washington, D.C., 1985), World Bank Staff Working Paper No. 728, pp. 2 and 16.

30. See the discussion in Ravenhill, 'Africa's Continuing Crises: the elusiveness of development', in Ravenhill (ed.), *Africa in Economic Crisis*, pp. 14–15.

31. Michael Lipton, 'The Place of Agricultural Research in the Development of Sub-Saharan Africa', in *IDS Bulletin*, 16, 3, 1985, p. 14.

32. Cathy L. Jabara, 'Agricultural Pricing Policy in Kenya', in *World Development*, 13, 5, May 1985, pp. 611–26. See also Jean-Jacques Faucher and Hartmut Schneider, 'Agricultural Crisis: structural constraints, prices and other policy issues', and Christian Morrisson, 'Agricultural Production and Government Policy in Burkina Faso and Mali', in Rose (ed.), op. cit. pp. 50–65 and 66–77, respectively.

33. Reginald H. Green and Caroline Allison, 'The World Bank's Agenda for Accelerated Development: dialectics, doubt and dialogue', in Ravenhill (ed.), op. cit. pp. 71–2; Reginald H. Green, 'Consolidation and Accelerated Development of African Agriculture: what agendas for action', in *African Studies Review*, 27, 4, December 1984, p. 23; and Mike Faber and Reginald H. Green, 'Sub-Saharan Africa's Economic Malaise: some questions and answers', in Rose (ed.) op. cit. p. 22.

34. Bruce F. Johnston, 'Governmental Strategies for Agricultural Development', and David K. Leonard, 'Putting the Farmer in Control: building agricultural institutions', in Berg and Whitaker (eds.), op. cit. pp. 155–83 and 184–214, respectively; and Green, 'Consolidation and Accelerated Development of African Agriculture', p. 27. For the contrary case, see Keith Hart, *The Political Economy of West African Agriculture* (Cambridge, 1982).

35. Robert H. Bates, *Markets and States in Tropical Africa* (Berkeley, 1981).

36. On Côte d'Ivoire, see Mathurin Gbetibouo and Christopher Delgado, 'Lessons and Constraints of Export Crop-Led Growth: cocoa in Ivory Coast', in I. William Zartman and Christopher Delgado (eds.), *The Political Economy of Ivory Coast* (New York, 1984), pp. 115–48; on Kenya, see Jabara, loc. cit.; on Malawi, see Ian Livingstone, 'Resource-Based Industrial Development: past experience and future prospects in Malawi', in *Industry and Development* (Nuremberg), 10, 1984, pp. 75–135, and Jonathan Kydd and Robert Christiansen, 'Structural Change in Malawi Since Independence: consequences of a development strategy based on large-scale agriculture', in *World Development*, 10, 5, May 1982, pp. 355–75.

37. Uma Lele, 'Rural Africa: modernization, equity and long-term development', in *Science* (Washington, D.C.), 211, 6 February 1981, p. 549.

38. Michael Bratton, 'Farmer Organizations and Food Production in Zimbabwe', in *World Development*, 14, 3, March 1986, pp. 367–84.

39. Helleiner, 'The Question of Conditionality', p. 76.

40. Green suggests in 'Consolidation and Accelerated Development of African Agriculture', pp. 23–4, that the record of private and public-sector organisations varies from crop to crop in Tanzania. Bratton, loc. cit. p. 367, comments that 'In many African countries, the capitalist market has even flimsier foundations that the state', and that peasant farmers, as the least accessible of all production units, often have to pay a premium for goods and services priced by markets.

41. Quoted in U.S. Congress, Office of Technology Assessment, *Africa Tomorrow: issues in technology, agriculture and U.S. foreign aid* (Washington, D.C., 1984), p. 78.

42. *Financing Adjustment with Growth*, p. 32.

43. Cf. Lipton, loc. cit. p. 22: 'National agricultural research in sub-Saharan Africa is, in general, not cost-effective. It concentrates heavily on a few export crops in price-inelastic demand, where, if it succeeds, the gains go largely to Western consumers. *Poor people's crops*—especially roots and cheap cereals, where on-

farm or local consumption (plus hunger) mean that there is little or no problem about inelastic demand—are generally neglected.'

44. Sven Kjellström and Ayite-Fily d'Almeida, 'Aid Coordination: a recipient's perspective', in *Finance and Development*, 23, 3, September 1986, p. 38.

45. Michael Lipton, 'Research and the Design of a Policy Frame for Agriculture', in Rose (ed.), op. cit. p. 87.

46. Eicher, 'Strategic Issues', p. 252.

47. See, for example, Caroline Allison, 'Women, Land, Labour and Survival: getting some basic facts straight', in *IDS Bulletin*, 16, 3, July 1985, pp. 24–30, 'What Alternatives for Women in Africa?', in Ndegwa, Mureithi, and Green (eds.), op. cit. ch. 10, and 'Health and Education for Development: African women's status and prospects', in Rose (ed.), op. cit. pp. 111–23. Also Winifred Weekes-Vagliani, 'Women, Food and Rural Development', in ibid. pp. 104–10; and Jane I. Guyer, 'Women's Role in Development', in Berg and Whitaker (eds.), op. cit. pp. 393–421.

48. Green, 'Consolidation and Accelerated Development of African Agriculture', p. 25.

49. See, for example, Philip Daniel, 'Zambia: structural adjustment or downward spiral?', in *IDS Bulletin*, 16, 3, July 1985, pp. 52–60.

50. U.N.I.D.O., 'Africa in Figures', Geneva, 6 February 1985, Table 1.

51. Larry Westphal, *Empirical Justification for Infant Industry Protection* (Washington, D.C., 1981), World Bank Staff Working Paper No. 445.

52. Manfred Bienefeld, 'The Lessons of Africa's Industrial 'Failure'', in *IDS Bulletin*, 16, 3, July 1985, pp. 69–77. For a discussion of some classic externally-financed 'white elephants', see Andrew Coulson, *African Socialism in Practice: Tanzania* (Nottingham, 1979).

53. Robert J. Berg, 'The Long-Run Future of Donor Planning Monitoring and Evaluation', in *Development* (Washington, D.C.), 22, 2–3, 1980. p. 72.

54. The World Bank has cited with approval the Kenya Tea Authority; and Livingstone, loc. cit., reported that parastatals in Malawi were run according to strict commercial criteria and, if anything, were too conservative in their activities. On the negative contribution to economic development of many state-owned enterprises, see Tony Killick, 'The Role of the Public Sector in the Industrialization of African Developing Countries', in *Industry and Development*, 7, 1983, pp. 57–88.

55. For instance, Goran Hyden, 'African Social Structure and Economic Development', in Berg and Whitaker (eds.), op. cit. ch. 2.

56. Nicola Swainson, *The Development of Corporate Capitalism in Kenya, 1918–1977* (Berkeley, 1980), p. 191, noted that 'the use of official positions within the State to advance business interests . . . is indeed the hallmark of the present stage of indigenous capitalism'.

57. Elliot Berg, 'The Potentials of the Private Sector in Africa', in Rose (ed.), op. cit. pp. 135–44.

58. Thomas M. Callaghy, 'The Political Economy of African Debt: the case of Zaïre', in Ravenhill (ed.), op. cit. ch. 12.

59. Faber and Green, loc. cit. p. 21.

60. For further discussion, see Ravenhill, 'Africa's Continuing Crises', pp. 16–18.

61. *Financing Adjustment with Growth*, p. 38.

62. United Nations, *Progress in the Implementation of the United Nations Programme of Action for African Economic Recovery and Development, 1986–1990* (New York, 1987), p. 20.

63. International Monetary Fund, *World Economic Outlook, 1986* (Washington, D.C., 1986), p. 261.

64. Gbetibouo and Delgado, loc. cit.

65. Livingstone, loc. cit. p. 116.

66. For an example of the failure of this strategy, see Steven Langdon, 'Industrial Dependence and Export Manufacturing in Kenya', in Ravenhill (ed.), op. cit. pp. 181–212.

67. John Ravenhill, 'Aid Through Trade: reforming the international trade regime in the interests of the least developed', in *Third World Quarterly* (London), 8, 2, April 1986, pp. 449–85.

68. Eduard H. Brau, 'African Debt: facts and figures on the current situation', in Lancaster and Williamson (eds.), op. cit. pp. 11–19 and statistical annex, pp. 30–46—this publication contains the most comprehensive discussion of the issue. Other useful sources include Callaghy, 'The Political Economy of African Debt', and 'Between Scylla and Charybdis: the foreign economic relations of sub-Saharan African states', in *The Annals* (Philadelphia), January 1987; Reginald H. Green and Stephany Griffith-Jones, 'External Debt: sub-Saharan Africa's emerging iceberg', in Rose (ed.), op. cit. pp. 211–30; Chandra S. Hardy, 'Africa's Debt: structural adjustment with stability', in Berg and Whitaker (eds.), op. cit. pp. 453–75; and Alwyn B. Taylor, 'The African Debtors: the decimating effects of pro-cyclical movements in concessional and non-concessional flows and the appropriate policy response', in *Journal of Development Planning* (New York), 16, 1985, pp. 143–64.

69. Callaghy, 'Between Scylla and Charybdis', loc. cit.

70. Hardy, loc. cit. p. 463.

71. See, for instance, Edward V. K. Jaycox, Ravi I. Gulhati, Sanjaya Lall, and Satya Yalamanchili, 'The Nature of the Debt Problem in Eastern and Southern Africa', in Lancaster and Williamson (eds.), op. cit. especially pp. 60–2.

72. *African Debt and Financing*, p. 170.

73. Helleiner, 'The Question of Conditionality', p. 67. See also Reginald H. Green, 'IMF Stabilisation and Structural Adjustment in Sub-Saharan Africa: are they technically compatible?', in *IDS Bulletin*, 16, 3, July 1985, p. 62.

74. O.A.U., 'Report of the Secretary General', p. 40. This provides a useful comparison of the projections by the Bank and the O.A.U. of Africa's estimated financing needs.

75. United Nations, op. cit. p. 20.

76. Gerald K. Helleiner, 'Economic Crisis in Sub-Saharan Africa: the international dimension', in *International Journal* (Toronto), 41, 4, Autumn, 1986, pp. 748–67.

77. Caroline Allison and Reginald H. Green, 'Editorial: toward getting some facts less snarled?', in *IDS Bulletin*, 16, 3, July 1985, p. 6, fn. 3.

78. Chester A. Crocker, 'FY 1987 Assistance Request for Sub-Saharan Africa', in *Current Policy* (Washington, D.C.), 814, 1986, p. 3.

79. Quoted in 'Concluding Appraisal', in Lancaster and Williamson (eds.), op. cit. p. 203.

80. Richard H. Carey, 'Prospects for Bilateral Aid', in ibid. p. 107. Cf. the statement by M. Peter McPherson, Administrator of U.S.A.I.D., 'Supporting African Economic Reform', in *Africa Report* (New Brunswick), 31, 3, May–June 1986, p. 11, that 'Donor budgets seem to be more constrained than at any time in the recent past, and the likelihood of substantially increased aid levels over the next few years is minimal at best'.

81. Anne O. Kreuger, 'Loans to Assist the Transition to Outward-Looking Policies', in *World Economy* (Oxford), 4, 3, September 1981.

82. Cf. Crawford Young, 'Africa's Colonial Legacy', in Berg and Whitaker (eds.), op, cit. p. 25–31.

83. Robert Cassen and Associates, *Does Aid Work?* (Oxford, 1986), p. 71.

84. Richard Feinberg, 'The Adjustment Imperative and U.S. Policy', in Feinberg and Valeriana Kallab (eds.), *Adjustment Crisis in the Third World* (New Brunswick, 1984), p. 17.

85. Reginald H. Green, 'Political-Economic Adjustment and IMF Conditionality: Tanzania, 1974–81', in John Williamson (ed.), *IMF Conditionality* (Washington, D.C., 1983), pp. 347–80.

86. Reginald H. Green, 'The IMF and Stabilisation in Sub-Saharan Africa: a critical review', I.D.S. Discussion Paper No. 216, Brighton, June 1986. For a restatement of the conventional I.M.F. argument for reduction in consumption, see the comments of Alassane D. Ouattara in 'A Panel Discussion', in Lancaster and Williamson (eds.), op. cit. pp. 185–9.

87. For example, Stanley Please, *The Hobbled Giant* (Boulder, 1984); and Tony Killick et al., *The Quest for Economic Stabilisation* (London, 1984).

88. Joan M. Nelson, 'The Politics of Stabilization', in Feinberg and Kallab (eds.), op. cit. p. 109.

89. Tony Killick et al., 'The IMF: the case for a change in emphasis', in ibid. p. 76.

90. See, particularly, Please, op. cit.

91. Comments in Lancaster and Williamson (eds.), op. cit. pp. 97–8.

92. See Cassen et al., op. cit. ch. 4; Kydd and Hewitt, loc. cit.; Edmar L. Bacha and Richard E. Feinberg, 'The World Bank and Structural Adjustment in Latin America', in *World Development*, 14, 3, March 1986, pp. 333–46. A Bank representative admitted that 'Various indicators of the Bank's work suggest that, in some respects, the extraordinary pressures of the early 1980s indeed led to a decline in the share of Bank activity specifically directed toward the reduction of poverty', and concluded that 'In some respects, the political climate of the 1980s does not favour the poor'; David Beckman, 'The World Bank and Poverty in the 1980s', in *Finance and Development*, 23, 3, September 1986, pp. 26 and 28, respectively. Cf. Reginald H. Green, 'Sub-Saharan Africa: poverty of development, development of poverty', I.D.S. Discussion Paper No. 218, Brighton, July 1986.

93. Helleiner, 'Policy-Based Programme Lending', p. 57.

94. Kydd and Hewitt, loc. cit., and Cassen et al., op. cit. p. 93. Cf. David Kimble, *Farewell Thoughts on the University* (Zomba, 1986).

95. Justin B. Zulu and Saleh M. Nsouli, *Adjustments Programs in Africa: the recent experience* (Washington, D.C., 1985), I.M.F. Occasional Paper No. 34, p. 14.

96. Williamson (ed.), op. cit. p. 638. John Loxley argues in *The IMF and the Poorest Countries* (Ottawa, 1984) that exogenous factors have swamped the effects of internal policy reforms in many African countries.

97. See, particularly, Green, 'The IMF and Stabilisation in Sub-Saharan Africa'.

98. Henry S. Bienen and Mark Gersovitz, 'Economic Stabilization, Conditionality, and Political Stability', in *International Organization* (Cambridge, Mass.), 39, 4, Autumn 1985, pp. 729–54.

99. Nelson, loc. cit. p. 94.

100. Edward V. L. Jaycox, 'Africa: development challenges and the World Bank's response', in *Finance and Development*, 23, 1, March 1986, p. 22.

101. Cassen et al. op. cit. p. 83.

102. Cf. Green, 'The IMF and Stabilisation in Sub-Saharan Africa', p. 19: 'The failure of the Fund to favour parallel—as opposed to subsequent—negotiations with the Bank (for structural adjustment or sectoral programmes) and bilateral sources (for import support and debt rescheduling) clearly endangers the viability of the programmes since they are usually dependent on significant increases in net external resource inflows—and quick ones at that if the early quarterly 'trigger clauses' are not to be pulled.'

103. Quoted in the *Christian Science Monitor* (Boston), 3 June 1986, p. 1.

104. 'Africa's Strong Case for Help', in *Financial Times* (London), 2 June 1986.

105. 'Transforming Africa's Economies', in *Africa Report*, 31, 3, May–June 1986, p. 8. For a review of the limitations of the Lomé Convention's Stabex scheme, see John Ravenhill, 'What Is to Be Done for Third World Commodity Exporters? An Evaluation of the STABEX Scheme', in *International Organization*, 38, 3, Summer 1984, pp. 537–74.

106. Sidney Dell, 'The Fifth Credit Tranche', in *World Development*, 13, 2, February 1985, pp. 245–9; and Nihad Kaibni, 'Evolution of the Compensatory Financing Facility', in *Finance and Development*, 23, 2, June 1986, pp. 24–7.

107. Report of the Committee on African Development Strategies, 'Compact for African Development', Council on Foreign Relations/Overseas Development Council, n.d.

108. Robert J. Berg, 'Foreign Aid in Africa: here's the answer—is it relevant to the question', in Berg and Whitaker (eds.), op. cit. p. 513.

109. *The Guardian* (London), 3 June 1986.

110. See John Ravenhill, *Collective Clientelism: the Lomé Conventions and North-South relations* (New York, 1985); also, Trevor W. Parfitt, 'Equals, Clients, or Dependents? A.C.P. Relations with the E.E.C under the Lomé Conventions, in *The Journal of Modern African Studies* (Cambridge), 25, 4, December 1987, pp. 717–23.

111. For a review of Japan's aid policies towards Africa, see Joanna Moss and John Ravenhill, *Emerging Japanese Economic Influence in Africa: implications for the United States* (Berkeley, 1985).

18

The Structural Adjustment of Politics in Africa

Jeffrey Herbst

1. Introduction

The structural adjustment programs currently being proposed by the World Bank and the International Monetary Fund (IMF) in Africa have important political consequences. Given that these programs entail significant income transfers among different groups (e.g., from food importers in the cities to peasants growing export crops) and that one of the major obstacles to adopting the new programs has been the violent objections of those who lose out in domestic economic reform, it is clear that, for African leaders, restructuring of their economies is as much a political as an economic question. However, there has been almost no attention devoted to the political implications of structural adjustment in African nations. The failure to examine the long-term consequences of economic reform for politics is particularly surprising given that the major instruments of structural adjustment—public sector reform, devaluation, elimination of marketing boards—threaten to change not only the constituencies that African leaders look to for support but the way in which leaders relate to their supporters in the countries south of the Sahara. Understanding the ultimate political logic of structural adjustment is also important because the state's position in an economy subject to a long-term reform program may be so unattractive to African elites that they may refuse to reform their economies after a certain point, even if they can withstand the short-term shocks that instruments such as devaluation impose. The implications of the analysis for donors are also discussed.

Reprinted with permission from *World Development* 18 (1990): 949–958. Elsevier Science Ltd., Oxford, England.

2. The Political Logic of State Intervention in Africa

Most African leaders operate in political systems where votes do not matter. Instead, rulers try to institutionalize their regimes by establishing webs of patron-client relations to garner the support necessary to remain in power. However, African governments are often not able to make direct transfers to those they would like to reward because of their weak tax bases. Indeed, given their dependence on import and export taxes, African countries as a group probably have the weakest tax bases in the world (Anderson, 1987, p. 6). As a result, it is sometimes extremely difficult for leaders to reward important constituencies with direct transfers or the kind of "pork barrel" projects that are so familiar in the West. Instead, African regimes often rig markets through direct state intervention in order for resources to flow to constituencies important to their continued tenure in office. To illustrate the political logic of state intervention in African markets, I will examine three areas that the World Bank (1981, p. 4) noted were in need of significant reform in its major 1981 document *Accelerated Development in Sub-Saharan Africa:* the public sector, exchange rates, and agricultural policies.

The paradigmatic example of state intervention in the economy to cement patron-client relations is the state-owned enterprises which blossomed throughout Africa as soon as countries began to receive their independence in the 1960s. For instance, in Tanzania, the number of public enterprises increased from 80 in 1967 to 400 in 1981 (d'Almeida, 1986, p. 56). Similarly, public enterprises in nominally capitalist Kenya grew in number from 20 at independence to 60 in 1979. In Ghana, parastatals also expanded in number from virtually zero prior to independence in 1959, to over 100 in the early 1960s. Other countries such as Zambia, Tanzania, Senegal, Mali, Côte d'Ivoire, Mauritania, and Madagascar have also experienced tremendous growth in their public enterprise sectors (Hyden, 1983, p. 97; Nellis, 1986, p. 56; Constantin *et al.,* 1979; Dutheil de la Rochère, 1976, pp. 49–51). Accordingly, Short's data suggest that the share of public enterprises in the gross domestic product (GDP) of African countries is roughly twice as high as in developing countries generally (17.5% compared to 8.6%) and that the African public enterprises' share in gross fixed capital formation is roughly 20% higher (32.4% versus 27.0%) than that in the average developing country (Short, 1984, p. 118).

Indeed, state-owned corporations are a particularly good source of patronage for African leaders because they can employ large numbers of people (by African standards); they can also direct important resources to specific areas and operate in greater secrecy than the government in general. As early as 1962 the Coker Commission found that the Action Group in Western Nigeria was siphoning off money from parastatals to fund political activities (Coker Commission, 1962). Since then, control of public enterprises has become an important part of the power structure for many African leaders. As Rondinelli, Nellis and Cheema note:

> Many political leaders emphasize the primacy of the public sector, which provides positions in the civil service and parastatal institutions with which to reward loyal political followers. They keep under central government control those factors—such as wages, prices, tariffs, food subsidies, and import and export regulations—that are considered to be most important for maintaining political stability. Clearly, policies promoting centralization usually pay off, at least in the short run, in material and political returns for the dominant elites.[1]

Precisely because they are such good conduits for patronage, however, African state-owned enterprises have performed exceptionally poorly since independence. Not surprisingly, their political functions cause African state-owned enterprises to be "pressured to increase employment, to deliver outputs at low prices to key groups, and to shape investment decisions other than with economic and financial returns in view" (World Bank, 1981, p. 38). What little systematic analysis there is reinforces the conclusion that African state-owned enterprises have performed extremely poorly. For instance, in one study of West African countries, 62% of the public enterprises showed net losses while 36% had negative net worth (Nellis, 1986, p. 17). Similarly, a study of state-owned transport enterprises in 18 Francophone countries found that only 20% generated enough revenue to cover operating costs, depreciation and finance charges; 20% covered operating costs plus depreciation; 40% barely covered operating costs; and a final 20% were far from covering operating costs. Thus, in Kenya the average rate of return of public enterprises was .2%, while in Niger the net losses of public enterprises amounted to 4% of the country's GDP in 1982. In Tanzania in the late 1970s one-third of all public enterprises ran losses (Nellis, 1986, p. 20). Other studies indicate that in Benin, Mali, Sudan, Nigeria, Mauritania, Zaïre, Sierra Leone and Senegal public enterprises have accumulated losses which sometimes amount to a significant percentage of the total economy (Nellis, 1986, pp. 17–19).

The second area where African governments have tended to intervene in the economy for political reasons has been the import regime. Countries have two basic ways of controlling imports so that they do not exhaust their foreign exchange reserves: the market (i.e., a correctly valued exchange rate) or administrative controls (e.g., tariffs and quotas).[2] African countries have consistently chosen to control imports administratively, in large part because this type of import regime yields greater political benefits. Under a market-determined import regime, no importer can be discriminated for or against because all face the same prices. However, in a system of tariffs and quotas, a government is able to selectively allocate import licenses and apply different levels of protection to different industries in order to reward clients. Indeed, in impoverished African countries, allocation of an import permit is almost a license to print money because those few who are able to bring in foreign goods will be assured of making a large profit.

Unfortunately, reliance on an administrative system to control imports almost inevitably leads in practice to an overvalued exchange rate. If leaders rely on administrative controls rather than the exchange rate to ration imports, they do not feel compelled to adjust the exchange rate to reflect differences between domestic inflation and the inflation rates of their trading partners. Indeed, in a perverse manner, use of administrative import regimes actually encourages overvaluation of exchange rates. The more the exchange rate becomes overvalued, the greater the benefit a government can bestow on those few who gain access to foreign goods. As the World Bank noted:

> Governments have relied increasingly on import restrictions rather than devaluation to conserve foreign exchange. More and more countries have imposed higher tariffs, quotas, and bans on "nonessential" imports. Quantitative restrictions have been the favored means of import restriction (World Bank, 1986, p. 24).

As is now well recognized, these overvalued exchange rates have a significant deleterious impact on African economies. The overvalued exchange rates make it extremely difficult for exporters to remain competitive in world markets that are priced in US dollars. The World Bank noted in 1981 that "trade and exchange-rate policy is at the heart of the failure to provide adequate incentives for agriculture production and for exports in much of Africa" (World Bank, 1986, p. 24). Overvalued exchange rates are particularly damaging for African countries because exports account for such a high percentage of the total economy. Exports of goods and nonfactor services accounted for 23% of GDP across all of sub-Saharan Africa in 1979, compared to 20% for all middle-income countries and 11% for all low-income countries (World Bank, 1986, p. 147).

The third area where African governments have widely intervened for political reasons has been agricultural producer prices. African governments have consistently adopted monopsonistic systems to buy food from peasant growers. Governments often set these prices below the true market price in order to subsidize urban customers who are politically important to African regimes. Peasants are usually unable to pressure the government to change prices for several reasons. They are fragmented; the state has the ability to crush most rural protests; and the state's control of the marketing system as well as the supply of inputs allows it to give selective "side-payments" to potential leaders of rural protests in order to buy them off (Bates, 1981). These low producer prices lead to underproduction by peasants for the market, and thereby contribute to the agricultural crisis affecting most countries in sub-Saharan Africa (World Bank, 1981, p. 55).

The incentive to intervene in the market for political reasons has been reinforced by several other coincidental factors. First, African governments inherited inverventionist state structures from the colonialists. As Nellis (1986, pp. 12–13) notes, "the national elites which came to power in the 1960's were thoroughly accustomed to legally strong, hierarchically organized and centralized, and economically intrusive governing systems." Second, the prevailing conventional wisdom in the 1960s and 1970s, endorsed by the World Bank, favored significant state intervention in the economy in order to foster development. Third, state intervention in the economy was attractive to African leaders because their regimes were insecure; greater control of the economy through administrative regulation and outright government ownership was a means of countering powerful foreign agents—multinational corporations and minority groups such as the Lebanese—that were perceived as operating against the national interest (see, for instance, Biersteker, 1987, p. 91).

The logic of political intervention in the economy had other important ramifications for the development of patronage systems in Africa. In particular, African leaders had little need to strengthen the weak political parties with which they began the independence period (Bretton, 1973, p. 3; Bienen, 1967). Given the state's own intervention in the economy and its distribution of extensive resources to the leader's clients, there was little reward for most African leaders to devoting time to building their party's administrative structure and mobilizing support through the party. The state already controlled the really important levers in society. Zolberg's early use of the phrase "party-states" to describe West African regimes is indicative of how much the patronage functions that might normally be carried out by parties had been taken over by the governments (Zolberg, 1966). In systems where votes do not count, there were no other compelling reasons for African politicians to devote significant resources to the development of political parties.

African regimes therefore created political economic systems that worked from the perspective of the leaders. While the perversion of state-owned enterprises, administrative controls of imports, and regulated and low agricultural producer prices brought disastrous consequences for African economies and a large proportion of the population, they did establish "arrangements by which uncertainty and potential instability can be reduced and some degree of political predictability obtained" (Jackson and Rosberg, 1982, p. 38). Indeed, the impetus for economic reform, which the Organization of African Unity now officially recognizes as necessary, came largely from outside Africa. The reluctance of African leaders to adopt changes in their political systems can best be seen by *The Lagos Plan of Action* which blamed all of the continent's problems on the outside world and looked to fanciful international economic unions to reverse the economic decline, even while the World Bank was making incisive criticisms of the policy failure of African governments (Organization of African Unity, 1981). However, the fact that African leaders were able to tolerate economic decline for so long should suggest just how well the patron-client systems worked for them.

3. What Is the Political Logic of Structural Adjustment?

As has now been widely recognized, structural adjustment programs of the type commonly prescribed for Africa can impose severe economic shocks which may have important political implications. Reform of public enterprises or privatization usually entails the loss of thousands of jobs when unemployment is already quite high; devaluation (routinely done in large shocks to prevent speculation) may raise food prices and the cost of other imports by 20% or more overnight; and increases in agricultural producer prices will also boost the cost of food. Analysis of the politics of structural adjustment has therefore concentrated on the question of how these shocks can be survived and which ones different types of governments are able to absorb. For instance, as Haggard and Kaufman (1989, p. 210) noted, "the central political dilemma is that stabilization and adjustment policies, no matter how beneficial they may be for the country as a whole, entail the imposition of short-term costs and have distributional implications" (see also, Nelson, 1984; Bienen and Gersovitz, 1986). Understanding the immediate political ramifications of structural adjustment is, in fact, exceptionally important because the consequent alienation of important constituencies may imperil economic reform programs at birth.

Yet, there is clearly a political logic beyond the initial stabilization shocks of structural adjustment. Structural adjustment involves not only the switching of constituencies by African governments (a feat that most governments find exceptionally difficult) but an entirely new mechanism through which leaders relate to their clients. Under the political systems established after independence, governments were able to provide a variety of resources—jobs, low prices for basic goods, preferential access to government projects—to favored constituencies. The whole point of structural adjustment is to eliminate, or at least significantly curtail, governments' ability to offer these kinds of advantages to their constituencies. As Elliott has noted, there is a fundamental asymmetry between the way the political system [in African countries] actually operates and the way economic decision-making would have to operate if the demanding conditions of equilibrium—i.e., noninflationary balances on internal and external account—were to be achieved (Elliott, 1988, p. 218).

Changing the way in which leaders relate to their constituencies is qualitatively more difficult than simply changing the constituencies that they look to for support. For instance, the African Development Bank and the Economic Commission for Africa noted that the reforms in the public sector that are now being implemented amount to nothing less than "[a] fundamental change in the economic structure itself" (African Development Bank and Economic Commission for Africa, 1988, p. 14).

At a more abstract level, state intervention in Africa led to systems where goods were allocated through state coercion, a process which inhibited the market from providing information. Structural adjustment requires states to cede much of their coercive powers over the economy, and pay much more attention to the information that real prices provide. As Apter noted in his discussion of the requisites of government, "the mixture of coercion and information that a government employs has an effect on the type of system, because if the proportions are substantially altered the structural relations of government will also be altered" (Apter, 1965, p. 240).

The point is not simply that all African countries will now adopt structural adjustment programs and therefore be forced to change the basis of their political systems. Clearly, many will not. Yet it is obvious that the logic of structural adjustment must be understood because some countries may adopt the program and others will partially adjust their economies. Therefore, many political systems across the continent which had as a central feature the ability to distribute patronage will be threatened to some degree by structural adjustment. At the very least, the disadvantages and advantages that structural adjustment poses to leaders will be a consideration in the adoption of programs of economic reform throughout the continent.

There has been very little speculation about the long-term functioning of the state under structural adjustment, even though the World Bank and many other commentators have traced much of Africa's current economic crisis to the present role of the state in African economies. The World Bank is reluctant to explicitly outline the role of the state under a long-term program of structural adjustment. The Bank is already sensitive about the political implications of structural adjustment, and the charges that foreigners are determining too many domestic policies in African countries. Still, given the Bank's incisive analysis of many of the current problems of the African state, it should make some suggestions as to what the state in Africa would look like during long-term structural adjustment. If a vision of the economic role of the state under structural adjustment is presented, it should then be possible to infer both the political functions of the state during a program of long-term economic reform and how the state will relate to its constituencies in the future.

· The World Bank's general writings on the role of the state in Third World countries during economic reform has been remarkably vague. For instance, in the 1983 *World Development Report* which focused on "management in development" the World Bank did try to outline its conception of the proper role of the state. The result, unfortunately, is not much more instructive than an introductory economics text:

> Markets may not perform perfectly because of insufficient information or because they do not take adequate account of indirect losses and benefits (the so-called externalities such as pollution or worker training). Nor can free markets handle public goods (such as national defense), where the cost of supply is independent of the number of beneficiaries, or natural monopolies. Finally, markets do not act to correct inequalities in income wealth. Some market failures are so evident that they cannot be ignored; in addition, governments will always have legitimate noneconomic objectives that can be pursued only by intervention (World Bank, 1983, p. 52).

This kind of statement means little in Africa where market failure is relatively common, information does not flow well, and there are many structural bottlenecks. Indeed, all the Bank seems to suggest is that the trajectory of state growth should be negative, but no desired vision of the proper economic role of the state is expressed. Without an understanding of the economic role of the state, it is impossible to set the parameters of its political functioning in the future and, in particular, how it will relate to important constituencies.

In publications specific to Africa, the World Bank is even vaguer as to what the role of the state should be. For instance, the Bank's influential report, *Accelerated Development in Sub-Saharan Africa* (1981), presents cogent criticisms of many states' interventions in the economy but does not outline what the role of the state should be. Other general reports have been equally vague. Similarly, the 1984 report *Towards Sustained Development in Sub-Saharan Africa* claimed only that:

> The need for flexibility and adaptability is the single most important lesson of experience. Economic institutions should be responsive to fast-changing circumstances: prescriptions and policy signals need to be assessed, analyzed, and internalized in the country's decision-making process (World Bank, 1984b, p. 39).

Also, the 1986 report *Financing Adjustment with Growth in Sub-Saharan Africa* noted with approval that the size of the state across Africa was shrinking, but coupled that statement with the somewhat paradoxical warning that cuts in the size of the state had led to excessive reductions in equipment, maintenance, operating funds, and materials (World Bank, 1986, p. 22). The recent report by the United Nations Development Program and the World Bank also does not comment on what the actual role of the state should be in Africa (United Nations Development Program and World Bank, 1989).

Nor does the World Bank develop a fuller picture of what the state should look like during a process of long-term structural adjustment in its specific country reports. For instance, in its report on Ghana, the World Bank does not describe a vision of the future state at all except to list what liberalization entails:

> Removing controls and regulation in factor, commodity and foreign exchange markets; de-regulating domestic commodity markets; reducing tariff and non-tariff barriers; elimination of price controls, nonprice allocation of credit, interest rate ceilings; and reducing restrictions on financial intermediation (World Bank, 1984a, p. 68).

In its report on Guinea-Bissau, the Bank notes nothing about the future of the state except that, due to the large public sector deficit, the government should endeavour to price all services according to cost and that expenditures should be reduced in real terms (World Bank, 1984b, p. 14). At no point does the Bank actually detail what the limits of state intervention in the market should be, and thereby establish at least the parameters of how the state is going to interact with its constituencies.

African organizations involved in economic reform might also be expected to address the issue of the long-term effects of structural adjustment on African states. These sources, however, are also exceptionally vague about eventual state functions and future relationships with constituencies. For instance, in the Economic Commission for Africa's (ECA) important report, *ECA and Africa's Development, 1983–2008,* the ECA notes repeatedly how important it will be to change the political environment in Africa but specifies only that:

> What is required from African Governments is to make it possible for the population to interrelate positively with all the development variables: natural and financial resources, development institutions, local and foreign technologies (ECA, 1983, p. 97).

Similarly, the Organization of African Unity's submission to the United Nations on the continent's economic crisis does not detail the future role of the state in Africa except to say:

> In many countries of the region, new measures are actively being pursued to increase government revenues through selective increases in consumption

taxes and charges, and taxes on travel. . . . Many Governments, in the circumstances, are focusing attention on the improvement and development of
appropriate institutional machinery in order to improve tax collection and to
encourage domestic savings (OAU, 1986, p. 74).

There is no real vision of the state here. Nor is the absence of such a vision
surprising given that it is not in the interests of African leaders to acknowledge that the economic reforms to which they are now nominally
committed also entails significant political reforms which might weaken
their power structures further.

The US government, which has been at the ideological forefront of the
push to convince African governments to fundamentally change the role
of the state, has a slightly more detailed vision of the state, but one which
does not suggest how it would work politically under long-term structural adjustment. In the end, the US prescription simply supports state
shrinkage along the lines of the World Bank's proposals: agricultural pricing and marketing reforms, privatization of parastatals, and better access
to markets (Whitehead, 1985, p. 39). The United States only suggests the
areas in which the state should begin to withdraw. The actual extent of
the state is left as a vague residual to be determined after programs such
as privatization have been adopted. This vagueness is really not surprising, because the US government is aware how sensitive African governments are to even its current statements on how African economies
should be restructured. Also, although former President Reagan certainly
used his bully pulpit to press for market-oriented reforms throughout the
world, the United States has only recently developed a special initiative
that would press for structural adjustment and that would have the analytical capacity to formulate an alternative vision of the role of the African
state in the economic and political spheres.

4. The Political Consequences
of Structural Adjustment

Structural adjustment has important consequences for the way that politics is conducted in Africa even if the World Bank and others who recom-
mend reforms are unwilling, or unable, to describe them. At the most basic
level, reductions in the size of the state and severe curtailments in its ability to provide patronage will make the state much less flexible in dealing
with a political crisis. True adoption of structural adjustment policies will
prevent the state from offering subsidies or some other political good if a
group becomes disaffected or if a leader suddenly needed to garner public
support. For instance, Luke explains that the parastatal sector in Sierra
Leone expanded after the death of Prime Minister Sir Milton Margai be-

cause the new Prime Minister (his brother, Albert Margai) needed to "consolidate his political base (via the patron-clientelist network of the Sierra Leone People's Party) by opening up new areas for the award of contracts and for appointments to positions in the new or expanded organizations" (Luke, 1984, p. 77). This option would not have been open to the new Prime Minister under a long-term structural adjustment program designed to reduce the absolute size of state-owned enterprises. Similarly, governments often use the levers provided by parastatals to influence the population when public support is necessary. For instance, it took the deficit-ridden National Railways of Zimbabwe 26 months to have a lower than requested fare increase approved by the government because of ministerial interference and a reluctance on the part of national leaders to raise rates before an election (Smith Commission, 1987, p. 74). This kind of price manipulation will be much more difficult if countries do adopt the public sector reforms that are an integral part of structural adjustment.

From the perspective of African leaders, structural adjustment creates a volatile political climate in which the threat of even minor disruptions must be taken very seriously. Without the recourse to parastatals and extensive control of price mechanisms, African leaders will not be able to provide side-payments to restive populations in order to prevent unrest. For instance, further subsidy of foodstuffs or other basic commodities of the urban population can no longer be used to prevent urban riots. Similarly, given the pressures that an IMF program places on government revenue (especially the emphasis of decreasing the fiscal deficit), it may not be as possible for governments to buy off restive militaries through increases in defense budgets and perks as it was in the past. The fundamental problem is that the urban population and the military will still be important to African politicians because leaders must retain physical control of the cities in order to stay in power. However, leaders will not be able to reward groups that can threaten violence, as they did in the past, even though those groups continue to be important to the leaders' political stability. Just as the particular forms of market intervention that African countries adopted made sense given the political needs and vulnerabilities of leaders, the political ramifications of structural adjustment are particularly dangerous to African leaders who cannot change the nature of their political systems in the short or medium terms. Certainly, structural adjustment poses fewer dangers to regimes that remain in power through votes and have gained a certain legitimacy than regimes that have to depend on a combination of coercion and patronage to endure.

African governments may therefore have to use even more coercion than before structural adjustment to remain in power. Indeed, given that there may be no way to continue previously established clientelistic networks in the new environment, African leaders may have no choice other than to procure future stability by repressing their former clients. The real repression that results from structural adjustments may not be from quelling food riots when IMF packages are first instituted, but from the elimination of some of the noncoercive measures that African governments could previously use to keep potentially threatening groups under control.

In other parts of the world, the liability of reducing patronage would be at least partially compensated for by the fact that groups would no longer look to the state for resources. Clearly, the logic of privatization in the United Kingdom and elsewhere is to deflect popular criticism from the state by reducing its economic role. For instance, consumers no longer protest against the government if a privatized gas company raises prices. Thus, the Ghanaian Finance and Economic Planning Secretary, Kwesi Botchwey, initiated an auction of foreign exchange, instead of the retaining the previous system of formal government control over the exchange rate, in order to "depoliticize" currency adjustments (Agyeman-Duah, 1987, p. 635).

In Africa, however the state will continue to have a dominant economic role, given the poverty of most countries' private sectors. The population will thus continue to look to the state as the only organization that can have an immediate impact on their lives. Also, the long tradition of supporting clientelistic politics through the state and the impossibility of reproducing those relations in the private sector means that the political demands will inevitably be directed at the state for the foreseeable future, even if politicians no longer have the means to address those demands. African states will be caught in the particularly frustrating position of being the dominant economic organizations within the country, but being limited in the extent to which they can actually intervene in the economy.

It is possible that ethnic tensions could subside if a significant number of economic decisions were removed from the government, resulting in a net decrease in instability. One of the factors promoting ethnic strife is the need different groups feel to mobilize in order to press the state on important allocation issues. A system where many more allocation decisions were made through the market could therefore decrease the perceived need to mobilize around ethnic symbols. This judgment, however, needs to be tempered. First, ethnic groups with close ties to the current leadership will suffer effective status reversals during structural adjustment because their privileged access to patronage and goods will be lost. Status reversals have in the past sometimes created heightened ethnic consciousness within the newly disadvantaged group. Feelings of resentment can be channeled into stronger attachments to group identities. Second, if one ethnic group were perceived as dominating new economic structures, ethnic strife could increase. There is already tremendous ill-will against Indians and Lebanese because of the perception that these groups dominate the retail sector and some industrial sectors in certain countries. Since the economic growth fostered by structural adjustment may not be ethnically neutral, groups that do particularly well could also become the victims of new ethnic strife. Structural adjustment will certainly change the patterns of ethnic conflict, but it will not automatically raise or lower the degree of group consciousness and division within a society.

In the long term, governments under structural adjustment will be less able to buy ethnic peace through the distribution of patronage and resources. Some governments have established a more or less effective *modus vivendi* among ethnic groups by distributing resources through parastatals and rigging markets so that the major groups do not feel too alienated. As Sandbrook (1985, p. 80) notes, African leaders will condemn discrimination on the basis of ethnicity, but resort to "ethnic arithmetic" in order to "suppress divisive tendencies." Structural adjustment would make this kind of ethnic balancing much more difficult because the opportunities to provide patronage will be more limited. Further, when the ethnic balance is disturbed for factors outside of government control (e.g., changes in population distribution, natural disasters, fluctuations in the international market), African leaders will find it much more difficult to intervene in economies to restore the old ethnic order or to establish a new one favorable to them.

African leaders will therefore face a much riskier political environment if they do enact long-term programs of structural adjustment. They will have fewer means of buying off restive groups, but they will still be vulnerable to violent confrontation with the urban population and the military. Ethnic groups that have been consciously discriminated against for years in order to appease the majority may suddenly become conspicuously wealthy from government instituted reform packages. Repression, which could in the past be used by intelligent politicians alongside patronage to promote stability, will now become much more of a blunt instrument. Governments will have to resort to repression more frequently with the attendant risk that significant segments of the population will become even more alienated.

In the long term, if structural adjustment does promote economic growth, the political situation may become more stable because all groups will receive more resources than before. The proposed reforms, however, will take many years to implement and, moreover, the structural weaknesses in African economies and governments will inhibit immediate, dramatic improvements in the economy (see, Callaghy, 1989, pp. 132–133). The persuasive argument for structural adjustment is not that it will turn African countries into high-growth economies but that, by removing some of the state-imposed distortions, structural adjustment will allow the economy to grow faster than it otherwise would have. Those who were once bought off by government side-payments may find the fact that the economy is not as weak as it would otherwise have been to be insufficient motivation to conform to government policies and demands. At the very least, governments will recognize that structural adjustment poses grave new risks for them because they cannot guarantee that increases in economic performance will produce political quiescence as effectively as direct transfers did in the era before structural adjustment.

A second aspect of African politics that is threatened by structural adjustment is the concentration of political power. In systems where the role of prices was largely abrogated by high-level political authorities, centralized political power was not only inevitable but logical. Leaders felt that they could readily effect economic developments and could observe how their economy was functioning without decentralized systems of administration. In economic systems where prices count, however, governments will be forced to decentralize political structures if they hope to monitor developments and understand what is happening in their economies. Also, given that structural adjustment has as one of its highest priorities reorienting resources to the countryside, governments will want to extend administrative structures to the new rural groups that will benefit from official policies.

However, African governments have yet to face up to this reality. The speculation in Africa and by outside observers has always been whether the current centralized political systems can withstand the shocks of structural adjustment but the long-term threat to the kind of centralized control that African leaders have developed is clear. As the Chinese have discovered, a profound tension develops when economic decentralization is attempted without a corresponding devolution of political power. Since the problem of incompatibility between highly centralized political structures and decentralized market structures has yet to become apparent, it is uncertain how African leaders will react to this profound challenge to their system of rule. It may well be that rulers will balk at shedding some of their political power in order to conform to their new economic systems. In this case, structural adjustment will flounder because of the threats it presents to leaders, not to vulnerable population groups.

One way for leaders to decentralize power while not challenging their own rule would be to reinvigorate their parties. In many countries political parties were previously not viewed as important, in part because leaders in highly centralized states had so many ways of developing support through government intervention. However, the removal of these political levers and the need to monitor economic developments in a more decentralized manner could create the conditions for new energy in, and resources devoted to, political parties. Parties would seem to be one of the few avenues political leaders would have left after structural adjustment to communicate with supporters. Parties could also play an important role in developing ties with the groups that will benefit from structural adjustment and that will therefore be potential new constituencies for the government. Indeed, parties might be especially relevant for African leaders newly interested in developing ties to the countryside, where formal government structures are weak and previous clientelistic networks irrelevant.

Similarly, redirection of resources to the countryside might occasion the development of stronger peasant associations. In many African countries peasants have been unable to organize effectively because of their atomistic nature and because governments did not encourage, or actively discouraged, smallholder associations. Leaders did not always nurture political ties with the peasantry in the past because development of peasant political power threatened the system of collaboration and support between leaders and the urban population. Under a system of long-term structural adjustment, however, information from and ties with the countryside could become much more important to leaders. Ghana, which has proceeded the farthest in Africa with structural adjustment, is also attempting to decentralize at least some aspects of public administration by establishing new local structures in the country's districts.

A few analysts have gone a step further and argued that the kind of economic decentralization implied by structural adjustment demands that countries move toward some sort of electoral democracy. It is true that at some point political centralization, even with a reinvigorated single party, would almost inevitably interfere with continued structural adjustment because leaders would still be tempted to exercise political power through market interference. However, when a contradiction does develop between structural adjustment and the centralization of political power, surely it will be the structural adjustment process that will be halted. Given that the state will remain the only economically significant prize for a long time, it is hard to imagine African leaders submitting themselves to the vagaries of the electoral process simply in order to foster long-term development. Leaders would also be far more likely to decentralize if they were relatively confident of staying in power. While structural adjustment demands that African leaders radically change their power structures, it cannot guarantee that they will be more secure in power. Politicians will remain vulnerable to groups that threaten violence. The causality between structural adjustment and movement toward any kind of electoral system is problematic when looking at the fragile position in which most African leaders find themselves.

5. Implications for Aid Donors

The implication of this analysis for multilateral and bilateral donors who seek to encourage structural adjustment is that there is an inherent dilemma in trying to impose conditionality on African countries. In the short term, the strict tying of further resource flows to proposed reforms will probably be necessary because the political incentives not to implement a structural adjustment program, or to do so haltingly, are very strong. At the same time, for African leaders to carry out a program which is so politically risky requires assurance of long-term flows of concessional aid. African governments cannot be assured of long-term resource flows if donors' further aid is conditional on achieving ambitious goals in the short term. Aid donors will therefore have to walk a very dangerous tightrope between nudging African leaders toward reform and assuring them that politically dangerous reforms will be rewarded in the long term. For countries that have made clear their commitment to structural adjustment, this tension will probably mean that donors should pay less attention to quarterly economic indicators and more attention to helping insure aid flows large enough to moderate some of the long-term risk of structural adjustment.

6. The Dangers of Structural Adjustment to African Leaders

If structural adjustment programs are actually carried out, the logic of economic reform suggests that African leaders will be put in an even more precarious position than they are now. African governments will be faced with a risky political environment as they will be forced to adopt more decentralized forms of government. Indeed, structural adjustment may impose so many limits on politicians' ability to direct resources to clients that the old networks of support may no longer be viable. At the very least, political life will become much more difficult for African leaders who attempt to reform their economic systems without structurally adjusting their polities. Some leaders may find the necessary political changes so unattractive that they actually balk at the economic reforms being suggested. The real losers in structural adjustment may be African leaders themselves.

Notes

1. The political importance of centralized economic institutions was noted early on by W. Arthur Lewis (1965, pp. 47–55).

2. This analysis follows from Charles Lindblom's (1977, p. ix) insight that there are only two ways to regulate a good: through the market or through administrative controls.

References

African Development Bank and Economic Commission for Africa, *Economic Report on Africa 1988* (Abidjan and Addis Ababa: African Development Bank and Economic Commission for Africa, 1988).

Agyeman-Duah, Baffour, "Ghana, 1982–6: The politics of the P.N.D.C." *The Journal of Modern African Studies,* Vol. 25 (1987).

Anderson, Dennis, "The public revenue and economic policy in African countries," World Bank Discussion Paper No. 19 (Washington, DC: The World Bank, 1987).

d'Almeida, Ayité-Fily, "La privatisation des enterprises publiques en Afrique au sud du Sahara—Premiere partie," *Le Mois en Afrique,* No. 245–246 (1986).

Apter, David E., *The Politics of Modernization* (Chicago: University of Chicago Press, 1965).

Bates, Robert H., *Markets and States in Tropical Africa* Berkley: University of California Press, 1981).

Bienen, Henry S., *Tanzania: Party Transformation and Economic Development* (Princeton: Princeton University Press, 1967).

Bienen, Henry S., and Mark Gersovitz, "Consumer subsidy cuts, violence, and political stability," *Comparative Politics,* Vol. 19 (1984).

Biersteker, Thomas J., *Multinationals, the State, and Control of the Nigerian Economy* (Princeton: Princeton University Press, 1987).

Bretton, Henry L., *Power and Politics in Africa* (Chicago: Aldine Publishing Co., 1973).

Callaghy, Thomas M., "Toward state capability and embedded liberalism in the Third World: Lessons for adjustment," in Joan M. Nelson (Ed.), *Fragile Coalition: The Politics of Economic Adjustment* (Washington, DC: Overseas Development Council, 1989).

(Coker Commission) Commission of Inquiry into the Affairs of Certain Statutory Corporations in Western Nigeria, *Report of Coker Commission of Inquiry into the Affairs of Certain Statutory Corporations in Western Nigeria,* Volume 1 (Lagos: Federal Ministry of Information, 1962).

Constantin, F., *et al., Les Enterprises Publiques en Afrique Noire,* Volume 1 (Paris: Centre d'Étude d'Afrique Noire, 1976).

Dutheil de la rochère, Jacqueline, *L'État de la Dévelopment Économique de la Côte d'Ivoire* (Paris: Centre d'Étude d'Afrique Noire, 1976).

Economic Commission for Africa, *ECA and Africa's Development, 1983–2008* (Addis Ababa: Economic Commission for Africa, 1983).

Elliott, Charles, "Structural adjustment in the longer run: Some uncomfortable questions," in Stephen K. Commins (Ed.), *Africa's Development Challenges and the World Bank* (Boulder, CO: Lynne Rienner Publishers, 1988).

Haggard, Stephan, and Robert Kaufman, "The politics of stabilization and structural adjustment," in Jeffrey D. Sachs (Ed.), *Developing Country Debt and the World Economy* (Chicago: University of Chicago Press, 1989).

Hyden, Goran, *No Shortcuts to Progress* (Berkeley: University of California, 1983).

Jackson, Robert H., and Carl G. Rosberg, *Personal Rule in Black Africa* (Berkeley: University of California Press, 1982).

Lewis, W. Arthur, *Politics in West Africa* (London: George Allen and Unwin, 1965).

Lindbloom, Charles E., *Politics and Markets* (New York: Basic Books, 1977).

Luke, David Fashole, *Labour and Parastatal Politics in Sierra Leone* (New York: University Press of America, 1984).

Nellis, John R., "Public enterprises in sub-Saharan Africa," World Bank Discussion Paper No. 1 (Washington, DC: World Bank, 1986).

Nelson, Joan M., "The political economy of stabilization: Commitment, capacity, and public response," *World Development* Vol. 12, No. 10 (1984).

Organization of African Unity, *Africa's Priority Programme for Economic Recovery* (Addis Ababa: Organization of African Unity, 1986).

Organization of African Unity, *Lagos Plan of Action for the Economic Development of Africa 1980–2000* (Geneva: International Institute for Labour Studies, 1981).

Rondinelli, Dennis A., John R. Nellis, and G. Shabbir Cheema, "Decentralization in developing countries," World Bank Staff Working Paper No. 581 (Washington, DC: World Bank, 1984).

Sandbrook, Richard, with Judith Barker, *The Politics of Africa's Economic Stagnation* (Cambridge: Cambridge University Press, 1985).

Short, R. P., "The role of public enterprises: An international statistical comparison," in Robert H. Floyd *et al.*, *Public Enterprises in Mixed Economies* (Washington, DC: International Monetary Fund, 1984).

(Smith Commission) Committee of Inquiry into Parastatals, *National Railways of Zimbabwe* (Harare: Government Printers, 1987).

United Nations Development Program and the World Bank, *Africa's Adjustment and Growth in the 1980's* (Washington, DC: The World Bank, 1989).

Whitehead, John C., "Statement of John C. Whitehead," in US Senate Committee on Foreign Affairs, *African Debt Crisis* (Washington, DC: Ninety-ninth Congress, First Session, October 24, 1985).

World Bank, *Guinea-Bissau: A Prescription for Comprehensive Adjustment* (Washington, DC: World Bank, 1987).

World Bank, *Financing Adjustment with Growth in Sub-Saharan Africa, 1986–1990* (Washington, DC: World Bank, 1986).

World Bank, *Ghana: Policies and Program for Adjustment* (Washington, DC: World Bank, 1984a).

World Bank, *Toward Sustained Development in Sub-Saharan Africa* (Washington, DC: World Bank, 1984b).

World Bank, *World Development Report 1983* (New York: Oxford University Press, 1983).

World Bank, *Accelerated Development in Sub-Saharan Africa* (Washington, DC: World Bank, 1981).

Zolberg, Aristide R., *Creating Political Order: The Party-States of West Africa* (Chicago: University of Chicago Press, 1966).

Suggestions for Further Reading

Ake, Claude. *A Political Economy of Africa*. London: Longman, 1981.

Allen, Chris, and Gavin Williams, eds. *The Sociology of the "Developing Countries": Sub-Saharan Africa*. New York: Monthly Review Press, 1982.

Bates, Robert H. *Markets and States in Tropical Africa*. Berkeley and Los Angeles: University of California Press, 1981.

Biersteker, Thomas J. *Multinationals, the State, and Control of the Nigerian Economy*. Princeton: Princeton University Press, 1987.

Brett, E. A. *Colonialism and Underdevelopment in East Africa*. London: Heinemann, 1973.

Callaghy, Thomas, and John Ravenhill, eds. *Hemmed In: Responses to Africa's Economic Decline.* New York: Columbia University Press, 1992.

Cooper, Frederick. "Africa and the World Economy." *African Studies Review,* 24, no. 2/3 (1981).

Hopkins, Anthony. *An Economic History of West Africa.* New York: Columbia University Press, 1973.

Hyden, Goran. *No Shortcuts to Progress.* Berkeley and Los Angeles: University of California Press, 1983.

Leys, Colin. *Underdevelopment in Kenya.* Berkeley and Los Angeles: University of California Press, 1974.

Ravenhill, John, ed. *Africa in Economic Crisis.* New York: Columbia University Press, 1986.

Rosberg, Carl, and Thomas Callaghy, eds. *Socialism in Sub-Saharan Africa: A New Assessment.* Berkeley: University of California, Institute for International Studies, 1979.

Sandbrook, Richard. *The Politics of Africa's Economic Stagnation.* Cambridge: Cambridge University Press, 1985.

_____. *The Politics of Africa's Economic Recovery.* Cambridge: Cambridge University Press, 1995.

World Bank. *Sub-Saharan Africa: From Crisis to Sustainable Growth.* Washington, D.C.: World Bank, 1989.

Young, Crawford. *Ideology and Development in Africa.* New Haven: Yale University Press, 1982.

About the Editor
and Contributors

Victor Azarya is associate professor of sociology and anthropology at the Hebrew University of Jerusalem.

Catherine Boone is associate professor of political science at the University of Texas at Austin.

Michael Bratton is professor of political science at Michigan State University.

Thomas M. Callaghy is professor of political science at the University of Pennsylvania.

Naomi Chazan is professor of political science and African studies at the Hebrew University of Jerusalem.

Larry Diamond is senior research fellow at the Hoover Institution, Stanford University.

Peter P. Ekeh is professor and chair of African American studies at the State University of New York at Buffalo.

Jeffrey Herbst is associate professor of politics at Princeton University.

Robert H. Jackson is professor of political science at the University of British Columbia.

Richard A. Joseph is professor of political science and fellow for African studies at Emory University.

Tony Killick is research fellow in the International Economic Development Group of the Overseas Development Institute.

Peter Lewis is assistant professor in the School of International Service, American University.

John Ravenhill is senior fellow in the Department of International Relations, Research School of Pacific Studies, Australian National University.

Pearl T. Robinson is associate professor of political science and director of the Program in International Relations at Tufts University.

Carl G. Rosberg, until his death in 1996, was professor of political science at the University of California at Berkeley.

Donald Rothchild is professor of political science at the University of California at Davis.

Richard Sandbrook is professor of political science at the University of Toronto.

Richard L. Sklar is professor emeritus of political science at the University of California at Los Angeles.

450

Aili Mari Tripp is assistant professor of political science and women's studies at the University of Wisconsin at Madison.

Nicolas van de Walle is associate professor of political science at Michigan State University.

Crawford Young is professor of political science at the University of Wisconsin at Madison.

Index